Fishes of the World

2nd edition

JOSEPH S. NELSON

Professor of Zoology
Department of Zoology
The University of Alberta, Edmonton

A WILEY-INTERSCIENCE PUBLICATION

JOHN WILEY & SONS
New York • Chichester • Brisbane • Toronto • Singapore

Library of Congress Cataloging in Publication Data:

Nelson, Joseph S.
  Fishes of the world.

  "A Wiley-Interscience publication."
  Bibliography: p.
  Includes index.
  1. Fishes—Classification.   I. Title.

QL618.N4   1984   597'.001'2   83-19684
ISBN 0-471-86475-7

Printed in the United States of America

10 9 8 7

Preface

One purpose dominated the writing of the first edition of this book—to present a modern introductory systematic treatment of all major fish groups. The same objective prevailed in doing the research and writing for this enlarged revision. The acceptance of the previous edition as a guide and reference to fish classification by many teachers for courses in ichthyology or fish biology and by many ichthyologists and other zoologists has been very gratifying. Many important works have been published since the last edition, and we have a better understanding of relationships than we had a decade ago; however, only further work will enable us to judge whether all of our new ideas are advances. To some extent, this greater understanding has led us to conclude that many postulated relationships are not as secure as once thought and that more work is needed to resolve differences in conclusions. In this edition I have made a total revision of the classification in light of recent work, given more references to recent systematic works, listed more genera under the families, enlarged many family descriptions, given more biological and systematic information, and attempted to synthesize more of the differing conclusions of various workers. Many new fish figures have also been included.

The introduction deals in an elementary way with various aspects of fish diversity, systematics, and zoogeography. The lower chordates and fishes are presented in linear order in a manner that would best seem to reflect their postulated evolutionary relationships in a synthetic classification. Alternative schemes of classification in recent literature, primarily cladistic, are referred to often. Evolutionary trends are mentioned for some of the groups. Categories are given down to at least family level and frequently lower. A relatively large number of categories are recognized in order to provide a better presentation of postulated relationships. The categories used, and their endings in parentheses when consistent, are as follows: phylum, subphylum, superclass, grade, subgrade, class, subclass, infraclass, division, subdivision, infradivision, superorder, series, order (*iformes*), suborder (*oidei*), infraorder (*oidea*), superfamily (*oidea*), family (*idae*), subfamily (*inae*), tribe (*ini*), genus, and subgenus. Not all categories are employed within a particular taxon. A dagger denotes those at the level of suborder or higher that do not contain living species. Users who find the number of categories given to be a cumbersome proliferation may wish to use only class, order, suborder, and family (as given in Appendix I).

For each family the most appropriate common name known to me, if any, and a mention of its general range are given. An outline drawing illustrates most of the families, and sometimes more than one is given; it must be remembered, however, that there is much variation in body shape within many of the illustrated groups. A short description is given for most categories; some are inconsistently brief, usually as a consequence of the lack of diagnostic features or my lack of information on them. I have tried to be more consistent in giving information than previously but have also felt it better to explore differing areas of particular interest in a group rather than produce a uniform but limited text. For some families the number of abdominal and caudal vertebrae are given in parentheses after the total vertebral number, for example, 25 (10 + 15). Interesting life-history or biological notes and the maximum length of the largest species are often given. Estimated numbers of recognized (valid) genera and species are given (in some cases the number of species in each genus is also given). These figures are always for living forms, never fossil unless so stated. The degree of agreement by others with these figures will vary from group to group (in part due to the subjective matter of lumping and splitting); for example, everyone would agree that there are but two valid species of described percopsids, but disagreement can be found on whether there is only one gonorynchid, and considerable disagreement would be found on the number of valid described species of gobiids that should be recognized. I have tried to represent current but conservative thinking in arriving at these numbers. I adhere to the biological species concept, although the evolutionary species concept of Wiley (1981:24–25) would be acceptable. I reject any redefinition of a species, however, which would essentially equate it with that of a subspecies or of any other lower recognizable unit. Examples of recognized generic names are given for each family; if the number is relatively small I have tried to list them all. (When this is not done it is usually because there is doubt about which of a number of nominal generic names should be recognized.) In choosing examples of generic names to list for large families I have tried to choose those that represent the following: (1) especially speciose genera, (2) the type of a subfamilial category or that of a nominal family not recognized here, (3) genera whose species exhibit some extreme biological diversity, and (4) genera whose species are commonly found or are important in commercial, sports fishery, or aquarium use. Names preceded by an equal sign and placed in parentheses after a generic name, in what is an unconventional practice, denote a variety of things: junior synonyms (objective or subjective and sometimes regarded as subgenera), junior homonyms, and names found in the literature which have been emended. This is done only when I feel that a name is relatively well known or was used as a valid generic name in the previous edition, and no attempt has been made to recognize all commonly used junior synonyms.

It is assumed that a knowledge of fish anatomy, if not already acquired, will be obtained elsewhere. (In the osteological descriptions I use the terms circumorbital, infraorbital, and suborbital synonymously and the lachrymal is the first bone in the series—i.e., it is synonymous with the first suborbital bone.) I originally hoped to include a section on fish osteology, but this idea has been put aside temporarily at least. The generalized maps in Appendix II are based primarily on the acknowledged sources. Limits are often based on scattered populations of one species. The maps are intended to show basic distributions only and are not necessarily accurate in detail.

Numerous minor and major changes have been made in the classification of the previous edition. For example, the Myxini are recognized as the most primitive fish group, and the Ostariophysi are changed in position and in internal classification. These and many of the other changes do not meet with universal acceptance. In order to keep the book within reasonable length I have not always given reasons for decisions in making changes. However, in preparing this edition I have again attempted to be relatively conservative in making changes while, at the same time, accepting new and often radically different schemes, or parts thereof, within a synthetic framework when they seem to be well founded. (I hasten, however, to beg forgiveness for overlooking or misjudging those references that I ought not to have.) It is very naive to accept the latest proposals as the best in postulating systematic relationships, regardless of the methodology used and even if the study gives sound comparative information. All new proposals should be critically evaluated. It is good to be innovative in doing systematic research but changes in a classification such as this, I feel, should be made only when the evidence for it is relatively strong.

As long as there are active, creative ichthyologists there will be major disagreements in our classification in the foreseeable future (similarly there is disagreement in almost all important fields of biology). Fish classification is in a dynamic state, and the student pursuing ichthyology will find that all groups can be reworked. There are many challenges, both in developing the theory of classification and in its actual practice. Because particular classifications eventually become obsolete (as will most biological information), they should be regarded as frameworks that will provide a basis for building as advances are made. If, however, anyone should question the value of learning a classification, it should be remembered that they are useful vehicles on which to base an understanding of biology. We do not stop using objects or acquiring the present state of knowledge merely because our technical knowledge is going to improve.

The spelling of some names above the generic level has been changed from the previous edition following Steyskal (1980) except for the following: Dasyatidae (vs. Dasyatididae), Carapidae (vs. Carapodidae), Anarhichadidae (vs. Anarhichantidae), and provisionally Grammidae (vs. Grammatidae). The decision to change family names in order to make them grammatically correct according to the stem of the generic name, strictly following the International Code of Zoological Nomenclature, was taken reluctantly. I originally felt it best to continue to use spellings that are in general usage, in the interests of stability, even if they are grammatically incorrect. However, ichthyologists appear to be accepting the spirit of Steyskal's proposals and probably will continue to do so (although some of the same ichthyologists do not accept the code's recommendations regarding the use of the terminal ending of *i* or *ii* in spelling masculine patronyms). I therefore have followed the proposals, except where valid reasons were given to me for not doing so, even when an awkward-sounding name is the result (e.g., Echeneididae). Unfortunately, there continues to be disagreement over various spellings in the modern literature.

It is the eventual hope to produce a standardized common name for each family. This will be achieved in the future with the help of such people as Drs. R. M. Bailey, C. R. Robins, and W. Fischer. In this regard, such publications as "A list of common and scientific names of fishes from the United States and Canada" (Robins et al., 1980) and "FAO species identification sheets for fishery purposes" (edited primarily by W. Fischer) are especially useful.

The ichthyologist is a student of fish systematics. Ichthyology courses may be designed for students interested in ichthyology or fisheries biology as a career and for the general biology student wishing to learn something of those animals who comprise one-half of the species of vertebrates. The laboratories usually demonstrate the diversity of fishes and their probable course of evolution, show systematically important characters, provide insight into how ichthyologists determine which characters to use, and provide training in identification. Stress may be given to the local fish fauna. For this purpose there are many fine regional books. However, it is desirable to have a broad look at fish classification and to place one's local fauna in perspective to all fishes. Depending on the time available, students may, for example, attempt to explain the biological significance of the differences we consider to be systematically important and to learn how morphology determines function and how ways of life can determine morphology. Fishes provide good examples in showing how diverse adaptations to common functions can be brought about by natural selection. Collecting trips, curatorial functions, and special projects (e.g., skeletal preparation and cleaning and staining specimens) may also be involved. The laboratory can be a good place to discuss taxonomic problems as well. The student of ichthyology must be well versed in the methods and theories of systematic biology. An understanding of how systematic relationships are postulated (hypothesized) and knowing the strengths and weaknesses of various approaches so that classification can be critically evaluated are far better than just learning the end results (which are likely to be short-lived). Meetings such as the American Society of Ichthyologists and Herpetologists and the Congress of European Ichthyologists provide excellent forums for learning and exchanging ideas.

JOSEPH S. NELSON

Edmonton, Alberta, Canada
November 1983

Acknowledgments

I am grateful to many individuals who have helped me in various ways with the preparation of this edition. I apologize to those I do not name here.

Much literature and research work was done at the Carl L. Hubbs Library and the Vertebrate Museum at Scripps Institution of Oceanography. I thank Laura Hubbs, Betty Shor, and Dick Rosenblatt, who made my trips to San Diego that much more enjoyable. The friendliness and help received during visits to many other museums, especially that from Bob Carveth, Graham Hardy, and Don McAllister, and, in addition, that from Wayne Roberts of the University of Alberta Museum of Zoology at my own university, are valued. I express my gratitude to the many museum curators and colleagues who have been so patient with overdue loans and collaborative research projects, respectively, while this work was completed. I appreciate the thoughtfulness of researchers from around the world who have kindly sent me reprints of or references to their systematic works. Many have taken time at meetings to discuss their work with me. I shall be thankful to those who send me referenced corrections and materials for future revisions.

I have benefited from comments and information from many individuals, including students and professors. It would be difficult to know where to stop if I attempted to name them (some are mentioned in the text as providing information by personal communication). However, I wish to thank Tyson Roberts, who has been particularly generous with his knowledge of tropical fishes. I would also be remiss not to mention valued discussions over the years with Reeve Bailey, Jack Briggs, Carl Hubbs, Bob Miller, and Donn Rosen. Bruce Collette and Craig Weatherby have given me useful suggestions. I am especially thankful to the following persons who, in addition to being helpful in a variety of ways, have critically read various parts of the manuscript and provided many useful suggestions: Dick Robins, who has been particularly encouraging, Bill Smith-Vaniz, and Vic Springer, who commented on substantial sections on the higher teleosts, Bill Eschmeyer and Stuart Poss on the Scorpaeniformes, Bob McDowall on the galaxioids, Peter Castle on the Anguilliformes, and my Alberta colleagues Dick Fox and Mark Wilson on the last two sections of the Introduction. As is often the case, anonymous reviewers provided many helpful suggestions. I also thank reviewers of the first edition for their corrections. I value the earlier training and continued interest from Peter Larkin, Don McPhail, Tom Northcote (whose darkroom turned on the lights), Ralph Nursall, and Norman Wilimovsky. I feel a special indebtedness to Casimir Lindsey, teacher, scholar, and friend.

I appreciate all those who helped with the various technical aspects of preparing the manuscript. Most of the new figures were prepared by Pauly Wong. The Zoology Department of The University of Alberta generously provided office assistance for which I thank Fu-Shiang Chia and Paul Pearlstone. For dedicated typing of the manuscript I thank Phyllis Miller, Julie Scheinas, Rose Sproule, and most especially Kay Baert, a tremendous person. Assistance with the manuscript was also ably provided at the start by Della Wells and toward the end by Marg Harris and Annemarie Mobach. The staff at John Wiley & Sons have again been extremely helpful and a great pleasure to work with. In particular I thank Mary Conway for all her help, advice, and faith in the book.

Financial support of the National Research Council of Canada, grant #5457, was invaluable, primarily in allowing me to visit research museums and attend ichthyological meetings.

Finally, I thank my wife Claudine and children Brenda, Janice, Mark, and Karen for making it all worthwhile—a work I dedicate to the cherished memory of my parents, Walter Innes Nelson and Mary Elizabeth Nelson (nee Schieser), brothers Walter and Bill, and aunt Anne Sorenson (nee Nelson).

J. S. N.

Contents

Fishes of the World

Introduction

Fish exhibit enormous diversity in their morphology, in the habitats they occupy, and in their biology. Unlike the other commonly recognized vertebrate groups, fish are a heterogeneous assemblage. From lamprey and hagfish to lungfish and flatfish, they include a vast array of distantly related vertebrates. Many are even more closely related to mammals than to certain other fish. Despite this diversity and the dilemma that evolution does not always make definitions easy, fish can be simply defined as aquatic poikilotherm vertebrates that have gills throughout life and limbs,if any, in the shape of fins. The body of information known about them is so vast that their study can include all facets of biology. On the other hand, they are attractive to the researcher because of the wealth of inforation still to be found. The field of ichthyology, the study of fish systematics, is enormously active and exciting. Many controversies exist and ichthyologists are split on fundamental issues on principles of zoogeography and systematics.

NUMBERS

Fishes constitute almost half the total number of vertebrates. An estimated 21,723 living species compared with 21,450 extant tetrapods (a total of about 43,173 recognized vertebrate species) have been described. Other workers, for various reasons, have arrived at different estimates, most of which range between 17,000 and 30,000, for the numbers of currently recognized fish species. The number arrived at here is somewhat larger than Cohen's (1970) 20,600 (mean of his extremes). Some groups are expanding with newly described species, whereas others are decreasing, for species are being synonymized faster than the new ones are described. However, a net increase is shown every year, and the number of new species of fishes described annually exceeds that of the new tetrapods. Bird and mammal species are not likely to rise much above the present 12,600. Amphibians and reptiles may increase significantly (perhaps at a relatively slow rate because herpetologists are far fewer than other vertebrate systematists). The eventual number of extant fish species may be close to 28,000. In contrast to amphibians, reptiles, and mammals, the known diversity of living fishes exceeds that of known fossil taxa. On the other hand, there is a much richer and more informative fossil fish record than is known for birds (even relative to their numbers).

Of the 445 fish families with living species recognized herein, the seven largest contain approximately 30% of the species (some 6411). These families, in order of numbers of species, are Cyprinidae, Gobiidae, Characidae, Cichlidae, Labridae, Loricariidae, and Serranidae. Interestingly, about 63% of the species in the seven largest families are freshwater ones (in contrast, about 39% of all fishes occur in or almost always in fresh water).

In the present classification some 66 families contain only one species, while 57 families have 100 or more species recognized in them, of which two have over 1000. The average number of species per family is 49, whereas the median number is only 10.

In most fish groups it appears that the number of taxa at any one level is not randomly distributed in the taxa at the next highest level within any one group; that is, the majority of lower-level taxa (e.g., species) are found in a relatively few higher-level taxa (e.g., genera) within that particular lineage (e.g., family). This does not seem to be an artifact of the classification, although some workers prefer to split some very speciose groups into groups more equal in size, while others lump monotypic offshoots with the ancestral family. It does not seem to be an artifact of a synthetic versus a cladistic classification either, although the details would vary. This observation, which is also apparent in other vertebrate groups (e.g., *Rana* and *Bufo* contain a disproportionately high number of amphibians as colubrids do for reptiles), may mean that there is a non-random relationship between the amount of diversity and divergence within a lineage. However, it is not clear to me what statistical test would be appropriate in this problem to determine whether or not there actually is randomness in the distribution of taxa; speculating on the biological meaning if it is nonrandom is another matter.

Approximate numbers of recognized extant families, genera, and species in the 50 orders of fishes that contain living representatives. The number of freshwater species is an estimate of the species always or almost always confined to fresh water (or inland lakes, regardless of salinity). It basically includes all species in Darlington's (1957) primary division families, most in his secondary division families, and many in his peripheral division families. It excludes commonly diadromous fishes that may have landlocked populations.

Order	Families	Genera	Species	Freshwater species
Myxiniformes	1	6	32	0
Petromyzontiformes	1	6	41	32
Chimaeriformes	3	6	30	0
Hexanchiformes	2	4	5	0
Heterodontiformes	1	1	8	0
Lamniformes	7	65	239	0
Squaliformes	3	21	87	0
Rajiformes	9	54	424	14
Ceratodontiformes	1	1	1	1
Lepidosireniformes	2	2	5	5
Coelacanthiformes	1	1	1	0
Polypteriformes	1	2	11	11
Acipenseriformes	2	6	25	15
Lepisosteiformes	1	1	7	7
Amiiformes	1	1	1	1
Osteoglossiformes	6	26	206	206
Elopiformes	3	4	11	0
Notacanthiformes	3	6	25	0
Anguilliformes	19	147	597	0
Clupeiformes	4	68	331	26
Gonorynchiformes	4	7	27	25
Cypriniformes	6	256	2,422	2,422
Characiformes	10	252	1,335	1,335
Siluriformes	31	400	2,211	2,155
Gymnotiformes	6	23	55	55
Salmoniformes	15	90	320	95

(*Continued*)

Order	Families	Genera	Species	Freshwater species
Stomiiformes	9	53	248	0
Aulopiformes	12	40	188	0
Myctophiformes	2	35	241	0
Percopsiformes	3	6	9	9
Gadiformes	7	76	414	1
Ophidiiformes	4	86	294	4
Batrachoidiformes	1	19	64	5
Lophiiformes	16	64	265	0
Gobiesociformes	2	36	114	2
Cyprinodontiformes	13	120	845	675
Atheriniformes	5	48	235	85
Lampriformes	11	20	39	0
Beryciformes	14	38	164	0
Zeiformes	6	21	36	0
Gasterosteiformes	3	8	10	2
Indostomiformes	1	1	1	1
Pegasiformes	1	1	5	0
Syngnathiformes	6	63	257	3
Dactylopteriformes	1	4	4	0
Synbranchiformes	1	4	15	11
Scorpaeniformes	20	269	1,160	90
Perciformes	150	1,367	7,791	1,107
Pleuronectiformes	6	117	538	3
Tetraodontiformes	8	92	329	8
Totals	445	4,044	21,723	8,411

Numbers of species of fishes in Canada and the United States as determined from Robins et al. (1980), excluding species introduced into the two countries, occurring in freshwater (FW; the number in parentheses indicates those species found only in fresh water in the area and is given only if not all are normally confined to fresh water); the Atlantic Ocean and eastern Arctic (Atl.); the Pacific Ocean and western Arctic (Pac.); those in both the Atlantic and Pacific Oceans (Atl. and Pac.), whether or not introduced into one from the other; and the total number occurring in the area. Species in the ocean which occur to as deep as the edge of the continental shelf (200 m depth) are included. Species with at least some individuals occurring both in fresh water and in the ocean (e.g., diadromous ones) are included in each of the four habitat categories. The number of fish families (Fam.) represented in the various orders are as recognized in this book.

Order	Fam.	Species				Total
		FW	Atl.	Pac.	Atl. and Pac.	
Myxiniformes	1	0	1	2	0	3
Petromyzontiformes	1	17(13)	1	3	0	17
Chimaeriformes	1	0	0	1	0	1
Hexanchiformes	2	0	1	3	1	3
Heterodontiformes	1	0	0	1	0	1
Lamniformes	7	1(0)	35	26	14	47
Squaliformes	2	0	9	4	1	12
Rajiformes	7	1(0)	30	22	1	51
Acipenseriformes	2	8(4)	2	2	0	8
Lepisosteiformes	1	5	0	0	0	5
Amiiformes	1	1	0	0	0	1
Osteoglossiformes	1	2	0	0	0	2
Elopiformes	2	3	3	2	1	4
Notacanthiformes	1	0	1	0	0	1
Anguilliformes	9	1(0)	60	8	1	67
Clupeiformes	2	11(0)	33	11	3	41
Cypriniformes	2	273	0	0	0	273
Characiformes	1	1	0	0	0	1
Siluriformes	2	40(39)	2	1	0	42
Salmoniformes	7	53(35)	12	21	6	62
Stomiiformes	2	0	0	2	0	2
Aulopiformes	7	0	14	5	2	17
Myctophiformes	1	0	0	9	0	9
Percopsiformes	3	9	0	0	0	9
Gadiformes	3	2(1)	24	7	1	31
Ophidiiformes	3	0	19	4	0	23
Batrachoidiformes	1	0	4	2	0	6
Lophiiformes	6	0	17	3	0	20
Gobiesociformes	1	0	3	6	0	9
Cyprinodontiformes	6	59(44)	41	12	3	94
Atheriniformes	1	3(2)	7	3	0	12
Lampriformes	5	0	8	7	4	11
Beryciformes	2	0	12	0	0	12
Zeiformes	3	0	5	1	0	6
Gasterosteiformes	2	4(1)	4	3	2	6
Syngnathiformes	4	1(0)	27	8	1	34
Dactylopteriformes	1	0	1	0	0	1

(Continued)

Order	Fam.	Species				
		FW	Atl.	Pac.	Atl. and Pac.	Total
Scorpaeniformes	8	28(23)	73	205	11	290
Perciformes	72	235(168)	511	223	36	866
Pleuronectiformes	4	4(0)	55	32	1	86
Tetraodontiformes	6	0	42	12	6	48
Totals	194	762(621)	1057	651	95	2234

IMPORTANCE TO PEOPLE

Fishes, like many other forms of life, are of immense value to mankind. They have long been a staple item in the diet of many peoples. Today they form an important element in the economy of many nations while giving incalculable recreational and psychological value to the naturalist, sports enthusiast, and home aquarist. They are also the subject of international and domestic agreements and disagreements. Adverse effects (e.g., from poisonous and man-eating species) are of immense concern in some areas. Many government institutions are devoted to the study of their biology and propagation. Particular aspects of phenomena of various species have lent themselves to studies in behavior, ecology, evolution, genetics, and physiology. They are used as general indicators or summators of pollution, partly to the direct benefit of mankind and partly to protect what people consider a valuable and necessary part of their heritage and life. We consider it desirable to maintain the diversity that the systematist studies.

BIOLOGICAL DIVERSITY

The diversity in fish behavior is as great as in their morphology. Some species travel in schools, others are highly territorial, some exhibit parental care for their offspring, and others scatter millions of eggs to the hazards of predation. Interesting commensal relationships exist with other fish and other animals. Fish are adapted to a wide variety of foods. Some are specialized or highly adapted to feed on plants, zooplankton, or coral. Almost all classes of animal can serve as food. A few species are parasitic on other species or on the female of their own. Some produce venom, electricity, sound, or light, and a few are known to be hermaphrodites or to exhibit sex reversal. Fish in all types of aquatic environment may migrate phenomenal distances, a field rich in research on homing mechanisms. The larvae and early juveniles of some oceanic species (e.g., the many flyingfishes and the dolphins) regularly inhabit shore waters, whereas the larvae of many shore fishes inhabit oceanic waters. In fresh water, *Oncorhynchus keta* and *O. tshawytscha* migrate 3000 km up the Yukon River to their spawning grounds without feeding. Many other fish are known to live out their lives in very restricted areas.

HABITAT DIVERSITY

Fishes live in almost every conceivable type of aquatic habitat. They are found in South America's Lake Titicaca, the world's highest large lake (3812 m), where a group of cyprinodontids have undergone much radiation, in Lake Baikal, the world's deepest (at least 1000 m), and 7000 m below the surface of the ocean. Some species live in almost pure fresh water of 0.01‰ (parts per thousand) total dissolved solids (most lakes are between 0.05 and 1‰) or in very salty lakes of 100‰ (ocean water is close to 35‰). They may be confined to total darkness in caves, or as in Tibet, China, and India, to fast torrential streams. In Africa a *Tilapia* occurs in hot soda lakes which have temperatures as high as 44°C, whereas under the Antarctic ice sheet *Trematomus* lives at about −2°C. Many species have acquired air-breathing organs and find a living in stagnant, tropical swamps; others demand well-oxygenated waters to sustain life. An individual species may tolerate a wide range of temperatures, in which case it is said to eurythermal, or a narrow range (stenothermal). Similarly, it may tolerate a wide range of salinity (euryhaline) or only a narrow range (stenohaline). Recently, new fish species have been taken near unlighted hot-water volcanic vents in the eastern Pacific Ocean.

MORPHOLOGICAL DIVERSITY

Fishes range in size from the recently found 8–10 mm adult goby in the Indian Ocean to the giant 15 m whale shark. They have stringlike to ballshaped bodies. Some species are brilliantly colored; others are drab (e.g., see Burgess and Axelrod, 1972–1976). Some are sleek and graceful, moving with little resistance through the water (which is 800 times denser than air); others are described by the general public as ugly and grotesque, their livelihood not depending on speed.

About 50 species of teleosts lack eyes (mostly cyprinids, siluriforms, amblyopsids, bythitids, and gobiids). Scales may be present or absent in closely related species. Fins may be missing (particularly the pelvic fins, especially in eellike, burrowing species and some teleosts lack the pelvic and pectoral fins and scales) or be highly modified into holdfast organs or as a lure for attracting prey. Their bodies may be inflatable or encased in inflexible bony armor. Internal anatomical diversity in hard and soft parts is also enormous. Many bizarre specializations exist. Some insight into morphological diversity will be found throughout the text.

CLASSIFICATION AND SYSTEMATICS

Classification is the practice of arranging items into groups or categories, and a classification is the arrangement which results. Taxa (singular taxon) are groups of organisms recognized in a classification and given biological names (e.g., Salmoniformes, Salmonidae, and *Oncorhynchus*). A category is the level or rank at which the taxon is placed (e.g., order, family, and genus). The objective in constructing a classification of a group of organisms is generally agreed to be to show in a hierarchical system the relationships of the various taxa. We may agree that the kind of relationship we wish to show, as best we can in a listing of names, is an evolutionary one. However, there are differences of opinion as to what evolutionary relationship means and how it should be determined, and there are also different ways of expressing evolutionary relationships or phylogeny in a classification. On a broad level, one way is to base a classification entirely on genealogical branching points. Another, as is attempted in this book, is to consider also degrees of divergence.

The fundamental unit in a biological classification is that of the species and those involved with constructing classifications must deal with species definitions. I adhere to the biological species concept (Mayr, 1969) and regard the species as the only taxonomic unit with evolutionary reality. A classification can also include subspecies. However, the following discussion is confined to classification above the species level. The science of systematics is the study of the diversity of organisms in order to understand their relationships, and biological classification is based on systematic studies. Taxonomy can be regarded as that part of systematics dealing with the theory and practice of describing diversity and erecting classifications.

The study of fish systematics, ichthyology in the limited sense of the word, has had a long and interesting history; its makers have often been dynamic figures. The history of Canadian and American ichthyology is reviewed by J. R. Dymond, G. S. Myers, and C. L. Hubbs in *Copeia* for 1964 (No. 1). Throughout the history of ichthyology numerous classifications of fishes have been proposed (e.g., see Patterson, 1977). Recent ones have been built on the studies of many past biologists (e.g., G. Cuvier, A. Valenciennes, T. N. Gill, B. A. Boulenger, A. Günther, D. S. Jordan, and C. T. Regan). Contemporary ichthyologists, such as P. H. Greenwood and D. E. Rosen, continue to make important contributions; the field is nevertheless rich in problems for future research.

During the past few decades there has been an impressive accumulation of descriptive information on extant and fossil material and the development of many new concepts applicable to fish systematics. More work is needed before a sound understanding is reached of how evolution has produced the diversity of fishes that exists. Although there is general agreement on many aspects of fish classification there is also much disagreement. This is true even among those following the same philosophical approach to classification. Numerous families of fishes are very poorly classified.

Students of ichthyology should know the principles of the major approaches to classification. These are the cladistic (=phylogenetic) and the synthetic (=evolutionary) approaches, both of which have various modifications. I prefer the terms cladistic, as opposed to phylogenetic, and synthetic, as opposed to evolutionary, because these terms seem appropriately descriptive and because in both one attempts to construct phylogenies with the intent of showing evolutionary history. Thus both are phylogenetic and evolutionary in the usual senses of the words (contrary to what proponents of each may claim of the other, or define words so as to exclude the other). Both cladistics and synthetics have been undergoing significant changes since the early 1970s, when they became widely used in ichthyology, and, especially in cladistics, new methodologies are continuing to be developed. The synthetic approach is the older of the two, although most ichthyologists undertaking revisionary work employ a cladistic methodology. A third approach, phenetics or numerical classification, is not as important in classification above the level of species or genus although it does have useful applications at lower levels. Many works discuss the different approaches (e.g., Ball, 1981; Mayr, 1969, 1981; Nelson and Platnick, 1981; Schultze, 1981; Wiley, 1981).

In simple terms, the cladistic method seeks to resolve which two taxa of a group of three or more are each other's closest genealogical relatives. A dichotomously branching cladogram (diagram) is constructed in which paired lineages, called sister groups, are recognized on the basis of sharing derived character states (termed synapomorphies in cladistics, with a particular derived character state being termed apomorphic; plesiomorphies are the primitive states and do not indicate the existence of sister groups). The sister group possessing more apomorphic character states relative to the other is the derived group, while the other is the primitive one; each is given the same taxonomic rank. A common source of disagreement is over which character states are apomorphic; consequently, a good understanding of character-state distribution is essential to a cladistic analysis. As with any approach, care must be taken that characters are not arbitrarily chosen or their states arbitrarily polarized, consciously or subconsciously, for the express purpose of either producing a change in existing classification or supporting preconceived ideas of relationships (perhaps to provide systematic evidence to support a favored zoogeographic hypothesis). In a cladistic analysis there is usually a clear presentation of the characters and character states employed (but, unfortunately for those wishing to appraise the work, characters discarded from analysis are usually not given). Polarity of morphoclines or of character states is usually determined by reference to what is called the outgroup (the nearest presumed related taxon—a character state widely distributed in related taxa is often taken to be primitive) with the group under consideration being called the in-group. Cladists often argue that their approach is more scientific than the synthetic approach in that they claim to be erecting testable or falsifiable hypotheses employing powerful techniques. The issue, I think, is more complicated than that. However, followers of the synthetic school now generally agree that only shared derived character states should be used in determining branching points for a phylogeny.

In some cladistic studies, new classifications are constructed on the basis of only a few presumed synapomorphies which are small osteological differences. In addition, often not all species are examined, resulting in a poor knowledge of character distribution. Such practices are not likely to produce a sound evolutionary classification (certainly not a utilitarian one), any more so than is a synthetic study based on ill-chosen characters or a phenetic study based on overall similarity. Apart from methodological problems or problems resulting from poor practice, there appears in some groups to be such a mosaic of character states of uncertain polarity that I suspect a good cladistic analysis may be more difficult to carry out than is commonly acknowledged. Carroll (1982) and Halstead (1982) give some serious criticisms of cladistic methodology and practice. However, cladistics has many strengths and has brought about many advances in the way in which we do systematics. For a good review of its procedures, I recommend the work of Wiley (1981), one of its advocates.

Perhaps the major inherent difference between cladistics and synthetics is in how a phylogeny is translated into a classification. In cladistics the classification is based solely on the hypothesized genealogical relations such that one is faithfully derivable from the other. Each taxon is strictly monophyletic or holophyletic, in that all groups sharing a common ancestry and only those groups, including the common ancestor itself, are included in the taxon. In contrast, in the synthetic school the classification is based on a synthesis of knowledge concerning both the genealogical relationships and the perceived degree of evolutionary or genetic similarity or divergence from other groups. Taxa may be holophyletic or paraphyletic (i.e., not all derivative groups are included in the taxon), but, of course, should never be polyphyletic (i.e., all members included within the taxon must share a common evolutionary origin). This has the advantage that one can recognize common levels of similarity but has the disadvantage that one cannot reconstruct the phylogeny directly from the classification. As well, not demanding that only holophyletic groups be recognized results in a loss of information for certain kinds of evolutionary or zoogeographical studies. In the synthetic school there is variation in the extent to which workers classify related groups together which through parallel evolution have achieved a common level or grade of evolution. The choice in these circumstances is therefore between adapting a so-called horizontal classification and recognizing grades of evolution as taxa or a vertical classification, which tends to be more similar to a cladistic classification although it may still involve paraphyly. Most workers would not consider taxa that represent only grade evolution to be fully acceptable in a synthetic classification.

I adhere to the synthetic school of classification and rely on annotated comments to indicate phylogenetic relations (or sister group relations). I believe that it is desirable to recognize degrees of divergence in classification and that employing inferences about divergence is no less valid than employing inferences about sister group relations. When accompanied by annotated comments or diagrams there is no loss of information. Many parts of the classification given here are more similar to a cladistic classification than to past ones based on synthetics (in part because when a choice must be made I tend to favor a vertical classification). I regard cladistic methodology as basically sound for determining relative phylogenetic branching points. The results of a cladistic analysis are highly compatible with synthetics; differences need only arise in the classification when we find what are perceived to be marked degrees of evolutionary divergence. Indeed, most of the changes in this classification are based on cladistic studies. For example, *Alabes* is removed from the synbranchiforms and aligned with the gobiesocids on the basis of a cladistic analysis. However, it is not combined with the gobiesocids as would be required in a cladistic classification and could be done in a synthetic system with a higher degree of lumping than I have chosen to employ.

Mormyroids are placed in a separate suborder from notopterids and hiodontids even though, cladistically, notopterids and mormyroids are sister groups; hiodontids and notopterids are placed in a suborder to the exclusion of mormyroids and would be whether or not the latter ever evolved. The butterfly fish, *Pantodon buchholzi*, is placed in a separate family from the Osteoglossidae even though one of the subfamilies of the latter, the Osteoglossinae, and *Pantodon* are probably sister groups. Similarly, should a known perciform group be identified as the sister group of pleuronectiforms it would not necessarily be removed from the perciforms. As has classically been done, sequencing is used to reflect primitive to derived relationships; however, this is not always possible (e.g., tetraodontiforms do not immediately follow their presumed ancestral group, the acanthuroids).

I consider fossils to be critical in understanding evolutionary relationships. Unfortunately, the fossil record in fishes is very incomplete and many decisions must be made without any evidence from fossils. However, I believe that many critical questions of interrelationship of higher categories will be answered only with a study of new fossils and not, conclusively at least, of extant material. Fossils are ranked along with extant taxa in the following classification. However, in order to avoid problems inherent in cladistics as it is generally practiced, where new fossil finds and new information on known fossils can require a restructuring of a cladistic classification, Patterson and Rosen (1977) have proposed, as a convention, that fossils not be ranked with extant material but that they be placed in sequenced groups called plesions within a classification. The position of plesions can be changed without altering the rank of taxa containing extant material.

DISTRIBUTION AND ZOOGEOGRAPHY

Fishes occur in lakes, streams, estuaries, and oceans throughout the world. In most species of fishes all individuals live entirely either in fresh or in marine waters. A few are diadromous, regularly living part of their lives in fresh water and part in the oceans. Among these most are anadromous, spawning in fresh water but spending much of their time in the sea. A few are catadromous, spawning in the oceans but returning to fresh water. Classification as marine, diadromous, estuarine, or freshwater is impossible, except as a generalization, for some species. Just as in an otherwise marine family there may be one species confined to fresh water so in some species there are populations that occur in an environment opposite to that of most of the others. Individuals of some otherwise marine species ascend rivers for short distances in part of their range, and those of some species that are usually freshwater are anadromous in some areas. Many freshwater and marine species are also common in brackishwater estuaries. Well over one-third of the 445 families have at least one species with individuals that live at least part of their life in fresh water. Berra (1981) gives distribution maps for the major freshwater fish families. About 8411 species or about 39% of all species normally live in the freshwater lakes and rivers that cover only about 1% of the earth's surface and account for a little less than 0.01% of its water (the mean depth of the lakes is only a few meters). About 13,160 usually live all their lives in the oceans, which cover about 70% of the earth's surface, account for 97% of its water, and have a mean depth of about 3700 m.

Many environmental factors influence just where a certain species will predominate. Competition and other biological interactions may exert a strong influence along with physicochemical factors. In freshwater environments species may show a preference for lakes or streams and variation may exist in this over the range of a species. Between lakes they may show a preference for deep, cold, oligotrophic lakes or for shallower, warmer, and more productive eutrophic lakes. In lake waters they may show a preference (horizontal and vertical) for the open-water limnetic zone, the benthic area, or shallow littoral areas. They may even be restricted to certain types of bottom or do best under certain physicochemical conditions. Stream fishes may prefer riffle or quiet areas, and a zonation of species is usually found from the headwaters to the mouth. In the oceans the vast majority of fishes, perhaps 10,200 species in all, are coastal or littoral. Most of those living beyond the 200 m deep continental shelf (oceanic species) are deep-sea (mesopelagic, bathypelagic, abyssopelagic, or benthic at various depths) and number about 2700; only a small minority, perhaps 250, regularly live close to the surface in the well-lighted upper 200 m zone (epipelagic), a region much larger in volume than the coastal waters. The epipelagic and mesopelagic fishes, which consist of both large predators and small plankton feeders, are varied, whereas most of the bathypelagic and abyssal fishes are relatively small.

Many species, both geologically young and old, have small ranges; the smallest is perhaps that of the Devils Hole pupfish, *Cyprinodon diabolis*, found only in one spring in Nevada. Many areas have a high degree of endemism. Marine fish have the obvious land (notably the New and Old World land masses) and mid-ocean barriers as well as many ecological and physiological barriers; freshwater species are limited by marine and land barriers. Some species have remarkably large ranges, and it would be interesting to know why some of their relatives have small ranges.

About 110 marine species extend around the world in tropical or subtropical waters. Many genera are represented in both the Pacific and Atlantic but, almost always, different species are involved. Representatives of many marine genera occur in the temperate and polar faunas of both hemispheres. Some are surface-bound, others are deep-water. This complete equatorial discontinuity or bipolarity has been termed antitropicality by Hubbs (1952). The vast majority of genera, however, are tropical; most of the rest occur either in the Northern or the Southern Hemisphere. We know little of the abyssal depths and their species composition. Many abyssal species have been found at widely separated localities, which suggests that some may be virtually worldwide. No freshwater species is circumtropical, but two species, *Esox lucius* and *Lota lota,* are circumpolar and several others are almost so. No genus of freshwater fish has an antitropical distribution. Many freshwater fishes have shown a remarkable ability to disperse across newly exposed land areas following glaciation. In addition, they may occur in isolated waters in deserts as a result of a reduction in range with reduction of waters from times when drainage systems were connected.

In both fresh and marine waters the largest number of species occurs in the tropics and there is a reduction toward the polar areas, although numbers of individuals in certain northern species are large. A great many species of freshwater fishes occur in southeastern Asia, and the Amazon, the world's largest river, has almost as many (at least 1500). Gilbert (1976) estimates that there are 950 species in fresh water in North America, 2200 in South America, 250 in Europe, 1800 in Africa, 1500 in Asia, and 230 in Australia. I think that the Asian figure should be much higher, while the Australian figure, according to McDowall (1981), should be closer to 170, with most of the species being marine derivatives. In contrast, New Zealand has only about 27 species native to its fresh waters and the majority of these are diadromous and all are closely related to marine or diadromous species (in contrast, probably over 600 marine species occur in the upper 500 m of the contiguous shelf region, the ratio of freshwater to marine species being far different from that found, for example, in North and South America). For a tropical region, Central America has relatively few freshwater species because of the physiography and geological history of the area. There are nearly 500 species recorded from fresh or nearly fresh water and only 354 primary and secondary division freshwater species (Miller, 1982). Most oceanic islands lack indigenous fishes confined to fresh water, and continental areas recently exposed from the last ice age tend to have a relatively sparse fish fauna, for example, northern regions of North America, Europe (especially western Europe), and Asia. In tropical areas, Africa exhibits the most diversity of nonostariophysan freshwater fishes; South America exhibits surprisingly little. In temperate areas, eastern North America shows the greatest diversity in nonostariophysan fishes. In marine waters, the Indo-West Pacific (Red Sea and Indian Ocean to northern Australia and Polynesia) is the richest, the most species occurring in the New Guinea to Queensland area. In terms of diversity, southeast Africa and Queensland appear to have the largest number of families of marine shorefishes (Springer, 1982). The West Indian or Caribbean fauna (southern Florida to northern Brazil) is also a rich one. The west African fauna, however, is relatively poor. Arctic and Antarctic faunas are depauperate. In all, then, the greatest number of fish species in the world inhabit the southeastern Asian region. An account of the various zoogeographic regions may be found in Briggs (1974) and Moyle and Cech (1982).

In the science of zoogeography we attempt to document the geographic distribution of animal taxa (descriptive zoogeography) and to explain their distributional patterns (interpretive zoogeography). It is an active field of study in ichthyology and is rich in problems. There are two extreme approaches to interpretive zoogeography. First, ecological zoogeography attempts to determine the environmental factors limiting the distribution of individuals of a species within a body of water or over the range of the species, such as oxygen concentration, temperature, silt, salinity, currents, and competition. Second, historical zoogeography attempts to explain the origin of distributional patterns and is usually done in conjunction with, and is based upon, systematic studies. Of course, presumed paleoclimatic changes, etc., are often invoked in historical zoogeography, especially when postulating that discontinuous distributions result from dispersal events. Aspects of both ecological and historical zoogeography, combined with a knowledge of geology, geography, and systematics (usually at below the species level), has the attention of many ichthyologists in studies such as that of species dispersal following glaciation (e.g., in northern Eurasia, North America, and New Zealand), or uplift of land from the ocean (e.g., Central America), or of dispersal through drainages submerged following glaciation (e.g., Indonesia). Ecological as well as historical factors must also be considered in studies of higher taxa that attempt to understand the reasons for complementary distributions [the occurrence in different areas of dominant, ecologically equivalent, and presumably competing groups; see Darlington (1957)].

There is much controversy in methodological and philosophical approach in explaining the origin of distributional patterns of fishes, as well as that of all animals and plants. Disagreement exists over the importance of such things as centers of origin and areas of endemism in

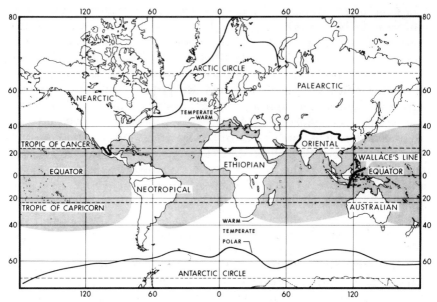

Commonly recognized zoogeographical regions of the continents (based on work of A.R. Wallace) and broad thermal zones of the ocean. The zoogeographical regions are useful summators of numbers and proportion of endemic organisms and help in understanding the evolutionary and geographic history of a group. The Nearctic and Palearctic are frequently combined into one region, the Holarctic. The thermal divisions of the sea denote warm water, temperate water, and polar water regions (based on part of a figure given in Hesse, Allee, and Schmidt, 1951). Zoogeographic regions, which express degrees of endemism, are also recognized in the oceans (e.g., Indo-West Pacific, tropical western Atlantic, tropical eastern Atlantic, North Pacific, North Atlantic, Mediterranean–East Atlantic). As in continental zoogeographic regions, marine oceans share different similarities with one another; for example, in many families the tropical eastern Pacific shows a greater resemblance to the western Atlantic than to the Indo-West Pacific because of the mid-Pacific barrier and the relatively recent marine connection across the Isthmus of Panama (see Briggs, 1974 for details and Springer, 1982, for an approach relating distribution to lithospheric plates).

understanding distributional patterns. The major source of controversy, however, concerns the relative importance of dispersal versus vicariant events, and in ichthyology this topic has been hotly debated since the early 1970s. Therefore, within historical zoogeography, there is that which can be broadly recognized as the classical dispersal school and the newer vicariant school. Dispersal is regarded here as the movement, active or passive, of individuals to areas new to the existing population of the individuals. Barriers of varying effectiveness may be involved as well as varying degrees of chance for reaching particular sites. It is of greatest zoogeographic significance if the breeding range of the species as it exists at that point of time is increased. Vicariance is the fragmentation of a former continuous distribution of the ancestral group into geographically separated units through the appearance of a barrier—a classic example is the appearance of a barrier as a result of plate tectonics. Both dispersal and vicariant approaches are used to explain disjunct distributions (the occurrence of a taxon in different areas with a marked geographical gap between them). Examples of disjunct distributions include the following: occurrence of *Prosopium coulteri* in western North America and in Lake Superior; *Geotria australis* and *Galaxias maculatus* in Australia, New Zealand, and South America; both cottids and agonids in cool temperate waters of the Northern and Southern hemispheres; characids in Africa and South America; and salmonoids in temperate waters of the Northern and Southern hemispheres.

In dispersal zoogeography, distributional patterns are postulated to be largely the result of dispersal events and each taxon is generally postulated to have had an identifiable center of origin, in theory at least [e.g., Darlington (1957), Briggs (1974), McDowall (1978a), and Hennig (1966)]. Differing generalities exist regarding centers of origin. The classical Matthew-Simpson-Darlington-Briggs group believes that recently evolved and competitively superior species usually arise in the center of origin of the taxon while primitive species occur in the periphery. Its followers generally employ the synthetic approach to systematics but the two are not tied together in principles; the cladistic approach could well be adopted. The Hennig group employs cladistics and postulates that primitive species generally occur at the center of origin.

The vicariant approach as practiced by many ichthyologists is a variable combination of the generalized track panbiogeographic method of Leon Croizat [e.g., Croizat (1982), which also gives a revealing insight into humanistic problems occurring during the development of the various approaches] and cladistics. Disjunct distributions are postulated to be the result of fragmentation of former continuous distributions and to be causally related to sister-group relationships [e.g., Nelson and Platnick (1981), Rosen (1975, 1978), and Wiley (1976, 1981)]. This new approach is undergoing much development. As an example of an interesting and innovative study, Springer (1982) examines many patterns of distribution of shore fishes in oceanic islands on and adjacent to the Pacific Plate and explores various vicariant explanations. He suggests that postulated vicariant events can be tested by determining if the postulated geological and oceanographic patterns of events fits cladistic patterns of relationships among the organisms concerned.

Although not readily apparent, there has been a certain amount of coming together of the dispersal and vicariant approaches since the early 1970s. For example, many ichthyologists adhering to the dispersal school recognize that plate tectonics had profound effects on the distribution of freshwater and marine fishes (e.g., it probably explains the occurrence of characins in South America and Africa—interestingly, this was advocated by some ichthyologists even when geologists believed the continents to be stable). Future workers in the dispersal school will probably develop more of a rigorous approach to their work as a result of criticism from vicariant zoogeographers. Alternatively, in the vicariant school, unlike at first with some workers, dispersal events are acknowledged as occurring if not of being of some importance [e.g., Wiley (1976) and Rosen (1978)].

I believe that distributional patterns are the result of both dispersal and vicariant events, with some individual disjunct distributions having components of both dispersal and vicariance. We must, despite the existence of common patterns, deal with each case, at least at first, on its own merits (this includes a consideration of fossils). Uncritical works exist in both schools and is not an inherent problem with the dispersal school. It is not clear why the occurrence of organisms with differing abilities of movement on South Sea islands (especially volcanic ones), for example, must be explained by vicariance and could be explained by dispersal, but with differing details [see Nelson and Platnick (1981: 46–59) and Wiley (1981) for a discussion of testing hypotheses of dispersal versus vicariance]. Perhaps, in the case of similarities between, for example, Australia and New Zealand, both dispersal and vicariant events were important. Surely it is absurd to believe that all disjunct distributions must be similarly explained despite the claim that only the vicariant school can erect falsifiable hypotheses and therefore qualify as science. The view that the common occurrence of *Geotria australis* or *Galaxias maculatus* (both with a marine form) in Australia, New Zealand, and South America (and on some small islands in the case of the latter species) dates back to the breakup of Gondwanaland and is a more parsimonious hypothesis than that of dispersal by existing ocean currents seems untenable. Dispersal in this case may not be falsifiable (and I doubt if the fish were concerned with this), but it seems to me to be the most reasonable explanation for their distribution.

Semantic problems play a part in the controversy between the dispersal and vicariant schools and one must be aware of how terms are defined. The term dispersal, for example, is regarded by Nelson and Platnick (1981:46) as only movement across a barrier resulting in immediate isolation, as opposed to enlargement of range prior to the appearance of a barrier. Colonization of a new area with the subsequent appearance of a barrier is considered to be a vicariant event, the distinction between dispersal and vicariance being made on the relative timing of movement of the organism, appearance of a barrier, and subsequent disjunction. However, barriers are not all-or-nothing entities, and I see no reason to insist that the barrier be so complete that speciation is the inevitable consequence, apart from defining the term dispersal to give it limited importance. According to the above definition there could be two ways to explain the distribution of *Galaxias maculatus* in nondispersal terms. One would be, as noted, to postulate that the distribution dates back to a breakup of Gondwanaland while the other would be to argue that it is a more recent event with movement of larvae by currents across the ocean in the absence of effective barriers. A change in ocean currents preventing further movement, like a continental ice sheet splitting a species' range into two, would result in a vicariant event. Surely the first biologically important question from a zoogeographic perspective concerns whether the distribution of the species resulted from modification or movement of the habitat (i.e., continental drift in the case of the galaxiid) or from movement of individuals from one area to another. If allopatric speciation results, then effective barriers to gene flow would have to have come into play anywhere from the geographic origin of the parental stock to the final site. I see no comparable biological difference relative to zoogeography between a species reaching a new area with barriers being completely absent and breeding occurring along the way (which, however, could not be the case with *Galaxias*) and the same area being reached by highly improbable crossings being successful in enough individuals to establish a population over a long time period. Ultimately the zoogeographer must study the biology of the situation without arguing for one extreme view or the other.

How to demonstrate that dispersal has not been a historical event in a given case and how to decide if correlations between cladistic and geological events are necessarily causal will probably continue to be unresolved. Future workers in the exuberance of exploring the new vicariant methodology must guard against the temptation of placing so much faith in a causal (rather than only a congruent) relationship between vicariant events and evolution that geological events unknown to geologists are postulated on the basis of a particular cladogram. Alternatively, care must be exercised that vicariant events are not first conceived and phylogenetic relationships interpreted accordingly (at least without a disclosure that this was the case).

Students should read widely on the subject and avoid becoming mentally locked into only the dispersal or the vicariant school. Both approaches and their assumptions, which were not discussed here, should be understood and both must be considered in doing good zoogeography. Some followers of vicariance have claimed that it represents the modern view which has overturned authoritarianism and dogma of the classical dispersal school. The danger is that one dogma, if it was that, can be prematurely replaced by another. References to the subject of zoogeography with differing viewpoints include Briggs (1974), Croizat (1982), Croizat et al. (1974), McDowall (1978a, 1980), Nelson and Platnick (1981), Rosen (1975, 1978), Springer (1982), Wiley (1981, Chapter 8), and numerous recent papers in the journal *Systematic Zoology*. The fields of systematics and zoogeography are attracting much exciting activity. There is every reason to believe that future ichthyologists will keep the field alive and we will achieve a stronger understanding than presently available of relationships and explanations of distributional patterns.

Phylum Chordata

The phylum Chordata has been used by most workers to encompass members of the subphyla Hemichordata (acorn worms), Urochordata (tunicates or sea-squirts), Cephalochordata (lancelets), and Vertebrata (fishes, amphibians, reptiles, birds, and mammals). The first three are commonly called the protochordates. On the basis of Jefferies' (1968, 1981a) work, the subphylum Calcichordata, known only from fossils, is included here in the Chordata. The five groups are thought to have shared a general common ancestry from, or at least with, the echinoderms.

As is true for many groups, a great deal of disagreement exists concerning the interrelationships and classification of the Chordata and its subphyla. The Pogonophora and Conodontophorida, included in the first edition of this book, are no longer thought to have chordate affinities. The Hemichordata should perhaps also be removed and they are excluded from Chordata by some authors (e.g., Barrington, 1965; Jefferies, 1981b). In accepting that calcichordates are chordates, Jefferies (1981b) concludes that similarities between echinoderms and calcichordates which are lacking in hemichordates suggest that echinoderms and chordates are more closely related to each other than either is to the hemichordates. He combines the former two into a group of higher rank termed the Dexiothetica to the exclusion of hemichordates.

21

Despite agreement by most recent workers that chordates had an echinoderm ancestry (e.g., Bone, 1960; Tarlo, 1960; Dillion, 1965; Romer, 1970; Denison, 1971a; Jefferies, 1981b), some authors believe there is evidence which contradicts our classical echinoderm–chordate scheme and supports or may support other groups (i.e., mollusks, arthropods, and nemertines) as being the ancestral group (e.g., Sillman, 1960; Jensen, 1963; Willmer, 1974, 1975; Løvtrup, 1977). These groups, along with others, also had their supporters in the last century as chordate ancestors. As at any level in taxonomic categories, evidence, both morphological and nonmorphological, is interpreted in many ways when critically examined. It is part of the scientific spirit to keep challenging our viewpoints; as Kerkut (1960) makes clear, we have often been naive in our outlook. However, the echinoderm–chordate theory seems to be the best founded view; attempts to demonstrate the contrary on biochemical grounds or otherwise are less secure than are attempts to demonstrate an echinoderm–chordate relationship. Chordates, echinoderms, and perhaps chaetognaths (arrow worms) may be placed in the superphylum Deuterostomia.

†SUBPHYLUM CALCICHORDATA (Class Stylophora, Class Caroidea)

Calcichordates are interpreted to be a primitive chordate with strong echinoderm affinities [placed by many in the phylum Echinodermata (Denison, 1971a)] and believed to be ancestral to all other chordate groups by Jefferies (1968, 1981a) and Jefferies and Prokop (1972). Eaton (1970) agrees with Jefferies that they are closer to chordates than to echinoderms and further believes that ostracoderms probably arose from certain mitrates in perhaps the early Ordovician. (This time must be pushed back because what are thought to be fossil agnathans are now known from the Late Cambrian and primitive urochordates or cephalochordates, and myxines might be involved in such a transition. Unfortunately, only cornutes and not the more vertebratelike mitrates are known from the Cambrian.) Some workers believe that calcichordates are aberrant echinoderms and not ancestral to chordates (e.g., Jollie, 1982a). Despite Jefferies' (1981a) defense of his calcichordate–chordate hypothesis, the criticisms of Jollie (1982a) leave it as being very questionable and it is only provisionally accepted here.

Calcichordates are thought to have had functional gill slits and, like echinoderms, a calcite skeleton (presumably their skeleton was lost before the phosphate skeleton of vertebrates was acquired). Jefferies (1981b) speculates that both mitrates and myxines possibly had an adenohypophysis of endodermal origin in contrast to vertebrates other than myxines, where it is of ectodermal origin (being derived from the roof of the stomodeum). Jefferies (1981a,b) gives a detailed discussion of possible homologies in the various groups thought to be ancestral to the higher chordates. The subphylum contains two orders, Cornuta and Mitrata, and is known from Cambrian to Devonian times.

SUBPHYLUM HEMICHORDATA

Hemichordates possess pharyngeal gill openings (absent in *Rhabdopleura*) but lack an endostyle (homologous with the thyroid gland) and notochord. When the embryology is known, they are clearly deuterostomes (the anus develops from the blastopore and the mouth represents a new opening; the coelom is enterocoelic). Some workers prefer to recognize hemichordates as a separate phylum because of the differences with other chordates but they are retained here simply to express the view (hypothesis) that they have closer affinities with the chordates than with any other group. Their classification is provisional.

The biology of living forms is reviewed by Barrington (1965).

Five classes, two of which are known only as fossils, and about 85 living species.

†Class GRAPTOLITHINA (Graptolites)

Cambrian to Mississippian forms, which, according to Kozlowski (1966) and Bulman (1970), are related to the pterobranchs. Graptolites were colonial, marine organisms which secreted a sclerotized exoskeleton with characteristic growth bands. There were both sessile and pelagic forms. Bulman (1970) recognizes six orders: the sessile Upper Cambrian-Mississippian Dendroidea; the sessile Upper Cambrian-Silurian Tuboidea; the encrusting Ordovician Camaroidea; the encrusting Ordovician Crustoidea; the sessile or encrusting Ordovician Stolonoidea; and the planktonic Ordovician-Lower Devonian Graptoloidea.

†Class ACANTHASTIDA

Colonial, sessile Lower Ordovician forms up to 5 mm in diameter; their upper surface is convex and bears long spines; thought to be related to the graptolites (Kozlowski, 1966; Bulman, 1970:138). This group, based on the only known genus *Acanthastus*, was described by R. Kozlowski in 1949.

Class PLANCTOSPHAEROIDEA

Based on two specimens taken in the Bay of Biscay and described in 1936 (Bulman, 1970:17). *Planctosphaera* may be the larvae of an unknown type of hemichordate.

Class ENTEROPNEUSTA (Acorn Worms)

Wormshaped marine animals with a proboscis, collar, and trunk which live mostly in burrows in shallow waters. They possess gill slits and a dorsal nerve cord (with a primitive nerve net lying within the epidermis) and have a microscopic ciliated tornaria larvae which has many echinoderm characteristics. Acorn worms lack an external skeleton (coenoecium) and there are no certain fossils. Maximum length about 2.5 m, attained in *Balanoglossus gigas;* most less than 30 cm.

About 12 genera (e.g., *Balanoglossus*, *Ptychodera*, and *Saccoglossus*) with about 65 species.

Class PTEROBRANCHIA

Small (body up to 7 mm) colonial or pseudocolonial sedentary marine animals with a ciliated lophophore; an external cuticular skeleton is present. Known as fossils from the Lower Ordovician, Upper Cretaceous, and Eocene (Bulman, 1970). Eaton (1970) believes that some early members may have been the ancestral forms to echinoderms and chordates (through the mitrates). The class contains two orders with about 20 living species.

Order CEPHALODISCA. Zooids free; no true colonies; living forms with four to nine pairs of arms with tentacles. Contains the fossil *Eocephalodiscus* and *Pterobranchites* and the living *Atubaria* (one species from near Japan) and *Cephalodiscus* (four subgenera; most species in the Antarctic).

Order RHABDOPLEURIDA. Zooids attached; true colonies; living forms with two tentacular arms. Contains the fossil *Rhabdopleurites* and

Rhabdopleuroides and the living *Rhabdopleura* (eastern Atlantic, South Pacific, and Antarctic).

SUBPHYLUM UROCHORDATA (Tunicata: the Tunicates)

Their tadpole larvae possess gill slits, dorsal hollow nerve cord, notochord, and a muscular, unsegmented tail; the adults are usually sessile filter feeders and usually lack the preceding features. Feeding is by means of a mucous trap inside the pharynx as in cephalochordates and ammocoete larvae. An endostyle, homologous with the thyroid, is present.

The urochordates are postulated to be more closely related to the vertebrates than are the cephalochordates by Jefferies (1979, 1981b). In urochordates and vertebrates the locomotory muscles are supplied by nerves from the dorsal nerve cord or from the brain and this is interpreted to be a shared derived character. In cephalochordates and echinoderms, however, the skeletal muscles are innervated through a muscle process extending from the muscle cells of the somites to the dorsal nerve cord.

The following classification is based largely on Berrill (1950). There is no fossil record. About 1600 species are known.

Class ASCIDIACEA

Larvae free-swimming, tadpolelike (short-lived and nonfeeding); adults sessile benthic, solitary or colonial, and without a tail.

Ascidians are marine and worldwide, extending from the intertidal to well into the abyssal-benthic region, occurring on almost any substrate; for example, *Ascidia, Boltenia, Botryllus, Ciona, Corella, Molgula, Pyura,* and *Styela.*

Class THALIACEA (Salps)

Larvae and adults transparent; pelagic (adults may be solitary or colonial). They tend to be planktonic but are generally capable of weak movements. Remarkable life cycles are characteristic of this group, with sexual and asexual reproductive stages occurring. The most complex cycle occurs in *Doliolum.*

Order PYROSOMIDA.   Marine seas except the Arctic. Tubular colonies
with a common atrial chamber. They can emit a strong phosphorescent
light. The colonies usually vary in length from about 3 cm to 1 m.
One genus, *Pyrosoma*.

Order DOLIOLIDA (Cyclomyaria).   Marine; primarily tropical to temperate. Generally barrel-shaped with eight or nine muscle bands around
the body; for example, *Doliolum*.

Order SALPIDA (Hemimyaria).   Marine, all seas. Cylindrical or prism-
shaped; for example, *Iasis, Thalia,* and *Salpa*.

Class APPENDICULARIA (Larvacea)

Pelagic; Arctic to Antarctic. Larval characteristics (such as the tail) are
retained in the adult; for example, *Appendicularia* and *Oikopleura*.

SUBPHYLUM CEPHALOCHORDATA (Acrania, in part)

The notochord extends to the anterior end of the body, in front of the
brain. Cranium is absent; no vertebrae; no cartilage or bone; heart consisting of a contractile vessel; no red corpuscles; liver diverticulum; segmented musculature; epidermis with a single layer of cells; protonephri-
dia with solenocytes for excretion; endostyle present (with iodine-fixing
cells; it may be homologous with the thyroid of vertebrates); true brain
absent, but two pairs of cerebral lobes and nerves present; sexes separate.

About 20 species; no fossil record. The Lower Ordovician mitrate *La-
gynocystis* is thought by Jefferies (1981b) to be related to ancestral cephalochordates.

At most, members of the subphyla Cephalochordata and Vertebrata
(Agnatha and Pisces only) are normally considered as fish or fishlike and
treated in "fish" books. Some workers restrict the term fish, in the nar-
rowest sense, to the Osteichthyes. It is the ichthyologist who generally
studies the lancelets and "fish."

Cephalochordates and vertebrates share the following attributes: notochord present (at least in embryo), a dorsal tubular central nervous
system, paired lateral gill slits (at least in embryo), postanal tail, hepatic
portal system, and endostyle (homologous with the thyroid).

Order AMPHIOXIFORMES (Lancelets).   The lancelets (or am-
phioxus) are small (up to 8 cm long), slender, fishlike animals, probably

close to the ancestral vertebrate lineage. They spend most of their time buried in sand or coarse shell gravel and occur primarily in shallow-water tropical and subtropical seas with some species extending into temperate waters as far north as Norway and as far south as New Zealand; they are particularly common off China. Feeding occurs by straining minute organisms from the water that is constantly drawn in through the mouth.

The present classification is based on Wickstead (1974, 1975, 1980, and pers. comm. 1982). It should be noted that Wickstead uses the generic name *Asymmetron* and the family name Asymmetrontidae, but *Epigonichthys*, regardless of its vague description, does have priority (as does the family name Epigonichthyidae, established by C. L. Hubbs) and is recognized in some recent works (e.g., Paulin, 1977).

Family BRANCHIOSTOMATIDAE.   Marine; Atlantic, Indian, and Pacific.

Double row of gonads; metapleural folds symmetrical, located laterally along ventral side and ending near the atriopore, neither fold connected with the median ventral fin.

One genus, *Branchiostoma*, with about 15 species.

Family EPIGONICHTHYIDAE.   Marine; Atlantic, Indian, and Pacific.

Gonads present along right side only; metapleural folds asymmetrical, right fold continuous with ventral fin, which passes to the right of the anus, and left fold ending behind atriopore.

One genus, *Epigonichthys* (= *Asymmetron, Heteropleuron*), with about 5 species, occurring primarily in the Indo-West Pacific.

SUBPHYLUM VERTEBRATA (Craniata)

The notochord never extends in front of brain; cranium present; vertebrae usually present; cartilage or bone or both are present; heart chambered; red blood corpuscles usually present; brain well developed; 10 to 12 pairs of cranial nerves; dorsal and ventral nerve roots usually uniting; nephridia absent; epidermis with several cell layers; endostyle only in larval lampreys (ammocoetes) and transformed into thyroid tissue in all others; sensory capsules present; neural crest formation present. Ectodermal embryonic cells giving rise to, for example, various structures of the nervous system, adrenal medulla, and much of the pharyngeal arch skeleton and neurocranium.

28   Fishes of the World

Instead of regarding the terms Vertebrata and Craniata as synonyms, Janvier (1981) uses them for different levels of classification. He places the following groups in Craniata (in reference to their possessing a cranium) and excludes Myxini from the Vertebrata because they lack arcualia (embryonic or rudimentary vertebral elements). This assumes that hagfishes are not degenerate forms of one of the vertebrate groups and the evidence supports this. The separation of hagfishes from all remaining groups is not formally recognized here. The superclass Agnatha is retained for those forms representing a primitive grade of vertebrate evolution. The term Vertebrata, although descriptively inappropriate for a group including hagfishes, is employed rather than Craniata because it is the more familiar of the two terms. In addition, Janvier (1981) uses the term Myopterygii for those vertebrates with true paired fins, muscularized unpaired fins, and large eyeballs with extrinsic musculature. This would include the Cephalaspidomorphi and Gnathostomata and exclude the Myxini and Pteraspidomorphi.

Divergent views exist on the interrelationships of the agnathans and gnathostomes. Jarvik (1968a:502) postulates that these two basic branches evolved independently from a common acraniate ancestor in the Cambrian or earlier. Attempts to derive gnathostomes from an agnathan line usually postulate the pteraspidiforms (= heterostracans) to be the ancestral form, and this continues to be effectively argued by Halstead (1982). However, I accept Janvier's (1981) arguments that the cephalaspidiforms (= osteostracans) are the nearest agnathan ancestor of the jawed vertebrates. It seems that the closest ancestral type of the vertebrates would be the cephalochordates, although Jefferies (1979, 1981b) postulates that urochordates come closest, or in cladistic terms are the sister group. The phylogenetic diagram of p. 29 expresses one view of the interrelations of the major groups of fishes.

SUPERCLASS AGNATHA (Cyclostomata, Marsipobranchii)

Jaws absent (a biting apparatus, not derived from gill arches, is present in some fossil forms); no pelvic fins; one or two vertical semicircular canals (one canal but two ampullae reported in myxiniforms, at least two in pteraspidiforms); vertebral centra never present (only the notochord); gills covered with endoderm and directed internally; gill arch skeleton fused with neurocranium, external to gill lamellae; gills opening to surface through pores rather than through slits; bony exoskeleton in most.

Possible agnathan remains first appear in the fossil record in the Late

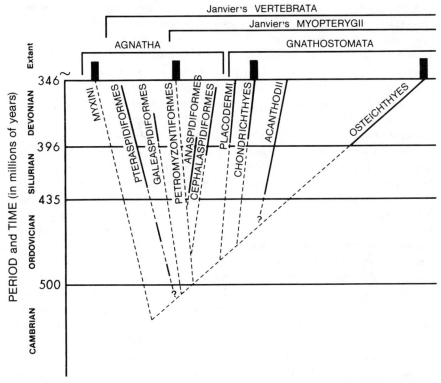

One speculative view on the affinities and time of divergence of the major groups of fishes. The solid line for each group denotes the extent in time of known fossils. The Agnatha and Gnathostomata are recognized here as comprising the subphylum Vertebrata; thelodonts are omitted. Janiver's (1981) use of the category Vertebrata and a newly proposed category, Myopterygii, are shown. The question marks denote possible fossil remains.

Cambrian, and definite remains occur in the middle Ordovician. The jawless fishes have their greatest radiation in the Silurian and Lower Devonian.

The interrelationships of the agnathans have been subject to many differences of opinion. Most workers now agree that the cyclostomes, the living naked agnathans, and ostracoderms, the extinct heavily armored agnathans, are not natural evolutionary categories. In the first edition of this book, the view of Stensio (1968) that hagfish may be derivatives of the pteraspidomorphs and lampreys of the cephalaspidomorphs was accepted. Moy-Thomas and Miles (1971) postulated different relations and placed the hagfishes in the Cephalaspidomorphi, but in a taxonomic unit of their own (the Hyperotreti) as opposed to the cephalaspidiforms, petromyzontiforms, and anaspidiforms (the Hyperoartii). Growing evidence suggests that hagfishes are probably the most primitive agnathan and that lampreys, while related to fossil cephalaspidomorphs, are more closely related in the cladistic sense to gnathostomes than to hagfishes (Løvtrup, 1977; Hardisty, 1979; Janvier and Blieck, 1979). However, in a critical examination of agnathan interrelationships, Halstead (1982) argues that the determination of primitive and advanced character states in agnathans is more complex than previously thought, and he believes that pteraspidiforms are the closest agnathan relatives of gnathostomes. In the study of Janvier and Blieck (1979) and Janvier (1981), the cephalaspidomorphs and gnathostomes are combined into the Myopterygii to the exclusion of hagfishes and pteraspidiforms to reflect this view. The current view favors the hypothesis that the morphological and physiological similarities shared between lampreys and gnathostomes, but not hagfishes (e.g., highly differentiated kidney tubules, absence of a persistent pronephros, more than one semicircular canal, large exocrine pancreas, photosensory pineal organ, vertebral elements, histological structure of the adenohypophysis, and composition of the body fluid), are due to common ancestry and not convergent evolution. Most similarities between hagfishes and lampreys involve superficial or primitive characters and cannot be convincingly used to support a hypothesis of a group containing only hagfishes and lampreys being monophyletic (Janvier, 1981, gives an analysis of this problem). Lampreys almost certainly have had a secondary loss of calcified tissue, but there is less certainty for hagfish ancestors having had bone. Just how unrelated hagfishes are to other fishes is open to question. It is interesting to note the view of Jensen (1963), which has never gained acceptance, that hagfishes have been derived from hoplonemertines.

Selley and Beamish (1977) and Tandler et al. (1979) present an annotated bibliography to hagfishes and lampreys, and their biology is reviewed by Hardisty (1979).

There are about 12 genera and 73 extant species in two families (some authors recognize five families). The recognition of five orders for the fossil jawless fishes with a bony exoskeleton is conservative. Many paleoichthyologists recognize more; that is, they would give higher taxonomic rank to the present orders and give ordinal status to many groups recognized here as families.

Class MYXINI

Order MYXINIFORMES (Hyperotreti).   One semicircular canal; single olfactory capsule with few folds in sensory epithelium, and olfactory nerves with separate bundles; no bone; eye musculature absent; 1–16 pairs of external gill openings; adenohypophysis with undifferentiated cellular elements, not divided into distinct regions (unlike in other vertebrates); body naked, eellike; no paired fins.

One family (the two subfamilies recognized here are given family status in some works), Recent. Janvier (1981) speculates that the fossil *Gilpichthys*, of Mississippian age, might have affinities with the myxiniforms.

Family MYXINIDAE—hagfishes.   Marine; temperate zones of the world (and Gulfs of Mexico and Panama).

The dorsal fin is absent (the caudal fin extends onto part of dorsal surface); eyes are degenerate; barbels present around biting mouth; teeth only on tongue, plus one on "palate"; dorsal and ventral nerve roots united; nasohypophyseal sac not blind, opening into pharynx; no spiral valve or cilia in intestinal tract; numerous mucous pores along body (shown in sketch); no cerebellum; ovaries and testes in same individual but only one gonad functional (not hermaphrodite); eggs large, yolky, up to 30 per individual; no metamorphosis. In stating that their eyes are degenerate it is assumed that hagfishes evolved from an ancestor with eyes. There is some variation in the structure of their eyes, but the lens is absent in all species. In *Eptatretus,* generally in shallower water than *Myxine,* the eye has a vitreous body and well differentiated retina and lies beneath unpigmented skin (presumably the more primitive state), whereas the deepwater *Myxine* lacks a vitreous body, has a poorly differentiated retina, and is not visible externally (Fernholm and Holmberg, 1975). The external nasohypophysial opening is terminal and it is through this opening that respiratory water passes backward to the gills (unlike lampreys).

Hagfishes are scavenger feeders, mostly eating the insides of dying or dead invertebrates and other fishes. They are the only vertebrate in which the body fluids are isosmotic with seawater. The mucous pores occur in two ventrolateral lines, each with about 70–200 slime glands that contain mucous cells and thread cells. The thread from the discharged thread cell of hagfishes probably gives tensile strength to the slime. The thread cell itself is not known from any other family of animals (Fernholm, 1981a). The secreted slime may be important in feeding and for defense, where it may clog the gills of other fishes and cause suffocation. The ability of hagfishes to go through knotting movements to free themselves from entanglement in slime, escape capture, or tear off food is shown in Hardisty (1979). Maximum length is up to about 0.8 m.

Six genera with about 32 species. The following classification is based largely on Adam and Strahan (1963), Strahan (1975), Hardisty (1979), Fernholm (1981b, 1982), and Fernholm and Hubbs (1981).

SUBFAMILY MYXININAE.   Efferent branchial ducts open by a common external aperture on each side. The pharyngocutaneous duct, which exits the pharynx behind the gills, is present only on the left side and probably functions to permit the pharynx to be flushed, thus clearing particles too large for the afferent branchial ducts.

Myxine. Anal fin ending posterior to branchial aperture; five or six pairs of gill pouches. Atlantic and Pacific; about nine species.

Notomyxine tridentiger. The pharyngocutaneous duct opens separately to the exterior, leaving two apertures on the left side instead of one as in all other Myxininae (in which it opens into the left common branchial aperture). Buenos Aires to Tierra del Fuego.

Neomyxine biplinicata. A pair of short ventrolateral finfolds behind the branchial region (finfolds are absent in other hagfishes). Cook Strait, New Zealand.

Nemamyxine elongata. Anal fin extending anterior to branchial apertures. New Zealand.

SUBFAMILY EPTATRETINAE.   Efferent branchial ducts open separately to the exterior with 5–16 external gill openings.

Two genera, *Eptatretus* (= *Bdellostoma* and *Polistotrema*) in the Atlantic and Pacific, and *Paramyxine,* limited to southeastern Asia (Fernholm and Hubbs, 1981); about 20 species.

Class PTERASPIDOMORPHI (Diplorhina)

At least two semicircular canals (Halstead, 1982, observes that a third or horizontal canal, if present in pteraspidiforms, would not have left any trace); bone present, true bone cells absent. The acellular nature of the bone may be a primitive rather than a secondary condition, unlike acellular bone in higher fishes, which is derived from cellular bone.

†**Order PTERASPIDIFORMES (Heterostraci).**   Exoskeleton consisting of plates covering the branchiocephalic region and scales covering the

trunk and tail; cancellous (honeycomblike structure) in middle layer of exoskeleton (a similar structure may be present in the Galeaspidi-formes—Janvier, 1981); photosensory pineal organ absent; single exter-nal lateral gill opening; eyes lateral, extremely small; sclerotic ring ab-sent; movable paired fins absent; anal fin absent; tail weakly hypocercal to externally symmetrical (see Denison, 1971b and Janvier, 1981); prob-ably two olfactory capsules (diplorhinal condition) with only an internal opening into the mouth area. The presence of two olfactory capsules, which has been used to suggest that pteraspidiforms are ancestral to gnathostomes, is not firmly established (Janvier and Blieck, 1979). Maxi-mum length is 1.5 m, usually much smaller.

Eleven families; including, Amphiaspidae, Cyathaspidae, Drepanaspi-dae, and Pteraspidae (e.g., *Pteraspis*).

The earliest known vertebrates are pteraspidiforms. Remains of pre-sumed pteraspidiforms of early Ordovician age are known from Spits-bergen, Greenland, and the United States and are placed in the genus *Anatolepis* (Bockelie and Fortey, 1976; Repetski, 1978). Those from Aus-tralia (and more likely to be pteraspidiform remains) are placed in the genera *Arandaspis* and *Porophoraspis* (Ritchie and Gilbert-Tomlinson, 1977). Of slightly younger age are *Astraspis* and *Eriptychius* known from the middle Ordovician of North America. Repetski (1978) interprets bony plate fragments found in the United States from Late Cambrian times to be of *Anatolepis*. If these are indeed remains of vertebrates, then it would push their first known occurrence in the fossil record back to about 510,000,000 years ago. Apart from the above, pteraspidiforms are well known from the Lower Silurian to the Upper Devonian. The presumed Cambrian and the Ordovician species were marine; some later members of the order were freshwater.

†Order GALEASPIDIFORMES.   The cephalic shield, though variable in shape, resembles that of the cephalaspidiforms, but they have a large opening on the dorsal face of the shield in front of the eyes. Janvier and Blieck (1979) and Janvier (1981) do not believe that this opening is a dorsal mouth but rather that it is a nasohypophysial opening connecting to the orobranchial chamber and retaining an inhalent function (with the mouth being ventral). These fishes had a large number of branchial openings, lacked paired fins, and may have had a hypocercal tail. Their affinities are uncertain.

Many genera have been described (e.g., *Duyunaspis* and *Polybranchiaspis*). Lower and Middle Devonian of southern China.

†**Order THELODONTIFORMES (Coelolepida).** Position uncertain. Anal fin present; tail hypocercal; one dorsal fin; lateral flaps present; orbits small; head depressed; body covered with placoidlike denticles; bone probably acellular. This group is basically unknown and most species are described only from isolated scales. It is not certain that they were jawless; they are probably not a monophyletic group.

Two families, Thelodontidae (e.g., *Thelodus* and *Turinia*) and Katoporidae (= Phlebolepidae) (e.g., *Lanarkia* and *Phlebolepis*). The theolodontids have some characteristics which suggest affinity to the pteraspidiforms while the katoporids may bear a closer relationship to the cephalaspidiforms (see Janvier, 1981). Lower Silurian to Upper Devonian. Early Ordovician fragments from the U.S.S.R. may be thelodontiform, but this is regarded as unlikely.

Palaeospondylus. Position uncertain; Middle Devonian of Scotland. Paired fins are evident in this fish, which has a maximum length of 5 cm. Its affinities are completely unknown. Various workers have postulated it to be the larval form of some preceding group (e.g., myxiniforms) or of one of several gnathostome groups. There is some evidence that true jaws existed, but it is retained in Agnatha following Moy-Thomas and Miles (1971).

Class CEPHALASPIDOMORPHI (Monorhina)

Two semicircular canals; some bony regions in cephalaspidiforms with true bone cells (the dermal skeleton of anaspidiforms lacks bone cells); single median nostril (nasohypophysial) opening between eyes with pineal eye behind; pectoral fins sometimes present.

Order PETROMYZONTIFORMES (Hyperoartii). No bone; seven pairs of external lateral gill openings; eyes lateral (except in *Mordacia*); tail isocercal in adults, hypocercal in ammocoete larvae; body naked, eellike; no paired fins.

One family, Recent and fossil. Janvier (1981) believes that *Jamoytius kerwoodi* (Silurian) and *Endeiolepis aneri* (Upper Devonian) show more affinity to petromyzontids than to the anaspidiforms. They could well be placed in the petromyzontiforms, but with it redefined, as separate sub-orders and families (Jamoytiidae and Endeiolepidae). *Jamoytius* lacks a dermal skeleton and *Endeiolepis* has a reduced one.

Although the petromyzontids and myxinids sometimes have been classified together, to the exclusion of fossil agnathans (e.g., Romer, 1966), it is now well established that they are phylogenetically far apart (Stensio, 1968; Janvier and Blieck, 1979). Both the cephalaspidiforms (Stensio, 1968) and anaspidiforms (Halstead, 1969; Janvier and Blieck, 1979; Janvier, 1981) have been postulated as having the closest affinity with the petromyzontids. The latter view is accepted here.

Family PETROMYZONTIDAE (Petromyzonidae)—lampreys. Anadromous and freshwater; cool zones of the world (see map on p. 402).

One or two dorsal fins are present; eyes well developed in adult; barbels absent; teeth on oral disc and tongue (except in fossil form); dorsal and ventral nerve roots separated; nasohypophyseal sac with external opening only; spiral valve and cilia in intestinal tract; small cerebellum; sexes separate; eggs small, not yolky, occurring in the thousands; larval stage (ammocoete) undergoes radical metamorphosis in fresh water. Ripe female lampreys can have an anal finlike fold, but Vladykov (1973) and Vladykov and Kott (1980) note the presence of a true anal fin in two female *Petromyzon* in tributaries to Lakes Erie and Huron. Lampreys of the Northern Hemisphere, Petromyzontinae, have a diploid chromosome number of 164–168 (*Geotria* may be even higher), the highest number of chromosomes of any vertebrate group. All lampreys die shortly after spawning.

Lampreys are either parasitic or nonparasitic and both life-history types may exist in individuals of the same species or characterize individuals of closely related species. It is believed that most nonparasitic species have been independently derived from a parasitic species. The parasitic phase, after metamorphosis from the ammocoete larvae but before reproducing, goes through a period of feeding on blood from other fish (very rarely on other animals) by rasping through their skin. The nonparasitic phase reproduces, without feeding, after metamorphosis. It is always confined to fresh water, whereas the parasitic form may be freshwater or anadromous. No parasitic freshwater lampreys are known from the Southern Hemisphere. Maximum length of larvae about 10 cm and parasitic adult about 0.9 m.

The spelling of suprageneric names based on *Petromyzon* has varied between authors. In 1981 the International Commission on Zoological Nomenclature ruled that the correct stem name is Petromyzont. Differences of opinion exist in lamprey classification, as they do in many other groups, regarding the subjective decision of what rank of classification to give the various groups. Recent works agree that there are three major lines of living lampreys, but whereas the classical view has been to recognize these in one family, with three subfamilies, the most recent major systematic studies of lampreys recognize three extant families (Hubbs and Potter, 1971; Potter, 1980). Arguments can be presented for a split classification, including the argument that the time of branching of the three lines from a common ancestor is probably much older than the time of origin of most other fish families, or for a lumped classification which emphasizes the conservative nature of their evolution. The latter course of action was followed in the first edition of this book and is in this one. Similar differences of opinion exist at lower levels of lamprey classification. For example, Vladykov and Kott (1979) place *Lampetra* and *Entosphenus* in different subfamilies (Lampetrinae and Entospheninae), while Potter (1980) recognizes *Entosphenus* as a subgenus of *Lampetra*, as is done here. For a debate on lumping versus splitting and on other areas of disagreement in lamprey systematics, see Bailey (1980, 1982) and Vladykov and Kott (1982).

I recognize four subfamilies, one known only from fossils (which is accorded family status by Hubbs and Potter, 1971) and six genera with 41 extant species. (A list of 39 species given in Potter, 1980; Beamish, 1982, describes a new species from Vancouver Island, while Vladykov et al., 1982, describe a new one from Greece.) Of the 41 species, 32 are almost always confined to fresh water and 18 are parasitic. Vladykov and Kott (1979) discuss the phenomenon of various parasitic species independently giving rise to nonparasitic species, termed satellite species. The first subfamily listed below is restricted to the Northern Hemisphere, generally north of 30°N, whereas the next two are restricted to the Southern Hemisphere, south of 34°S.

SUBFAMILY PETROMYZONTINAE. Supraoral plate single (immediately anterior to the front edge of the esophageal opening), and rarely with more than three cusps; transverse lingual lamina (extending across the tongue), straight or incurved; largest cusp, if developed, median; slight lateral bulge in midgut.

TRIBE PETROMYZONTINI. Supraoral tooth plate narrow, with two or three (rarely four) adjacent cusps; regularly arranged teeth throughout entire oral disc in curvilinear radiating rows.

Ichthyomyzon. Freshwater; eastern North America; three pairs of species (i.e., six species), each pair with an ancestral parasitic species and a nonparasitic derivative.

Petromyzon marinus. Anadromous (landlocked in Great Lakes region); Atlantic drainages of Canada, United States, Iceland, and Europe (including the Mediterranean); parasitic.

Caspiomyzon wagneri. Caspian Sea basin; probably parasitic.

TRIBE LAMPETRINI. Supraoral tooth plate broad (extending width of esophageal opening), with enlarged cusp at either end (one or more small intermediate cusps may be present); no regularly arranged curvilinear rows of teeth throughout entire oral disc.

Lampetra. Six subgenera recognized here which are variously recognized as genera in other works. *Eudontomyzon*—freshwater; Black Sea drainage (primarily Danube basin), China, and Korea; parasitic and nonparasitic, six species. *Tetrapleurodon*—freshwater; Rio Lerma system of Mexico; parasitic and nonparasitic; two species. *Entosphenus*—anadromous and freshwater; coastal regions of North Pacific in North America and Asia; parasitic and nonparasitic; seven species (one recently extinct). *Lethenteron*—anadromous and freshwater; circumarctic drainage basins, eastern Pacific coast south to Japan, coastal regions of western Alaska, and eastern North America; parasitic and nonparasitic; six species. *Okkelbergia*—freshwater; southeastern United States; one nonparasitic species. *Lampetra*—coastal regions of Europe and western North America; parasitic and nonparasitic; seven species.

SUBFAMILY GEOTRIINAE. Supraoral plate single, with four cusps; transverse lingual lamina strongly trident, bident at maturity; two well-developed diverticulae in midgut; caudal and second dorsal fins well separated in the immature (continuous or contiguous in other lampreys).
Geotria (= *Exomegas*) *australis.* Anadromous; southern Australia, Tasmania, New Zealand, Chile, Argentina, and the Falkland and South Georgia islands; parasitic.

SUBFAMILY MORDACIINAE. Supraoral plate paired, each plate with three cusps; transverse lingual lamina incurved, largest cusp at each lateral edge; one well-developed diverticula in midgut; eyes dorsolateral in immature and dorsal in mature (lateral in other lampreys).

Mordacia. Anadromous and freshwater; southeastern Australia, Tasmania, and Chile; parasitic and nonparasitic; three species.

SUBFAMILY MAYOMYZONTINAE.   Teeth absent (except on tongue). Its only species, *Mayomyzon pieckoensis*, is known from the Pennsylvanian Period in the State of Illinois (Bardack and Zangerl, 1968, 1971; Bardack, 1979). The nearly 20 specimens now known are all small in size but have adult characteristics. They are known from marine beds but need not have been marine themselves.

A second species of fossil lamprey, *Hardistiella montanensis*, of Mississippian age, is known from Montana (Janvier and Lund, 1983). This species retains a distinct hypocercal tail, has rays in the anal fin, and appears to lack an oral sucker. The number of gill openings cannot be determined. Phylogenetically, it is thought to belong between *Mayomyzon* and *Jaymoytius*. Other possible fossil cyclostomes, *Gilpichthys* and *Pipiscius*, are described in Bardack (1979).

†**Order ANASPIDIFORMES (Birkeniae).**   Six to 15 pairs of external lateral gill openings; branchial region posteriorly placed with first gill pouch well behind eye (as in lampreys); eyes lateral; tail hypocercal with large epichordal lobe; dorsal fin absent, replaced by series of scutes; body usually covered with dorsoventrally elongated scales (which are virtually absent in *Lasanius*); body fusiform and somewhat compressed; mouth terminal; bone cells absent. Maximum length about 15 cm.

Two families, Birkeniidae and Lasaniidae. Lower Silurian to Devonian (primarily Upper Silurian), predominantly freshwater.

†**Order CEPHALASPIDIFORMES (Osteostraci).**   Dorsal and lateral areas of cephalic shield with depressed areas in exoskeleton and associated canals present (this may have been an electric or sensory organ); usually 10 pairs of gill chambers and 10 pairs of external ventral gill openings; branchial region anteriorly placed (first gill arch at least level with eye); eyes dorsal; sclerotic ring present; endolymphatic duct present; tail heterocercal, with a pair of horizontal caudal flaps in ventral position (Heintz, 1967); body with dorsoventrally elongated scales; head depressed anteriorly, triangular posteriorly; body slightly compressed; mouth ventral; long rostral process present in species of *Boreaspis* (Janvier, 1977). Maximum length about 60 cm, but most are much smaller. These are the best known of the fossil agnathans.

Seven families; for example, Cephalaspidae, Hemicyclaspidae, Kia-eraspidae, and Tremataspidae. Upper Silurian to Upper Devonian, pre-dominantly freshwater (Janvier, 1981, gives references to phylogenetic studies on this order).

SUPERCLASS GNATHOSTOMATA

Jaws present, derived from modified gill arches; paired limbs usually present; three semicircular canals; vertebral centra usually present; gills covered with ectoderm and directed externally; gill arches not fused with neurocranium—internal to gill lamellae; gills opening to surface in Pisces through slits (opercular opening, when present, may be porelike); bony exoskeleton rarely developed; myelinized nerve fibers.

The first jawed vertebrate, the acanthodians, appear in the Middle Silurian.

Two grades: Pisces, with four classes (as follows), and Tetrapoda, with four classes: Amphibia, Reptilia, Aves, and Mammalia. These eight classes are as classically recognized in a synthetic or evolutionary classification; cladistic classifications based on the sister group model of W. Hennig recognize the gnathostomes in a markedly different way. As estimated, there are about 21,650 species of jawed fishes (i.e., currently recognized living valid species of Pisces). This is slightly more than the estimated 21,450 species of tetrapods.

GRADE PISCES

The jawed aquatic vertebrates in this grade have gills throughout life and paired limbs, if any, in the shape of fins, which are not polydactylous.

The interrelations of the various major groups of jawed fishes are unknown. All appear distinct when first present in the fossil record (Up-per Silurian to Lower Devonian).

Grade Pisces contains two subgrades and four classes with a total of about 21,650 extant species. Two major but poorly defined phyletic lines are recognized: the Elasmobranchiomorphi with 793 species and the Teleostomi with 20,857 species.

SUBGRADE ELASMOBRANCHIOMORPHI

Although placoderms share some characteristics with chondrichthyans, there are also many basic differences, and the two groups cannot be closely related. Their placement together in this subgrade merely serves to indicate continued but provisional support of the view of E. Stensiö and E. Jarvik (based on weak evidence) that their origins may have been relatively close. Miles and Young (1977) do not feel it possible to distinguish between the hypotheses that placoderms are the sister group of all other gnathostomes or are more closely related to chondrichthyans than to other gnathostomes. However, Schaeffer (1975) suggests, on the basis of feeding mechanisms, that placoderms are a separate and distinct group not more closely related to chondrichthyans than to teleostomes (e.g., that in cladistic terms they are the sister group to all other gnathostomes, a position that Forey, 1980, gives to the acanthodians). Furthermore, Zangerl (1981) notes that the Chondrichthyes, Teleostomi, and Tetrapoda share a specific mode of tooth formation which is not present in placoderms. This strongly suggests that chondrichthyans are more closely related to the latter group than are placoderms and they are sequenced here accordingly. (Zangerl, 1981, combines them with the higher groups to the exclusion of placoderms in his Teleostomi.) An earlier view of a diphyletic origin of chondrichthyans from placoderms with elasmobranchs being derived from the petalichthyiforms via the cladoselachimorphs and holocephalans being derived from the ptyctodontiforms via the iniopterygiforms is doubtful.

†Class PLACODERMI

Head and shoulder girdle with dermal bony plates (with bone cells in most groups); head shield usually movably articulated with the trunk shield; gill chamber extending anteriorly under neurocranium and covered laterally by opercula; probably five gill arches, no good evidence for spiracles; notochord unconstricted with vertebrae consisting only of neural and haemal arches and spines; tail diphycercal or slightly heterocercal; anal fin probably absent. Lower to Upper Devonian with a few into Lower Mississippian.

Most primitive groups of placoderms and a few advanced ones were marine. Many arthrodiriforms, most antiarchiforms, and all phyllolepidiforms were freshwater. Most were bottom-living fish with depressed bodies; only two families had species with compressed bodies. A rapid replacement of placoderms by the chondrichthyans occurred at the end of the Devonian. Maximum length 6 m, but most are much shorter.

The classification of this group is based on Denison (1978). Miles and Young (1977) favor a different arrangement that allows an easier diagnosis of the groups. They recognize three superorders with seven orders, regard arthrodires as the most primitive group, and do not feel that the stensioelliforms are known well enough to be put in the classification. Their arrangement is (using their stem endings) as follows: superorder Dolichothoracomorpha, with the orders Arthrodira (and the two suborders Actinolepidoidei and Phlyctaenioidei), Antiarcha, and Phyllolepida; superorder Petalichthyomorpha and the orders Petalichthyida, Rhenanida, and Pseudopetalichthyida; and the superorder Ptyctodontomorpha.

†Order STENSIOELLIFORMES. Considered to be the most primitive placoderms with one family and one genus known from the Lower Devonian (marine) of Germany.

†Order PSEUDOPETALICHTHYIFORMES. One family, Paraplesiobatidae, with two genera from the Lower Devonian (marine) in Europe.

†Order RHENANIFORMES. One family, Asterosteidae (including Gemuendinidae), with a raylike body, and several genera from the Lower to Upper Devonian (marine) in the United States, Germany, Turkey, and Australia.

†Order PTYCTODONTIFORMES. Large sexually dimorphic pelvic fins with claspers in males (fertilization was probably internal); many resemblances with living holocephalans. One family, Ptyctodontidae (e.g., *Ctenurella* and *Rhamphodopsis*), from Lower Devonian to possibly Lower Mississippian (primarily marine) in North America, Europe, Asia, Libya, and Australia.

†Order ACANTHOTHORACIFORMES. One family, Palaeacanthaspidae, with several genera (e.g., *Romundina*) from Lower Devonian (marine) in Europe, Asia, and Arctic Canada.

†Order PETALICHTHYIFORMES

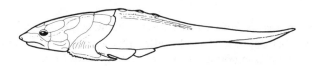

One family, Macropetalichthyidae, with several genera (e.g., *Lunaspis*) from Lower to Upper Devonian (marine) in North America, Europe, Asia, and Australia.

†**Order PHYLLOLEPIFORMES.** Two Upper Devonian (freshwater) families with one genus each, one in Antarctica and the other in Europe, Greenland, and Australia.

†**Order ARTHRODIRIFORMES**

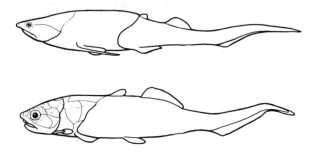

Six suborders and 21 families; for example, Phlyctaeniidae (e.g., *Arctolepis*—upper figure), Coccosteidae (lower figure), Dinichthyidae, and Titanichthyidae. This group, the largest in number of genera and best known of the placoderms, occurs from Lower Devonian to Lower Mississippian and is found on all major land masses.

†**Order ANTIARCHIFORMES.** In addition to gills, a pair of sacs are thought to be lungs; bottom feeders with mouth subterminal, and eyes dorsal and closely placed; pineal organ between eyes. Maximum length about 1.2 m.

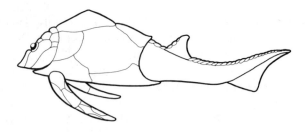

Three families, Bothriolepidae, Asterolepidae (= Pterichthyidae) (in figure), and Sinolepidae from Middle Devonian to Lower Mississippian (primarily freshwater) on, as a group, all major land masses.

Class CHONDRICHTHYES—Cartilaginous Fishes

The cartilagenous skeleton is often calcified but seldom if ever ossified, and the skull lacks sutures in living forms. (Hall, 1982, reports on the finding of bone in the vertebrae of *Scyliorhinus canicula* by Peignoux-Deville et al.) Teeth are usually not fused to jaws and replaced serially; horny, soft fin rays unsegmented and epidermal in origin (ceratotrichia); nasal openings on each side usually single (imperfectly divided by a flap into incurrent and excurrent openings) and more or less ventral; biting edge of upper jaw formed by palatoquadrate; swim bladder and lung absent; intestinal spiral valve present; internal fertilization in modern forms—males with pelvic claspers which are inserted in the female cloaca and oviduct(s); embryo encapsulated in a leatherlike case (gestation periods of two years are known, the longest of any vertebrate); high blood concentration of urea and trimethylamine oxide (converted from toxic ammonia) allows water to be drawn freely into the body.

Two main lines of evolution can be recognized: the holocephalans and elasmobranchs (ranked as subclasses). They are considered here as belonging to a monophyletic unit, with holocephalans being the most primitive lineage following Schaeffer (1981). It is considered unlikely that they had separate origins among the placoderms as has been previously suggested. Indeed, there are hyostylic, operculate chondrichthyans (Petalodontiformes) which appear to be evolutionary intermediates of the two lineages (Lund, 1977a), but they are assigned to the Holocephali. The ancestral group of chondrichthyans is unknown. There is no good evidence to postulate a derivation from either placoderms or acanthodians, although they are postulated here to be most closely related to the placoderms. The oldest chondrichthyan remains are denticles of placoid scale character from the Upper Silurian (Zangerl, 1981:5). A good fossil record is known from the Devonian onwards.

Extant taxa constitute six orders, 25 families, 151 genera, and about 793 species.

Subclass HOLOCEPHALI

Gill cover over the four gill openings, leaving one opening on each side; palatoquadrate usually fused to cranium (holostylic); branchial basket mostly beneath the neurocranium; no spiracle opening; tooth replacement slow; teeth as a few grinding plates in extant and many fossil forms; no cloaca, separate anal and urogenital openings; skin in adult naked (except in the fossil *Echinochimaera*); no stomach; no ribs; males with clasping organ on head (in addition to the pelvic claspers). The anatomy of the group is discussed in detail by Patterson (1965) and Stahl (1967). Other references include Bendix-Almgreen (1968), Patterson (1968a), Moy-Thomas and Miles (1971), Lund (1977b,c), and Zangerl (1979). Upper Devonian to Recent.

Two names have recently been proposed to replace Holocephali on the grounds that the present term refers to fusion of the palatoquadrate and neurocranium (holocephaly or holostyly), a condition which is not found in all members of the group. Some members of at least three groups, edestids, iniopterygians, and petalodonts, have a free palatoquadrate, and holocephaly has probably arisen independently several times within the subclass. Lund (1977b) uses the term Bradyodonti for this subclass, which describes the condition of slowness of tooth replacement in contrast to rapid tooth replacement in elasmobranchs. This term has been used before at different levels, and Lund (1977b) uses the term holocephalan at a lower level. On the other hand, Zangerl (1979, 1981) proposes the new name Subterbranchialia for this subclass, recognizing the category Holocephali at a lower level. I retain the well-known term Holocephali, believing it undesirable to change the names of higher categories just because they become descriptively inaccurate with new finds.

Lund (1977b) divides the subclass Holocephali (his Bradyodonti) into two main groups (with my endings) as follows: (1) the superorder Paraselachimorpha, with the dentition similar to selachians and palatoquadrate not fused to the cranium in all forms, and (2) the superorder Holocephalimorpha, with the dentition consisting of a few large permanent grinding tooth plates (selachianlike teeth may also be present) and palatoquadrate fused to cranium (holostyly). This is provisionally accepted here. It must be stressed that the relationships of the groups are very poorly known.

†Superorder PARASELACHIMORPHA

Dentition similar to selachians and palatoquadrate not fused to cranium in all forms. Upper Devonian to Permian.

Five orders: Iniopterygiformes, Edestiformes (e.g., Edestidae and Helicoprionidae), Helodontiformes (Helodontidae), Petalodontiformes (Petalodontidae), and Chondrenchelyiformes (Chondrenchelyidae). The iniopterygiforms of the Pennsylvanian period in North America appear to be morphological intermediates (but not strict phylogenetic intermediates as the petalodontiforms may be) between chimaeroids and elasmobranchs (Zangerl and Case, 1973; Zangerl, 1973). Lund (1982) reviews the chondrenchelyiforms and describes a new Mississippian species with large paired, distally biramous claspers (similar to crab claws) on the ethmoid region.

Superorder HOLOCEPHALIMORPHA

Dentition consisting of a few large permanent grinding tooth plates (selachianlike teeth may also be present) and palatoquadrate fused to cranium (holostyly). The Copodontiformes (Copodontidae) and Psammodontiformes (Psammodontidae) probably also belong in this superorder.

†**Order MYRIACANTHIFORMES.** Three families, Jurassic.

Order CHIMAERIFORMES. Lund (1977c) restricts this class to the last two suborders.

†*Suborder Cochliodontoidei.* Known only from the mandible and dentition.
   One family, Cochliodontidae (e.g., *Cochliodus*, *Deltodus*, and *Sandalodus*). Upper Devonian to Permian.
   This group is placed in the bradyodonts in most older works.

†*Suborder Menaspoidei.* One family, Menaspidae (e.g., *Menaspis* and *Deltoptychius*). Mississippian to Upper Permian.

†*Suborder Squalorajoidei.* One family, Squalorajidae, Jurassic.

†*Suborder Echinochimaeroidei.* One monotypic family. Mississippian. Differs from the chimaeroids in having a dermal cranial armor of denticles, placoid squamation, a tuberculated first dorsal spine, and no frontal clasper in males (Lund, 1977c).

Suborder Chimaeroidei. Two dorsal fins, the first erectile, with short base, and preceded by an erectile spine, the second nonerectile, low, and with long base; mouth inferior. In living forms, at least, fertilization is internal; the deposited egg is encased in a brown horny capsule. Water for breathing is chiefly taken in through the nostrils.
   Six extant genera with about 30 species. Many authors place all species into one family, Chimaeridae, rather than in three as is done here. Jurassic to Recent.

Family CALLORHYNCHIDAE—plownose chimaeras. Marine; Southern Hemisphere (off southern South America, New Zealand, southern Australia, southern Africa, etc.).

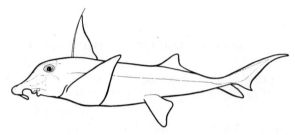

Snout with elongate, flexible, hooklike process; tail heterocercal.
One genus, *Callorhynchus,* with as many as four species.

Family CHIMAERIDAE—shortnose chimaeras or ratfishes. Marine; Atlantic and Pacific.

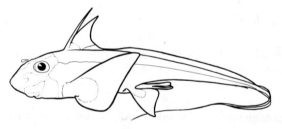

Snout short and rounded; tail diphycercal. Egg capsule tadpole-shaped with rearward filament. A poison gland is associated with the dorsal spine and the venom is painful to humans.

Two genera, *Chimaera* (with anal fin separate from caudal fin) and *Hydrolagus* (with anal fin joined to caudal fin) and about 20 species. *Chimaera* has six species and occurs in the northern Atlantic, Japan and northern China, and South Africa, whereas *Hydrolagus* has about 14 species and occurs primarily in the northern Atlantic, off South Africa, and in many areas in the Pacific (e.g., California to Alaska, Japan, New Zealand, and Australia).

Family RHINOCHIMAERIDAE—longnose chimaeras. Marine; Atlantic and Pacific.

Snout long and pointed, not hooklike; tail diphycercal; anal fin separated from caudal in *Neoharriotta* and joined with it in the other genera.

Three genera: *Harriotta* of the western and eastern Atlantic, Japan, New Zealand, and lower California, with possibly two species; *Neoharriotta* of the southern Caribbean Sea and West Africa with two species; and *Rhinochimaera* of Japan, New Zealand, Peru, both sides of North Atlantic, and southeastern Atlantic with two species (Bigelow and Schroeder, 1953; Bullis and Carpenter, 1966; Leim and Scott, 1966; Penrith, 1969; Garrick, 1971; Inada and Garrick, 1979). Of the six species, four are in the Atlantic and two in the Pacific.

Subclass ELASMOBRANCHII

Five to seven separate gill openings on each side; dorsal fin(s) and spines, if present, are rigid; males without clasper organ on head; dermal placoid scales often present; palatoquadrate (upper jaw) not fused to cranium (suspension amphistylic or hyostylic); branchial basket mostly behind the neurocranium; tooth replacement relatively rapid; teeth numerous; some ribs usually present; spiracle opening (remains of hyoidean gill slit) usually present. Middle Devonian to Recent.

Elasmobranchs are typically predaceous fishes that rely more on smell (the olfactory capsules are relatively large) than sight (the eyes are relatively small) for obtaining their food.

Compagno's (1973, 1977) classification differs considerably from that given here. Research in progress by other workers, most notably by G. Dingerkus, will probably result in changes from Compagno's detailed work. For this reason, the following classification, especially of the selachimorphs, largely follows that previously given (the few changes are based on Compagno, 1973, and that of others' works as noted).

Extant taxa constitute 5 orders, 22 families, 145 genera, and about 763 species.

†Superorder CLADOSELACHIMORPHA

Cladodont-type tooth (tall central cusp and one or more pairs of lateral cusps on a broad base); claspers usually absent; amphistylic jaw suspension; no anal fin; paired fins in shape of triangular flaps; radials of fins unsegmented and extending almost to the edge of the fin.

Schaeffer (1981) presents evidence favoring aligning *Cladodus* on the *Xenacanthus–Tamiobatis* lineage with *Cladoselache* being the primitive sister group for all elasmobranchs.

†**Order CLADOSELACHIFORMES.**   Two dorsal fins, each with a spine.
One family.

Family CLADOSELACHIDAE.   Upper Devonian to Mississippian.

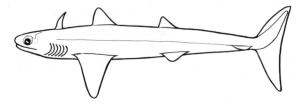

Maximum length about 2 m.
Includes the well-known *Cladoselache*.

†**Order CLADODONTIFORMES.**   One dorsal fin, without a spine.
One family.

Family CLADODONTIDAE.   Middle Devonian to Mississippian (? Permian).

Includes *Cladodus* (a genus to which a number of primitive but unrelated
species have been assigned), *Denaea*, and *Symmorium*.

†**Superorder XENACANTHIMORPHA (Pleuracanthodii)**

†**Order XENACANTHIFORMES.**   Pleuracanth-type tooth (three cusps
of variable size, usually two prominent lateral cusps and a smaller median
one). Claspers in male; amphistylic jaw suspension; elongate dorsal fin
base; diphycercal tail; two anal fins; cephalic spine; radials of pectorals
jointed and ending well before fin margin.
    One family. Schaeffer (1981) gives a detailed description of the neu-
rocranium.

Family XENACANTHIDAE.   Freshwater; Late Devonian to Triassic.

For example, *Xenacanthus*, *Orthacanthus*, and *Tamiobatis*.

Superorder SELACHIMORPHA (Pleurotremata)—Sharks

Gill openings mainly lateral. Anterior edge of pectoral fin not attached to side of head; anal fin present or absent; pectoral girdle halves not joined dorsally (fused ventrally).

The well-known terms for vertebral types (astrospondylic, tectospondylic, and cyclospondylic) lump unrelated groups, and Applegate (1967) has proposed a new system.

Thirteen families with about 91 genera and 339 species. Compagno (1973) gives a much more split classification than that given here and recognizes a total of 49 families. The number of species in various units is generally from L. J. V. Compagno (pers. comm. 1977).

†Order CTENACANTHIFORMES.   Two dorsal fins, each with a spine. Anal fin near caudal fin; cladodont-type tooth; amphistylic jaw suspension.

One family.

Family CTENACANTHIDAE.   Upper Devonian and Mississippian.

Maximum length about 2.5 m.

Bandringa, Ctenacanthus, Goodrichthys, and *Tristychius* are included.

†Order HYBODONTIFORMES.   Hybodontids have the features given above for the closely related ctenacanthids. They differ, among other features, in their internal fin structure. Males have hooked spines above the eye which may have functioned as cephalic claspers during copulation.

It is generally believed that modern sharks are derived from hybodontidlike fishes. The amphistylic jaw suspension is transformed to a hyostylic one in the majority of living sharks (correlated with their protrusible jaws).

Four families (e.g., Coronodontidae and Hybodontidae). Pennsylvanian to Cretaceous (the dominant selachians of the Triassic and Jurassic).

Order HEXANCHIFORMES (Notidanoidei).   One dorsal fin, without spine; anal fin present; six or seven gill slits; eyes without nictitating fold; spiracle present.

Family CHLAMYDOSELACHIDAE—frill shark.   Marine; Japan, California, and Europe.

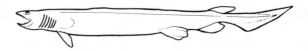

Six gill openings, margin of first gill continuous across throat; mouth terminal.

One species, *Chlamydoselachus anguineus*.

Family HEXANCHIDAE—cow sharks.   Marine; Atlantic, Indian, and Pacific.

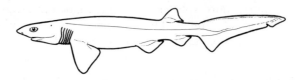

Six or seven gill openings, margin of first gill not continuous across throat; mouth ventral. Three genera and four species: *Hexanchus* with six gill openings, and *Heptranchias* and *Notorynchus* with seven gill openings.

Order HETERODONTIFORMES.   Two dorsal fins, each with a spine; anal fin present; five gill slits; eyes without nictitating fold; spiracle present; nostrils connected with mouth by deep groove.

Family HETERODONTIDAE—bullhead, horn, or Port Jackson sharks.   Marine; tropical Indian and Pacific (South Africa to Japan and Australia and New Zealand; eastern Pacific from California to Galapagos Islands and Peru).

Compagno (1973) aligned this family with the lamniforms (which he recognized in three orders) in his superorder Galeomorphii.

One genus, *Heterodontus*, with eight species.

Order LAMNIFORMES (Galeoidea).   Two dorsal fins (one dorsal fin in the scyliorhinid *Pentanchus*), without spines; anal fin present; five gill slits; gill rakers absent except as noted; spiracle present except as noted.

Seven families with about 65 genera and 239 species. In addition, this order probably contains a new but undescribed family with one species, the Pacific large-mouth shark or "megamouth," known from one specimen caught off Oahu. It has an enormous mouth with protrusile lips; the skin in the interior of the mouth is thought to be luminescent (Tinker, 1978).

Suborder Lamnoidei (Isurida).   Eyes without nictitating membrane.

Family RHINCODONTIDAE—whale shark.   Marine; pelagic tropical.

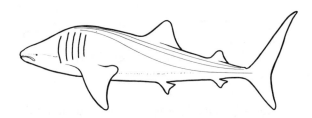

Mouth terminal; gill openings exceptionally large; fifth gill opening behind origin of pectoral, over fin base; gill rakers elongate, plankton feeders; teeth reduced.

World's largest fish with lengths up to 15.2 m (perhaps up to about 18 m).

One species, *Rhincodon typus,* first described under the generic name *Rhiniodon* in 1828 (Penrith, 1972), but the well-known name *Rhincodon* is best retained.

Family ORECTOLOBIDAE—carpet or nurse sharks.   Marine; all oceans.

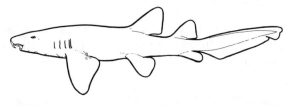

Mouth ventral; fourth and fifth gill openings behind origin of pectoral, over fin base; nostril connected to mouth by a deep groove, with a well-developed barbel; first dorsal fin posteriorly placed. Young born alive in some; in others the females lay eggs.

Maximum length about 4.2 m, attained in several species (e.g., *Ginglymostoma cirratum*).

About 11 genera (e.g., *Brachaelurus, Ginglymostoma, Hemiscyllium, Orectolobus, Parascyllium,* and *Stegostoma*) with about 28 species.

Family ODONTASPIDIDAE (Carchariidae)—sand tigers. Marine; Atlantic, Indian, and Pacific.

Mouth ventral; fifth gill opening well in front of pectoral fin.

SUBFAMILY ODONTASPIDINAE (SAND SHARKS). Jaws not greatly protrusible.

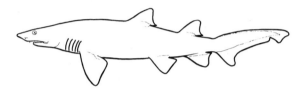

Two genera, *Odontaspis* and *Pseudocarcharias,* with about five species.

SUBFAMILY SCAPANORHYNCHINAE (GOBLIN SHARKS). Jaws greatly protrusible; rostral projection.

One species, *Scapanorhynchus (= Mitsukurina) owstoni.* The living species, known only from a few specimens, is usually placed in *Mitsukurina* with the earlier discovered fossil form placed in *Scapanorhynchus.*

Family LAMNIDAE. Marine; all oceans.

The following subfamilies are given family status by some workers.

The Alopiinae bears some relationship to Odontaspidae, whereas the Cetorhinae has a close affinity to the Lamninae.

SUBFAMILY ALOPIINAE (THRESHER SHARKS). Upper lobe of caudal fin greatly elongate, caudal fin almost one-half of total length; third to fifth gill openings over origin of pectoral fin.

One genus, *Alopias,* with three species.

SUBFAMILY CETORHININAE (BASKING SHARKS).   Gill openings exceptionally large; gill rakers elongate, plankton feeders, teeth reduced; tail nearly symmetrical with keel on caudal peduncle; fifth gill opening in front of pectoral fin.

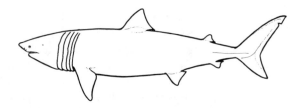

World's second largest fish, attains lengths up to 13.6 m.
One genus, *Cetorhinus*, with two species.

SUBFAMILY LAMNINAE (ISURIDAE) (MACKEREL SHARKS).   Caudal peduncle with a distinct keel; teeth large; fifth gill opening in front of pectoral fin; spiracle sometimes absent.

Some are maneaters (e.g., the dreaded white shark, *Carcharodon carcharias*) and reach lengths of at least 6.4 m.
Three genera, *Carcharodon*, *Isurus*, and *Lamna*, and about five species.

Suborder Scyliorhinoidei.   Nictitating fold or membrane usually present.

Family SCYLIORHINIDAE—cat sharks.   Maine; temperate, and tropical.

Nictitating membrane absent, but longitudinal fold along lower eyelid usually present; fifth gill opening over origin of pectoral fin.
About 20 genera with about 94 species.

SUBFAMILY PSEUDOTRIAKINAE.   First dorsal fin base longer than tail length and well anterior to origin of pelvics.

One genus, *Pseudotriakis*, with two species.

SUBFAMILY SCYLIORHININAE.   First dorsal fin base shorter than tail length; teeth in upper and lower jaws similar in shape, multicuspid, except in adult males of two species where they have one cusp; fourth gill opening over origin of pectoral fin in some. Maximum length about 1.5 m. Most species live in cool waters of the upper continental slope, while a few species are known from warm or cool shallow waters or from mid-water (e.g., some species of *Parmaturus*). Given family status in S. Springer (1979).

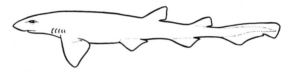

About 17 genera; for example, *Apristurus* (the most speciose genus with 21 species), *Atelomycterus*, *Cephaloscyllium*, *Galeus*, *Halaelurus*, *Parmaturus*, *Pentanchus* (its only species has only one dorsal fin), *Poroderma* (= *Conoporoderma*) (has distinct cone-shaped barbels), *Schroederichthys*, and *Scyliorhinus*. There are about 86 species (S. Springer, 1979).

SUBFAMILY PROSCYLLIINAE.   Two genera, *Eridacnis* and *Proscyllium*, with about six species.

Family CARCHARHINIDAE.   Marine; all oceans.

Fifth gill opening over or behind origin of pectoral fin.
    About 24 genera and 91 species.

SUBFAMILY TRIAKINAE (SMOOTH DOGFISHES).   Teeth usually low with three or more cusps.

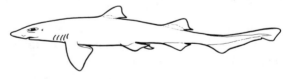

Thirteen genera with about 41 species.

TRIBE LEPTOCHARIINI.   One species, *Leptocharias smithii*.

TRIBE TRIAKINI.   Eight genera (e.g., *Galeorhinus, Iago, Mustelus, Triakis,* and *Scylliogaleus*) with about 35 species.

TRIBE HEMIGALEINI.   Four genera, *Dirrhizodon, Chaenogaleus, Hemigaleus,* and *Paragaleus,* with about five species.

SUBFAMILY CARCHARHININAE (REQUIEM SHARKS).   Teeth usually bladelike with one cusp.

Carcharhinus leucas, the bull shark, of the Atlantic and Pacific oceans, is found in some lakes and streams in Mexico, Central America, and northern South America; it also occurs inland up the Amazon River as far as Peru (Thorson, 1972).

Eleven genera with about 50 species.

TRIBE GALEOCERDONINI.   One genus, *Galeocerdo* (tiger sharks), with perhaps two species.

TRIBE SCOLIODONTINI.   One genus, *Scoliodon,* with several species.

TRIBE CARCHARHININI.   Nine genera, *Carcharhinus, Hypoprion, Isogomphodon, Lamiopsis, Loxodon, Negaprion, Prionace, Rhizoprionodon,* and *Triaenodon,* with about 45 species. Garrick (1982) revised *Carcharhinus* (25 species).

Family SPHYRNIDAE—hammerhead sharks.   Marine (occasionally brackish); all oceans (primarily in warm coastal waters).

Lateral expansion of the head (with the eyes and nasal openings farther apart than in other sharks, which may confer an advantage in homing in on food); spiracle absent. A great deal of variation between species in the development of the lateral lobes is illustrated in Gilbert (1967). *Sphyrna (Eusphyra) blochii*, sometimes placed in its own genus, *Eusphyra*, has an extremely wide and hammerlike head (with narrow extensions), whereas in *S. tiburo* it is evenly rounded and spadelike.

These sharks are closely related to the Carcharhininae but differ in many cranial characters associated with the sphyrnid cephalic hydrofoil or "hammer." Large individuals are highly dangerous and there are many records of fatal attacks on humans. Maximum length 4.5 m, attained in *Sphyrna tudes*.

One genus, *Sphyrna*, with nine species (Gilbert, 1967).

Order SQUALIFORMES (Tectospondyli). Two dorsal fins, with or without spines; anal fin absent; five or six gill slits. Members of the first two suborders have a sharklike body with lateral eyes, while members of the last have a raylike body and dorsal eyes.

About 21 genera and 87 species.

Suborder Squaloidei

Family SQUALIDAE—dogfish sharks. Marine; Atlantic, Indian, and Pacific.

Snout not produced into a flat blade and without lateral teeth or barbels; dorsal fin spines present or absent; five gill openings (all anterior to the pectoral fin).

Bigelow and Schroeder (1957) favor placing *Oxynotus* in its own family apart from other squalids, while Compagno (1973) favors placing *Echinorhinus* in its own family apart from the others. Bass et al. (1976) give family status to all four subfamilies recognized here. There may have been considerable parallelism in the loss of the fin spines in the Dalatiinae, and the relationships of the genera placed here in Squalidae are too poorly known to erect any but a provisional classification.

Several members of this family, such as *Isistius, Euprotomicrus, Centroscyllium, Squaliolus,* and *Etmopterus,* are luminescent. The spiny dogfish, *Squalus acanthias,* commonly used in comparative anatomy laboratories, is one of the most cosmopolitan fish species, being widespread in the Northern and Southern hemispheres, with transoceanic movements (e.g., from Washington to Japan and Scotland to Newfoundland—Jones and Geen, 1976).

Maximum length 6.3 m, attained by *Somniosus microcephalus.* The world's smallest sharks belong to this family. The largest specimen of the smallest species, *Squaliolus laticaudus* (revised by Seigel, 1978), is 24.3 cm (this species also has the lowest number of vertebrae for any shark: 55–62). *Euprotomicrus bispinatus,* the next smallest, has a maximum known length of 26.5 cm and weight of 67.6 g (Hubbs et al., 1967). *Etmopterus hillianus* reaches about 35 cm.

Eighteen genera with about 71 species.

SUBFAMILY ECHINORHININAE (BRAMBLE SHARKS).   No dorsal fin spines; both jaws with multicuspid teeth (except in juveniles), teeth similar between upper and lower jaws; precaudal pits present; caudal fin without a subterminal notch.

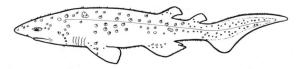

Two species, *Echinorhinus brucus* from most oceans and the rare *E. cooki* from the Pacific (Garrick, 1960).

SUBFAMILY SQUALINAE (DOGFISH SHARKS).   Each dorsal fin preceded by a spine (may be short).

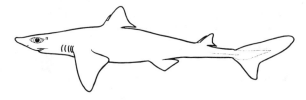

Eight genera with about 54 species.

TRIBE CENTROPHORINI.   Laterally grooved fin spines; unicuspid teeth, lower teeth broader than uppers and dissimilar in shape.

Four genera, *Deania, Centrophorus, Centroscymnus,* and *Symnodon,* with about 26 species.

TRIBE ETMOPTERINI.   Laterally grooved fin spines; multicuspid teeth in upper jaw.

Two genera, *Centroscyllium* and *Etmopterus,* with about 21 species.

TRIBE SQUALINI.   Dorsal fin spines lacking lateral groove; teeth in upper and lower jaws with single cusps.

Two genera, *Aculeola* (one) and *Squalus* (= *Cirrhigaleus*) (six), with seven species.

SUBFAMILY DALATIINAE (SLEEPER SHARKS). Second dorsal and usually the first without spines; both jaws with unicuspid teeth, upper teeth slender and lanceolate and lower teeth broad and overlapping; precaudal pits absent. The first four genera listed below have a distinct subterminal notch on the caudal fin while the remaining four lack a subterminal notch on the caudal fin.

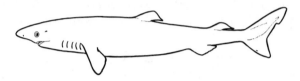

About 8 genera, *Isistius, Somniosus, Scymnodalatias, Dalatias, Squaliolus, Euprotomicroides, Euprotomicrus,* and possibly *Heteroscymnoides* (known only from the small holotype), with about 11 species.

SUBFAMILY OXYNOTINAE. Each dorsal fin with a spine; precaudal pits absent; trunk approximately triangular in cross section, with a pronounced ventrolateral ridge on each side between the pectoral and pelvic fins. (Sharks placed in Echinorhininae, Squalinae, and Dalatiinae have a trunk approximately cylindrical in cross section and any marked lateral ridges are confined to the caudal peduncle.)

One genus, *Oxynotus,* with four species.

Suborder Pristiophoroidei

Family PRISTIOPHORIDAE—saw sharks. Marine; South Africa and Indo-Pacific (Australia to Japan).

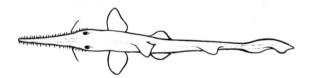

Snout producd in a long flat blade with teeth on each side (teeth unequal in size, usually alternating large and small, and weakly embedded); one pair of long barbels; no dorsal fin spines (sometimes present as internal rudiments).

Pristiophorids have many raylike characters and probably have a relatively close affinity to the Batoidimorpha, as do the squatinids.

Two genera, *Pristiophorus* (five gill openings) and *Pliotrema* (six gill openings), with five species.

Suborder Squatinoidei

Family SQUATINIDAE—angel sharks.   Marine; Atlantic and Pacific.

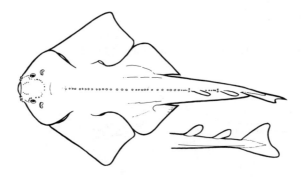

Two spineless dorsal fins; no anal fin; five gill openings; spiracle large; mouth almost terminal; nostrils terminal with barbels on anterior margin.

One genus, *Squatina*, with 11 species.

Superorder BATIDOIDIMORPHA (Hypotremata)—Rays

Gill openings ventral; anterior edge of the greatly enlarged pectoral fin attached to side of head, anterior to the five gill openings (six in *Hexatrygon*); anal fin absent; eyes and spiracles on dorsal surface; anterior vertebrae fused to form a synarcual; suprascapulae of pectoral girdles joined dorsally over vertebral column and articulating with column or synarcual or fused with synarcual; nictitating membrane absent, cornea attached directly to skin around the eyes; body generally strongly depressed; ceratotrichia reduced; jaws protrusible; teeth pavementlike; in most, water for breathing taken in chiefly through the spiracle rather than the mouth (except for those living off the bottom); habitat generally benthic; most give birth to live young (Rajidae, however, have eggs encased in a horny capsule); no electric organs in head region except in Torpedinidae. Upper Jurassic to Recent.

Order RAJIFORMES. The recognition of four major categories and their sequence follows Heemstra and Smith (1980), while the generic composition of various units generally follows Compagno (1973). Both these works give ordinal status to the four lineages given as suborders here. Compagno (1973) gives a much more split classification than that given here and recognizes a total of 20 families. The number of species in various units is generally from L. J. V. Compagno (pers. comm. 1977).

Nine families with 54 genera and about 424 species.

Suborder Pristoidei

Family PRISTIDAE—sawfishes. Marine; Atlantic, Indian, and Pacific; freshwater in some areas.

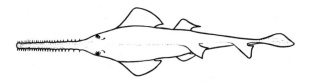

Snout produced in a long flat blade with teeth on each side (teeth of equal size and embedded in deep sockets); barbels absent; body somewhat sharklike, although the head is depressed; two distinct dorsal fins and a caudal fin.

One genus, *Pristis* (with two subgenera, *Anoxypristis*, for *P. cuspidatus*, and *Pristis*), with six species.

Suborder Torpedinoidei

Family TORPEDINIDAE—electric rays. Marine; Atlantic, Indian, and Pacific.

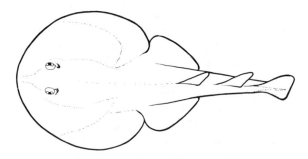

Powerful electric organs, derived from branchial muscles, in head region; skin soft and loose; eyes small to obsolete; caudal fin well developed;

dorsal fins 0–2 (on which basis some workers have recognized three families or subfamilies).

Four species are blind; the two species of *Typhlonarke* endemic to New Zealand and *Benthobatis moresbyi* off southern India have concealed eyes, whereas *Narke impennis* of the Bay of Bengal has minute sunken eyes (Garrick, 1951).

Ten genera with about 38 species.

SUBFAMILY TORPEDININAE.   Disc truncate or emarginate anteriorly; jaws extremely slender; no labial cartilages; rostrum absent or reduced.

TRIBE TORPEDININI.   Tail and dorsal and caudal fins well developed. One genus, *Torpedo*, with about 13 species.

TRIBE HYPNINI.   Tail and dorsal and caudal fins very small. One Australian species, *Hypnos subnigrum*.

SUBFAMILY NARCININAE.   Disc rounded anteriorly; jaws stout; strong labial cartilages; rostrum present.

TRIBE NARCININI.   Deep groove around mouth and lips; jaws long and strongly protractile; rostrum broad; usually two dorsal fins.

Four genera, *Benthobatis*, *Diplobatis*, *Discopyge*, and *Narcine*, with about 15 species.

TRIBE NARKINI.   Shallow groove around mouth; jaws short and weakly protractile; rostrum narrow; usually a single dorsal fin.

Four genera, *Heteronarce* (has two dorsal fins), *Narke*, *Typhlonarke*, and *Temera* (lacks dorsal fin), with about 9 species.

Suborder Rajoidei

Family RHINOBATIDAE—guitarfishes.   Marine; Atlantic, Indian, and Pacific.

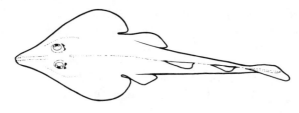

Body intermediate between sharklike and skatelike; tail stout, not defi-

nitely marked off from body; two distinct dorsal fins and a caudal fin; denticles over body form a row on midline of back; tail without spine.
Nine genera and about 48 species.

SUBFAMILY RHINOBATINAE. Caudal fin not bilobed; origin of first dorsal behind pelvics.

TRIBE RHINOBATINI. Four genera, *Aptychotrema, Rhinobatos, Trygonorrhina,* and *Zapteryx,* with about 40 species.

TRIBE PLATYRHININI. Three genera, *Platyrhina, Platyrhinoidis,* and *Zanobatus,* with about five species.

SUBFAMILY RHYNCHOBATINAE. Caudal fin bilobed; origin of first dorsal over or in front of pelvics.

TRIBE RHYNCHOBATINI. One genus, *Rhynchobatus,* probably with two species.

TRIBE RHININI. One Indo-Pacific species, *Rhina ancylostoma.*

Family RAJIDAE—skates. Marine, all oceans.

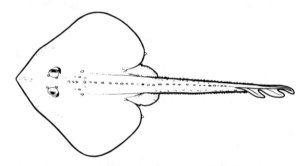

Caudal fin reduced or absent; tail extremely slender; weak electric organs derived from caudal muscles; dorsal fins 0–2; most with prickles on skin, often with a row along midline of back. Eggs encased in horny capsule with four long tips.
    Fourteen genera and about 190 species. The following subfamilies are given family status in some works (e.g., Bigelow and Schroeder, 1962, and Compagno, 1973), while *Gurgesiella* is placed in its own family by Hulley (1972).

SUBFAMILY ANACANTHOBATIDINAE. No dorsal fin; caudal fin well-developed or not; upper surface smooth; pelvic fins divided into two distinct lobes, the anterior lobe limblike; tip of snout with a filament (expanded terminally in *Springeria*).

Two genera, *Anacanthobatis* and *Springeria*, with six species. Known from South Africa, Natal, and tropical western Atlantic.

SUBFAMILY ARHYNCHOBATIDINAE. One dorsal fin; caudal fin complete.

One species, *Arhynchobatis asperrimus*, endemic to New Zealand and known from between 90–750 m (Garrick and Paul, 1974).

SUBFAMILY PSEUDORAJINAE. No dorsal fin; snout terminating in a short rostral filament.

Two genera, *Gurgesiella*, with two species having pelvic fins with pointed outer angles, known from the tropical western Atlantic and off Chile, and *Pseudoraja*, with one species having pelvic fins with broadly rounded outer angles, known from the gulfs of Mexico and Honduras.

SUBFAMILY RAJINAE. Two dorsal fins; caudal fin usually poorly developed.

Nine genera, *Bathyraja*, *Breviraja*, *Cruriraja*, *Dactylobatus*, *Pavoraja*, *Psammobatis*, *Raja* (the most speciose elasmobranch genus and containing several subgenera), *Rhinoraja*, and *Sympterygia*, with about 180 species. The genera are discussed in Bigelow and Schroeder (1953), Ishiyama (1967), Garrick and Paul (1974), and McEachran and Fechhelm (1982a,b).

Suborder Myliobatidoidei

Family DASYATIDAE (Trygonidae)—stingrays. Marine; Atlantic, Indian, and Pacific (a few species occasionally occur in brackish and fresh water).

Outer anterior margin of pectorals continuous along side of head; no separate cephalic or subrostral fins; no distinct dorsal fin (completely absent in most species); most species with one or more long poisonous spines on tail (pain said to be excruciating to humans).

Ten genera and about 90 species.

SUBFAMILY DASYATINAE (STINGRAYS OR WHIPRAYS). Disc less than 1.3 times as broad as long; no caudal fin; tail long (distance from cloaca to tip much longer than breadth of disc).

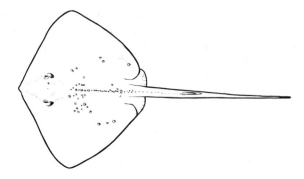

Six genera, *Dasyatis, Himantura, Hypolophus, Taeniura, Urogymnus,* and *Urolophoides,* with about 50 species. Several species are known only from fresh water (Compagno and Roberts, 1982).

SUBFAMILY GYMNURINAE (BUTTERFLY RAYS). Disc extremely broad (more than 1.5 times as broad as long); no caudal fin; tail short (distance from cloaca to tip much shorter than breadth of disc).

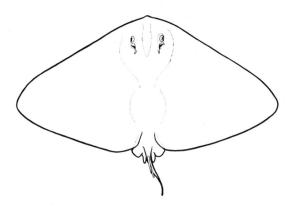

Two genera, *Aetoplatea* and *Gymnura,* with about 10 species.

SUBFAMILY UROLOPHINAE (ROUND RAYS). Disc less than 1.3 times as broad as long; well-developed caudal fin; tail moderately long.

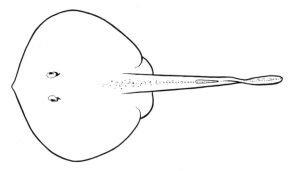

Two genera, *Urolophus* (= *Trygonoptera*), with a relatively short tail and confluent caudal fin lobes, and *Urotrygon*, with a relatively long tail and separated caudal fin lobes. About 30 species.

Family POTAMOTRYGONIDAE—river stingrays.   Freshwater; South America (Atlantic drainage).

Similar to the Dasyatinae; the major difference is the long, median, anteriorly directed process from the pelvis, which is absent in the Dasyatidae (but present in the Myliobatidae and Mobulidae). T. B. Thorson and his colleagues have found these rays to have low urea concentrations in the blood, unlike other members of the class Chondrichthyes.

Freshwater stingrays reported from Africa and Laos (e.g., Castex, 1967) apparently belong to Dasyatidae (T. R. Roberts, pers. comm. 1980).

Two genera, *Disceus* and *Potamotrygon*, with about 14 species.

Family HEXATRYGONIDAE.   Marine; off South Africa.

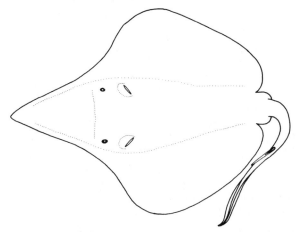

Six gill openings and six gill arches; snout elongate, thin (depressed), translucent (the snout may function as an electroreceptive organ); no supraorbital crests on cranium; spiracles large, well behind eyes, with external flaplike valve (the spiracle of other rays is closed by an internal valve); brain very small, posteriorly placed in large cranial cavity; tail with two serrate spines; disc longer than broad; nostrils wide apart, anterior nasal flaps short.

One species, *Hexatrygon bickelli*, described from one specimen washed up on a beach on the south coast of South Africa (Heemstra and Smith, 1980).

Family MYLIOBATIDIDAE—eagle rays. Marine; Atlantic, Indian, and Pacific.

Head elevated and distinct from disc; eyes and spiracles lateral on head; gill openings about length of eye; tail much longer than disc; venomous spine(s) present in some; small dorsal fin; no caudal fin; pectoral fins reduced or absent opposite the eyes, but with an anterior subdivision that unites below the tip of the snout forming a subrostral lobe. Some are famous for their ability to leap high into the air from the water.

SUBFAMILY MYLIOBATIDINAE (EAGLE RAYS). Anterior face of cranium nearly straight; subrostral fin not incised.

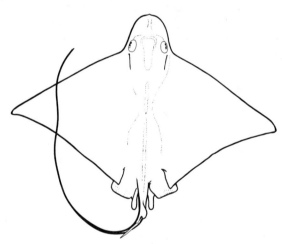

Four genera, *Aetobatus, Aetomylaeus, Myliobatis,* and *Pteromylaeus,* with about 24 species.

SUBFAMILY RHINOPTERINAE (COW-NOSED RAYS). Anterior face of cranium concave; subrostral fin incised (bilobed).

One genus, *Rhinoptera,* with about three species.

Family MOBULIDAE—manta rays and devil rays. Marine; Atlantic, Indian, and Pacific.

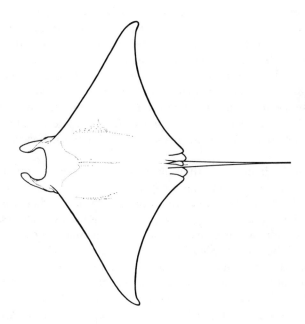

Head distinct from disc; eyes and spiracles lateral on head; gill openings much longer than eye; tail much longer than disc; spine(s) present in some; small dorsal fin; no caudal fin. Members of this family are the only living vertebrates with three functional paired limbs. (The cephalic pair assist in feeding and are essentially the anterior subdivision of the pectorals.)

Some mantas grow to a width of about 6.1 m and a weight of more than 1360 kg; largest members of the superorder (and like the whale shark and basking shark, strain their food out of the water).

Two genera, *Manta* with mouth terminal and *Mobula* with mouth ventral, and 10 species.

SUBGRADE TELEOSTOMI

This is a poorly defined group. Its only merit is to indicate that acanthodians probably bear a closer relation to the osteichthyans than to the chondrichthyans.

†Class ACANTHODII

True bone present; jaws formed by palatoquadrate and Meckel's cartilage, both ossified; mandibular arch (palatoquadrate), probably closely
associated with hyoid arch, with the spiracular gill cleft (homologous with
spiracle of other fish and eustachian tube of tetrapods) virtually closed;
dermal operculum (associated with hyoid arch); five gill arches; notochord generally persistent; ganoid scales present; stout spines present
before the dorsal, anal, and paired fins (up to six paired spines present
between the pectorals and pelvics in some); caudal fin heterocercal. Lower
Silurian to Lower Permian. Fish spines which may be from an acanthodian are known from marine beds of the Upper Ordovician (Harper,
1979).

The acanthodians, with their large anterior eyes, terminal or near
terminal mouth, and small nasal capsules, were probably mid- and sur-
face-water feeders. Many were microphagous in their diet while others,
especially the ischnacanthids, were probably highly predaceous. The Silurian acanthodians were marine but the Devonian ones were mainly
freshwater. They are the earliest known true jawed fishes. Maximum
length estimated at about 2.5 m, most less than 20 cm.

A variety of views have been expressed about acanthodian relationships. Watson (1937), in his review of the group, felt that they were the
most primitive known gnathostomes. He placed them in the Aphetohyoi-
dea, along with several other groups, which had equal rank as the Pisces.
In many classifications of the 1930s to 1950s they were placed in the class
Placodermi. Berg (1940) recognized acanthodians in their own class and
placed them immediately before his class Elasmobranchii. Romer (1966)
provisionally considered them as the most primitive subclass of the Osteichthyes because of certain resemblances to the actinopterygians, but
Nelson (1968a) felt that their closest relationship was with the elasmo-
branchiomorphs. Jarvik (1968a:517) favored placing them between the
Chondrichthyes and Osteichthyes. The view of Moy-Thomas and Miles
(1971) and Miles (1973) that they are more closely related to the latter is
accepted here as the most probable hypothesis. This opinion, however,
has had subsequent opponents. Jarvik (1977) interpreted numerous morphological characters to suggest that acanthodians should be regarded as
elasmobranchs, sharing a common ancestry with selachians. Forey (1980),
as did Watson, postulates that acanthodians are the most primitive gnathostome, the sister group to chondrichthyans, placoderms, and osteichthyans.

The classification of this group follows Denison (1979). The climatii-
forms appear to be closest to the presumed ancestral acanthodian, and

the ischnacanthiforms and acanthodiforms are probably independently derived.

†**Order CLIMATIIFORMES.** Dermal bones in shoulder girdle (other acanthodians possess only endoskeletal elements); two dorsal fins, each with a spine; teeth absent or if present not fused to jaws. Middle Silurian to Pennsylvanian (North America, Greenland, Europe, Asia, Australia, and Antarctica).

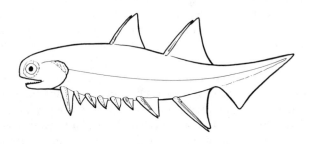

Three families: Climatiidae, with three to six paired spines between the pectoral and pelvic fin spines [e.g., *Brachyacanthus, Climatius* (usually reached only 7.5 cm, shown in figure), *Erriwacanthus, Euthacanthus, Nostolepis, Parexus* (had exceptionally long dorsal spines), *Ptomacanthus, Sabrinacanthus,* and *Vernicomacanthus*]. Diplacanthidae, with two paired intermediate spines *(Diplacanthus* and *Gladiobranchus)*. And Gyracanthidae, with no intermediate spines (e.g., *Gyracanthus, Gyracanthides,* and *Oracanthus*).

†**Order ISCHNACANTHIFORMES.** Two dorsal fins, each with a spine; teeth fixed to strong dermal jaw bones; 0–2 paired spines between the pectoral and pelvic fin spines. Upper Silurian to Pennsylvanian (North America, Europe, and Asia).
One family, Ischnacanthidae (e.g., *Gomphonchus, Ischnacanthus, Uraniacanthus,* and *Xylacanthus*).

†**Order ACANTHODIFORMES.** One posterior dorsal fin with spine; teeth absent; intermediate spines absent or limited to one pair. Lower Devonian to Lower Permian (North America, Europe, Asia, South Africa, Australia, and Antarctica).
One family, Acanthodidae (e.g., *Acanthodes, Cheiracanthus,* and *Mesacanthus*).

Class OSTEICHTHYES—Bony Fishes

Skeleton, in part at least, with true bone (endochondral or membrane bone); skull with sutures; teeth usually fused to the bones; soft fin rays usually segmented and dermal in origin (lepidotrichia); nasal openings on each side usually double and more or less dorsal; biting edge of upper jaw usually formed by dermal bones, the premaxillae and maxillae; swim bladder or functional lung usually present; intestinal spiral valve in only a few lower groups; internal fertilization relatively rare—pelvic copulatory device in only one group (phallostethoids); embryos not encapsulated in a case, with effective elimination of ammonia allowed; low blood concentration of urea and trimethylamine oxide (except in dipnoans and *Latimeria*)—osmotic balance maintained only by an energy demanding transfer process.

This class is divided here into four subclasses. The distinctiveness of the first two, dipnoans and crossopterygians, may not be as great as is generally thought. Chang (1982) describes a lower Devonian fossil, *Youngolepis*, which appears to be intermediate between these two groups but which lacks choana. Some workers have previously combined the two into the Sarcopterygii, a move which is strengthened with this new find in China. (C. L. Hubbs, in 1919, proposed the term Amphibioidei for such a union.) The last two subclasses, Brachiopterygii and Actinopterygii, are combined by some workers. In addition to this, the major groups of the Osteichthyes are classified in a variety of ways by other workers.

The Osteichthyes, in cladistic classifications, includes all derivative groups and as such includes the tetrapods. The latter are excluded in the present classification. Two recent cladistic classifications of the group are given below, the first by Wiley (1979) and the second by Rosen et al. (1981). Jollie (1982a) notes that some anatomical details in the former study are incorrect.

Superclass Teleostomi—according to Wiley (1979).
   Class Actinistia
         Order Coelacanthiformes *(Latimeria)*
   Class Euosteichthyes
     Subclass Sarcopterygii
     Infraclass Dipnoi
     Infraclass Choanata
       Superdivision Amphibia
       Superdivision Amniota
     Subclass Actinopterygii

Infraclass Brachiopterygii
Infraclass Chondrostei
Infraclass Neopterygii
Class Osteichthyes—according to Rosen et al. (1981)
　　Subclass Actinopterygii
　　　Infraclass Cladistia
　　　Infraclass Actinopteri
　　　　Series Chondrostei
　　　　Series Neopterygii
　　Subclass Sarcopterygii
　　　Infraclass Actinistia
　　　Infraclass Choanata
　　　　Series Dipnoi
　　　　Series Tetrapoda

Primitive (and advanced) states in the three major subclasses of Osteichthyes:

	Dipneusti	Crossopterygii	Actinopterygii
Tail	heterocercal (diphycercal)	heterocercal (diphycercal)	heterocercal (homocercal)
Dorsal fins	double (single)	double (double)	single (single or double)
Scales	cosmoid (cycloid)	cosmoid (cycloid)	ganoid (cycloid or ctenoid)
Presence of pineal foramen	common (rare)	common (lost)	rare (lost)

　　The category Sarcopterygii is used by Wiley (1979) and Rosen et al. (1981) in a different way from that classically employed (i.e., for the dipnoans and crossopterygians, in the strict sense as used here—the lobe-finned fishes, e.g., Romer, 1966). Nelson (1969a) employed the subclass Sarcopterygii to include his infraclasses Brachiopterygii, Coelacanthini, Dipnoi, and Choanata (rhipidistians and the tetrapods), while Miles (1975) used it to include the Dipnoi and Crossopterygii (which, in turn, included the Actinistia and Choanata). Various views on the transformation from fishes to amphibians may be found in Panchen (1980) and Rosen et al. (1981).

　　The dipnoans, crossopterygians, and actinopterygians are all repre-sented in the Lower Devonian.

　　The class, as used here, contains 42 orders, 418 families, about 3881 genera, and about 20,857 species.

Subclass DIPNEUSTI—Lungfishes (see map on p. 403)

It has generally been thought that the many similarities between dipnoans and amphibians are the result of convergent evolution and not due
to phylogenetic relationship. However, a view of many early workers that
dipnoans are more closely related to the tetrapods than is any other fish
group has been put forth by Gardiner (1980) and Rosen et al. (1981).
This view is based partly on their conclusion that the internal (excurrent)
nostril of Recent lungfishes is a true choana. Bertmar (1968), in an
embryological study, had concluded that the dipnoans internal excurrent
nostril is a ventrally migrated external excurrent nostril. According to
Gardiner (1980), the cladistic sequence, proceeding from primitive to
advanced, is as follows: coelacanths, porolepiforms, *Eusthenopteron*, osteo-
lepidids, panderichthyids, lungfishes, and tetrapods. Jarvik (1981), in a
review of Rosen et al. (1981), defends the view that it is the rhipidistians
and not the lungfishes that are ancestral to the tetrapods. Furthermore,
Vorobyeva (1975) and Janvier (1980) regard the Osteolepiformes as the
ancestral group of the tetrapods, although Janvier (1980) admits that the
Osteolepiformes and Dipnoi may have shared an immediate common
ancestor with both being the sister group of tetrapods. General acceptance as to whether dipnoans or crossopterygians gave rise to amphibians
will probably not be easily reached. However, the problem probably will
be resolved only through the study of fossils, and the viewpoint is accepted here that the present weight of evidence favors the crossopterygians as being the ancestral group.

   Miles (1977) does not believe it possible, with available information, to
develop a phylogenetic classification of the lungfishes and recognizes a
sequence of 10 families. *Neoceratodus* is given under the new family name
Neoceratodontidae, and *Lepidosiren* and *Protopterus* are placed together in
Lepidosirenidae. Work in progress by such paleontologists as K.S.W.
Campbell holds promise of establishing a sound classification.

   Lungfishes probably arose in the Lower Devonian.

†Superorder DIPTERIMORPHA

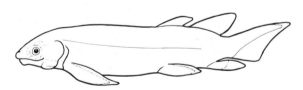

Branchiostegal rays 0–3, gular plates present; caudal fin heterocercal or diphycercal.

Devonian to Triassic.

Moy-Thomas and Miles (1971) recognize six distinct assemblages as orders: Dipteriformes, Holodipteriformes, Rhynchodipteriformes, Phaneropleuriformes, Uronemiformes, and Ctenodontiformes (endings modified).

Superorder CERATODONTIMORPHA

Branchiostegals and gulars absent; caudal fin diphycercal, confluent with dorsal and anal fins; premaxilla and maxilla absent; functional lungs.

Extensive fossil record since the Lower Triassic in addition to the following three extant genera and six species.

Order CERATODONTIFORMES. Body compressed; pectoral and pelvic fins flipperlike; scales large; air bladder unpaired; larvae without external gills; adults do not estivate.

Family CERATODONTIDAE—Australian lungfish. Freshwater; Queensland, Australia.

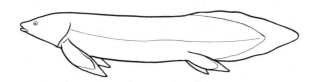

One species, *Neoceratodus forsteri*. Campbell (1981) notes the existence of Cretaceous tooth plates identical with this species.

Order LEPIDOSIRENIFORMES. Body cylindrical; pectoral and pelvic fins filamentous, without rays; scales small; air bladder paired; larvae with external gills; adults estivate in dry season.

Family LEPIDOSIRENIDAE—South American lungfish. Freshwater; Brazil and Paraguay.

Five gill arches and four gill clefts; body very elongate.
One species, *Lepidosiren paradoxa*.

Family PROTOPTERIDAE—African lungfishes.   Freshwater; Africa.

Six gill arches and five gill clefts; body moderately elongate.
One genus, *Protopterus*, with four species.

Subclass CROSSOPTERYGII—Fringe-Finned or Tassel-Finned Fishes

Two dorsal fins; paired fins lobate; "cosmoid" scales; hyomandibular involved in suspensorium.

Differing views exist in the interrelationships of the crossopterygians with various authors employing different characters or placing differing interpretations on given characters. Andrews (1973) provisionally places the osteolepiforms, rhizodontiforms, and struniiforms together in one superorder and the porolepiforms and coelacanthiforms in another. Bjerring (1973), however, suggests that the relationships of the coelacanthiforms are problematical and he retains them in their own superorder. Wiley (1979) regards *Latimeria* as the primitive sister group of all other osteichthyans. Some authors have suggested that *Latimeria*, because of various similarities with the chondrichthyans, are more closely related to the chondrichthyans than to the osteichthyans. Forey (1980), however, presents arguments for retaining *Latimeria* in the Osteichthyes.

†Superorder OSTEOLEPIMORPHA—Rhipidistians

Caudal fin heterocercal or diphycercal, but not with three lobes; internal nostrils (choanae); branchiostegals 4–13; lepidotrichia (fin rays) branched; many more lepidotrichia in caudal fin than radials. Middle Devonian to Lower Permian. This group probably gave rise to the tetrapods.
Maximum length 4 m.

†Order POROLEPIFORMES (Holoptychiiformes).   Body plump; pectorals inserted relatively high on body; thick rhombic cosmoid scales to thin cycloid scales; no pineal foramen.

Jarvik (1968a) reviews the evidence that suggests that the urodeles were derived from porolepids, whereas the other tetrapods were derived from the osteolepids.

Two families, Porolepidae and Holoptychiidae. Devonian.

†**Order OSTEOLEPIFORMES.** Body slender; pectorals usually inserted low on body; thick rhombic scales; pineal foramen present.

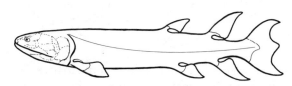

Five families, Osteolepidae, Tristichopteridae, Eusthenopteridae (*Eusthenopteron* is one of the best known of all fossil fishes—see Andrews and Westoll, 1970, and Moy-Thomas and Miles, 1971), Rhizodopsidae, and Panderichthyidae (this group closely resembles *Ichthyostega* and many other labyrinthodonts, the most primitive amphibians, in the form of the teeth and skull-roofing bones—Gardiner, 1980). Rosen et al. (1981) reject the generally accepted view that *Eusthenopteron* is close to the ancestral tetrapod, believing it to be too primitive, and propose that dipnoans are the ancestral group.

†**Order RHIZODONTIFORMES.** One family, Rhizodontidae, containing *Rhizodus, Sauripterus,* and *Strepsodus.* This group is too poorly known for its relationships to be considered.

†**Order STRUNIIFORMES (Onychodontiformes).** Position uncertain. A poorly known Middle to Upper Devonian group known from two genera (*Onychodus* and *Strunius*), which appears to resemble most closely the rhipidistians (Jarvik, 1968a).

Superorder COELACANTHIMORPHA (Actinistia)

Order COELACANTHIFORMES. Caudal fin diphycercal, consisting of three lobes; external nostrils, no choana; branchiostegals absent; lepidotrichia never branched; lepidotrichia in tail equal to number of radials or somewhat more numerous; anterior dorsal fin in front of center of body. Maximum length about 1.5 m (1.8 m in *Latimeria*).

Several families known only from fossils, Devonian to Cretaceous. One family with a living representative.

Family LATIMERIIDAE—gombessa. Marine; South Africa and Comores Archipelago.

First specimen trawled off East London, South Africa, in 1938. Since 1952 numerous other specimens have been taken, all in the Comores Archipelago, northwest of Madagascar. This species is ovoviviparous, with eggs up to 9 cm diameter and young in the oviduct up to about 33 cm in total length. Length of adults up to 1.8 m.

One species, *Latimeria chalumnae* (J. L. B. Smith, 1940; McAllister, 1971; Thomson, 1973; Millot and Anthony, 1958; Millot et al., 1978; Smith et al., 1975; McCosker and Lagios, 1979; Forey, 1980).

Subclass BRACHIOPTERYGII (Cladistia)

Rhombic ganoid scales; spiracle present; dorsal fin consisting of 5–18 finlets, each with a single spine to which is attached one or more soft rays; pectoral fin rays supported by numerous ossified radials which attach to a cartilaginous plate and two rods, thence to the scapula and coracoid; no interopercle; a pair of gular plates, no branchiostegals; maxilla firmly united to skull; intestine with spiral valve; lungs partially used in respiration.

Two views are currently held concerning the relationship of the brachiopterygians (or cladistians): one, that they are allied to the Dipnoi, and the other, more generally accepted view, that they are allied to the Chondrostei. The former view is favored, for example, by Nelson (1969a), who places them in his subclass Sarcopterygii, a group coordinate with Actinopterygii and including lungfishes and crossopterygians, and Mok

(1981), who feels that they shared a common ancestry with the Dipnoi. Most authors, however, place their affinities with or near the Chondrostei and include them in the Actinopterygii. Schaeffer (1973), for example, believes that brachiopterygians may have been derived from an early palaeoniscid line. Patterson (1982) reviews various proposals on their affinities and presents an analysis of their characters; he lists several characters uniting the brachiopterygians and actinopterygians such as the presence of ganoid scales and absence of a squamosal. Rosen et al. (1981) and Patterson (1982) regard this group as the primitive sister group of the Actinopterygii (see below for their use of this category).

Order POLYPTERIFORMES

Family POLYPTERIDAE—bichirs. Freshwater; Africa (see map on p. 403).

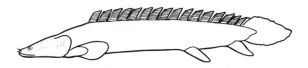

Extensive fossil record in addition to the 11 extant species placed in two genera. Maximum length about 1.2 m, most species less than 30 cm.

Calamoichthys (= *Erpetoichthys*) *calabaricus* (reedfish or ropefish), body eellike; pelvics absent.

Polypterus (bichirs), body elongate; pelvics present; 10 species.

Subclass ACTINOPTERYGII—Ray-Finned Fishes

Scales ganoid, cycloid, or ctenoid (absent in many groups); spiracle usually absent; finlets, if present, with rays attached to body, not to a fin spine; pectoral radials (actinosts) attached to the scapulo-coracoid complex; interopercle and branchiostegal rays usually present; gular plate usually absent; internal nostrils absent; nostrils relatively high up on head. Patterson (1975) describes the braincase of various primitive actinopterygians. A review of the occurrence of bioluminescence in fishes, primarily actinopterygians, is presented in Herring and Morin (1978).

Rosen et al. (1981) and Patterson (1982), in recognizing polyteriforms (in their category Cladistia) as the primitive sister group of the following groups, use the term Actinopterygii to include the polypteriforms and higher categories and Actinopteri (= Actinopterygii as used here) for

Chondrostei and Neopterygii. In Rosen's et al. (1981) classification, Cladistia and Actinopteri are recognized as infraclasses.

Lauder and Liem (1983) have produced a detailed critical review of our understanding of the relationships of actinopterygian fishes.

A cladistic relationship of the higher categories of actinopterygians is shown.

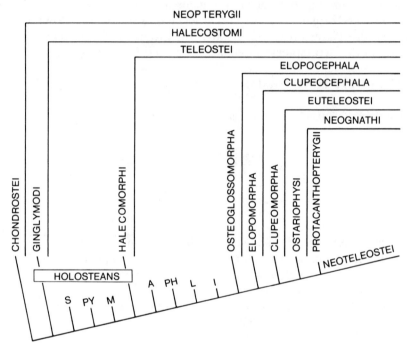

Cladistic relationships of the higher actinopterygian groups with the composition of the holosteans (previously recognized as the infraclass Holostei) indicated. The categories Elopocephala and Clupeocephala of Patterson and Rosen (1977) and Neognathi of Rosen (1973a) are not recognized in the text. Abbreviations for fossil groups: S—Semionotiformes; PY—Pycnodontiformes; M—Macrosemiiformes; A—Aspidorhynchiformes; PM—Pholidophoriformes; L—Leptolepidiformes; I—Ichthyodectiformes (many of these are of uncertain position).

Infraclass CHONDROSTEI

Interoperculum absent; premaxilla and maxilla rigidly attached to the ectopterygoid and dermopalatine; spiracle usually present; myodome usually absent.

Extant taxa in two families, six genera, and 25 species.

The classification of this group is very insecure. It is a group of great structural diversity. Classification of the fossil groups is based largely on parts of Schaeffer (1973), Moy-Thomas and Miles (1971), and Romer (1966). The latter author presented most of the following orders as suborders under the order Palaeonisciformes.

†Order PALAEONISCIFORMES. In many primitive palaeoniscids the cheekbones form a solid unit (the maxilla, preopercles, and suborbitals are firmly united), the hyomandibular is oblique, the eyes are large and far forward, and the tail is strongly heterocercal. More advanced forms had a hyomandibular in the vertical plane and a breakup of the cheekbones. This permitted more flexibility in the oral-branchial chamber. The dorsal lobe of the tail became reduced to an abbreviated heterocercal tail. Numerous other evolutionary trends can be noted in proceeding from the chondrostean level of organization to the holostean level.

Suborder Palaeoniscoidei. This is a heterogenous group of primitive chondrosteans. Some classifications recognize as many as 42 families. It includes the Devonian Cheirolepididae with one genus, *Cheirolepis* (studied by Pearson and Westoll, 1979 and Pearson, 1982), and the Lower Permian Aeduellidae. Patterson (1982) argues that *Cheirolepis* is one of the stem group forms of what is given here as the Brachiopterygii and Actinopterygii.

Lower Devonian to Lower Cretaceous.

Suborder Platysomoidei. Body deep and compressed (zeidlike).

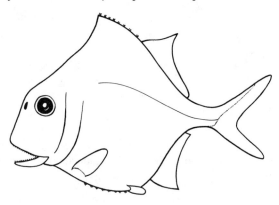

Three families, Bobastraniidae, Chirodontidae, and Platysomidae. Marine and freshwater.
Mississippian to Lower Triassic.

†**Order HAPLOLEPIDIFORMES.** Body fusiform; fin rays few in number and not branched.
Three Pennsylvanian genera recognized. Included in the Palaeoniscoidei in Romer (1966).

†**Order TARRASIIFORMES.** Dorsal and anal fins continuous with the diphycercal caudal fin; pelvic fins absent; scales variously reduced or absent; body elongate; pectoral fins with a rounded fleshy lobe; frontal bones distinct.
Only a few Mississippian genera are recognized (Lund and Melton, 1982).

†**Order PHANERORHYNCHIFORMES.** Body superficially like that of a sturgeon.
One Pennsylvanian genus, *Phanerorhynchus*. Questionably placed in the Acipenseriformes in Romer (1966).

†**Order DORYPTERIFORMES.** Body deep and mostly scaleless; pelvic fin in front of pectorals (jugular); caudal peduncle very narrow.

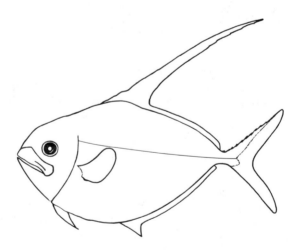

One Upper Permian genus, *Dorypterus*. Placed in the Platysomoidei in Romer (1966).

†**Order PTYCHOLEPIFORMES.**   Triassic and Jurassic.

Order ACIPENSERIFORMES.   Caudal fin heterocercal; one branchiostegal ray; gulars absent; skeleton largely cartilagenous; fin rays more numerous than their basals; intestine with spiral valve.

Includes several extinct families from Pennsylvanian to Cretaceous times. Two families with living representatives.

Suborder Acipenseroidei

Family ACIPENSERIDAE—sturgeons.   Anadromous and freshwater; Northern Hemisphere (see map on p. 404).

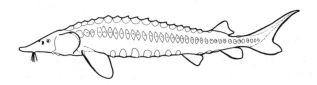

Five rows of bony scutes on body; four barbels in front of mouth; mouth inferior and protrusible; gill rakers fewer than 50; teeth absent in adults; swim bladder large. The freshwater kaluga, *Huso dauricus*, and the anadromous beluga, *H. huso*, are among the largest if not the largest fish in fresh water. *H. huso* definitely reaches 4.2 m and longer lengths have been reported for both species.

Four genera with 23 species.

SUBFAMILY ACIPENSERINAE.   Spiracle present; snout and caudal peduncle subconical.

Acipenser. Range of family. Gill membranes joined to isthmus, mouth transverse. Sixteen species.

Huso. Adriatic Sea to Amur River. Gill membranes joined to one another, mouth crescentic. Two species.

SUBFAMILY SCAPHIRHYNCHINAE.   Spiracle absent; snout depressed.

Pseudoscaphirhynchus (= Kessleria). Aral Sea basin. Caudal peduncle short, slightly depressed, and not completely armored. Three species.

Scaphirhynchus. Mississippi basin. Caudal peduncle long, depressed, and completely armored. Two species.

†*Suborder Chondrosteoidei.*   Two families known from Triassic to Cretaceous times. Errolichthyidae (mouth nearly terminal) and Chondrosteidae (mouth subterminal), have generally been placed together. Schaeffer (1973), however, believes that chondrosteids and acipenserids may be sister groups but excludes the errolichthyids from this order.

Suborder Polyodontoidei

Family POLYODONTIDAE—paddlefishes.   Freshwater; China and United States (see map on p. 404).

Snout paddlelike; body naked except for a few scales on caudal peduncle; minute barbels on snout; gill rakers long and in the hundreds in the plankton-feeding *Polyodon;* teeth minute; spiracle present; gill cover greatly produced posteriorly.

Two living species, *Polyodon spathula* with a nonprotrusible mouth from the United States (Mississippi drainage) and *Psephurus gladius* with a protrusible mouth from China (Yangtze River).

†**Order ASAROTIFORMES.**   Cretaceous.

†**Order PHOLIDOPLEURIFORMES.**   Triassic.

†**Order LUGANOIIFORMES.**   Triassic.

†**Order REDFIELDIIFORMES.**   Triassic.

†**Order PERLEIDIFORMES.**   Triassic and Lower Jurassic.

†**Order PELTOPLEURIFORMES.**   Triassic.

†**Order CEPHALOXENIFORMES.**   Triassic.

Infraclass NEOPTERYGII

Fin rays equal in number to their supports in dorsal and anal fins; premaxilla with internal process lining the anterior part of nasal pit; symplectic developed as an outgrowth of hyomandibular cartilage (Patterson and Rosen, 1977).

It seems generally agreed that the neopterygian fishes are a monophyletic group. Among the major groups with extant species, the gars (Ginglymodi) comprise the most primitive group with the bowfin (Halecomorphi) and the teleosts forming a derived monophyletic group (Halecostomi) (e.g., Patterson, 1973; Wiley, 1976, 1981). However, the interrelationships of the fossil groups are poorly known. The category Holostei, which includes the gars and bowfin and allied fossil groups, is not a monophyletic group, but the term holostean is still useful in describing a particular stage or grade of evolution. In the following classification, up to the Teleostei, I have used parts of the differing systems of Gardiner (1967) and Patterson (1973). Many of the taxa are known to be nonmonophyletic (e.g., see Patterson and Rosen, 1977) and much more work will be required before the phylogenetic relationships are known. I have not included all holostean families in the following classification.

Division GINGLYMODI

Interoperculum absent; two or more supratemporal bones on each side; maxilla small and immobile; supramaxilla absent; myodome absent.

Order LEPISOSTEIFORMES. One family with extinct genera and one extant genus with seven species. Upper Cretaceous to Recent.

Family LEPISOSTEIDAE—gars. Freshwater, occasionally brackish, very rarely in marine water; eastern North America, Central America (south to Costa Rica), and Cuba (see map on p. 405).

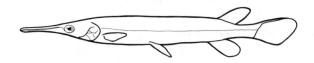

Body and jaws elongate; mouth with needlelike teeth; abbreviated heterocercal tail; heavy ganoid scales, about 50–65 along lateral line; dorsal fin far back, with few rays; three branchiostegal rays; no gular or interopercle; vomer paired; swim bladder vascularized (thus permitting aerial respiration); vertebrae opisthocoelous (anterior end convex, posterior end concave, as in some reptiles and unlike all other fish except the blenny *Andamia*).

The heavily armored predaceous gars usually occur in shallow, weedy areas. Maximum length about 3.0 m, attained in *Lepisosteus spatula*.

The northernmost limit is reached by *Lepisosteus osseus* in southern Quebec, whereas the southernmost limit is reached by *L. tropicus* in Costa Rica. This is also the only species that ranges to Pacific slope drainages (from southern Mexico to Honduras). *Lepisosteus tristoechus* is known to enter marine water around Cuba and the Isle of Pines (Vergara, 1980).

One genus, *Lepisosteus*, with two subgenera are recognized here following Suttkus (1963). The subgenus *Lepisosteus* has four species, with about 14–33 small pear-shaped gill rakers, and the subgenus *Atractosteus* has three species, with about 59–81 large laterally compressed gill rakers. Wiley (1976), in a detailed phylogenetic study of extant and fossil material, prefers to give generic rank to these two lineages. Wiley (1976:4) also refers to a possible new species from the coastal plain of Texas. Fossil species (primarily Cretaceous and Eocene) of the subgenus *Lepisosteus* are known from North America, Europe, and India (extant species are restricted to North America). Fossil species of the subgenus *Atractosteus* are known from North America, Europe, and Africa (extant species are restricted to North America, Cuba, and Central America).

Division HALECOSTOMI

Interoperculum present; one supratemporal bone on each side; mobile maxilla; supramaxilla and large myodome present.

Holostean fossil families that are omitted here include Oligopleuridae, Paracentrophoridae, Catervariolidae, and Promecosominidae.

†Order SEMIONOTIFORMES.   Position uncertain.

Family SEMIONOTIDAE (Lepidotidae)
Mouth small.

Patterson (1973) feels that this group bears more affinity to the halecostomes than to *Lepisosteus* and places it as a basal grade in his Halecostomi. The family may be polyphyletic.

SUBFAMILY SEMIONOTINAE.   Upper Permian to Cretaceous. Body fusiform; dorsal and anal fins usually short; gular absent.

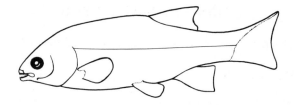

About 16 genera (e.g., *Acentrophorus, Lepidotes,* and *Semionotus; Dandya* and *Heterostrophus* probably also belong to this subfamily rather than to the Dapediinae). Among all holosteans only *Acentrophorus* is known from the Palaeozoic (Permian).

SUBFAMILY DAPEDIINAE.   Upper Triassic to Lower Jurassic; in marine and freshwater deposits; North America, Europe, and India.

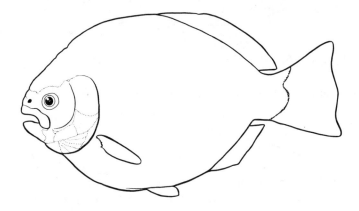

Body deep; dorsal and anal fins long; gular present.
Four genera, *Hemicalypterus, Tetragonolepis, Dapedium,* and *Paradapedium* (Jain, 1973).

†**Order PYCNODONTIFORMES.**   Position uncertain.
Several families (e.g., Pycnodontidae). Upper Triassic to Eocene.

†**Order MACROSEMIIFORMES.**   Position uncertain.
Two families known from the Upper Triassic to Lower Cretaceous, Uarbryichthyidae and Macrosemiidae, are recognized here. Bartram (1977) revised the macrosemiids and concluded that they could not be shown to belong to any other halecostome group.

Subdivision HALECOMORPHI

Symplectic forms an auxillary articulation with the lower jaw.

Order AMIIFORMES

†*Suborder Parasemionotoidei.* The Triassic to Cretaceous Parasemiono-
tidae and Caturidae are placed here. They represent a grade of evolution
and it has generally been felt that parasemionotids are ancestral to catur-
ids with the latter being ancestral to the amioids.

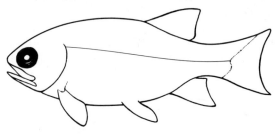

Suborder Amioidei

Family AMIIDAE—bowfin.   Freshwater; eastern North America (see map on p. 405).

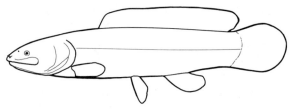

Caudal fin abbreviate heterocercal; dorsal fin base long, with about 48
rays; large median gular plate and 10–13 branchiostegal rays; swim bladder can function as a lung; no pyloric caeca. Maximum length about 90
cm. Lauder (1979) found that the feeding mechanism of the bowfin is of
a fundamentally different nature than that of primitive teleost fishes;
branchiostegal expansion and hyoid depression reach a maximum only
well after the jaws have begun to close.

One species, *Amia calva.* Fossil amiids are known from marine and
freshwater deposits from North America, Brazil, Europe, Asia, and Saudi
Arabia (on the African continental plate); the oldest fossils are of Jurassic
age (Patterson, 1973; Boreske, 1974; Chalifa and Tchernov, 1982; Wilson, 1982, 1983).

Subdivision TELEOSTEI

The composition of this group follows Patterson and Rosen (1977), who define it as a group of halecostomes with the ural neural arches elongated as uroneurals, basibranchial toothplates unpaired, and premaxilla mobile.

Patterson (1977) reviews various attempts to classify the teleosts as well as changes in the philosophy of classification and in definitions and composition of the group. (He presents a controversial view on the contribution of fossils to classification, advocating that the interpretation of fossils is of subsidiary importance to that of Recent organisms.) Several groups of primitive fossil teleosts of uncertain affinities are listed here, while several other early fossil groups such as Crossognathidae, Pachycormidae, and *Tharsis* are omitted. These are followed by the four lineages, given as infradivisions, that I recognize following Nelson (1973a,b) and Patterson and Rosen (1977). They are the Osteoglossomorpha, Elopomorpha, Clupeomorpha, and Euteleostei. Patterson and Rosen (1977), in reflecting a sister group relationship in their classification, recognize the Clupeomorpha and Euteleostei as sister groups in the Clupeocephala. The latter group and its primitive sister group, the Elopomorpha, is recognized as the Elopocephala and given equal rank as the Osteoglossomorpha. In contrast, Greenwood et al. (1966, 1967) provisionally allied the Clupeomorpha with the Elopomorpha in a group termed the Taeniopaedia, while Greenwood (1973) allied the Osteoglossomorpha with the Clupeomorpha and the Elopomorpha with the Euteleostei. Other recent studies on teleostean evolution include Gosline (1980) and Rosen (1982). The muscles of teleosts are described by Winterbottom (1974a).

Teleosts are by far the most abundant (in species) and diversified group of all the vertebrates. About 20,812 extant species placed in 35 orders, 409 families, and 3876 genera represent about 96% of all extant fishes.

†Order ASPIDORHYNCHIFORMES. Position uncertain.
One family.

Family ASPIDORHYNCHIDAE. Jurassic and Cretaceous.

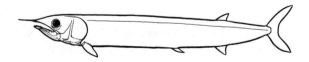

Body elongate with a long, slender snout; dorsal and anal fins opposite one another and placed posteriorly. Appearance superficially like needlefishes. All were probably marine, with lengths up to 1 m.

Two genera, *Aspidorhynchus* and *Belonostomus*.

†Order PHOLIDOPHORIFORMES. Position uncertain. This group may have given rise to the leptolepidiforms in the Triassic and, independently, the elopomorph and osteoglossomorph teleostean lines in the Triassic or Jurassic. All major teleostean lines radiate in the Cretaceous.

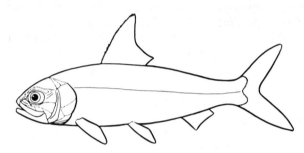

Schaeffer (1972) gives references to studies on various families of the order and describes a Lower Jurassic species (of about 179–161 million years age) from the Antarctica of the presumed freshwater family, Archaeomaenidae, previously known only from Australia.

†Order LEPTOLEPIDIFORMES. Position uncertain.

Family LEPTOLEPIDIDAE. Probably marine, Triassic to Cretaceous.

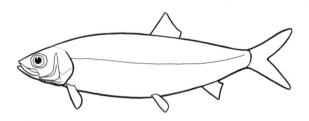

This family has been revised by Nybelin (1974). The type species of the type genus, *Leptolepis coryphaenoides* (redescribed in detail by Wenz, 1967), probably belongs elsewhere (Patterson and Rosen, 1977).

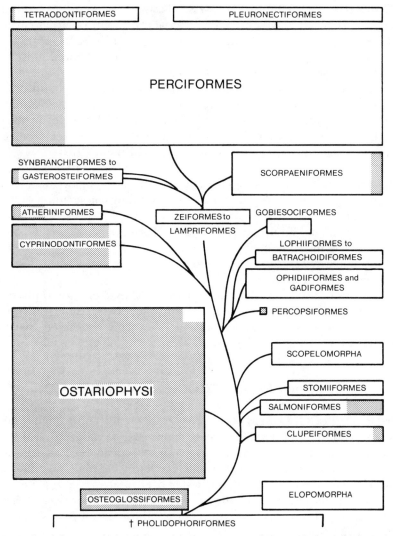

Generalized diagram of relationships of the major groups of extant teleosts. All lines indicating postulated relationships are shown as the same regardless of whether the affinity is considered highly speculative or relatively certain. The area of the blocks is roughly proportional to the number of species recognized in the indicated group; the black area represents the percentage of species normally confined to fresh water.

†**Order ICHTHYODECTIFORMES.** Position uncertain. An endoskeletal ethmo–palatine bone in floor of nasal capsule; uroneurals covering lateral faces of preural centra; anal fin long, usually with 24–37 rays and opposite the posteriorly situated dorsal fin of 10–18 rays. Most were marine and probably predators of other fishes.

Contains three families: Allothrissopidae with the Upper Jurassic *Allothrissops*, Ichthyodectidae with nine nominal genera (e.g., *Ichthyodectes*, *Xiphactinus*, *Gillicus*, *Cladocyclus*, and *Thrissops*) from the Upper Jurassic to the Upper Cretaceous, and Saurodontidae with the two Cretaceous genera *Saurodon* and *Saurocephalus* (Patterson and Rosen, 1977).

†*Suborder Tselfatoidei.* Position uncertain. Body deep; mouth bordered by premaxilla and maxilla; dorsal fin extending along most of back; pectoral fins inserted high on body; pelvics absent or present with six or seven rays; caudal fin deeply forked with 18 principal rays; palate toothed; most fin rays unsegmented.

This suborder includes several Cretaceous genera, such as *Tselfatia*, *Protobrama*, and *Plethodus*.

McAllister (1968) felt that the majority of characters would place this group near the Elopoidei, Albuloidei, and Clupeoidei. Patterson (1967b) placed them in the Osteoglossomorpha but later concluded that they belong elsewhere (see Greenwood, 1973).

Infradivision OSTEOGLOSSOMORPHA

Order OSTEOGLOSSIFORMES. Parasphenoid and tongue bones usually with well-developed teeth; no supramaxilla; caudal fin with 16 or fewer branched rays; caudal fin skeleton, except in *Hiodon*, with large first ural centrum and no urodermals; nasal capsule rigid, no antorbital-supraorbital system for pumping water over olfactory epithelium; epipleural intermuscular bones absent; intestine passes posteriorly to left of esophagus and stomach (in most other gnathostomes it passes to right); one or two pyloric caeca.

The following classification is based largely on the study of Greenwood (1973). The most significant difference is that he places the Mormyridae and Gymnarchidae in the superfamily Notopteroidea on the basis of shared specializations, whereas I, agreeing with the phylogenetic relationship, recognize the two families in separate suborders because of the inferred substantial genetic divergence of the two from their closest known relative, as judged from the presence of electric organs and an enlarged brain. I follow Nelson (1968b) and Kershaw (1976) in placing *Arapaima* and *Heterotis* in the same subfamily. Kershaw (1976), in a detailed study of osteoglossoid cranial anatomy, lists many unique characters for *Pantodon* but suggests that it might be included in the Osteoglossinae. Although it may be most closely related to this subfamily I do not accept such a lumping here. Additional studies on osteoglossiform systematics include Nelson (1969b, 1972a) and various studies of L. P. Taverne.

Six families, 26 genera, and about 206 species.

Suborder Osteoglossoidei.   Maxilla toothed; no intracranial penetration of swim bladder; six pelvic rays; lateral line scales 21–55.

Seven species.

Family OSTEOGLOSSIDAE—osteoglossids or bonytongues.   Freshwater; circumtropical (see map on p. 406).

Pelvic fins distinctly behind base of pectoral fins; some possess a suprabranchial organ and can utilize atmospheric air; 60–100 vertebrae.

Most osteoglossids are omnivorous or carnivorous. Lowe-McConnell (1975) notes that even little river bats are included in the diet of the relatively small *Osteoglossum*.

The fossil record includes *Phareodus* from the Eocene of Wyoming and specimens resembling *Phareodus* and *Heterotis* from the Paleocene of Alberta.

SUBFAMILY HETEROTIDINAE.   No mandibular barbels; branchiostegal rays 10 or 11 *(Arapaima)* or 7–9 *(Heterotis)*.

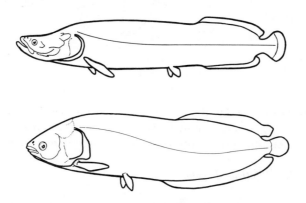

Two species, *Arapaima gigas* (pirarucú) of South America (upper figure) and *Heterotis (= Clupisudis) niloticus,* which lacks parasphenoid teeth and has reduced tongue teeth, of western Africa (lower figure). *A. gigas* of South America, one of the world's largest species of scaled freshwater fish, grows to about 2–2½ m in length. Although larger specimens probably existed before the modern fisheries, the much larger sizes of 3 m or over, given in earlier reports, are probably in error (Roberts, 1982a).

SUBFAMILY OSTEOGLOSSINAE.   Mandibular barbels present; 10–17 branchiostegal rays.

Osteoglossum bicirrosum (arawana) and *O. ferreirai* occur in South America and have 42–57 dorsal rays; *Scleropages leichardti* and *S. formosus* occur in northern Australia and Southeast Asia and have about 20 dorsal rays.

Family PANTODONTIDAE—butterflyfish.   Freshwater; tropical western Africa.

Pelvic fins located under the pectoral fins; swim bladder can act as an air-breathing organ; eight branchiostegal rays; greatly enlarged pectoral fins; suboperculum absent; interoperculum sometimes absent; 30 vertebrae. Length up to 10 cm.

One species, *Pantodon buchholzi.*

Suborder Notopteroidei.   Maxilla toothed; anterior prongs of the swim bladder pass forward to the ear lateral to the skull (intracranially in *Xenomystus* and *Papyrocranus*).

Eight species.

Superfamily Hiodontoidea

†**Family LYCOPTERIDAE.**   Upper Jurassic to Lower Cretaceous; freshwater; eastern Asia.

This family has usually been associated with the Cyprinidae, of Berg's (1940) basal Clupeiformes, and the Leptolepidae. Its placement here in a superfamily with Hiodontidae follows Greenwood (1970).
   Includes the well-known genus *Lycoptera* and several poorly known genera.

Family HIODONTIDAE—mooneyes.   Freshwater; North America (see map on p. 406).

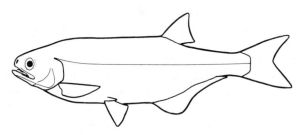

Anal fin moderately long (23–33 rays) and not confluent with the well-developed forked caudal fin; pelvic fins distinct, with seven rays; 7–10 branchiostegal rays; subopercular present; lateral-line scales about 54–61. Length up to 50 cm.
   Two species: *Hiodon tergisus* (mooneye) with 11 or 12 principal dorsal fin rays and no keel in front of pelvics; and *Hiodon alosoides* (goldeye) with 9 or 10 principal dorsal fin rays and a keel in front of pelvics.
   Several species of the fossil *Eohiodon* are known from Eocene deposits in western North America (e.g., Cavender, 1966; Grande, 1979; Wilson, 1977) and specimens resembling *Eohiodon* and *Hiodon* are known from the Paleocene of Alberta (Wilson, 1980).

Superfamily Notopteroidea

Family NOTOPTERIDAE—featherbacks or knifefishes.   Freshwater, sometimes brackish; Africa to Southeast Asia (see map on p. 407).

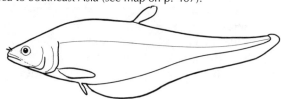

Anal fin long (85–141 rays or 100 or more rays in anal and caudal combined) and confluent with a reduced caudal fin; pelvic fins small (3–6 rays) to absent; subopercular absent; lateral-line scales 120–180; ventral scutes 25–45. Length up to 80 cm.

Three genera: *Notopterus* (about four species) occurs in India and Southeast Asia and has a small dorsal fin with 8–10 rays and eight or nine branchiostegal rays; *Papyrocranus afer* occurs in tropical Africa and has six or seven rays in the dorsal fin and 6–9 branchiostegal rays. *Xenomystus nigri* is confined to tropical Africa; it lacks a dorsal fin and has three branchiostegal rays. *Papyrocranus* and *Xenomystus* probably belong on the same phyletic line (and may be placed in the subfamily Xenomystinae, as opposed to the Notopterinae).

Suborder Mormyroidei.   Maxilla toothless; enormous cerebellum; eyes usually small; electric organs derived from caudal muscles; intracranial penetration of swim bladder.

Some mormyrids and the one gymnarchid are known to transmit weak electric currents and to be capable of detecting extremely weak charges. They are primarily nocturnal fishes and may use these currents to locate objects (see Lissman, 1963). Mormyrids, at least, appear to have considerable learning ability. Their brain size (largely cerebellum), relative to body weight, is comparable to that of humans.

Family MORMYRIDAE—elephantfishes.   Freshwater; tropical Africa and Nile (see map on p. 407).

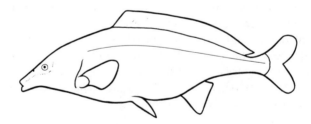

Anal, caudal, and pelvic fins present; caudal peduncle narrow; caudal fin deeply forked; teeth present on parasphenoid and tongue; 6–8 branchiostegal rays; dorsal fin rays 12–91; anal rays 20–70; dorsal and anal fins usually opposite and placed back on body; vertebrae 37–64.

The mouth is extremely variable in mormyrids. In some there is a very elongate proboscislike snout with a terminal mouth (e.g., *Gnathonemus curvirostris*); in a few there is an elongate lower jaw (e.g., *Gnathonemus petersii*), whereas in others there is a rounded snout with an undershot mouth (e.g., *Marcusenius*). The fish shown on p. 94 has a moderately developed proboscislike snout. Some bottom-feeding mormyrids have a chin barbel which is absent in the midwater species. Taverne (1968) gives an osteological description of several species and Taverne (1972) reviews the family. Length reported up to 1.5 m; the maximum length in most species is 9–50 cm.

About 16 genera (e.g., *Gnathonemus, Marcusenius, Mormyrops, Mormyrus,* and *Petrocephalus*) and about 190 species.

Family GYMNARCHIDAE.   Freshwater; tropical Africa and Nile.

Anal, caudal, and pelvic fins absent; teeth absent from parasphenoid and tongue; four branchiostegal rays; elongate body; long dorsal fin (183–230 rays), which can be used for locomotion. (They can move forward or backward equally well by passing reversible wavelike movements along the fin while keeping the body rigid.) Vertebrae 114–120. Mok (1981) reports an interesting difference between the circulatory system of *Gymnarchus* and that of other members of the order. In most osteoglossiforms the left neoposterior cardinal vein is much longer than the right, while in *Gymnarchus*, as in most other teleosts, the right neoposterior cardinal vein is the major vein. (But in *Gymnarchus* the small left one arises from the right one.) Length reported up to 1.5 m but usually less than 0.9 m.

One species, *Gymnarchus niloticus.*

Infradivision ELOPOMORPHA

Leptocephalous larva (ribbonlike, totally unlike the adult); swim bladder not connected with ear (in *Megalops,* however, it does lie against the skull); no *recessus lateralis;* hypurals, when present, on three or more centra; branchiostegal rays usually more than 15; parasphenoid toothed (except in some Notacanthiformes). During metamorphosis from the leptocephalous to the juvenile body form the fish shrinks greatly in length (Hollister, 1936, describes the shrinkage in *Albula*). Larvae commonly reach 10 cm and may be as long as 1.8 m. Smith (1979) gives keys and descriptions for the leptocephali of this group.

The recognition of a relationship between the elopiforms and anguilliforms, based largely on the common occurrence of a leptocephalous larval stage, has only recently been accepted following the classification of Greenwood et al. (1966) which has formed the basis for further work. They recognized three orders in the superorder Elopomorpha, the Elopiformes (with Elopoidei and Albuloidei), Anguilliformes (Anguilloidei and Saccopharyngoidei), and Notacanthiformes. Subsequent changes, employing cladistic principles, largely involved rearranging groups within the superorder (Forey, 1973a,b; Nelson, 1973a,b; Patterson and Rosen, 1977; Greenwood, 1977). Not all authors accept the larva as a valid indicator of affinity. For example, Blot (1975), in a study of Upper Cretaceous and Lower Eocene eel fossils, proposes that anguilliforms may be derived from Amiidae and should, perhaps, be excluded from the teleosteans. The characters that Blot employs in proposing an amiid–eel relationship are probably, however, primitive characters which are not valid indicators of phylogenetic relationship.

The classification of Greenwood (1977) is basically similar to that of Nelson (1973a,b). His cohort Taeniopaedia is equivalent to what is given here as the infradivision Elopomorpha. Greenwood (1977) recognizes two superorders, the Elopomorpha (Elopidae and Megalopidae) and the Anguillomorpha (with the orders Albuliformes and Anguilliformes). He places the suborders Albuloidei and Halosauroidei (Halosauridae and Notacanthidae) within the Albuliformes. I accept the sequencing given by Greenwood but do not follow the cladistic classification, preferring, for example, to recognize the primitive relationship of Elopidae and Albulidae by placing them in the same order. Below, the elopomorphs with herringlike bodies are placed in Elopiformes and those with eellike bodies are placed in Notacanthiformes and Anguilliformes.

Twenty-five families, 157 genera, and about 633 species.

Order ELOPIFORMES. Pelvic fins abdominal; body slender, usually compressed; gill openings wide; caudal fin deeply forked; scales cycloid; mesocoracoid and postcleithra present. Leptocephali with a well developed, forked, caudal fin and a posterior dorsal fin (pelvic fins in older larvae).

Four genera with about 11 species. Forey (1973b) provides a detailed account of the fossil and extant forms.

Suborder Elopoidei. Gular plate well developed (median); branchiostegal rays 23–35; mouth bordered by premaxilla and toothed maxilla; upper jaw extending past eye; tip of snout not overhanging mouth (mouth terminal or superior); caudal fin with seven hypurals; no sensory canal extending onto the small premaxilla.

Forey (1973a) postulates that albulids and megalopids were probably derived from elopids but that the megalopid lineage is older than the albulid lineage. I recognize the greater divergence of albulids by placing them in a separate suborder from the elopids and megalopids. Although I agree that elopids and megalopids are closely related, placement of them in the same family (as in Bailey et al., 1970; Gosline, 1971; Robins et al., 1980) seems as inappropriate as placing them in separate orders (as in Patterson and Rosen, 1977).

Family ELOPIDAE—tenpounders.   Mainly marine (rarely brackish and freshwater); tropical and subtropical oceans.

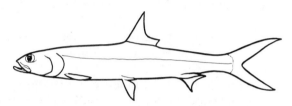

Body rounded (little compressed); mouth terminal; pseudobranchiae large; branchiostegal rays 27–35; dorsal fin rays usually 20–25, the last ray not elongate; anal fin rays usually 13–18; pelvic rays usually 12–16; no conus arteriosus; lateral line tubes unbranched; lateral line scales usually 95–120; insertion of pelvic fin beneath or posterior to origin of dorsal fin; vertebrae 63–79.

One genus, *Elops*, with about five species. Whitehead (1962) presents a key to the six species he recognizes. J. L. B. Smith has speculated that only one valid species exists. Forey (1973b) recognizes the fossil genera *Davichthys* and *Anaethalion*. The latter is a generic complex in which some species show a close affinity to other elopoids. The oldest known elopiform is *A. vidali*, found in the Upper Jurassic.

Family MEGALOPIDAE—tarpons.   Mainly marine (enters fresh waters); tropical and subtropical oceans.

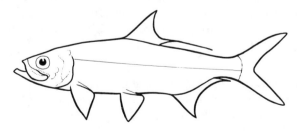

Body compressed; mouth terminal or superior; pseudobranchiae absent; branchiostegal rays 23–27; dorsal fin rays 13–21, the last ray elongate; anal fin rays usually 22–29; pelvic rays 10 or 11; conus arteriosus present; lateral line tubes branched (radiating over surface of lateral line scales); only elopiforms with the swim bladder lying against the skull (there is no intimate association between the swim bladder and the perilymphatic cavity as in clupeoids and notopteroids). Maximum length about 2.2 m, attained in *Megalops atlanticus.*

Two species, *Megalops cyprinoides* of the Indo-West Pacific (Africa to Society Islands) and *Megalops atlanticus* (= *Tarpon atlanticus*) of the western Atlantic (Nova Scotia to Brazil and offshore) and off tropical West Africa. The two species can be distinguished as follows:

M. cyprinoides. Insertion of pelvic fin beneath origin of dorsal fin; dorsal fin rays 17–21; lateral line scales 37–42; vertebrae 67 or 68.

M. atlanticus. Insertion of pelvic fin in advance of origin of dorsal fin; dorsal fin rays 13–16; lateral line scales 41–48; vertebrae 53–57.

Forey (1973b) recognizes the following fossil genera: *Protarpon, Promegalops, Elopoides, Sedenhorstia,* and possibly *Pachythrissops.*

Suborder Albuloidei. Gular plate reduced to a thin median splint or absent; branchiostegal rays 6–16; pelvic rays 10–14; mouth bordered primarily by the premaxilla (maxilla toothed only in Pterothrissinae); upper jaw not extending as far as front of eye; tip of snout overhanging mouth (mouth inferior); caudal fin with six hypurals; infraorbital lateral line canal extending onto premaxilla, which is rare among living teleosteans.

Greenwood (1977) rejects Forey's (1973a,b) proposal that Notacanthiformes and the Pterothrissinae shared a common ancestry with the Albulidae. However, he regards the albuloids and notacanthiforms as sister groups.

Forey (1973b) erected the family Osmeroididae for the extinct *Osmeroides* and *Dinelops* and placed it in this suborder. *Albula* and *Pterothrissus* probably evolved from an osmeroidid, which may in turn have been derived from an elopid.

Family ALBULIDAE—bonefishes.   Marine; tropical seas.

Maximum length about 105 cm, attained in *Albula vulpes.*

SUBFAMILY ALBULINAE.   Most tropical seas (rarely brackish and fresh-water).

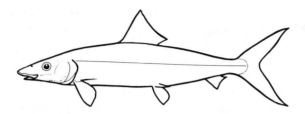

Dorsal fin base short, 16–21 rays (last ray of dorsal fin prolonged into a filament in *Albula nemoptera*); branchiostegal rays 10–16; gill rakers 15–17; lateral line scales 66–84; vertebrae 69–80; small median gular plate; maxilla toothless.

Two species, *Albula vulpes* (most tropical seas) and *A. nemoptera* (= *Dixonina nemoptera*) (Panama to Venezuela in the Atlantic and Mexico to Panama in the Pacific (Rivas and Warlen, 1967). However, several species may be represented in what is recognized here as *A. vulpes;* Shaklee and Tamaru (1981) note the existence of two additional species which appear to be genetically more distinct than many genera of fishes.

Several fossil *Albula* exist and Forey (1973b) describes *Lebonichthys*.

SUBFAMILY PTEROTHRISSINAE.   Eastern Atlantic (Gulf of Guinea) and Japan.

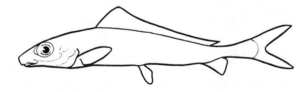

Dorsal fin base long, about 55–65 rays; branchiostegal rays six; lateral line scales 85–112; vertebrae about 107; gular plate absent; maxilla each with six or seven small teeth.

One genus, *Pterothrissus*, with two species: *P. belloci* (from tropical west Africa) and *P. gissu* from Japan.

Forey (1973b) recognizes the fossil genus *Istieus* and possibly *Hajulia*.

Order NOTACANTHIFORMES (Lyopomi and Heteromi).   Body eel-like; posteriorly directed spine on dorsal edge of rear of maxilla; pre-maxilla and maxilla bordering upper jaw; gill membranes separate; pectoral fins relatively high on body; pelvic fins abdominal, with 7–11 rays (the two fins are usually connected by a membrane); anal fin base long and merged with what remains of the caudal fin; caudal fin skeleton reduced or absent; tail easily regenerated when lost (analogous to loss of tail in lizards?); branchiostegal rays 5–23; swim bladder present. Some have photophores (Marshall, 1962).

Mead (1965), Harrisson (1966), Smith (1970, 1979), and Castle (1973) describe the leptocephalous larva. A normal caudal fin is absent but there is a postcaudal filament. The dorsal fin is short, consisting of about 10 rays, and is located in the anterior half of the body. Older larvae have small pelvic fins. The larvae, which can be exceptionally large, reach a length of up to 1.8 m before metamorphosis.

Greenwood (1977), on the basis of assumed shared derived specializations, postulates that *Lipogenys* and *Polyacanthonotus* had a common ancestry and he places both in his subfamily Polyacanthonotinae of the family Notacanthidae.

Members of this deep-sea order have been taken between 125 and 4900 m but most seem to occur at depths of 450–2500 m.

Six genera with about 25 species (McDowell, 1973; Sulak, 1977a; Paulin and Moreland, 1979a).

Suborder Halosauroidei

Family HALOSAURIDAE—halosaurs. Deep-sea; worldwide.

Maxilla and premaxilla toothed; branchiostegal membranes completely separate, rays 9–23; dorsal fin entirely anterior to anus, with 9–13 soft rays, no spines; lateral line cavernous and extending full length of body, lateroventrally; scales relatively large, fewer than 30 longitudinal rows on each side.

Three genera with 15 species. *Halosaurus*, with eight species, occurs in many areas of the Atlantic, Indian, and Pacific, usually confined to continental margins. *Halosauropsis macrochir* is in the Atlantic, southwestern Pacific, and Indian. *Aldrovandia*, with six species, is in the Atlantic, Indian, and western and central Pacific. In addition, some fossils, such as the Upper Cretaceous *Echidnocephalus*, are known.

Suborder Notacanthoidei. Branchiostegal membranes at least partly joined; at least part of the dorsal fin posterior to the anus; lateral line not cavernous and well up on the side; scales relatively small, more than 50 longitudinal rows occur on each side; some have the unique feature of having as many as three spinelike rays in each pelvic fin.

Family NOTACANTHIDAE—spiny eels. Deep-sea; worldwide.

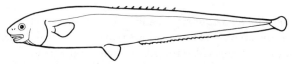

Mouth normal in size, maxilla toothless but premaxilla and dentary are toothed; branchiostegal rays 6–13; well-developed gill rakers; cleithrum and supracleithrum well ossified; dorsal fin with 6–40 isolated spines and no conspicuous soft rays.

Two genera with nine species. *Polyacanthonotus* (= *Macdonaldia*), with three species, has 26–40 dorsal spines and is known from the southern Bering Sea, North Pacific, New Zealand, Caribbean, Mediterranean, and North Atlantic. *Notacanthus*, with six species, has 6–15 dorsal spines and is probably worldwide.

Family LIPOGENYIDAE. Deep-sea; western North Atlantic.

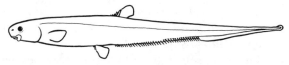

Mouth small, toothless, and suctorial; lower jaw short, lying within the suckerlike opening; branchiostegal rays 5–7; gill rakers absent; pectoral girdle somewhat degenerate, cleithrum and supracleithrum absent; dorsal fin base short, with 9–12 rays (the first few spinelike); anal fin base long, with the first 32–44 rays spinelike, total rays about 116–136; pyloric caeca 5–7; vertebrae about 228–234.

Specimens of the one species are described by McDowell (1973) and Templeman (1973).

One species, *Lipogenys gilli*.

Order ANGUILLIFORMES. Pelvic fins absent (present only in the fossil eel genera *Anguillavus*, which had eight-rayed pelvic fins, and *Enchelurus*); pectoral fins and skeleton entirely absent in some; body elongate (eellike); anal fin usually elongate; gill openings narrow; the two premaxillae, the vomer (usually), and the ethmoid united into a single bone; maxilla toothed, bordering gape; no posttemporal; mesocoracoid and postcleithra absent. Leptocephali with rounded or pointed posteriors and with a many-rayed dorsal fin which is continuous with the caudal but so inconspicuous that it is easily missed.

Eels are primarily specialized for wedging through small openings. Some, in addition, are adapted to burrowing in soft bottoms or to a bathypelagiac existence.

Nineteen families, 147 genera, and about 597 species.

Suborder Anguilloidei (Apodes). Scales, if present, cycloid; symplectic usually absent (hyomandibular united with quadrate); swim bladder present and with a duct; oviducts absent; gills displaced posteriorly; 6–49 branchiostegal rays. Nelson (1966) gives a detailed discussion of the gill arches.

Considerable morphological diversity exists among the pelagic leptocephali larvae, more so than among the adults. Selective pressures on larval characters have generally been different than on adult characters; the larvae and adults give the appearance of having evolved independently. Problems still exist in determining which leptocephali are the young of which adult and the larval forms of some families have not yet been recognized. Most leptocephali are less than 20 cm long before metamorphosis (when there is a loss of certain characters and a contraction in length) but a few are known to exceed 50 cm. Castle (1969) gives an index to the literature of eel larvae and Smith (1979) gives a guide to their identification.

The recognition of two categories in this suborder, based on the presence or absence of fused frontal bones, is based on advice from D. G. Smith (pers. comm. 1982). Superfamilies could be recognized within each infraorder but they are not given here (for example, the Xenocongridae, Myrocongridae, and Muraenidae are closely related).

Sixteen families, 144 genera, and about 586 species.

Infraorder Anguilloidea.   Frontals divided (sutured).
Eight families, 30 genera, and about 171 species.

Family ANGUILLIDAE—freshwater eels. Usually catadromous; tropical and temperate seas except eastern Pacific and south Atlantic (see map on p. 408).

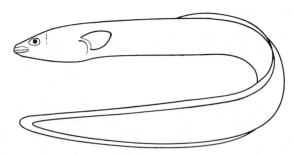

Minute scales present.

The North American and European freshwater eels originate in the Sargasso Sea area. It has been suggested that they do not represent two distinct species but that European eels are strays from the North American *Anguilla rostrata* which develop in cooler regions. (See Vladykov 1964, D.G. Smith, 1968, and Tesch, 1977, for a review of this problem.) This hypothesis, however, is doubtful. Despite much effort, many mysteries remain concerning the life history of *A. rostrata*. For example, adults have only very rarely been taken in the open ocean after they leave the estuaries on their spawning migration. It was not until 1977 that the first evidence of adults occurring off the continental shelf was obtained when two were photographed on the bottom at about 2000 m depth near the Bahamas (Robins et. al., 1979).

One genus, *Anguilla*, with 16 species (Ege, 1939, Tesch, 1977).

Family HETERENCHELYIDAE. Marine; tropical Atlantic (and Mediterranean) and Pacific (Panama Bay only).

Pectoral fin absent; mouth large. Members of this family appear to live in mud.

Two genera, *Panturichthys* (with inner row of maxillary teeth complete or nearly so and 109–136 vertebrae), with four species and *Pythonichthys* (with inner row of maxillary teeth imcomplete and 141–227 vertebrae), also with four species (Rosenblatt and Rubinoff, 1972).

Family MORINGUIDAE—worm or spaghetti eels. Marine; Indo-Pacific and western Atlantic.

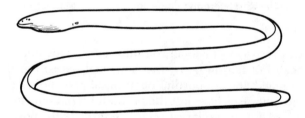

Body extremely elongate, threadlike; no scales; gill openings low on body; dorsal and anal fins reduced to low folds, posteriorly, and confluent with caudal fin; pectorals feeble or absent; eyes small and covered with skin. Marked sexual differences exist, although it is not always certain which males and females are conspecific.

Two genera, *Moringua* and *Neoconger* (Smith and Castle, 1972), with about 10 species.

Family XENOCONGRIDAE—false morays.   Marine; Atlantic, Indian, and Pacific.

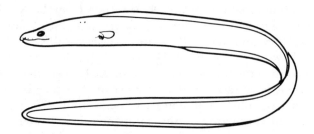

Gill openings restricted to small roundish lateral openings; lateral line pores on head but not on body; one or two branchial pores; no scales; pectoral fins absent in some; all but *Kaupichthys nuchalis* with posterior nostril opening into the lip.

Seven genera, *Chilorhinus*, *Chlopsis*, *Catesbya*, *Kaupichthys*, *Powellichthys*, *Robinsia*, and *Xenoconger*, with 15 species, some known only from single specimens. Böhlke (1956) gives a key to most of the species but recognizes only four genera, and Böhlke and Smith (1968) give a key to the presently recognized genera.

Family MYROCONGRIDAE.   Marine; Atlantic.

One species, *Myroconger compressus*, known from only one specimen described by A. Gunther in 1870 and redescribed by Robins and Robins (1966).

Family MURAENIDAE (Heteromyridae)—moray eels.   Marine; tropical and temperate seas.

Gill openings restricted to small roundish lateral openings; lateral line pores on head but not on body; two branchial pores; fourth branchial arch strengthened and supporting pharyngeal jaws; no scales; pectorals absent (some other eels have lost the pectoral fin but only morays have a greatly reduced fin in the larval stage—Smith, 1979); posterior nostril high in head (usually above front portion of eye); most with long fanglike teeth.Maximum length 3.0 m.

Some morays are involved in ciguatera fish poisoning. This disease occurs largely between 35° N and 34° S and results from eating any one of a large variety of fish species which are ciguatoxic (Halstead, 1967–1970). It is suspected that plant-feeding fishes acquire the toxicity first by feeding on a certain benthic alga; they then pass it on to carnivorous fishes which are the most likely to be poisonous (e.g., *Sphyraena, Caranx, Mycteroperca,* and *Lutjanus*). Randall (1979) found ciguatoxin in many species from Enewetak and Bikini islands in the Pacific in a survey of ciguatera. Randall et al. (1981) note the presence of a skin toxin in an Indo-Pacific moray eel, and note that skin toxins have been demonstrated for at least some species of 10 other families (e.g., trunkfishes, soapfishes, gobies, soles, toadfishes, and clingfishes).

Twelve genera with about 110 species.

SUBFAMILY UROPTERYGIINAE. Ossified hypobranchials in first and second arches; vertical fins reduced, rays confined to tip of tail (the dorsal and anal fins in the larvae are also confined to the posterior end).

Three genera, *Anarchias, Uropterygius,* and *Channomuraena,* with about 19 species (P. H. J. Castle, pers. comm. 1983).

SUBFAMILY MURAENINAE. No ossified hypobranchials; vertical fins not confined to tip of tail. (Usually the dorsal fin origin is above the gill opening or forward, but in three species it begins over the anus or behind.)

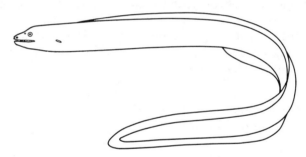

About nine genera, *Echidna* (= *Gymnomuraena*), *Enchelycore, Enchelynassa, Gymnothorax* (= *Lycodontis, Rabula, Strophidon*), *Muraena, Pseudechidna, Rhinomuraena, Siderea,* and *Thyrsoidea* (= *Evenchelys*) (P. H. J. Castle, pers. comm. 1983).

Family NEMICHTHYIDAE—snipe eels. Marine (bathy- and mesopelagic): Atlantic, Indian, and Pacific.

Extremely long, nonocclusible upper and lower jaws (except in ripe males), with upper jaw longer than lower; body very elongate; pectoral fin present; dorsal and anal fins confluent with caudal; eyes large; preopercle absent; frontals partially fused; lateral line complete; vertebrae 170–220 in *Labichthys* and *Avocettina* to over 750 in *Nemichthys* (species of this genus have a caudal filament which is frequently lost and thus precluding accurate counts).

Male snipe eels undergo a marked transformation at sexual maturity with, for example, the jaws undergoing a drastic shortening and loss of teeth. The two sexes of some species were at one time placed in separate genera and even in separate suborders.

Three genera, *Labichthys*, *Avocettina* (= *Avocettinops*, *Borodinula*), and *Nemichthys*, with nine species (Nielsen and Smith, 1978).

Family CYEMATIDAE—bobtail snipe eels.   Marine (bathypelagic); Atlantic, Indian, and Pacific.

Body relatively short; lateral line pores absent; eye small to vestigial; branchiostegal rays and opercular bones absent; gill arches greatly reduced.

Two monotypic genera, *Cyema* (long, nonocclusible upper and lower jaws) and *Neocyema* (body bright red, pectoral skeleton absent—probably neotenic) (Castle, 1977a).

Infraorder Congroidea.   Frontals fused.
    Eight families with 114 genera and about 415 species.

Family SYNAPHOBRANCHIDAE—cutthroat eels.   Marine; Atlantic, Indian, and Pacific.

Larvae with telescopic eyes.
    Ten genera and about 28 species. The recognition of three subfamilies, previously recognized as families, and their included genera follows Robins and Robins (1976).

SUBFAMILY DYSOMMATINAE (MUSTARD OR ARROWTOOTH EELS).   Body scaleless (except in *Ilyophis brunneus*); pectoral fin absent in two species; head shape depressed and relatively rounded; some teeth relatively long.

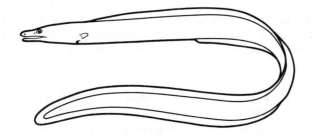

Five genera, *Dysomma* (= *Dysommopsis* and *Nettodarus*), *Dysommina, Atrac-todenchelys, Meadia,* and *Ilyophis,* with about 16 species.

SUBFAMILY SYNAPHOBRANCHINAE. Body scaled (naked in *Haptenchelys texis*); head shape compressed and relatively pointed; teeth small and needlelike; branchial apertures confluent or only slightly separated in most; ventral region dark-colored and dorsal region pale.

Four genera, *Haptenchelys, Diastobranchus, Synaphobranchus,* and *Histio-branchus,* with about 11 species.

SUBFAMILY SIMENCHELYINAE (SNUBNOSE PARASITIC EEL). Body slimy, with scales embedded in skin; snout blunt and rounded with terminal slitlike mouth; pectoral fin moderate in size; complete palatopterygoid arcade (absent or only a splinterlike pterygoid present in members of the other subfamilies). Maximum length about 60 cm.

This eel occurs most commonly between 500 and 1400 m. It is known from the western North Atlantic, the Azores off Africa, Japanese waters, and Cook Strait, New Zealand (Castle, 1961; Leim and Scott, 1966). Although this eel is reported to be parasitic on other fishes (especially halibut), little is known of its feeding habits and food. Adults probably cut or rasp chunks of tissue from moribund fishes and feed on inverte-brates (Solomon-Raju and Rosenblatt, 1971; Robins and Robins, 1976).

One species, *Simenchelys parasiticus.*

Family OPHICHTHIDAE—snake eels. Marine; coastal areas of tropical to warm temperate oceans.

Posterior nostril usually within or piercing the upper lip; tongue not free; branchiostegal rays numerous (15–49 pairs) and overlapping along the midventral line, forming a basketlike structure termed a jugostegalia in the ventral wall of the throat; neural spines poorly developed or absent; hyomandibulae usually vertical or backwardly inclined (inclined obliquely forward in *Benthenchelys*); pectoral fins present or absent; vertebrae 110–270.

McCosker (1977a) recognizes two subfamilies, one with two tribes and the other with four, with a total of 49 genera and 236 species. (Almost one-third of the species are placed in two genera, *Ophichthus* and *Muraenichthys*.) Formerly, subfamily designation was based largely on whether the caudal fin was present, and continuous with the dorsal and anal fins, (Echelinae—the worm eels) or absent, with the tip of the tail hard and pointed, allowing the fish to burrow tailfirst, with the dorsal and anal fins discontinuous externally (Ophichthinae). In the present arrangement, based on McCosker (1977a), greater emphasis is placed in osteological characters. The New Zealand eel *Aotea acus*, upon which the family Aoteidae was based, is a damaged *Muraenichthys* (Castle, 1976). Castle (1972) feels that *Benthenchelys* is a structural intermediate with the Heterocongrinae (family Congridae—particularly with the relatively primitive *Gorgasia*), which also shows some affinity with *Derichthys*.

Subfamily Myrophinae. Gill openings midlateral, opening constricted; caudal fin rays conspicuous, confluent with dorsal and anal, tail tip flexible; coloration uniform or darkened dorsally.

Eight genera, *Benthenchelys*, *Ahlia*, *Muraenichthys*, *Myrophis*, *Neenchelys*, *Pseudomyrophis*, *Schismorhynchus*, and *Schultzidia*, with a total of 37 species.

Subfamily Ophichthinae. Gill openings midlateral to entirely ventral, unconstricted; tail tip is a hard or fleshy finless point, rudimentary rays visible in some genera; coloration variable (usually spotted or striped) or uniform.

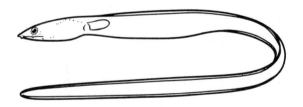

Forty-one genera [e.g., *Callechelys*, *Letharchus*, *Apterichtus* (= *Verma*), *Caecula* (= *Sphagebranchus*), *Ichthyapus*, *Yirrkala*, *Bascanichthys*, *Phaenomonas*,

Cirrhimuraena, Echelus, Myrichthys, Ophichthus, Pisodonophis] with about 199 species.

Family NETTASTOMATIDAE—duckbill eels.   Marine; Atlantic, Indian, and Pacific.

Head and snout elongate and narrow; mouth enlarged; tail greatly attenuated, pectoral fin usually absent in adults. This family of tropical and warm temperate waters is poorly known; eventually, it may be shown to be best combined with Congridae (Smith, Böhlke, and Castle, 1981). *Hoplunnis* is placed in this family, following Smith (1979), and *Gavialiceps* is removed, following Castle (1977b).

Six genera, *Nettastoma* (= *Metopomycter)*, *Nettenchelys*, *Facciolella*, *Hoplunnis*, *Saurenchelys*, and *Venefica*, with about 25 species and at least another 10 undescribed species (Smith and Castle, 1982).

Family COLOCONGRIDAE.   Marine; Atlantic, Indian, and Pacific.

One genus, *Coloconger*, with three species.

Family MACROCEPHENCHELYIDAE.   Marine; Macassar Strait (between Borneo and Celebes).

Body elongate; pectoral fins well developed; mouth subterminal.

One species, *Macrocephenchelys brachialis*, known only from two specimens collected in 1909 (Fowler, 1933:275; Robins and Robins, 1971).

Family CONGRIDAE—conger eels.   Marine; Atlantic, Indian, and Pacific.

Body scaleless; pectoral fin usually present; branchiostegal rays 8–22.

The recognition of Muraenesocidae as a subfamily of Congridae follows Smith (1979). The families Nettastomatidae, Macrocephenchelyidae, and Colocongridae are closely related to the Congridae and may eventually be found to be best placed with it.

Four subfamilies with 42 genera and about 109 species.

SUBFAMILY CONGRINAE.   Pectoral fin well developed.

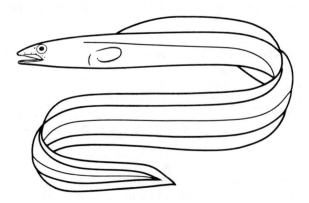

About 25 genera (e.g. *Conger, Gnathophis, Hildebrandia, Rhechias,* and *Uroconger*).

SUBFAMILY BATHYMYRINAE. About five genera, *Alloconger, Ariosoma, Bathymyrus, Leptocephalus,* and *Paraconger.*

SUBFAMILY HETEROCONGRINAE (GARDEN EELS). Pectoral fin minute or absent; body very elongate. Garden eels have the interesting habit of hovering above their sand burrows in large colonies (giving the appearance of a garden), with their tail down and the body relatively straight up.

Four genera, *Gorgasia, Heteroconger, Nystactichthys (= Nystactes),* and *Taenioconger,* with at least 14 species (Böhlke, 1957; Cowan and Rosenblatt, 1974; Böhlke and Randall, 1981). Böhlke and Randall (1981) tentatively regard *Nystactichthys* and *Taenioconger* as junior synonyms of *Heteroconger.* Species in the latter genus are distinguished from those of *Gorgasia* in having a free upper labial flange continuous around the snout to include the anterior nostrils, as opposed to other congrids, that have the labial flanges restricted anteriorly and anterior nostrils on the snout tip before the labial flanges.

SUBFAMILY MURAENESOCINAE (PIKE CONGERS). Pectorals well developed; eyes large and covered with skin; dorsal fin origin over pectoral base; lateral line conspicuous; teeth well developed, especially on the vomer.

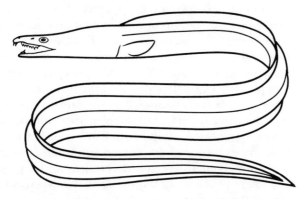

Eight genera, *Congresox, Cynoponticus, Gavialiceps, Muraenesox, Oxycon-ger, Paraxenomystax, Sauromuraenesox,* and *Xenomystax,* with about 14 species (e.g., Castle and Williamson, 1975; Castle, 1977b; Smith, 1979).

Family DERICHTHYIDAE—longneck eels. Bathypelagic; Atlantic, Indian, and Pacific.

Series of parallel striations on the head forming part of a sensory system.
Two genera, the monotypic *Derichthys* with a short snout (Castle, 1970) and *Nessorhamphus* containing two circumtropical species with relatively long snouts. The two genera have been recognized in separate families but Robins and Robins (1971:148) place them together in the same family.

Family SERRIVOMERIDAE—sawtooth eels. Bathypelagic; Atlantic, Indian, and Pacific.

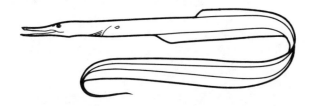

Jaws elongate; vomerine teeth bladelike.
Three genera, *Platuronides, Serrivomer (= Spinivomer),* and *Stemonidium,* with about 10 species.

Suborder Saccopharyngoidei (Lyomeri). Highly aberrant fishes, lacking symplectic bone, opercular bones, branchiostegal rays, scales, pelvic fins, ribs, pyloric caeca, and swim bladder; caudal fin absent or rudimentary; gill openings ventral; dorsal and anal fins long; jaws, hyomandibular, and quadrate greatly elongate; highly distensible pharynx (accommodating extremely large prey); eyes small and placed far forward.

The saccopharyngoids and anguilloids share a relatively close relationship (Böhlke, 1966, and others), but some earlier authors (e.g., V. V. Tchernavin) have questioned whether they are true bony fishes at all. Orton (1963) describes the saccopharyngoid leptocephalous larvae.

Three genera with about 11 species. References to this group include Böhlke (1966), Raju (1974), and Smith (1979). The species of this suborder are perhaps the most anatomically modified of all vertebrate species.

Family SACCOPHARYNGIDAE—swallowers. Marine; Atlantic, Indian, and Pacific.

Gill openings closer to end of snout than to anus; mouth large; jaws with curved teeth; pectoral fins well developed.

One genus, *Saccopharynx*, with four species known from a total of 16 specimens.

Family EURYPHARYNGIDAE—gulpers. Marine; Atlantic, Indian, and Pacific.

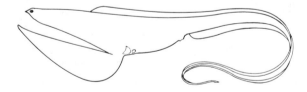

Gill openings small, closer to anus than to end of snout; only teleosts with five gill arches and six visceral clefts; mouth enormous; jaws with minute teeth; pectoral fins minute.

One species, *Eurypharynx pelecanoides*.

Family MONOGNATHIDAE. Marine; Atlantic and Pacific.

Upper jaw absent (i.e., no maxilla or premaxilla); pectoral fins absent; dorsal and anal fins without skeletal supports.

One genus, *Monognathus*, with six species.

Infradivision CLUPEOMORPHA

Second hypural fused with first ural centrum in all stages of development, and the first hypural free from first ural centrum; otophysic connection involving a diverticulum of the swim bladder that penetrates the exoccipital and extends into the prootic within the lateral wall of the braincase (unlike that occurring in any other group); branchiostegal rays usually fewer than 15; body compressed in most; all but Engraulidae with swim bladder opening into stomach; jaws not protrusile. The first two diagnostic characters are from Patterson and Rosen (1977), who align this group with the Euteleostei in their Clupeocephala.

Several lines of clupeomorphs, both fossil and extant, have members which are double-armored, that is, they have both dorsal and ventral scutes. In some of these there is only one or two dorsal scutes (including the several double-armored engraulids), while in others there is a series (e.g., *Diplomystus, Knightia, Hyperlophus, Potamalosa, Ethmidium,* and *Clupanodon*). The double-armored feature has evolved independently several times. Grande (1982a) gives a systematic list of the double-armored clupeomorphs. Studies on the fossil forms include Schaeffer (1947) and Grande (1980, 1982a,b).

Four families, 68 genera, and about 331 species.

†Order ELLIMMICHTHYIFORMES. No *recessus lateralis* (infraorbital canal not merging with preopercular canal but extending through dermosphenotic); patch of teeth on the parasphenoid similar to that in *Osteoglossum;* large foramen in the anterior ceratohyal; parietals in contact between the supraoccipital and the frontals.

The fossils *Ornategulum* and *Armigatus* appear to be related to this group. The recognition of this order and its one family follows Grande (1982a). Its members were formerly considered to be clupeoids.

Family ELLIMMICHTHYIDAE. Lower Cretaceous to Middle Eocene; freshwater and marine.

Subrectangular dorsal scutes; pelvic fin, as far as known, in advance of dorsal fin; ventral scutes extending from isthmus to anus; two supramaxillary bones; parhypural fused to vertebral column; lateral line complete. The monotypic Lower Cretaceous *Ellimmichthys* of Brazil and one of the three species of *Diplomystus* (*D. dubertreti* of the Upper Cretaceous in Lebanon) appear to have had very deep bodies.

Two fossil genera, *Diplomystus* and *Ellimmichthys* (Grande, 1982a).

Order CLUPEIFORMES. *Recessus lateralis* present (infraorbital canal merges with preopercular canal within a chamber of the neurocranium; not known from any other group); parasphenoid teeth absent; no large foramen on the anterior ceratohyal; parietals separated by the supraoccipital; no leptocephalous larvae. Most are plankton feeders with numerous long gill rakers which serve as efficient straining devices.

Suborder Denticipitoidei

Family DENTICIPITIDAE—denticle herring.   Freshwater; southwest Nigeria, Africa.

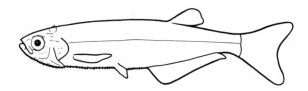

Denticles (odontodes) on all roofing bones of skull; no supramaxilla; 16 principal caudal fin rays; five branchiostegal rays, median pair with denticles on anterior edge; ventral half of head with "furred" appearance from small denticles; lateral line complete.

Family erected in 1959 (Clausen, 1959). A fossil denticipitid *(Palaeodenticeps)* is known from the Oligocene or Miocene from Tanzania, East Africa (Greenwood, 1968).

One species, *Denticeps clupeoides.*

Suborder Clupeoidei.   Lateral line not extending onto body (canals do extend over the gill cover); parhypural usually separate from the first preural centrum. Whitehead (1963a) reviews the groups and Whitehead (1967, 1974) gives keys to the Indo-Pacific genera.

Family CLUPEIDAE—herrings (shads, sardines, and menhadens).   Primarily marine, some freshwater and anadromous; worldwide (mostly tropical).

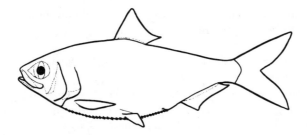

Lateral line existing on a few scales behind the head in some species, absent in others; head scaleless; dorsal and pelvic fins rarely absent (both absent in *Raconda*); mouth inferior, superior, or terminal; teeth small or absent; abdominal scutes usually present [the Dussumieriinae (round herrings) usually lack abdominal scutes, except for a single pelvic scute]; usually 5–10 branchiostegal rays (6–20 in Dussumieriinae). See Svetovidov (1952), Berry (1964), and Nelson (1967, 1970a) for an account of the family. Maximum length 75 cm.

A valuable commercial fishery exists for clupeids in many parts of the world. Most species form schools and swim near the surface, usually in coastal waters, feeding on plankton.

Seven subfamilies, some given family status (e.g., Greenwood, 1968, recognizes Dussumieriidae, Congothrissidae, and Pristigastridae), with living representatives recognized. (Whitehead, 1974, recognizes an eighth subfamily, the Spratelloidinae, for those dussumieriines with only 6 or 7 branchiostegal rays.) About 50 genera and 190 species. The following genera are examples:

Dussumieriinae (Whitehead, 1963b, recognized seven genera and 10 species of round herrings and gave the group family status): *Dussumieria, Etrumeus, Ehirava, Gilchristella, Sauvagella, Spratelloides,* and *Jenkinsia.*

Clupeinae: *Clupea, Harengula, Opisthonema, Sardina, Sardinella,* and *Sprattus.*

Pellonulinae: *Hyperlophus, Pellonula,* and *Potamalosa.* Grande (1982b) places the double-armored fossil *Knightia* in this subfamily (largely on the basis of it having only one supramaxilla, while the majority of members of the other subfamilies have two). This genus contains three species and is known from presumed freshwater deposits of the Middle Paleocene to Middle Eocene from western North America. Material of possible affinity to *Knightia* exists from elsewhere. This is possibly the most common complete vertebrate fossil known, and Grande (1980) estimates that 20,000 complete *Knightia* specimens were excavated in Wyoming in 1978 alone, mainly by commercial and amateur collectors.

Alosinae: *Alosa (= Pomolobus), Brevoortia,* and *Ethmidium.*

Dorosomatinae (Nelson and Rothman, 1973, recognize five genera and 17 species of gizzard shads; 12 species are Indo-Pacific and the five *Dorosoma* are North American): *Anodontostoma, Gonialosa, Nematalosa, Clupanodon (= Konosirus),* and *Dorosoma (= Signalosa).*

Pristigastrinae (Berry, 1964, recognized eight genera): *Ilisha, Odontognathus, Opisthopterus, Pellona, Pristigaster,* and *Raconda.* Several species lack the pelvic fins.

Congothrissinae (has one genus in Africa and was given family status by Poll, 1964): *Congothrissa.*

Family   ENGRAULIDIDAE   (Stolephoridae)—anchovies. Marine,   occasionally freshwater; Atlantic, Indian, and Pacific.

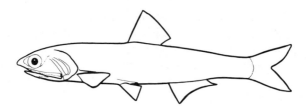

Tip of snout overhanging mouth; upper jaw extending well beyond eye; gill rakers 10–50 or more on lower limb of first arch, 90 or more in some; teeth on jaws absent to well developed; 7–19 branchiostegal rays; body translucent with a silvery stripe down the side. The vast majority of Old World anchovies possess abdominal scutes, while all New World anchovies lack them (except for a single pelvic scute which lacks a keel). Luminescent organs have been reported in one species of *Coilia* (Berry, 1964:722).

   Most species filter feed on zooplankton, but a few large species are piscivorous. Most of the freshwater species occur in South America. The maximum size is about 50 cm but most species are less than 15 cm.

   Two subfamilies with 16 genera and about 139 species (Nelson, 1970a and G. J. Nelson, pers. comm. 1982).

SUBFAMILY COILINAE.   One genus, *Coilia,* with 13 Indo-West Pacific species.

Subfamily Engraulidinae. The Indo-Pacific tribe Stolephorini contains six genera (e.g., *Setipinna, Stolephorus,* and *Thryssa*) with 46 species, while the tribe Engraulini, which is worldwide but primarily in the New World, contains nine genera (e.g., *Anchoa, Anchovia, Anchoviella, Engraulis,* and *Lycengraulis*) with 80 species.

Family CHIROCENTRIDAE—wolf herring. Marine; Indian (west to South Africa and the Red Sea) and western Pacific (Japan to New South Wales).

Body elongate and compressed; fanglike teeth in the jaws (highly predacious fish); spiral valve in intestine; 17–22 gill rakers; no pyloric caeca; scales small; dorsal fin with 16–18 rays; anal fin with 32–35 rays; pelvic fins small, with six or seven rays; pectoral fin with 13–15 rays; 6–8 branchiostegal rays; vertebrae 70–74.

Wolf herrings are voracious carnivores, unlike all other clupeoids. Maximum length 3.6 m.

Bardack (1965) gives a detailed description of *Chirocentrus.*

One species, *Chirocentrus dorab.* (Another species, *C. nudus,* is recognized by some authors.)

Infradivision EUTELEOSTEI

This group, containing all the remaining fishes, is very poorly characterized and there is no convincing evidence that it is monophyletic. There seems to be no known unique character present in all its species. Much more work remains to be done before a sound classification of euteleosteans can be erected, whether employing cladistic or evolutionary principles. Many changes in the alignment and composition of the major groups within it have been made since its recognition by Greenwood et al. (1966; as Division III).

The basic arrangement given in Rosen (1973a) has generally been found acceptable by other cladists. However, some presumed synapomorphic characters upon which the classification is based need thorough analysis before acceptance as such. For example, Greenwood and Lauder (1981) found one synapomorphy which was thought to be characteristic of the Eurypterygii, the protractor pectoralis muscle, to be widely distributed in the Teleostei and perhaps to be present in some other fish groups as well. This muscle, probably homologous with the trapezius of tetrapods, can be present or absent in closely related groups, for example, it is present in *Dallia* but absent in *Umbra* and *Novumbra*, and it is present in some species of *Galaxias* but not in others. In addition, Travers (1981) found the interarcual cartilage, an element between the first epibranchial and the second pharyngobranchial, that was previously thought to be found only in the perciform gill arch skeleton, to be present in several other higher euteleostean groups (and to be ossified in the synbranchids and carapids).

Rosen's (1973a) proposed cladistic classification for the Euteleostei is as follows:

Division Ostariophysi
Division Neognathi
  Subdivision Protacanthopterygii
  Subdivision Neoteleostei
    Section Stenopterygii (Stomiiformes)
    Section Eurypterygii
      Subsection Cyclosquamata (Aulopiformes)
      Subsection Ctenosquamata
        Sept Scopelomorpha (Myctophiformes)
        Sept Acanthomorpha
          Superorder Paracanthopterygii
          Superorder Acanthopterygii

A major realignment of groups within the Ostariophysi has been proposed by Fink and Fink (1981), and a reduction in the membership of the Protacanthopterygii is suggested from the work of Fink and Weitzman (1982). They recognize the esocoids at the base of euteleostean evolution. Esocoids retain a toothplate over the fourth basibranchial which is lacking in ostariophysans and all other non-esocoid euteleosts. The esocoids are retained here with the salmoniforms until further work corroborates the view that ostariophysans are more closely related to nonesocoid salmoniforms than the esocoids. In their cladogram, Fink and Weitzman (1982) suggest that the relationships of Ostariophysi, Argentinoidei plus Osmeroidea (and Galaxioidea), and Salmonidae are uncertain. However, Fink and Weitzman suggest that the Salmonidae is more closely related to the neoteleosts than are the other groups. This is based on two shared features. First, in both salmonids and neoteleosts, both the exoccipital and the basioccipital articulate with the anterior vertebra, whereas in other examined teleosts only the basioccipital articulates with the anterior vertebra. (*Hiodon* has the exoccipital included but the nature of the articulation is different and the similarity is thought to be due to convergence.) Second, the presence of a cartilage structure between the ethmoid and the premaxillae (the rostral cartilage of neoteleosteans) is thought to be homologous in salmonids and neoteleosteans.

It is generally accepted that the stomiiforms are derivatives of the salmoniforms and, because of the many shared primitive characters, it would not be inconsistent in an evolutionary classification to recognize them in the Protacanthopterygii (e.g., with the superorder containing two orders, Salmoniformes and Stomiiformes). However, I have placed them in their own superorder following the Protacanthopterygii with the neoteleostean level recognized as beginning with the stomiiforms but not given formal rank.

The Ostariophysi is recognized here at the start of the Euteleostei following Rosen (1973a) and Greenwood and Lauder (1981). However, probably both the Ostariophysi and Protacanthopterygii have equally primitive beginnings with the neoteleosts being derived from the Protacanthopterygii.

Thirty orders, 374 families, 3625 genera, and 19,642 species. The five largest families, Cyprinidae, Gobiidae, Characidae, Cichlidae, and Labridae, contain about 26% of the species of the Euteleostei.

Superorder OSTARIOPHYSI

Upper jaw protractile in many species; pelvic fins, if present, abdominal; basisphenoid absent; orbitosphenoid present, except in gonorynchiforms; mesocoracoid usually present; postcleithrum absent in gonorynchiforms and siluriforms, one in most cypriniforms, and three in some characiforms and gymnotiforms; swim bladder present (except in *Gonorynchus*) and usually divided into a smaller anterior chamber, which is partially or completely covered by a silvery peritoneal tunic and a larger posterior chamber (reduced or absent in some groups); minute, unicellular, horny projections, termed unculi, commonly present on various body parts (e.g., mouth region or ventral surface of paired fins), known only from ostariophysans (Roberts, 1982b); multicellular horny tubercles (= breeding or nuptial tubercles or pearl organs) with keratinous cap well developed (not restricted to a thin cuticle as in other euteleosts) (Wiley and Collette, 1970; Roberts, 1982b).

Fishes of this group possess a fright reaction elicited by an alarm substance. This was first documented by Karl von Frisch and later described in detail by Pfeiffer (1963, 1977). Such a reaction is otherwise known in fishes only from some percids where it results in reduced activity (Smith, 1982). The alarm substance (Schreckstoff) is a pheromone which is chemically similar or identical in all ostariophysans and is produced from epidermal club cells. Injuries to the skin release the alarm substance which is detected by the sense of smell and causes a fright reaction in members of the same species (or sometimes in related species) in proximity. Some members of this superorder lack the fright reaction but possess an alarm substance (e.g., Serrasalminae) or lack both the alarm substance and the fright reaction to alarm substances of other species (e.g., Loricariidae and Gymnotiformes).

The recognition of five major lineages and their sequencing follows the cladistic study of Fink and Fink (1981), although they recognize the siluriforms and gymnotiforms as suborders of the order Siluriformes. Their classification presents a major change from our previous concept of ostariophysan interrelationships in that they postulate gymnotiforms to be siluriform derivatives and characiforms to be the primitive sister group of both, with cypriniforms being more primitive than this assemblage. Previously, gymnotiforms were considered characiform derivatives and the characiforms and cypriniforms were placed in the same order, Cypriniformes, with characiforms thought to be the more primitive group. The new arrangement of Fink and Fink (1981) should be regarded as provisional. A consideration of other characters may well support our earlier concept, especially with respect to whether cypriniforms are more primitive than characiforms. The five major lineages, recognized as orders, are therefore considered here as being distinct and of uncertain interrelationships but the innovative arrangement of Fink and Fink (1981) seems, at present, more acceptable than our previous one. A detailed description of many characters may be found in Fink and Fink (1981). A freshwater fish from Borneo with certain resemblances to Kneriidae and Cobitidae, *Ellopostoma megalomycter,* cannot be assigned any firm systematic position (Roberts, 1972).

Five orders, 57 families, 938 genera, and about 6050 species. The three largest families, Cyprinidae, Characidae, and Loricariidae, account for 3361 (or 56%) of the species. The ostariophysans contain about 28% of the known fish species in the world while accounting for about 72% of the freshwater species. They are present on all continents and major land masses except Antarctica, Greenland, and New Zealand (Australia has a few catfishes secondarily derived from marine groups). Differing theories concerning the time of origin and zoogeography of the Ostariophysi are discussed by Gosline (1975a), Briggs (1979), and Fink and Fink (1981).

Series ANOTOPHYSI

Order GONORYNCHIFORMES. Suprabranchial (= epibranchial) organ present (consisting of lateral pouches in the posterior part of the branchial chamber behind the fourth epibranchials); mouth small; jaws toothless (except in phractolaemids); orbitosphenoid absent; parietals small; teeth absent on fifth ceratobranchial; first three vertebrae specialized and associated with one or more cephalic ribs (this represents a primitive Weberian apparatus—see Rosen and Greenwood, 1970); 5–7 hypural plates.

Several features suggest some affinity between this order and the clupeiforms. Thus they may represent an evolutionary link between clupeiforms (where many earlier workers placed them) and other ostariophysans.

Four families, seven genera, and about 27 species.

Suborder Chanoidei. Branchiostegal rays three or four; swim bladder present.

Family CHANIDAE—milkfish. Marine and brackish (occasionally freshwater); Indian and tropical Pacific.

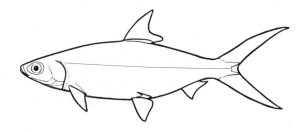

Body compressed; mouth terminal; nonprotractile upper jaw; cycloid scales; dorsal fin rays 13–17; anal fin rays 9–11; pelvic fin rays 11 or 12; branchiostegal rays four; swim bladder present.

Chanos is of considerable importance as a food fish in Southeast Asia. In the Philippines (where they are known as bangos, bangus, or sabalo), Indonesia, and Taiwan, especially, there is an extensive fishpond culture for them. Young are caught close inshore and reared in coastal ponds. Breeding, however, does not occur in the ponds. Females are highly fecund and can lay millions of eggs. Adults feed primarily on algae. Maximum length 1.7 m, usually 1.0 m.

One species, *Chanos chanos*.

Suborder Gonorynchoidei.

Family GONORYNCHIDAE (Gonorhynchidae). Marine; Indo-Pacific.

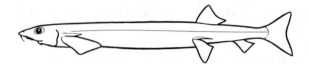

Body elongate; mouth inferior; protractile upper jaw; single barbel at tip of pointed snout; ctenoid scales on body and head; branchiostegal rays four or five; no swim bladder. Maximum length 60 cm.

Among the more recent fossil finds is that of a form similar to the widespread freshwater *Notogoneus* reported from the Paleocene of Alberta (Wilson, 1980). The oldest fossil assigned to the family is the Upper Cretaceous *Charitosomus*.

Probably only one variable species, *Gonorynchus gonorynchus*.

Suborder Knerioidei. Branchiostegal rays usually three; swim bladder present and used in respiration in some species at least.

Family KNERIIDAE. Freshwater; tropical Africa and Nile.

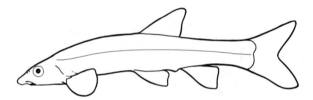

Mouth inferior or subterminal; protractile upper jaw; pelvic rays 6–9. *Kneria* and *Parakneria* have cycloid scales and a lateral line, whereas the small and transparent species of the monotypic *Cromeria* and *Grasseichthys* have a naked body and lack a lateral line. Maximum length about 15 cm. The species generally occur only in rivers and streams.

Four genera, *Cromeria, Grasseichthys, Kneria,* and *Parakneria,* with about 24 species (e.g., Jubb and Bell-Cross, 1974; Lenglet, 1973; Penrith, 1973; Peters, 1967; Poll, 1967, 1969, 1973, and 1976).

Family PHRACTOLAEMIDAE. Freshwater; tropical Africa.

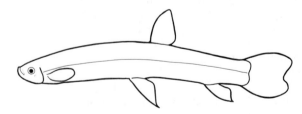

Mouth superior; protractile upper jaw; pelvic rays six; cycloid scales; body elongate; jaws with ony two teeth (at symphysis of lower jaw); dorsal and anal fin rays about six; swim bladder divided into numerous small alveoli and adapted to airbreathing. Maximum length about 18 cm.

One species, *Phractolaemus ansorgei*, found in the Congo and Niger basins (Thys van den Audenaerde, 1961).

Series OTOPHYSI

Distinctive modification of anterior four or five vertebrae; movable bony parts (ossicles) which connect the swim bladder to the inner ear for sound transmission. (The ossicles are known as the Weberian ossicles and their ligaments and the associated vertebrae are defined here as being the Weberian apparatus; see Rosen and Greenwood, 1970, for a discussion of its evolution.) Air-breathing members in the Amazon basin are noted in Kramer et al. (1978).

Order CYPRINIFORMES. Mouth usually protractile and always toothless; adipose fin absent (except in some cobitidids); head scaleless; teeth on fifth ceratobranchial ankylosed to the bone (bound by collagenous fibers to the bone in other ostariophysans with such teeth); branchiostegal rays three; spinelike rays in dorsal fin of some species.

This group is given subordinal status in most classifications. Ordinal status is given here following Fink and Fink (1981). The interrelationship of the families has been studied by Lundberg and Marsh (1976) and Wu et al. (1981). The present classification is based largely on the latter study which, however, unlike earlier authors and the present work, regards the Catostomoidea as the primitive sister group based on the classical assumption that characiforms are primitive relative to cypriniforms. I tentatively accept Fink and Fink's (1981) conclusion that cypriniforms are more primitive than characiforms and therefore regard Cyprinoidea as more primitive than Catostomoidea. Sawada (1982), on the basis of a few presumed synapomorphic characters found in a detailed osteological study, favors a realignment of members of the cobitidids and homalopterids. In his superfamily Cobitoidea, he recognizes the family Cobitid[id]ae with the subfamilies Botiinae and Cobit[id]inae and the family Homalopteridae with the subfamilies Noemacheilinae and Homalopterinae (which includes the gastromyzontines).

Six families, 256 genera, and about 2422 species. The greatest diversity is in southeastern Asia. Wu et al. (1981) estimate that there are 580 species of this group in China alone. Members of this order are popular aquarium fishes, especially the minnows and loaches.

Superfamily Cyprinoidea

Family CYPRINIDAE—minnows or carps.   Freshwater; North American (northern Canada to Mexico), Africa, and Eurasia (see map on p. 408).

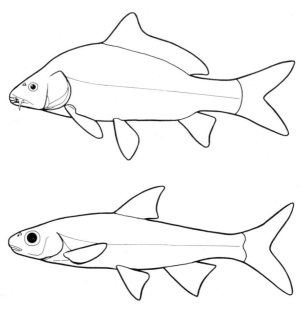

Pharyngeal teeth in one to three rows, never more than eight teeth in any one row; lips usually thin, not with plicae or papillae; upper jaw usually bordered only by premaxilla; spinelike rays in dorsal fin in some. One species from the Iberian Peninsula has an exceptionally high number of gillrakers, 82–130 (Collares-Pereira, 1980). Recent studies on the osteology of this family include Howes (1978, 1980, 1981, and 1982a). The largest species is probably the barbine *Catlocarpio siamensis* of Thailand which is known to reach at least 2.5 m and probably 3 m; many species are under 3 cm.

There are about 194 genera and 2070 species, making it the largest family of fishes. (Only the gobiids come close to containing as many species, and they may well eventually be shown to be more speciose.) Of this figure, some 1850 species are known from Eurasia and Africa (G.J. Howes, pers. comm., 1982) and about 220 from North America (Robins et al., 1980; Barbour and Miller, 1978). This is the most abundant family in most areas within its distribution. Their greatest diversity is in southeastern Asia. They extend southward in North America only to southern Mexico (Barbour and Miller, 1978) and are absent from South America, where characins dominate, and from Madagascar, Australia, New Guinea, and New Zealand. Some species occur in desert areas (e.g., Hubbs et al., 1974). In North America the dominant genus is *Notropis* (with about 110 species) while *Rasbora*, *Barbus*, and *Puntius* are the dominant genera in the Old World.

North American genera include (total of 37 genera with native species) *Campostosma*, *Couesius*, *Gila*, *Hybognathus*, *Hybopsis*, *Nocomis*, *Notropis*, *Phoxinus* (also in Eurasia), *Pimephales*, *Rhinichthys*, and *Semotilus*. Old World genera include *Abramis*, *Alburnus*, *Barbus* (barbels), *Barilius*, *Brachydanio*, *Carassius* (goldfish), *Ctenopharyngodon* (grass carp), *Cyprinus* (common carp), *Danio*, *Garra*, *Gobio* (gudgeons), *Idus*, *Labeo*, *Leuciscus*, *Osteochilus* (= *Osteocheilus*), *Puntius*, *Rasbora*, *Rhodeus* (bitterlings), *Rutilus* (roach), *Scardinius* (rudd), *Schizothorax*, *Tinca* (tench), *Xenocypris*, and *Zacco*. The recognition of subfamilies is very unsatisfactory; relationships are poorly known. Some of the subfamilies often recognized include Cyprininae, Garrinae, Barbinae (the largest subfamily and found in Africa and Eurasia), Schizothoracinae (snow minnows, occurring in fast flowing streams), Hypophthalmichthyinae (small eye set low on head and with gill membranes joined to each other), Acheilognathinae (Rhodeinae) (bitterlings—eggs laid in mantle cavity of clams), Gobioninae (Gobiobotiinae—gudgeons), Rasborinae (Danioinae), Leuciscinae (which includes all North American minnows, except *Notemigonus*, and some Old World members), Abramidinae, Chondrostominae, Cultrinae, Xenocyprininae (e.g., Banarescu and Nalbant, 1973; Gosline, 1978; Jayaram, 1981; Wu, 1964, 1977). Additional subfamilies may be recognized, although Gosline (1978) places all minnows in only five subfamilies.

Family PSILORHYNCHIDAE. Freshwater mountain streams; India and Nepal to Burma.

Mouth small, subterminal; jaws with sharp horny edges, lips fleshy; barbels absent; gill openings narrow; dorsal fin with 10–12 rays (7–9 branched) and anal fin with five branched rays; pectoral fin with at least four unbranched rays; lateral line complete, with 32–50 scales; pharyngeal bone with one row of four teeth; swim bladder reduced. Maximum length about 8 cm. Wu et al. (1981) combine this group with Cyprinidae.

One genus, *Psilorhynchus*, with at least four species (Chandra, 1976; Jayaram, 1981).

Family HOMALOPTERIDAE—hillstream loaches. Freshwater torrential streams; India to China, Malaya, and Borneo.

Mouth subterminal; three or more pairs of barbels present; pelvic fin separate or united under belly; gill opening restricted or not. Their paired fins act as adhesive organs. Maximum length about 12 cm. Additional information may be found in Alfred (1969) and Silas (1953). An earlier view, that the homalopterines were derived from cyprinids while the gastromyzontines were derived from cobitidids (and therefore requiring placement in separate families), is probably not correct (Wu et al., 1981). Twenty-seven genera and about 110 species.

SUBFAMILY HOMALOPTERINAE.   Two or more unbranched anterior rays in both pectoral and pelvic fins. India to China and Borneo regions.

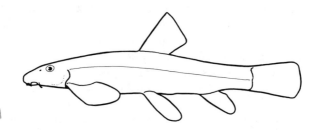

Twelve genera (e.g., *Balitora, Bhavania, Hemimyzon, Homaloptera,* and *Sinogastromyzon*) with about 58 species.

SUBFAMILY GASTROMYZONTINAE.   Single unbranched anterior ray in pectoral and pelvic fins. China, Borneo, and perhaps Vietnam.

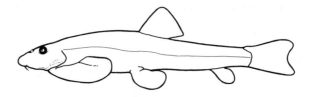

About 15 genera (e.g., *Beaufortia, Crossostoma, Gastromyzon, Glaniopsis,* and *Protomyzon*) with about 52 species (Roberts, 1982c).

Superfamily Catostomoidea

Family COBITIDIDAE—loaches.   Freshwater; Eurasia, Morocco, and Ethiopia (see map on p. 409).

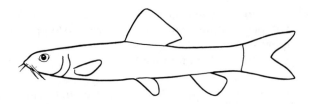

Body wormlike to fusiform; mouth subterminal; 3–6 pairs of barbels present; some members of noemacheilines with an adipose fin; botines and cobitidines with erectile spine near eye; one row of pharyngeal teeth. Greatest diversity in southern Asia; bottom dwellers. Maximum length about 35 cm. Popular aquarium species belong to such genera as *Acantho-phthalmus* (e.g., coolie loaches), *Botia*, *Noemacheilus*, and *Misgurnus* (e.g., weatherfishes, including a color form of the Japanese weather loach called the golden dojo—see Axelrod and Burgess, 1982).

Twenty-one genera and at least 175 species.

SUBFAMILY NOEMACHEILINAE. No spine under or before eye. Eurasia and Etheopia. About four genera (e.g., the very speciose *Noemacheilus*) with about 115 species. The genus *Noemacheilus* is a composite one and additional genera are probably warrented (e.g., Banarescu and Nalbant, 1975).

SUBFAMILY COBITIDINAE. One pair of rostral barbels (rarely absent); caudal fin usually rounded or slightly emarginate. Eurasia and Morocco. About 15 genera (e.g., *Acanthophthalmus, Acanthopsis, Cobitis, Lepidoce-phalus*, and *Misgurnus*) with about 40 species.

SUBFAMILY BOTIINAE. Two pairs of rostral barbels; caudal fin deeply forked; body compressed. Asia. Two genera, *Botia* and *Leptobotia*, with about 20 species.

Family GYRINOCHEILIDAE—algae eaters. Freshwater mountain streams; Southeast Asia.

Pharyngeal teeth absent; ventral mouth modified into a sucking organ for attaching onto objects; inhalent aperture above gill opening entering into gill chamber; no barbels. Feeds exclusively on algae. Size up to 30 cm. These fishes are used extensively in home aquaria.

One genus, *Gyrinocheilus*, with two or three species.

Family CATOSTOMIDAE—suckers. Freshwater; China, northeast Siberia, North America (see map on p. 409).

One row of 16 or more pharyngeal teeth; lips usually thick and fleshy with plicae or papillae; upper jaw usually bordered by premaxilla and maxilla; tetraploids. Anatomical studies include Eastman (1977, 1980) and Ramaswami (1957). Maximum length about 1.0 m, less than 60 cm for most species.

Twelve genera with 61 species (41 species placed in the genera *Catostomus* and *Moxostoma*). The recognition of three subfamilies follows Miller (1958). Fossils include the Eocene-Oligocene genus *Amyzon* with seven species from western North America (Wilson, 1977; Grande et al., 1982). *Amyzon* may be related to the Ictiobinae.

Subfamily Cycleptinae

TRIBE MYXOCYPRINI.   Twelve to 14 anal rays; 52–57 dorsal rays; 47–55 lateral line scales.

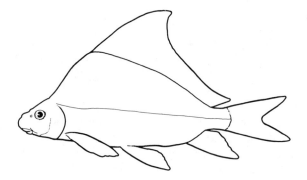

One species, *Myxocyprinus asiaticus* in Yangtse Kiang, China.

TRIBE CYCLEPTINI.   Seven anal rays; 30–37 dorsal rays; 51–59 lateral line scales; southern United States and Mexico.

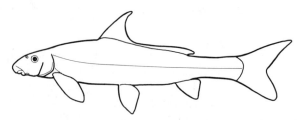

One species, *Cycleptus elongatus.*

Subfamily Ictiobinae.   Seven to 11 anal rays; 22–32 dorsal rays; 33–43 lateral line scales; 115–190 pharyngeal teeth (the highest of all catostomids). Canada to Guatemala (absent from Pacific drainages). Northernmost species is *Carpiodes cyprinus* (North Saskatchewan and Red Deer rivers, Alberta); southernmost is *Ictiobus meridionalis* (Guatemala).

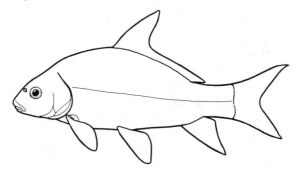

Two genera, *Carpiodes* and *Ictiobus*, with six species.

SUBFAMILY CATOSTOMINAE. Seven anal rays; 10–18 dorsal rays; 30–120 lateral line scales. Northeastern Siberia, Alaska, and northern Canada to Mexico. Northernmost species is *Catostomus catostomus* (rivers adjacent to Arctic coastline); southernmost is probably *Moxostoma congestum* (northeastern Mexico).

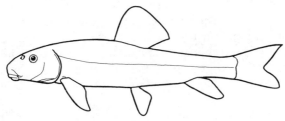

Various species of sucker are known to hybridize as do species of many other families (Schwartz, 1972, 1981), primarily those in north temperate freshwaters. C. L. Hubbs, in numerous papers, has contributed the most to our knowledge of the extent of this hybridization. Nelson (1968) discusses isolating mechanisms and problems of identifying hybrids in a study of hybridization under natural environmental conditions in two species of *Catostomus*.

TRIBE ERIMYZONTINI. Lateral line incomplete or absent.
Two genera, *Erimyzon* and *Minytrema*, with four species, in eastern and southern United States.

TRIBE MOXOSTOMATINI. Lateral line present; fewer than 50 lateral line scales.

Most of the species live in eastern North America. One, *M. macrolepi-dotum*, which is particularly widespread, extends from easternmost United States to Alberta. *Lagochila* is undoubtedly extinct.

Three genera, *Lagochila*, *Moxostoma* (with several subgenera, e.g., *Thoburnia* and *Scartomyzon;* Lee et al., 1980), and *Hypentelium*, with 23 species.

TRIBE CATOSTOMINI. Lateral line present; more than 50 lateral line scales. Most suckers are benthic feeders and have a ventral mouth, but species of *Chasmistes* (lakesuckers) are midwater planktivores and have a large, terminal mouth (Miller and Smith, 1981).

Most of the species live in western North America. Two are particularly widespread, *Catostomus catostomus* (longnose sucker) extends from New York to eastern Siberia and *C. commersoni* (white sucker) extends from Georgia to British Columbia.

Three genera, *Catostomus* (with the subgenera *Catostomus*, *Pantosteus*, and *Deltistes*), *Chasmistes*, and *Xyrauchen*, with 26 species.

Order CHARACIFORMES. Teeth usually well developed (most are carnivores); adipose fin usually present; body almost always scaled (very rarely absent in South American species, e.g., the tetra *Gymnocharacinus bergi* of Argentina is naked, lacks an adipose fin, and is the most southerly known characiform); pelvic fin present (with 5–12 rays); anal fin short to moderately long (fewer than 45 rays); lateral line often decurved; upper jaw usually not truly protractile; pharyngeal teeth usually present, but not specialized as in cypriniforms; barbels absent; branchiostegal rays 3–5; first hypural separated from the centrum by a gap in adults (most other primitive teleosts lack such a gap); usually 19 principal caudal fin rays.

Members of this order are usually small and often extremely colorful (many are silvery); they are popular aquarium fishes. Members exhibit a great deal of diversity; for example, terrestrial spawning has been observed (Kramer, 1978) and some members are scale-eaters (Sazima, 1977).

Workers disagree on the number of families to recognize and the classification of this order is very unsatisfactory. Weitzman (1962) and Gosline (1971) recognize one family, Géry (1977) 14, and Greenwood et al. (1966) 16. There is a great deal of morphological diversity, convergent evolution is common, and interrelationships are poorly known. The present classification is a synthesis based on several recent revisions referred to under family descriptions and the work of Géry (1977). The latter work has been used for much descriptive information including estimates for the number of species in various groups. Géry (1972, 1977) provides keys to the groups.

Ten families with about 252 genera and at least 1335 species. About 176 species occur in Africa with the remainder in Mexico and Central and South America. Included here, in the counts of genera and species, are five genera of the South American darters (e.g., *Characidium, Elachocharax,* and *Geisleria*) that contain about 55 species usually found on river bottoms and, less commonly, among immersed tree roots. They are recognized by Géry (1977) in their own family, Characidiidae. However, their relationship to other characiforms is very uncertain and I have provisionally left them unassigned to a family.

Family CITHARINIDAE.   Freshwater; Africa.

Neural arch of fourth vertebra autogenous; premaxillary ascending process absent; scales ctenoid (cycloid in *Citharinus*); pelvic fin rays relatively numerous.

Fink and Fink (1981) postulate this group to be the primitive sister group to all other characiforms, with *Xenocharax* being the most primitive member. The groups monophyly has been demonstrated by Vari (1979), although he recognized two families; the placement of all species in one family (rather than three in Nelson, 1976) follows Géry (1977) and the implications of Vari (1979).

Seventeen genera and about 77 species.

SUBFAMILY DISTICHODONTINAE

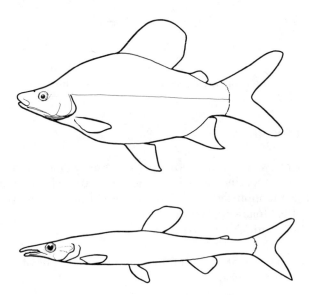

Two evolutionary grades can be recognized. One line consists of those members with nonprotractile upper jaws which are micropredators and herbivores; their body shape is variable, ranging from deep (as in upper figure) to shallow. This grade consists of eight genera (e.g., *Xenocharax, Neolebias, Distichodus, Nannocharax,* and *Hemigrammocharax*) with about 52 species. The other grade consists of species with a movable upper jaw which eat the fins of other fishes or the whole fish; their body is usually elongate (as in lower figure). This grade consists of seven genera (e.g., *Ichthyborus, Mesoborus, Paraphago, Phago,* and *Belonophago*) with about 17 species.

SUBFAMILY CITHARININAE.   Body deep; dorsal and anal fins relatively long, dorsal with 16–24 rays and anal with 19–31 rays. Maximum length about 80 cm.

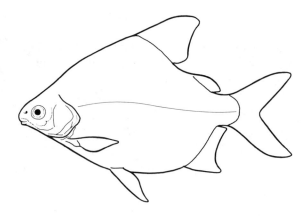

Two genera, *Citharinus* with seven species and the monotypic *Cithari-dium.*

Family HEMIODONTIDAE.   Freshwater; South America.

Mouth variably subterminal; most species with small lower jaw that lacks teeth. The parodontines and hemiodontines are related, but whether they form a monophyletic unit is uncertain (Roberts, 1974). They are placed together following Géry (1977).
    Nine genera with about 50 species.

SUBFAMILY PARODONTINAE.   Benthic; mountain streams of eastern Panama and South America.

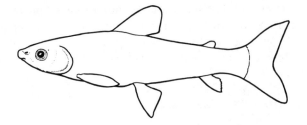

Peculiar fishes with ventral mouths and teeth modified for scraping algae off rocks; premaxillaries highly mobile and greatly enlarged; adipose eyelid absent; lateral line scales 35–43; pectoral fins expanded and flattened; vertebrae 35–41. Maximum length usually 15 cm.

Two genera, *Parodon* (= *Apareiodon*) and *Saccodon*, with about 23 species (Roberts, 1974, Géry, 1977).

SUBFAMILY HEMIODONTINAE.   Usually pelagic.

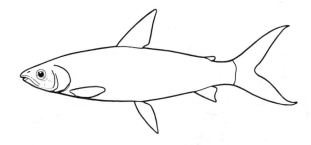

Body subcylindrical to fusiform (and swift swimming fishes); gill membranes free; adipose eyelid present; lateral line scales 50–125; pectoral fin rays 18–23; vertebrae 40–45. Maximum length about 30 cm.

Seven genera with about 27 species (Roberts, 1974).

TRIBE HEMIODONTINI.   Two genera, *Hemiodus* (= *Hemiodopsis*) and *Pterohemiodus*, with about 19 species.

TRIBE BIVIBRANCHINI.   The only characoid with a highly protrusible upper jaw with a unique mechanism of protrusion; premaxilla minute and firmly attached to anterior end of maxilla. Three genera, *Argonectes*, *Atomaster*, and *Bivibranchia*, with about five species.

TRIBE MICROMISCHODONTINI.   Only hemiodontid with teeth on lower jaw throughout life. One species, *Micromischodus sugillatus* (Roberts, 1971a).

TRIBE ANODONTINI.   Jaw teeth absent; numerous elongate gillrakers, up to 200 on first arch (more than any other characoid) depending on fish size; pharyngeal structures specialized for filter feeding on plankton. One genus, *Anodus* (= *Eigenmannina*) with two species previously placed in Curimatidae.

Family CURIMATIDAE.   Freshwater; South America.

Teeth usually absent; typically herbivorous.
    About 30 genera and at least 138 species. The following three subfamilies are sometimes given family status. The classification here follows Géry (1977), while the removal of *Anodus* follows Roberts (1974).

SUBFAMILY CHILODONTINAE.   Seven to 10 branched dorsal fin rays; lateral line scales about 25–31; highly modified pharyngeal apparatus; few teeth present in jaws. Often swim in oblique head-down position (similar to many anostomids—both groups having members called headstanders). Maximum length 18 cm.

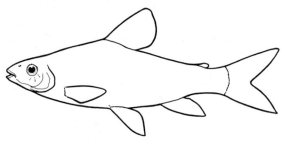

    Two genera, *Caenotropus* (= *Tylobranchus*) and *Chilodus*, with three species.
SUBFAMILY PROCHILODONTINAE.   Mouth protractile, forming a sucking disc (lips enlarged); predorsal spine present. Superficially resemble the cyprinid *Labeo*. Maximum length about 45 cm.

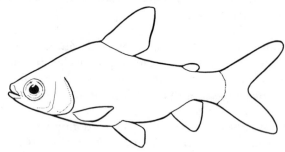

Three genera, *Ichthyoelephas, Semaprochilodus,* and *Prochilodus,* with about 30 species (Roberts, 1973b).

SUBFAMILY CURIMATINAE (CURIMATAS). Mulletlike fishes; jaw teeth absent; gillrakers absent or poorly developed; four branchiostegal rays; strong flange on lateral surface of upper opercle; branchiostegal membranes united to isthmus; vertebrae usually 30–36.

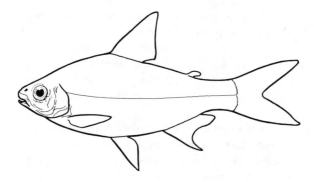

About 25 genera (e.g., *Acuticurimata, Cruxentina, Curimata, Curimatopsis, Curimatorbis, Gasterotomus,* and *Suprasinelichthys*) with about 105 species (Roberts, 1974; Géry, 1977; Vari, 1982).

Family ANOSTOMIDAE. Freshwater; South America.

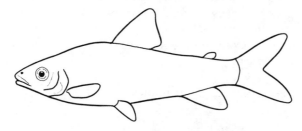

Mouth small, nonprotractile (upturned in many species); body usually elongate; anal fin short, usually with less than 10 branched rays. Many of these species swim in a head-down position and most are herbivores or detritovores. Maximum length 40 cm.

Ten genera (e.g., *Abramites, Anostomus, Leporinus, Leporellus, Rhytiodus,* and *Schizodon*) with about 105 species. Winterbottom (1980) revises one of the two recognized subfamilies.

Family ERYTHRINIDAE—trahiras. Freshwater; South America.

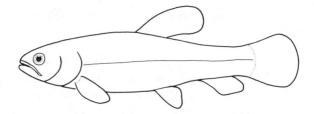

Gape long, extending beyond anterior margin of orbit; body cylindrical; five branchiostegal rays; pectoral fin rays relatively few, 9–14; dorsal fin with 8–15 rays (plus three rudimentary ones), origin in front of anal fin and usually over pelvic fins (males of *Erythrinus* can have an elongated dorsal fin); anal fin short, 10–12 rays; adipose fin absent; caudal fin rounded; scales relatively large, 32–47 in lateral line; numerous teeth on palate.

Some are predators. Some can breath air and move across land between ponds. They show some resemblance to *Amia* in anatomy and, in the case of at least one species, in nest construction. Maximum length about 1.0 m, attained in *Hoplias macrophthalmus* of the Guianas.

Three genera, *Erythrinus*, *Hoplerythrinus*, and *Hoplias*, with about five species.

Family LEBIASINIDAE.   Freshwater; South America.

Gape short, usually not reaching orbit; three or four branchiostegal rays; adipose fin present or absent; anal fin with 8–14 rays; dorsal fin in front of anal fin, usually over pelvic fins (often behind in the Pyrrhulinini, which also have an elongate upper caudal fin lobe); scales large, 18–30 in longitudinal series.

SUBFAMILY LEBIASININAE.   Four branchiostegal rays.

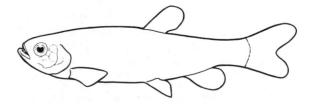

Two genera, *Lebiasina* and *Piabucina*, with about 11 species.

SUBFAMILY PYRRHULININAE.   Three branchiostegal rays.

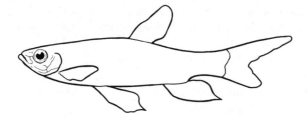

Two tribes are recognized: Pyrrhulinini, with about 25 species, in *Copeina, Copella,* and *Pyrrhulina;* and Nannostomini, which contains about 14 species in the one genus of pencilfishes, *Nannostomus (= Poecilobrycon)* (Weitzman 1964, 1978).

Family GASTEROPELECIDAE—freshwater hatchetfishes. Freshwater; Panama and South America.

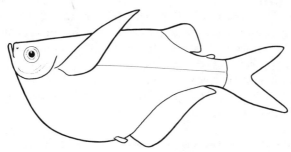

Strongly compressed head and body with protruding muscular breast region; lateral line extremely short, extending to tail, or curved downward to approach origin of anal fin; dorsal fin rays 8–17; anal fin rays 22–44; four or five branchiostegal rays; adipose fin present or absent; posttemporal and supracleithrum fused into a single bone; cleithra of each side fused.

These fishes are capable of making short flights out of the water and are the only fish known to "fly" with a propulsive force while in the air.

Three genera, *Carnegiella, Gasteropelecus, Thoracocharax,* with nine species (e.g., Weitzman, 1960).

Family CTENOLUCIIDAE (Xiphostomidae)—pike-characids. Freshwater; Panama and South America.

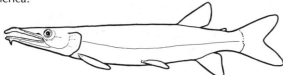

Elongate pikelike body; carnivorous; dorsal and anal fins set far back on body; scales ctenoid; pelvic fin with eight rays. Maximum length about 1.0 m.

Two genera, *Ctenolucius*, with one species having 42–50 strongly ctenoid scales along the lateral line, and *Boulengerella*, with three species having 78–110 finely denticulated scales along the lateral line.

Family HEPSETIDAE.   Freshwater; tropical Africa.

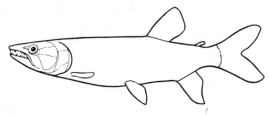

Elongate pikelike body; long snout and large mouth with a few large canines and smaller pointed teeth; dorsal fin with nine rays placed before origin of anal fin which has 11 rays; pelvic fin with nine rays; lateral line scales 49–60, cycloid. Maximum length 30 cm. Eggs are laid in a nest of floating foam. This species is considered to be a gamefish.

One species, *Hepsetus odoe*. It appears to be most closely related to the ctenolucids of South America (Roberts, 1969).

Family CHARACIDAE—characins.   Freshwater; southwestern Texas, Mexico, Central and South America, and Africa (see map on p. 410).

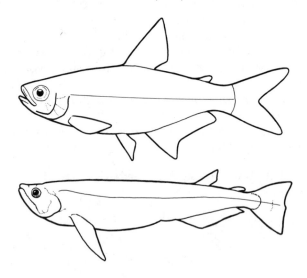

This is a large and diversified family. In it are the potentially dangerous Amazon piranhas (*Serrasalmus*), the South American tetras (e.g., *Hemigrammus* and *Hyphessobrycon*), a blind cavefish in Mexico (forms of *Astyanax mexicanus*, formerly *Anoptichthys jordani*) and Brazil (*Stygichthys typhlops*), and a species that has dispersed into the southwestern United States (*Astyanax mexicanus* = *A. fasciatus mexicanus*). Within *A. mexicanus* there are eyed surface fish (with relatively high genetic variability) and eyeless cave forms (with relatively low genetic variability); in at least one cave the two forms interbreed (Avise and Selander, 1972). Some characins lack the adipose fin. Osteological studies include Howes (1976) and Weitzman (1962). Maximum length about 1.4 m, attained by *Hydrocynus goliath* of the Congo.

This and the osteoglossids are the only completely freshwater fish families indigenous to both Africa and South America (some nandids enter brackish water, and cyprinodontids and cichlids have a few members that enter marine water).

Géry (1977) gives family rank to several groups that are given subfamily status here. These groups are as follows: Alestiinae, from Africa (African tetras), with 13 genera (e.g., *Alestes*, *Brycinus*, *Micralestes*, *Phenacogrammus*, *Petersius*, and *Hydrocynus*) and about 98 species; Crenuchinae, from northern South America, with two genera and three species; and Serrasalminae, from South America (pacus, silver dollars, and piranhas), with nine genera (e.g., *Myleus*, *Metynnis*, *Serrasalmus*, and *Catoprion*—see Géry, 1976) and about 55 species. The subfamily Characinae (ranked as a family by Géry, 1977, and divided into 12 subfamilies, including the South American tetras) is endemic to South America and contains about 142 genera [e.g., *Acestrorhynchus*, *Agoniates*, *Astyanax*, *Brycon* (reviewed by Howes, 1982b), *Characinus*, *Cheirodon*, *Cynodon*, *Gymnocorymbus*, *Hemigrammus* (in upper figure), *Hydrolycus*, *Hyphessobrycon*, *Moenkhausia*, *Rhaphiodon* (in lower figure), *Salminus*, and *Tetragonopterus*] with about 685 species. The family, as recognized here, contains 166 genera and 841 species.

Order SILURIFORMES (Nematognathi). Symplectic, subopercular, and intermuscular bones absent; parietals probably present but fused to supraoccipital; mesopterygoid very reduced; preopercle and interopercle relatively small; posttemporal probably fused to supracleithrum but thought by some to be present as a separate element in many families; vomer usually toothed (as is the pterygoid and palatine); adipose fin usually present; spines often present at the front of the dorsal and pectoral fins; body either naked or covered with bony plates; maxilla rudimentary (except in Diplomystidae), supporting a barbel; principal caudal fin rays 18 or fewer (most with 17); caudal skeleton varying between having six separate hypural plates to complete fusion of caudal elements; eyes usually small (barbels are important in detecting food); air-breathing organs in Clariidae and Heteropneustidae. The Weberian apparatus of catfishes is described in detail by Alexander (1964) and Chardon (1968).

Several species of the catfish order are known to be venomous (Halstead, 1970). They can inflict severe wounds with their spines (primarily those of the pectoral fin) and inject a poison produced by glandular cells in the epidermal tissue covering the spines. Most species are passive stingers (e.g., *Noturus*), and presumably the toxicity of their stings has developed as a protective device in response to predation pressure (Birkhead, 1972). Some, such as *Heteropneustes fossilis* of India, which has a painful and potentially dangerous sting, have an aggressive behavior with records of attacks on humans and other fishes. Stings from *Plotosus lineatus* may result in death.

In many areas catfishes are a popular sports fish and a valued food item. They are also widely used as a tropical aquarium fish. The largest catfish is *Silurus glanis* which commonly reaches 3 m in length. Many catfishes have a maximum length of under 12 cm.

The classification of catfishes is not settled and disagreement exists on the interrelationships of the families. Works on their zoogeography and systematics include Chardon (1967, 1968), Gosline (1975b), and Lundberg and Baskin (1969).

Thirty-one families with about 400 genera and about 2211 species. Of these, about 1300 species occur in the New World. Two families, Ariidae and Plotosidae, consist largely of marine species but have representatives that are frequently found in brackish and coastal waters. Other catfish families are freshwater, although some have species which can invade brackish water.

Family DIPLOMYSTIDAE—diplomystid catfishes. Freshwater; southern South America, Chile and Argentina.

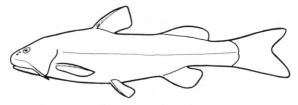

The only catfish family with teeth on a well-developed maxilla, 18 principal caudal fin rays, and lagenar otolith equal in size to or larger than the utricular otolith. There are only maxillary barbels present.

One genus, *Diplomystes*, with two species.

Family ICTALURIDAE (Ameiuridae)—North American freshwater catfishes.
Freshwater; North America (southern Canada to Guatemala) (see map on p. 410).

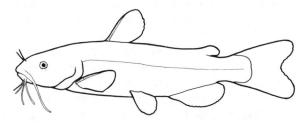

Eight barbels on head (two nasal, two maxillary, four chin); skin naked; dorsal (except in *Prietella*) and pectoral fins with spine on leading edge; dorsal usually with six soft rays; palate toothless. Three species of unrelated blind (eyeless) catfishes are known; two (*Satan* and *Trogloglanis*) from deep artesian wells and associated ditches near San Antonio, Texas and one (*Prietella*) from a well in northeastern Mexico. The aberrant *Trogloglanis pattersoni* is probably allied to the primitive *Ictalurus* lineage, *Prietella phreatophila* is related to the genus *Noturus*, and *Satan eurystomus* is allied to *Pylodictis olivaris* (Hubbs and Bailey, 1947; Taylor, 1969; Lundberg, 1982). Maximum length about 1.6 m, attained in *Ictalurus furcatus* and *Pylodictis olivaris*.

Six genera: *Ictalurus*, with about 16 species recognized in two subgenera, *Ictalurus* (about five species of which occur only in Mexico and Guatemala) and *Ameiurus* (species placed in the latter subgenus are generally called bullheads); *Noturus*, with about 25 species (stonecat and madtoms which have a poison gland at base of pectoral spine); and *Trogloglanis, Prietella, Satan,* and *Pylodictis* (flathead catfish), each with one species, with a total of about 45 species in the family. The various genera and their interrelationships are discussed by Taylor (1969) and Lundberg (1982). Fossil ictalurids are known back to the Paleocene (Lundberg, 1975).

Family BAGRIDAE—bagrid catfishes.   Freshwater; Africa and Asia (see map on p. 411).

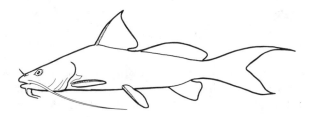

Dorsal fin preceded by a spine, usually with 6 or 7 soft rays (rarely 8–20); adipose fin present and highly variable in size between species; pectoral spine serrated; body naked; usually four pairs of well-developed barbels. Some species are kept as aquarium fishes, while others are large and important as food fishes.

Twenty-seven genera [e.g., *Auchenoglanis*, *Bagrichthys*, *Bagroides*, *Chrysichthys*, *Clarotes*, *Gephyroglanis*, *Leiocassis* (= *Liocassis*), *Mystus*, *Pelteobagrus*, *Porcus* (= *Bagrus*), *Pseudobagrus*, and *Rita*] with roughly 205 species (e.g., Jayaram, 1968, 1976). About 13 genera are endemic in Africa, seven in India, four in Malaysia, and three in China and Japan. Five subfamilies are recognized in Jayaram (1976).

Family CRANOGLANIDIDAE—armorhead catfishes. Freshwater; Asia

Placed in Bagridae in Berg (1940).

Dorsal fin short, six (rarely five) branched rays and one spine; anal fin with 35–41 rays; pectoral with a spine; caudal fin deeply forked; body naked; rough bony plates on top of head; four pairs of barbels. Similar to *Pseudobagrus*.

One genus, *Cranoglanis*, with one to three species (e.g., Nichols, 1943; Lundberg and Baskin, 1969).

Family SILURIDAE—sheatfishes. Freshwater; Europe and Asia (see map on p. 411).

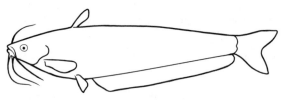

Dorsal fin usually with fewer than seven rays, sometimes absent, not preceded by a spine; adipose fin absent; pelvic fins small, sometimes absent; anal fin base very elongate (up to 90 anal rays).

The largest species of siluriform is the commercially important European wels, *Silurus glanis*, which commonly reaches 3 m (maximum recorded length is 5 m and weight 330 kg). This species is native in Europe, east of the Rhine, and in some areas occurs in brackish water and in inland saline seas.

About 15 genera [e.g., *Kryptopterus* (glass catfish), *Ompok*, *Silurus*, and *Wallago*] with roughly 70 species.

Family SCHILBIDAE—schilbid catfishes.   Freshwater; Africa and southern Asia.

Dorsal fin present (with short base and a spine) or absent; adipose fin usually present; anal fin base very long, not confluent with caudal; usually 2–4 pairs of barbels.

About 20 genera [e.g., *Ailia*, *Clupisoma*, *Eutropius*, *Physailia* (African glass catfish), *Schilbe*, and *Silonia*] with roughly 60 species.

Family PANGASIIDAE.   Freshwater; southern Asia (Pakistan to Borneo).

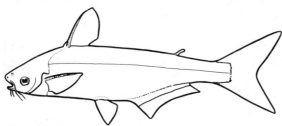

Usually two pairs of barbels (nasal barbels absent and only one pair of chin barbels present); body compressed; adipose fin present, small, never confluent with caudal fin; dorsal fin far forward with one or two spines; anal fin with 28–44 rays. Maximum length about 2.5 m, attained in the plant-eating, toothless (in adults) *Pangasianodon gigas* (Smith, 1945).

About eight genera (e.g., *Pangasianodon*, *Pangasius*, and *Pteropangasius*) with about 25 species.

Family AMBLYCIPITIDAE—torrent catfishes.   Freshwater; southern Asia (Pakistan to southern Japan).

Dorsal fin covered by thick skin; adipose fin present; anal fin base short, with 9–13 rays; four pairs of barbels; lateral line absent. These small fish inhabit swift streams.

Two genera, *Amblyceps* and *Liobagrus*, with about five species.

Family AMPHILIIDAE—loach catfishes.   Freshwater; Africa.

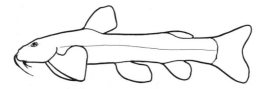

Three pairs of barbels; dorsal and anal fin bases short; dorsal fin spine absent (weakly developed in *Trachyglanis*); pectoral spine absent in most; adipose fin sometimes with a short spine (modified scute); pterygoid and posttemporal absent. Widespread in Africa but usually limited to streams at high elevations. Maximum length 18 cm, attained in *Phractura scaphirhynchura*, but most species are less than 12 cm. Seven genera with 47 species (Harry, 1953).

SUBFAMILY AMPHILIINAE.   Body relatively short, appearing similar to homalopterids; bony plates and nuchal shield absent; mouth subterminal.

Two genera, *Amphilius* and *Paramphilius*, with 27 species.

SUBFAMILY DOUMEINAE.   Body elongate; bony plates often developed along body, nuchal shield present; mouth inferior.

Five genera, *Doumea*, *Andersonia*, *Phractura*, *Trachyglanis*, and *Belonoglanis*, with 20 species.

Family AKYSIDAE—stream catfishes.   Freshwater; southern Asia.

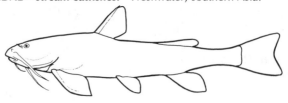

Dorsal fin preceded by a spine and with short base; adipose fin present or absent; pectoral fin with strong spine; gill openings relatively narrow; body usually with longitudinal row of tubercles.

About three genera, *Acrochordonichthys*, *Akysis*, and *Breitensteinia*, with about eight species.

Family SISORIDAE (Bagariidae)—sisorid catfishes.   Freshwater; southern and western Asia.

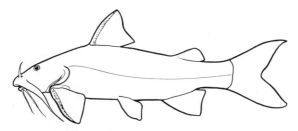

Four pairs of barbels; adipose fin present and usually large (confluent with caudal in some genera and consisting of a small spine in the elongate *Sisor*); dorsal fin base short, fin with or without a spine; adhesive apparatus in thoracic region present or absent. Mostly small forms occurring in mountain rapids; maximum length 2 m.

About 20 genera (e.g., *Bagarius*, *Exostoma*, *Euchiloglanis*, *Gagata*, *Glyptosternum*, *Glyptothorax*, *Hara*, *Nangra*, and *Sisor*) with at least 65 species (e.g., Hora and Silas, 1952; Jayaram, 1981; Misra, 1976).

Family CLARIIDAE—airbreathing catfishes.   Freshwater; Africa, Syria, and southern and western Asia (Philippines to Java) (see map on p. 412).

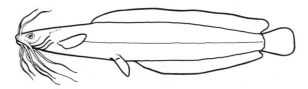

Dorsal fin base very long, usually with more than 30 rays, not preceded by a spine, separate or continuous with caudal fin; caudal fin rounded; gill openings wide; four pairs of barbels; air-breathing labyrinthic organ arising from gill arches (see Greenwood, 1961).

Some members of this family can move short distances over land. One species of walking catfish, *Clarias batrachus* (which is found almost throughout the range of the family), has been introduced into southern Florida waters, where it thrives. Members of three African genera (*Gymnallabes*, *Channallabes*, and *Dolichallabes*) have a marked burrowing habit and have small eyes and reduced or absent pectoral and pelvic fins. *Uegitglanis* of Somali Republic, *Horaglanis* of India, and one species of *Clarias* in South-West Africa, are blind (Menon, 1951a,b).

About 13 genera (e.g., *Clarias, Dinotopterus, Heterobranchus, Horaglanis,* and *Uegitglanis*) with about 100 species (e.g., Poll, 1977).

Family HETEROPNEUSTIDAE (Saccobranchidae)—airsac catfishes. Freshwater; Pakistan to Thailand (primarily India, Ceylon, and Burma).

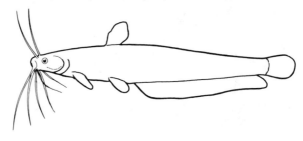

Body elongate, compressed; head greatly depressed; four pairs of barbels; long air sac, serving as a lung, extends posteriorly from the gill chamber; dorsal fin short, without a spine; adipose fin absent or represented as a low ridge.

The pectoral spines have an associated venom gland and the fish is considered dangerous to persons wading in their territory.

One genus, *Heteropneustes,* with two species, *H. fossilis* and *H. microps* (Hora, 1936).

Family CHACIDAE—squarehead or angler catfishes. Freshwater; India to Borneo.

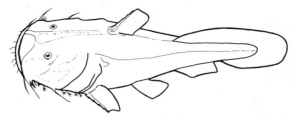

Head broad and depressed, body compressed posteriorly; mouth terminal, very wide; eyes very small; dorsal fin with one short spine and four soft rays; anal fin with 8–10 soft rays; pectoral fin with one serrated spine and four or five soft rays; pelvic fins large, with six rays; adipose fin confluent with caudal fin; branchiostegal rays 6–8; vertebrae 31–35 (14–16 abdominals). Maximum length about 24 cm. On occasions, *Chaca* uses its maxillary barbels to lure prey fish closer to its large mouth.

One genus, *Chaca,* with two species with disjunct ranges, one in eastern India to Burma and the second in the southern Malay Peninsula and Indonesia (Roberts, 1982d).

Family OLYRIDAE. Freshwater; India and Burma.

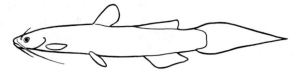

Body elongate, naked; four pairs of barbels; eyes small and subcutaneous; dorsal fin without spine, with seven or eight soft rays; anal fin with 16–23 rays; adipose fin low; caudal fin long, pointed or forked; vertebrae 48–53.

One genus, *Olyra,* with about four species (e.g., Hora, 1936; Jayaram, 1981).

Family MALAPTERURIDAE—electric catfishes. Freshwater; tropical Africa and Nile.

No dorsal fin, adipose fin far back. Produce strong stunning electrical currents.

Two species, *Malapterurus electricus* of the Congo and Nile basins and adjacent areas and *M. microstoma* of the Congo basin (Poll and Gosse, 1969).

Family ARIIDAE (Tachysuridae)—sea catfishes. Mainly marine; tropical and subtropical.

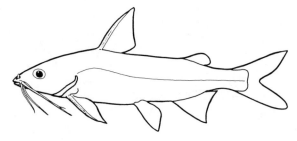

Caudal fin forked; adipose fin present; usually three pairs of barbels (no nasal barbels); some bony plates on head and near dorsal fin origin; pectoral and dorsal fins with a spine; many species of the sea catfishes enter freshwater and some only occur in freshwater.

About 20 genera (e.g., *Ariopsis, Arius, Bagre, Cathorops, Hexanematichthys, Netuma, Potamarius,* and *Doüchthys*) with about 120 species (e.g., Jayaram and Dhanze, 1978). Wheeler and Baddokway (1981) give reasons for not recognizing *Tachysurus* as the senior synonym of the speciose and commercially important *Arius.*

Family PLOTOSIDAE—eeltail catfishes.　Marine, brackish, and freshwater; Indian Ocean and western Pacific from Japan to Australia (see map on p. 412).

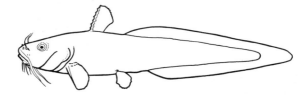

Body eellike, tail pointed or bluntly rounded; usually four pairs of barbels; no adipose fin; caudodorsal fin rays may extend far forward, and lower procurrent caudal rays join the long anal fin to form a continuous fin; branchiostegal rays 7–14. As with some other catfishes, some of these can inflict painful wounds.

About eight genera (e.g., *Cnidoglanis, Euristhmus, Neosilurus, Paraplotosus, Plotosus,* and *Tandanus*) with about 30 species (M. N. Feinberg and G. Nelson, pers. comm. 1982). About half of the species are freshwater.

Family MOCHOKIDAE (Synodidae)—squeakers or upside-down catfishes. Freshwater; Africa.

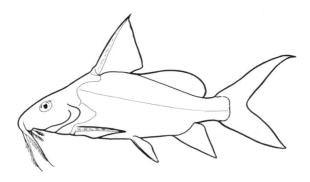

Ossified rays in adipose fin; anal fin with fewer than 10 rays.

About 10 genera (e.g., *Chiloglanis*, *Euchilichthys*, and *Synodontis*) with about 150 species.

Family DORADIDAE—thorny catfishes.   Freshwater; South America.

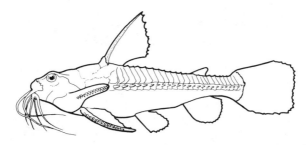

Body with a row of lateral bony plates, most with spines. *Liosomadoras morrowi* lacks lateral bony plates and *Doraops zuloagai* has them only on the posterior portion of the body. Three pairs of barbels (no nasals); adipose fin usually present.

About 37 genera, 25 with head wider than long (e.g., *Acanthodoras*, *Anadoras*, *Doraops*, *Liosomadoras*, and *Platydoras*), and 12 with head longer than wide (e.g., *Doras*, *Hemidoras*, and *Leptodoras*—pers. comm. D. W. Greenfield, 1981) with about 80 species. This family and the auchenipterids are sometimes placed in the same family.

Family AUCHENIPTERIDAE.   Freshwater; tropical South America (to Argentina) and Panama.

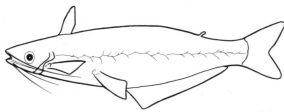

Body naked; three pairs of barbels (except one species with one pair); maxillary pair longest; strong spine in pectoral and dorsal fins; adipose fin present or absent.

About 19 genera (e.g., *Auchenipterus*, *Centromochlus*, *Glanidium*, *Tatia*, and *Trachycorystes*) with about 60 species (Mees, 1974).

Family PIMELODIDAE—long-whiskered catfishes.   Freshwater; Central and South America (north to southernmost Mexico) (see map on p. 413).

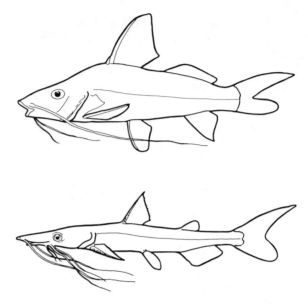

Body naked; adipose fin present; three pairs of barbels.

About 56 genera (e.g., *Calophysus, Heptapterus, Pimelodus, Pimelodella, Pseudopimelodus, Rhamdia, Sorubim, Zungaro,* and *Luciopimelodus*) and about 290 species (e.g., Mees, 1974).

Family AGENEIOSIDAE—bottlenose or barbelless catfishes.   Freshwater; Panama and tropical South America (to Argentina).

Only maxillary barbels present (which are sometimes rudimentary); adipose fin very small; 14 branchiostegal rays.

Two genera (e.g., *Ageneiosus*) with about 25 species.

Family HELOGENIDAE.   Freshwater; tropical South America.

Dorsal fin base short, with about five soft rays and no spine; adipose fin, if present, small; anal fin with 31 or more rays. Maximum length about 10 cm.

Two genera, *Helogenes* (three species in Amazon drainage) and *Levaichthys* (one species in Orinoco drainage of Colombia), with four species (Glodek and Carter, 1978).

Family CETOPSIDAE—whalelike catfishes.   Freshwater; South America.

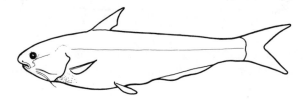

Body naked; three pairs of barbels (no nasals); no adipose fin; swim bladder highly reduced and enclosed in bony capsule.

Four genera, *Cetopsis*, *Cetopsogiton*, *Hemicetopsis*, and *Pseudocetopsis*, with about 12 species.

Family HYPOPHTHALMIDAE—loweye catfish.   Freshwater; tropical South America.

Body naked; three pairs of barbels; eyes set low on a broad head; adipose fin small; pelagic and probably filter feeders. Maximum length about 60 cm.

One species (possibly more), *Hypophthalmus edentatus*.

Family ASPREDINIDAE—banjo catfishes.   Freshwater (some brackish); tropical South America.

Body naked except for large tubercles; no adipose fin; body depressed anteriorly. Maximum length about 42 cm, attained in *Aspredo aspredo;* most species less than 15 cm. Gradwell (1971) describes a form of jet propulsion in these fishes caused by the rapid expulsion of water from the opercular cavity.

About eight genera and 25 species (e.g., Myers, 1960a).

SUBFAMILY BUNOCEPHALINAE.   Anal fin with 12 or fewer rays; body relatively short; always freshwater (Venezuela to Argentina).

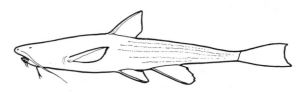

Five genera, *Agmus* (two species), *Amaralia* (one species), *Bunocephalus* (about 15 species), *Hoplomyzon* (two species), and *Xyliphius* (one species), with about 21 species.

SUBFAMILY ASPREDININAE.   Anal fin with 50 or more rays; body relatively elongate; freshwater and brackish water in the Guiana Mangrove province (perhaps rarely extending into marine water).

Three genera, *Aspredinichthys* (one species), *Aspredo* (two species), and *Chamaigenes* (one species), with four species.

Family   TRICHOMYCTERIDAE   (Pygidiidae)—pencil   or   parasitic   catfishes. Freshwater; Costa Rica, Panama, and South America.

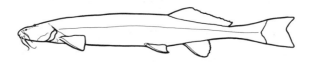

Body naked and elongate; chin barbels usually absent, usually two pairs of maxillary barbels; no adipose fin.

About 27 genera (e.g., *Pygidium, Trichomycterus, Hatcheria, Homodiaetus, Branchioica,* and *Stegophilus*) with about 175 species (e.g., Tchernavin, 1944a). Some members pierce the skin of living fish or other animals and gorge themselves on blood. *Branchioica* and *Vandellia* live on blood within the gill cavities of other fish. In addition, individuals of *Vandellia* (a candiru) of Brazil are known to enter the urethra of humans with serious consequences (Eigenmann, 1917; Norman and Greenwood, 1963; Masters, 1968).

Family CALLICHTHYIDAE—callichthyid armored catfishes. Freshwater; South America and Panama.

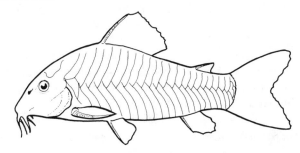

Body with bony plates; swim bladder encased in bone; spine at anterior border of adipose fin. Some species can move short distances on land by utilizing air in vascular hindgut.

Eight genera [e.g., *Aspidoras, Callichthys, Corydoras* (with about 70 species), and *Hoplosternum*] with about 110 species (e.g., Gosline, 1940; Nijssen and Isbrücker, 1979).

FAMILY LORICARIIDAE—suckermouth armored catfishes. Freshwater; Costa Rica, Panama, and South America.

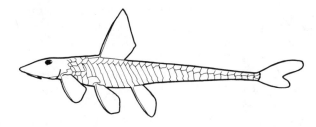

Body with bony plates, rarely naked; mouth ventral without noticeable barbels; ventral lip papillose; adipose fin, when present, with a spine at anterior border; relatively long intestine; 23–38 vertebrae.

About 70 genera (e.g., *Ancistrus, Chaetostoma, Farlowella, Hypostomus, Loricaria, Otocinclus, Plecostomus, Rineloricaria, Sturisoma,* and *Xenocara*) with about 450 species. Isbrücker (1978, 1980) discusses the classification of this family and lists the 600 or so nominal species.

Family ASTROBLEPIDAE (Argidae).   Freshwater; South America and Panama.

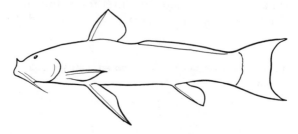

Body naked; mouth disc present as in virtually all loricariids; adipose fin present or absent; dorsal fin spine lacking locking mechanism (a locking mechanism is present in the related callichthyids and loricariids); relatively short intestine; 34 vertebrae (17 + 17).

This family is placed in the Loricariidae by many workers.

One genus, *Astroblepus*, with about 35 species.

Order GYMNOTIFORMES (see map on p. 413).   Body eellike (compressed or rounded); pelvic girdle and fins absent; dorsal fin absent; anal fin extremely long (more than 140 rays and extending from near pectoral fin origin to near tip of body), and employed in forward and backward movements; caudal fin absent or greatly reduced; restricted gill openings; anal opening under head or pectorals; basal pterygiophores to anal fin with only one section (radial) and a hemispherical cartilaginous head that articulates the fin rays (allowing them to move in a circular motion); electric organs present; suboperculum and palatine absent; maxilla rudimentary. They are thought now, on the basis of a cladistic study by Fink and Fink (1981), to be derived from siluriforms and not the characoids as previously thought (e.g., Mago-Leccia and Zaret, 1978). Like catfishes, gymnotiforms are nocturnal. They probably arose in the Neotropical region.

Six families, 23 genera, and about 55 species. The recognition of six families placed in two suborders follows Mago-Leccia (1978).

Suborder Sternopygoidei.   Body compressed; precaudal vertebrae 12–26.

Family STERNOPYGIDAE.   Freshwater; South America.

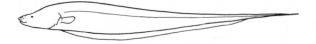

Villiform teeth present on the upper and lower jaws; snout relatively short; three pectoral radials (four in *Sternopygus*); infraorbital bone series complete and with an enlarged sensory canal.

Five genera, *Sternopygus*, *Archolaemus*, *Eigenmannia*, *Distocyclus*, and *Rhabdolichops*, with about 11 species (Mago-Leccia, 1978).

Family RHAMPHICHTHYIDAE.   Freshwater; South America.

Teeth absent on lower jaw; snout long, tubular; nostrils relatively close together. These fish burrow in sand and mud.

Two genera, the monotypic *Rhamphichthys* and *Gymnorhamphichthys* (e.g., Nijssen et al., 1976).

Family HYPOPOMIDAE.   Freshwater; South America.

Teeth absent on lower jaw; snout usually relatively short, not tubular (except in *Parupygus*); nostrils well separated.

Four genera, *Hypopomus*, *Hypopygus*, *Parupygus*, and *Steatogenys*, with about 12 species.

Family APTERONOTIDAE.   Freshwater; South America.

Small caudal fin present which is not united to the anal fin (the only gymnotiform to have a distinct caudal fin).

Ten genera (e.g., *Apteronotus*, *Sternarchella*, *Sternarchorchynchus*, and *Ubidia*) with about 25 species.

Suborder Gymnotoidei.   Body rounded or partially so; precaudal vertebrae 33–43.

Family GYMNOTIDAE—naked–back knifefishes.   Freshwater; Central and South America.

Scales small; anal fin terminating to a point at the tip of the tail; body subcylindrical; vertebrae about 100 (34–43 precaudals); weak electrical charge. Maximum length 60 cm.

One genus, *Gymnotus*, with three species (Miller, 1966). *G. carapo* is the most widespread; the other two occur in the northern portion of the families' range.

Family ELECTROPHORIDAE—electric knifefish. Freshwater; South America (Orinoco and Amazon).

Scales absent; anal fin continuing to the tip of the tail; body rounded; vertebrae about 240 (33 precaudals); large electric organs producing lethal charges for killing prey. Length up to 2.3 m.

One species, *Electrophorus electricus*. (The validity of a second nominal species from Peru needs confirmation—D. J. Stewart, pers. comm. 1982.)

Superorder PROTACANTHOPTERYGII

The membership of the Protacanthopterygii with its one order, Salmoniformes, has been markedly reduced from that recognized in Greenwood et al. (1966), largely as a result of the work of Rosen (1973a). Rosen removed several groups; namely, what he recognized and what are herein recognized as the orders Stomiiformes, Aulopiformes, and Myctophiformes (the latter group was removed by Rosen and Patterson, 1969). The giganturids, formerly recognized as a suborder of the salmoniforms, is placed in the aulopiforms following Rosen (1973a). Rosen (1974) reviews the remaining groups of the salmoniforms; namely, the suborders Esocoidei (including Lepidogalaxiidae), Argentinoidei, and Salmonoidei.

Fink and Weitzman (1982) cast serious doubt on the monophyly of the Salmoniformes as recognized by Rosen (1974) and herein. They find no evidence to consider the esocoids as closely related to the other members of the order, and they suggest that it is the most primitive euteleostean, with both the ostariophysans and the other salmoniforms given here being derived groups. The view that esocoids are relatively distantly related to the other salmoniforms was also expressed by Nelson (1970b) and Rosen (1974) and indeed is expressed in Berg's (1940) classification. In the present classification, it would not be inappropriate to recognize the esocoids as a separate order (Rosen, 1974, gave it as the infraorder Esocae).

Rosen (1974), in his cladistic classification based on gill arch and caudal skeleton anatomy and secondary sexual characters, postulated argentinoids to be the plesiomorphic (primitive) sister group of salmonoids and osmeroids. Fink and Weitzman (1982) suggest that osmeroids and galaxioids form a monophyletic group on the basis of sharing the following characters: (1) specialized "tongue bite" mechanism in which food is manipulated between the basihyal teeth and mesopterygoid teeth, similar to osteoglossomorphs, and (2) absence of basisphenoid and orbitosphenoid bones. They find evidence for a relationship between argentinoids, osmeroids, galaxioids, and salmonoids in the presence of enlarged teeth along the margin of the basihyal and platelike bone on some neural and hemal spines.

The suborders are placed in sequence, from primitive to advanced (i.e., closest to the stomiiforms): Esocoidei, Argentinoidei, and Salmonoidei. I consider the relationship of *Lepidogalaxias* to be uncertain and recognize it in its own suborder before the salmonoids.

Order SALMONIFORMES.   Maxilla included in gape of mouth. (The toothless maxilla is excluded from the gape in *Prototroctes* and *Lovettia* and almost in *Aplochiton*.)

All salmoniforms spawn in fresh water except the Argentinoidei and *Osmerus eperlanus;* only some salangids, sundasalangids, and *Nesogalaxias* occur in tropical regions (Rosen, 1974; Roberts, 1981).

In commenting on salmoniform zoogeography, Rosen (1974) relies largely on continental drift in explaining the amphitropical distribution of his suborder Esocoidei (Esocidae and Umbridae versus Lepidogalaxiidae), superfamily Salmonoidea (Salmonidae versus Galaxiidae), and superfamily Osmeroidea (Osmeridae, Salangidae, and Plecoglossidae versus Retropinnidae). He also prefers the continental drift model over the dispersal model (e.g., see McDowall, 1970, 1971a, 1973a, 1978a, 1980) in explaining panaustral distributions within the Galaxiidae (including the Aplochitoninae as used here). In all, events some 90 to 180 million years ago are involved in the theory. The relative importance of continental drift versus dispersal, however, is unresolved.

Currently recognized with one order, four suborders, 15 families, 90 genera, and 320 species.

Suborder Esocoidei (Haplomi).   No adipose fin; maxilla toothless but in gape of mouth; dorsal and anal fins located posteriorly; no pyloric caeca; no mesocoracoid. Four genera and 10 species.

Family ESOCIDAE—pikes.   Freshwater; Northern Hemisphere (see map on p. 414).

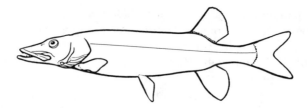

Snout produced; caudal fin forked, with 40–50 rays (17 branched, rarely 16); lateral line complete; infraorbital canal with eight or more pores; 10–20 branchiostegal rays; nasals present; vertebrae 43–67. Maximum length 1.4 m, obtained in *Esox masquinongy.*

One genus, *Esox*, with one circumpolar species (*E. lucius*, the northern pike), one species in Siberia (*E. reicherti*, the Amur pike), and three species restricted to eastern North America (*E. masquinongy* the muskellunge, *E. niger* the chain pickerel, and *E. americanus*, with two subspecies, the redfin pickerel and the grass pickerel) (Crossman, 1978).

The oldest known fossils are from Paleocene formations of about 62 million years ago in Alberta and are relatively similar in appearance to *E. lucius*, more so than Tertiary *Esox* species from Eurasia (Wilson, 1980).

Family UMBRIDAE—mudminnows.   Freshwater; parts of Northern Hemisphere (see map on p. 414).

Snout not produced; caudal fin rounded, with 20–30 rays (8–19 branched); lateral line faint or absent; infraorbital canal with three or fewer pores; 5–8 branchiostegal rays; nasals absent; vertebrae 32–42. Maximum length 20 cm.

One genus of this family, *Dallia*, has been placed in its own order (Jordan and Evermann, 1896) or family (e.g., McPhail and Lindsey, 1970). Most recent authors place *Dallia, Novumbra,* and *Umbra* in the same family but there is much disagreement on the interrelations. Beamish et al. (1971) feel that this lumping may be ill-advised because of the highly variable chromosome number in the group, which ranges from 22 in *Umbra* to 78 in *Dallia* (all *Esox* have 50). Little is known, however, about the evolutionary stability, and thus the systematic value, of karyotypes. Cavender (1969) claimed that *Dallia* is closer to *Novumbra* than to any other living esocoid but felt it best not to recognize subfamilies. Nelson (1972b) regarded *Dallia* and *Umbra* as relatively close (and placed them in the subfamily Umbrinae, whereas *Novumbra* was put in its own subfamily). In a detailed osteological study of extant species, Wilson and Veilleux (1982) also conclude that *Dallia* is more closely related to *Umbra* than to *Novumbra*. Based on the assumption that *Esox* shows the primitive character states for the characters employed, they favor regarding *Novumbra* as the most primitive genus and the European species of *Umbra* as the primitive sister group of the two North American ones.

Three genera with five species. Fossils include *Proumbra* of Oligocene in western Siberia, *Palaeoesox* of Eocene in Germany, and *Novumbra* of Oligocene in North America.

Novumbra

Pectoral rays 18–23; pelvic rays six or seven; dorsal rays 12–15; anal rays 11–13; lateral scales 52–58; vertebrae 37–40.

One species, *Novumbra hubbsi,* confined to the Olympic Peninsula in western Washington, occurring primarily in the Chehalis system.

Dallia

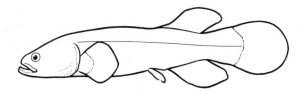

Pectoral rays 32–36; pelvic rays usually two or three (rarely 0 or 1); dorsal rays 10–14; anal rays 12–16; lateral scales 76–100; vertebrae 40–42; Baudelot's ligament ossified (only esocid with it ossified).

One species, *Dallia pectoralis* (Alaska blackfish), freshwater, northeast Siberia and Alaska.

Umbra

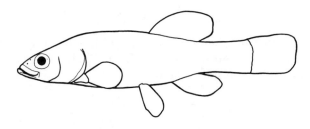

Pectoral rays 11–16; pelvic rays 5–7; dorsal rays 13–17; anal rays 7–10; lateral scales 30–36; vertebrae 32–37.

Three species, two in central and eastern United States and one in southeastern Europe.

Suborder Argentinoidei. Complex posterior branchial structure ("epibranchial" organ), termed the crumenal organ.

Classification of this group is based partly on Marshall (1966a), Gosline (1969), and Greenwood and Rosen (1971).

Five families, 50 genera, and about 160 species.

Superfamily Argentinoidea. Adipose fin usually present; caudal fin forked; dorsal fin near body center; maxillae and premaxillae (when present) toothless; branchiostegal rays 2–7; lateral line scales 40–70; swim bladder, when present, physoclistic; mesocoracoid present or absent. Many are bathypelagic. Color silvery.

Twelve genera and about 65 species.

Family ARGENTINIDAE—argentines or herring smelts.   Marine; Atlantic, Indian, and Pacific.

SUBFAMILY ARGENTININAE.   Eyes not tubular; adipose fin over anal fin base; dorsal fin origin in front of pelvics; pectoral fin base on ventrolateral surface; mouth small.

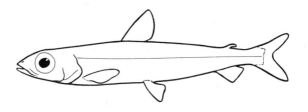

Two genera, *Argentina* and *Glossanodon,* with about 18 species (Cohen and Atsaides, 1969; Parin and Shcherbachev, 1982).

SUBFAMILY XENOPHTHALMICHTHYINAE.   Eyes tubular (protruding anteriorly); no adipose fin; dorsal fin origin behind pelvic fin insertion; pectoral fin base well up on side; mouth small.

One genus, *Xenophthalmichthys,* with two species.

Family BATHYLAGIDAE—deep-sea smelts.   Marine; Atlantic, Indian, and Pacific.

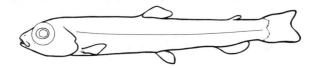

SUBFAMILY BATHYLAGINAE.   Adipose fin present or absent; pectoral fin base near ventral surface; swim bladder absent; no orbitosphenoid.

One genus, *Bathylagus* (= *Leuroglossus*), with about 27 species. *Leuroglossus* is recognized as a separate genus by some workers (e.g., Peden, 1981).

SUBFAMILY MICROSTOMATINAE.   Lateral line and lateral line scales extending onto tail; pectoral fin base on side; mesocoracoid absent; orbitosphenoid present.

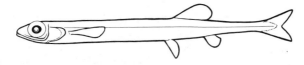

Two genera with about eight species.

Microstoma: no adipose fin; dorsal fin behind pelvics.

Nansenia: adipose fin present; dorsal fin in front of pelvics.

Family OPISTHOPROCTIDAE—barreleyes or spookfishes.   Marine; Atlantic, Indian, and Pacific.

Eyes usually tubular; pectoral fin base on side; pelvic fin base on side in some; adipose fin in some; photophores in some; most lack swim bladder; 2–4 branchiostegal rays.

Six genera, *Bathylychnops, Dolichopteryx, Macropinna, Opisthoproctus, Rhynchohyalus,* and *Winteria,* with about 10 species (Cohen, 1964).

Superfamily Alepocephaloidea. Dorsal fin inserted well back on body; no adipose fin; no swim bladder; dark colored fishes.
About 38 genera with 95 species.

Family ALEPOCEPHALIDAE—slickheads. Deep-sea; all oceans.

Pelvic fins absent in some; teeth usually small; gill rakers long and numerous; shoulder sac apparatus absent; 5–13 branchiostegal rays. Most commonly found below 1000 m.

SUBFAMILY ALEPOCEPHALINAE. Photophores present; 7–18 pectoral rays; 5–8 branchiostegal rays; scales absent in some.

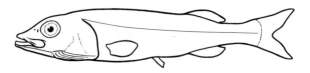

About 22 genera (e.g., *Alepocephalus, Asquamiceps, Ericara, Narcetes, Photostylus, Rinoctes, Rouleina,* and *Xenodermichthys*) with at least 60 species (e.g., Markle, 1980; Markle and Merrett, 1980).

SUBFAMILY BATHYPRIONINAE. Body pikelike in shape; relatively large, widely spaced maxillary teeth; 10 pectoral rays; 12 branchiostegal rays.
One species, *Bathyprion danae* (Marshall, 1966a).

SUBFAMILY BATHYLACONINAE. Premaxilla minute, maxilla extending well behind eyes; 4–11 pectoral rays (higher in *Herwigia*); 7–10 branchiostegal rays, upper ones forming part of posterior gill cover; large cycloid scales.

Two genera, *Bathylaco* and *Herwigia,* with three species known from few specimens from circumtropical waters (Nielsen and Larsen, 1968; Iwamoto et al., 1976).

SUBFAMILY LEPTOCHILICHTHYINAE. Expanded and toothless maxilla; 13 branchiostegal rays.

One genus, *Leptochilichthys*, with perhaps two species.

Family SEARSIIDAE. Marine; all oceans.

Shoulder sac apparatus (beneath the cleithrum) produces luminous fluid with conspicuous opening through tubular papilla; light organs present in many species (directed ventrally in adults); 14–28 pectoral rays; 4–8 branchiostegal rays.

About 12 genera (e.g., *Holtbyrnia, Maulisia, Mentodus, Mirorictus, Normichthys, Persparsia, Platytroctes, Sagamichthys,* and *Searsia*) with at least 29 species (Parr, 1960; Matsui and Rosenblatt, 1979).

Suborder Lepidogalaxioidei

Family LEPIDOGALAXIIDAE. Freshwater; Western Australia.

Dorsal fin posterior to pelvic fin, above anal fin; no adipose fin; nine principal caudal fin rays, unbranched; scales very thin; males with modified anal fin rays and a sheath of scales over anal fin base.

The one species was described in 1961 as a galaxiid. Nelson (1972b:36) noted some similarity with *Dallia* in the pitlines. Rosen (1974) found similarities with galaxioids and osmeroids but considered it most closely allied to the esocoids.

One species, *Lepidogalaxias salamandroides.* This small fish is known only from a small creek tributary to the Shannon River of southwestern Western Australia (Lake, 1971).

Suborder Salmonoidei. Seven families, 35 genera, and about 149 species.

Superfamily Osmeroidea. Adipose fin usually present. Fourteen genera and 27 species.

Family OSMERIDAE—smelts. Marine, anadromous, and coastal freshwater; Northern Hemisphere in Atlantic and Pacific (see map on p. 415).

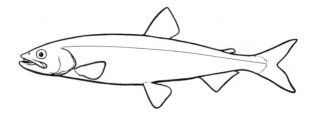

Pelvic axillary process absent; eight pelvic rays and 19 principal caudal rays (17 branched); branchiostegal rays 6–10; teeth on premaxillae, maxillae, dentary, and inner mouth bones; mesocoracoid present; orbitosphenoid absent; pyloric caeca 0–11; last vertebra turned up. Color silvery. Maximum length about 40 cm; most species less than 20 cm.
McAllister (1963) gives a revision of the family.

SUBFAMILY HYPOMESINAE. Two genera, *Hypomesus* and *Mallotus* with four species.

SUBFAMILY OSMERINAE. Four genera, *Allosmerus, Osmerus, Spirinchus, and Thaleichthys*, with six (possibly seven) species.

Family PLECOGLOSSIDAE—ayu fish. Anadromous; Japan, Korea, and China.

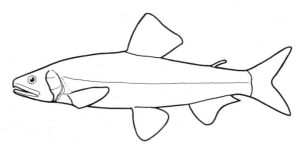

No pelvic axillary process; last vertebrae not turned up; more than 300 pyloric caeca; dorsal rays 10–12; anal rays 9–17; five or six branchiostegal rays; vertebrae usually 59–64.
One species, *Plecoglossus altivelis*.

Family SALANGIDAE—icefishes or noddlefishes. Anadromous and freshwater; Sakhalin, Japan, Korea, China, and perhaps Vietnam.

Body transparent or translucent, body scaleless except for one row above anal fin base in adult males; head strongly depressed; pelvic fins with seven rays; maxilla with numerous teeth; branchiostegal rays three or four; skeleton poorly ossified. Possibly neotenic.

Six genera (e.g., *Protosalanx*, *Salangichthys*, and *Salanx*) and about 14 species (Wakiya and Takahasi, 1937; T. R. Roberts, pers. comm. 1982).

Family SUNDASALANGIDAE—Sundaland noodlefishes. Freshwater; Borneo and southern Thailand.

Body transparent and scaleless; adipose fin absent; olfactory organs each with a single nasal opening; pelvic fin with five rays; dorsal and anal fins posteriorly placed, dorsal with 11–14 rays and anal with 15–21 rays; symplectic, circumorbital, and interopercle bones absent; branchiostegal rays four; vertebrae 37–43.

This family was erected by Roberts (1981). Although its species resemble the salangids in many characters they apparently have several features of the pectoral skeleton, pelvic skeleton, and gill arches which are not known from any other teleost. The two known species are from Thailand and Borneo. The one from Thailand is sexually mature at only 14.9 mm, making it the smallest known adult salmoniform.

One genus, *Sundasalanx*, with two species (Roberts, 1981).

Superfamily Galaxioidea. Usually no pyloric caeca; no mesocoracoid; no supramaxillae; 18 or fewer principal caudal fin rays; no upturned vertebrae. These cold-water fishes form the dominant element in the freshwater fish fauna of the Southern Hemisphere. Eleven genera and about 54 species.

McDowall (1969) and Nelson (1972b) conclude that *Prototroctes* is more closely related to *Retropinna* than to *Aplochiton* (with which it was formerly classified in the family Aplochitonidae) and that *Aplochiton* shows affinities to the Galaxiidae. I recognize this relationship in two families, each with two subfamilies. Nelson (1972b), however, places all of them in the same family, Galaxiidae, recognizing two subfamilies, Galaxiinae and Retropinninae, while McDowall (1979a), in the opposite extreme, gives family status to each of the four subfamilies given here. In contrast to McDowall (1969), who believes that the northern and southern groups of Salmonoidei represent separate radiations, Rosen (1974), on the basis of hyobranchial and caudal skeleton evidence, concludes that the two main southern lineages are polyphyletic and associates the galaxiids with the salmonids and the retropinnids with the osmerids.

Family RETROPINNIDAE—New Zealand smelts. Fresh and brackishwater (some partially marine); New Zealand, Chatham Islands, southeastern Australia, and Tasmania.

Adipose fin present; caudal fin forked, with 16 branched rays; cycloid scales present, but no lateral line on body; small horny keel along midventral abdomen, in front of anus; vomerine, palatine, and basibranchial teeth present; branchiostegal rays usually five or six; pyloric caeca absent; only left gonad present; cucumber odor to body in most species when captured (this has also been detected in some osmerids; see Berra et al., 1982, for its probable identification).

Three genera with about five species.

SUBFAMILY RETROPINNINAE (SOUTHERN SMELTS). Dorsal fin posterior to pelvics and a little in front of anal fin origin; maxilla sometimes with teeth; vertebrae 45–63. Maximum length about 15 cm, usually less than 10 cm. These small silvery fishes occur in coastal seas, estuaries and lowland rivers, and inland lakes and rivers.

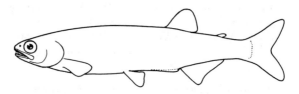

Two genera, *Retropinna* and *Stokellia*, with about four species. *Retropinna* has about three highly variable species, one in Australia (southern Queensland to eastern South Australia), one in Tasmania, and one in New Zealand (including the Chatham Islands); *Stokellia anisodon* is endemic to the South Island of New Zealand (McDowall, 1979a; McDowall and Whitaker, 1975).

SUBFAMILY PROTOTROCTINAE (SOUTHERN GRAYLINGS). Dorsal fin forward, above pelvic fin; maxilla toothless; horny shelf surrounding lower jaw; vertebrae 62–72. Length up to 35 cm.

One species, *Prototroctes maraena*, in southeastern Australia and Tasmania. Another species of this genus in New Zealand is apparently now extinct (McDowall, 1976a, 1978b; Bell et al., 1980).

Family GALAXIIDAE—galaxiids. Freshwater and diadromous; Australia, New Zealand, New Caledonia, southernmost Africa, and southern South America.

Caudal fin with 12–14 branched rays; scales absent, but lateral line present; no horny keel along abdomen; maxillary, vomerine, palatine, and basibranchial teeth absent; gonads paired; no cucumber odor.
Eight genera and about 49 species.

SUBFAMILY APLOCHITONINAE. Adipose fin present; dorsal fin anteriorly placed, above pelvic fin; caudal fin forked; branchiostegal rays 3–6; pyloric caeca 0–2; vertebrae 52–72. *Aplochiton* has pyloric caeca but lacks the postcleithrum. Maximum length 24 cm.

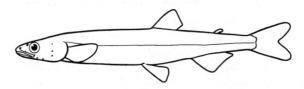

McDowall (1971a) reviews the life history and distribution of the species and describes their morphology. Certain life history stages may be marine.

Two genera, *Aplochiton* and *Lovettia*, with perhaps four species. *Aplochiton* (with two or three species) occurs in Chile, Argentina, Tierra del Fuego, and the Falkland Islands; *Lovettia sealii* is confined to Tasmania. The genera are very different in their morphology and it is not entirely certain that they share a common ancestry. *Lovettia* and a few *Galaxias* comprise the Tasmanian whitebait fishery.

SUBFAMILY GALAXIINAE. No adipose fin; dorsal fin posteriorly placed near tail (originating above pelvics in *Paragalaxias*); caudal fin usually truncate to emarginate (forked or rounded in some); pelvic fins absent in most *Neochanna*; branchiostegal rays 5–9; pyloric caeca 0–6 (usually two); vertebrae 37–66.

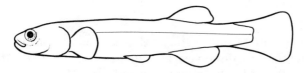

Most members are confined to fresh water, although some species are partially anadromous, having larvae that descend streams after hatching and spend some time in the ocean. The 16 cm *Galaxias maculatus* is peculiar among galaxiids in that ripe adults migrate down streams and spawn in esturine grasses in the upper tidal flats at spring tides. The eggs usually hatch after two weeks in future high tides when they are reimmersed in water and the larvae are washed out to sea (they have been found as far as 700 km from shore). The species is marginally catadromous (with a lunar rhythm), although landlocked populations are known. The term whitebait is applied to the transparent young which move from the sea into rivers at approximately six months of age. In New Zealand, several species of *Galaxias* constitute the whitebait commercial and recreational fishery. McDowall and Eldon (1980) describe the ecology of whitebait migrations.

Maximum length 58 cm, attained in *Galaxias argenteus* of New Zealand; most species are less than 20 cm.

Six genera, *Brachygalaxias*, *Galaxias* (= *Saxilaga*), *Galaxiella*, *Neochanna*, *Nesogalaxias*, and *Paragalaxias*, with about 45 species. Species abundance is greatest in Australia, especially in Tasmania and southeastern Australia. There are 20 species in Australia (13 *Galaxias*, three *Galaxiella*, and four *Paragalaxias;* McDowall and Frankenberg, 1981), 13 species in New Zealand (10 *Galaxias* and three *Neochanna;* McDowall, 1978b), and four species in South America (three *Galaxias* and one *Brachygalaxias;* McDowall, 1971b). Only *Galaxias zebratus* occurs in South Africa, and the only species of *Nesogalaxias* occurs in the uplands of New Caledonia. The most widespread species, *G. maculatus*, occurs in Australia, Tasmania, Lord Howe Island, New Zealand, Chatham Islands, and southern South America (Chile, Patagonia, Tierra del Fuego, and Falkland Islands) (McDowall, 1972, 1976b). McDowall (1970, 1971b, 1973a, 1978b) and McDowall and Frankenberg (1981) give detailed descriptions of many of the species.

Superfamily Salmonoidea.   Adipose fin present; mesocoracoid present; pyloric caeca present.

Family SALMONIDAE—salmonids.   Freshwater and anadromous; Northern Hemisphere.

Gill membranes extending far forward, free from isthmus; pelvic axillary process present; last three vertebrae turned up; 11–210 pyloric caeca; 7–20 branchiostegal rays. Maximum length up to 1.5 m. This family has tremendous value in sport and commercial fisheries.

Ten genera with about 68 species.

As suggested in Behnke (1972), the biological diversity in this family is much greater than recognized in our current taxonomy with its nomenclatorial limits. Many biological species exist that are not named. Several "species," such as *Coregonus lavaretus*, *Coregonus artedii*, and *Salvelinus al-*

pinus, are each best described as a species complex. Perhaps our realization that salmonid classification, like gasterosteid classification, cannot adequately express evolutionary reality is due to the numerous detailed studies of the family (because of its economic importance), and the problems in trying to express their diversity in binomial taxonomy may not be so unique.

Classification of this group is based largely on Behnke (1968, 1970, 1972), Lindsey and Woods (1970), Norden (1961), and Vladykov (1963).

SUBFAMILY COREGONINAE. Fewer than 16 dorsal fin rays; scales large, fewer than 110 along lateral line; no teeth on maxilla; orbitosphenoid present; suprapreopercular absent.

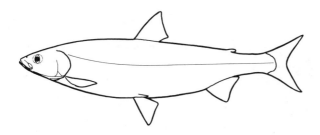

Stenodus leucichthys (inconnu). Large mouth with many small teeth on jaws, vomer, and palatine; two flaps between nostrils. Anadromous; Arctic Asia and North America.

Prosopium (whitefishes). Small mouth with weak or no teeth; single flap between nostrils; basibranchial plate present; young with parr marks. Freshwater; northern Northern Hemisphere; six species. One species occurs in northern North America and Siberia; three are endemic to Bear Lake, Utah-Idaho, one of which is ciscolike.

Coregonus (whitefishes and ciscoes). Small mouth with weak or no teeth; two flaps between nostrils; no basibranchial plate; young without parr marks. Freshwater (occasionally anadromous along Arctic coastline), northern Northern Hemisphere; 25 species (17 ciscoes and eight lake whitefishes).

The two subgenera may not be strictly monophyletic. In North America there is good separation between the two groups in gill raker number; the lake whitefishes almost always have 35 or fewer gill rakers, the ciscoes 36 or more. In Eurasia, however, one lake whitefish (*C. muksun*) usually has 51–56 gill rakers, whereas one cisco (*C. tugun*) has 25–39.

Subgenus *Leucichthys* (ciscoes). Mouth superior or terminal; maxillae normally extending beyond front margin of eye. Usually plankton feeders.
  Circumpolar but most species in eastern North America in Great Lakes.

Subgenus *Coregonus* (lake whitefishes). Mouth subterminal; maxillae usually not extending beyond front margin of eye. Bottom and plankton feeders.
  Circumpolar but most species in northwestern Eurasia.
  The dominant ones are *C. lavaretus* complex in Eurasia and *C. clupeaformis* complex in North America.

SUBFAMILY THYMALLINAE.   More than 17 dorsal fin rays; teeth on maxilla; orbitosphenoid absent; suprapreopercular absent.

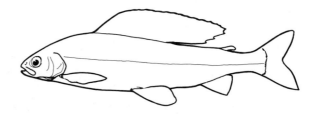

  One genus, *Thymallus* (graylings), freshwater; Northern Hemisphere; four species (one in Europe, two in Mongolia, and probably one widespread across northern Asia and North America).

SUBFAMILY SALMONINAE.   Fewer than 16 dorsal fin rays; scales small, more than 110 along lateral line; teeth on maxilla; orbitosphenoid present; suprapreopercular present.

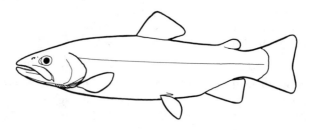

  Certain species, such as *Salvelinus fontinalis, Salmo trutta,* and *S. gairdneri,* have been introduced virtually throughout the world.
  Rounsefell (1962) gives meristic and other data on North American species. Fossils include the large Pliocene *Smilodonichthys* from Oregon and California which had over 100 gill rakers and probably lived at the

same time as its presumed closest relative, *Oncorhynchus*. This extinct fish is thought to have reached 1.9 m in length (Cavender and Miller, 1972).

Brachymystax lenok (lenok). Freshwater; northern Asia to Korea. Two subspecies are recognized (Li, 1966).

Salmothymus. Freshwater; southern Yugoslavia; three species.

Hucho (huchen or taimen). Freshwater and anadromous; northern Asia to Japan, Danube basin of Europe; four species (Holčík, 1982).

Salvelinus. Much biological information on the species of this genus is given in Balon (1980).

Subgenus *Salvelinus* (chars). Freshwater and anadromous; Northern Hemisphere. Six or seven species (e.g., Arctic char, Dolly Varden, and bull trout). Cavender (1978) recognizes the bull trout as a valid species separate from the more coastal Dolly Varden.

Subgenus *Baione*. Freshwater and anadromous; eastern North America. One species, *S. fontinalis*, the brook trout.

Subgenus *Cristivomer*. Freshwater; North America. One species, *S. namaycush*, the lake trout.

Salmo (trouts): Subgenus *Salmo*. Freshwater and anadromous; North Atlantic basin (northeastern North America and Europe) and European Arctic. Fall spawning. About five species (e.g., Atlantic salmon and brown trout, both with anadromous and freshwater populations).

Subgenus *Parasalmo*. Freshwater and anadromous; North Pacific basin (eastern slopes of parts of Rocky Mountains in North America) and south to Mexico and Arizona. Spring spawning. About five species (e.g., rainbow and cutthroat trout). Behnke (1979) provides a detailed taxonomic review of the various species.

Oncorhynchus (Pacific salmon). Usually anadromous, occasionally freshwater; North Pacific coastal areas from Japan to California and adjacent parts of Arctic Ocean (see map on p. 415). Fall spawning. Six or seven species (five of which occur in North America).

Pacific salmon are a rich source of material for studies in raciation (e.g., Simon and Larkin, 1972). They have a strong homing ability, usually returning to their natal streams for spawning. Many studies have been conducted on the mechanisms of various aspects of their migration and that of *Salmo* (e.g., Brannon, 1972; Brannon et al., 1981; Kelso et al., 1981). *O. gorbuscha* (pink salmon) have a rigid two-year life span, with the even- and odd-year stocks existing alone or together (allochronously in the same stream, with, of course, no gene flow between them). Other species have variable lifespans: *O. nerka* (sockeye) lives as long as eight years in its northern range (Alaska). In one species, *O. nerka,* the anadromous form (sockeye) has throughout most of its range given rise to freshwater populations (kokanee) which occur in sympatry or allopatry (usually in "landlocked" lakes) with the parental anadromous form. *O. gorbuscha* and *O. keta* (chum salmon) usually spawn in the lower reaches of rivers and are the most "marinelike" of all Pacific salmon. All die after spawning.

Bulletins of the International North Pacific Fisheries Commission (Vancouver, Canada), contain many excellent articles on the biology of Pacific salmon. Bulletin 16 for 1965 contains articles on the life history of *O. kisutch* (coho), *O. tschawytscha* (chinook), and *O. masou* (masu); Bulletin 18 for 1966 contains articles on the life history of *O. nerka, O. gorbuscha,* and *O. keta.* Several articles on the biology of *Oncorhynchus* (and other salmonids) are given in Northcote (1969) and osteological information is provided by Hikita (1962), Norden (1961), and Vladykov (1962).

NEOTELEOSTS.   The following four superorders belong to the Neoteleostei, a group not given formal rank here. The category was recognized by Nelson (1969a) as having equal rank to his Protacanthopterygii and Ostariophysi.

According to Rosen (1973a), the characters shared in the following orders, which are lacking in the salmoniforms, are the possession of (1) a retractor arcuum branchialium muscle (RAB) (the anterior end of this muscle inserts on the dorsal gill–arch elements while the posterior end usually originates on vertebrae 1–16, (2) ascending and articular premaxillary processes and crossed rostral ligaments, and (3) an advanced type of internal maxillary muscle with a deep origin in the pterygoquadrate complex.

Superorder STENOPTERYGII

This group is recognized for the order Stomiiformes, a group whose ancestral form was probably allied to the salmonoids and may not have been far from the aulopiform ancestor. The order retains some of the primitive characters of the salmoniforms and was formerly recognized in that order.

Order STOMIIFORMES (Stomiatiformes).   Luminescent organs (photophores) present; chin barbel present in some; premaxilla and maxilla in gape of mouth—both have teeth; mouth extending past eye in most; scales, if present, cycloid and easily lost; pectoral, dorsal, or adipose fins absent in some; ventral adipose fin present in some; pelvic fin rays 4–9; branchiostegal rays 5–24. Color in most is dark brown or black; some are silvery (primarily some Gonostomatoidei). Mostly tropical to temperate; many are deep-sea.

The classification of the order here partly follows an arrangement proposed by Weitzman (1974) for his suborder Stomioidei, rather than the one formerly employed based on Weitzman (1967a) and Gosline (1971). The major changes are (1) removal of most genera of the shallow-bodied Gonostomatidae, placing some of them (the maurolicins) in the expanded Sternoptychidae and others in a new family, the Photichthyidae, and (2) recognition of two main phyletic branches, the Gonostomatoidei and the Photichthyoidei. Although the Gonostomatidae and Photichthyidae are recognized as belonging to separate phyletic lines, they are relatively closely related. Primitive genera in both share many features and the two families cannot be separated on external characteristics. Certain parts of the classification are provisional.

Nine families, 53 genera, and about 248 species.

Suborder Gonostomatoidei (Heterophotodermi, in part).   Four pectoral fin radials (except in *Cyclothone*); serial photophores with lumen or duct; true gillrakers present; jaw teeth small, all about equal in size. Generic composition of the families is based on Weitzman (1974).

Sixteen genera with 67 species.

Family GONOSTOMATIDAE—lightfishes or bristlemouths.   Marine; Atlantic, Indian, and Pacific.

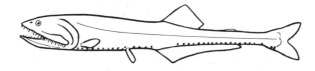

Body elongate, never extremely compressed; adipose fins present or absent; 16–68 anal fin rays; 12–16 branchiostegal rays, 4–6 on epihyal; 8–16 branchiostegal photophores; photophores on isthmus.

Six genera, *Bonapartia, Diplophos* (=*Mandurus*), *Triplophos, Gonostoma, Margrethia,* and *Cyclothone,* with about 26 species. *Cyclothone,* with 12 species, occurs in virtually all seas including the Antarctic and has, perhaps, the greatest abundance of individuals of any fish genus in the world.

Family STERNOPTYCHIDAE.   Marine; Atlantic, Indian, and Pacific.

Ten branchiostegal rays (six in *Sternoptyx*), three on epihyal; 3–7 (usually six) branchiostegal photophores; pseudobranch present (reduced or lost in most other stomiiforms).

According to Weitzman (1974), the first two or three genera listed in the Maurolicinae form a phyletic branch separate from the other sternoptychids. The subfamily division adopted here recognizes the greater divergence of the three genera of hatchetfishes (which form a derived sister group of *Argyripnus* and *Sonoda*).

SUBFAMILY MAUROLICINAE. Body elongate, never extremely compressed; adipose fin present or absent; 19–38 anal fin rays; photophores present on isthmus, six on branchiostegal membrane.

Seven genera, *Thorophos* (= *Neophos*), *Araiophos*, *Maurolicus*, *Danaphos*, *Valenciennellus*, *Argyripnus*, and *Sonoda*, with about 14 species.

SUBFAMILY STERNOPTYCHINAE (MARINE HATCHETFISHES). Body deep and extremely compressed; mouth nearly vertical; preopercular spine; eyes sometimes telescopic; abdominal keellike structure; blade in front of the dorsal fin composed of specialized dorsal pterygiophores; anal fin sometimes divided, rays 11–19; dorsal fin rays 8–17; vertically orientated pelvic bones.

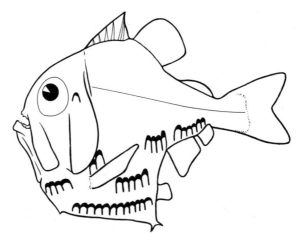

Three genera, *Argyropelecus* (seven species, broadly worldwide, high-sea pelagic, usually 100–600 m), *Sternoptyx* (three species, broadly worldwide, high-sea pelagic, 500–1500 m), and *Polyipnus* [17 species, usually coastal (50–400 m); most species in the western Pacific], with 27 species (Baird, 1971).

Suborder Photichthyoidei. Three pectoral fin radials (rarely 0–2 in some genera with reduced pectoral fins); branchiostegal rays 10 (*Bathophilus*) to 28 (*Heterophotus*).
About 37 genera and 181 species.

Superfamily Photichthyoidea. Serial photophores having a lumen and a duct.

FAMILY PHOTICHTHYIDAE. Marine; Atlantic, Indian, and Pacific.

General body shape similar to the gonostomatids; gillrakers well developed in adults; usually two supramaxillaries; adipose fin present except in *Yarrella;* 10–16 dorsal fin rays; 12–33 anal fin rays; 11–22 branchiostegal rays, 4–7 on epihyal.
Seven genera, *Ichthyococcus, Photichthys, Pollichthys, Polymetme, Vinciguerria, Woodsia,* and *Yarrella,* with about 18 species.

Superfamily Stomioidea (Lepidophotodermi). Scales present (or body marked with scalelike pattern); no true gillrakers in adults; one or no supramaxillaries; photophores without ducts or lumen.

Family CHAULIODONTIDAE—viperfishes. Marine; Atlantic, Indian, and Pacific.

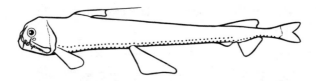

Dorsal fin well in advance of pelvics, shortly behind head; first dorsal fin ray greatly elongated; fanglike teeth on premaxilla and lower jaw; short chin barbel present in some; adipose fins present behind dorsal fin and in front of anal fin; dorsal fin rays 5–7; anal fin rays 10–13.
One genus, *Chauliodus,* with six species (Morrow, 1964a).

Family STOMIIDAE—scaly dragonfishes. Marine; Atlantic, Indian, and Pacific.

Body elongate; dorsal fin origin far behind pelvics, above anal fin; long barbel on chin; no adipose fin.

Two genera, *Stomias* with eight species and *Macrostomias longibarbatus* (Morrow, 1964b).

Superfamily Astronesthoidea (Gymnophotodermi). Scales absent; no true gillrakers in adults; one or no supramaxillaries; photophores without ducts or lumen.

Family ASTRONESTHIDAE—snaggletooths. Marine; Atlantic, Indian, and Pacific.

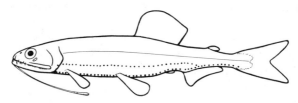

Dorsal fin origin over or behind pelvic fin insertion but well ahead of anal origin; dorsal adipose fin present except in *Rhadinesthes decimus;* ventral adipose fin present in many, in front of anal fin; no scales; barbel on chin; dorsal fin rays 9–21; anal fin rays 12–28.

Maximum length about 30 cm.

Six genera, *Astronesthes, Borostomias, Diplolychnus, Heterophotus, Neonesthes,* and *Rhadinesthes,* with 27 species (Gibbs, 1964a).

Family MELANOSTOMIIDAE—scaleless black dragonfishes. Marine; Atlantic, Indian, and Pacific.

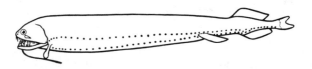

Dorsal fin origin far behind pelvic fin, over anal fin; dorsal adipose fin absent except in *Chirostomias;* no scales; most with barbel on chin; pectoral fins absent in some.

Sixteen genera, *Bathophilus, Chirostomias, Echiostomias, Eustomias, Flagellostomias, Grammatostomias, Leptostomias, Melanostomias, Odontostomias, Opostomias, Pachystomias, Photonectes, Photonectoides, Tactostoma, Thysanactis,* and *Trigonolampa,* with about 104 species (primarily from Morrow and Gibbs, 1964). More than one-half of the species are contained in *Eustomias* and *Bathophilus.*

Family MALACOSTEIDAE—loosejaws. Marine; Atlantic, Indian, and Pacific.

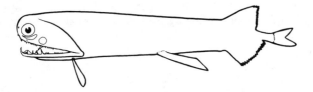

Jaws elongated, longer than skull; dorsal fin origin far behind pelvic fin, over anal fin; adipose fin and scales absent; chin barbel in most; pectoral fins absent in some; dorsal fin rays 14–28; anal fin rays 17–32.

Four genera, *Aristostomias*, *Malacosteus*, *Photostomias*, and *Ultimostomias*, with 13 species (Morrow, 1964c).

Family IDIACANTHIDAE—black dragonfishes. Marine; Atlantic, Indian, and Pacific.

Body eellike; dorsal fin extremely elongate, more than one-half the body length and with 54–74 rays; anal fin rays 29–49; each dorsal and anal fin ray flanked by a spur; no scales; pectoral fins absent in adult; chin barbel only in females.

One genus, *Idiacanthus*, with about four species (Gibbs, 1964b).

Superorder SCOPELOMORPHA (Iniomi, in part)

The premaxilla form the gape of the mouth (maxilla excluded); the upper jaw is not protrusible; adipose fin is usually present; photophores often present; caudal fin usually forked; pelvic fins usually abdominal, with 8–12 rays (eight or nine in most families); usually 19 principal caudal fin rays; branchiostegal rays 6–26; swim bladder, when present, closed (physoclistic); vertebrae 28–121. Several families have species that are hermaphrodites (with self-fertilization).

The families of this superorder (the inioms) were formerly recognized in the order Myctophiformes. The view that the distinctive specialization of the gill arches of the aulopiforms warrants their separation from myctophids and neoscopelids in an evolutionary classification is doubtful but is followed here. The composition of the two recognized orders basically follows Rosen (1973a). However, Rosen recognizes his sept Scopelomorpha only for the two myctophiform families and places that order and the paracanthopterygians and acanthopterygians in his Ctenosquamata, a group coordinate with the more primitive Cyclosquamata (containing only the Aulopiformes). This is based on several shared derived characters (together, the Cyclosquamata and Ctenosquamata comprise Rosen's Eurypterygii).

Two orders with 14 families, 75 genera, and about 429 species.

Order AULOPIFORMES. Second pharyngobranchial greatly elongated posterolaterally, extending away from third pharyngobranchial, with uncinate process of second epibranchial contacting third pharyngobranchial. This specialization in the gill arches is apparently not known in any other teleost (Rosen, 1973a).

The classification of the aulopiforms is based on the works of Rosen (1973a), Sulak (1977b), and Johnson (1982). Rosen (1973a) placed the 14 families that he recognized into two lineages, the suborders Aulopoidei and Alepisauroidei (recognized here with modified composition). Sulak (1977b), in his study of benthic forms, lumps two previously recognized families into the Chlorophthalmidae and two into the Synodontidae because of similarities in osteology; this is accepted here. His concept of Synodontidae contains elements of both of Rosen's (1973a) suborders, with the bathysaurines being in Rosen's aulopoid lineage and the synodontines and harpadontines being in his alepisauroid lineage. Johnson (1982) retains a split classification but does recognize Sulak's Synodontidae (as recognized here) as probably being a monophyletic group and in the alepisauroid lineage. He recognizes the Scopelarchidae, previously associated with Evermannellidae, as being close to the Chlorophthalmidae as is accepted here. However, he does not believe it possible to demonstrate that any two of this Scopelarchidae + Chlorophthalmidae + Ipnopidae are more closely related to each other than is either to the third. He also casts doubt on the advisability of separating the myctophids and neoscopelids from the aulopiform families.

The families Aulopidae, Chlorophthalmidae, and Synodontidae, as recognized here after Sulak (1977b), are benthic. Species in the remaining nine families tend to be pelagic to bathypelagic. Many aulopiforms are synchronous hermaphrodites.

Twelve families with 40 genera and about 188 species.

†Suborder Enchodontoidei. Maxilla a narrow strut in gape (excluded in the other members of this order). Rosen (1973a) gives reasons for rejecting Goody's (1969) placement of his four suborders in Salmoniformes.

Suborder Aulopoidei

Family AULOPODIDAE—aulopus. Marine; tropical and subtropical waters except eastern Pacific.

Body slender; fulcral scales on caudal peduncle; dorsal fin origin in front third of body, fin with 14–21 rays; anal fin rays 9–13; pelvic fin thoracic, nine rays; pectoral fin lateral, 11–14 rays; scales in head and body, cycloid or ctenoid; two supramaxillae; orbitosphenoid present; vertebrae 41–53.

This family is considered to be the most primitive one of the order. It probably gave rise, independently, to the chlorophthalmid and synodontid lineages.

One genus, *Aulopus* (includes *Hime* and *Latropiscis*), with seven species.

Family CHLOROPHTHALMIDAE—greeneyes.   Marine; Atlantic, Indian, and Pacific.

Single elongate supramaxilla; branchiostegal rays 8–13; monoecious mode of reproduction; vertebrae 38–80.

Seven genera with 38 species (Sulak, 1977b).

SUBFAMILY CHLOROPHTHALMINAE (GREENEYES).   Eyes large, normal; pseudobranch present; tip of upper jaw not extending beyond orbit; pyloric caeca present; dorsal fin rays 9–13; anal fin rays 7–11; pectoral fin rays 15–17.

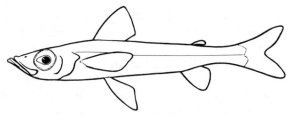

Three genera, *Chlorophthalmus, Parasudis, and Bathysauropsis,* with 12 species.

SUBFAMILY IPNOPINAE.   Eyes minute (first three genera listed here) or large, directed dorsally, and lensless (*Ipnops*); pseudobranch absent in adult; tip of upper jaw extending past orbit; pyloric caeca absent; dorsal fin rays 8–16; anal fin rays 7–19; the 18 species of *Bathypterois* (spider-fishes) have elongated pectoral, pelvic, and caudal rays.

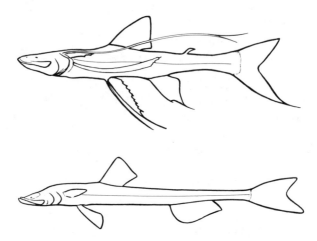

Four genera, *Bathypterois* (= *Benthosaurus*) (upper figure), *Bathymicrops*, *Bathytyphlops* (= *Macristiella*), and *Ipnops* (lower figure), with 26 species.

Family SCOPELARCHIDAE—pearleyes. Marine; Antarctic; Atlantic, Indian, and Pacific.

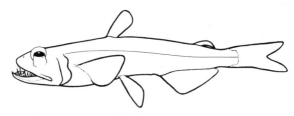

Cycloid scales present on entire body and postorbital region, 40–65 along lateral line; strong teeth on tongue, usually hooked; large tubular eyes, directed upward or slightly dorso-anteriad; dorsal fin rays 5–10; anal fin rays usually 17–27 (up to 39); pectoral fin rays 18–28; no swim bladder; vertebrae 40–65. Adults usually occur between 500–1000 m, larvae of most species usually between 100–200 m. Maximum length about 23 cm, attained in two species of *Benthalbella*.

Four genera, *Benthalbella* (= *Neoscopelarchoides*), *Rosenblattichthys*, *Scopelarchoides*, and *Scopelarchus*, with 17 species (Johnson, 1974a,b; 1982).

Family NOTOSUDIDAE (Scopelosauridae)—waryfishes. Marine; Subarctic to Subantarctic.

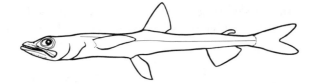

Dorsal fin rays 9–14; anal fin rays 16–21; pectoral fin rays 10–15; lateral line scales 44–65; no swim bladder; no photophores; larvae with maxillary teeth (all other larvae of the order lack teeth); vertebrae 42–66.

Three genera, *Ahliesaurus*, *Scopelosaurus* (*=Notosudis*), and *Luciosudis*, with 19 species (Bertelsen et al., 1976).

Suborder Alepisauroidei

Family SYNODONTIDAE (Synodidae)—lizardfishes. Marine (rarely brackish); Atlantic, Indian, and Pacific.

Supramaxilla small (two in *Saurida* and one in *Harpadon*) or absent; branchiostegal rays 12–26 (except eight in the neotenous *Bathysaurus mollis*); vertebrae 49–63; most with dioecious mode of reproduction (only *Bathysaurus* is monoecious).

Dutt (1973) notes that the family name Synodontidae is based on the African freshwater catfish *Synodontis* (recognized here in Mochokidae), and that the correct family name for the lizardfishes, based on *Synodus*, is the seldom used Synodidae. In the interests of stability, the family name Synodontidae is retained for lizardfishes.

Five genera with about 39 species.

SUBFAMILY SYNODONTINAE (LIZARDFISHES). Scales along lateral line not enlarged; dorsal fin rays 10–14; anal fin rays 14–16; adipose fin usually present. Maximum length about 60 cm.

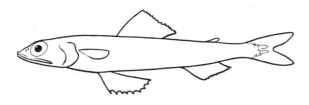

Two genera, *Synodus* (*=Xystodus*) and *Trachinocephalus*, with about 25 species (e.g., Cressey, 1981).

SUBFAMILY HARPADONTINAE (BOMBAY DUCKS).   Nine pelvic fin rays (eight in other members of family); dorsal and anal fin rays 9–14.

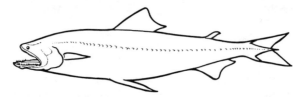

Two genera, *Harpadon* (shown in figure) (3) and *Saurida* (9), with 12 species. *Harpadon* is secondarily pelagic and has a naked head and body except for scales along the lateral line and on part of the posterior half of the body.

SUBFAMILY BATHYSAURINAE.   Scales along lateral line enlarged; dorsal fin rays 15–18; anal fin rays 11–14; adipose fin present or absent.
    One genus, *Bathysaurus* (= *Macristium*), with two species.

Family GIGANTURIDAE—giganturids.   Marine; Atlantic, Indian, and Pacific.

Eyes large, tubular, and directed forward; mouth large, extending well behind eyes; sharp depressible teeth in mouth; pectoral fins high on body, above gill opening; body scaleless, no pelvic or adipose fins; caudal fin forked with some rays in lower lobe greatly elongated; no premaxilla, orbitosphenoid, parietal, symplectic, branchiostegal rays, gill rakers, posttemporal, supratemporal, or cleithrum; no swim bladder. Color silvery. The loss of many characters that generally appear late in fish morphogenesis suggests a neotenous condition for these fish.
    Two genera, *Bathyleptus* and *Gigantura*, with five species (Walters, 1964). *Rosaura*, based on a single specimen 8.4 mm long (Tucker, 1954), may be based on the young of a giganturid although it does have an adipose fin.

Family PARALEPIDIDAE—barracudinas.   Marine; all oceans, Arctic to Antarctic.

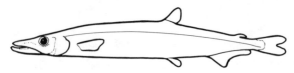

Dorsal fin origin in middle of trunk, fin rays 7–16; anal fin base long, with 20–50 rays; pectoral fin rays 11–17; body scales present or absent; no swim bladder; vertebrae 53–121. Superficially resemble sphyraenids.

Eleven genera (e.g., *Lestidium, Paralepis, Stemonosudis,* and *Sudis*) with 50 species. Rofen (1966) recognizes the genera in three subfamilies and considers *Anotopterus* to be a derivative of the family.

Family ANOTOPTERIDAE—daggertooth. Marine; Antarctic, Atlantic, and Pacific.

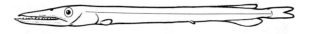

No dorsal fin (adipose fin well developed); no scales; no photophores; pelvic fin minute, with 9–11 rays; pectoral rays 12–15; vertebrae 78–83.

One species, *Anotopterus pharao* (Hubbs et al., 1953; Rofen, 1966).

Family EVERMANNELLIDAE—sabertooth fishes. Marine; Atlantic, Indian, and Pacific.

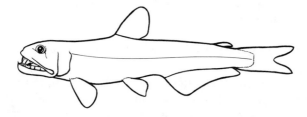

Normal scales lacking on head and body; three distinct bands of muscle tissue, epaxial, midlateral, and hypaxial, externally visible on the tail; teeth absent on tongue; anteriormost palatine tooth very elongate; eyes small to large, tubular in most species; dorsal fin rays 10–13; anal fin rays 26–37; pectoral fin rays 11–13; no swim bladder; vertebrae 45–54. The sabertooth fishes are mesopelagic predators, occurring primarily in tropical and subtropical waters and absent from cold water areas.

Three genera, *Coccorella, Evermannella,* and *Odontostomops,* with seven species (Johnson, 1982).

Family OMOSUDIDAE. Marine; Atlantic and Indian.

No scales; an enormously enlarged fang on each dentary; no body pores; dorsal fin rays 9–12; anal fin rays 14–16; pectoral fin rays 11–13; no swim bladder; vertebrae 39–41.

One species, *Omosudis lowei.*

Family ALEPISAURIDAE—lancetfishes.   Marine; Atlantic and Pacific.

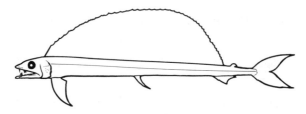

Body slender, covered with pores; scales and light organs absent; dorsal fin high and extending along most of body (originating over opercle and with 36–48 rays); anal fin low with 13–18 rays; pelvics abdominal with 8–10 rays; mouth large; teeth well developed, palatines especially long; vertebrae 50; swim bladder absent. Length up to 2 m.

One genus, *Alepisaurus,* with three species.

Family PSEUDOTRICHONOTIDAE.   Marine; Izu Peninsula, Japan.

Body slender and cylindrical; mouth relatively small, upper jaw bordered only by premaxillaries; lateral line complete, midlateral; cycloid scales, 46–48 in lateral line; dorsal fin single, with about 33 soft rays; anal fin rays 14 or 15; pelvic fin beneath origin of dorsal, with seven long rays; caudal fin with 17 principal rays; adipose fin absent; photophores absent; swim bladder absent; orbitosphenoid and mesocoracoid absent; six branchiostegal rays; 23 or 24 abdominal vertebrae and 25 or 26 caudal vertebrae. It has been observed to dive into the sand.

This new family is noted by Yoshino and Araga (1975) to resemble the Trichonotidae but is placed in the Myctophiformes (of former usage). However, as noted by Johnson (1982), many of its reported characters differ from all known scopelomorphs (e.g., 17 vs. 19 principal caudal rays) and its relationship may well belong elsewhere. It is only provisionally placed here in the Aulopiformes.

One species, *Pseudotrichonotus altivelis.*

Order MYCTOPHIFORMES.   Differs from the Aulopiformes in having the upper pharyngobranchials and retractor muscles like those of generalized paracanthopterygians (Rosen, 1973a:452). Other characteristics of the group are as follows: head and body compressed; eye lateral (dorsolateral in the myctophid *Hierops*); mouth usually large and terminal; adipose fin present; usually 8 pelvic fin rays; usually 7–11 branchiostegal rays. All are deep-sea pelagic and benthopelagic fishes.

Two families, 35 genera, and about 241 species.

Family NEOSCOPELIDAE. Marine; Atlantic, Indian, and Pacific.

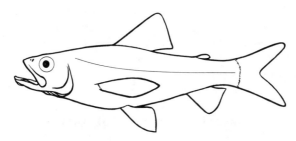

Head and body compressed; long slender supramaxilla present; subocular shelf absent; origin of anal fin far behind dorsal fin base; photophores present in *Neoscopelus;* scales cycloid except in *Solivomer,* which has ctenoid scales on body; swim bladder absent only in *Scopelengys;* vertebrae 29–35. Maximum length about 30 cm.

Three genera, *Neoscopelus, Scopelengys,* and *Solivomer* (with one species known only from the Philippine Islands), with six species (Nafpaktitis, 1977).

Family MYCTOPHIDAE—lanternfishes. Marine; all oceans, Arctic to Antarctic.

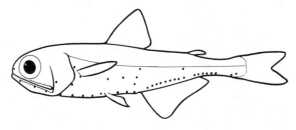

Small supramaxilla present in some genera; subocular shelf present; origin of anal fin under or short distance behind dorsal fin base; small photophores arranged in groups and rows on head and body (except in one species); scales usually cycloid (ctenoid in four species); swim bladder present (except in adults of a few species); vertebrae 28–45.

Myctophids are heavily consumed by numerous marine fishes and mammals. Most undergo a diurnal migration of several hundred meters.

During the daytime the peak abundance of most species is between 300 and 1200 m, while at night it is between 10 and 100 m.

About 32 genera with about 235 species (Paxton, 1972, 1979; Nafpaktitis et al., 1977; Nafpaktitis, 1978). The largest genera are *Diaphus* and *Lampanyctus*, which total about 105 species.

SUBFAMILY MYCTOPHINAE. About 14 genera (e.g., *Diogenichthys, Gonichthys, Hygophum, Myctophum, Protomyctophum,* and *Tarletonbeania*).

SUBFAMILY LAMPANYCTINAE. About 18 genera (e.g., *Ceratoscopelus, Diaphus, Gymnoscopelus, Lampanyctus, Notolychnus, Notoscopelus, Scopelopsis, Stenobrachius,* and *Triphoturus*).

Superorder PARACANTHOPTERYGII

The Paracanthopterygii was first proposed by Greenwood et al. (1966). In redefining the group, Rosen and Patterson (1969) largely employ the caudal skeleton and jaw muscles (particularly the levator maxillae superioris), while Freihofer (1970), arrives at somewhat different conclusions using nerve patterns. Fraser (1972a) and Rosen (1973a) discuss the group further and critically evaluate earlier works.

The superorder comprises forms of early origin thought to be derivatives of the neoscopelid–myctophid or the ctenothrissiform lineage via the Percopsiformes. It represents a side branch in teleost evolution with the remaining fishes (Acanthopterygii) either sharing a common ancestry or being derivatives of a related lineage. The membership of the Paracanthopterygii and Acanthopterygii, however, is very much a problem and will certainly be subject to future revision.

There is a close interrelationship between the Batrachoidiformes and Lophiiformes (they are included together in the same order by Gosline, 1971), but the interrelationships of these orders and of the Gadiformes and Ophidiiformes are questionable. Groups that I recognize in the Acanthopterygii but that are placed in the Paracanthopterygii by others include the Polymixiiformes (Rosen and Patterson, 1969), Gobioidei (Freihofer, 1970), and Indostomiformes (Banister, 1970).

The 1160 or so living species are placed in about 287 genera, 33 families, and six orders.

†**Order CTENOTHRISSIFORMES.** Contains the marine Upper Cretaceous genera *Aulolepis* and *Ctenothrissa* (Rosen, 1973a). The previous inclusion of *Pateroperca* and *Pattersonichthys* is without foundation. Rosen

(1973a) considers it possible that the ctenothrissiforms are the "primitive sister group of the paracanthopterygian–acanthopterygian assemblage" and classifies them with that assemblage under the category of Sept Acanthomorpha.

The family Macristiidae was formerly placed in this order. Rosen (1971) presents evidence that its two "species" may be larval or juvenile scopelomorphs, and Sulak (1977b) recognizes them in the families Synodontidae and Chlorophthalmidae.

Order PERCOPSIFORMES. Premaxilla forms the entire margin of the upper jaw, nonprotractile; ectopterygoid and palatine with teeth; pelvic fins, if present, behind pectorals and with 3–8 soft rays; spines (normally weak) usually present in dorsal fin; many species with ctenoid scales; six branchiostegal rays; 16 branched caudal rays; orbitosphenoid, basisphenoid, and suborbital shelf absent; vertebrae 28–35.

Three families and nine species.

†Suborder Sphenocephaloidei. Adipose fin present.

The one family, Sphenocephalidae with the marine *Sphenocephalus*, is known from the Upper Cretaceous of Europe and is thought to be ancestral to the living North American freshwater groups.

Suborder Percopsoidei. Adipose fin present; anus in front of anal fin; lateral line complete; vomer toothless.

Family PERCOPSIDAE—trout-perches. Freshwater; northern North America (see map on p. 416).

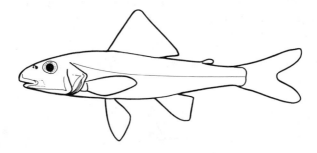

Ctenoid and cycloid scales; head naked; dorsal fin with one or two spines and 9–12 soft rays; anal fin with one or two spines and six or seven soft rays; pelvic fin subthoracic, with eight rays. Maximum length 20 cm, attained in *Percopsis omiscomaycus*.

Two species, the widespread *Percopsis omiscomaycus* and *P.* (= *Columbia*) *transmontana* of Columbia River drainage. The family was well represented in Eocene times with such genera as *Amphiplaga*, *Erismatopterus*, and *Libotonius* (Wilson, 1979).

Suborder Aphredoderoidei.   Adipose fin absent; anus between gill membranes in adults; lateral line absent or incomplete; vomer toothed.

Family APHREDODERIDAE—pirate perch.   Freshwater; eastern United States (see map on p. 416).

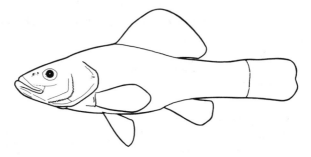

Ctenoid scales; sides of head scaly; eyes normal; dorsal fin with three or four spines and 10 or 11 soft rays; anal fin with two or three spines and 5–7 soft rays; pelvic fin subthoracic, with seven rays.

The anus is in the normal position in juveniles, just ahead of the anal fin, and moves forward during the growth of the fish. Also, in young pirate perch the third anal ray becomes transformed from a soft ray to a spine during growth. Young individuals thus appear to have two spines and eight soft rays; adults have three spines and seven soft rays (Mansueti, 1963). Maximum length about 13 cm.

One species, *Aphredoderus sayanus*.

Family AMBLYOPSIDAE—cavefishes.   Freshwater; southern and eastern United States (see map on p. 417).

Cycloid scales; head naked; eyes small to rudimentary; dorsal fin with 0–2 spines and 7–12 soft rays; anal fin with 0–2 spines and 7–11 soft rays; pelvic fins usually absent (present only in *Amblyopsis spelaea* where they are small, abdominal, and with 0–6 rays); sensory papillae in rows on the head, body, and tail; vertebrae 27–35. Rosen (1962) compares the Amblyopsidae with *Aphredoderus* and the Cyprinodontoidei (with which they were formerly thought to be related). Woods and Inger (1957) and Poulson (1963) give biological information on the group.

All the species, except *Chologaster cornuta* of the Atlantic coastal plains, usually live in caves in limestone formations. *C. cornuta* and *C. agassizi* are the only species with functional eyes. The other four species are blind. Maximum length about 9 cm, attained in *Amblyopsis spelaea*.

Four genera, *Amblyopsis* (two), *Chologaster* (two), *Speoplatyrhinus*, and *Typhlichthys*, with six species (Cooper and Kuehne, 1974).

Order GADIFORMES.   Pelvic fins, when present, inserted below or in front of pectorals (thoracic or jugular, rarely behind in Macrouridae) with up to 17 rays; no true spines in the fins; most with long dorsal and anal fins; cycloid scales; premaxilla forms the entire margin of upper jaw, protractile in some; ectopterygoid toothless; orbitosphenoid and basisphenoid absent; branchiostegal rays 5–8; posterior vertebral reduction results in posterior dorsal and anal pterygiophores exceeding the number of caudal vertebrae; swim bladder without pneumatic duct.

Different concepts of the composition of Gadiformes exist as a result of various hypotheses of relationship and philosophy of classification. Berg (1940) recognized it as a relatively compact group, containing only the suborders Muraenolepidoidei and Gadoidei. At the opposite extreme, it was recognized in Nelson (1976), following Greenwood et al. (1966) and Rosen and Patterson (1969), as including two additional suborders, the Ophidioidei (=Ophidiiformes) and Zoarcoidei, which are recognized here as not being closely related to this group (following, e.g., Gosline, 1971; Cohen and Nielsen, 1978; Shaklee and Whitt, 1981).

Three suborders, seven families, 76 genera, and about 414 species. They are commonly referred to as the anacanthine fishes.

Suborder Muraenolepidoidei.   Caudal fin connected with anal and second dorsal fins; gill openings narrow, extending upward only to level of pectoral bases; pectoral radials 10–13; pelvic fin in front of pectoral.

Family MURAENOLEPIDIDAE.   Marine; Southern Hemisphere.

Two dorsal fins (the first with only one ray) and one anal fin; chin barbel present; head of vomer toothless; no pyloric caeca.

One genus, *Muraenolepis*, with four species.

Suborder Gadoidei. Caudal fin separate from dorsal and anal fins, only rarely partly connected; gill openings wide, extending above base of pectoral fins; pectoral radials 4–6; pelvic fin in front of pectoral.

Svetovidov (1948) reviews the group.

About 45 genera and 150 species.

Family MORIDAE (Eretmophoridae)—morid cods. Marine, deep-water; all seas.

One or two, rarely three dorsal fins; one or two anal fins; chin barbel present or absent; head of vomer toothless or with minute teeth; swim bladder in contact with auditory capsules (otophysic connection).

What appears to be a remarkable case of disjunct distribution occurs in *Halargyreus*, in which individuals of what may be the same species have been collected in New Zealand and the North Atlantic (Templeman, 1968).

About 17 genera (e.g., *Antimora, Halargyreus, Laemonema, Lepidion, Lotella, Mora, Physiculus, Salilota,* and *Tripterophycis*) with about 70 species (some based on only one specimen) (e.g., Paulin, 1983).

Family MELANONIDAE—melanonids. Marine, bathypelagic; southern Atlantic and southern Pacific.

Two dorsal fins, the second united with the pointed caudal; barbel absent; moridlike in most features but lacks otophysic connection.

One genus, *Melanonus*, with two species.

Family BREGMACEROTIDAE—codlets. Marine; tropical and subtropical seas.

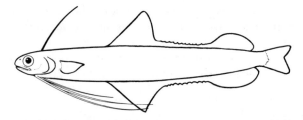

Two dorsal fins and one long anal fin (first dorsal fin on nape and consisting of one elongate ray, second dorsal and anal fins with large notch in middle); no chin barbel; relatively large scales, 40–89 along side; head of vomer toothed; pelvic fins with five rays, outer three are elongate free filaments; lateral line adjacent to second dorsal fin, reported as absent in some works; a few pyloric caeca; swim bladder not in contact with auditory capsules; 43–59 vertebrae. Maximum length about 12 cm.

One genus, *Bregmaceros* (= *Auchenoceros*) with seven species (d'Ancona and Cavinato, 1965).

Family GADIDAE—cods. Marine with one Holarctic freshwater species; Arctic, Atlantic, and Pacific (see map on p. 417).

First dorsal fin posterior to head; head of vomer toothed; swim bladder not connected with auditory capsules. Maximum length about 1.8 m, attained by the Atlantic *Gadus morhua*.

About 55 species.

SUBFAMILY GADINAE (CODS AND HADDOCK). Three dorsal fins and two anal fins; chin barbel usually present; caudal fin truncate or slightly forked; egg without an oil globule.

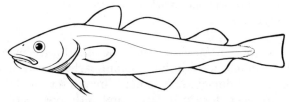

Twelve genera (e.g., *Arctogadus, Boreogadus, Eleginus, Gadus, Melanogrammus, Microgadus,* and *Theragra*) with about 25 species.

SUBFAMILY LOTINAE. One to three dorsal fins (in those species with three, the first two are modified and are not as in Gadinae) and one anal fin; chin barbel always present; caudal fin rounded; egg with oil globule.

Markle (1982) recognizes a relationship among the genera different from
that given here. He places the genera *Brosme*, *Lota*, and *Molva* in the
Lotinae (myomeres relatively numerous and egg diameter 1.0 mm or
larger) and the remaining genera given here in another subfamily, the
Phycinae (myomeres fewer in number than in Lotinae and egg diameter
1.0 mm or smaller).

TRIBE LOTINI (HAKES AND BURBOT). One or two (first may be rudimentary) dorsal fins; no barbels on snout.

Six genera, *Brosme*, *Lota*, *Molva*, *Phycis*, *Raniceps*, and *Urophycis*, with
about 15 species. *Lota lota*, found in northern parts of Eurasia and North
America, is the only freshwater member of the family.

TRIBE GAIDROPSARINI (ROCKLINGS). Three dorsal fins barely separated from each other (the first with a single thickened unsegmented ray,
the second with small, unsegmented rays in a fleshy ridge that rises
within a groove, and the third with segmented rays in an elongate fin);
2–4 prominent individual barbels on snout (rudimentary barbels may
also be present), in addition to the one at the tip of the lower jaw.
    Three genera, *Gaidropsarus* (= *Antonogadus* and *Onogadus*), *Ciliata*, and
Enchelyopus (= *Rhinonemus*) (Cohen and Russo, 1979), with about 15 species.

Family MERLUCCIIDAE—merluccid hakes. Marine; Atlantic, eastern Pacific, Tasmania, and New Zealand.

Two dorsal fins (one in *Lyconodes*) and one anal fin (second dorsal and
anal fins with a notch posteriorly); no chin barbel; head of vomer with
teeth; first principal dorsal ray is spinous; mouth terminal (in *Merluccius*
the lower jaw projects forward), large, and with long teeth; 7–9 pelvic
rays; seven branchiostegal rays; no pyloric caeca.
    The membership of this family follows, in modified form, Marshall
(1966b). Marshall and Cohen (1973) give family status to *Steindachneria*.
Many workers prefer to recognize the Merlucciidae as a subfamily of
Gadidae. The common names usually applied to various species of *Mer-*

luccius throughout the world are hake and whiting. However, as is often the case with common names, they are also variously applied to species of other families (Cohen, 1980).

SUBFAMILY MACRURONINAE. Long tapering tail; dorsal and anal fins confluent with caudal fin or with each other.

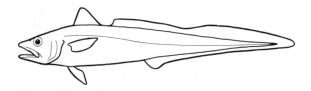

Three genera, *Lyconodes* (one), *Lyconus* (two), and *Macruronus* (five), with eight species.

SUBFAMILY STEINDACHNERIINAE. Anus between pelvic fins and far forward of urogenital pores, which are immediately anterior of the anal fin; elaborate light organ system on head and body; caudal fin absent.

One species, *Steindachneria argentea,* confined to the tropical western Atlantic (primarily the Gulf of Mexico).

SUBFAMILY MERLUCCIINAE. Caudal fin truncate, not confluent with dorsal and anal fins; no fanglike teeth.

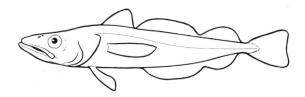

One genus, *Merluccius,* with about seven species.

Suborder Macrouroidei. Okamura (1970) reviews the Japanese forms and recognizes two families, Macrouroididae (with only two genera, *Macrouroides* and *Squalogadus,* which lack the first, short dorsal fin) and Macrouridae.

Family MACROURIDAE (Coryphaenoididae)—grenadiers or rattails. Marine; deepwater, Arctic to Antarctic.

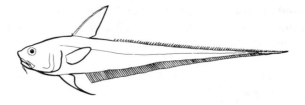

Second dorsal and anal fins continuous with tail, which tapers to a sharp point; no true fin spines (first dorsal fin ray may be spinous); chin barbel usually present; pelvic fins more or less thoracic (under, behind, or in front of pectoral fin base), with 5–17 rays (absent in *Macrouroides*); caudal fin absent (present in one species of *Trachyrhynchus*); scales small; light organ, if present, subdermal along midline of abdomen with opening just before anus; 6–8 branchiostegal rays; 10–16 abdominal vertebrae. Length normally up to 0.8 m.

About 30 genera (e.g., *Trachyrhynchus, Macrouroides, Squalogadus, Bathygadus, Gadomus, Cetonurus, Chalinura, Coelorhynchus, Coryphaenoides, Hymenocephalus, Hyomacrurus, Lepidorhynchus, Lionurus, Macrourus, Malacocephalus, Mataeocephalus, Mesobius, Nematonurus, Nezumia, Paracetonurus, Sphagemacrurus,* and *Ventrifossa*) with a total of about 260 species (e.g., Iwamoto, 1970; Marshall and Iwamoto, 1973; Hubbs and Iwamoto, 1977; Iwamoto, 1979; McCann and McKnight, 1980). Three genera, *Coelorhynchus, Coryphaenoides,* and *Nezumia,* have over half of the species. Most species are benthopelagic, occur in tropical and subtropical latitudes, and live at depths between 200 and 2000 m.

Order OPHIDIIFORMES.   Pelvic fins, when present, inserted at level of preopercle or farther anterior (mental or jugular), one or two soft rays in each, and occasionally with a spine; dorsal and anal fins long, extending to and usually joined with caudal fin; nostrils paired on each side; dorsal and anal fin pterygiophores more numerous than adjacent vertebrae.

There is much disagreement about the phyletic relationships and taxonomic rank of this group. Rosen and Patterson (1969) place it in the order Gadiformes along with the zoarcids. Gosline (1968, 1971) places the group in the Perciformes and includes the Gadopsidae (which appear morphologically intermediate between the percoids and ophidiforms) in his suborder Ophidioidei. It is given ordinal status here, following Cohen and Nielsen (1978) and others, because of its compact nature and uncertain position. The following classification is based on Cohen and Nielsen (1978).

Four families, 86 genera, and about 294 species (in addition, numerous undescribed species are known).

Suborder Ophidioidei. Anterior nostril well above upper lip in most species; oviparous, males lack an external intromittent organ; caudal fin usually present and connected with dorsal and anal fins (appearing as one continuous fin and tapering to a point).

Family OPHIDIIDAE—cusk-eels. Marine, rarely freshwater; Atlantic, Indian, and Pacific.

Dorsal fin rays usually equal to or longer than opposing anal fin rays; anus and anal fin origin usually behind tip of pectoral fin; scales present; some with one or more spines on opercle; supramaxillary present; larvae without a vexillum; pelvics rarely absent. Maximum length about 1.5 m, attained in South Africa by *Genypterus capensis*.

Four subfamilies with 48 genera and about 164 species.

SUBFAMILY BROTULINAE. Barbels present on chin and snout.

One circumtropical genus, *Brotula*, with about five species.

SUBFAMILY BROTULOTAENIINAE. No barbels on chin or snout; scales in the form of small prickles.

One circumtropical genus, *Brotulotaenia*, with four species.

SUBFAMILY OPHIDIINAE. No barbels on snout or chin; cycloid scales present (in regular rows or at oblique angles to each other); slender, elongate filament of bone extending anteriorly from junction of ventral arms of cleithra.

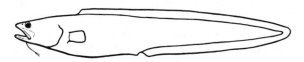

About eight genera, *Cherublemma, Genypterus, Lepophidium, Chilara, Ophidion (=Rissola), Otophidium, Parophidion,* and *Raneya,* with about 50 species.

SUBFAMILY NEOBYTHITINAE. No barbels on snout or chin; cycloid scales present; no filament of bone extending anteriorly from junction of ventral arms of cleithra. Members of this group range from the littoral to the greatest depths at which fish have been obtained. One abyssal species has eyes so small that they may not be visible at the surface.

About 38 genera (e.g., *Bassogigas, Bassozetus, Dicrolene, Monomitopus, Neobythites, Petrotyx, Porogadus,* and *Sirembo*) with about 105 species.

Family CARAPIDAE—carapids. Marine; Atlantic, Indian, and Pacific.

Anal fin rays longer than opposing dorsal fin rays; anus of adults and anal fin origin far forward, behind head and usually beneath pectoral fin (which is rarely absent); scales absent; gill openings wide and extending far forward; teeth on jaws, vomer, and palatines; no spines on opercular bones; branchiostegal rays 6–7; supramaxillary absent; about 85–145 vertebrae; larvae (planktonic vexillifer stage) with a vexillum (long, threadlike process anterior to dorsal fin).

The correct spelling of the family name is accepted here to be Carapidae (based on the opinion of G. S. Myers in letter to C. R. Robins, 1982) and not Carapodidae (as reasoned by Steyskal, 1980).

SUBFAMILY CARAPINAE (FIERASFERIDAE)—PEARLFISHES. Occur in tropical and temperate seas.

Pectoral fin usually much shorter than head length and with 20 or fewer rays (absent in the three species of the subgenus *Encheliophis* of the genus *Encheliophis*); pelvic fins and girdle absent; upper jaw nonprotractile; precaudal vertebrae 17–27.

Many species have the interesting habit of hiding in living animals. Some live in sea cucumbers and eat the cucumber's internal organs in a parasitic fashion. (They and some species of the unrelated Trichomycteridae are the only two groups of jawed fishes known to have developed parasitic members.) Others are commensal with star fish, sea cucumbers, clams, and tunicates with a few appearing to be free living. Pearlfishes (also known as fierasfers) pass through two distinct larval stages. The first larval, or vexillifer, stage is pelagic; the second larval, or tenuis, stage is benthic. (In this stage the vexillum is gone and the head is relatively small.) Except in the free-living species, individuals can enter the host in the tenuis stage. Arnold (1956), Trott (1970, 1981), and Olney and Markle (1979) describe their life history and present other information.

Maximum length about 30 cm, attained by *Echiodon drummondii* and *Carapus bermudensis.*

Four genera, the free-living *Echiodon*, the commensal *Carapus* (= *Disparichthys*, with one species known only from the holotype that was collected from a brook in New Guinea and described in 1935 as an eel in its own family) and *Onuxodon*, and the parasitic *Encheliophis* (= *Jordanicus*), with a total of about 24 species. Unlike Cohen and Nielsen (1978), who I follow here, Trott (1981) places the one species of parasitic carapid with pectoral fins in its own genus, *Jordanicus* (rather than in a separate subgenus).

SUBFAMILY PYRAMODONTINAE—PYRAMODONTINES. Basically circumtropical, north to Japan and south to New Zealand.

Pectoral fin nearly as long as head, rays 24–27; upper jaw protractile; precaudal vertebrae 12–15. Trott (1981) recognizes this group, with free-living species, as a separate family.

Two genera, *Pyramodon* (pelvics present) and *Snyderidia* (pelvics absent), with three species (Robins and Nielsen, 1970; Markle and Olney, 1980).

Suborder Bythitoidei. Anterior nostril immediately above upper lip in most species; viviparous, males with an external intromittent organ; caudal fin connected with dorsal and anal fins or separate.

Family BYTHITIDAE—viviparous brotulas. Marine (rarely in brackish and fresh waters); Atlantic, Indian, and Pacific.

Scales usually present; swim bladder present; opercular spine usually present and strong; pyloric caeca present; precaudal vertebrae 9–22.

SUBFAMILY BYTHITINAE. Caudal fin united with dorsal and anal fins.

About 14 genera (e.g., *Bythites*, *Cataetyx*, *Diplacanthopoma*, *Oligopus*, and *Stygnobrotula*) with about 50 species.

SUBFAMILY BROSMOPHYCINAE. Caudal fin separate from dorsal and anal fins. The three species of *Lucifuga* live in limestone caves and sinkholes in waters ranging in salinity from fresh to highly saline; two species of the subgenus *Stygicola* occur in Cuba and are blind, while the other species of the subgenus *Lucifuga* occurs in the Bahamas and has small eyes (Cohen and Robins, 1970). Some species of *Ogilbia* live in freshwater caves in the Yucatan and brackish water in the Galapagos.

Thirteen genera (e.g., *Brosmophycis*, *Dinematichthys*, *Gunterichthys*, *Lucifuga*, and *Ogilbia*) with 35 species.

Family APHYONIDAE.   Marine; Atlantic, Indian, and Pacific.

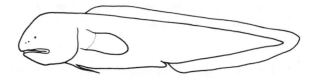

Scales absent; swim bladder absent; dorsal and anal fins confluent; eyes poorly developed; opercular spine weak or absent; pyloric caeca absent; pelvics jugular, one ray in each (absent in a few species); precaudal vertebrae 26–48 (total of 68–86 vertebrae). A number of neotenic characters are present. Most species occur in depths exceeding 700 m. Nielsen (1969) discusses the biology of the group.

Five genera, *Aphyonus*, *Barathronus*, *Meteoria*, *Nybelinella*, and *Sciadonus* (= *Leucochlamys*), with 18 species.

Order BATRACHOIDIFORMES (Haplodoci).   Body usually scaleless (small cycloid scales in some); head large with eyes more dorsal than lateral; mouth large and bordered by premaxilla and maxilla; pore (foramen) in axil of pectoral fin in some; pelvic fins jugular (in front of pectorals), with one spine and two or three soft rays; three pairs of gills; gill membrane broadly joined to isthmus; branchiostegal rays six; four or five pectoral radials; swim bladder present; upper hypurals with peculiar intervertebrallike basal articulation with rest of caudal skeleton; no ribs, epiotics, or intercalars; no pyloric caeca.

Some members can produce audible sounds with the swim bladder and can live out of water for several hours. Most are drab colored.

Family BATRACHOIDIDAE—toadfishes.   Marine (primarily coastal benthic; rarely entering brackish waters, a few species confined to fresh water); Atlantic, Indian, and Pacific.

Three subfamilies with 19 genera and 64 species (Collette and Russo, 1981).

SUBFAMILY BATRACHOIDINAE.   Off coasts of the Americas, Africa, Europe, southern Asia, and Australia.

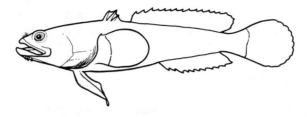

Three solid dorsal spines and solid opercular spine, no venom glands; subopercular spines present; body with or without scales (cycloid); no photophores; axillary gland at pectoral base present or absent; canine teeth absent; usually one or three lateral lines.

Toadfishes generally occur on sand and mud bottoms, although species of *Sanopus* occur in coral reefs. The greatest diversity of this worldwide subfamily is in the New World where there are seven genera and 25 species in the western Atlantic (and three of Atlantic origin in freshwater) and four genera and 15 species in the eastern Pacific. The most speciose genus, *Batrachoides*, with nine species, is the only one in the family to have species in both the Old and New Worlds (Collette and Russo, 1981).

The composition of this subfamily is based primarily on Smith (1952a), Greenfield and Greenfield (1973), Hutchins (1976, 1981), and Collette and Russo (1981).

Fifteen genera, *Amphichthys, Austrobatrachus, Barchatus, Batrichthys, Batrachoides, Batrachomoeus, Chatrabus, Halobatrachus, Halophryne, Opsanus, Parabatrachus, Riekertia, Sanopus, Tharbacus,* and *Triathalassothia* with about 41 species.

SUBFAMILY PORICHTHYINAE. Eastern Pacific and western Atlantic.

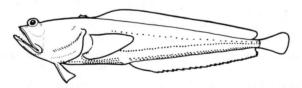

Two solid dorsal spines and solid opercular spine, no venom glands; no subopercular spines; body scaleless; photophores present or absent; axillary gland absent; canine teeth present; several lateral lines.

Two genera with about 12 species.

Aphos. Lacks photophores; one southeastern Pacific (Peru and Chile) species.

Porichthys (midshipmen). Numerous photophores (this is one of the few shallow-water fishes that possess photophores). Eleven species (includes *Nautopaedium*) (Gilbert, 1968), six along the eastern Pacific (southeastern Alaska to Colombia) and five along the western Atlantic (Virginia to Argentina, but generally absent from the West Indies).

SUBFAMILY THALASSOPHRYNINAE.   Eastern Pacific and western Atlantic.

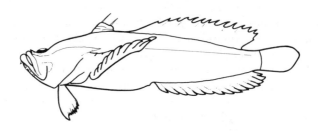

Two hollow dorsal spines and hollow opercular spine (serving as a venom-injecting apparatus capable of producing extremely painful wounds, shown in Halstead, 1970) connecting with venom glands; no subopercular spines; body scaleless; no photophores; no canine teeth; lateral line single or absent.

Two genera with 11 species (Collette, 1966, 1973).

Daector. Second dorsal rays 22–33; anal rays 21–30; distinct glands present between bases of uppermost pectoral fin rays. Four tropical eastern Pacific marine species and *D. quadrizonatus* from fresh water, Colombia (Atrato basin, Atlantic drainage).

Thalassophryne. Second dorsal rays 17–22; anal rays 16–20; no distinct glands present on pectoral fin (they are located distally on the upper pectoral rays). Five western Atlantic marine species (Panama and South America) and *T. amazonica,* known only from the Amazon River.

Order LOPHIIFORMES (Pediculati)–anglerfishes.   First ray of spinous dorsal, if present, on head and transformed into illicium [line and bait (esca) device for attracting prey to mouth]; pelvic fins, if present, in front of pectorals and with one spine and four (rarely) or five soft rays; gill opening small, tubelike, at or behind (rarely partly in front of) pectoral fin base; five or six branchiostegal rays; no ribs; pectoral radials 2–4, narrow and elongate; swim bladder, when present, physoclistic.

Sixteen families with about 64 genera and 265 species. All are marine. Most species occur in deep water.

Suborder Lophioidei. Pelvic fins present; pseudobranch present; body scaleless; frontals united.

Family LOPHIIDAE—goosefishes. Marine; Arctic, Atlantic, Indian, and Pacific.

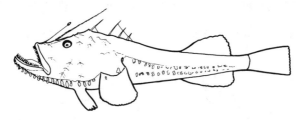

Huge, wide, flattened head; teeth well developed; fringe of small flaps extending around lower jaw and along sides of head onto the body.

The movable "fishing pole" device has a flap of flesh at its tip which acts like a flag, apparently attracting prey within easy reach of its large mouth. Size up to 1.2 m.

Four genera, *Lophiodes* (= *Chirolophius*), *Lophiomus*, *Lophius*, and *Sladenia*, with 25 species (Caruso, 1981).

Suborder Antennarioidei. Pelvic fins present; pectorals usually muscular and armlike; pseudobranch and swim bladder present (Antennariinae only) or absent; body usually scaleless (minute dermal spines may be present); frontals united posteriorly but usually separated from each other anteriorly. Most species are benthic; some are epipelagic.

The classification of this suborder follows Pietsch (1981) except that he places *Tetrabrachium* and *Lophichthys* each in their own family. Chaunacidae and Ogcocephalidae are particularly close and form a separate lineage from the other families. Four families with 26 genera and 130 species.

Family ANTENNARIIDAE—frogfishes. Marine; all tropical and subtropical seas.

Body covered with loose skin, naked or with denticles; first three dorsal spines separate (one or two illicia, the third spine may be ornamented or inconspicuous); gill opening below base of pectoral. Species pelagic; its unusual prehensile pectoral fin is used for "clasping" or moving on algal mats.

The "fishing pole" of frogfishes, a modification of the first dorsal fin, is particularly pronounced and highly variable between species. Maximum length 36 cm, some only 3 cm.

Fifteen genera and about 60 species.

SUBFAMILY ANTENNARIINAE.   Deep-bodied (globularlike); mouth large;
eyes lateral; swim bladder present; nape not conspicuously humped; soft
dorsal fin rays 11–16; soft anal fin rays 6–10; pectoral fin rays 7–14;
palatine teeth present. A case of aggressive mimicry, in which the lure of
an *Antennarius* resembles a small fish, is noted by Pietsch and Grobecker
(1978).
    Reviewed by Schultz (1957).

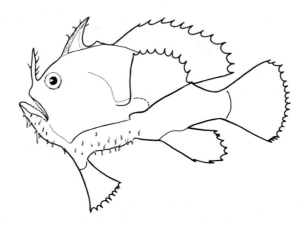

    Thirteen genera (e.g., *Antennarius, Antennatus, Echinophryne, Histio-
phryne, Histrio, Lophiocharon, Phrynelox,* and *Tathicarpus*) with about 58
species (perhaps fewer).

SUBFAMILY TETRABRACHIINAE.   Body elongate and strongly compressed; mouth small; eyes small and superior; swim bladder absent;
nape humped; soft dorsal fin rays 16 or 17; anal fin rays 11 or 12;
pectoral fin rays 9, fin divided into two portions; palatine teeth absent.
Maximum length about 7 cm.
    One species, *Tetrabrachium ocellatum,* known from the western and
northern coasts of Australia, southern coast of New Guinea, and the
south Molucca Islands of Indonesia (Pietsch, 1981).

SUBFAMILY LOPHICHTHYINAE.   Nape not humped; soft dorsal fin rays 12
or 13; anal fin rays nine; pectoral fin rays seven; palatine teeth present.
    One species, *Lophichthys boschmai,* from the Arafura Sea, western New
Guinea (Pietsch, 1981).

Family BRACHIONICHTHYIDAE—warty anglers (handfishes). Marine; southern Australia.

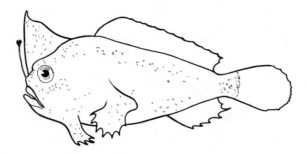

Body deep; skin covered with denticles; second and third dorsal spines united by a membrane; gill opening behind base of pectoral; soft dorsal fin rays about 17; anal fin rays about seven.

One genus, *Brachionichthys* (= *Sympterichthys*), and about four species. A fossil, very similar to the extant species, is known from the Eocene of Italy (Pietsch, 1981).

Family CHAUNACIDAE—sea toads. Marine; Atlantic, Indian, and Pacific.

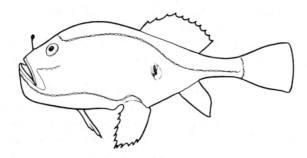

Body balloon-shaped; illicium, but no other spinous dorsal rays; mouth oblique; gill opening behind base of pectoral.

One genus, *Chaunax*, with about nine species.

Family OGCOCEPHALIDAE—batfishes. Marine; all main tropical and many sub-tropical seas.

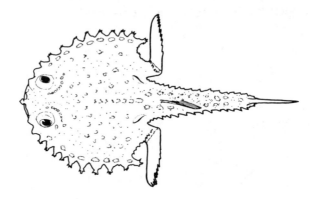

Body usually much depressed and flattened ventrally (somewhat box-shaped in five Indo-West Pacific species); relatively short illicium (comprised primarily of the modified pterygiophore of a normal first fin spine) but no other spinous dorsal rays; illicial cavity, opening anteriorly, which houses the esca when illicium is retracted; mouth nearly horizontal; gill opening in or above pectoral base; two or two and one-half gills (first arch reduced and lacking filaments); well-developed tuberclelike scales. The first four genera given here have conicallike tubercles; the last four, excluding *Halieutichthys*, which has pitted tubercles in adults, have multispined structures called bucklers (spines arranged in a radiating pattern) in addition to having very small tubercles. All have a modified type of scale associated with the lateral line organs.

Batfishes walk about on the bottom on their large armlike pectoral fins and smaller pelvic fins. They are awkward swimmers. Size normally 20 cm; up to 40 cm in *Ogcocephalus nasutus*.

Nine genera, *Coelophrys* (four), *Halieutopsis* (seven), *Dibranchus* (13), *Halieutaea* (eight), *Halicmetus* (two), *Malthopsis* (seven), *Halieutichthys* (two), *Ogcocephalus* (12), and *Zalieutes* (two), with 57 species (Bradbury, 1967, 1980). Species of the first six genera predominate in the Indo-West Pacific and eastern Pacific while members of the last three predominate in the western Atlantic. Only *Dibranchus* is circumtropical, one species of which is the only batfish known from the eastern Atlantic.

Suborder Ceratioidei.   Pelvic fins absent; pseudobranch absent; body scaleless (prickles, spines, or plates may be present); frontals not united; lower pharyngeals reduced and toothless; pectoral fin rays 13–30; eight or nine caudal fin rays; only females with illicium, the tip of which usually has a light organ (undoubtedly increasing its function in attracting prey; light organs may also be present elsewhere).

Marked sexual dimorphism is characteristic of the ceratioids. The longest known female in each family is 3 to 13 times longer than the longest known male (within species the difference can be much greater). The adult males of all species in at least four families are parasitic on the larger females. These males actively seek out females after metamorphosis into the parasitic stage (probably through a female emitted, species-specific pheromone), attach to their bodies, and feed on their blood. (A vascular connection may exist in all such parasitic relationships.) Males are generally different in appearance from females (which are pictured and utilized for the family descriptions), although dorsal and anal fin ray counts are the same. Pietsch (1976) concludes that the sexually mature males of the Ceratiidae, Linophrynidae, and perhaps the Neoceratiidae are obligatory sexual parasites (nonparasitized females never have developed ovaries and free-living males never have developed testes nor undergo postmetamorphic growth), while parasitism in the Caulophrynidae and one oneirodid genus may be facultative (most other taxa are known to be nonparasitic). In the past, males, females, and larva of the same species have been described as different species. Some species are still known only from males, females, or larva and often only from a few specimens.

Larval life is spent in the upper, food-rich oceanic layer; adults are bathypelagic (usually occurring between 1500 and 2500 m). Ceratioids extend from the subarctic to the subantarctic but are absent from the Mediterranean Sea.

Maximum size in most species is seldom longer than 8 cm; however, the largest specimen is a 1.2 m *Ceratias holbroelli*.

Eleven families, 34 genera, and about 110 species. Major references to this group include Bertelsen (1951) and Pietsch (1974, 1976). The order of families follows Pietsch (1979, figure 26). Bertelsen (1951) noted many similarities between caulophrynids and ogcocephalids. Pietsch (1979) concludes, when considering both shared primitive and derived character states, that caulophrynids represent the most primitive ceratioid and that sexual parasitism has evolved independently in at least two separate lineages.

Family CAULOPHRYNIDAE. Marine; Atlantic, Indian, and Pacific.

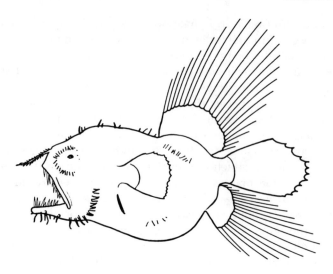

No distal bulb with light organ on illicium; mature males parasitic on females; pelvic fins in larvae (only ceratioid with pelvics at some stage); two pectoral radials (all other ceratioids have 3–5); dorsal fin with 6 (in *Robia*) or 14–22 normal rays, and anal fin with 5 (in *Robia*) or 12–19 rays (other ceratioids have 13 or fewer anal fin rays); extremely elongate dorsal and anal rays; eight caudal fin rays.

Two genera, *Robia*, monotypic, and *Caulophryne*, with three species (plus an undescribed one) (Pietsch, 1979).

Family CERATIIDAE—seadevils.   Marine; Atlantic, Indian, and Pacific.

Females with two or three rays modified into caruncles (low fleshy appendages) in front of soft dorsal fin; mature males parasitic on females; dorsal and anal fin soft-rays usually four, rarely five.

Two species, *Cryptopsaras couesi* and *Ceratias holboelli*.

Family GIGANTACTINIDAE.   Marine; Atlantic, Indian, and Pacific.

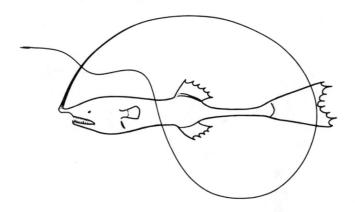

Body elongate in females; illicium almost as long as or longer than body; upper jaw extending slightly beyond lower jaw; five pectoral radials; dorsal fin with 3–10 rays and anal fin with 3–8 rays; nine caudal fin rays.

Two genera, *Gigantactis* with 17 species and the monotypic *Rhynchactis* (Bertelsen et al. 1981). In addition, Uwate (1979: 138) places *Laevoceratias liparis* in this family.

Family NEOCERATIIDAE.   Marine; Atlantic, Indian, and Pacific.

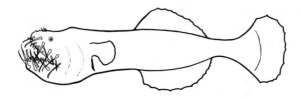

Illicium absent; long movable teeth outside jaws in females; mature males parasitic on females; dorsal fin with 11–13 rays and 10–13 anal rays.

One species, *Neoceratias spinifer.*

Family LINOPHRYNIDAE.   Marine; Atlantic, Indian, and Gulf of Panama.

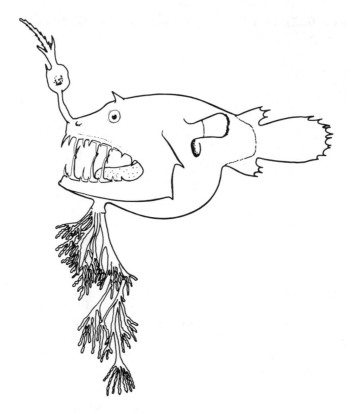

Mature males parasitic on females; dorsal and anal fin soft-rays usually three; hyoid barbel in female *Linophryne*.

Five genera, *Linophryne* with 13 species, and the monotypic *Acentrophryne, Borophryne, Edriolychus,* and *Photocorynus* with 17 species (Pietsch, 1976).

Family ONEIRODIDAE. Marine; Atlantic, Indian, and Pacific.

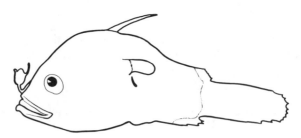

Skin naked or with short spines in some females; dorsal fin with 4–8 rays and 4–7 anal fin rays; jaws equal anteriorly.

Fifteen genera (e.g., *Oneirodes*, *Chaenophryne*, *Lophodolos*, *Dolopichthys*, *Microlophichthys*, and *Puck*) with about 50 species (e.g., Bertelsen and Pietsch, 1977; Pietsch, 1974, 1975, 1976, 1978a). The genus *Oneirodes* has about one-half the species.

Family THAUMATICHTHYIDAE.   Marine; Atlantic and Pacific.

Similar to Oneirodidae, but with upper jaw extending far beyond lower jaw.

Two genera, *Lasiognathus* and *Thaumatichthys* (= *Amacrodon*), with about five species (Nolan and Rosenblatt, 1975; Pietsch, 1976).

Family CENTROPHRYNIDAE—deep-sea anglerfish.   Marine; Atlantic, Indian, and Pacific.

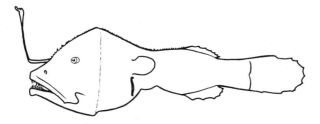

Small hyoid barbel present in young; skin with numerous small spines; dorsal fin with 5–7 rays and five or six anal fin rays.

One species, *Centrophryne spinulosa* (Pietsch, 1972).

Family DICERATIIDAE.   Marine; continental shelf or slope of tropical and subtropical seas, Atlantic and Indo-West Pacific.

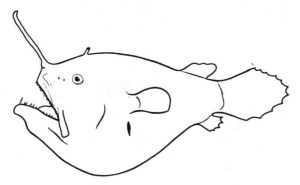

Females distinguished from all other ceratioids in having second cephalic ray externally exposed, clubshaped, with distal light organ; skin spines present; dorsal fin with five to seven rays and anal fin with four rays; small pelvic bone present, connected with cleithrum.

Two genera, *Diceratias* (= *Paroneirodes*) (illicial length less than 50% of standard length) and *Phrynichthys* (illicial length greater than 80% of standard length), each with two species (Uwate, 1979).

Family HIMANTOLOPHIDAE—footballfishes.   Marine; Atlantic, Indian, and Pacific.

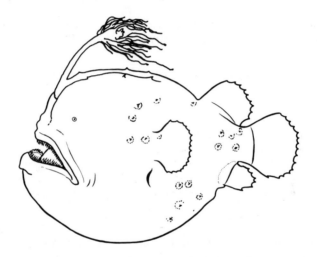

Females with some bony plates, each with a median spine, over body; dorsal fin with five or six rays and four or five anal fin rays.

One genus, *Himantolophus*, with four species.

Family MELANOCETIDAE.   Marine; Atlantic, Indian, and Pacific.

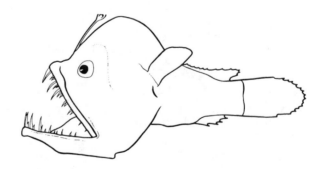

Dorsal fin with 12–17 rays and three or four anal fin rays.

One genus, *Melanocetus*, with about five species (Pietsch and Van Duzer, 1980).

Order GOBIESOCIFORMES (Xenopterygii). Pelvic fins usually present and modified into a sucking disc; spinous dorsal fin absent; head and body scaleless; branchiostegal rays 5–7 (three in *Alabes*); no circumorbital bones behind the lachrymal; articular process of premaxilla either fused with ascending process or absent; basibranchials one and two probably absent; supracleithrum with concave process that articulates with condyle on cleithrum (not known from other fishes); basisphenoid and orbitosphenoid absent; genital papilla behind anus; three or three and one-half gills; hypurals fused into a single plate; no swim bladder. Most species are shallowwater bottom dwelling fishes.

Springer and Fraser (1976) provided evidence that the correct systematic relationship of Alabetidae, placed formerly as a "loose end" in Synbranchiformes, lies with Gobiesocidae. On the basis of many shared characters thought to be specializations, they synonymized the Alabetidae (= Cheilobranchidae) with the Gobiesocidae and concluded that *Alabes* has been derived from gobiesocids through a reduction of various character states. Although no specializations are known which unite all gobiesocids to the exclusion of *Alabes* the latter is retained in its own family here, largely because of the differences between *Alabes* and the gobiesocids. Rosen and Greenwood (1976) also removed Alabetidae from the Synbranchiformes, believing it to have a closer affinity with blennylike fishes (where Greenwood, 1975, placed it).

About 36 genera with 114 species in two families.

Family GOBIESOCIDAE—clingfishes. Marine; primarily shallow water or intertidal; few in fresh water; Atlantic, Indian, and Pacific.

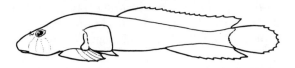

Pelvic fins modified into a thoracic sucking disc (permitting fish to adhere to substrate), with underlying pelvic bones specialized for supporting disc; each pelvic fin with one small spine and four soft rays (rarely five); single dorsal fin without spines; scapula and four pectoral radials and 16–31 pectoral fin rays; usually two postcleithra (rarely one); either common gill opening or separate opening on each side; pleural ribs attached to the epipleural ribs (an opposite relationship to that found in most fish); total caudal fin rays 16–27 (8–14 articulating on hypural fan); vertebrae 25–54 (11–20 abdominal + 13–33 caudal). Maximum length normally 7 cm; two species, however, reach 30 cm or slightly more, *Chorisochismus dentex* of South Africa (Smith, 1964a) and *Sicyases sanguineus* of Chile (pers. comm. A. R. Palmer).

The large amphibious marine clingfish of Chile, *Sicyases sanguineus*, is unique in its high intertidal foraging habits and in its breadth of diet (Paine and Palmer, 1978). This species can forage on vertical rock walls in areas of strong surf action, consuming such items as algae, bivalves, gastropods, and barnacles.

About 35 genera [e.g., *Arcos, Aspasma, Chorisochismus, Diademichthys, Diplecogaster, Gobiesox* (four species of which occur in freshwater streams in Central America), *Haplocylix, Lepadogaster, Rimicola, Tomicodon,* and *Trachelochismus*] with about 110 species. Briggs (1955) recognized eight subfamilies identifiable by the following character states: sucking disc single or double; gill arches three or three and one-half; gill membranes free or attached to isthmus.

Family ALABETIDAE (Cheilobranchidae)—singleslits. Marine; Australia (primarily southern parts including Tasmania) and Norfolk Island (one specimen).

Pelvic bones absent in three species and present in one behind the gill opening (jugular) with three reduced rays (vestigial "sucking disc" in some specimens of one species); no rays in dorsal and anal fins; scapula and pectoral fin radials and rays absent; no postcleithra; single gill opening to both gill chambers situated on midventral side of head; pleural ribs absent (epipleurals attached to vertebral centra); total caudal fin rays 8–11 (seven or eight articulating on hypural fan); vertebrae 60–78 (18–25 abdominal; 39–55 caudal). Maximum length 12 cm, attained in *Alabes dorsalis.*

Springer and Fraser (1976), who provide a detailed description of the group, suggest that *Gastrocymba* is the gobiesocid most closely related to the eellike *Alabes*. In the interests of stability, the generally accepted Alabetidae (first used in 1906) is retained over the senior family name Cheilobranchidae, thereby keeping the tautonymous relationship with the accepted senior generic name, *Alabes.*

One genus, *Alabes (= Cheilobranchus)* with four species (Springer and Fraser, 1976).

Superorder ACANTHOPTERYGII

Greenwood et al. (1966) gave equal rank to the Atherinomorpha and Acanthopterygii (=present Percomorpha); Rosen and Patterson (1969) combined them under the category Acanthopterygii. According to Rosen (1973a), the group can be defined as having the retractor arcuum branchialum (RAB) muscle inserted principally or entirely on the third pharyngobranchial, and the articular surface of the fourth epibranchial reduced with the second and third epibranchials enlarged as the principal support of the upper pharyngeal dentition.
Fifteen orders and 246 families.

Series ATHERINOMORPHA

Opercular and preopercular margin without spines or serrations; ctenoid scales rare; branchiostegal rays 4–15; no orbitosphenoid; ligamentous support of pectoral skeleton (Baudelot's ligament) to basicranium; four cuboidal pectoral actinosts; caudal skeleton usually with two large triangular hypural plates, never more than four; swimbladder physoclistic. The protrusible upper jaw differs from that of other acanthopterygians in lacking a ball and socket joint between the palatine and maxilla (a feature which prevents the premaxillaries from being locked in the protruded position) and in lacking crossed rostral ligaments extending between the palatines and the heads of the premaxillaries.

Most species of this group are surface-feeding fishes and about 75% live in fresh or brackish water. The eggs of the oviparous members have a long, chorionic filament which adheres to the spawning substrate and, except in most exocoetoids, have conspicuous oil droplets which coalesce at the vegetal pole.

The present classification basically follows Rosen (1964) with some changes based, in part, on Rosen and Parenti (1981) and Parenti (1981). In the cladistic scheme of Rosen and Parenti (1981) two divisions are recognized, the first for the Atheriniformes and the second for the remaining groups. In the latter, their division II, they recognize two orders, Cyprinodontiformes (recognized here as the suborder Cyprinodontoidei) and Beloniformes (containing the suborders Adrianichthyoidei and Exocoetoidei). Rosen and Parenti (1981) list the atheriniforms first in order to present the most parsimonious arrangement for the derived characters they employ. For example, they argue that if their spineless cyprinodontiforms and beloniforms are primitive to the spined atheriniforms (as is recognized here), then spines would have to have been lost once and regained by the atheriniforms.

Two orders with 18 families, 168 genera, and about 1080 species.

Order CYPRINODONTIFORMES.   Single dorsal fin; spines very rarely present in fins; second circumorbital bone absent.

Three suborders, Exocoetoidei, Adrianichthyoidei, and Cyprinodontoidei, with a total of 13 families, 120 genera, and about 845 species.

Suborder Exocoetoidei.   Lateral line low on body (absent in some hemiramphids and in *Elassichthys*); narial opening single; branchiostegal rays 6–15; elongate lower jaw at least in some stage of life history; dorsal, anal, and pelvic fins placed far back on body; pelvic fin with six rays; caudal fin usually with 13 branched rays.

This group is given ordinal status, Beloniformes, by some workers (e.g., Berg, 1940; Gosline, 1971; Parin and Astakhov, 1982).

Four families with 34 genera and 164 species.

Superfamily Exocoetoidea.   Scales large, usually 38–60 in lateral line; mouth opening small; no isolated finlets; dorsal and anal fins usually with 8–16 rays each; teeth small.

Family EXOCOETIDAE—flyingfishes.   Marine; Atlantic, Indian, and Pacific.

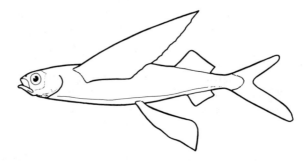

Jaws relatively short and equal in length (lower jaw produced in some juveniles); exceptionally large pectoral fins (gliding flights can be made out of water with the pectorals spread like wings); pelvic fins exceptionally large in some species (thus two-winged and four-winged types can be recognized); lower lobe of caudal fin longer than dorsal lobe (fin deeply forked); juveniles of many have a pair of long, flaplike whiskers. Maximum length 45 cm (attained in *Cypselurus californicus*); most species are less than 30 cm.

Eight genera, *Cypselurus, Cheilopogon, Hirundichthys, Prognichthys, Danichthys, Exocoetus, Fodiator,* and *Parexocoetus,* with at least 48 species.

Family HEMIRAMPHIDAE—halfbeaks.   Marine and freshwater; Atlantic, Indian, and Pacific.

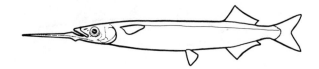

Upper jaw much shorter than lower (lower jaw elongate in most); pectoral and pelvic fins short; some species with lower lobe of caudal fin longer than upper lobe (fin rounded, truncate, or forked). Maximum length about 45 cm.

Twelve genera, *Arrhamphus*, *Chriodorus*, *Dermogenys* (a freshwater halfbeak with internal fertilization; gives birth to live young), *Euleptorhamphus* (with about 20 dorsal and anal fin rays and 105–125 lateral line scales), *Hemiramphus*, *Hemirhamphodon*, *Hyporhamphus* (= *Reporhamphus*), *Melapedalion*, *Nomorhamphus*, *Oxyporhamphus* (shows many intermediate characters between flyingfishes and halfbeaks), *Rhynchorhamphus*, and *Zenarchopterus*, with up to 80 species (e.g., Collette, 1974, 1982a; Parin et al., 1980). Most of the 16 or so freshwater species are in the Indo-Australian region, whereas most of the 11 freshwater needlefishes are in the Neotropical region (Collette, 1982b).

Superfamily Scomberesocoidea.   Scales small, 70 to over 350 in lateral line; mouth opening usually relatively large.

Family BELONIDAE—needlefishes.   Marine and freshwater (e.g., South America, India, and Southeast Asia); epipelagic tropical and temperate waters.

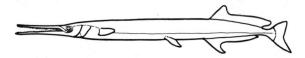

Scales small (usually 130–350 in lateral line); mouth opening large; no isolated finlets; dorsal fin rays usually 10–26; anal fin rays usually 14–23; both upper and lower jaws elongate with numerous needlelike teeth (two South American freshwater species have a short upper jaw, similar to halfbeaks); general body shape superficially resembling *Lepisosteus*. Some species are capable of high jumps out of water. Maximum length about 1.0 m, attained in several species, such as *Tylosurus crocodilus*.

Nine or 10 genera (e.g., *Ablennes*, *Belone*, *Belonion*, *Platybelone*, *Potamorrhaphis*, *Strongylura*, *Tylosurus*, and *Xenentodon*) with 32 species (Collette, 1982b).

Family SCOMBERESOCIDAE—sauries.   Marine; epipelagic tropical and temperate seas.

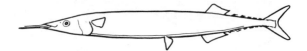

Scales small (70–91 along midline in two dwarf species and 107–148 in two large species); mouth opening relatively small, jaws varying in length from both produced into long, slender beaks (as in *Scomberesox* shown in figure) to relatively short beaks with lower jaw only slightly produced (small juveniles of all species have short jaws); 5–7 finlets after both dorsal and anal fins; dorsal fin rays 14–18; anal fin rays 16–21; teeth relatively small; swim bladder absent and ovary single in two dwarf species; vertebrae 54–70 (32–43 precaudal). Maximum length about 46 cm, attained in *Scomberesox saurus.*

Four species in monotypic genera: the relatively large *Scomberesox* (North Atlantic and Southern Hemisphere) and *Cololabis* (North Pacific), and the more tropical and dwarf *Nanichthys* (Atlantic and small portion of Indian) and *Elassichthys* (eastern central Pacific) (Hubbs and Wisner, 1980).

Suborder Adrianichthyoidei. Lateral line absent on body; narial opening paired; branchiostegal rays 4–7; vomer, supracleithrum, metapterygoid, and ectopterygoid absent; premaxilla not protractile.

Three families with four genera and 11 species. Rosen and Parenti (1981) place all species in the family Adrianichthyidae.

Family ORYZIIDAE—medakas or ricefishes. Fresh- and brackish water; India and Japan to Indo-Australian Archipelago.

Jaws not tremendously enlarged; dorsal and anal fins of male (shown in figure) usually more pronounced than in female; almost always egg layers. Maximum length about 9 cm.

One genus, *Oryzias*, with seven species (Rosen, 1964).

Family ADRIANICHTHYIDAE—adrianichthyids. Freshwater; Celebes Island.

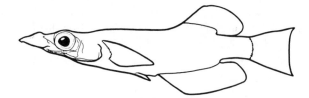

Jaws tremendously enlarged; scoop-shovel type mouth; egg layers. Maximum size up to 20 cm.

Two genera, *Adrianichthys* and *Xenopoecilus,* with three species.

Family HORAICHTHYIDAE.   Fresh- and brackish water; coastal western India.

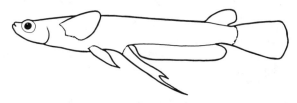

Body thin and translucent; dorsal fin small, near caudal fin; anal fin elongate; right pelvic fin absent in females; maxilla absent. Superficially similar to the poeciliid *Tomeurus.* Certain similarities in fin structure with the phallostethids has been noted by Hubbs (1944) to be due to convergence. Maximum length about 3 cm.

One species, *Horaichthys setnai,* found in 1937, occurs along coastal India from near the Gulf of Kutch (northwestern India) to Trivandrum near the southern tip (Hubbs, 1941; Silas, 1959).

Suborder Cyprinodontoidei (Microcyprini).   Lateral line chiefly on head, not on body; narial opening paired; branchiostegal rays 3–7; pelvic fins and girdle present or absent; upper jaw bordered by premaxilla only, protrusible; vomer usually present and supracleithrum always present; metapterygoid usually absent and ectopterygoid always absent; parietals present or absent; vertebrae 24–54. The males are often brightly colored. Parenti (1981) describes several shared derived characters of the group in, for example, the following structures: the caudal skeleton, upper jaw, gill arches, and position of the first pleural rib.

Members of this suborder are popular aquarium and experimental fishes. Rosen (1973b) presents a key to the salt-tolerant species, and Parenti (1981) gives a key to genera of most of the families.

Parenti (1981) recognizes a markedly different arrangement to that previously followed and to that employed here. Much of the following information is based on her detailed study, which should be consulted for a description of the derived character states for the various groups. The families that she recognizes in this suborder, given in her study as the order Cyprinodontiformes, and some of the higher categories, are as follows:

Suborder Aplocheiloidei
    Families Aplocheilidae and Rivulidae
Suborder Cyprinodontoidei
    Section 1
        Family Profundulidae
    Section 2
      Division 1
        Family Fundulidae
      Division 2
        Families Valenciidae, Anablepidae, Poeciliidae, Goodeidae, and Cyprinodontidae

Six families with 82 genera and about 670 species. Members of the first two families are oviparous, while those of the last four are viviparous (except for *Tomeurus*, which has internal fertilization but the fertilized eggs are layed). According to the postulated phylogenetic scheme of Parenti (1981), the viviparous families do not form a monophyletic group and viviparity is postulated to have arisen at least three times within the group.

Family APLOCHEILIDAE—rivulines.   Freshwater; Africa, southern Asia, southern North America, and South America (see map on page 418).

Pelvic fin bases inserted close together; metapterygoid present; three basibranchials; a dorsal ray on each of the first two dorsal radials. In all other members of the suborder the pelvic fin bases are not inserted close together and they possess two basibranchials, lack the metapterygoid, and have one dorsal ray articulating with the first two radials.

Parenti (1981) gives this group subordinal rank and places those species with the supracleithrum fused to the posttemporal and possessing the first postcleithrum in the family Aplocheilidae (the panchax group— found in Africa and southern Asia to Java). Those with the supracleithrum not fused to the posttemporal and lacking the first postcleithrum she places in the family Rivulidae (found from southern Florida, through much of Middle America, to Uruguay). Members of this group are, in an alternative and classical system of classification, placed in the subfamily Rivulinae of Cyprinodontidae.

One species, *Rivulus marmoratus*, consists of individuals which have simultaneously functional ovary and testis (self-fertilizing hermaphrodites). Fertilization is internal and then eggs are layed (Harrington, 1961). Two species of the South American genus *Cynolebias* have internal fertilization and one species has a gonopodium. Some members of the family are termed annuals. In these, adults spawn during the rainy season and the eggs survive dry periods buried in the substrate. Hatching normally occurs during the next rainy season. According to Parenti (1981), the true annuals do not form a monophyletic group.

Many species of the large, nonannual genus *Aphyosemion* of western and central Africa are particularly colorful.

About 15 genera (e.g., *Aplocheilus, Aphyosemion, Epiplatys, Fundulopanchax, Nothobranchius, Cynolebias*, and *Rivulus*) with about 210 species.

Family CYPRINODONTIDAE—killifishes (toothcarps).   Fresh- and brackish water, rarely coastal marine; southeastern Canada to South America, Africa, Madagascar, southern Europe, and southern Asia (see map on p. 418).

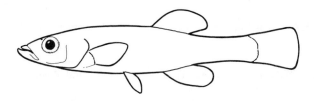

Egg layers (males lack gonopodium) which have pelvic fin bases (when fins are present) relatively far apart, lack the metapterygoid, and have one dorsal ray articulating with the first two radials. Maximum length about 16 cm.

The members of Cyprinodontidae that are recognized here include those groups formerly placed in this family excluding those now placed in the Aplocheilidae. Parenti (1981) recognizes the forms given here in the following categories:

Family Profundulidae—One genus with five species in Middle America.

Family Fundulidae—Five genera, *Adinia, Fundulus, Leptolucania, Lucania*, and *Plancterus*, with about 40 species in Middle America.

Family Valenciidae—One genus with two species in Europe.

Subfamily Oxyzygonectinae of the expanded family Anablepidae—One species in Costa Rica.

Subfamily Fluviphylacinae of the expanded family Poeciliidae—One species in the Amazon basin.

Subfamily Aplocheilichthyinae of the expanded family Poeciliidae— Eight genera (e.g., *Lamprichthys, Pantanodon,* and *Procatopus*) with about 110 species in Africa (including Madagascar).

Subfamily Empetrichthyinae of the expanded family Goodeidae—Two genera, *Crenichthys* and *Empetrichthys,* with four species that lack the pelvic fins in the Death Valley system and eastern Nevada, United States.

Family Cyprinodontidae—About 10 genera (e.g., *Cubanichthys, Aphanius, Kosswigichthys, Orestias, Cyprinodon, Floridichthys, Jordanella,* and *Megupsilon*) with about 105 species in the New World and Mediterranean Anatolian regions. Of these, pelvic fins are absent in the North American *Cyprinodon diabolis* and *Megupsilon aporus,* the South American *Orestias* (which is found in high altitude lakes in western Bolivia and southern Peru and also lacks a vomer and a first postcleithrum; Tchernavin, 1944b, gives a key to 20 species in Lake Titicaca), and the Old World *Aphanius apodus.* About 30 species of pupfishes of the genus *Cyprinodon* inhabit deserts of the southwestern United States and northern Mexico (Miller, 1981). Much information on the biology of the species of this genus is given in Naiman and Soltz (1981).

As recognized here, the family contains 29 genera and about 268 species.

Family GOODEIDAE—goodeids.   Freshwater; west central Mexico.

Internal fertilization; bear young alive; anterior rays of anal fin in male crowded, shortened, and slightly separated from rest of fin (primitive gonopodium?, termed a pseudophallus); ovaries partly united into a single median organ; embryos and newborn young usually have a placentalike trophotaeniae (ribbonlike extensions from anal region associated with nutrition and respiration). Reviewed by Miller and Fitzsimons (1971).

This family, centered in the Lio Lerma basin, has species of many diverse body forms (deep-bodied to long-bodied) and feeding habits (carnivores to herbivores). Maximum length up to 20 cm.

About 14 genera [e.g., *Ameca, Ataeniobius, Characodon, Ilyodon, Girardinichthys* (= *Lermichthys*), *Skiffia* (= *Neotoca* and *Ollentodon*), and *Xenotoca*] with about 36 species.

Family ANABLEPIDAE—four-eyed fishes. Fresh- and brackish water, rarely coastal marine; southern Mexico to northern South America.

Eyes elevated above top of head and divided longitudinally into upper and lower portions giving two pupils on each side (water line in surface-swimming individuals in center of eye, and images can be focused simultaneously from above and below water with their unusual double vision); most rays of the anal fin modified into tubelike gonopodium for intromission; first three anal fin rays (excluding anteriormost, rudimentary ray of males) unbranched (as in Poeciliidae); dorsal fin with 7–10 rays and lying well behind anal fin; lateral line scales 50–96; vertebrae 45–54 (more than in other Cyprinodontoidei); bear young alive.

In some males the gonopodium can move only to the left; in others, only to the right. In females the genital aperture is open to the right or to the left. It is thought that in mating a left-handed (sinistral) male must copulate with a right-handed (dextral) female and vice versa. Both sexes are divided equally into dextral and sinistral mating types. Maximum length up to 32 cm, usually somewhat less (females much larger than males).

One genus, *Anableps,* with three species (Zahl et al., 1977; Miller, 1979). Parenti (1981) includes *Jenynsia* and *Oxyzygonectes* in this family.

Family JENYNSIIDAE—jenynsiids. Freshwater; southern South America.

Tubular gonopodium formed from anal fin rays; bear young alive. Dextral and sinistral mating types occur as in the Anablepidae. Maximum size up to 12 cm.

One genus, *Jenynsia,* with about three species.

Family POECILIIDAE—livebearers. Fresh- and brackish water; low elevations from eastern United States to northeastern Argentina (see map on p. 418).

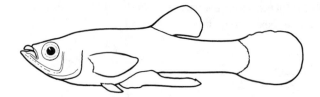

First three anal rays unbranched. Male with elongated anterior anal fin rays (gonopodium, primarily formed from the third, fourth, and fifth rays) with internal fertilization; bear young alive (except in *Tomeurus*). Reviewed by Rosen and Bailey (1963). Rosen (1979) revises the genera *Heterandria* and *Xiphophorus*, and in rejecting the biological species concept (by defining a species as "a population or group of populations defined by one or more apomorphous features . . .") and raising previously recognized subspecies to species status, recognizes a total of 24 species (rather than the previous 14) in these two genera. Thibault and Schultz (1978) present information on the wide range of adaptations accompanying viviparity in poeciliids.

The world-famous guppy, *Poecilia reticulata*, and mosquitofish, *Gambusia affinis*, are popular for aquariums and mosquito control, respectively. All-female forms are known from *Poeciliopsis* (Moore et al., 1970; Schultz, 1973) in northwestern Mexico, whereas in *Poecilia* (= *Mollienesia*) *formosa* virtually all individuals are females. In the latter species (and in some *Poeciliopsis*) the spermatozoan of another species stimulates egg development but does not contribute any genetic material. Maximum size about 18 cm; most species are much smaller.

SUBFAMILY POECILIINAE. About 20 genera (e.g., *Cnesterodon, Gambusia, Girardinus, Heterandria, Poecilia*, and *Xiphophorus*) with 148 species.

SUBFAMILY TOMEURINAE. Gonopodium under pectoral fins; female lays eggs. One species, *Tomeurus gracilus*, in northeastern South America.

SUBFAMILY XENODEXIINAE. Most of the scales ctenoid (with needle-sharp ctenii on the margin); adult male with complex structure, presumably of copulatory function, in axillary region of right pectoral fin (pectoral clasper). One species, *Xenodexia ctenolepis*, in Guatemala (Hubbs, 1950).

Order ATHERINIFORMES. Usually two dorsal fins, the first, if present, with flexible spines; anal fin usually preceded by a spine; lateral line absent or very weak; branchiostegal rays 5–7; narial openings paired; parietals present.

Gosline (1971) views the affinity of this group to be with the members of his perciform suborder Mugiloidei. Unlike the other major atherinomorph groups, shared derived characters are poorly known for the atheriniforms and they cannot be defined cladistically (Rosen and Parenti, 1981). The characters given in the above description and additional ones given in Rosen (1964) are regarded as being primitive.

Five families with 48 genera and about 235 species.

Superfamily Atherinoidea. Pelvic fins present and abdominal, subabdominal, or thoracic in position, not modified into clasping organ.

Family ATHERINIDAE—silversides. Marine; tropical to temperate seas; some in fresh water.

Two widely separated dorsal fins; no lateral line, broad silvery lateral band (black in preserved specimens); pelvic fins usually abdominal; scales relatively large (usually 31–50 in lateral series, more in *Labidesthes*); vertebrae 32–60.

The small grunion, *Leuresthes tenuis,* of southern California has the peculiar adaptation of spawning high on beaches at night during the period of the highest tides, usually from March to August (Walker, 1952). The young hatch out in future high tides.

Most atherinids are marine. There are, however, many species in fresh water; for example, 18 species of *Chirostoma* live in fresh water in the southern portion of the Mexican plateau (Barbour, 1973), whereas *Labidesthes sicculus* is spread across most of the eastern United States. *Bedotia,* which occurs in streams in Madagascar, and its presumed relatives are recognized in their own family (Bedotiidae) and placed after Atherinidae by Rosen and Parenti (1981). In addition, they recognize the several species of *Telmatherina,* which occur in lakes and streams in the Celebes in their own family (Telmatherinidae) which is placed after Phallostethidae.

Maximum length 60 cm.

About 29 genera (e.g., *Allanetta, Atherinops, Atherion, Bedotia, Chirostoma, Craterocephalus, Labidesthes, Leuresthes, Membras, Menidia, Pranesus, Stenatherina,* and *Telmatherina*) with about 160 species.

Family ISONIDAE. Marine; South Africa, India, Japan, Australia, Hawaii, and Chile.

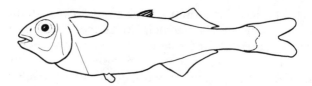

Upper jaw teeth confined to symphyseal portion of premaxilla; pelvis with lateral spur extending upward between pleural ribs almost to vertebral column; epurals absent; autopalatine present. Maximum length about 5 cm.

Two genera with six species: *Iso* with five species, and *Notocheirus hubbsi* (known from Chile) (Rosen, 1964).

Family MELANOTAENIIDAE—rainbowfishes. Freshwater , some in brackish water; northern and eastern Australia and New Guinea and some nearby islands.

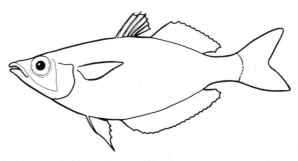

Body compressed; dorsal fins narrowly separated, the first with 3–7 spines and the second with 6–22 rays (the first being a stout spine in some species); anal fin with 10–30 rays, the first a stout spine in some species; lateral line absent or weakly developed; scales relatively large, 28–60 in lateral series; innermost pelvic ray attached to abdomen by membrane along its entire length. (This is a useful character in separating rainbowfishes from silversides, but the membrane is easily broken.) Vertebrae 27–38. Most rainbowfishes exhibit some sexual dimorphism with, for example, males usually being more colorful than females. Maximum length about 12 cm.

Eight genera, *Pseudomugil* (some species can enter marine water and one species extends along the eastern Australian coastline to New South Wales), *Popondetta*, *Cairnsichthys*, *Rhadinocentrus*, *Iriatherina*, *Melanotaenia* (which contains about one-half the species), *Glossolepis*, and *Chilatherina*, with about 50 species (Allen, 1980a; Allen and Cross, 1982).

Superfamily Phallostethoidea. Body somewhat translucent in life, compressed, and moderately elongate; mouth protractile; muscular and bony copulatory organ (priapium) under throat of male (a complicated internal structure that contains ducts from kidney and gonads as well as terminal parts of intestine); priapium sometimes has a slender anterior, curved bony projection (toxactinium) and one or two posterior projections (ctenactinia) which may be used as claspers; pelvic fins modified to form part of a complex thoracic clasping organ in male (serving to clasp female during copulation; pelvics absent in female); internal fertilization; anus below or in front of pectorals; usually two dorsal fins, the first with one or two tiny spines and the second (completely separated from the first) with 5–10 soft rays; anal fin with one short spine and 11–29 soft rays; caudal fin forked; pectoral fins high, with 10 to 11 rays; two pectoral radials; scales cycloid, 31–58 in lateral series; vertebrae 34–38; no orbitosphenoid; eggs with a filamentous process as in Atherinidae.

Two families with nine genera and 19 species (Bailey, 1936; Herre, 1939, 1953; Roberts, 1971b,c). This group probably originated from the atherinids, the most closely related ones being in the subfamily Taeniomembrasinae (e.g., *Stenatherina*) (Roberts, 1971c).

Family NEOSTETHIDAE.   Brackish and freshwater (rarely coastal marine); Southeast Asia.

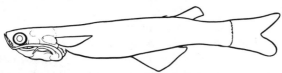

Toxactinium absent; one or two long, curved, nonserrated ctenactinia; usually five branchiostegal rays. Maximum length about 3.7 cm, attained in *Gulaphallus eximus*.

Two subfamilies, seven genera, and 16 species.

Subfamily Neostethinae.   Philippines, Borneo, Malay Peninsula, and adjacent areas. Anterior end of ctenactinium exposed.

Five genera, *Ceratostethus, Solenophallus, Plectrostethus, Neostethus,* and *Manacopus,* with 13 species.

Subfamily Gulaphallinae.   Luzon, Philippines. Anterior end of ctenactinium fits into a fleshy sheath in the anterior end of the priapium.

Two genera: *Gulaphallus* (two species) and *Mirophallus* (one species).

Family PHALLOSTETHIDAE.   Brackish and freshwater; Malaya and Thailand.

Toxactinium present (long bony process projecting from anterior of priapium); ctenactinium single, serrated or not; four branchiostegal rays.

Members of this family probably arose from a *Neostethus* lineage. Maximum length about 2.3 cm.

Two genera: *Phallostethus* (with one species, *P. dunckeri*, known only from the four type specimens collected before 1904 from the mouth of the Muar River, Malaya) and *Phenacostethus* (with two species, one from fresh water in Thailand and the other from the Indian Ocean coast of Thailand).

Series PERCOMORPHA

The first three orders, Lampriformes, Beryciformes, and Zeiformes, seem to have a relatively close relationship. Problems in the classification of these groups and in defining the boundary with Perciformes are discussed by Rosen (1973a).

ORDER LAMPRIFORMES. No true spines in fins; premaxilla excludes maxilla from gape; unique type of protrusible upper jaw (maxilla, instead of being ligamentously attached to the ethmoid and palatine, slides in and out with the highly protactile premaxilla in at least the first four suborders); pelvic fins with 0–17 rays; swim bladder, when present, physoclistic; orbitosphenoid present in some.

The scope of this order has been increased over the years. Berg (1940) placed only the first five families in the Lampriformes (Allotriognathi). Greenwood et al. (1966) added Stylephoridae. The last four families, added by Rosen and Patterson (1969), are retained only provisionally. Rosen's (1973a) study suggests that the Mirapinnidae, Eutaeniophoridae, and Megalomycteridae are better placed in the related order Beryciformes. With the Ateleopodidae he finds that their gill arch structure does not support a lampriform alignment (indeed, their fragmented pharyngeal tooth plates, which are separated from their endoskeletal support, are secondarily similar to that of elopomorphs and osteoglossomorphs). In the absence of a more plausible alignment they are retained in the lampriforms on the basis of having a lampriformlike upper jaw specialization. Members of the Trachipteroidei and Stylephoroidei, with a long ribbonlike body with a dorsal fin extending from the head to the tail, are referred to as the taeniosomes.

Eleven families with 20 genera and about 39 species.

Suborder Lamproidei

Family LAMPRIDAE—opah. Marine pelagic; Atlantic and Pacific.

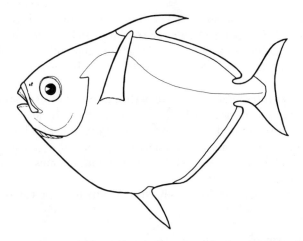

Body oval-shaped and compressed; lateral line arched high in front; dorsal and anal fins long (dorsal usually with 50–55 rays and anal usually with 34–41 rays); pelvic fin rays 15–17; minute cycloid scales. Its food consists primarily of squids, octopuses, and crustaceans. Maximum size up to 1.8 m. In an anatomical study, Rosenblatt and Johnson (1976) concluded that normal cruising is probably accomplished by pectoral swimming.

One species, *Lampris guttatus (= regius)* (Palmer and Oelschläger, 1976).

Suborder Veliferoidei.   Walters (1960) reviews this group.

Family VELIFERIDAE.   Marine; Indian and western and mid-Pacific.

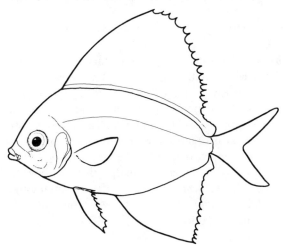

Body deep and compressed; pelvic fins with eight or nine rays; dorsal and anal fins long; swim bladder extending far beyond anus; six branchiostegal rays; vertebrae 33 or 34 (16 abdominal and 17 or 18 caudal). One genus, *Velifer (= Metavelifer)*, with two or three species.

Suborder Trachipteroidei. Body very thin and ribbonlike; anal fin short or absent; pelvic fin rays 0–10; six or seven branchiostegal rays; swim bladder, when present, does not extend past the anus; each dorsal fin ray has a lateral spine at its base; suborbital series absent except for the lachrymal and second suborbital (jugal); frontal bones separated by a groove; vertebrae 62–200.

Walters and Fitch (1960) review this group (except for the Radiicephalidae).

Family LOPHOTIDAE—crestfishes.   Marine; most oceans.

Body with small deciduous cycloid scales (sometimes appearing naked); anal fin present (short and posterior); caudal fin normal; pelvic fin, if present, with 1–9 rays; dorsal fin very long with about 220–392 rays and originating above or before tip of snout; swim bladder present; ink sac present which discharges into cloaca. The extinct *Protolophotus* is known from Oligocene deposits in Iran.

Perhaps only two species, *Lophotus capellei* and *L. (= Eumecichthys) fiski*.

Family RADIICEPHALIDAE.   Marine; central and eastern Atlantic.

Body elongate and laterally compressed, tapering to a thin caudal filament (caudal fin with small upper lobe of four rays and long, slender lower lobe of seven rays); dorsal fin with 152–159 rays; anal fin with seven rays; pectorals and pelvics each with nine rays (pelvic rays tend to be lost with development); scales along lateral line but absent on rest of body; ribs present; swim bladder well developed; brown ink sac, which discharges into the cloaca (the ink, like that of *Lophotus*, may serve to blind would-be predators); cloaca about one-third along total length from snout; vertebrae 114–118 (36–39 + 77–79), of equal length.

One species, *Radiicephalus elongatus*, known from only a few specimens (Harrisson and Palmer, 1968).

Family TRACHIPTERIDAE—ribbonfishes. Marine; Arctic, Atlantic (including Mediterranean), Indian, and Pacific.

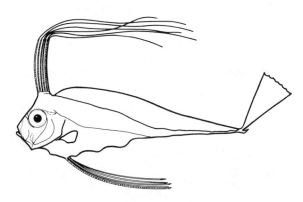

Body naked, with deciduous cycloid scales, or with deciduous modified ctenoid scales (tubercles may also be present); no anal fin; caudal fin long and at a right angle to the body, consisting of upper lobe only (*Desmodema* has the few caudal rays parallel to the caudal peduncle); pelvic fins with 1–10 rays; dorsal fin very long, originating distinctly behind tip of snout; eye large; teeth present; ribs absent; swim bladder rudimentary or absent; vertebrae 62–111. Allometric growth results in various body shapes during growth (including the loss of the pelvic fins during metamorphosis in *Desmodema*). Maximum length about 1.7 m, attained in *Trachipterus altivelis.*

Palmer (1961), Fitch (1964), and Rosenblatt and Butler (1977) discuss various members of the group.

Three genera, *Desmodema* (two), *Trachipterus* (about five—including king-of-the-salmon), and *Zu* (one), with about eight species.

Family REGALECIDAE—oarfishes. Marine; all oceans.

Scales absent; no anal fin; pelvic fin very elongate, slender, with 1–5 rays; dorsal fin very long, originating distinctly behind tip of snout; first few rays are elongate and bright red; eye small; no teeth; swim bladder absent. *Regalecus glesne* (king-of-the-herring) has 40–58 gill rakers; *Regalecus (= Agrostichthys) parkeri* has about 8–10 gill rakers. This group is probably responsible for many sea-serpent stories. Maximum length up to about 8 m.

One genus, *Regalecus* (= *Agrostichthys*), with two species.

Suborder Stylephoroidei

Family STYLEPHORIDAE—tube-eye or thread-tail.   Marine abyssal; most oceans.

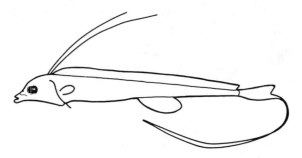

Body ribbonlike; dorsal fin extending from nape to tail, with 110–122 rays; anal fin short, 16 or 17 rays; pectoral fin rays 10 or 11; pelvic fin with only one ray; caudal fin in two parts, upper with five rays and lower with two extremely elongate rays; eyes large, telescopic, may be directed forward or upward; mouth small and protractile; teeth small; no swim bladder. This fish swims in a vertical position, head uppermost. Maximum body size 31 cm. This fish has an unusual feeding mechanism in which the volume of the buccal cavity can rapidly increase up to 38 times from the closed position, thereby effectively sucking in small planktonic organisms through the elongate, tubular snout (Pietsch, 1978b).

Perhaps only one species, *Stylephorus chordatus.*

Suborder Ateleopodoidei

Family ATELEOPODIDAE.   Marine; Caribbean Sea, eastern Atlantic, and Indo-Pacific.

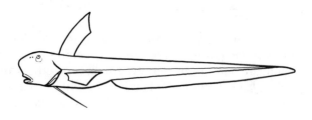

Caudal fin reduced, united with the long anal fin; pelvic fin of adults with single ray on throat (young specimens and *Guentherus* have several rays, and the pelvics of the latter are behind the pectorals); dorsal fin with 3–13 rays.

Four genera (Walters, 1963), *Ateleopus, Ijimaia, Parateleopus,* and *Guentherus,* with about 12 species.

Suborder Mirapinnatoidei. No scales; gill membranes separate and free from isthmus; fins without spines; dorsal and anal fins opposite one another; pelvic fins jugular, 4–10 rays; 3–5 branchiostegal rays.

The first specimen of this group was collected in 1911. Bertelsen and Marshall (1956) placed the two families in a new order, Miripinnati, placed here in the order Lampriformes as advised by Rosen and Patterson (1969). All specimens are immature and 5 cm or less.

Family MIRAPINNIDAE—hairyfish. Marine; Atlantic.

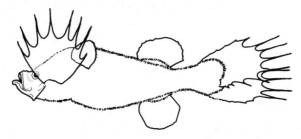

Body moderately elongate, covered with short hairlike pile; two halves of caudal fin overlapping; large, winglike pelvic fins; pectoral fins relatively small and placed high on body.

One species, *Mirapinna esau.*

Family EUTAENIOPHORIDAE (Taeniophoridae)—tapetails or ribbonbearers. Marine; Atlantic, Indian, and western Pacific.

Body very elongate, smooth; caudal fin in juveniles with extremely long tapelike streamer (several times body length); dorsal and anal fins near caudal fin; dorsal and anal fins each with 15–31 rays.

Bertelsen and Marshall (1958) give reasons for erecting the name *Eutaeniophorus* to replace *Taeniophorus* and present distributional records. Two genera, *Eutaeniophorus* and *Parataeniophorus*, with three species.

Suborder Megalomycteroidei. This suborder and the one included family were erected and described by Myers and Freihofer (1966). Five species (Goodyear, 1970).

Family MEGALOMYCTERIDAE—largenose fishes. Marine, deep-sea; Atlantic and Pacific.

Olfactory organs exceptionally large; pelvic fin usually absent [present and inserted slightly ahead of the pectorals in *Megalomycter* (three rays) and *Ataxolepis henactis* (one ray)]; fins without spines; dorsal and anal fins near caudal fin; vertebrae 45–52.

Four genera, *Ataxolepis*, with two species (one in the Atlantic and one in the tropical eastern Pacific), and the monotypic *Cetomimoides*, *Megalomycter*, and *Vitiaziella*.

Order BERYCIFORMES. Mucous cavities on head usually well developed; 17 branched caudal rays (or 19 principal rays, one less in *Cleidopus*); maxilla usually partially included in gape of mouth; orbitosphenoid present or absent; pelvic fins, when present, usually with more than five soft rays.

There is little agreement in the composition of this order. Parts of the present classification are based on the somewhat different systems of Rosen (1973a), Woods and Sonoda (1973), and Zehren (1979). The beryciforms, as recognized here, are probably related to the Mirapinnatoidei, Megalomycteroidei, and some Zeiformes. This order may come closest to representing the ancestral stock from which many other more advanced acanthopterygians evolved, in particular the Perciformes.

Fourteen families with about 38 genera and 164 species. Two families, the Melamphaidae and Holocentridae, comprise well over half of the species.

Suborder Berycoidei. Mouth large, usually oblique; body usually compressed; teeth usually on vomer and palatine; orbitosphenoid present;

subocular shelf present (except in Anoplogastridae); supramaxillae one or two; branchiostegal rays six or seven. Berycoids are usually deep-sea benthic or occur in tropical reefs. There is a well-known fossil record with their first appearance being at the base of the Upper Cretaceous (Patterson, 1964).

The families Sorosichthyidae (with *Sorosichthys*) and Paradiretmidae (with *Paradiretmus*) are not treated here. They were erected by G. P. Whitley of Australia and placed in the Beryciformes by Patterson (1964), McAllister (1968), and Rosen (1973a). They are thought to be related to the Trachichthyidae.

Seven families with 22 genera and about 104 species.

Superfamily Anoplogastroidea.

Family MONOCENTRIDIDAE—pinecone fishes.   Marine; Indo-Pacific.

Body covered with large, heavy platelike scales; pelvic fin with one large spine and two or three small soft rays; dorsal fin spines alternating from side to side; two phosphorescent light organs under lower jaw; anal fin with 10 soft rays (no spines). Maximum length about 21 cm.

Two genera, *Cleidopus* and *Monocentris*, with about three species. They occur primarily off South Africa, Japan, and Australia.

Family TRACHICHTHYIDAE—slimeheads.   Marine; Atlantic, Indian, and Pacific.

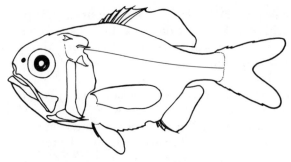

Distinct spine at angle of preopercle; pelvic fin with one normal spine and six or seven soft rays; dorsal fin spines 3–8; abdomen with median ridge of scutes; scales variable between species (e.g., thick and spiny to thin and cycloid); body very deep in the Australian *Trachichthys* and the widespread *Gephyroberyx* and *Hoplostethus* (shown in figure) to only moderately deep; some species with luminescence.

Five genera, *Gephyroberyx*, *Hoplostethus* (= *Korsogaster* and *Leiogaster*), *Optivus*, *Paratrachichthys*, and *Trachichthys*, with about 26 species. About half of the species are placed in *Hoplostethus*. Most species occur in deep water.

Family ANOMALOPIDAE—lanterneye fishes.   Marine; scattered warm-water localities, primarily Indo-Pacific.

Light organ beneath eye with rotational and shutter mechanism for controlling light emission (hence the common name, lanterneye or flashlight fishes); pelvic fin with one spine and five or six soft rays; dorsal fin with 2–6 spines, spinous and soft portions continuous (*Photoblepharon* only) or with notch; anal fin spines two or three; short subocular shelf. The mechanical means of controlling light emission from the subocular organ with luminous bacteria and the advantage of the blinking action in avoiding predation is discussed by Rosenblatt and Montgomery (1976). Maximum length about 30 cm, attained by the shallow-water pelagic planktivore, *Anomalops katoptron*.

Three genera, the Indo-West Pacific *Anomalops* and *Photoblepharon* and the New World *Kryptophanaron* (with one species from Jamaica and another from the Gulf of California), with four species (Rosenblatt and Montgomery, 1976; McCosker, 1977b; Colin et al., 1979).

Family DIRETMIDAE—spinyfins.   Marine; Atlantic, Indian, and Pacific.

No lateral line; dorsal and anal fins without spines, dorsal rays 25–28 and anal rays 19–22; pelvic fin with laminar spine and six soft rays;

sharp edge to abdomen formed by ventral scutes; vertebrae 30 or 31. Maximum size 37 cm.

One genus, *Diretmus*, with two species (Woods and Sonoda, 1973).

Family ANOPLOGASTRIDAE—fangtooth. Marine, bathypelagic.

Body short and deep; numerous long fanglike teeth on jaws in adults; eye small, diameter less than snout length; scales small or minute; lateral line an open groove (partly covered by scales); fins without spines, dorsal with 17–20 rays and anal usually with 8 or 9 rays; Baudelot's ligament absent; about 28 vertebrae. Maximum length about 15 cm.

One species, *Anoplogaster (= Caulolepis) cornuta* (Woods and Sonoda, 1973).

Superfamily Berycoidea

Family BERYCIDAE—alfonsinos. Marine; Atlantic, Indian, and Pacific.

Pelvic fin with one spine and 7–13 soft rays; dorsal fin without notch, with 4–7 spines increasing in length from first to last, and 12–19 soft rays; anal fin with four spines and 12–17 *(Centroberyx)* or 25–29 *(Beryx)* soft rays; lateral line scales 39–51 *(Centroberyx)* or 66–82 *(Beryx);* 24 vertebrae.

Two genera, *Beryx* and *Centroberyx (= Hoplopteryx)*, with about 8 species.

Superfamily Holocentroidea

Family HOLOCENTRIDAE—squirrelfishes. Tropical marine; Atlantic, Indian, and Pacific.

Pelvic fin with one spine and 5–8 (usually seven) soft rays; long dorsal fin with spiny portion (10–13 spines) and soft-rayed portion divided by a notch; caudal fin forked, with 18 or 19 principal rays; scales large and ctenoid (extremely rough); eyes large; opercle with spiny edge; vertebrae 26 or 27; color usually reddish.

Squirrelfishes are mostly nocturnal, usually hiding in crevices or beneath ledges of reefs in the daytime (along with cardinalfishes, bigeyes, and sweepers). Unlike most beryciforms, which are deep-sea, most species occur between the shoreline and 100 m. Adults tend to remain close to the bottom (the very young are planktonic). Maximum length about 61 cm, attained in *Sargocentron spinifer*.

Eight genera with about 61 species.

SUBFAMILY HOLOCENTRINAE (SQUIRRELFISHES). A strong spine present at angle of preoperculum (sometimes a toxin is associated with this spine); longest anal spine usually longer than or equal to longest dorsal spine; swim bladder tubular, extending entire length of body (contacting the skull in a few species).

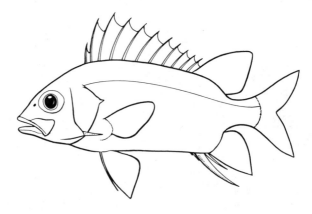

Three genera, *Holocentrus* (two), *Sargocentron* (=*Adioryx*) (24), and *Flammeo* (five), with 31 species (Woods and Sonoda, 1973; Matsuura and Shimizu, 1982). In an osteological study, Li et al. (1981) erect the new genus *Dispinus* for *S. ruber*.

SUBFAMILY MYRIPRISTINAE (SOLDIERFISHES). No enlarged preopercular spine (except in the Atlantic *Corniger spinosus* which has two enlarged spines at the corner of the preopercle); longest anal spine usually shorter than longest dorsal spine; swim bladder constricted in anterior third to form two more or less separate chambers (anterior section with two anterolateral projections).

In this subfamily, *Myripristis* with 18 species, is the largest genus. As in many other circumtropical genera, most species occur around the Indo-Australian Archipelago. The genus is absent from the Mediterranean, and the most wide-ranging species, *M. murdjan*, extends from the Galapagos Islands to the Red Sea (Greenfield, 1968, 1974; Randall and Guézé, 1981).

Five genera, *Myripristis, Ostichthys, Plectrypops (=Holotrachys), Corniger,* and *Pristilepis* (Randall et al., 1982), with about 30 species. The monotypic *Beanea* of the Red Sea, previously allied with this subfamily, may be an apogonid.

†Suborder Dinopterygoidei. This group contains four extinct (Upper Cretaceous) families, Dinopterygidae, Pycnosteroididae, Aipichthyidae, and Pharmacichthyidae (Patterson, 1964; McAllister, 1968).

Suborder Polymixioidei. This suborder has been removed from the paracanthopterygians where it was originally placed by Rosen and Patterson (1969). These authors felt the group to be particularly close to the ancestral percopsiforms (including *Sphenocephalus*), largely on the basis of presumed similarities in the caudal skeleton. This view was rejected by Fraser (1972a) and Rosen (1973a). The one included family is placed in the Beryciformes in Berg (1940), Greenwood et al. (1966), Gosline (1971), Woods and Sonoda (1973), Rosen (1973a), and Zehren (1979).

Family POLYMIXIIDAE—beardfishes. Marine; tropical and subtropical Atlantic, Indian (primarily off Natal), and western Pacific.

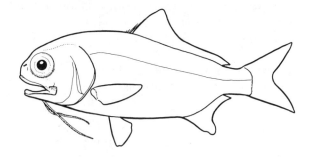

Body moderately elongate and compressed; pair of hyoid barbels; dorsal fin continuous, with 4–6 spines and 26–38 soft rays; anal fin with four short spines and 13–17 soft rays; pelvic fins subabdominal, with one spinelike ray and six soft rays; 16 branched caudal rays; about 33–38 lateral line scales; four branchiostegal rays; 11–21 gillrakers; two supramaxillae; subocular shelf, orbitosphenoid, and basisphenoid present; three epurals; usually 29 or 30 vertebrae. Maximum length 38 cm. Beardfishes usually occur between 180 and 640 m.

One genus, *Polymixia*, with five species (Lachner, 1955; Zehren, 1979). Fossils include such Upper Cretaceous genera as *Berycopsis* and *Omosoma*.

Suborder Stephanoberycoidei (Xenoberyces, in part). Body usually roundish; palate toothless; skull bones, in general, exceptionally thin; orbitosphenoid absent; subocular shelf absent; supramaxilla absent or reduced. Species of this suborder attain a maximum length of about 13 cm. Three families with about 38 species.

Family STEPHANOBERYCIDAE—pricklefishes. Marine; tropical and subtropical western parts of Atlantic, Indian, and Pacific.

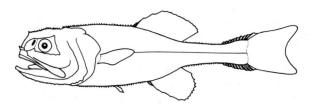

Spines, if any, in dorsal and anal fins, weak; each fin with about 10–14 soft rays; pelvic fin abdominal or subabdominal, with five soft rays, no spine; caudal fin with 8–11 procurrent spines (these precede the principal rays dorsally and ventrally); scales smooth or spiny; lateral line faint; 30–33 vertebrae.

Three monotypic genera: *Acanthochaenus* (Atlantic and Indian), *Malacosarcus* (Pacific), and *Stephanoberyx* (Atlantic) (Ebeling and Weed, 1973). All are known from relatively few specimens.

Family MELAMPHAIDAE—bigscale fishes or ridgeheads. Marine, bathypelagic; most oceans (absent from Arctic and Mediterranean).

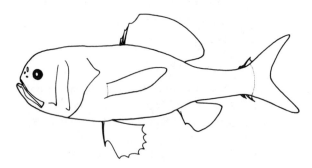

Dorsal fin single, 1–3 weak spines preceding the soft rays; pelvic fin thoracic or subthoracic, with one spine and 6–8 soft rays; caudal fin with three or four procurrent spines; scales usually large, cycloid, and deciduous; no lateral line (one or two pored scales at most); 24–31 vertebrae.

Five genera, *Melamphaes* (19), *Poromitra* (five), *Scopeloberyx* (about five), *Scopelogadus* (three), and *Sio* (one), with about 33 species (Ebeling and Weed, 1973; Parin and Ebeling, 1980).

Family GIBBERICHTHYIDAE—gibberfishes. Marine; tropical western Atlantic, western Indian, and western and southwestern Pacific.

Pelvic fin subabdominal, with one spine and five or six soft rays (prejuvenile with elongate appendage off third pelvic ray); adults with semi-isolated series of 5–8 short spinous rays before soft dorsal fin and four or five before anal fin (about 7–9 soft rays in each fin); scales cycloid, about 28–34 in lateral line; vertical rows of papillae on sides of body over the vertical lateral line tubes; swim bladder present and partially filled with fat; 28–31 vertebrae. Maximum length about 12 cm. Prejuveniles have been found between near-surface waters and 50 m, while adults have been captured primarily between 400 and 1000 m.

Kasidoron, formerly given family status (Kasidoridae), is the larva of *Gibberichthys pumilus* (Robins, 1973; Ebeling and Weed, 1973:412; de Sylva and Eschmeyer, 1977).

One genus, *Gibberichthys*, with two species known from relatively few specimens (de Sylva and Eschmeyer, 1977).

Suborder Cetomimoidei (Cetunculi, Xenoberyces, in part). Body whale-shaped; mouth very large and stomach highly distensible; eyes well-developed to degenerate; lateral line made up of enormous hollow tubes; luminous tissue on body; dorsal and anal fins far back on body and opposite one another; no fin spines; no swim bladder; orbitosphenoid absent; supramaxilla absent or reduced; color usually orange and red on a black body. Bathypelagic. Size up to 15 cm.

Greenwood et al. (1966) placed a heterogeneous assemblage of poorly known oceanic fish together in their order Cetomimiformes of the superorder Protacanthopterygii. Gosline (1971) recognized a different composition in the order (he excluded the giganturoids and included the megalomycterids and gibberichthyids) but acknowledged its composite origin. Rosen and Patterson (1969) placed the three families in a suborder of the Beryciformes and placed other members of the Cetomimiformes (of Greenwood et al., 1966) in the Lampriformes or elsewhere in the Beryciformes. Ebeling and Weed (1973) give evidence suggesting a close relationship to the Stephanoberycoidei, while Rosen (1973a) postulates an affinity with the three families included here and the three of the Stephanoberycoidei with the Anoplogastridae, Mirapinnidae, Eutaeniophoridae, and Megalomycteridae, on the basis of pharyngobranchial, jaw, and caudal similarities. (I place the latter three at the end of the Lampriformes.) Zehren (1979) excludes this group from the Beryciformes.

Six genera and about 16 species (all rare). Harry (1952), Rofen (1959), and Paxton (1974) discuss the families.

Family RONDELETIIDAE—redmouth whalefishes.   Marine; oceanic.

Box-shaped head; skin smooth; lateral line system composed of a number of pores in each of a series of 14–26 vertical rows; pelvics subabdominal; three epurals and six hypurals; vertebrae 24–27.

Two species, *Rondeletia bicolor* and *R. loricata*.

Family BARBOURISIIDAE.   Marine; Gulf of Mexico, off South Africa, near Madagascar, and western North Pacific.

Pelvic fins present, subabdominal; skin spiny; dorsal fin rays 20–22; anal fin rays 16–18; vertebrae 42.

One species, *Barbourisia rufa* (Rofen, 1959; Penrith, 1969).

Family CETOMIMIDAE—flabby whalefishes.   Marine; oceanic.

Pelvic fins absent; skin loose and scaleless; eyes reduced or rudimentary; three or four gills; no photophores present, but luminous organ often present around anus and dorsal and anal fin bases; vertebrae 51 or 52. Live color brown or orange with brilliant orange or red jaws and fins.

Four genera, *Ditropichthys*, *Cetomimus*, *Cetostoma*, and *Gyrinomimus*, with about 13 species, most known from only a few specimens (Rofen, 1959; Maul, 1969). The genera *Cetomimoides* and *Vitiaziella*, at one time placed in this family, are now recognized in Megalomycteridae.

Order ZEIFORMES.   Pelvic fin with one spine and 5−9 soft rays; caudal fin usually with 11 branched rays (13 in grammicolepidids); dorsal fin spines 5−10; anal fin spines 0−4; soft rays of dorsal, anal, and pectoral fins not branched; body usually thin and deep; jaws usually greatly distensible; no orbitosphenoid; simple posttemporal fused to skull; swim bladder present; branchiostegal rays 7 or 8; vertebrae 21−46. Caproids have the lowest number of vertebrae and grammicolepidids the highest; both groups have had their inclusion in zeiforms questioned.

The classification of this order is based largely on Mead (1957), Myers (1937, 1960b), Smith (1960), and Heemstra (1980) and is particularly weak. The Pacific genera *Capromimus* and *Cyttomimus* are of uncertain position. Rosen (1973a) presents evidence that caproids might be better placed in Perciformes than in Zeiformes. For example, their caudal skeleton is of percoid type in having three epurals and the parhypural and five hypurals articulating with a terminal half-centrum, whereas the other zeiforms have only one or two epurals and the hypurals fused together into large plates. Heemstra (1980) questions the inclusion of both Grammicolepididae and Caproidae in this order. Most zeiform species are deep-sea. The zeids, however, tend to be midwater.

About 21 genera and 36 species (including the genera *Capromimus* and *Cyttomimus*).

Family PARAZENIDAE—parazen.   Marine; Japan and Cuba.

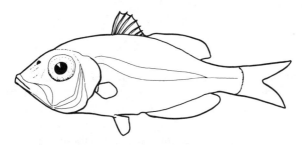

Body compressed and elongate; premaxillaries extremely protractile; two lateral lines, uniting behind the soft dorsal fin; two dorsal fins, the first with eight spines, second with 26−30 soft rays; anal fin with one spine and 31 soft rays; pectoral fin with 15 or 16 rays; pelvic fins thoracic, with one unbranched ray and six branched rays; principal caudal rays 11; scales weakly ctenoid; three and one-half gills, 34 vertebrae.

One species, *Parazen pacificus.* Mead (1957) stated, however, that the Japanese and Cuban populations are probably specifically or subspecifically distinct.

Family MACRUROCYTTIDAE.   Marine; primarily off southern Africa and tropical western Pacific.

Pelvic fin with one long, strong, highly serrated spine (and soft rays); one lateral line; anal fin with or without one or two weak spines.

SUBFAMILY MACRUROCYTTINAE.   Luzon (Philippines).

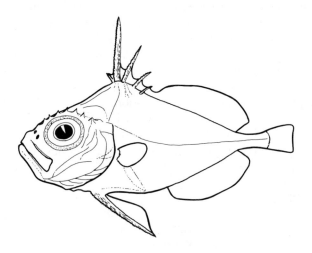

Pelvic fin, in addition to the spine, with two inconspicuous soft rays; spinous dorsal elevated, with five spines (strong, but all but one relatively short); soft dorsal rays 27, and anal fin with 22 soft rays; pectoral rays 15.

One species, *Macrurocyttus acanthopodus*, described by Fowler (1933).

SUBFAMILY ZENIINAE.   Pelvic fin, in addition to the spine, with five or six branched soft rays; dorsal fin with six or seven spines and 25–29 soft rays; vertebrae 25–27.

Two genera, *Cyttula* and *Zenion*, with about three species.

Family ZEIDAE—dories.   Marine; Atlantic, Indian, and Pacific.

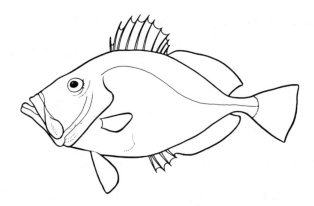

Small spines or bucklers at base of dorsal and anal fin rays; eight or nine spinous plates along abdomen; some with large round black spot surrounded by a yellow ring in center of body; long trailing filaments extending from the 10 or so spines in adults; scales small, rudimentary, or absent; no spines or serrae on opercular bones.

Five genera, *Zeus*, *Zenopsis*, *Cyttus* (= *Cyttoidops*), *Cyttopsis* (= *Zen*), and *Stethopristes*, with 10 species. Heemstra (1980) gives a map showing locality records; the regions of greatest diversity are the eastern Atlantic, Japan, southern Australia, and New Zealand.

Family OREOSOMATIDAE—oreos. Marine; Antarctic, Atlantic, Indian, and Pacific. Known primarily from off South Africa and southern Australia.

Body very deep and compressed; mouth upturned, protractile; scales small, cycloid or ctenoid; young with conical scutes on parts of body; pelvic fin with one spine and 5–7 soft rays; dorsal fin with 5–8 spines and 29–35 soft rays; anal fin with 2–4 spines and 28–33 soft rays.

Five genera, *Allocyttus*, *Neocyttus*, *Pseudocyttus*, *Oreosoma* (= *Cyttosoma*), and *Xenocyttus* (known from only two specimens, the first taken from the stomach of an Antarctic whale—Abe, 1957; Svetlov, 1978), with about nine species. Karrer (1968) gives locality records for the species.

Family GRAMMICOLEPIDIDAE—grammicolepidids. Marine; scattered parts of Atlantic and Pacific.

Scales vertically elongate; mouth small, nearly vertical; dorsal fin with 5–7 spines and 27–34 soft rays; anal fin with two spines and 27–35 soft rays; row of spines along each side of dorsal and anal fin bases; pelvic fin with one spine and six soft rays; caudal fin with 13 branched rays; verte-brae 37–46.

Three genera, *Grammicolepis* (= *Vesposus*—the one species, *G. brachius-culus*, is known only from Cuba and Hawaii, where one specimen was brought to the surface in a lava flow in 1919), *Xenolepidichthys* (with one species known from such widely separated areas as South Africa, Japan, Philippines, Gulf of Maine, western Caribbean, British Hondurus, and southern Brazil—DeWitt et al., 1981), and *Daramattus* (with two species).

Family CAPROIDAE—boarfishes.   Marine; Atlantic, Indian, and Pacific.

Body covered with small ctenoid scales; dorsal fin spines 7–9; two or three anal fin spines; pelvic fin with one spine and five soft rays; caudal fin rounded; vertebrae 21–23.

SUBFAMILY ANTIGONIINAE.   Red colored fishes with extremely deep and slim bodies (rhomboid shape); dorsal fin with eight or nine spines and 26–38 soft rays; three anal spines, separate from the anal soft rays.

In the western Atlantic they range from the northern United States to southern Brazil between approximately 70–600 m (Berry, 1959). Both Berry (1959) and Fraser-Brunner (1950) have studied *Antigonia*.

One genus, *Antigonia,* with five species.

SUBFAMILY CAPROINAE.   Similar to Zeidae except that there are no ab-dominal spinous plates.

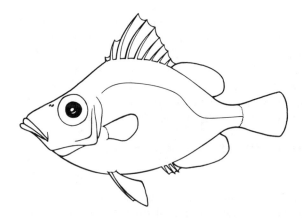

One species, *Capros aper.*

Order GASTEROSTEIFORMES (Thoracostei). Upper jaw protractile, ascending process of premaxilla well developed; postcleithrum absent; circumorbital bones, in addition to lachrymal, present; nasals and parietals present; anterior vertebrae not elongate.

Eight genera with about 10 species. The family Hypoptychidae is placed here with reservation. I agree with Ida (1976) that this monotypic family is not related to Ammodytidae, as previously thought, but I have reservations in accepting the hypothesis that its closest affinities are with sticklebacks (Nelson, 1978a).

Many workers combine the Syngnathiformes and Gasterosteiformes, either under the former ordinal name (e.g., Gosline, 1971; Ida, 1976) or the latter (e.g., Greenwood et al., 1966; Bailey and Cavender, 1971; Greenwood, 1975; Pietsch, 1978c; Robins et al., 1980). Monophyly has not been established and McAllister (1968) has the two groups on different lineages. Until their relationships are clarified I prefer to recognize them in separate orders.

Family HYPOPTYCHIDAE—sand eel. Marine; Japan and Korea to Sea of Okhotsk.

Body elongate, scutes and scales absent; spines absent; dorsal and anal fins posteriorly placed, each with about 20 soft rays; pelvic girdle and fins absent; pectoral fin rays 9; caudal fin with 13 principal rays (11 branched); four branchiostegal rays; circumorbital ring incomplete; premaxillary teeth present in males but absent in females; about 29 pairs of pleural ribs, epipleurals absent; vertebrae about 55–57; hypural plate divided into upper and lower halves (all other gasterosteiforms except *Gasterosteus*, which also has a split hypural, have a fused hypural plate). Maximum length about 8.5 cm. The osteology of the one included species has been studied by Gosline (1963b) and Ida (1976). Before Ida's work it was thought to be allied to Ammodytidae; indeed, Berg (1940) and Robins and Böhlke (1970) placed it in Ammodytidae as a separate subfamily.

One species, *Hypoptychus dybowskii.*

Family AULORHYNCHIDAE—tubesnouts. Coastal marine; North Pacific.

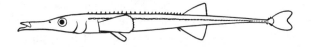

Body elongate, with lateral bony scutes; series of 24–26 very short isolated dorsal spines, followed by a normal dorsal fin with about 10 soft rays; pelvic fin with one spine and four soft rays; caudal fin with 13 rays; four branchiostegal rays; circumorbital ring complete posteriorly; epipleurals absent; vertebrae 52–56. Maximum length 17 cm, attained in *Aulorhynchus flavidus*.

Two species, *Aulichthys japonicus* and *Aulorhynchus flavidus* (Nelson, 1971).

Family GASTEROSTEIDAE—sticklebacks. Marine, brackish, and freshwater; Northern Hemisphere (see map on p. 419).

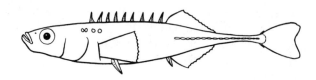

Body elongate or not, with lateral bony scutes or naked; series of 3–16 well-developed isolated dorsal spines (very rarely fewer than three) followed by a normal dorsal fin with 6–14 rays; pelvic fin (rarely absent) with one spine and one or two soft rays; caudal fin usually with 12 rays; three branchiostegal rays; circumorbital ring incomplete posteriorly; epipleurals present; vertebrae 28–42. Maximum length about 18 cm; attained in *Spinachia spinachia*.

This family is famous for the numerous studies made of its species, especially by ethologists and physiologists. The mating behavior and nest-building activity of the males has attracted much attention. Wootton (1976) reviews stickleback biology and Coad (1981a) gives an extensive bibliography of the family.

The recognition of only seven species in this family fails to account for the enormous genetic diversity and biological species that exist (but form taxonomic problems) in the *Gasterosteus aculeatus* complex and perhaps in the *Pungitius pungitius* complex (e.g., see Hagen and McPhail, 1970; Nelson, 1971; Bell, 1976). A high proportion of individuals of three species in certain localities fail to develop the pelvic skeleton (e.g., see Bell, 1976; Nelson, 1977; Reimchen, 1980). Five genera with about seven species: *Spinachia spinachia* (fifteenspine stickleback), marine, Atlantic of northern Europe; *Apeltes quadracus* (fourspine stickleback), usually marine and brackishwater, Atlantic coast of central North America; *Gasterosteus wheatlandi* (blackspotted stickleback), usually marine, Atlantic coast of central North America; *Gasterosteus aculeatus* complex (threespine stickleback), marine, anadromous, and freshwater, Atlantic and Pacific coastal areas of North America and Eurasia and part of Arctic, seldom above 100 m elevation; *Pungitius pungitius* complex (ninespine stickleback), anadromous and freshwater, Atlantic, Pacific, and Arctic coastal areas of North America and Eurasia and across much of above continental areas up to about 600 m (certain subspecies are sometimes given species status); *Pungitius platygaster,* primarily in the Black Sea to Aral Sea area; *Culaea inconstans* (brook stickleback), freshwater, North America. Among the various known fossil sticklebacks, Sychevskaya and Grechina (1981) describe two species of Miocene *Gasterosteus* from eastern Siberia, one of which possesses four dorsal spines and three branched pelvic fin rays, while the other has 38 scutes (characters which differ from that known in extant species). Miocene *Gasterosteus aculeatus* are known from California (Bell, 1977).

Order INDOSTOMIFORMES.   The systematic position of the one included species is very uncertain. It has generally been placed in the presumed gasterosteiform–syngnathiform lineage and thought to be related to syngnathoids until Bolin (1936) speculated that its closest relationship was with the aulorhynchids or aulostomids. Banister (1970), in the first osteological study of the species, concluded that it was a paracanthopterygian, probably with some affinity to the batrachoid–lophiid–gobiesocid lineage. However, the characters of the species does not firmly establish a relationship in the paracanthopterygians nor preclude it from being allied to the gasterosteiform–syngnathiform group (Pietsch, 1978c). I place it between the groups to which it seems to come closest.

Family INDOSTOMIDAE.   Freshwater; Upper Burma in Lake Indawgyi.

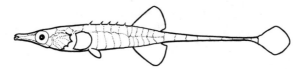

Body slender and covered with bony scutes; upper jaw not protrusible; opercle with six spines; dorsal and anal fins each with six rays, five isolated spines preceding the dorsal fin; 23 pectoral fin rays; pelvic fin with four soft rays, no spine; five branchiostegal rays; no ribs; usually 21 vertebrae; swim bladder physoclistic. Maximum length of Banister's (1970) specimens was 2.7 cm.

This species, along with certain other fishes, has apparently been transported along drug trade routes in Southeast Asia as a cover in smuggling operations and released in various waters. Whether or not reproductive populations are established is not yet known (pers. comm. 1982, K. E. Banister).

One species, *Indostomus paradoxus.*

Order PEGASIFORMES (Hypostomides). Most workers have thought pegasids to be related to the syngnathiforms, agonids, or some ancestral scorpaeniform. Pietsch (1978c), in an anatomical study and contribution to the systematics of gasterosteiform–syngnathiform fishes, concluded that they are most closely related to the solenostomid–syngnathid lineage and placed them in his order Gasterosteiformes, suborder Syngnathoidei. He also believes them to be closely related to the lower Eocene *Ramphosus* of Italy and Denmark (and recognizes the fossil family Ramphosidae in the same superfamily). Pegasids are retained here in a separate order until confirmatory evidence is obtained that their closest relatives are syngnathoids.

Family PEGASIDAE—seamoths.   Marine; Indo-West Pacific.

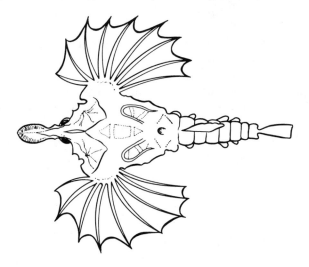

Body oddly shaped (broad and depressed), encased in bony plates; mouth small and toothless, beneath a long flattened rostrum (formed by fused nasals), with an unusual mechanism for protrusion of the jaws (described by Pietsch, 1978c); tufted and lobelike gill filaments; opercle and subopercle minute (widely separated from the interopercle), preopercle greatly enlarged; dorsal and anal fins short, each usually with five soft rays only; pectoral fins relatively large, horizontal, with 10–18 unbranched rays; pelvics abdominal, with one spine and 1–3 soft rays; caudal fin with eight rays; caudal peduncle quadrangular; five filamentous branchiostegal rays; supracleithrum and postcleithrum absent; three circumorbital bones, lachrymal largest; no swim bladder; 19–22 vertebrae (anterior six of the seven abdominal ones elongate). Maximum size about 13 cm.

One genus, *Pegasus* (= *Zalises*), with five species. Several nominal genera exist.

Order SYNGNATHIFORMES (Solenichthys). Mouth small, at end of tube-shaped snout (except in the "finless" pipefish *Enchelyocampus*, which lacks even a short tubiform snout); tufted lobelike gills in some; pelvic fins, when present, abdominal; upper jaw not protractile; lachrymal usually present, other circumorbital bones usually absent; ribs absent; anterior 3–6 vertebrae elongate; aglomerular kidney in at least some.

Six families with 63 genera and about 257 species. The lumping of this order with Gasterosteiformes by some authors is discussed under that order.

Suborder Aulostomoidei. Teeth small or absent; lateral line well developed to absent; usually four or five (rarely three) branchiostegal rays; gills comblike; postcleithrum present.

Superfamily Aulostomoidea. Anterior four vertebrae elongate; three median, well-developed bones dorsally behind head (nuchal plates); usually six (rarely five) soft pelvic rays.

Family AULOSTOMIDAE—trumpetfishes. Tropical marine; Atlantic and Indo-Pacific.

Body compressed, elongate, and scaly; fleshy barbel at tip of lower jaw; series of 8–12 isolated dorsal spines followed by a normal dorsal fin or 23–28 soft rays; anal rays 25–28; caudal fin rounded; anus far behind pelvics; lateral line well developed; abdominal vertebrae with two transverse processes of equal size (or a divided process); body musculature with a network of bony struts that forms an interwoven pattern (observed in *Aulostomus chinensis* from Easter Island); vertebrae 59–64 (24–26 + 35–38).

Trumpetfishes are predators and are usually seen on reefs. They often swim alongside larger fish or lie with their bodies at odd angles such as vertical with the head downward. Maximum length up to 80 cm.

One genus, *Aulostomus*, probably with three species (Wheeler, 1955).

Family FISTULARIIDAE—cornetfishes. Tropical marine; Atlantic, Indian, and Pacific.

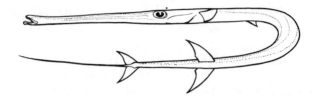

Body depressed, elongate, and naked or with minute prickles and linear series of scutes (no scales); no barbel on jaw; no dorsal spines; anal and dorsal fins each with 13–20 soft rays; caudal fin forked with elongate filament produced by middle two caudal rays; anus short distance behind pelvic fins; lateral line well developed, arched anteriorly almost to middle of back and continuing onto caudal filament; abdominal vertebrae with two transverse processes but the posterior ones reduced; vertebrae 76–87.

Cornetfishes usually inhabit shallow waters of tropical and subtropical seas. They are predatory on other fishes, feeding both in open water and in coral reefs. (Their long tubular snout, which functions as a pipette, is an excellent adaptation for feeding among reefs.) Maximum length up to 1.8 m, attained in *Fistularia tabacaria*, usually less than 1 m.

One genus, *Fistularia*, with four species (Fritzsche, 1976).

Superfamily Centriscoidea.   Anterior five or six vertebrae elongate; pelvic fins with one spine and four soft rays.

Family MACRORHAMPHOSIDAE—snipefishes.   Tropical and subtropical marine; Atlantic, Indian, and Pacific.

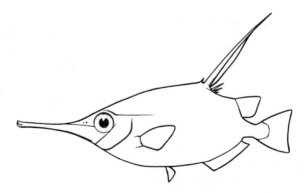

Body compressed, deep, and usually with bony plates on each side of back; no barbel on jaw; 4–8 dorsal spines, second spine very long, all joined by a membrane; second dorsal fin has about 11–19 soft rays; lateral line present or absent. Maximum length up to 30 cm.

First known in the fossil record from the Upper Cretaceous (Sorbini, 1981), the earliest record of any syngnathiform. The species involved, *Gasterorhamphosus zuppichinii*, resembles *Macrorhamphosus* in body shape but, among various differences, has some characters suggesting an affinity with the Gasterosteiformes.

Three genera, *Centriscops*, *Macrorhamphosus*, and *Notopogon*, with 11 species.

Family CENTRISCIDAE—shrimpfishes.   Marine; Indo-Pacific.

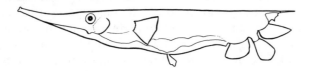

Extremely compressed, razorlike body with sharp ventral edge; body almost entirely encased by thin bony plates which are expansions of the vertebral column; first dorsal spine long and sharp at extreme end of body, followed by two shorter spines; soft dorsal fin and caudal fin displaced ventrally; no lateral line; mouth toothless. Swimming is in a vertical position, snout down. Maximum length up to 15 cm.

Two genera, *Aeoliscus* and *Centriscus*, with four species.

Suborder Syngnathoidei (Lophobranchii).   No teeth; no lateral line; branchiostegal rays 1–3; gills tufted and lobelike; anterior three vertebrae elongate; postcleithrum absent.

Family SOLENOSTOMIDAE—ghost pipefishes.   Marine; tropical Indo-Pacific.

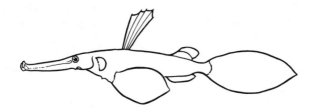

Body short, compressed and with large stellate bony plates; two separate dorsal fins, the first with five long feeble spines and the second with 18–23 soft rays on an elevated base; pelvic fins relatively large, with one spine and six soft rays, opposite spinous dorsal; gill openings moderately large; females with brood pouch formed by the pelvics. Maximum length up to 16 cm.

One genus, *Solenostomus* (= *Solenichthys* and *Solenostomatichthys*), with five species.

Family SYNGNATHIDAE—pipefishes and seahorses. Marine, some species in brackish and fresh water; Atlantic, Indian, and Pacific.

Body elongate and encased in a series of bony rings; one dorsal fin, usually with 15–60 soft rays, anal fin very small and usually with 2–6 rays, and pectoral fin usually with 10–23 rays. (The dorsal, anal, and pectoral fins may be absent in adults of some species.) No pelvic fins; caudal fin absent in some; tail (caudal peduncle) may be prehensile and employed for holding onto objects when caudal fin is absent; gill openings very small; 1–3 branchiostegal rays; supracleithrum and basisphenoid absent; kidney present only on right side, aglomerular. Some species are very colorful. Maximum length about 60 cm.

Syngnathids are usually confined to shallow water. Most species occur in warm temperate to tropical waters but some pipefishes range into relatively cool water, occurring from southwestern Alaska to Tierra del Fuego in the New World; six species are known from New Zealand. A few species are confined to fresh water but most are marine or euryhaline. Males care for the eggs which are attached to them by the female in a special area in the undersurface of the trunk or tail, which may or may not be developed into a pouch. Two tribes may be recognized based on whether the brood organ is on the tail (syngnathines), as in most genera, or on the trunk (doryrhamphines). Genera such as *Amphelikturus* and *Acentronura* are, to a certain extent, morphological intermediates, if not evolutionary links, between pipefishes and seahorses. The intermediate forms and the various genera of seadragons of Australia, which resemble seahorses but reach a larger size and have leaflike appendages, are placed in the pipefish subfamily. Herald (1959) discusses the various trends of brood pouch closure in pipefishes in relation to the seahorse condition.

SUBFAMILY SYNGNATHINAE (PIPEFISHES).   Marine and brackish water; some in freshwater.

Fifty-four genera (e.g., *Amphelikturus, Acentronura, Bombonia, Corythoichthys, Cosmocampus, Dermatostethus, Doryichthys, Doryrhamphus, Enchelyocampus, Heraldia, Micrognathus, Nerophis, Nannocampus, Oostethus, Penetopteryx, Phyllopteryx, Siokunichthys, Solegnathus, Syngnathoides,* and *Syngnathus*) with about 200 species (e.g., Dawson and Allen, 1978; Dawson, 1980a,b, 1981a,b, 1982a; Fritzsche, 1980; Lee, 1983. Paxton, 1975; pers. comm. C. E. Dawson, 1982).

SUBFAMILY HIPPOCAMPINAE (SEAHORSES). Marine.

One genus, *Hippocampus,* with about 30 species (pers. comm. C. E. Dawson, 1982). Myers (1979) notes the possible occurrence of a seahorse in fresh water in Thailand. Bellomy (1969) presents an account of their natural history.

Order DACTYLOPTERIFORMES. Pietsch (1978c) gives reasons to believe that this group may bear some affinity with the pegasids and syngnathiforms.

Family DACTYLOPTERIDAE (Cephalacanthidae)—flying gurnards. Marine tropical; Indo-Pacific and Atlantic.

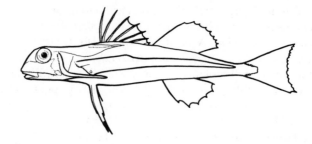

Large, blunt, bony head (with spines and keels); body covered with scute-like scales; tremendously enlarged pectoral fins with inner rays free (once thought capable of gliding short distances); two free spines (the first may be on the nape) before the two dorsal fins; pelvic fins thoracic, each with one spine and four soft rays; no lateral line; 22 vertebrae. Maximum length about 50 cm.

These benthic fishes, which superficially resemble triglids, produce sounds by stridulation by utilizing the hyomandibular bone and "walk" on the sea floor by alternately moving the pelvic fins.

About four genera (e.g., *Dactyloptena*, *Dactylopterus*, and *Daicocus*) and about four species.

Order SYNBRANCHIFORMES (Symbranchii). The membership of this order has been reduced from three families to the present one. Rosen and Greenwood (1976) and Springer and Fraser (1976) removed the Alabetidae from the Synbranchiformes. The former felt it to have a closer affinity with blennylike fishes, whereas the latter synonymized it under the Gobiesocidae (Liem, 1968, also did not believe Alabetidae and Synbranchidae to be related). Rosen and Greenwood (1976) placed the Amphipnoidae in the Synbranchidae in their revision of the group.

Family SYNBRANCHIDAE—swamp-eels. Tropical and subtropical freshwater, some species occasionally in brackish water; west Africa, Liberia, Asia, Indo-Australian Archipelago, Mexico, and Central and South America (see map on p. 419).

Body eellike; pectoral and pelvic fins absent (pectorals present in early development of some species); dorsal and anal fins vestigial (reduced to a rayless ridge); caudal fin small (in *Macrotrema caligans*) or vestigial to absent; scales absent except in the species of the subgenus *Amphipnous* of *Monopterus;* eyes small (some species functionally blind with eyes sunken below skin); gill membranes united; small gill opening as slit or pore under head or throat (*Macrotrema* has normal size gill openings continuous with each other under throat); branchiostegal rays 4–6; swim bladder absent; ribs absent; vertebrae 98–188 (51–135 abdominal).

Most species are capable of air breathing. Many have burrowing habits, while some live in caves. Rosen (1975) discusses the highly disjunct distribution of the pantropical *Ophisternon* (particularly of one species found in isolated centers in northern South America, northern Central America and southern Mexico, and Cuba) in light of plate tectonics, vicariance, and generalized distributional tracks (see Croizat et al., 1974). Maximum length over 70 cm, attained in *Ophisternon aenigmaticum* (formerly part of *Synbranchus marmoratus*) of the New World.

Rosen and Greenwood (1976), whose major revision forms the basis of the material here, place the Amphipnoidae in synonymy with the genus *Monopterus*. However, generic recognition could be retained for *Amphipnous* (the cuchias—revised by Silas and Dawson, 1961), with three species from India, Bangladesh, Nepal, and Burma (one record from Queensland was probably the result of an introduction), because of the presence of paired lunglike suprabranchial pouches (with respiratory function) and the partially scaled body. These species are highly evolved as air-breathing fish. Rosen and Greenwood (1976) recognize two subfamilies of synbranchids, Macrotreminae (for *Macrotrema caligans*) and Synbranchinae (for the other species).

Four genera, *Macrotrema* (one species, in fresh and brackish water, in Thailand and Malay Peninsula), *Ophisternon (= Furmastix)* (six: two New World and four Old World), *Synbranchus* (two: Mexico and Central and South America), *Monopterus (= Amphipnous* and *Typhlosynbranchus)* (six: Liberia and India to Japan), with 15 species.

Order SCORPAENIFORMES.   (Cataphracti in part, Scleroparei in part). This order contains the "mail cheeked" fishes, distinguished by the suborbital stay, a posterior extension of the third suborbital bone (counting the lachrymal), which extends across the cheek to the preoperculum. Head and body tend to be spiny or have bony plates; pectoral fin usually rounded, membranes between lower rays often incised; caudal fin usually rounded (occasionally truncate, rarely forked).

Twenty families with 269 genera and about 1160 species. The classification and placement of this order is very provisional. Indeed, it is uncertain whether or not the one diagnostic character of the order, the presence of a suborbital stay, defines a monophyletic unit. The five suborders recognized are undefined and serve only to group families thought to bear a closer relationship with one another than with those placed in other suborders. The arrangement of families and family boundaries is subject to much disagreement.

Suborder Scorpaenoidei. Contains the world's most venomous fishes. Usually brightly colored. Seven families with about 109 genera and 482 species.

Family SCORPAENIDAE—scorpionfishes (rockfishes). Marine (rarely in fresh water); all tropical and temperate seas.

Body compressed; head usually with ridges and spines (usually with two opercular and five preopercular spines); suborbital stay usually securely fastened to preopercle (no attachment in some); scales, when present, usually ctenoid; dorsal fin usually single (often with a notch), usually with 11–17 spines and 8–18 soft rays; anal fin with 1–3 spines (usually three) and 3–9 soft rays (usually five); pelvic fin with one spine and 2–5 soft rays (usually five); pectoral fin well developed (usually with 15–25 rays), rarely with one free lower ray; gill membranes free from isthmus; swim bladder absent in some; vertebrae 24–40. Venom gland in dorsal, anal, and pelvic spines. Most have internal fertilization, and some give birth to live young (e.g., *Sebastes*). Some lay eggs on a gelatinous balloon, and *Scorpaena guttata* is reported to have an egg balloon that may be as much as 20 cm in diameter. Many species are commercially important.

About 60 genera with about 310 species. Most species are in the Indian and Pacific oceans; only 58 species in 11 genera are recognized from the Atlantic Ocean (Eschmeyer, 1969). Other taxa are recognized in this family by some workers as follows: Matsubara (1943) and Eschmeyer and Rao (1973) include the Synanceiidae; Chen (1981), in his study (including a key to the 64 Taiwan species), retained inclusion of the Aploactinidae after Matsubara (1943); Eschmeyer, Hirosaki, and Abe (1973:307) include the Congiopodidae (as a subfamily). These groups, as in Greenwood et al. (1966), are given family status here. Several subfamilies can be recognized (see Matsubara, 1943, and Eschmeyer, 1969). A provisional listing follows. The first three and the last one are Indo-Pacific only.

SUBFAMILY APISTINAE. For example, *Apistops, Apistus,* and *Cheroscorpaena.*

SUBFAMILY PTEROIDICHTHYINAE. For example, *Rhinopias.* Eschmeyer, Hirosaki, and Abe (1973) discuss this group.

SUBFAMILY PTEROINAE. Includes about six genera, *Brachirus, Brachypterois, Dendrochirus, Ebosia, Parapterois,* and *Pterois* (highly venomous lionfishes and turkeyfishes) (Eschmeyer and Rama-Rao, 1977; Kanayama and Amaoka, 1981).

SUBFAMILY SCORPAENINAE

About 12 genera (e.g., *Idiastion, Neomerinthe, Phenacoscorpius, Pontinus, Scorpaena,* and *Scorpaenodes*).

SUBFAMILY SEBASTOLOBINAE. One North Pacific genus: *Sebastolobus,* with 15–17 dorsal spines (highest for the family) and 27–30 vertebrae. Two other genera, *Trachyscorpia* (Eschmeyer, 1969:47) and *Adelosebastes* (Eschmeyer et al., 1979), show some affinity to this group.

SUBFAMILY SEBASTINAE. Four genera: *Helicolenus, Sebastes* (= *Sebastodes*), *Sebastiscus,* and *Hozukius.* The first two occur in all oceans, whereas the latter two occur only in the western Pacific. The live bearing genus *Sebastes* is the largest in the family with about 100 species (almost all of them occurring in the North Pacific).

SUBFAMILY SETARCHINAE. Three genera (e.g., *Setarches* and *Ectreposebastes*) with four species. This subfamily is treated in detail by Eschmeyer and Collette, 1966).

SUBFAMILY TETRAROGINAE (SAILBACK SCORPIONFISHES)

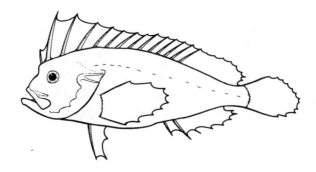

About 11 genera (e.g., *Ablabys, Cottapistus, Paracentropogon, Tetraroge*, and *Vespicula*) with about 40 species (S. G. Poss, pers. comm. 1982). Tetrarogines show some resemblance to the Aploactinidae.

Family SYNANCEIIDAE (Synancejidae). Tropical marine (rarely brackish and freshwater); coastal Indo-Pacific (including the Red Sea), South Africa east to Japan, Society Islands, and Australia.

Body scaleless (except for buried scales along the lateral line and other parts of the body), usually covered with skin glands; head large; swim bladder usually absent; venom glands present near base of hypodermiclike dorsal fin spines. The neurotoxin of these fishes is the most deadly of the fish venoms and can be fatal to man (Halstead, 1970; Munro, 1967). The fish is particularly dangerous because it usually rests in a half-buried position, looking much like a rock. Maximum length about 32 cm.

Nine genera with about 30 species. Eschmeyer and Rao (1973) give reasons for recognizing the following three subfamilies in the Scorpaenidae; placement with the scorpaenids is recognized in more recent works of W. N. Eschmeyer and his collaborators. They are retained here in a separate family because of the belief that they may be each other's closest relatives (and derivatives of Scorpaenidae).

SUBFAMILY SYNANCEIINAE (STONEFISHES). No free pectoral rays; skin glands present (appearing as "warts" in most species) and usually scattered over the body; dorsal fin with 11–17 spines and 4–14 soft rays; anal fin with 2–4 spines and 4–14 soft rays; pelvic fin with one spine and 3–5 soft rays; pectoral fin rays 11–19; vertebrae 23–30.

Two species, *Erosa erosa* (Japan to Australia) and *Dampierosa daruma* (northwestern Australia), have a terminal mouth which is slightly oblique and lateral eyes which are directed outward. The remaining species have a vertical or superior mouth and dorsal eyes that are directed outward and upward or only upward. Some species are known from rivers.

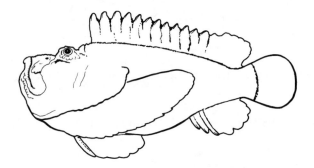

Six genera, the monotypic *Erosa*, *Dampierosa*, *Pseudosynanceia*, *Leptosynanceia*, and *Trachicephalus* and *Synanceia* (with five species), with a total of 10 species.

SUBFAMILY CHORIDACTYLINAE (INIMICINAE).   Two *(Inimicus)* or three *(Choridactylus)* lowermost pectoral rays separated from rest; body often with warts or lumps (caused by buried scales); dorsal fin with 12–18 spines and 5–10 soft rays; anal fin with two spines and 8–13 soft rays; pelvic fin with one spine and five soft rays; most soft fin rays branched; vertebrae 26–30. Members of this group occur on sand and silty bottoms from near shore to about 90 m in the western Pacific and Indian oceans.

Two genera, *Inimicus* (= *Pelor*) with eight species and *Choridactylus* with two species (Eschmeyer and Rama-Rao, 1979).

SUBFAMILY MINOINAE.   Lowermost ray of pectoral fin separated from the other 11 rays, fitted at its tip with a peculiar "cap"; body smooth; dorsal fin with 8–12 spines and 10–14 soft rays; anal fin with two spines and 7–11 soft rays; pelvic fin with one spine and five soft rays; soft fin rays unbranched; swim bladder present or absent; vertebrae 24–27. Maximum length usually 15 cm. Members of this group occur on mud and sand bottoms from about 10 to 420 m in the western Pacific and Indian oceans. They are thought to use the free pectoral ray for "walking" on the bottom.

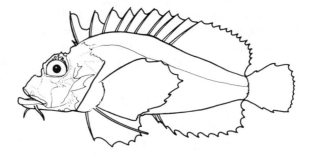

One genus, *Minous*, with 10 species (reviewed by Eschmeyer et al., 1979).

Family CARACANTHIDAE—orbicular velvetfishes.   Marine; Indian and Pacific.

Body oval, extremely compressed, and covered with small rough papillae; mouth small and terminal; one dorsal fin with a notch, origin on nape, with 6–8 spines and 11–13 soft rays; anal fin with two spines and 11–14 soft rays; pelvic fins inconspicuous, with one spine and usually two small soft rays; gill openings restricted to sides. Members of this genus have been described as scaleless, but Mizuno and Tominaga (1980) found scales below the dorsal fin base and on the dorsal surface of the head (the latter are minute and bear a single spine) and tubelike scales on the lateral line. Maximum length only 5 cm.

One genus, *Caracanthus*, with about three species.

Family APLOACTINIDAE—velvetfishes.   Marine; primarily coastal parts of western Pacific and Indian oceans.

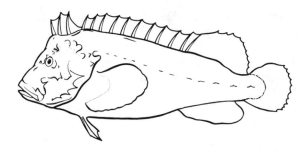

Body usually covered with modified, prickly scales giving a velvety appearance (some species lack the prickles and have a smooth skin); head armed with knoblike lumps (rarely with pungent spines); all fin rays unbranched; anal fin spines usually indistinct (rarely pungent) or absent; origin of dorsal fin far forward, above eye or almost so (except in *Adventor* and *Peristrominous*); anterior 3–5 dorsal fin spines usually divergent, either elevated or largely devoid of connecting membrane; four species with three or four anterior spines forming a separate fin; pelvic fin with fewer than four soft rays; most species with fleshy extension on the anterior isthmus; palatine teeth absent; no gill slit behind the last arch. Most species occur in the Indonesian and Australian regions. This family is thought to be closely related to the venomous Tetraroginae and Synanceiidae.

About 17 genera (e.g., *Adventor, Aploactis, Aploactisoma, Cocotropus, Erisphex, Kanekonia, Paraploactis,* and *Xenaploactis*) with about 40 species (Poss and Eschmeyer, 1978, 1979, 1980; S. G. Poss, pers. comm. 1982). Two subfamilies may be recognized. Aploactininae, with gill slits not restricted, has 14 genera and about 36 species. Bathyaploactininae, with gill slits restricted by fusion of the branchiostegal membranes to the isthmus, tubed anterior nostrils far forward on the snout, scales with a central spine that is strongly curved posteriorly, has two genera, *Bathyaploactis (= Karumba)* and *Acanthosphex (= Kleiwegia),* and about three species. A species of the South China Sea, *Prosoproctus pataecus,* has some features of both subfamilies and is unique among scorpaenoid fishes in having the anus far forward, immediately behind the pelvic fin base (Poss and Eschmeyer, 1979).

Family PATAECIDAE.   Marine; Australia.

Body scaleless (smooth or with tubercles or papillae); all fin rays unbranched; fleshy extension on the anterior isthmus. This family is probably closely related to the aploactinids. The inclusion of *Gnathanacanthus* is provisional.

SUBFAMILY PATAECINAE (PROWFISHES).   No pelvic fins; very long continuous dorsal fin, extending from head to tail (connected with or free from caudal fin).

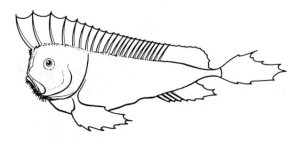

Three monotypic genera, *Aetapcus*, *Neopataecus*, and *Pataecus* (S. G. Poss, pers. comm. 1982).

SUBFAMILY GNATHANACANTHINAE (RED VELVETFISH).   Pelvic fins present, with one spine and five soft rays; two separate dorsal fins of about equal length, the first with seven spines, the second with three spines and 10 or 11 soft rays; anal fin with three spines and eight or nine soft rays.

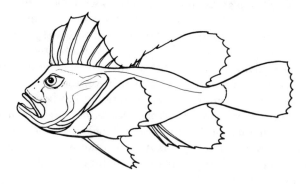

One species, *Gnathanacanthus goetzeei*, known from Western Australia, South Australia, Victoria, and Tasmania (Scott et al., 1974).

Family CONGIOPODIDAE—racehorses (pigfishes). Marine; Southern Hemisphere.

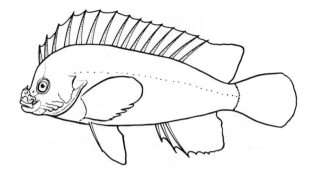

Snout relatively long; body without scales, skin sometimes granular; only one nostril on each side; gill opening reduced, above pectoral base; lateral line usually well developed; dorsal fins joined (separate in *Zanclorhynchus*), with 8–21 spines; anal fin with 0–3 spines. One species in South Africa is reported to cast its skin, like reptiles.

Four genera, *Congiopodus* (= *Agriopus*) with six species and the monotypic *Alertichthys*, *Perryena*, and *Zanclorhynchus*, with nine species (Hureau, 1971; Paulin and Moreland, 1979b).

Family TRIGLIDAE—searobins. Marine; all tropical and temperate seas.

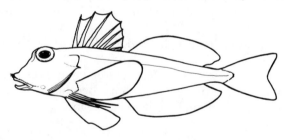

Two separate dorsal fins; casquelike, bony head; lower two or three pectoral rays enlarged and free, used for detecting food. Benthic habitat. Triglids are good sound producers. Maximum length up to 1 m.

The following two subfamilies are sometimes recognized as separate families (e.g., Evans, 1975; Heemstra, 1982).

SUBFAMILY TRIGLINAE (UNARMORED SEAROBINS). Body with scales or covered by long plates; preorbitals usually produced forward, with spines; barbels sometimes present. Benthic in habitat.

Ten genera (e.g., *Bellator*, *Lepidotrigla*, *Prionotus*, and *Trigla*) with about 69 species.

SUBFAMILY PERISTEDIINAE (ARMORED SEAROBINS).   Body entirely encased in heavy spine bearing plates; preorbitals each with a forward projection; barbels on lower jaw.

About four genera, *Gargariscus, Heminodus, Peristedion,* and *Satyrichthys,* with about 17 species.

Suborder *Platycephaloidei*

Family PLATYCEPHALIDAE—flatheads.   Marine (some brackish); Indo-Pacific.

Body elongate and cylindrical; head depressed, usually with ridges and spines; mouth large, lower jaw projects forward; ctenoid scales cover body; two dorsal fins, the first with 6–9 spines and the second with 11–14 soft rays; anal fin with 11–14 soft rays; gill openings wide; pelvic fins widely separated, with one spine and five soft rays; pectoral fins without free rays; no swim bladder; 27 vertebrae.

L. W. Knapp, who is working on the systematics of this group, prefers to give family status to the following two subfamilies (e.g., Knapp, 1979). The bembradines occur in deeper water than most platycephalines.

SUBFAMILY BEMBRADINAE.   Head moderately depressed; pelvics below pectoral base; spinous dorsal fin not preceded by an isolated spine. Most are small red fishes.

About four genera (e.g., *Bembras* and *Parabembras*) with several species.

SUBFAMILY PLATYCEPHALINAE.   Head extremely depressed; pelvics behind pectoral base; first dorsal spine short. Benthic habitat, often burying in the bottom. Maximum length about 1.1 m.

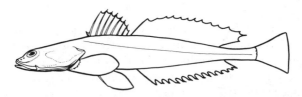

About 18 genera (e.g., *Cociella, Elates, Grammoplites, Onigocia, Platycephalus, Sorsogona, Suggrundus,* and *Thysanophrys*) with about 60 species. Hughes (1981) studied the development of cteni in the scales in about one-half the species (virtually all in *Platycephalus*).

Family HOPLICHTHYIDAE (Oplichthyidae)—ghost flatheads.   Marine; Indo-Pacific.

Body elongate; head extremely depressed and very wide, with spines and ridges; no scales, row of spiny scutes along side; lower pectoral rays (three or four) free; pelvic fins widely separated, with one spine and five soft rays; no anal spines; 26 vertebrae (8 + 18).

One genus, *Hoplichthys*, with about 10 species (Matsubara and Ochiai, 1950).

Suborder Anoplopomatoidei. Quast (1965) notes that the family Anoplopomatidae has little affinity to other scorpaeniforms and speculates that the only uniting character, the suborbital stay, may have originated independently.

Family ANOPLOPOMATIDAE—sablefishes. Marine; North Pacific.

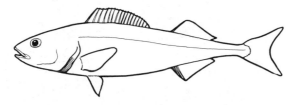

Head without spines, ridges, or cirri; two dorsal fins; anal fin with three weak spines and 11–19 soft rays; pelvic fins with one spine and five soft rays; two well-developed nostrils on each side; gill membranes attached to isthmus; lateral line single. Maximum length about 1.8 m, attained in *Erilepis zonifer* (the skilfish).

Two species, *Anoplopoma fimbria* (with well-separated dorsal fins and 17–22 spines in first dorsal) and *Erilepis zonifer* (with closely spaced dorsal fins and 12–14 spines in first dorsal). Both species range from California to Japan.

Suborder Hexagrammoidei

Family HEXAGRAMMIDAE—greenlings. Marine; North Pacific.

Head with cirri but without ridges or spines; lateral lines one or five; scales cycloid or ctenoid; one dorsal fin (but with a notch) with 16–27 spines and 11–24 soft rays; pelvic fin with one spine and five soft rays;

well-developed anterior nostril on each side, posterior nostril (if present) reduced to a small pore; anal fin with 0–3 spines followed by soft rays; six or seven branchiostegal rays; swim bladder absent. Maximum length up to 1.5 m, attained in *Ophiodon elongatus;* most other species less than 45 cm.

Although small, this is the most speciose family endemic to the North Pacific. Most species are primarily littoral.

Four subfamilies, four genera, and nine species. The following classification is based on Rutenberg (1962), except for a few changes, including the recognition of family status for *Zaniolepis* (the combfishes), following Quast (1965).

SUBFAMILY HEXAGRAMMINAE.   Dorsal fin divided approximately in the middle by a notch into an anterior spinous portion and a posterior soft portion; anal fin without spines; head covered with scales; caudal fin rounded, truncate, or slightly emarginate; no large ridges on skull; vertebrae 47–56; single lateral line (in the one species of the subgenus *Agrammus, H. agrammus* of Japan, Korea, and North China) or five.

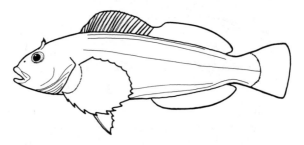

One genus, *Hexagrammos* (= *Agrammus*), with six species, from western and eastern coasts of the North Pacific.

SUBFAMILY PLEUROGRAMMINAE.   Dorsal fin without a notch but with 47–51 hard rays; anal fin without spines (24–30 soft rays); scales partly covering head; caudal fin forked; strongly developed ridges on upper surface of skull; vertebrae 59–62; five lateral lines on body. Primarily pelagic.

One species, *Pleurogrammus monopterygius,* in the northwestern Pacific and southern Bering Sea.

SUBFAMILY OPHIODONTINAE.   Dorsal fin divided into two parts by a deep notch, first portion with 24–27 spines and second portion with 21–24 soft rays; anal fin without spines but first three rays are nonsegmented;

head not covered with scales; only member with cycloid scales on body, others may have cycloid scales on head; caudal fin truncate or slightly emarginate; 57 vertebrae; single lateral line; mouth large; jaws with small teeth interspersed with large fanglike teeth; feeds primarily on fishes, crustaceans, and squids and is extremely voracious.

One species, *Ophiodon elongatus* (lingcod), of eastern Pacific from southern Alaska to Mexico.

SUBFAMILY OXYLEBIINAE. Dorsal fin divided by a shallow notch; anal fin usually with three large spines, of which the second is longest; scales covering the head; caudal fin rounded; one lateral line.

One species, *Oxylebius pictus*, of eastern Pacific from southern British Columbia to California.

Family ZANIOLEPIDIDAE—combfishes. Marine; eastern North Pacific.

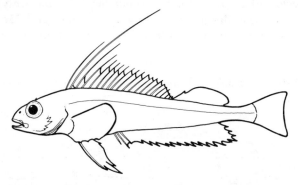

Dorsal fin with deep notch in posterior third of fin; first three dorsal fin spines elongate, the second greatly prolonged in *Zaniolepis latipinnis;* ctenoid scales; first two pelvic fin rays thickened and extending past origin of anal fin; one lateral line. This group is placed in the hexagrammids by most workers. Primarily benthic. Maximum length about 30 cm.

Two species, *Zaniolepis latipinnis* and *Z. frenata*, found from California to British Columbia.

Suborder Cottoidei. The family Psychrolutidae (including Cottunculidae) is included in Cottidae by many workers. Jordan (1923), on the other hand, split the present family Cottidae into several families. The relations of the family Normanichthyidae are uncertain.

I recognize eight families with about 130 genera and 585 species.

Family NORMANICHTHYIDAE. Marine; off Chile.

Body covered with ctenoid scales; head unarmed; pelvic fin with one
spine and five soft rays; no ribs.

One species, *Normanichthys crockeri*, described by Clark (1937).

Family EREUNIIDAE. Marine; deep-water, Japan.

Four lower pectoral fin rays free (similar to triglids); body with spinous
ctenoid scales; prootic forms part of posterior margin of orbit, pterosphenoid and parasphenoid not in contact. (In cottids the pterosphenoid
and parasphenoid are in contact and form the posterior margin, excluding the prootic.) Preopercle with simple spines (uppermost never antler-
like); six branchiostegal rays; two slender postcleithra; vertebrae 36–39
(13 precaudal vertebrae). The two genera recognized here were formerly
placed, along with *Icelus*, in Icelidae. Yabe (1981) gives reasons for recognizing the family Ereuniidae and placing *Icelus* in Cottidae.

Two species, *Ereunias grallator* (without pelvic fin but with underlying
pelvis and variously developed rudimentary spine) and *Marukawichthys
ambulator* (pelvic fin present with one spine and four soft rays) (Yabe,
1981).

Family COTTIDAE—sculpins. Marine and freshwater; Northern Hemisphere and
near New Zealand.

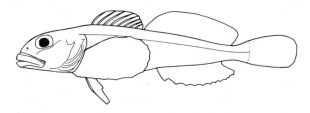

Body often appearing naked, commonly with scales or prickles (never
completely encased in heavy bony armor); eye usually large and placed
high on the head; lateral line present, single; pelvic fins (absent in one
species) with one spine and 2–5 soft rays; no spines in anal fin; adults
without swim bladder. Maximum length about 78 cm (e.g., *Scorpaenichthys
marmoratus*).

Detailed studies on this family include those by Bolin (1947—and reference therein to his 1944 review), Taranets (1941), and Watanabe (1960).
Wilimovsky (1979) gives a key and annotated listing of the genera (with
nominal species). Regional studies such as Hart (1973) give an account
of many species. The implications of larval characters to sculpin systematics are being studied by S. L. Richardson (e.g., Richardson, 1981).

Most species are marine with the greatest diversity occurring along the

North Pacific coastline. About 130 species are known from fresh and marine waters in North America and about 75 species are known from Japan. Two species, of the genus *Antipodocottus*, are known from New Zealand (DeWitt, 1969; Nelson, 1975).

About 70 genera [e.g., *Artediellus, Artedius, Ascelichthys* (lacks pelvics), *Blepsias, Chitonotus, Clinocottus, Cottus* (a large circumpolar, freshwater group), *Enophrys, Gymnocanthus, Hemilepidotus, Hemitripterus, Icelinus, Icelus, Jordania, Leptocottus, Myoxocephalus, Nautichthys, Oligocottus, Pseudoblennius, Radulinus, Rhamphocottus, Scorpaenichthys, Sigmistes, Synchirus,* and *Triglops*] with about 300 species.

Family COTTOCOMEPHORIDAE.   Freshwater; primarily Lake Baikal (USSR); some species in other USSR drainages.

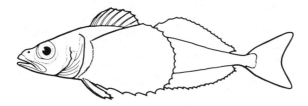

Postcleithra reduced or absent. Some species are pelagic.

The taxonomy and biology of this and the next family are discussed by Taliev (1955) and briefly reviewed by Kozhov (1963), both of whom placed the following two subfamilies in the Cottidae. In the present classification all sculpins in Lake Baikal are placed in this and the following family and account for 26 of its 50 known fish species. Maximum length about 18 cm.

SUBFAMILY ABYSSOCOTTINAE.   Three genera, *Abyssocottus, Asprocottus,* and *Cottinella*, with about 12 species. Species formerly placed in *Limnocottus* are now placed in the first two genera.

SUBFAMILY COTTOCOMEPHORINAE.   Five genera, *Batrachocottus, Cottocomephorus, Metacottus, Paracottus* (similar to *Cottus*), and *Procottus*, with about 12 species.

Family COMEPHORIDAE—Baikal oilfishes.   Freshwater; Lake Baikal (USSR).

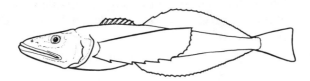

Body naked; pectoral fins very long; no pelvic fins (pelvic bones present); postcleithra absent; body glassy—dull and translucent in living fish; body usually high in fat content; vertebrae 48–50; viviparous. Maximum length about 20 cm.

One genus, *Comephorus*, with two species.

Family PSYCHROLUTIDAE.   Marine; Atlantic, Indian, and Pacific.

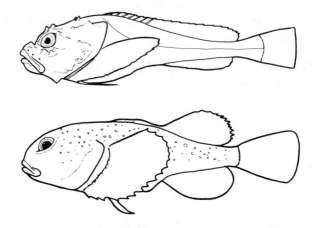

Body naked or with plates bearing prickles; interorbital space usually greater than exposed eye diameter (much smaller in *Malacocottus*); lateral line reduced, with 20 or fewer pores; pelvic fin with one spine and three soft rays; dorsal fins usually continuous with spinous dorsal, often partially hidden by skin (bases separate or nearly so in *Malacocottus* and *Dasycottus*); branchiostegal rays seven; vomerine teeth present or absent, palatine teeth always absent; one or two postorbitals (if two, they are usually ringlike; cottids have two or three elongate postorbitals); system of well-developed bony arches, which may bear spines, on the cranium over the lateral line system with wide intervening space (described in Nelson, 1982a).

About seven genera, *Dasycottus, Malacocottus, Cottunculus, Eurymen, Ebinania, Psychrolutes* (= *Cottunculoides, Gilbertidia*), and *Neophrynichthys*, with 29 species currently recognized (Nelson, 1982a). Additional genera may belong here. Two subfamilies are recognized, one for those species with a relatively rigid interorbital region and with spines often developed on the head (as in the upper figure of *Cottunculus*), and one for those with a soft interorbital region and always lacking spines on the head (and having the general appearance of an overgrown tadpole—as in the lower figure of *Psychrolutes*).

Family AGONIDAE—poachers. Marine; North Atlantic, North Pacific, and southern South America.

Body usually elongate and covered with bony plates; pelvic fins thoracic, each with one spine and two soft rays; one or two dorsal fins.
About 20 genera and 50 species.

SUBFAMILY ASPIDOPHOROIDINAE (ALLIGATORFISHES). One dorsal fin.

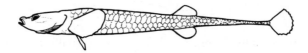

Two genera, *Anoplagonus* and *Aspidophoroides*, with five species. The distribution and characteristics of the two species of *Anoplagonus* are given by Kanayama and Maruyama (1979).

SUBFAMILY AGONINAE. Two dorsal fins.

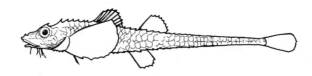

About 18 genera (e.g., *Agonopsis, Agonus, Bathyagonus (= Asterotheca), Bothragonus, Hypsagonus, Occella, Odontopyxis, Pallasina, Sarritor, Stellerina,* and *Xeneretmus*).

Family CYCLOPTERIDAE—lumpfishes and snailfishes. Marine; Antarctic, Arctic, Atlantic, and Pacific.

Pelvic fins, when present, modified into a sucking disc, thoracic; lateral line usually absent; gill opening usually small.
The snailfishes are frequently recognized in their own family, Liparididae (e.g., Able and McAllister, 1980; Stein, 1978a; Andriashev et al., 1977).
Twenty-one genera with about 177 species.

SUBFAMILY CYCLOPTERINAE (LUMPFISHES OR LUMPSUCKERS). Cooler regions of Northern Hemisphere.

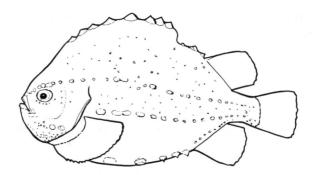

Body globose, usually covered with tubercles; usually two short dorsal fins, the first spinous, the second soft rayed (the spinous is "absent" in some), never confluent with caudal; anal fin short. Maximum length up to 60 cm.

The following classification is based on Ueno (1970) who recognized its tribes as subfamilies. Among its members *Cyclopterus* shows some affinity to the Cottidae and Psychrolutidae, whereas *Aptocyclus* is the most closely related to the Liparinae.

TRIBE CYCLOPTERINI.   First dorsal fin projecting above the upper profile of the back; skin with large conical bony tubercles or dermal cirri or warts. (Skin naked in *Lethotremus* which has long dermal tubes on underside of head.)

Five genera, *Cyclopterus, Eumicrotremus, Cyclopteropsis, Cyclopsis,* and *Lethotremus,* with 24 species.

TRIBE APTOCYCLINI.   First dorsal fin embedded under thick skin, not visible without dissection; skin without bony or dermal appendages.

Two species, *Aptocyclus ventricosus* and *Pelagocyclus vitiazi.* The latter leads a pelagic life and has a rudimentary sucking disc.

SUBFAMILY LIPARIDINAE (SNAILFISHES).   Primarily Northern Hemisphere and Antarctic.

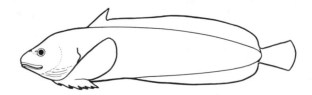

Body elongate, scaleless (small prickles in some) and skin jellylike; dorsal and anal fins long, confluent, or nearly so, with caudal fin; pelvic fin absent in some. Maximum length about 50 cm.

TRIBE LIPARINI. About 13 genera [e.g., *Careproctus, Cyclogaster, Liparis, Paraliparis (= Psednos)*, and *Polypera*] and about 150 species. A few species are known from other than the Northern Hemisphere and Antarctica (e.g., South Africa and Macquarie Trench) and Smith (1968) notes the unexpected collection of one small specimen from the Red Sea. Stein (1978b) speculates that the group may be essentially worldwide in temperate and cold waters.

TRIBE RHODICHTHYINI. One species, *Rhodichthys regina*, which is found in the northern North Atlantic and adjacent Arctic in deep water. This species lacks pelvic fins and has elongate pectoral rays on the throat.

Order PERCIFORMES. (Percomorphi in part, Acanthopterygii in part, Labyrinthici in part, Jugulares in part, Beryciformes in part, and many more).

The order Perciformes is the most diversified of all fish orders. Indeed, it is the largest vertebrate order. Perciformes dominate in vertebrate ocean life and are the dominant fish group in many tropical and subtropical fresh waters.

The classification of this suborder is controversial and some workers would include other groups (e.g., Scorpaeniformes, considering them to be percoid derivatives) while excluding others (e.g., Mugiloidei). Monophyly for the group is by no means certain. Most families in many suborders are basically similar and are not currently defineable in terms of common shared derived characters.

The families of the suborder Blennioidei as previously recognized (Nelson, 1976) are placed in four suborders. The family arrangement is markedly different from Gosline (1968, 1971) and Greenwood et al. (1966). Whether the four suborders, representing hypothesized evolutionary lineages, are each other's closest relatives or might each have closer affinities with other groups is uncertain. The pelvic fin, when present, originates in front of the pectorals in all species of the four suborders. The advice of Dr. V. G. Springer has been particularly helpful in the decision to restrict the membership of the suborder Blennioidei and in many other matters relating to the classification of the blennylike perciforms.

Although they are a morphologically and ecologically diverse group with secondary losses and gains, the level of evolution reached, as contrasted with "typical" lower teleosts (Protacanthopterygii and Ostariophysi), can be generalized as follows. (Many exceptions to these generalizations occur; for example, the bodies of some perciforms are covered mainly by cycloid scales.)

	Lower teleosts	Perciformes
Spines in fins	Absent	Present
Dorsal fin number	One, adipose fin may also be present	Two, never an adipose fin
Scales	Cycloid	Ctenoid or absent
Pelvic fin position	Abdominal	If present, thoracic or jugular
Pelvic fin rays	Six or more soft rays	One spine and five soft rays, sometimes fewer
Pectoral fin base	Ventral and horizontal	Lateral and vertical
Upper jaw bordered by	Premaxilla and maxilla	Premaxilla
Swim bladder	Duct present (physostomes)	Duct absent (physoclists)
Orbitosphenoid	Present	Absent
Mesocoracoid	Present	Absent
Intermuscular bones	Present	Absent
Bone cells in bone of adult	Present	Absent
Principal caudal fin ray number	Often 18 or 19	Never more than 17, often fewer

The Perciformes contains 22 suborders, 150 families, about 1367 genera, and about 7800 (7791 by counts herein) species. Two suborders, Percoidei and Gobioidei, account for about two-thirds of the species. The eight largest families of this, the largest fish order, are Gobiidae, Cichlidae, Labridae, Serranidae, Blenniidae, Pomacentridae, Sciaenidae, and Apogonidae. Together they constitute slightly over 50% of the species. About three-fourths of all perciforms are marine shore fishes while about 14% (primarily cichlids and percids) normally occur only in fresh water.

Suborder Percoidei. This suborder, the largest of the Perciformes, contains 73 families, 589 genera, and about 3524 species. Of the 73 families, 10 are monotypic and 11 have 100 or more species. The six largest families, Cichlidae, Serranidae, Pomacentridae, Sciaenidae, Apogonidae, and Lutjanidae, contain more than 50% of the species. About 930 or 26% of the species normally occur only in fresh water (the majority of these being cichlids and percids). This suborder contains many highly colorful fishes.

This is probably the basal evolutionary group from which the other perciform groups and the remaining two orders have been derived.

Superfamily Percoidea. Most of the 65 families are very similar and poorly separated from one another; some are very distinctive and have been allied with other orders or placed in their own order. Several groups of families form distinct lineages and are given superfamilial rank (e.g., Johnson, 1980). Major changes in the classification, including in the placement of genera in particular families and the inclusion of families in higher groups, may be expected with further family revisions and detailed studies of particular anatomical features throughout the group.

Family CENTROPOMIDAE—snooks. Marine (often brackish); Atlantic, Indian, and Pacific, some in fresh water (especially in Africa).

Lateral line extending onto tail, reaching posterior margin of fin in all but one species of Centropominae and Latinae. (Three rows exist on the tail of some species.) Scaly process usually in pelvic axis; dorsal fin in two portions (either with a deep notch or a distinct gap), the first with 7–9 spines and the second with one spine and 8–15 soft rays; anal fin with three spines and 6–17 soft rays (subfamilies Centropominae and Latinae have 6–9 soft rays); pelvic fin with one spine and five soft rays; caudal fin rounded, truncate, or forked; seven branchiostegal rays; 24 or 25 vertebrae. Maximum length about 2.0 m.

Six genera recognized in three subfamilies with about 35 species. Greenwood (1976) reviews the family (recognizing only the Centropominae and Latinae) and gives an anatomical description of several species. The subfamily Centropominae contains *Centropomus* with nine species in tropical and subtropical waters of the New World (individuals may enter fresh water). The subfamily Latinae contains *Psammoperca* with one Indo-West Pacific species and *Lates* (= *Luciolates*) with eight species, seven in fresh water in Africa (including the large Nile perch), and one in the Indo-West Pacific (and the lower Eocene fossil *Eolates*). The subfamily

Ambassinae contains *Chanda* (= *Ambassis*), *Parambassis*, and *Priops*. *Chanda*, the Asiatic glassfishes, are popular aquarium fishes that are marine and freshwater. H. M. Smith, 1945, gives reasons for regarding *Ambassis*, along with several other nominal genera, as a junior synonym of *Chanda*, but some authors recognize *Ambassis* as a generic name. Ambassinae is often recognized as a separate family, either Ambassidae or Chandidae (e.g., Johnson, 1975; Greenwood, 1976). Its relationships are uncertain so it is retained here (where it is also placed by Berg, 1940; Norman, 1957; Greenwood et al., 1966; Lindberg, 1971) until evidence demonstrating a relationship elsewhere is forthcoming.

Family PERCICHTHYIDAE—temperate basses.   Marine, brackish, and freshwater; tropical and temperate regions of world.

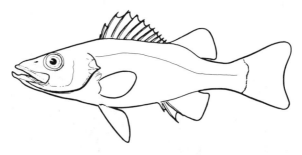

Opercle with two rounded spines—no spine below the main spine (except in *Niphon*, which has three); lateral line complete and continuous; caudal fin usually forked; no scaly process in pelvic axis; pelvic fin with one spine and five soft rays; not hermaphroditic, sexes separate.

This family, which is one of the most generalized percoids, was erected from the family Serranidae by Gosline (1966). It is a poorly defined group and its composition is subject to change.

About 20 genera: the marine *Acropoma*, *Dicentrarchus* (two European species which enter fresh water), *Doderleinia*, *Malakichthys*, *Neoscombrops*, *Niphon*, *Polyprion*, *Stereolepis*, *Synagrops*, and *Verilus*; the freshwater *Morone* (= *Roccus*), from North America, Europe, and North Africa, *Percichthys* and *Percilia*, from South America, *Ctenolates*, *Macquaria*, *Maccullochella*, and *Percalates*, from Australia, and *Coreoperca*, *Lateolabrax*, and *Siniperca*, from Asia. About 50 species. *Priscacara*, a freshwater Middle Eocene fish, probably also belongs in this family (F. Cichocki and G. R. Smith, pers. comm. 1982). The three distinctive species of *Acropoma* (formerly comprising the family Acropomatidae) have light organs and the anus near the pelvic fin base—the only other perciform with such an anterior anus is the serranid *Bullisichthys*. Greenwood (1977) has confirmed the placement of *Niphon* in this family, rather than in Centropomidae; however, its placement in Serranidae cannot be ruled out. The genus *Verilus*, formerly placed in Lutjanidae, is placed here following Johnson (1980). Johnson (1975) rejects Fraser's (1972b) placement of *Howella* and *Bathysphyraenops* in the Percichthyidae and retains them in the Apogonidae. Fraser and Fourmanoir (1971) tentatively placed *Scombrosphyraena* in the Percichthyidae, but its stated affinity to *Howella* puts this placement in doubt.

Family SERRANIDAE—sea basses. Marine (a few freshwater); tropical and temperate seas.

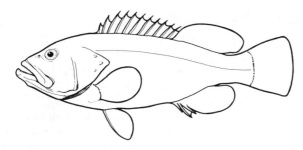

Opercle with three spines—the main spine with one above it and one below it. (The lower opercular spine is also found in Grammistidae and *Niphon.*) Scales usually ctenoid, cycloid in some; lateral line complete and continuous (absent in one species), not extending onto caudal fin (running close to dorsal fin base in Anthiinae); dorsal fin generally continuous, may be notched, with 7–12 spines; three anal fin spines; caudal fin usually rounded, truncate, or lunate (rarely forked); tip of maxilla exposed, not slipping beneath sheath when mouth closed; no scaly axillary pelvic process; pelvic fin with one spine and five soft rays; usually seven branchiostegal rays; 24–26 vertebrae; hermaphroditic, although the two sexes usually do not develop at the same time (most *Serranus* and their immediate relatives are functional hermaphrodites). Maximum length up to about 3 m (and weight up to about 400 kg); some species, however, grow no longer than 10 cm.

The hamlets *(Hypoplectrus)* provide an unusually interesting puzzle in evolution and taxonomy. There are about 12 morphospecies in the New World tropics of these small synchronous hermaphroditic fish which differ in color pattern but very little, if at all, in morphometry, meristics, ecology, or reproductive behavior. As many as seven of the color morphs have been observed on the same reef. In an electrophoretic study, Graves and Rosenblatt (1980) concluded that of the ten color morphs from the Caribbean that they examined there was no reason to recognize more than one species. However, in making observations on pairing during mating using SCUBA gear along with other evidence, Fischer (1980) concluded that they form a multispecies complex (and not a single polymorphic species) with restricted gene exchange among sympatric morphospecies. The hamlets are carnivorous, and the color patterns in some cases are similar to that of sympatric noncarnivorous fishes. Whether this is aggressive mimicry, as has been postulated, or the result of similar selective pressure in both the putative model and mimic seems to be an open question (Fischer, 1980). The interrelationships of the morphospecies are unanswered, but many exciting questions are posed by what is known.

Systematic revisions of component groups include Kendall (1979), Randall (1980a), and C. L. Smith (1971). Several subfamilies are usually recognized (e.g., Serraninae, Anthiinae, Epinephelinae, and Liopropominae). There is a continuing question as to what the limits of the family Serranidae should be and whether or not grammistids and pseudogrammatids arose independently from serranids. Kendall (1976) studied the interface of the liopropomine line with groups he believes to be derived from it. He concludes, on the basis of the arrangement of predorsal and associated bones, that *Aulacocephalus* and *Diploprion* (considered here as grammistids) are similar to epinephelines, and that the liopropomines, grammistids, pseudogrammatids, and *Rainfordia* form a lineage derived from the epinephelines. Later, in also considering larval characters, Kendall (1979) formally recognized the families Grammistidae and Pseudogrammatidae and the genus *Liopropoma* as a subfamily of Serranidae (the Grammistinae).

Approximately 35 genera [e.g., *Alphestes, Anthias, Caesioperca, Centropristis, Cephalopholis, Dermatolepis, Diplectrum, Epinephelus* (groupers), *Gonioplectrus, Hemanthias, Hypoplectrus* (hamlets), *Liopropoma, Mycteroperca* (groupers), *Ocyanthias, Paralabrax, Paranthias, Pikea, Plectranthias, Promicrops, Pteranthias, Schultzea, Serraniculus,* and *Serranus*] and about 370 species.

Several genera are of uncertain position. They have generally been thought to have serranid or other percoid affinities and include the following:

Symphysanodon: this genus has been considered a serranid or lutjanid. Johnson (1975, 1980) believes that it may occupy a very primitive position within the percoids. It contains about five species found in the western Atlantic and the Indo-West Pacific (Anderson, 1970).

Caesioscorpis: the characters of this western Australian fish exclude placement in Lutjanidae, where it was originally placed, but its percoid affinities are unknown (Johnson, 1980).

Callanthias: usually placed in Serranidae (Subfamily Anthiinae). It lacks many serranid specializations and may have a pseudochromid affinity.

Centrogenys: placed in its own family but bears a superficial resemblance to the cirrhitids.

Ostracoberyx: this genus, with a relatively small oblique mouth and a prominent spine extending backward from the preopercle, was placed in its own family in Beryciformes by Berg (1940). It may be related to *Niphon*.

Family GRAMMISTIDAE—soapfishes. Marine; Atlantic and Indo-Pacific.

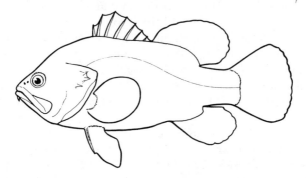

Dorsal fin with 2–9 spines and 12–27 soft rays; anal fin with two or three short spines or none at all and 8–17 soft rays; lower jaw projecting and chin usually with terminal appendage; opercle with three distinct spines (two in one species); pelvic fins inserted below or slightly in front of pectoral base; innermost pelvic ray attached to abdomen by a membrane; scales mainly ctenoid and not embedded or cycloid and often embedded, small with about 75–140 rows along the side; body mucus can create a soapsudslike effect (with toxin grammistin) in the subfamily Grammistinae. Maximum length about 30 cm.

The families Grammistidae and Pseudogrammatidae have been combined here following Gosline (1966), Robins et al. (1980), and, to some extent, Kendall (1976, 1979). As discussed under Serranidae, Kendall (1979) considers this lineage to be a subfamily of Serranidae. Smith and Atz (1969), however, in an examination of gonads, and Randall et al. (1971) postulate that pseudogrammatids and grammistids arose independently from serranids.

Ten genera with about 24 species. Two subfamilies may be recognized. The Grammistinae (Grammistidae as recognized by Randall et al., 1971, 1980), shown in the figure, have a complete lateral line and 24 or 25 vertebrae. There are seven genera, *Aulacocephalus, Belonoperca, Diploprion, Grammistes, Grammistops, Pogonoperca,* and *Rypticus,* with about 18 species. The Pseudogrammatinae have 6–8 dorsal fin spines (first vestigial), an anal fin with three spines and generally 16 or 17 soft rays, a lateral line which is interrupted or divided into upper and lower portions, and 26–28 vertebrae. It contains *Pseudogramma (= Rhegma), Aporops,* and *Suttonia,* with about six species. They are small fishes which only reach about 10 cm in length.

Family PSEUDOCHROMIDAE—dottybacks.   Marine; Indo-Pacific.

Dorsal and anal fins each with one to three spines (often inconspicuous), in addition, dorsal with 21–37 soft rays and anal usually with 13–21 soft rays; pelvic fin with one spine and three to five soft rays, inserted below or in front of pectoral fin base; lateral line variable; six branchiostegal rays; no interarcual cartilage between uncinate process of the first epibranchial and the second infrapharyngobranchial ligamentous attachment, unlike most percoids; vertebrae 26–35 (10 − 13 + 16 − 25). Maximum length about 20 cm (obtained in *Labracinus*), most less than 11 cm.

Springer et al. (1977) synonymize the Pseudochromidae, Pseudoplesiopidae, and Anisochromidae. The latter two are considered to be each others closest relatives. Springer et al. (1977) do not recognize subfamilies, but they are given here as an aid to identification and as a provisional statement on general affinities. The Pseudochrominae may be polyphyletic.

About eight genera and at least 60 species.

SUBFAMILY PSEUDOCHROMINAE (DOTTYBACKS)

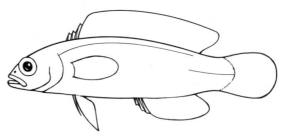

Pelvic fin with one spine and five branched soft rays; head scaled; teeth on palatine; pectoral fin rays 16–20; lateral line interrupted, two parts (one dorsoanteriorly, one midlateral posteriorly).

Genera include *Pseudochromis* (with 39 species—Lubbock, 1975, 1976a,b), *Labracinus*, and probably *Dampieria*, *Nesiotes*, and *Nematochromis*.

SUBFAMILY PSEUDOPLESIOPINAE.   Pelvic fin with one spine and three or four simple soft rays; head scaled; teeth on palatine; pectoral fin rays 17–19; lateral line with one anterior pored scale.

Two genera, *Chlidichthys* with six species (Lubbock, 1975, 1976b) and *Pseudoplesiops* with several species.

SUBFAMILY ANISOCHROMINAE.   Pelvic fin with one spine and four soft rays (three branched and one simple), inserted distinctly in front of pectoral base; head naked; teeth absent on palatine; pectoral fin rays 13–15; single lateral line along base of dorsal fin; dorsal fin with one weak spine.

One genus, *Anisochromis*, with two species in the western Indian Ocean (Smith, 1954; Springer et al., 1977).

Family GRAMMIDAE (Grammatidae)—basslets.   Marine; tropical western Atlantic and western Pacific.

Lateral line on body interrupted or absent; pelvic fin with one spine and five soft rays; spines in dorsal fin 11–13. Maximum length about 10 cm.

Species of *Gramma* and *Lipogramma* and some members of the above few families (e.g., *Pseudochromis* and *Liopropoma*) are especially colorful and are popular as marine aquarium fishes.

About five genera with 13 species: includes *Gramma* (three species in the West Indies—Starck and Colin, 1978), *Liopogramma* (six species in the tropical western Atlantic—Robins and Colin, 1979), *Stigmatonotus australis* (Western Australia), *Grammatonotus laysanus* (known only from the small holotype obtained in deep water off Hawaii), and possibly *Fraudella carassiops* (Queensland).

Family PLESIOPIDAE—roundheads.   Marine; Indo-Pacific, south to Tasmania.

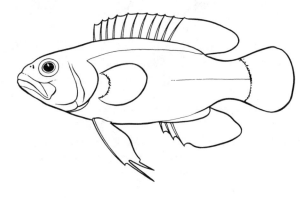

Dorsal fin with 11–15 spines; anal fin with three spines; pelvic fin with one spine and four soft rays; lateral line in two parts.

Five genera, *Assessor*, *Calloplesiops*, *Paraplesiops*, *Plesiops*, and *Trachinops*, with about 20 species.

Family ACANTHOCLINIDAE.   Marine; Indo-West Pacific (India to Marshall Islands and south to Queensland and New Zealand).

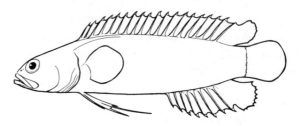

Dorsal fin with 18–21 spines; anal fin with 8–15 spines; pelvic fin with one spine and two soft rays; 1–4 lateral lines. Maximum length about 20 cm.

Three genera, *Acanthoclinus*, *Acanthoplesiops*, and *Belonepterygion*, and about five species.

Family GLAUCOSOMATIDAE.   Marine; western Pacific (Japan to Australia).

Dorsal fin with eight graduated spines and 12–14 soft rays; anal fin with three spines and 12 soft rays; maxillae scaled; lateral line nearly straight and extending to tail; caudal fin lunate or truncate. Maximum length at least 60 cm.

One genus, *Glaucosoma*, with five species.

Family TERAPONIDAE (Theraponidae)—grunters or tigerperches.   Marine coastal, brackish, and freshwater, Indo-West Pacific.

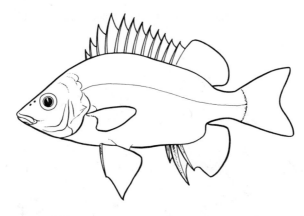

Body oblong to oblong-ovate, somewhat compressed; opercle with two spines, lower spine longer; dorsal fin with notch, 11–14 spines and 8–14 soft rays, spinous portion depressible into a groove formed by a sheath of scales; anal fin with three spines and 7–12 soft rays; pelvic fins inserted distinctly behind base of pectoral fins, with one spine and five soft rays; caudal fin rounded, truncate, or emarginate; lateral line continuous and extending onto caudal fin; vomer and palatines of most species lacking teeth; six branchiostegal rays; paired extrinsic swim bladder muscles arising from rear of skull or posttemporal and inserting on anterodorsal surface of the anterior chamber of the swim bladder (employed for sound production—a few other perciforms have sonic muscles but they differ in position); swim bladder transversely divided (Vari, 1978, gives details on these features of the swim bladder which are unique within the perciforms); 25–27 vertebrae. Maximum length about 80 cm.

Vari (1978) notes that the original spelling employed for the type genus by G. Cuvier was *Terapon*, which thus forms the stem for the family name Teraponidae. However, as Vari notes, this is an incorrect transliteration of the Greek word for slaves (the Japanese considered the fish fit only for slaves and it was termed "slave-fish" by the Europeans). According to current rules of zoological nomenclature applicable to this case and acceptance that Cuvier's incorrect spelling was not a *lapsus calami*, the spelling should, unfortunately, be *Terapon* and Teraponidae, rather than *Therapon* and Theraponidae.

Most of the freshwater species occur in Australia where they are the third largest freshwater fish group; they are most diverse in the northwestern section of Australia (Lake, 1971; Vari and Hutchins, 1978).

Fifteen genera [e.g., *Leiopotherapon*, *Pelates* (= *Helotes*), *Terapon*, *Mesopristes*, *Hephaestus*, and *Scortum*] with 39 species (Vari, 1978; Vari and Hutchins, 1978).

Family BANJOSIDAE.   Marine; coasts of China, southern Japan, and Korea.

Body deep, strongly compressed; head with steep, nearly straight profile; opercle spineless; dorsal fin with 10 flattened spines and 12 soft rays; anal fin with three spines, the second much longer than other anal rays, and seven soft rays; pelvics inserted behind base of pectorals; caudal fin slightly emarginate; lateral line continuous and complete; color brownish or olive with eight faint longitudinal darkish bands. This fish closely resembles the pomadasyids. Maximum length about 30 cm.

One species; *Banjos banjos* (= *typus*—Fowler, 1972:485).

Family KUHLIIDAE—aholeholes.   Marine, brackish, and freshwater; Indo-West Pacific.

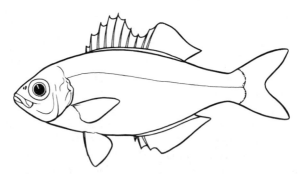

Dorsal and anal fins each with a well-developed scaly sheath; dorsal fin deeply notched; anal fin with three spines; no scaly pelvic axillary process. Maximum length up to 50 cm.

Four genera with about 17 species. Two subfamilies may be recognized. Kuhliinae contains one genus, *Kuhlia* (opercle with two spines), with about 12 species; most of the species are marine and brackish water but some are restricted to fresh water. Nannopercinae contains *Nannatherina* (status uncertain), *Nannoperca,* and *Edelia* with about five species; these species occur in brackish and fresh water in southern Australia (Lake, 1971; Llewellyn, 1974) and may not be as closely related to *Kuhlia* as is suggested here. These subfamilies are often given family status (e.g., Johnson, 1975, who places the Kuhliidae after Percichthyidae and the Nannopercidae between Teraponidae and Centrarchidae).

Family CENTRARCHIDAE—sunfishes. Freshwater; North America (see map on p. 420).

Three or more anal spines; pseudobranch small and concealed; branchiostegal rays 5–7; gill membranes separate.

Most sunfishes are nest builders. The male hollows out a small depression with his tail and then guards the eggs. Centrarchids are an important sports fish and have been introduced into many areas beyond their native range. Some, such as *Lepomis macrochirus,* the bluegill, have been used in physiological and ecological experimental work. Maximum length about 83 cm, attained in *Micropterus salmoides* (largemouth bass). At the other extreme species of *Elassoma* are not known to exceed 4 cm.

Nine genera with 30 species.

Subfamily Centrarchinae (sunfishes). Suborbital bones present in addition to the lachrymal; dentary and angular penetrated by lateral line; lateral line present on body, sometimes incomplete; anal fin spines usually three (or fewer) or five (or more); dorsal fin usually with 5–13 spines (most with about 10).

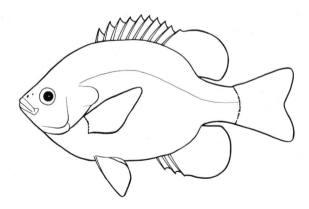

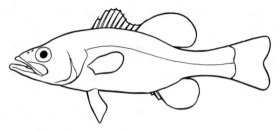

The 20 species typically with three anal spines are placed in *Enneacanthus*, *Lepomis* (figure p. 285), and *Micropterus* (basses) (upper figure). The seven species typically with more than three anal spines (usually five) are placed in *Acantharchus*, *Ambloplites*, *Archoplites* (one species, the Sacramento perch, is the only living centrarchid native west of the Rocky Mountains), *Centrarchus*, and *Pomoxis* (crappies).

SUBFAMILY ELASSOMATINAE (ELASSOMINAE) (PYGMY SUNFISHES). No suborbitals, except the lachrymal; dentary and angular not penetrated by lateral line; no lateral line on body; anal fin with three spines and 4–8 soft rays; dorsal fin with 3–5 spines and 8–13 soft rays.

The pygmy sunfishes are placed in their own family by some workers (e.g., Branson and Moore, 1962). The biochemical data of Avise et al. (1977) also suggests that *Elassoma* is the most distinct and genetically distant of the centrarchid genera. It is believed, however, that *Elassoma* has closer affinities to the centrarchids than to any other family and it is retained in it.

One genus, *Elassoma*, with at least three species.

Family PERCIDAE—perches. Freshwater; Northern Hemisphere (see map on p. 420).

Two dorsal fins, separate or narrowly joined (broadly joined in *Zingel*); one or two anal spines, if two, the second is usually weak; pelvic fins thoracic, with one spine and five soft rays; premaxilla protractile or nonprotractile; branchiostegal rays 5–8; branchiostegal membrane not joined to isthmus (may be united to each other or not); pseudobranchiae well developed to rudimentary; no subocular shelf; one or no predorsal bones (interneural before first pterygiophore); vertebrae 32–50. Maximum size up to 90 cm, attained in *Stizostedion vitreum* (walleye); most species much smaller. Much biological information on the economically important percids is contained in Volume 34, Number 10 of the *Journal of the Fisheries Research Board of Canada* for 1977.

Nine genera with 146 species (about 159 including known undescribed species). Collette (1963) and Collette and Bănărescu (1977) recognize two subfamilies, as shown here. Within each subfamily there is a lineage of small fishes with depressed or terete bodies and reduced or vestigial swim bladders that has been independently derived from larger fish with compressed bodies and possessing a swim bladder.

SUBFAMILY PERCINAE. Anteriormost interhaemal bone greatly enlarged; anal spines usually well developed; lateral line usually not extending onto tail.
Six genera with 137 species.

TRIBE PERCINI. Preopercle strongly serrate; usually seven or eight branchiostegal rays; body compressed; anal spines prominent; swim bladder well developed.

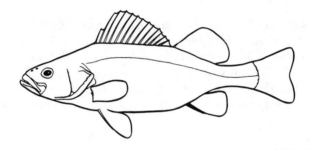

Three genera: the circumpolar *Perca* with three species (the Eurasian *P. fluviatilis* which has been introduced into South Africa, Australia, and New Zealand, the almost identical North American *P. flavescens*, and *P. shrenki* of the Balkhash and Alakul' lakes area of Asia); the European and western Asian *Gymnocephalus* (=*Acerina)* with four species; and *Percarina demidoffi* of the northern Black Sea area.

TRIBE ETHEOSTOMATINI. Preopercle margin smooth or partly serrate; usually five or six branchiostegal rays; body slightly compressed or fusiform; anal spines moderately prominent; swim bladder reduced or absent. Seldom over 11 cm.

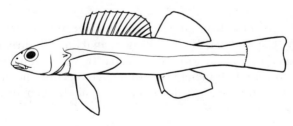

Three genera of North American darters: *Percina* with 31 species (about seven more are known but undescribed), *Ammocrypta* with seven species, and *Etheostoma* with 91 species (about 12 more are known but undescribed), giving a total of 129 described species (Page, 1981, 1983).

SUBFAMILY LUCIOPERCINAE.   Anteriormost interhaemal no larger than posterior ones; anal spines weak; lateral line extending onto tail.

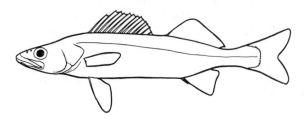

Contains the genus of predaceous pikeperches, *Stizostedion*, possessing a well-developed swim bladder, with three species in Europe (including the Caspian and Aral seas) and two species (sauger and walleye) in North America. It also contains two genera of European darterlike fishes lacking a swim bladder, *Zingel* (= *Aspro*), with three species, of the Danube, Rhone, and Vardar systems and the monotypic and very restricted *Romanichthys* of Romania.

Family PRIACANTHIDAE—bigeyes (catalufas).   Marine; tropical and subtropical; Atlantic, Indian, and Pacific.

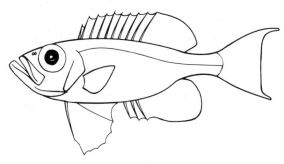

Eyes very large; mouth large, strongly oblique; dorsal fin continuous, usually with 10 spines and 10–15 soft rays; anal fin with three spines and 9–16 soft rays; caudal fin with 16 principal rays (14 branched), slightly emarginate to rounded; membrane present connecting the inner rays of the pelvic fin to the body; scales strongly ctenoid; color usually bright red.

Bigeyes are usually carnivorous and nocturnal. The tapetum lucidum, in at least one species, lies in the chorioid as it does in many "lower" fishes, whereas in all other teleosts investigated it lies, when present, in the retina (Nicol et al., 1973). Maximum length up to 60 cm.

Three genera, *Cookeolus*, *Priacanthus*, and *Pristigenys* (= *Pseudopriacanthus*), with about 18 species. The genus *Pseudopriacanthus* should perhaps be recognized; Fritzsche (1978) expresses doubt that the fossil genus *Pristigenys* is congeneric with any extant priacanthid genus.

Family APOGONIDAE—cardinalfishes.   Marine; Atlantic, Indian, and Pacific, some brackish water; a few in streams on tropical Pacific Islands.

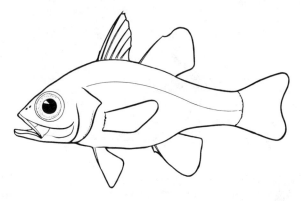

Two separated dorsal fins, the first with 6–8 spines and the second with one spine and 8–14 soft rays; anal fin with two spines and 8–18 soft rays; scales usually ctenoid, but cycloid in several groups and absent in *Gymnapogon*; seven branchiostegal rays; 24 or 25 vertebrae (10 + 14 or 15). Many of the species are mouthbreeders; it is suspected that in some only the males incubate the eggs, whereas in others it is only the females. Maximum length about 58 cm, attained in several species of the deepwater genus *Epigonus*; very few species of other genera reach 20 cm and most are less than 10 cm.

A confusing synonymy exists in this family in that the names Amiidae and *Amia* are used in some works (e.g., Fowler, 1959). Fraser (1972b) recognizes three subfamilies (Epigoninae, Apogoninae, and Pseudaminae) and gives a detailed review of the shallowwater forms.

About 26 genera (e.g. *Amiichthys*, *Apogon*, *Apogonichthyoides*, *Astrapogon*, *Cheilodipterus*, *Epigonus*, *Gymnapogon*, *Paramia*, *Phaeoptyx*, *Pseudamia*, and *Siphamia*) with about 192 species.

Family DINOLESTIDAE.   Marine; southern Australia.

Body shape much like *Sphyraena;* lower jaw extending beyond upper jaw; vomer and palatine with teeth, some teeth in mouth caninelike; head, including maxilla, snout, and occiput covered with scales; axillary scale at pelvic base; dorsal fins widely separated, first with four or five visible spines, second with one short spine and about 18 or 19 soft rays; anal fin with one short spine and about 26 soft rays; lateral line scales about 64–67, cycloid; lateral line continuing onto caudal fin; vertebrae 27 (10 + 17). Maximum length about 50 cm.

Fraser (1971) gives reasons for excluding this species from the Apogonidae where it has usually been placed. He believes it to have affinities with Centropomidae and Sciaenidae.

One species, *Dinolestes lewini.*

Family SILLAGINIDAE—smelt-whitings.   Marine and brackish water; Indo-Pacific.

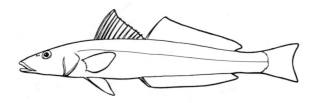

Body elongate; mouth small; two dorsal fins (little or no interspace), first with 9–12 spines and second with 16–26 soft rays; anal fin with two spines and 15–27 soft rays. Maximum length about 45 cm.

Three genera, *Sillaginodes, Sillaginopsis,* and *Sillago,* with about 16 species.

Family MALACANTHIDAE—tilefishes.   Marine; Atlantic, Indian, and Pacific.

Dorsal fin relatively long, continuous, and with spines and soft rays (total of 22–84 elements); anal fin relatively long, with one or two weak spines and 11–55 soft rays; pelvic fin with one spine and five soft rays; single opercular spine, sharp and strong in Malacanthinae and *Caulolatilus;* six branchiostegal rays; caudal fin truncate to variously forked; 24, 25, or 27 vertebrae (10 or 11 precaudal vertebrae); larvae with elaborate head and scale spination.

Although Dooley (1978) recognizes the tilefishes in two families, I prefer to retain the 34 species in one family as Robins et al. (1980) and Randall (1981a) also prefer to do. Dooley (1978) and Marino and Dooley (1982) demonstrate that many differences exist between the two lines, but they appear to be closely related and to be each other's closest relatives. I regard the matter of splitting or lumping these groups to be a subjective issue dependent on one's views of the degree of the difference relative to that between other percoid families. Robins et al. (1980) note that the family group names Malacanthidae and Latilidae (used here as a subfamily name) have priority over the previously used name Branchiostegidae.

SUBFAMILY MALACANTHINAE (SAND TILEFISHES). Predorsal ridge absent; enlarged spine at angle of preoperculum in some; body usually more streamlined than in Latilinae, head rounded in profile; dorsal fin with 1–4 spines and 43–60 soft rays *(Malacanthus)* or 3–10 spines and 13–34 soft rays *(Hoplolatilus);* anal fin with 12–55 soft rays in addition to the spines. Sand tilefishes, unlike members of Latilinae, are known to construct or inhabit mounds or borrows. They are usually found in depths less than 50 m, whereas latilines are usually found at depths more than 50 m.

Two genera, *Malacanthus* with three species and *Hoplolatilus* with eight species (Randall, 1981a).

SUBFAMILY LATILINAE. Predorsal ridge present; never an enlarged spine at angle of preopercle; body depth usually greater than in malacanthines; head rounded to squarish in profile; dorsal fin with 6–10 spines and 14–27 soft rays; anal fin with 11–26 soft rays in addition to the spines.

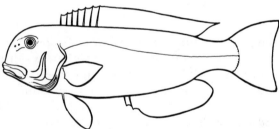

Three genera, *Caulolatilus, Lopholatilus,* and *Branchiostegus,* with 23 species (Dooley, 1978, 1981; Marino and Dooley, 1982).

Family LABRACOGLOSSIDAE. Marine; western and South Pacific.

Single dorsal fin, with spines and soft rays; soft-rayed portion of dorsal and anal fins covered with scales; jaws without canine teeth.

Three genera, *Bathystethus, Evistius,* and *Labracoglossa,* with about five species.

Family LACTARIIDAE—false trevallies. Marine; Indo-Pacific.

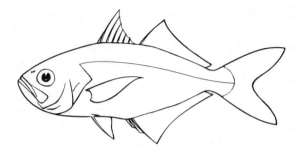

Dorsal fins separate; soft-rayed portion of dorsal and anal fins covered with scales (all scales easily shed); each jaw with two small canine teeth at front.

One genus, *Lactarius*, with one or two species.

Family POMATOMIDAE—bluefishes.   Marine; Atlantic, Indian, and Pacific.

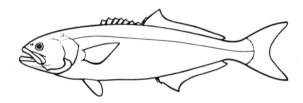

Dorsal fins separate, the first with seven or eight spines and the second with one spine and 13–28 soft rays; anal fin with two or three spines and with 12–27 soft rays; soft dorsal and anal fins covered with scales; preoperculum with a membrane flap over the suboperculum; black blotch at base of pectoral.

Pomatomus saltatrix is described as being extremely bloodthirsty, killing more fish than it can consume.

Two genera, *Pomatomus* and *Scombrops*, with about three species.

Family RACHYCENTRIDAE—cobia.   Marine; Atlantic and Indo-Pacific.

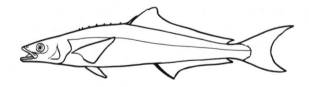

Body elongate, head depressed; 6–9 short free spines ahead of the long dorsal fin (1–3 spines and 26–33 soft rays); anal fin long, with two or three spines and 22–28 soft rays; three dark stripes on side of body. Maximum length up to 1.5 m.

One species: *Rachycentron canadum.*

Family ECHENEIDIDAE—remoras.   Marine; Atlantic, Indian, and Pacific.

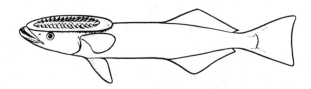

Body elongate, head flattened, and lower jaw projecting past upper jaw; scales small, cycloid; dorsal and anal fins lacking spines, each with about 18–40 soft rays; swim bladder absent; branchiostegal rays 8–11; sucking disc on head (developed from a transformed spinous dorsal fin, the spines of which are split to form 10–28 transverse movable lamina inside a fleshy margin). The remora presents the disc against other fish and creates a partial vacuum by operating the movable disc ridges like the slats in a Venetian blind, thereby causing the sucking action which permits it to obtain rides on larger animals. Remoras are found on sharks, bony fishes, sea turtles, and marine mammals; some species show considerable host specificity. A fully formed disc is present in specimens as small as 27 mm, while the beginnings of the disc are apparent in specimens as small as about 10 mm in length (Gudger, 1926). Maximum length about 1.0 m, attained in *Echeneis naucrates.* The smallest species is 17 cm.

This family is given ordinal status by several authors (e.g., Berg, 1940; McAllister, 1968; Gosline, 1971). Although various authors have allied it with a number of diverse groups, it does seem to be most closely related to *Rachycentron.*

Steyskal (1980) notes that the grammatically correct spelling is as given above. However, Robins et al. (1980) favor the spelling Echeneidae (which is much easier to pronounce).

Seven genera, *Echeneis, Phtheirichthys, Remora, Remorina, Remilegia, Remoropsis,* and *Rhombochirus,* with eight widespread species (Strasburg, 1964). Robins et al. (1980) favor recognizing only the first four genera for the eight species (placing four of the species in *Remora*).

Family CARANGIDAE—jacks and pompanos.   Marine (rarely brackish), Atlantic, Indian, and Pacific.

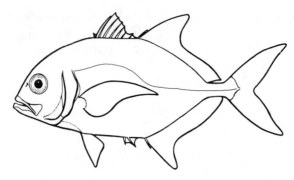

Body generally compressed (but ranging from very deep to fusiform); only small cycloid scales in most species, ctenoid in a few (scales on the lateral line are modified into spiny scutes in many species), naked areas variously developed; up to nine detached finlets sometimes present behind dorsal and anal fins (counts for these rays are included in following ray counts); two dorsal fins in large juveniles and adults, the first with 3–9 spines (which in a few species are very short and lack a continuous membrane) and the second with one spine and usually 18–37 soft rays; usually three anal spines with the first two detached from the rest of the anal fin and usually 15–31 soft rays; caudal fin widely forked; caudal peduncle slender; one species lacks pelvic fins (*Parona signata* from off southern Brazil to Argentina); vertebrae 24–27 (usually 24).

Carangids are extremely variable in body shape, ranging from the shallow-bodied *Decapterus* and *Elagatis* to the extremely thin and deep-bodied *Selene*. The family contains some very important food species.

Important systematic and osteological studies on species of this family include Smith-Vaniz and Staiger (1973) and Suzuki (1962). In a study of cranial nerve patterns, Freihofer (1978) states that carangids, rachycentrids, echeneidids, and coryphaenids have a shared, derived specialization in features of the two prenasal canals, apparently a rare specialization in teleosts. This provides further evidence that these groups are interrelated.

About 25 genera (e.g., *Alectis, Carangoides, Caranx, Chloroscombrus, Chorinemus, Citula, Decapterus, Elagatis, Gnathanodon, Megalaspis, Naucrates, Oligoplites, Scomberoides, Selar, Selene, Seriola, Trachinotus, Trachurus, Uraspis,* and *Vomer*) with about 140 species (pers. comm. W. F. Smith-Vaniz, 1982).

Family NEMATISTIIDAE—roosterfish.   Marine; tropical eastern Pacific.

Body compressed; small cycloid scales, about 120–130 in irregular series along lateral line (no scutes along lateral line); first dorsal with seven very elongate spines (which normally rest in a groove), second with one spine and 25–28 soft rays; anal fin with three spines (none detached from rest of fin) and about 15–17 soft rays; unique otophysic connection, swim bladder enters skull through large foramina in basioccipital and contacts inner ear (presumably increasing hearing sensitivity); 24 vertebrae (10 abdominal and 14 caudal).

Nematistius variously has been regarded as a member of Carangidae or placed in a separate family. Rosenblatt and Bell (1976) give reasons for accepting placement in a monotypic family. These authors also argue against attempts to derive carangids from beryciforms and believe that similarities with the Cretaceous *Aipichthys* are due to convergent evolution.

One species, *Nematistius pectoralis*, which is a popular gamefish ranging from southernmost California to Peru.

Family CORYPHAENIDAE—dolphins.   Marine; Atlantic, Indian, and Pacific.

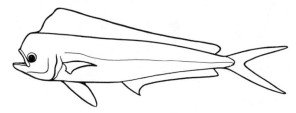

Dorsal fin originating on head, with 48–65 rays; no spines in dorsal and anal fins; caudal fin deeply forked; forehead prominent (steep and high) in adult males of the largest of the two species; color in life exceedingly beautiful; vertebrae 30–34. Maximum length 1.5 m, attained in *Coryphaena hippurus*.

One genus, *Coryphaena*, with two species.

Family APOLECTIDAE (Formionidae).   Marine; Indo-West Pacific (southern Africa and Gulf of Oman to southern Japan and Queensland).

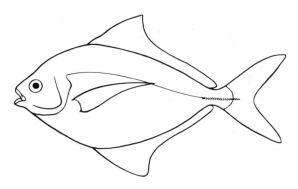

Pelvic fins lost in individuals over 9 cm; dorsal fin with 2–6 rudimentary spines and 41–46 soft rays; anal fin with two rudimentary spines and 35–40 soft rays; lateral line scales usually 108–112; a few enlarged scutes at end of lateral line in form of keel; vertebrae 24 (10 + 14).

One species, *Apolectus (= Formio) niger* (Witzell, 1977). Some authors place this species in the Carangidae.

Family MENIDAE—moonfish.   Marine; Indo-West Pacific.

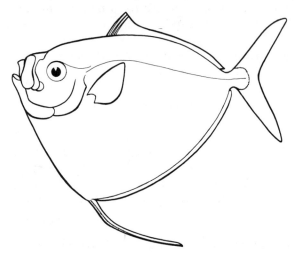

Body disclike, with sharp breast; dorsal contour nearly horizontal; dorsal fin with 43–45 soft rays, no spines; anal fin with 30–33 soft rays, no spines; first pelvic ray in adult prolonged.

One species, *Mene maculata (= anno-carolina)*.

Family LEIOGNATHIDAE—ponyfishes, slimys, or slipmouths.   Marine and brackish water; Indo-West Pacific.

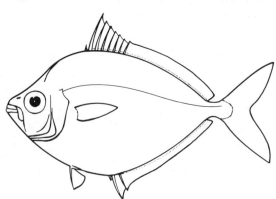

Body greatly compressed and slimy, with small scales; head naked, upper surface with bony ridges; gill membranes united with isthmus; mouth small and highly protrusible; no pseudobranchiae; single dorsal fin, the anterior portion usually with eight or nine spines that are more or less elevated; anal fin with three spines; both dorsal and anal fins fold into a basal scaly sheath. The dorsal and anal fin spines have a locking mechanism which is described by Seigel (1982).

Leiognathus klunzingeri, a former Red Sea endemic, is one of the 24 known species of fishes which, since the Suez Canal was opened in 1869, have passed from the tropical Red Sea, through the highly saline Great Bitter Lake, to the subtropical Mediterranean Sea; it is common in parts of the eastern Mediterranean and is the only leiognathid known to have dispersed through the Suez (Ben-Tuvia, 1966).

Berg (1940) and Norman (1957) lumped the family Gerreidae with this one.

Three genera, *Gazza*, *Leiognathus* (= *Equula*), and *Secutor*, with about 21 species.

Family BRAMIDAE—pomfrets.   Marine; oceanic, Atlantic, Indian, and Pacific.

Single dorsal fin (extending length of body in some) with unbranched anterior spines. *Eumegistus* is thought to be the most primitive genus. Maximum length 85 cm, attained in *Taractichthys longipinnis*.

Six genera with 18 species (Mead, 1972).

SUBFAMILY BRAMINAE.   Dorsal and anal fins of adults with scales and not wholly depressable; pelvic fins thoracic.

Four genera, *Brama*, *Eumegistus*, *Taractes*, and *Taractichthys*, with about 13 species.

SUBFAMILY PTERACLINAE.   Dorsal and anal fins high, scaleless, and completely depressable; pelvic fins often jugular or nearly so.

Two genera, *Pteraclis* and *Pterycombus*, with about five species.

Family CARISTIIDAE—manefishes.   Marine; oceanic.

Body deep; dorsal fin high and with long base (origin on head); pelvic fins elongate, in advance or behind pectoral fin base, with one spine and five soft rays; 15 branched caudal rays; seven branchiostegal rays.

Berg (1940) Norman (1957), McAllister (1968), and Gosline (1971) placed this poorly known family in the Beryciformes. Placement in Per-

ciformes by Greenwood et al. (1966) and Scott et al. (1970) is accepted
here.

One genus, *Caristius* (= *Elephenor, Platyberyx*), with about four species.

Family ARRIPIDAE—Australian salmon. Marine; South Pacific (southern Australia
and New Zealand region).

Three anal spines; gill membranes free from isthmus; anal fin much
shorter than the soft dorsal.

One genus, *Arripis*, with two species.

Family EMMELICHTHYIDAE—rovers. Marine; primarily tropical to warm temperate regions of Indo-Pacific, southern Pacific, eastern Atlantic, and Caribbean Sea.

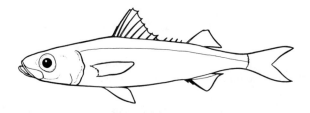

Jaws toothless or nearly so, very protractile; maxilla expanded distally,
scaled, and not covered by preorbital bone when mouth closed; supramaxilla well-developed; rostral cartilage large; dorsal fin continuous but
with slight notch (*Plagiogeneion*), divided to base (*Erythrocles*), or with an
apparent gap with intervening isolated short spines visible or not (*Emmelichthys*, as shown in figure); dorsal fin with 11–14 spines and 9–12 soft
rays; anal fin with three spines and 9–11 soft rays; caudal fin forked with
the two lobes folding in scissorlike fashion; seven branchiostegal rays; 24
vertebrae (10 + 14). Maximum length up to 50 cm. Adults are usually
near the bottom in depths of 100–400 m.

Several genera formally recognized in this family are now placed in
the families Caesionidae, Inermiidae, and Centracanthidae (Heemstra
and Randall, 1977; Johnson, 1980). The common name bonnetmouths,
formerly applied to this family, is now more appropriately applied to the
Inermiidae (Robins et al., 1980).

Three genera, *Plagiogeneion* (two), *Erythrocles* (four), and *Emmelichthys*
(four), with 10 species (Heemstra and Randall, 1977).

Family LUTJANIDAE—snappers. Marine (rarely in estuaries); Atlantic, Indian, and
Pacific.

Dorsal fin continuous or with a shallow notch, with 10–12 spines and 10–17 soft rays; anal fin with three spines and 7–11 soft rays; pelvic fins inserted just behind pectoral base; mouth terminal, moderate to large; most with enlarged canine teeth on jaws, small teeth on palatines and usually on vomer; maxilla slips beneath preorbital when mouth closed; seven branchiostegal rays; 24 vertebrae (10 + 14).

Snappers are important food fishes but are sometimes responsible for ciguatera, the tropical fish poisoning disease. They generally occur near the bottom in tropical and subtropical seas to depths of about 450 m. Maximum length about 1.0 m.

Seventeen genera (which are recognized in four subfamilies by Johnson, 1980) (e.g., *Aphareus, Etelis, Pristipomoides, Apsilus, Paracaesio, Symphorus, Hoplopagrus, Lutjanus, Ocyurus,* and *Rhomboplites*) with about 185 species (the number of species estimated for *Lutjanus,* over 140, is uncertain and may be too high).

Family CAESIONIDAE (Caesiodidae)—fusiliers.   Marine; Indo-West Pacific.

Dorsal fin continuous with 9–15 slender spines and 9–21 soft rays; anal fin with three spines and 9–13 soft rays; mouth upturned, small; jaw teeth small (absent in two species); caudal fin deeply forked; 24 vertebrae.

This family is recognized following Johnson (1975, 1980), who considers its closest relatives to be the lutjanids. They are planktivorous and have a highly protrusible jaw. Maximum length about 60 cm.

Four genera, *Caesio, Pterocaesio, Gymnocaesio,* and *Dipterygonotus,* with very approximately 30 species.

Family LOBOTIDAE—tripletails.   Marine, brackish, and freshwater; most warm seas.

Palatine and vomer toothless; caudal fin rounded; profile similar to centrarchids; rounded lobes on anal and second dorsal fins giving fish the appearance of having three tails.

The very young can camouflage themselves by turning sideways and floating like leaves. Maximum length about 1.0 m, attained in *Lobotes surinamensis.*

Two genera, *Datnioides* (fresh- and brackish water from India to Borneo and New Guinea) and *Lobotes* (marine), with about four species. The two species of *Datnioides* were at one time considered to be teraponids, and Vari (1978) agrees that they are more closely related to *Lobotes.*

Family GERREIDAE—mojarras.   Marine (occasionally brackish and rarely in fresh water); most warm seas.

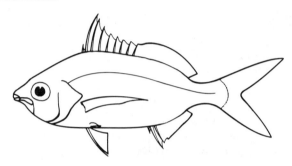

Mouth highly protrusible; head scaly, upper surface smooth; scaly sheath along bases of dorsal and anal fins; gill membranes free from isthmus; tail deeply forked.

The former family name, Gerridae, is preoccupied by the water striders of the insect order Hemiptera. Emendation of the orthography to Gerreidae to eliminate homonymy follows Böhlke and Chaplin (1968). Berg (1940) and Norman (1957) included this family with the Leiognathidae. Maximum length 35 cm.

Seven genera, *Diapterus, Eucinostomus, Gerres, Parequula, Pentaprion* (with five or six spines in anal fin), *Ulaema,* and *Xystaema,* with about 40 species.

Family HAEMULIDAE (Pomadasyidae)—grunts.   Marine (some in brackish water, rarely in fresh water); Atlantic, Indian, and Pacific.

Dorsal fin continuous, with 9–14 spines and 11–26 soft rays; anal fin with three spines and 6–18 soft rays; mouth small; teeth on jaws usually cardiform, generally absent on vomer; enlarged chin pores usually present; seven branchiostegal rays; 26 or 27 vertebrae (10 or 11 + 16). Maximum length about 60 cm.

Johnson (1980) recognizes two subfamilies: the Haemulinae, primarily of the New World with a short dorsal fin of 13–16 soft rays, and the Plectorhynchinae, of the Indo-West Pacific and eastern Atlantic with a long dorsal fin of 17–26 soft rays (comprises the last three genera listed below). Fishes in the last subfamily often have thick fleshy lips as adults (these are called the sweetlips) and are brightly colored (e.g., see Smith, 1962).

Seventeen genera [e.g., *Anisotremus, Conodon, Haemulon, Orthopristis, Pomadasys, Xenichthys, Xenistius, Plectorhynchus (= Gaterin), Diagramma,* and *Parapristipoma*] with about 175 species.

Family INERMIIDAE—bonnetmouths.   Marine; western tropical Atlantic.

Dorsal fins separated by a deep notch, first fin with 10 (first genus below) or 17 spines (second genus) and second fin with two spines and 10 soft rays or 9 soft rays, respectively; anal fin with three spines and 8 or 10 soft rays; teeth absent on jaws, vomer, and palatine; two enlarged chin pores; caudal fin deeply forked; 26 vertebrae (12 or 13 abdominal). These fishes are planktivorous and have a highly protrusible upper jaw. Maximum length about 25 cm. This family is recognized following Johnson (1980) and is probably a haemulid derivative.

Two monotypic genera, *Emmelichthops* (bonnetmouth) and *Inermia* (boga).

Family SPARIDAE—porgies.   Marine (very rarely brackish and fresh water); Atlantic, Indian, and Pacific.

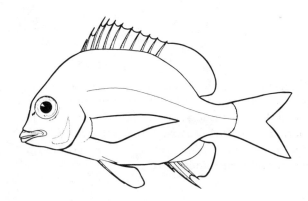

Dorsal fin continuous, usually with 10–13 spines and 10–15 soft rays; anal fin with three spines and 8–14 soft rays; maxilla covered by a sheath when mouth closed; six branchiostegal rays; 24 vertebrae (10 + 14). Maximum length about 1.2 m.

The continental western Atlantic sheepshead, *Archosargus probatocephalus*, which occasionally occurs in brackish water, is known to rarely enter fresh water in Florida (Lee et al., 1980). Four species of sparids occur in brackish water in Australia and one species of *Acanthopagrus*, which enters fresh water, is known to spawn in brackish water (Lake, 1971).

Twenty-nine genera (e.g., *Archosargus, Boops, Calamus, Chrysophrys, Dentex, Diplodus, Pagellus, Pagrus, Pimelepterus, Rhabdosargus, Sparus,* and *Stenotomus*) with about 100 species.

Family CENTRACANTHIDAE (Maenidae).   Marine; eastern Atlantic (including Mediterranean) and off South Africa.

Dorsal fin continuous, with 11–13 spines and 9–11 soft rays; anal fin with three spines and 9–10 soft rays. The species of this group of planktivorous fishes have a highly protrusible upper jaw and appear to be closely related to the sparids.

Two genera, *Centracanthus* (one) and *Spicara* (= *Coleosmaris, Merolepis, Pterosmaris,* and *Smaris*—six) with seven species (Heemstra and Randall, 1977).

Family LETHRINIDAE—scavengers or emperors.   Marine coastal; west Africa and Indo-West Pacific.

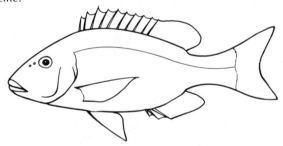

Dorsal fin continuous, with 10 spines and 8–10 soft rays; anal fin with three spines and 8–10 soft rays; no accessory subpelvic keel; reduced subocular shelf. Lethrinids are closely related to sparids (Johnson, 1980).

Four genera, *Lethrinus, Monotaxis, Gnathodentex,* and *Gymnocranius,* with about 25 species. The last three genera are placed here, rather than in the formerly recognized family Pentapodidae, following Johnson (1975,

1980). However, Lee (1982) places the three in their own family, Mono-taxidae, although he recognizes their affinity with Lethrinidae and Nem-ipteridae. They are differentiated from *Lethrinus*, which has a scaleless cheek, in having at least three transverse scale rows on each cheek.

Family NEMIPTERIDAE—threadfin breams.   Marine; Indo-West Pacific.

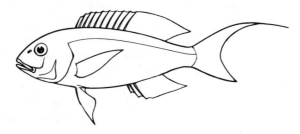

Dorsal fin continuous, with 10 spines and nine or 10 soft rays; anal fin with three spines and seven or eight soft rays; caudal fin in some with filament off upper lobe; subocular shelf and accessory subpelvic keel well developed; intercalar (-opisthotic of Johnson, 1980) present (lost or fused in the three related families). Nemipterids appear to be most closely related to lethrinids and are recognized in the superfamily Sparoidea with them and the sparids and centracanthids by Johnson (1980).

Three genera, *Nemipterus*, *Scolopsis*, and *Pentapodus*, with about 35 spe-cies. The last genus, the type for the formerly recognized family Penta-podidae, is placed here following Johnson (1975, 1980).

Family SCIAENIDAE—drums (croakers).   Marine, brackish, and freshwater (partic-ularly in South America); Atlantic, Indian, and Pacific.

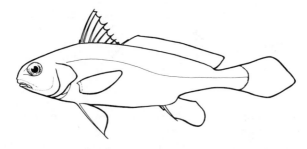

Dorsal fin long, with a deep notch separating spinous from soft portion (rarely separate), first with 6–13 spines and second with one spine and usually 20–35 soft rays; anal fin with one or two spines (both are usually weak but the second may be large) and 6–13 soft rays; lateral line scales extending to the end of caudal fin; caudal fin slightly emarginate to rounded; upper bony edge of opercle forked, bony flap present above gill opening; single barbel or a patch of small barbels on chin of some species; head with large cavernous canals (part of the lateral line system); conspicuous pores on snout and lower jaw; vomer and palatine without teeth; swim bladder (rarely rudimentary in adults) usually with many branches; otoliths (sagitta at least) exceptionally large; vertebrae 24–29.

Sciaenids occur in shallow water, usually near continental regions, and are absent from islands in the mid-Indian and Pacific oceans. They can produce sound by using the swim bladder as a resonating chamber. Some are important food fishes. Chao (1978) discusses the phylogenetic relationships of the western Atlantic sciaenids and gives a list of the four genera and 22 nominal species of New World freshwater species.

About 50 genera [e.g., *Aplodinotus* (freshwater, North America), *Bairdiella*, *Cynoscion*, *Equetus*, *Genyonemus*, *Larimus*, *Menticirrhus*, *Micropogon*, *Micropogonias*, *Ophioscion*, *Otolithes*, *Sciaena*, *Seriphus*, *Stellifer*, and *Umbrina*] with about 210 species.

Family MULLIDAE—goatfishes. Marine (rarely brackish water); Atlantic, Indian, and Pacific.

Body elongate; two widely separated dorsal fins, the first with 6–8 spines; soft dorsal fin shorter than anal fin; anal fin with one or two small spines; two long chin barbels (used in detecting food); caudal fin forked; 23 or 24 vertebrae.

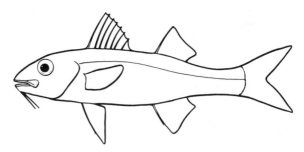

Goatfishes are important as a food fish. Many are brightly colored. Maximum length up to 60 cm.

Six genera, *Mulloidichthys*, *Mullus*, *Parupeneus*, *Pseudupeneus*, *Upeneichthys*, and *Upeneus*, with 55 species.

Family MONODACTYLIDAE—moonfishes (fingerfishes). Marine and brackish water (sometimes entering fresh water); west Africa and Indo-Pacific.

Body strongly compressed and deep (deeper than long in some); pelvic fins usually small or vestigial; dorsal fin single and with a long base, covered with scales and 5–8 short graduated spines; anal fin with three spines, long base; scales cycloid or ctenoid.

Moonfishes are occasionally sold as aquarium fishes. They are often of a silvery color.

Three genera, *Monodactylus*, *Psettias*, and *Schuettea*, with about five species. Most authors place *Schuettea* (with two species in New South Wales and Western Australia) in the Monodactylidae but Tominaga (1968) recommends placement in a family of its own. It differs from other monodactylids in a few characters (e.g., normally developed pelvic fins, cycloid scales, teeth absent from endopterygoid and ectopterygoid) but it is provisionally retained in the family as a conservative measure.

Family PEMPHERIDIDAE—sweepers. Marine and brackish water; western Atlantic, Indian, and Pacific.

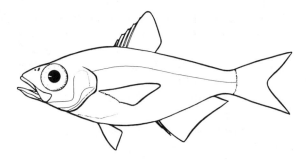

Body compressed and deep; maxillae not reaching beyond center of eye; preorbital smooth; eye large, without adipose lid; one short dorsal fin, originating before middle of body, with 4–7 graduated spines and 7–12 soft rays; anal fin with two (very rarely) or three spines and 17–45 soft rays; lateral line scales usually 40–82; tubes of lateral line usually short and wide; gill rakers long and usually 25–31; luminescent organs in a few species; pyloric caeca 9 or 10; swim bladder absent in one species *(Pempheris poeyi);* 25 vertebrae (10 + 15).

Tominaga (1968) presents a detailed description of their morphology and gives reasons for removing *Leptobrama* from this family. Maximum length about 30 cm.

Two genera: *Parapriacanthus* with about five species and *Pempheris* (= *Priacanthopsis)* with about 20 species.

Family LEPTOBRAMIDAE—beachsalmon. Marine and brackish water (occasionally entering rivers); coasts of southern New Guinea, Queensland, and Western Australia.

Body compressed and deep; maxillae reaching far behind eye; preorbital serrate; eye relatively small, with adipose lid; one short dorsal fin behind middle of body (above anal fin), with four spines and 16–18 soft rays; anal fin with three spines and 26–30 soft rays; lateral line scales about 75–77; tubes in lateral line long and narrow; gill rakers short, usually 10.

This family was included with the Pempheridae by such workers as Norman (1957) and Greenwood et al. (1966), but Tominaga (1965, 1968) has shown it to have no particular affinity with the pempherids. Maximum length about 35 cm.

One species: *Leptobrama muelleri.*

Family BATHYCLUPEIDAE. Marine oceanic; Indian, western Pacific, and Gulf of Mexico.

One dorsal fin in posterior half of body, without spines; anal fin long, with one spine; dorsal and anal fins covered with scales; premaxillae and maxillae bordering mouth; usually 31 vertebrae (10 + 21).

Berg (1940) placed this family in its own order, Bathyclupeiformes, between the Clupeiformes and Galaxiiformes.

One genus, *Bathyclupea,* with about four species.

Family TOXOTIDAE—archerfishes. Marine coastal, brackish, and freshwater; from India to Philippines and Australia and Polynesia (see map on p. 421).

Body deep and compressed, greatest body depth 1.8–2.5 in standard length; eye large; dorsal fin with 4–6 strong spines and 11–14 soft rays; anal fin with three spines and 15–18 soft rays; length of soft dorsal much shorter than soft portion of anal; mouth large, terminal (lower jaw protruding), and highly protractile; lateral line scales about 25–47; seven branchiostegal rays; 24 vertebrae (10 + 14).

Archerfishes are capable of forcefully ejecting squirts of water from their mouths and downing insects. The widespread *Toxotes jaculator,* extending from India to New Hebrides, is normally found in brackish water near mangroves while the others frequently occur in fresh water (often well inland). Maximum length 40 cm, attained in *T. chatareus;* usually under 16 cm.

One genus, *Toxotes,* with six species (Allen, 1978).

Family CORACINIDAE—galjoen fishes. Marine coastal and brackish water; South Africa and Madagascar.

Body relatively deep; mouth small; dorsal fin with 10 spines and usually 18–23 soft rays; anal fin with three spines and usually 13 or 14 soft rays; gill membranes fused with isthmus; some teeth incisiform.

One genus, *Coracinus (=Dichistius),* with about three species.

Family KYPHOSIDAE—sea chubs. Marine; Atlantic, Indian, and Pacific.

The following three subfamilies are often recognized as separate families or only the first two under Kyphosidae. Monophyly for the group has not been established. Members of the first two subfamilies are plant-feeding fishes, primarily consuming algae, while the scorpidines are primarily carnivorous. All are usually found near shore. Three spines in the anal fin.

Seventeen genera with about 45 species.

SUBFAMILY GIRELLINAE (NIBBLERS). Some incisiform teeth present; maxilla concealed beneath suborbital bone. Pacific (primarily Philippines to Australia but extending to California where the opaleye is a common species).

Six genera (e.g., *Girella, Graus,* and *Melambaphes*) with about 20 species.

SUBFAMILY KYPHOSINAE (CYPHOSINAE) (RUDDERFISHES). Some incisiform teeth; maxilla exposed. Atlantic, Indian, and Pacific.

Three genera, *Hermosilla, Kyphosus,* and *Sectator,* with 10 species.

SUBFAMILY SCORPIDINAE (HALFMOONS). No incisiform teeth; pelvics well behind pectorals. Indo-Pacific (to California).

Eight genera, *Atypichthys, Medialuna, Neatypus, Neoscorpis, Parascorpis,*

Scorpis, Microcanthus, and *Vinculum,* with about 15 species. The last two genera were at one time thought to be chaetodontids (Steene, 1978; Burgess, 1978).

Family EPHIPPIDIDAE—spadefishes.   Marine; Atlantic, Indian, and Pacific.

Three anal fin spines; gill membranes united to isthmus; body deep and laterally compressed; mouth small; no teeth on vomer or palatines; spinous portion of dorsal fin distinct from soft-rayed portion (except in *Platax*). Young may have black bands extending around body which are lost with growth. Five genera with about 17 species.

SUBFAMILY DREPANEINAE.   Mouth markedly protractile; pectoral fins longer than head, falcate; maxilla distally exposed; subocular shelf absent. Indo-West Pacific and West Africa.
   One genus, *Drepane,* with perhaps two species.

SUBFAMILY EPHIPPIDINAE (CHAETODIPTERINAE).   Mouth weakly protractile; pectoral fins shorter than head, rounded; maxilla distally hidden; subocular shelf present (may be weak). Atlantic, Indian, and Pacific.

   Three genera, *Chaetodipterus, Ephippus,* and *Tripterodon,* with about 12 species.

SUBFAMILY PLATACINAE.   Spinous portion of dorsal fin continuous with soft portion; dorsal and anal fins in young very elongate.

One genus, *Platax*, with about three species.

Family SCATOPHAGIDAE—scats.   Marine and brackish water; Indo-Pacific (see map on p. 421).

Body deep and compressed, resembling that of butterflyfishes; pelvic axillary process present; dorsal fin deeply notched, first dorsal spine procumbent; four anal fin spines; caudal fin with 16 branched rays; mouth not protractile; 23 vertebrae (11 + 12). Maximum length about 35 cm.

Two genera, *Selenotoca* and *Scatophagus*, with about four species.

Family RHINOPRENIDAE—threadfin scat.   Marine and brackish water; Gulf of Papua, New Guinea.

Body deep and compressed, quadrangular in outline; mouth small and inferior; second dorsal spine, fourth pectoral ray, and first pelvic ray greatly prolonged into free filaments which reach tail base or beyond; anal fin with three spines and 16 or 17 soft rays. Maximum length about 15 cm.

One species: *Rhinoprenes pentanemus* (Munro, 1964, 1967).

Family CHAETODONTIDAE—butterflyfishes.   Marine; tropical to temperate Atlantic, Indian, and Pacific (primarily tropical Indo-West Pacific).

Body strongly compressed; no spine at angle of preopercle (small serrations may be present on the preopercle); well-developed pelvic axillary process; head region in larval (tholichthys) stage covered with bony plates; dorsal fin continuous or with slight notch, with 6–16 spines and 15–30 soft rays, no procumbent spine; anal fin with 3–5 (usually 3) spines and 14–23 soft rays; caudal fin with 15 branched rays (17 principal), margin rounded to emarginate; scales extending onto the dorsal and anal fins; mouth small, terminal, protractile (the two species of the Indo-Pacific *Forcipiger* have a very elongate snout); gut coiled many times (various patterns and their taxonomic implications are given in Shen and Lam, 1979); swim bladder with two anteriorly directed processes; 24 vertebrae (11 + 13).

Most species of butterflyfish have brightly colored patterns. Also, most have a dark band running across the eye, and many have an "eyespot" on the dorsal or posterior part of the body; both patterns may serve to confuse predators. Butterflyfishes generally occur near coral reefs and at depths less than 20 m but a few go to at least 200 m. A few species occur in brackish water. Most species are in the Australian to Taiwan region. Only thirteen species occur in the Atlantic and four in the eastern Pacific. Butterflyfishes are known to feed on coral polyps (but are not known to break off coral) along with other invertebrates.

G. Cuvier in 1831 included chaetodontids and all other fishes with the proximal portion of the dorsal and anal fins covered with scales in the family Squamipennes. Various authors subsequently employed this category, usually at the subordinal level following Jordan and Evermann's 1898 work, with varying membership. The families given here from Toxotidae to Pentacerotidae would seem to have some relationship with one another and be part of the Squamipennes group. (If the families of the present superfamily Percoidea were to be recognized in many superfamilies, in a parallel manner to the groups discussed by Johnson, 1980, then this group might well be classified as the superfamily Chaetodontoidea.) Burgess (1978) reviews the history of various proposals on the relationships of chaetodontids.

Butterflyfishes and angelfishes were, until the mid-1970s, combined in the same family; however, Burgess (1974) gives reasons for recognizing them in separate families. He notes many morphological differences, including in osteology, between the two groups.

Ten genera (e.g., *Chaetodon*, *Chelmon*, *Coradion*, *Forcipiger*, *Hemitaurichthys*, and *Heniochus*) with 114 species (Burgess, 1978; Steene, 1978;

Allen, 1980b). Some 89 species are placed in the 13 subgenera of the genus *Chaetodon*.

Family POMACANTHIDAE—angelfishes.   Marine; tropical Atlantic, Indian, and Pacific (primarily in western Pacific).

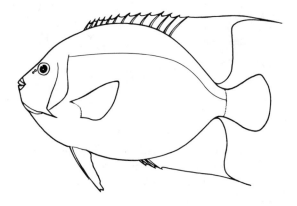

Body strongly compressed; strong spine at angle of preopercle; no well-developed pelvic axillary process; larval stage lacking bony plates; dorsal fin continuous, with 9–15 spines and 15–37 soft rays, no procumbent spine; anal fin with three spines and 14–25 soft rays; dorsal and anal fins with elongate extension on hind margin in many species (shown in figure); caudal fin with 15 branched rays, margin rounded to lunate (strongly lunate, often with produced lobes, in some species of *Genicanthus*); swim bladder lacking anteriorly directed processes; 24 vertebrae (10 + 14).

Angelfishes have striking color patterns and in many species the pattern in juveniles differs markedly from that of adults. They generally occur near coral reefs at depths of less than 20 m (very seldom below 50 m). Only nine species occur in the Atlantic and four in the eastern Pacific.

Seven genera, *Apolemichthys, Centropyge, Chaetodontoplus, Genicanthus, Holacanthus, Pomacanthus,* and *Pygoplites,* with 74 species (Allen, 1980b). Over half the species are placed in *Centropyge* and *Pomacanthus.*

Family ENOPLOSIDAE—oldwife.   Marine; southern half of Australia.

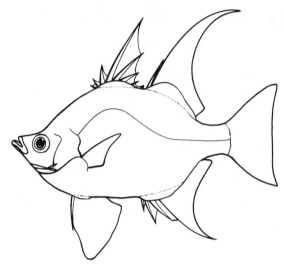

Pelvic fins unusually large, each with a strong spine; external bones of head not rough; supramaxilla present; two sharp spines on lower angle of preoperculum. The fish has black vertical bands on a silvery body.

One species, *Enoplosus armatus*.

Family PENTACEROTIDAE (Histiopteridae)—armorheads.   Marine; Indo-Pacific and southwestern Atlantic.

Body strongly compressed, ranging from very deep in *Pentaceros* (shown in figure) to only moderately deep in adult *Pentaceropsis;* head encased in exposed, rough, striated bone; no supramaxilla; single dorsal fin with 4–14 strong spines and 9–29 soft rays; anal fin with 2–5 strong spines and 7–13 soft rays; pelvic fins large, with one long, strong spine and five soft rays; scales small. These fishes are commonly called boarfishes in Australia.

Five genera in two subfamilies: *Histiopterus*, *Zanclistius*, and *Paristiopterus* in Histiopterinae (with a dorsal fin with fewer than nine spines and with 17–29 soft rays) and *Pentaceropsis* and *Pentaceros* (= *Pseudopentaceros* and *Quinquarias*) in Pentacerotinae (with a dorsal fin with 10–14 spines and 8–15 soft rays), with a total of about 11 species (Smith, 1964b).

Family NANDIDAE—leaffishes.   Fresh water (occasionally brackish water); northeast South America, West Africa, and Southern Asia (see map on p. 422).

Head usually large; mouth usually large and highly protrusible; dorsal fin continuous; caudal fin rounded; lateral line incomplete or absent; pelvic fin without scaly axillary process. Many are vicious predators. At rest, most look deceptively like drifting leaves.

As with many families, this one has been split in various ways by past authors. Recently Barlow et al. (1968), in a detailed and comprehensive study, erected a new family for *Badis badis* and concluded that it descended from a proto-anabantoid stock. Gosline (1971) recognized three families, Badidae, Nandidae, and Pristolepidae, and placed them at the start of his Percoidei. He believed them to be related to the Anabantoidei and perhaps even deserving of placement with them. Liem (1970), in a detailed myological and osteological study with a functional analysis of the feeding apparatus, argues convincingly that nandids (Nandinae here) and anabantoids show no phylogenetic affinity and considers nandids to resemble relatively advanced Percoidei. He also places *Badis* and *Pristolepis* in separate families and does not believe that they bear a close affinity to his Nandidae. Here, although acknowledging the diversity of the group and the fact that *Badis* may have some anabantoid affinity, the Nandinae, *Badis*, and *Pristolepis* are tentatively placed in the same family. Freihofer (1978) provides a detailed study of the cranial nerves of *Polycentrus* (and discusses some implications of nerve patterns to fish classification).

Maximum length about 21 cm, attained in *Pristolepis fasciata*.

Seven genera with about 10 species.

SUBFAMILY NANDINAE

TRIBE NANDINI.   Tropical west Africa, India, and southeast Asia (to Borneo).

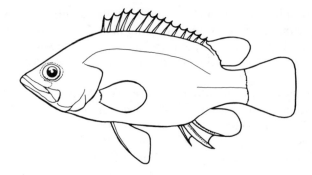

Anal fin with three spines in *Nandus* spp., four in *Afronandus sheljuzhkoi*, and 9–12 in *Polycentropsis abbreviata*. Maximum length about 20 cm, usually much smaller.

Three genera, *Afronandus* (springs in Ivory Coast), *Nandus* (India to Borneo), and *Polycentropsis* (West Africa), with four species.

TRIBE POLYCENTRINI.   Northeast South America. Dorsal fin with 16–18 spines, plus a soft-rayed portion; anal fin with 12 or 13 spines, plus a soft-rayed portion. Maximum length about 10 cm.

Two species: *Monocirrhus polyacanthus* (Guiana and the Amazon lowlands) and *Polycentrus schomburgkii* (Trinidad to Guiana).

SUBFAMILY PRISTOLEPIDINAE.   Small area of peninsular India and Sri Lanka, southeast Asia, and parts of Malay Archipelago (e.g., Sumatra, Java, and Borneo).

Mouth relatively small and only slightly protrusible; suborbital shelf present. The most widespread species, *Pristolepis fasciata*, has dorsal fin with 13–16 spines and 14–16 soft rays; anal fin with three spines and eight or nine soft rays; lateral line scales 26–28.

One genus, *Pristolepis*, with about three species.

SUBFAMILY BADINAE.   India and Burma.

Mouth relatively small and only slightly protrusible; no suborbital shelf; dorsal fin with six or seven spines and 6–10 soft rays; anal fin with three spines and 6–8 soft rays; lateral line scales 26–33.

This is a colorful fish, which can change its color quite rapidly. Its behavior has been studied in considerable detail by Dr. G. W. Barlow and others. Maximum length about 8 cm.

One species: *Badis badis*.

Family OPLEGNATHIDAE—knifejaws.   Marine; Japan, southern half of Australia including Tasmania, Galapagos and Peru, and South Africa.

Teeth in adult united to form a parrotlike beak (as in Scaridae, capable of crushing barnacle shells and sea urchins); spinous dorsal fin low in adults, basically as high as soft dorsal and continuous with it in juveniles; dorsal fin with 11 or 12 spines and 11–22 soft rays; anal fin with three spines and 11–16 soft rays; scales very small (unlike in scarids where they are large). Maximum length about 0.9 m. There is an old literature record of one specimen being obtained in Hawaii; no additional specimens have been captured (Tinker, 1978).

One genus, *Oplegnathus* (= *Hoplegnathus, Ostorhinchus*) with about six species.

Family CICHLIDAE—cichlids. Fresh- and brackish water; Central and South America (one species extending north to Texas), West Indies, Africa, Madagascar, Syria, and coastal India (see map on p. 422).

Single nostril on each side; lateral line interrupted, generally 20–50 scales in lateral lines but number may exceed 100; generally 7–25 spines and 5–30 soft rays in dorsal fin and 3 (in the majority of species)–15 spines and 4–15 soft rays in the anal fin. (*Etroplus* has about 12–15 anal spines, but most other species exceeding three spines have 4–9; a few cichlids may have more than 30 soft rays in the anal fin.) No subocular shelf. Maximum length about 80 cm, attained in *Boulengerochromis microlepis* of Lake Tanganyika.

As in many families, there is much variability in body shape between some species. Most cichlids have a moderately deep and compressed body similar to *Cichlasoma* shown in figure. However, the body can be disc-shaped and have extremely high, saillike fins, as in *Pterophyllum* (angel-fishes), or low fins, as in *Symphysodon* (discus fishes); it can also be elongate, as in *Crenicichla* (pike cichlids).

Cichlids form an important group of relatively large and often colorful aquarium fishes (e.g., Axelrod, 1973; Goldstein, 1973). Many color patterns have been developed through selective breeding in some of the species for the aquarium trade (e.g., see Norton, 1982, for a discussion of the various morphs of angelfishes). It should be kept in mind that the common names for the species of *Pterophyllum*, the angelfishes, can be confused with the pomacanthids, which are also known as angelfishes; the first group is freshwater and the latter is marine and, where confusion could arise, they should be referred to as either the freshwater or the marine angelfishes.

Species of the family have highly organized breeding activities (Breder and Rosen, 1966; Fryer and Iles, 1972; Smith-Grayton and Keenleyside, 1978; Keenleyside, 1979). Three forms of parental care may be recognized: in mouthbrooders usually only the female carries the fertilized eggs in the mouth; both sexes may care for the eggs in substratebrooders; a few species combine the above two methods, eggs are laid and cared for on the substrate, but the newly hatched young are carried in the parents' mouth. Mouthbrooding or oral incubation is common and appears to have arisen independently in several groups of African cichlids but is known from only a relatively few species in Central and South America. In most species of the mouthbrooding subgenus *Sarotherodon* of *Tilapia* (see below for discussion of its taxonomic status), it is the female that carries the eggs, but one species is known to be a paternal mouthbrooder and one to be biparental. (This last species seems to be somewhat intermediate between mouthbrooders and the substratebrooders of the subgenus *Tilapia*—Rothbard, 1979.) It is the species of the subgenus *Sarotherodon* that are commonly used in pond culture. Female discus fish secrete a whitish milklike substance from the skin to "nurse" their young.

Cichlids have attracted much attention in evolutionary biology because of the existence of species flocks in Africa (e.g., Greenwood, 1974). A wealth of information on the biology, adaptive radiation, and speciation of African cichlids is provided by Fryer and Iles (1972). Endemic cichlids make up most of the fish fauna in the three African lakes which contain the most species of fish of any lake in the world. Lake Malawi has more than 200 cichlids (all but four endemic; total of 42 noncichlids), Lake Victoria has at least 170 (all but six endemic; total of 38 noncichlids), and Lake Tanganyika has 126 (all endemic; total of 67 noncichlids). These cichlids exhibit a vast diversity of feeding habits, including species specialized to eat the scales of other fishes (e.g., see Liem and Stewart, 1976). New species are still being described, and Axelrod (1973), in a book with hundreds of excellent color photos, estimates that there are about 250 species of cichlids in Malawi and 150 species in Tanganyika. About 76 species of *Cichlasoma* (one of which, *C. cyanoguttatum*, ranges into Texas) are known from Mexico and Central America (Miller, 1966); other species occur in South America.

Studies of functional morphology in cichlids include Barel et al. (1976) and Liem (1978, 1979). Osteological and phyletic studies include Greenwood (1974, 1980), and Liem (1981). Stiassny (1981), in a study of muscles and the pharyngeal jaw apparatus, provides evidence for the monophyly of the group. Goldstein (1973) reviews the family.

About 84 genera: for example, *Aequidens, Apistogramma, Astronotus, Cichlasoma, Crenicichla, Geophagus, Pterophyllum,* and *Symphysodon,* from Central and South America; *Haplochromis, Hemichromis, Pelmatochromis, Pseudocrenilabrus* (Trewavas, 1973a), and *Tilapia* (ranges to Syria) from Africa; and *Tristramella,* endemic to Syria; *Iranocichla,* endemic to southern Iran (Coad, 1982); and *Etroplus,* from India and Ceylon. About 680 species. The majority of species are known from Africa. This is the second largest family of perciform fish. Trewavas (1973b) recommended giving generic rank to two subgenera of *Tilapia.* The mouthbrooders, which include widely introduced species, would be in the genus *Sarotherodon,* while the substratebreeders would be retained in the genus *Tilapia.* While this proposal has merits and is adopted by many researchers, I agree with the recommendations of Robins et al. (1980) that it is preferable to recognize the two groups in the one genus, the more familiar *Tilapia.* Subsequently, Trewavas (1981) has recommended giving generic rank to those species in the subgenus *Sarotherodon* that practice a "lek" system in breeding; if accepted, the common *Tilapia mossambica* would be recognized in *Orechromis.*

Family EMBIOTOCIDAE—surfperches. Coastal marine (rarely in fresh water); North Pacific.

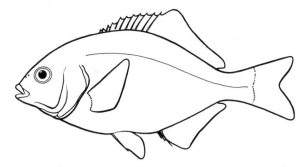

Dorsal fin continuous, with 6–11 spines (except 15–19 in *Hysterocarpus traski*) and 9–28 soft rays; anal fin with three spines and 15–35 soft rays; scales cycloid, generally 35–75 in lateral line; caudal fin forked. Viviparous (impregnation by the male is aided by the thickened forward end of the anal fin). Maximum length about 45 cm, attained in *Rhacochilus toxotes.* The family is reviewed by Tarp (1952).

Thirteen genera, *Amphistichus, Brachyistius, Cymatogaster, Ditrema, Embiotoca, Hyperprosopon, Hypsurus, Hysterocarpus* (with one species, *H. traski,* in streams in California), *Micrometrus, Neoditrema, Phanerodon, Rhacochilus,* and *Zalembius,* with about 23 species.

Family POMACENTRIDAE—damselfishes. Marine (rarely brackish); all tropical seas (primarily Indo-Pacific).

Nostril usually single on each side (*Chromis* and *Dascyllus* have species with double nostrils, a condition which may be difficult to see); body usually high (generally terete in the plankton-pickers) and compressed; mouth small; lateral line incomplete or interrupted; anal fin with two spines (very rarely three); subocular shelf present; palate toothless; single continuous dorsal fin with 9–14 spines (rarely more) and usually 11–18 soft rays (but base of spinous portion longer than soft). Maximum length about 35 cm.

Damselfishes present many problems to the taxonomist because of the many species complexes and color patterns which vary with individuals and between localities in a species. Considerable morphological diversity exists in many of the genera. The classification of this family is based primarily on the following studies: Allen, 1975a,b; Allen and Emery, 1973; Emery and Allen, 1980; Greenfield and Woods, 1980; Randall and Allen, 1977. Much information on the biology of damselfishes may be found in the *Bulletin of Marine Science,* Vol. 30, for March 1980.

Twenty-five genera with about 235 species.

SUBFAMILY AMPHIPRIONINAE (ANEMONEFISHES). Transverse scale rows 50–78 (most members of the following subfamilies have fewer than 40); all the opercles usually serrate (all the opercles not serrate in the other subfamilies); dorsal fin with 10 spines, rarely nine or 11 (most members of the following subfamilies have 12–14 spines) and usually 14–20 soft rays.

These fish live in coral reefs and show a commensal relationship with large sea anemones, living about and within them for protection (they probably have a factor in the skin inhibiting nematocyst discharge).

Two genera: *Premnas biaculeatus* (suborbital usually armed with two long spines; transverse scale rows 68–78; caudal fin rounded; body color usually reddish, ranging to dark brown, with three white transverse bands—found from northeastern Indian Ocean to the Philippines and northern Queensland) and *Amphiprion* (suborbital without spines, one or more serrations only; transverse scale rows 50–65; caudal fin usually truncate, or emarginate, or forked as in other pomacentrids; color variable, 0–3 white transverse bands—found in coastal tropical Indo-West Pacific waters, with about 26 species).

SUBFAMILY CHROMINAE.   Upper and lower edges of caudal peduncle usually with two or three short spiny procurrent caudal rays. *Dascyllus* appears to have a commensal relationship with coral.

Four genera, *Acanthochromis* (one), *Azurina* (two, tropical eastern Pacific, pers. comm. 1979 G. R. Allen), *Chromis* (51) and *Dascyllus* (nine), with about 63 species.

SUBFAMILY LEPIDOZYGINAE.   Body elongate; upper and lower edges of caudal peduncle without projecting spiny caudal rays; small papillalike structures on inner edge of posterior circumorbitals. Emery (1980) describes the osteology of the one species.

One species, *Lepidozygus tapeinosoma*, a plankton-picker found throughout much of the Indo-West Pacific.

SUBFAMILY POMACENTRINAE.   Body orbiculate to moderately elongate; upper and lower edges of caudal peduncle without projecting spiny caudal rays.

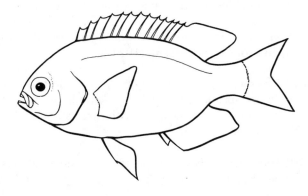

Eighteen genera, *Abudefduf* (sergeant-majors) (= *Glyphidodon, Glyphisodon*), *Amblyglyphidodon, Amblypomacentrus, Cheiloprion, Chrysiptera* (= *Glyphidodontops*), *Dischistodus, Hemiglyphidodon, Hypsypops, Microspathodon, Neopomacentrus* (one of the seven species, *N. taeniurus,* the freshwater demoiselle, penetrates freshwater streams of some islands in the tropical western Pacific), *Paraglyphidodon, Parma, Plectroglyphidodon, Pomacentrus, Pomachromis, Pristotis, Stegastes* (= *Eupomacentrus*—unfortunately, this name is well entrenched in the literature), and *Teixeirichthys,* with about 144 species. Only *Microspathodon* is endemic to the Atlantic. Genera similar to

Pomacentrus in having the hind margin of the preoperculum serrated were formerly placed in one tribe, and those similar to *Abudefduf* with the margin entire were placed in another.

Superfamily Gadopsoidea

Family GADOPSIDAE—blackfish.   Freshwater; eastern Australia and Tasmania.

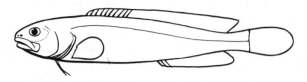

Body elongate and rounded; single long dorsal fin with 10–12 spines and 25–28 soft rays; anal fin with three small spines and 17–19 soft rays; pelvic fin with one ray in front of pectorals; body with small cycloid scales. Length up to 0.6 m.

One species, *Gadopsis marmoratus* (Lake, 1971, recognized the larger Tasmanian form as a separate species).

Rosen and Patterson (1969) feel that this species is perhaps more related to the Trachinoidei and Blennioidei than its present position in the Percoidei would suggest. Gosline (1968) felt that it should be placed in the Ophidioidei which he, in turn, felt should be in the Perciformes. It is placed in its own order by Scott et al. (1974).

Superfamily Cirrhitoidea.   Pelvics rather far behind pectorals; lower 5–8 rays of pectorals unbranched, usually thickened, and sometimes separate from one another; anal fin usually with three spines.

Five families and about 67 species.

Family CIRRHITIDAE—hawkfishes.   Marine; tropical western and eastern Atlantic, Indian, and Pacific (majority are Indo-Pacific).

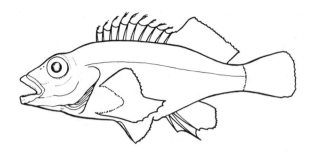

Dorsal fin continuous with 10 spines and 11–17 soft rays; cirri on inter-spinous membrane; anal fin with 5–7 soft rays; scales cycloid or ctenoid; vertebrae 26–28. Maximum length about 55 cm.

Hawkfishes are usually small and richly colored fishes that live in rocky and coral habitats. They have many features in common with the scor-paenids.

Nine genera (e.g., *Amblycirrhitus*, *Cirrhitichthys*, *Cirrhitops*, *Cirrhitus*, and *Paracirrhites*) with about 32 species (Randall, 1963; Randall and Heem-stra, 1978).

Family CHIRONEMIDAE—kelpfishes.   Marine; coastal Australia and New Zealand.

Dorsal fin with 14 or 15 spines and 16–21 soft rays; anal fin with 6–8 soft rays; vomer with teeth, palatines without teeth; jaw teeth conical or villiform. Maximum length about 40 cm.

Two genera, *Chironemus* and *Threpterius*, with about four species.

Family APLODACTYLIDAE (Haplodactylidae).   Coastal marine; southern Australia, New Zealand, Peru, and Chile.

Dorsal fin with 14–23 spines and 16–21 soft rays; anal fin with 6–8 soft rays; vomer with teeth; jaw teeth incisiform, lanceolate, or tricuspid.

Three genera, *Aplodactylus*, *Crinodus*, and *Dactylosargus*, with about five species.

Family CHEILODACTYLIDAE—morwongs.   Marine; parts of the Southern Hemi-sphere in Atlantic, Indian, and Pacific and in the Northern Hemisphere off coasts of China and Japan and reported from the Hawaiian Islands.

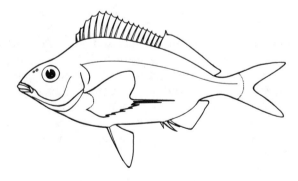

Dorsal fin continuous, may be almost separated, with 14–22 spines and 19–39 soft rays; anal fin with three spines (third may be difficult to detect) and 7–19 soft rays; vomer and palatines toothless; lower four to seven pectoral rays in adults usually thickened, elongated, and detached (free of rest of fin); usually 24 vertebrae. Maximum length about 1.0 m.

Five genera, *Acantholatris, Cheilodactylus [= Goniistius (= Gregoryina)]*, *Chirodactylus (= Palunolepis), Nemadactylus*, and *Sciaenoides*, with about 16 species (e.g., Smith, 1980, and references therein).

Family LATRIDIDAE—trumpeters.   Marine; coastal southern Australia, New Zealand, and Chile.

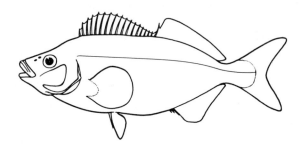

Dorsal fin with 14–23 spines and 23–40 soft rays; anal fin with 18–35 soft rays; vomer with or without teeth. Trumpeters form an important sport fishery and are known for their fine taste.

Three genera, *Latridopsis, Latris,* and *Mendosoma*, with about 10 species.

Superfamily Cepoloidea.   Dorsal fin continuous, with 0–4 spines (usually three); anal fin with 0–1 spines; vomer and palatine toothless; single postcleithrum; six branchiostegal rays; body color generally red or pink. Some workers prefer to recognize all members of this group in one family, the Cepolidae (Okada and Suzuki, 1956; Springer et al., 1977). However, whether they are closer to one another than many other perciform families are to each other seems uncertain. Springer et al. (1977) note certain specializations, thought to be the result of convergent evolution, shared between this group and the pseudochromids. About five genera and 19 species (however, W. F. Smith-Vaniz, pers. comm. 1983, finds there to be no valid reason for recognizing *Sphenanthias* as a valid taxon and considers it to be a junior synonym of *Owstonia*, a genus which would then have 11 species).

Family OWSTONIIDAE.   Marine deepwater; Indo-West Pacific.

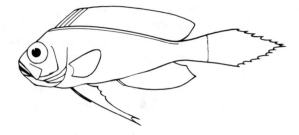

Body elongate and compressed; cycloid scales; caudal fin elongate; lateral line along base of dorsal fin.

Three genera, *Owstonia* (= *Parasphenanthias*), *Sphenanthias*, and *Pseudocepola*, with about 12 species.

Family CEPOLIDAE—bandfishes. Marine; eastern Atlantic (off Europe and in Mediterranean) and Indo-West Pacific (including New Zealand).

Body elongate, gradually tapering to tail, and highly compressed; scales minute; dorsal and anal fins very long and connected with caudal fin, without spines; lateral line along base of dorsal fin; vertebrae 65–100. Maximum length 70 cm attained in *Cepola rubescens* of Europe.

Two genera, *Acanthocepola* and *Cepola*, with about seven species.

Suborder Mugiloidei. Berg (1940) placed the three families Atherinidae, Mugilidae, and Sphyraenidae in the order Mugiliformes at the subperciform level. Gosline (1968, 1971) considered the suborder Mugiloidei as a perciform and included the families Polynemidae, Sphyraenidae, Mugilidae, Melanotaeniidae, Atherinidae, Isonidae, Neostethidae, and Phallostethidae (unlike Greenwood et al., 1966, followed here, who gave subordinal status to the first three families and placed the latter five in the preacanthopterygian order Atheriniformes). Gosline also considered his suborders Mugiloidei and Anabantoidei to be early perciform offshoots and listed them first in his perciform classification. He did this largely on the basis that all mugiloids and some anabantoids lack any direct articulation between the pelvic girdle and the cleithra (whereas in most other perciforms they are attached). It is not certain whether the lack of a pelvic–cleithral articulation is a primitive condition or whether it represents a secondary loss. Such information, however, would still leave the value of the characters in relation to the other characters in determining phylogenetic relationships open to question. McAllister (1968) placed Sphyraenidae and Mugilidae in Mugiloidei and Polynemidae in its own suborder and considered them all as perciforms, whereas he considered the Anabantoidei and its closest relatives (Luciocephalidae and Channidae) as preperciforms.

The next three families, which contain about 148 species, probably bear a closer relationship to one another than they do to any other family. It may eventually prove desirable to place them in the same suborder but in different infraorders or superfamilies.

Family MUGILIDAE—mullets.   Coastal marine and brackish water (some are freshwater); all tropical and temperate seas.

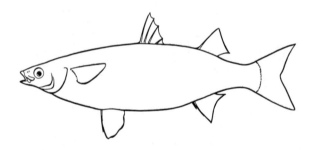

Widely separated spiny-rayed (with four spines) and soft-rayed dorsal fins; pelvic fins subabdominal, with one spine and five branched soft rays; lateral line absent or very faint; mouth moderate in size; teeth small or absent; gill rakers long; stomach muscular and intestine exceedingly long; vertebrae 24–26. Maximum length about 0.9 m.

About 13 genera (e.g., *Agonostomus, Cestraeus, Chaenomugil, Joturus, Liza, Mugil, Myxus, Rhinomugil,* and *Valamugil*) with about 95 species. Thomson (1964), in his bibliography of the mugilids, recognizes 13 generic names and 70 valid species (with 32 more of doubtful status) from a list of 281 nominal species.

Suborder Sphyraenoidei.   See taxonomic notes under Mugiloidei.

Family SPHYRAENIDAE—barracudas.   Marine; tropical and subtropical Atlantic, Indian, and Pacific.

Body elongate; mouth large, jutting lower jaw with strong fanglike teeth; upper jaw not protrusible (a secondary modification adapting the fish to feeding on large prey); lateral line well developed; gill rakers obsolete; pectoral fins relatively low; two widely separated dorsal fins, the first with five spines and the second with one spine and nine soft rays; vertebrae 24 (11 + 13).

Barracudas are known to attack humans and are feared more than sharks in some areas. Maximum length normally to 1.8 m but said to reach somewhat longer lengths.

One genus, *Sphyraena*, with 18 species.

Suborder Polynemoidei.   Berg (1940) placed the one family Polynemidae in its own order, Polynemiformes, and considered it to be a subperciform. Also see taxonomic notes under Mugiloidei.

Family POLYNEMIDAE—threadfins.   Marine and brackish water (some in rivers); all tropical and subtropical seas.

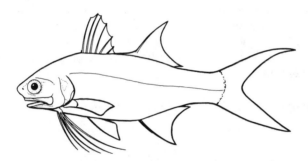

Mouth subterminal; pectoral fin divided into two sections, the upper with rays attached and the lower with 3–7 (but usually 14 or 15 in *Polistonemus*) long unattached rays; two widely separated dorsal fins (one spiny and one soft rayed); pelvics subabdominal, with one spine and five branched rays; caudal fin deeply forked; 24 or 25 vertebrae. Maximum length 1.8 m, attained in *Eleutheronema tetradactylum*.

Seven genera, *Eleutheronema, Filimanus, Galeoides, Pentanemus, Polistone-*

mus, Polydactylus, and *Polynemus,* with about 32 species provisionally recognized (pers. comm. 1981, R. M. Feltes).

Suborder Labroidei.   Toothplates of fourth pharyngobranchials absent and first pharyngobranchials absent or reduced; fourth epibranchials highly modified.

Most species of labrids and scarids are protogynous, that is, they can change their sex from female to male; there is a wide diversity of color patterns associated with sex and size (e.g., Robertson, 1972; Diener, 1977; Warner and Robertson, 1978; Robertson and Warner, 1978; Randall and Choat, 1980). Males may be primary (not capable of sex change) or secondary (resulting from a sex change of a female). Various populations may consist of only secondary males (monandry) or primary and secondary males (diandry). In coloration, individuals with a color pattern characteristic of small adults are said to be in the initial phase, while those having a color pattern characteristic of the largest males are in the terminal phase. Sexual dichromatism is common and refers to the situation where terminal phase males have a different color pattern from females. A definition of other terms associated with labroid coloration, sexuality, and mating patterns may be found in Warner and Robertson (1978).

Three families, 74 genera, and about 576 species. Kaufman and Liem (1982) combine the three families recognized here into the Labridae and postulate, on cladistic grounds, that Pomacentridae, Cichlidae, Embiotocidae, and Labridae comprise a monophyletic assemblage which they recognize as the Labroidei. Their group is characterized by possessing united or fused fifth ceratobranchials, diarthrosis between the upper pharyngeal jaws and the basicranium, and the presence of an undivided sphincter oesophagi muscle.

Family LABRIDAE—wrasses.   Marine; Atlantic, Indian, and Pacific.

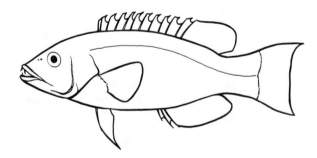

Mouth protractile; jaw teeth mostly separate, usually projecting outward; dorsal fin with 8–21 spines (usually fewer than 15) and 7–14 soft rays; anal fin with three spines (very rarely two) and 7–18 soft rays; scales cycloid, generally large to moderate with 25–80 along side (but may be small and exceed 100); lateral line continuous or interrupted; vertebrae 23–41. *Gomphosus* has an elongate snout.

This family is one of the most diversified of all fish families in shape, color, and size. Many species are highly colorful and several color patterns may exist within a species. Most species bury themselves in sand at night. Some small species clean larger fishes of their ectoparasites. Wrasses are popular aquarium fishes, particularly species of the genus *Coris*. Maximum size 3 m, although many species reach only 6 cm.

This is the second largest family of marine fishes and the third largest perciform family. Norman (1957) recognizes nine subfamilies. Recent systematic studies on the group include Randall (1978, 1980b, 1981b), Randall and Randall (1981), and Shen and Choi (1978).

About 57 genera (e.g., *Anampses, Bodianus, Cheilinus, Choerodon, Clepticus, Coris, Epibulus, Gomphosus, Halichoeres, Hemipteronotus, Hologymnosus, Julichthys, Labrus, Neolabrus, Pseudodax, Pseudojulis, Tautoga,* and *Thalassoma*) with approximately 500 species. Some undescribed species are known to exist, but some recognized species may just be color phases of other species.

Family ODACIDAE.   Coastal marine; Australia and New Zealand.

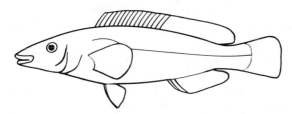

Mouth nonprotractile; jaw teeth coalesced (parrotlike teeth); dorsal fin with 14–23 spines; pelvic fins each with one spine and four soft rays (pelvic fins absent in the one species of *Siphonognathus*); scales usually small to moderate in size (about 30–87 in lateral line).

Six genera, *Neoodax (= Haletta)* with five species, *Odax (= Coridodax)* with two, and the monotypic *Heteroscarus, Olisthops, Parodax,* and *Siphonognathus,* with a total of 11 species (Ayling and Paxton, 1983). The two species of *Odax* are endemic to New Zealand while the other species are confined to southern Australia.

Family SCARIDAE (Callyodontidae)—parrotfishes.   Marine (mainly tropical); Atlantic, Indian, and Pacific.

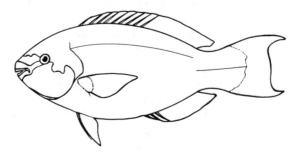

Mouth nonprotractile; jaw teeth coalesced (parrotlike teeth); dorsal fin with nine spines and 10 soft rays; anal fin with three spines and nine soft rays; pelvics each with one spine and five soft rays; branched caudal rays 11; scales large and cycloid, usually 22–24 in lateral line; 25 vertebrae.

Parrotfishes are herbivorous, usually grazing on dead coral substrates. Individuals of some species at night are known to secrete an envelope of mucus in which they rest. As with wrasses, sex change appears to be common in species of this family and males in most species that have been studied may be either primary or secondary. Unlike the wrasses, parrotfishes are remarkably uniform in most meristic characters. The living color pattern is important in identifying many species; however, in addition to fading quickly in preservation, the color pattern can vary greatly with growth and sex change. The wide diversity of bright colors in parrotfishes is shown in Schultz (1969) and Randall and Choat (1980).

SUBFAMILY SCARINAE.   Two to four rows of scales on cheek below eye; front edge of dental plate of lower jaw fits within that of upper jaw when mouth is closed. Four genera, *Scarops*, *Bolbometopon*, *Ypsiscarus*, and *Scarus* (= *Callyodon*) (which has the majority of species), with about 53 species.

SUBFAMILY SPARISOMATINAE.   Single row of 2–5 scales in cheek below eye; front edge of dental plate of upper jaw fits within that of lower jaw when mouth is closed. Seven genera (e.g., *Cryptotomus*, *Nicholsina*, and *Sparisoma*) with 15 species.

Suborder Zoarcoidei.   All have a single nostril but there is no known diagnostic character or simple combination of characters that distinguishes this group from the other blennylike perciforms. The nine included families with about 87 genera and 244 species occur primarily in the North Pacific.

Family BATHYMASTERIDAE—ronquils. Marine coastal; North Pacific.

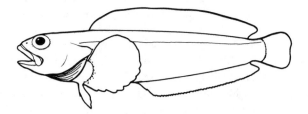

Dorsal fins continuous; pectoral fin base vertical; lateral line high, ending near end of dorsal fin; palate with teeth. Maximum length about 30 cm.

Three genera, *Bathymaster*, *Rathbunella* and *Ronquilus*, and seven species.

Family ZOARCIDAE—eelpouts. Marine; Arctic to Antarctic.

Body elongate; dorsal and anal fins long and confluent with caudal fin; mouth subterminal; pelvics, when present, small and in front of pectorals, jugular. (In *Derepodichthys*, a deepwater, eastern North Pacific species formerly placed in its own family, Derepodichthyidae, the cleithrum is extended far forward and the erectile pelvic fins are beneath the eyes.) Scales present or absent; gill membranes joined to isthmus; vertebrae 90–150. Some are viviparous. Length up to about 1.0 m in *Macrozoarces americanus*.

The placement of this family in higher classification is particularly uncertain. Greenwood et al. (1966) and Rosen and Patterson (1969) placed it in Gadiformes. Many workers, however, have placed it in Blennioidei (as used in the expanded and former sense of incuding what are herein recognized under four suborders, zoarcoids, notothenioids, trachinoids, and blennioids—e.g., Gosline 1968, 1971), a view that I now accept. Gosline (1971) stated that he did not regard the blennioids, as then conceived, as being strictly monophyletic, and he considered the zoarcids to be closely related to the Bathymasteridae. The arguments favoring a lack of affinity to Gadiformes (e.g., the number of rays in the dorsal and anal fins corresponds with the number of vertebrae, unlike in Gadiformes and Ophidiiformes where the fin rays outnumber the vertebrae in the area of overlap) are stronger than those supporting an affinity to the other families placed with it here in the same suborder.

About 40 genera (e.g., *Aprodon, Bothrocara, Derepodichthys, Gymnelis, Hadropareia, Leucobrotula, Lycenchelys, Lycodapus, Lycodes, Lycodonus, Lycodopsis, Macrozoarces, Maynea, Melanostigma, Pachycara, Parabrotula, Rhigophila,* and *Zoarces*) and about 150 species. The majority of species are in the Northern Hemisphere (15 species are known from Arctic Canada). Information on some of the species may be found in Anderson (1982), Anderson and Hubbs (1981), DeWitt (1977), Gosztonyi (1977), Markle and Sedberry (1978), McAllister et al. (1981), McAllister and Rees (1964), Nielsen (1968), Peden and Anderson (1981), and Yarberry (1965).

Family STICHAEIDAE—pricklebacks. Marine; primarily North Pacific, a few in North Atlantic.

At least some spinous rays in dorsal fin (entirely spinous in most species); dorsal fin long; pelvic fin rays, if present, branched; ribs present; distance from snout to anal origin usually equal to or less than distance from anal origin to caudal fin.

Each of the following eight tribes, placed in three subfamilies, was given subfamily status by Makushok (1958) from whom much of the following information is taken.

Thirty-one genera with about 60 species.

SUBFAMILY STICHAEINAE. Pelvic fins with one spine and three or four soft rays (*Gymnoclinus* has only two soft rays); pectoral fins large; vertebrae 46–71.

TRIBE STICHAEINI. North Pacific (primarily along the Asiatic coast) and northwestern Atlantic.

Five genera, *Ernogrammus, Eumesogrammus, Stichaeopsis, Stichaeus,* and *Ulvaria,* with about 11 species.

TRIBE CHIROLOPHINI. North Pacific with one species endemic to Atlantic.

Four genera, *Bryozoichthys, Chirolophis, Soldatovia,* and *Gymnoclinus,* with about 16 species.

SUBFAMILY LUMPENINAE. Pelvic fins with one spine and three soft rays to absent (fins and girdle absent in *Kasatkia*); pectoral fins large; vertebrae 53–94; lateral line usually indistinct or absent.

TRIBE LUMPENINI.   North Pacific, North Atlantic, and Arctic.
Six genera, *Acantholumpenus, Anisarchus, Leptoclinus, Lumpenella, Lumpenus,* and *Poroclinus,* with about nine species.

TRIBE OPISTHOCENTRINI.   Sea of Japan to Bering Sea and eastern North Pacific.
Six genera, *Allolumpenus, Ascoldia, Kasatkia, Lumpenopsis, Opisthocentrus,* and *Plectobranchus,* with about nine species.

SUBFAMILY XIPHISTERINAE.   Pectoral fins small; pelvic fins absent; vertebrae 62–81 (first two tribes) or greater than 100 (last two tribes).

TRIBE ALECTRIINI.   North Pacific.
Four genera, *Alectrias, Alectridium, Pseudalectrias,* and *Anoplarchus,* with about five species.

TRIBE XIPHISTERINI.   North Pacific. Three or four lateral lines present in *Phytichthys* and *Xiphister.*
Four genera, *Dictyosoma, Cebidichthys, Phytichthys,* and *Xiphister (= Epigeichthys),* with about seven species.

TRIBE AZYGOPTERINI.   Kuril Islands.
One species, *Azygopterus corallinus.*

TRIBE EULOPHIINI.   Sea of Japan.
One genus, *Eulophias,* with two species.

Family CRYPTACANTHODIDAE—wrymouths.   Marine; northwest Atlantic and northern Pacific.

Pelvic fins absent; mouth very oblique; lateral line obsolete.
The wrymouths were placed in the Stichaeidae in Greenwood et al. (1966) but are recognized as a separate family in most works (e.g., Makushok, 1958; Gosline, 1968; Bailey et al., 1970).
Four monotypic genera, *Cryptacanthodes, Cryptacanthoides, Delolepis,* and *Lyconectes.*

Family PHOLIDIDAE (Pholidae)—gunnels.   Marine; North Atlantic and North Pacific.

Dorsal fin with 75 to 100 spines, about twice as long as the anal fin; pectoral fins small, rudimentary, or absent; pelvic fins rudimentary (one spine and one soft ray in *Pholis*) or absent (along with pelvic girdle); vertebrae 84–107; ribs absent; distance from snout to anal origin usually more than distance from anal origin to caudal fin; lateral line short or absent.

Gunnels are small littoral fishes that, like some pricklebacks, are often found under rocks or in tide-pools at low tide.

Four genera with about 13 species.

SUBFAMILY PHOLIDINAE. Most are North Pacific, a few North Atlantic. One genus, *Pholis*, with about 10 species.

SUBFAMILY APODICHTHYINAE. Pacific coast of North America. Three monotypic genera; *Apodichthys*, *Xererpes*, and *Ulvicola*.

Family ANARHICHADIDAE—wolffishes. Marine; North Atlantic and North Pacific.

Body naked or with minute cycloid scales; no lateral line; gill membranes attached to isthmus; dorsal fin with spines only; pectoral fins large; pelvic fins absent (rudiments of girdle retained); caudal fin small or pointed; jaws with strong conical canines anteriorly and with large molariform teeth laterally; vertebrae 72–89 to more than 250. Maximum length about 2.5 m.

Two genera, *Anarhichas* (= *Lycichthys*) with six species (North Atlantic and Pacific) and *Anarrhichthys ocellatus* (Alaska to California).

Family PTILICHTHYIDAE—quillfish. Marine; Pacific North America (Puget Sound to northwestern Alaska).

Body extremely elongate and slender; caudal fin absent; pelvics absent; body naked; dorsal fin with 90 isolated low spines and 137–145 high soft rays; anal fin with 185–196 high soft rays; no lateral line; vertebrae about 238–240. Maximum length 33 cm.

One species, *Ptilichthys goodei*.

Family ZAPRORIDAE—prowfish. Marine; North Pacific (California to Alaska and Hokkaido).

No pelvic fins; gill membranes united; small cycloid scales on body; no lateral line; pectoral rays 24 or 25; dorsal fin long, with 54–57 spines; anal fin short, with three weak spines and 24–27 soft rays; large pores on head; vertebrae 61 or 62 (24–26 abdominal); pyloric caeca about 36. Maximum length 88 cm.

One species, *Zaprora silenus* (McAllister and Krejsa, 1961).

Family SCYTALINIDAE—graveldiver.   Marine; Pacific coast North America (southern California to northwestern Alaska).

No pelvic fins; gill membranes united; eyes very small and placed high on head; no scales; no lateral line; dorsal and anal fins on posterior half of back and confluent with caudal fin. Maximum length 15 cm.

One species, *Scytalina cerdale*.

Suborder Notothenioidei.   Pelvic fins each with one spine and five branched rays, jugular; one nostril on each side; dorsal fin spines usually nonpungent; principal caudal fin rays 10–19, usually fewer than 15; usually two or three lateral lines, occasionally one (as in all bovichthyids); body with ctenoid or cycloid scales or naked (except for lateral line scales); three platelike pectoral actinosts; pleural ribs poorly developed, floating or absent (the epipleurals are usually well developed); palatine teeth absent and vomerine teeth usually absent except in bovichthyids which have both; branchiostegal rays 5–9; swim bladder absent; primarily Antarctic in distribution.

Most of the species of coastal fishes in the Antarctic Region belong to this suborder. Some species live at an average temperature of − 1.9°C and have a glycoprotein in their blood which lowers the freezing point. Some species lack red blood cells and haemoglobin.

Five families with about 106 species. Andriashev (1965) and DeWitt (1971) review the suborder and Eakin (1981a) presents a key to and comparison of the families. Notothenioids are probably percoid derivatives.

Family BOVICHTHYIDAE (Bovictidae).   Marine; southern Australia, New Zealand, and southern South America regions and freshwater southeastern Australia and Tasmania.

Gill membranes free from isthmus, extending far forward; mouth protractile; spinous dorsal fin present; snout not produced.

Four genera, *Aurion, Bovichthys, Cottoperca,* and *Pseudaphritis,* with about six species.

Family NOTOTHENIIDAE—cod icefishes.   Marine (rarely brackish); coastal Antarctic and southern Southern Hemisphere.

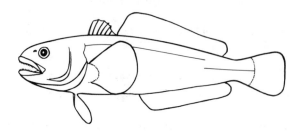

Body scaled; gill membranes forming a fold across the isthmus; mouth protractile; spinous dorsal fin present. Nototheniids show a certain similarity to hexagrammids.

The majority of notothenioids are benthic. However, several species of this family, such as the abundant and circumpolar plankton feeder *Pleurogramma antarcticum,* are pelagic. They utilize lipid deposits and reduced skeletal mineralization to attain near neutral buoyancy in the absence of a swim bladder (Eastman and DeVries, 1982). Some species are cryopelagic, living beneath the sea ice.

Eight genera, *Aethotaxis, Cryothenia, Dissostichus, Eleginops, Notothenia, Pagothenia, Pleurogramma,* and *Trematomus,* with as many as 50 species (Andriashev, 1965; Daniels, 1981). The most speciose genus, *Notothenia,* ranges northward to such regions as New Zealand, Macquarie Island, and Argentina. Most species of the family, however, occur in Antarctica.

Family HARPAGIFERIDAE—plunderfishes.   Marine; coastal Antarctic and peripheral islands to Falkland Islands.

Body naked; gill membranes broadly united to isthmus; all but *Harpagifer* have a chin barbel and a weakly armed gill cover; spinous dorsal fin present; mouth protractile. Wyanski and Targett (1981) note the striking similarity (convergent evolution) between harpagiferids and cottids in morphology, food habits, and feeding behavior. Maximum length about 30 cm.

Five genera, *Harpagifer, Artedidraco, Dolloidraco, Histiodraco,* and *Pogonophryne,* with 19 species (Eakin, 1981a,b). Species of the genus *Harpagifer* are generally present only on islands north of Antarctica (e.g., Kerguelen, Macquarie, and Falkland) while the others are generally confined to the Antarctic coastline (Andriashev, 1965).

Family BATHYDRACONIDAE—Antarctic dragonfishes. Marine; Antarctic.

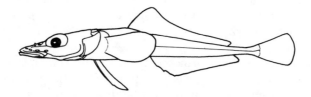

Gill membranes united; mouth usually nonprotractile; no spinous dorsal fin.

Eight genera, *Bathydraco, Cygnodraco, Gerlachea, Gymnodraco, Parachaenichthys, Prionodraco, Psilodraco,* and *Racovitzia,* with 15 species (Andriashev, 1965).

Family CHANNICHTHYIDAE (Chaenichthyidae)—crocodile icefishes. Marine; Antarctic and southern South America.

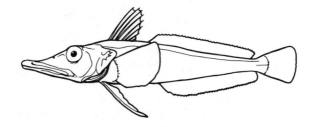

Gill membranes united; mouth nonprotractile; snout produced and depressed; spinous dorsal fin present.

Most or all species are without red blood cells. Survival is probably permitted by the fish living in extremely cold, well-oxygenated water and having a large volume of blood circulation and skin respiration.

Nine genera (e.g., *Chaenocephalus, Channichthys, Cryodraco,* and *Pagetopsis*) with 16 species.

Suborder Trachinoidei. Fifteen families with a total of 59 genera and 239 species, the majority of which are tropical marine fishes, are recognized in this suborder. The placement of the first six families, particularly that of the first two, in this suborder is very provisional. The affinities of the family Opistognathidae, being revised by Dr. W. F. Smith-Vaniz, are especially uncertain. Springer et al. (1977) note similarities between opistognaths and certain percoids with other than a single, un-interrupted lateral line. Drs. V. G. Springer and R. Winterbottom have evidence suggesting a close relationship between the Congrogadidae and Pseudochromidae (particularly Anisochrominae), and they should probably be placed together. However, it seems to be unresolved as to what the resultant group is allied to, although it is probably with the percoids. Pending further work on this problem I leave the families involved in their classical position.

Xenocephalus armatus (the armored blenny) from New Ireland, for which the family Xenocephalidae has been recognized, is thought to be the larval form of some other family of fishes (species unknown but possibly a dactylopterid, chaetodontid, or scatophagid) by V. G. Springer (pers. comm. 1982) and is not treated further.

Family OPISTOGNATHIDAE—jawfishes.   Marine; western and central Atlantic, Indian, and Gulf of California region.

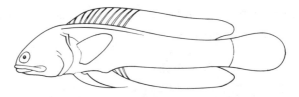

Mouth large; body with cycloid scales; head naked; pelvic fins ahead of pectorals, with one spine and five soft rays (inner three weak and branched and outer two stout and unbranched, unlike any other perciform); dorsal fin continuous, with 9–12 dorsal spines; lateral line high, ending near middle of dorsal fin (one species has both a ventral and a dorsal lateral line); palate without teeth. The species of Stalix are probably unique among fishes in having the anterior dorsal fin spines transversely forked (Smith-Vaniz, 1974). The males practice oral incubation. All jawfishes are burrow dwellers and use their large mouth to excavate their burrows.

Three genera, Opistognathus, Lonchopisthus (=Lonchistium), and Stalix, with at least 70 species (pers. comm. 1982, W. F. Smith-Vaniz).

Family CONGROGADIDAE—eelblennies.   Marine (rarely brackish); Indo-West Pacific.

Body elongate to eellike; body with small cycloid scales; one spine before dorsal fin (absent in *Congrogadus subducens*), no anal spines; dorsal and anal fins long; pelvic fin present (jugular and with one small spine and one to three soft rays) or absent; caudal fin confluent with dorsal and anal fins in a few species, slightly separated in most; mouth protractile; gill membranes united; opercle with strong, posteriorly directed spine on upper margin; one to three lateral lines, fully or partly complete (only *Halidesmus* has three and auxillary lines may be present); palatine teeth absent, vomerine teeth present or absent; cordlike ligament extending from ceratohyal to dentary symphisis. Maximum length about 50 cm. Eelblennies occur on coral reefs and on gravel and mud bottoms. One species is known to inhabit the insides of sponges in the Gulf of Carpentaria.

There is some suggestion that this family is closely related to pseudochromids (Springer et al., 1977; pers. comm. 1981, R. Winterbottom).

Eight genera with 17 species (pers. comm. 1981, R. Winterbottom; Winterbottom, 1982): *Blennodesmus* (one species, northeastern and northwestern Australia), *Congrogadoides* (three species, western Pacific from New Guinea to Australia), *Congrogadus* (two species, primarily Japan to Australia), *Halidesmus* (= *Pholioides*) (three species, India, Kenya, and South Africa), *Halimuraena* (three species, eastern and southern Africa), *Haliophis* (one species, Red Sea to Madagascar), *Natalichthys* (three species, South Africa), and *Rusichthys* (one species, western Indian Ocean off Kenya—this is the most primitive genus of the family).

Family CHIASMODONTIDAE.   Marine; oceanic.

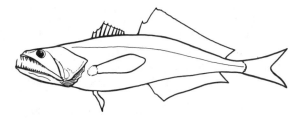

Premaxilla and maxilla long and slender, firmly united posteriorly; anterior tip of premaxilla expanded dorsally and diverging laterally; highly distensible mouth and stomach. Placed in its own division by Norman (1957) and in the Percoidei by Gosline (1971).

Four genera, *Chiasmodon*, *Dysalotus*, *Kali* (= *Gargaropteron*), and *Pseudoscopelus*, with about 15 species (e.g. Johnson and Cohen, 1974). The last genus bears photophores and is placed in its own family by Smith (1964c).

Family CHAMPSODONTIDAE.   Marine; Indo-Pacific.

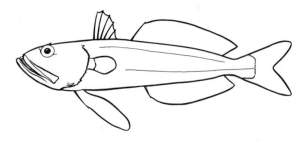

Pelvic fins large, in front of pectorals; pectoral fins small, base oblique; spinous dorsal short, soft dorsal and anal fins long.

Placed in its own division by Norman (1957). One genus, *Champsodon*, with about five species.

Family NOTOGRAPTIDAE.   Marine; southern New Guinea and northern Australia (south to northern Queensland).

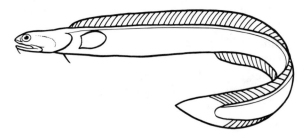

Dorsal, caudal, and anal fins confluent; dorsal fin with 64–68 spines and usually two soft rays; anal fin with 38–43 spines and usually two soft rays; caudal fin with 11 rays and a few rudimentary ones; pectoral fin rays 16–20; pelvic fin with one small, slender spine and two soft rays; median barbel on lower jaw (mental); vertebrae 71–75. Maximum length about 11 cm.

One genus, *Notograptus*, with about two species (e.g., Tyler and Smith, 1970).

Family PHOLIDICHTHYIDAE—convict blenny.   Marine, southwesternmost Philippines to Solomon Islands.

Body eelshaped; one nostril on each side; scales absent; pelvics below or slightly in front of pectoral base, with one thin spine and two or three soft rays; caudal fin rounded and joined with dorsal and anal fins; dorsal fin with 70–79 soft rays; anal fin with 55–62 soft rays; pectoral fin with 15 rays; lower pharyngeals fused into a single bone; septal bone present in interorbital area; vertebrae 71–79 (22–26 + 48–56).

This fish is of very uncertain position within the Perciformes. Springer and Freihofer (1976), in a detailed study of this aquarium fish, found it to have some similarity to certain tropical blennioids (e.g., clinids and blenniids) in the trunk lateral- line nerves but not in osteological specializations. However, the unusual presence of a septal bone in *Pholidichthys* is a similarity shared only with certain genera of Tripterygiidae among the perciforms (V. G. Springer, pers. comm. 1982).

One species, *Pholidichthys leucotaenia.*

Family TRICHODONTIDAE—sandfishes.   Marine; North Pacific.

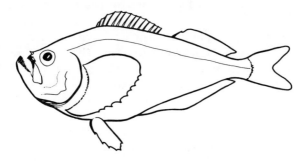

Mouth nearly vertical, with fringed lips; preopercle with five sharp spines; body scaleless; dorsal spines 10–15. Normal habitat is lying partly buried in the bottom. Maximum length about 30 cm.

Two species, *Arctoscopus japonicus* (Alaska to Korea) and *Trichodon tricho-don* (northern California to Alaska).

Family TRACHINIDAE—weeverfishes.   Marine; eastern Atlantic (commonest in Mediterranean), Black Sea, and off Chile.

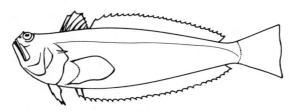

Body elongate; anal and second dorsal fins long; pelvic fins in front of pectorals; poisonous glands associated with gill cover spine and first dorsal spines; 34–43 vertebrae. These fish have a habit of burying in sand.

One genus, *Trachinus*, with at least four species. (Recently, Bentivegna, 1982, recognized Bleeker's *Echiichthys* as a valid genus.)

Family URANOSCOPIDAE—stargazers.   Marine; Atlantic, Indian, and Pacific.

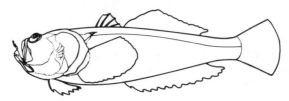

Head large and cuboid; body naked or covered with small smooth scales; mouth extremely oblique; lips fringed; eyes dorsal or nearly so; lateral line on upper part of side; pelvic fins narrowly separated, with one spine and five soft rays, located under the throat; dorsal and anal fins moderately long, spinous dorsal absent in many; some with small wormlike filament extending from floor of mouth used to lure prey fish; two large, double-grooved poison spines, with a venom gland at each base, just above the pectoral fin and behind the opercle; 24–26 vertebrae.

One genus, *Astroscopus*, has internal nares used during inspiration and electric organs derived from portions of eye muscle.

Nine genera (e.g., *Astroscopus*, *Gnathagnus*, *Ichthyscopus*, *Kathetostoma*, *Pleuroscopus*, and *Uranoscopus*) and 25 species.

Family TRICHONOTIDAE—sanddivers.   Marine; Indo-West Pacific.

Lower jaw projecting beyond upper jaw; anterior rays of dorsal fin often elongated; pelvic fin with one spine and five soft rays; lateral line on midside of body. The type species of the type genus, *Trichonotus setiger* (specimens studied in the Australian Museum, Sydney), shows many differences from species placed here in other families, including those of Creediidae which also burrow in sand or small gravel. *Trichonotus setiger* has a distinct dorsal iris flap (= dorsal operculum, iris lappet) consisting of numerous elongate strands extending over the lens. Many other benthic fish have an iris flap (creediids do not) but not of such a highly splintered type. The lateral line scales have a deep V-shaped notch in the posterior margin.

Three monotypic genera are recognized here, *Trichonotus* and, only very provisionally, *Trichonotops* of South Africa and *Lesueurina* of Victoria, Australia.

Family CREEDIIDAE (Limnichthyidae)—sandburrowers.   Marine; Indo-West Pacific (South Africa to Hawaii).

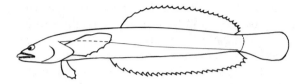

Row of cirri bordering lower jaw; dorsally projecting knob at symphysis of lower jaw; snout fleshy, projecting beyond lower jaw; lateral line descending abruptly or gradually to ventral surface; lateral line scales, except for anteriormost ones, with posterior extension, often trilobed; body largely scaleless in a few species (lateral line scales always present); dorsal fin continuous, with 12–43 unbranched soft rays; pelvic fin with one spine and 3–5 soft rays (fins absent in the one species of *Apodocreedia*), interpelvic space very small; eye with infolding of the cornea at cornea–skin junction, and eyes slightly protruding. (Eyes probably capable of chameleonlike movement in all species.) Bone of operculum highly splintered (can be revealed by passing light through the gill cover—this condition is present in some species of other families). Maximum length about 8 cm.

Seven genera, *Apodocreedia*, *Chalixodytes*, *Creedia*, *Crystallodytes*, *Limnichthys*, *Schizochirus*, and *Tewara*, with about 14 species (Nelson, 1979a, 1983).

Family LEPTOSCOPIDAE.   Marine; Australia and New Zealand.

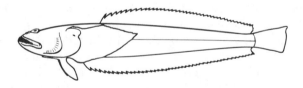

Mouth moderately oblique; lips fringed; eyes dorsal or nearly so; lateral line on middle of side; body with scales; pelvic fins widely separated; dorsal and anal fins long.

Two genera, *Crapatulus* and *Leptoscopus*, with at least three species.

Family PERCOPHIDAE—duckbills.   Marine; Atlantic and Indo-West Pacific.

Head depressed; eyes usually large and interorbital space narrow; spinous dorsal, if present, separate from soft dorsal; anal fin with or without a single spine; pelvic fin with one spine and five soft rays, interpelvic space wide.

Twelve genera and about 37 species.

SUBFAMILY PERCOPHINAE. Tropical western Atlantic. Dorsal fins with eight or nine spines and about 31 soft rays; anal fin with one weak spine and about 38–42 soft rays; lower jaw projecting past upper; caudal fin with 13 branched rays; dorsal iris flap absent; distinct flap above pectoral fin base; scales above lateral line ctenoid but lateral line scales not serrated, trilobed, or with keel; minute scales extending along rays of caudal fin.

One species, *Percophis brasiliensis.*

SUBFAMILY BEMBROPINAE. Atlantic and Indo-West Pacific. Dorsal fins with six spines (only first two crowded) and 13–18 soft rays; anal fin with 15–20 soft rays; lower jaw projecting past upper; caudal fin with 10 or 11 branched rays; maxillary tentacle present in *Bembrops;* scales ctenoid, with prominent keel on anterior few lateral line scales.

Two genera, *Bembrops* and *Chrionema* (= *Chriomystax),* with about 19 species (e.g., Iwamoto and Staiger, 1976; Nelson, 1978b). The nominal species of *Bembrops* are very poorly defined.

SUBFAMILY HEMEROCOETINAE. Western Pacific in Oceania and Japan to Australia with two species in South Africa. Spines in dorsal fin, if present, 2–6 and usually very crowded at base; jaws about equal or upper jaw slightly longer than lower; caudal fin with seven or eight branched rays; dorsal iris flap present in most species; medial barbel at tip of snout in some species (only in males in the species of *Hemerocoetes* that have it).

Two lineages may be recognized with 9 genera and about 17 species (e.g., Iwamoto, 1980; Nelson, 1979b, 1982b). *Squamicreedia, Enigmapercis,* and *Matsubaraea* (= *Cirrinasus)* lack protruding maxillary spines and a jet black membrane of the 2–4 spines of the first dorsal fin. They have trilobed lateral line scales (except in pectoral fin area) and one or more flaps or cirri in the anterior nostril. *Hemerocoetes* (a New Zealand endemic lacking the spinous dorsal fin), *Spinapsaron, Branchiopsaron, Osopsaron, Acanthaphritis,* and *Pteropsaron* have a spine protruding from the anterior face of the maxilla. The membrane of the 4–6 spines of the first dorsal fin is jet black for at least a portion of it (except in *Pteropsaron*) and spines are often elongated. They have a serrated posterior margin on the lateral line scales and lack flaps in the anterior nostril. The validity of these two lineages is cast into some doubt by the recent examination of a specimen in the Muséum National d'Histoire Naturelle in Paris (MNHN 90–106) collected with the types of *Acanthaphritis grandisquamis* Günther. This specimen, which represents an undescribed species, has maxillary spines present; three dorsal spines, the first very elongate (extending to the caudal fin) and much thicker than the others which are closely set, with a jet black membrane; trilobed lateral line scales (central lobe rounded or indented); and anterior nostril lacking cirri.

Family MUGILOIDIDAE (Parapercidae and Pinguipedidae)—sandperches. Marine; Atlantic coast of South America and Africa, Indo-Pacific (to New Zealand and Hawaii), and off Chile.

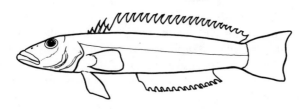

Pelvic fins below or slightly in front of pectorals; mouth protractile and terminal; caudal fin truncate to deeply crescentic, with 13 or 15 branched rays; dorsal fin continuous, with four or five short spines and 19–26 soft rays; anal fin with 17–25 rays, first one or two may be spinelike; lateral line continuous; gill membranes united, free from isthmus.

Four genera, *Mugiloides, Parapercis* (=*Neopercis*), *Pinguipes*, and *Prolatilus*, with at least 40 species. *Prolatilus* is included in this family following McCosker (1971).

Family CHEIMARRHICHTHYIDAE (Cheimarrichthyidae). Freshwater (young are known from the sea); rivers of New Zealand.

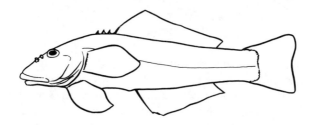

Pelvic fins well in front of pectorals, wide apart; mouth nonprotractile and inferior; caudal fin with 13–15 branched rays; dorsal fin usually has four or five spines and 19 or 20 soft rays, the anterior three or four spines are short and stout and separated from the remainder of the continuous fin; anal fin with one or two spines and 15 soft rays; 15 pectoral rays; about 50 scales along lateral line; vertebrae 31–33. Maximum length about 15 cm.

McDowall (1973b) provides an osteological description and because of the similarity with *Parapercis colias*, favors assigning *Cheimarrichthys* to the Mugiloididae.

One species, *Cheimarrichthys fosteri.*

Suborder Blennioidei.   Anal fin with one or two spines and all simple soft rays; pelvic fins with one spine and two to four simple soft rays, insertion ahead of pectorals; two nostrils on either side (except for some specimens of some species of *Enchelyurus*); cirri often present on head (variously on nape, above eye, on nostrils, or on margins of cephalic sensory pores); single bone representing infrapharyngobranchials 2–4; no autogenous parhypural (parhypural absent or indistinguishably fused to hypurals); hypurals 3 and 4 fused to each other and to urostylar centrum (pers. comm. V. G. Springer, 1982).

Six families are recognized in this group following George and Springer (1980), who considered them to be the sole members of their Blennioidei. The families Labrisomidae, Clinidae, and Chaenopsidae are treated as one family, Clinidae, in many works (e.g., Robins et al., 1980).

Six families, 127 genera, and about 675 species.

Family TRIPTERYGIIDAE—threefin blennies.   Marine (primarily tropical); Atlantic, Indian, and Pacific.

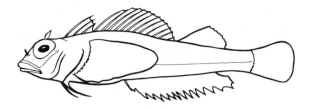

Dorsal fin divided into three distinct segments, the first two composed of spines and the third with never fewer than seven soft rays; anal fin spines one, two (usually), or none; pelvics jugular, spine present but reduced; branchiostegal rays six or seven; no cirri on nape; scales usually ctenoid, with radii on anterior field only; first gill arch attached to opercle by a membrane. Dr. V. G. Springer (pers. comm. 1982) has found a specialized character which separates tripterygiids from all other blennioids. In blennioids other than tripterygiids with both spines and soft rays in the dorsal fin the pterygiophore that supports the first soft ray also supports a spine. In tripterygiids, the pterygiophore that supports the first segmented dorsal fin ray does not support a dorsal fin spine, and there may be as many as three more pterygiophores anterior to the one supporting the first soft ray which do not support spines. Maximum length about 25 cm, most species less than 6 cm.

Nineteen genera (e.g., *Axoclinus, Enneanectes, Lepidoblennius, Forsterygion, Notoclinus, Trianectes,* and *Tripterygion*), with about 95 species (based on Rosenblatt, 1959; the number of valid species described to date is probably upwards of 110). The area of greatest diversity is probably New Zealand where many undescribed species are known to exist. The few species in the eastern Atlantic have been revised by Wirtz (1980).

Family DACTYLOSCOPIDAE—sand stargazers. Marine (rarely brackish); warm temperate to tropical in North and South America.

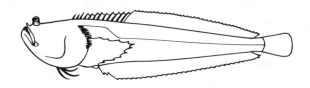

Mouth extremely oblique; lips usually fringed; upper edge of gill cover subdivided into fingerlike elements; eyes dorsal, somewhat protrusile (may be on stalk); pelvic fins with one spine and three soft rays, jugular; dorsal fin long, continuous or divided, with 7–23 spines and 12–36 soft rays; anal fin with 21–41 soft rays; lateral line scales 33–73; parasphenoid absent; abdominal vertebrae 10–13 and caudal vertebrae 23–42. Maximum length about 15 cm.

Sand stargazers frequently bury themselves in sand bottoms, similar to some trachinoids. However, unlike virtually all other teleosts which normally pump water over the gills by alternately expanding and contracting the buccal and opercular cavities, they have evolved a branchiostegal pump which replaces the opercular pump (other benthic fishes have both). Fingerlike labial and opercular fimbriae probably function to prevent particles from clogging the branchial chamber.

Nine genera, *Dactylagnus, Dactyloscopus, Gillellus, Heteristius, Leurochilus, Myxodagnus, Platygillellus, Sindoscopus,* and *Storrsia,* with 41 species (Dawson, 1974a, 1975, 1976, 1977, and 1982b). Seventeen species occur in the Atlantic (United States to Brazil) and 24 in the Pacific (Gulf of California to Chile). Subspecies are recognized for four species giving 29 subordinate Pacific taxa.

Family LABRISOMIDAE—labrisomids. Marine, mostly tropical; Atlantic and Pacific.

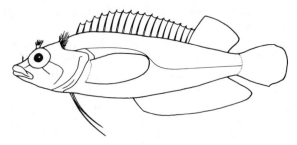

Scales with radii only on anterior margin (scales absent in five of the six species of *Stathmonotus* and one species of *Neoclinus* from Taiwan) and never small and imbedded; cirri often present on nape, nostril, and above eye; dorsal fin with more spines than soft rays (some species with only spines); only *Xenomedea* and eastern Pacific species of *Starksia* are viviparous, and only *Starksia* has intromittent organ in males (but of a different type than in clinids).

Sixteen genera, *Alloclinus, Auchenionchus, Calliclinus, Cryptotrema, Dialomus, Excerpes, Haptoclinus, Labrisomus, Malacoctenus, Mnierpes, Nemaclinus, Neoclinus, Paraclinus, Starksia, Stathmonotus,* and *Xenomedea* with about 102 species (e.g., Stephens and Springer, 1973; Böhlke and Springer, 1975; Greenfield and Johnson, 1981). Most species of this family occur in the tropics of North America (primarily in Central America) and South America: four species of *Neoclinus* are in the western Pacific (Taiwan to Japan), about 52 in the eastern Pacific, 45 in the western Atlantic, and two in the eastern Atlantic off Africa (one of which, a *Labrisomus,* is widespread in the western Atlantic). Miocene fossils of *Labrisomus* are present in the Mediterranean (Springer, 1970) where the family is no longer represented.

Family CLINIDAE—clinids.   Marine, primarily temperate; Atlantic, Indian, and Pacific.

Scales cycloid, with radii on all fields (scales absent only in *Clinoporus biporosus* of South Africa), and usually small and imbedded; nape cirri absent (cirri may be present elsewhere on head); dorsal fin with more spines than soft rays; all fin rays simple; cordlike ligament extending from ceratohyal to dentary symphysis. Maximum length about 60 cm, attained in *Heterostichus rostratus,* most much smaller.

Three tribes with about 20 genera and 75 species (George and Springer, 1980; V. G. Springer, pers. comm. 1982). The monophyly of the last two tribes is uncertain. Unlike related families, clinids are generally absent from the tropics; there are only about four species in the tropics (in the Indo-Pacific).

TRIBE OPHICLININI.   Southern Australia.

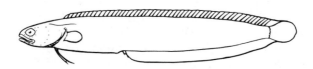

Dorsal and anal fins united to caudal fin; dòrsal fin continuous and without elongated anterior rays, with 36–84 spines and 1–4 soft rays; pectoral fins vestigial in several species, both pectoral and pelvic fins vestigial in *Peronedys;* no orbital cirri and nostril cirri usually absent; lateral line reduced; males with intromittent organ; ovoviviparous; body eelshaped, especially in *Peronedys* and *Sticharium;* vertebrae 48–96 (18–35 precaudal). Maximum length 16 cm.

Four genera, *Ophiclinops, Ophiclinus, Peronedys,* and *Sticharium (=Breona),* with 12 species (George and Springer, 1980).

TRIBE CLININI.   Widespread in temperate Indo-West Pacific (including New Zealand) with about four species in the tropics.

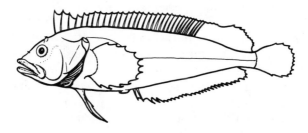

First three dorsal fin spines usually longer than remaining spines and separated from them by a small notch; anal fin rarely attached to caudal fin; orbital and nasal cirri usually present; males with intromittent organ; ovoviviparous.

About 11 genera, *Cancelloxus, Clinoporus, Clinus, Cologrammus, Ericentrus, Gynutoclinus, Heteroclinus, Neoblennius, Pavoclinus, Springeratus,* and *Xenopoclinus,* with 50 species.

TRIBE MYXODINI.   Temperate waters of Western Hemisphere and Mediterranean Sea. First three dorsal fin spines usually not separated from rest by notch (last two genera listed below have a deep notch between spines three and four); anal fin not attached to caudal fin; dorsal fin with 30–38 spines and 2–14 soft rays; anal fin with two spines and 18–36 soft rays; orbital and nasal cirri present; vomerine teeth present in first two genera listed below; males without an intromittent organ; oviparous; vertebrae 40–58 (precaudal 13–22).

Five genera, *Heterostichus*, *Gibbonsia*, *Myxodes*, *Ribeiroclinus*, and *Clinitrachus*, with about 13 species. *Clinitrachus* is known only in the Mediterranean, *Reibeiroclinus* from the western Atlantic coast of South America, and the others from the eastern Pacific from British Columbia to the tip of Baja California and Peru to southern Chile (Springer, 1970; Stephens and Springer, 1973).

Family CHAENOPSIDAE—pikeblennies, tubeblennies, or flagblennies.   Warm seas of North and South America.

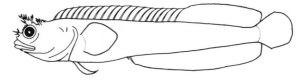

Body naked; no lateral line (three pores at most behind opercle); maxilla not visible externally; some species with anterior portion of dorsal fin much higher than rest; dorsal fin with 17–28 spines and 10–38 soft rays (total rays 29–57); anal fin with two spines and 19–38 soft rays; pectoral fin with 12–15 rays; caudal fin separate or variously united with dorsal and anal fins; orbital and nasal cirri variously present or absent (cirri on nape absent); head often spiny or rough; body usually elongate and compressed (as shown in figure), particularly slender (eellike) in *Chaenopsis*. Maximum length about 16 cm, attained in various species of *Chaenopsis*, most much less.

A symbiotic relationship, similar to that occurring between some pomacentrids and sea anemones, has been observed between a chaenopsid and a stony coral in the Caribbean (Butter et al., 1980).

Ten genera, *Acanthemblemaria*, *Emblemaria*, *Chaenopsis*, *Protemblemaria*, *Ekemblemaria*, *Emblemariopsis*, *Coralliozetus*, *Hemiemblemaria*, *Lucayablennius*, and *Mccoskerichthys*, with 56 species (Stephens, 1963, 1970; Smith-Vaniz and Palacio, 1974; Rosenblatt and Stephens, 1978; Greenfield and Johnson, 1981). The first three genera have more than one-half of the species. Six of the genera are amphi-American and there is a total of 32 Atlantic species (several more are being described) and 24 Pacific ones.

Family BLENNIIDAE—combtooth blennies.   Marine (rarely fresh- or brackish water, primarily tropical and subtropical); Atlantic, Indian, and Pacific.

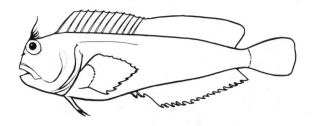

Body naked or with modified scales; head usually blunt; pelvic fins present (except in two species of *Plagiotremus*), anterior to the pectorals, and with one short imbedded spine (easily overlooked) and 2–4 segmented rays; palatines toothless, vomer may have teeth; jaws with comblike teeth, fixed or freely movable (occasionally with a canine tooth on each side of each jaw posteriorly); dorsal fin with 3–17 flexible spines and 9–119 segmented rays (fewer spines than soft rays in most species); pectoral rays not branched, 10–18; caudal fin rays branched (unbranched in one species); anal fin with two spines (the first is buried beneath genital tissue in females); basisphenoid present except in Nemophini; adults without swim bladder except in *Phenablennius, Omox,* and most Nemophini (Smith-Vaniz, 1976) where it may be minute and easily overlooked; vertebrae usually 28–44 (up to 135 in *Xiphasia*). Maximum length about 54 cm, most species under 15 cm.

Many species of blenniids are involved in mimetic associations with other fishes, being similar in external appearance to the other species (Springer and Smith-Vaniz, 1972a). Elements of Mullerian, Batesian, and aggressive mimicry are involved.

Fifty-three genera with about 301 species. Springer (1968) gives a listing of most of the nominal genera and a detailed osteological description of *Entomacrodus.*

TRIBE SALARIINI.   Marine, primarily Indo-West Pacific. Caudal fin rays branched or not; two, four, or five circumorbital bones; three or four segmented pelvic fin rays (the spine and innermost soft ray may be easily overlooked); dorsal fin with 9–17 spines (usually 11–14) and 9–24 soft rays; teeth on upper jaw usually over 80. Some species can spend much of their time out of water.

Twenty-six genera (e.g., *Ecsenius, Andamia, Alticus, Praealticus, Istiblennius, Ophioblennius, Cirripectes, Entomacrodus, Salarias, Rhabdoblennius,* and

Antennablennius), with about 160 species (Smith-Vaniz and Springer, 1971; McKinney and Springer, 1976; Springer and Spreitzer, 1978). The genus *Ecsenius*, with 25 species, is probably the most speciose genus of blenniid.

TRIBE BLENNIINI. Marine (rarely fresh- and brackish water). Caudal fin rays branched; five circumorbital bones; three or four segmented pelvic fin rays; dorsal fin usually with 10–14 spines and 12–22 soft rays; vertebrae 30–41 (usually $10+21-29$).

Fifteen genera (e.g., *Blennius, Chalaroderma, Chasmodes, Hypleurochilus, Hypsoblennius, Lipophrys, Lupinoblennius, Parablennius, Salaria,* and *Scartella*) with 70 species (Bath, 1977, 1982). The most speciose genus is the New World amphi–American *Hypsoblennius* (Smith-Vaniz, 1980). This tribe, unlike the others, is probably not monophyletic. Smith-Vaniz (1976) concludes that the genus *Blennius* (with three species used in the restricted sense of Bath, 1977) is more closely related to the following three tribes than to other blenniids.

TRIBE OMOBRANCHINI. Marine (rarely fresh- and brackish water). Caudal fin rays not branched; two segmented pelvic fin rays; 15–27 segmented dorsal fin rays.

Six genera, *Enchelyurus* (five), *Haptogenys* (one), *Laiphognathus* (one), *Omobranchus* (19), *Omox* (one), and *Parenchelyurus* (two), with 29 species (Springer, 1972; Springer and Gomon, 1975).

TRIBE PHENABLENNIINI. Fresh- and brackish water; Sumatra, Cambodia, and Sarawak, northern Borneo. Body similar in appearance to Omobranchini; all fin rays unbranched; three segmented pelvic fin rays; 14 or 15 segmented dorsal fin rays (12 or 13 spines); five infraorbital pores; labial flaps on both jaws; postcleithrum single (other blenniids have two postcleithra or 1–3 fragments); vertebrae 32–34 $(10+22-24)$.

One species, *Phenablennius heyligeri* (Springer and Smith-Vaniz, 1972b; Smith-Vaniz, 1975).

TRIBE NEMOPHINI (SABER-TOOTHED BLENNIES). Marine (including brackish and fresh water for *Meiacanthus anema*); Indian and Pacific oceans. All fin rays unbranched; total dorsal rays 25–133; pelvic fin with one imbedded spine and three segmented rays (fin absent in two species of *Plagiotremus*); swim bladder present (except in *Xiphasia*); circumorbital bones usually four, rarely three; basisphenoid absent; body eellike in *Xiphasia* (which has the highest number of dorsal and anal fin rays and vertebrae); unique toxic buccal glands in *Meiacanthus;* vertebrae 30–135 $(11-16+19-119)$.

Five genera, *Xiphasia* (= *Nemophis*) (two), *Meiacanthus* (16), *Plagiotremus* (11), *Petroscirtes* (10), and *Aspidontus* (two), with 41 species (Smith-Vaniz, 1976).

Suborder Icosteoidei (Malacichthyes).   The one included family and species are placed in their own order, Icosteiformes, by Berg (1940) and Gosline (1971).

Family ICOSTEIDAE—ragfish.   Marine; Pacific coast North America.

Body elliptical, highly compressed, and limp; skeleton largely cartilaginous; no spines in fins; no scales in adult; pelvic fins loosely attached in young, lost in adults; 70 vertebrae. Maximum length 2 m.

   One species, *Icosteus aenigmaticus.*

Suborder Schindlerioidei

Family SCHINDLERIIDAE.   Marine; oceanic.

Small neotenic fishes that show no adult characteristics. Some of the larval characteristics found in sexually mature individuals include functional pronephros, transparent body, and large opercular gills. Other characteristics are 15–20 dorsal fin rays, 11–17 anal fin rays, 15–17 pectoral fin rays, 13 principal rays in caudal fin, five short branchiostegal rays, 33–39 vertebrae, and rodlike terminal section on vertebral column.

   Gosline (1959) placed this family in its own suborder in the Perciformes, as is done here. Its relationships are highly speculative, although there is a possible relationship with the ammodytoids (Gosline 1963b, 1971).

   One genus, *Schindleria*, with two species.

Suborder Ammodytoidei.   Body elongate; premaxilla protractile; caudal fin forked; dorsal and anal fin spines absent; lower jaw projecting forward beyond upper jaw; no swim bladder.

   The family Hypoptychidae, formerly placed in this suborder, has been provisionally placed in Gasterosteiformes following Ida (1976).

Family AMMODYTIDAE—sand lances.   Marine; Atlantic, Indian, and Pacific.

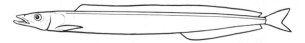

Scales cycloid, minute; pelvic fins usually absent (jugular and with one spine and three soft rays in *Embolichthys*); lateral line high, close to dorsal fin; no teeth; single long dorsal fin usually with 40–65 soft rays; seven branchiostegal rays; gill membranes separate. Length up to 30 cm.

Three genera, *Ammodytes* (= *Gymnammodytes* and *Hyperoplus*), *Bleekeria*, and *Embolichthys*, with about 12 species.

Suborder Callionymoidei.   Head usually broad and depressed; body scaleless; mouth small; usually two dorsal fins present and first with 1–4 flexible spines (spinous fin absent in *Draculo*); pelvic fin with one spine and five soft rays; basibranchials present; vertebrae 21–23.

In the previous edition I followed Gosline (1970) in placing the two families of this suborder along with Gobiesocidae in the Gobiesociformes. Gosline believed this group to be a notothenioid derivative and placed it after the Perciformes. It seems unlikely that callionymoids and gobiesocids are related, so I now follow the more conventional practice of placing the callionymoids between the Ammodytoidei and Gobioidei (e.g., Greenwood, 1975)and placing gobiesocids in the Paracanthopterygii.

Family CALLIONYMIDAE—dragonets.   Marine (two species enter rivers), benthic; all warm seas, primarily Indo-West Pacific.

Gill opening reduced to a small opening on upper side of head; preoperculum with a strong spine, operculum and suboperculum spineless; lateral line continued on body; three radials in pectoral skeleton; usually no basisphenoid or posttemporal; paired nasal bones; two postcleithra; hypurals fused into a single plate; dorsal fin spines usually four and soft rays 6–11; anal fin with 4–10 soft rays. Maximum length about 25 cm. Dragonets can be very colorful; sexual dimorphism is common.

About 10 genera (e.g., *Callionymus, Diplogrammus, Draculo, Pogonymus,* and *Synchiropus*) with about 130 species (Smith, 1963; Fricke, 1981, 1982).

Family DRACONETTIDAE. Marine; Japan to Hawaii, Atlantic, and Indian.

Gill opening comparatively broad; operculum and suboperculum each with a strong straight spine; preoperculum spineless; lateral line developed on head but degenerate on body (in a groove); four radials in pectoral skeleton; basisphenoid and posttemporal present; no nasal bone; one postcleithrum; two separate hypurals; three dorsal fin spines and 12–15 soft rays; anal fin with 12 or 13 soft rays; two nostrils on each side.

Draconettids are relatively rare. They occur primarily in tropical to warm temperate waters along the edge of the continental shelf or on seamounts in widely scattered areas.

Two genera, *Centrodraco* and the monotypic *Draconetta,* with seven species. Unlike Briggs and Berry (1959) who first revised this family, Nakabo (1982) recognizes *Centrodraco* as a valid genus. Species of *Centrodraco* have stout dorsal spines and usually 14 soft dorsal fin rays and 13 anal fin rays, while *Draconetta xenica* has soft dorsal spines and 12 soft rays in each of the dorsal and anal fins.

Suborder Gobioidei. Parietals absent; infraorbitals unossified or absent; lateral line system reduced to variably developed cephalic canals except in the primitive *Rhyacichthys*; swim bladder usually absent; gill membranes usually joined to isthmus; barbels on head in some; no pyloric caeca; spinous dorsal, when present, with 1–8 flexible spines; pelvic fins below pectorals, with one spine and four or five soft rays, often united; vertebrae 25–35 (exceptions to some characters occur in Microdesmidae).

Some authors give ordinal status to this group, while some treat most of the families recognized here as subfamilies of Gobiidae (e.g., Miller, 1973). The families Gobioididae and Trypauchenidae are sometimes combined under the family name Taenioididae, with the two lineages recognized at the subfamily level (e.g., Fowler, 1972:1400). Miller (1973) places them and the nominal subfamily Periophthalminae in his gobiid subfamily Gobionellinae. The Upper Oligocene fossil *Pirskenius* from freshwater deposits of Bohemia may warrent family status.

Seven families, about 263 genera, and approximately 1720 species.

Family RHYACICHTHYIDAE—loach gobies. Freshwater streams; Indo-Australian Archipelago (e.g., Java, Celebes, and New Guinea), Philippines, China, and Solomon Islands.

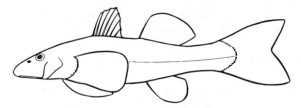

Head depressed, tail compressed; mouth inferior with fleshy upper lip; eyes small; pelvic fins widely separated; pectoral fins very broad, with 21 or 22 rays; lower surface of head and anterior part of body, with the paired fins, form an adhesive disc; dorsal fins well separated, first with seven feeble spines and second with one spine and eight or nine soft rays; anal fin with one feeble spine and eight or nine soft rays; lateral line scales (ctenoid) about 35–40; lateral line system on body and head well developed (presumably a unique primitive feature to the suborder); caudal fin lunate. The fish superficially resembles the homalopterids in appearance and habit. Maximum length about 32 cm.

One species, *Rhyacichthys* (= *Platyptera*) *aspro* (Herre, 1953; Munro, 1967; Fowler, 1972:1457; Miller, 1973).

Family ELEOTRIDIDAE—sleepers.   Marine, brackish, and freshwater; most tropical and subtropical areas (rarely temperate areas).

Pelvic fins separate (no sucking disc), bases close together or united (there is considerable variation in the degree of union or separation of the pelvic fins and sleepers and gobies cannot always be neatly separated on the basis of this character alone); mouth never inferior; spinous dorsal with 2–8 flexible spines; scales cycloid or ctenoid; vertebrae 25–28. Maximum length about 60 cm, attained in *Dormitator maculatus*.

Eleotridids extend as far north as the Atlantic coast of the United States and as far south as Stewart Island, New Zealand. Six species occur in New Zealand fresh waters in swift streams and the larvae are thought to generally drift downstream to the ocean (McDowall, 1975, 1978b).

About 40 genera (e.g., *Dormitator, Eleotris, Erotelis, Gobiomorphus, Gobiomorus,* and *Philypnodon*), with about 150 species.

Family GOBIIDAE—gobies.   Marine, brackish, and occasionally freshwater; most tropical and subtropical areas.

Pelvic fins, when well developed, united, usually forming an adhesive or sucking disc; spinous dorsal, when present, separate from soft dorsal and with 2–8 flexible spines; scales cycloid or ctenoid (rarely absent); some species with prominent head barbels (e.g., see Lachner and McKinney, 1978).

This is the largest family of marine fishes; they are often the most abundant fish in fresh water on oceanic islands. A few species are known even in the headwaters of rivers in mountains (Smith, 1945). Some species that occur in fresh water spawn in the ocean and are thus catadromous like the anguillids. Together with clinids and blennies, they form the dominant element in the small-fish fauna of benthic habit in tropical reefs. Some gobies live in close association with other animals (e.g., sponges, shrimps, and sea urchins). Some species of *Gobiosoma* feed on ectoparasites of other fishes. Several gobies live on wet beaches and may spend several days out of water. In at least one of these species, *Periophthalmus vulgaris*, the opercular chambers, which serve as a storehouse for the respiratory air in aerial respiration, are highly modified into saclike structures bounded by highly vascularized and folded epithelium (Singh and Datta Munshi, 1969). *Gillichthys mirabilis*, which usually remains in the water, comes to the surface, however, when the water is low in oxygen and gulps air which is held in the highy vascularized buccopharynx for respiratory exchange. Some of the land gobies, such as the mudskippers, *Periophthalmus* and *Periophthalmodon*, can move along with considerable speed. Their eyes, placed on top of the head on short stalks and capable of being elevated or retracted, are well adapted for vision in air. Their behavior in a mangrove swamp is described by Nursall (1981).

Maximum length up to 50 cm, most under about 10 cm. This family contains the world's smallest fishes (and vertebrates). The scaleless *Trimmatom nanus* of the Chagos Archipelago in the Indian Ocean is the shortest species, with mature females reaching only 8–10 mm in standard length (Winterbottom and Emery, 1981). Some species of the marine

Eviota and *Mistichthys* are only slightly larger. The freshwater *Pandaka pygmaea* of Luzon, Philippines, is the shortest freshwater fish with females maturing at about 10–11 mm.

Recent contributions to the systematics and taxonomy of gobiids include Birdsong (1975), who discusses the problems in recognizing subfamilies, Hoese and Winterbottom (1979), Lachner and Karnella (1980), Miller and Wongrat (1979), and Winterbottom and Emery (1981). Also, Crown Prince Akihito of Japan is doing extensive revisionary work (e.g., Akihito and Meguro, 1981). Chromosome number in various lineages are given by Nishikawa et al. (1974). Springer (1978) has shown that *Oxuderces*, upon which the family Oxudercidae has been recognized, is a gobiid.

About 200 genera (e.g., *Amblygobius, Apocryptes, Bathygobius, Benthophilus, Bollmannia, Clevelandia, Coryphopterus, Eucyclogobius, Gillichthys, Gobionellus, Gobiopsis (= Pipidonia), Gobiosoma, Gobius, Lebetus, Lepidogobius, Lethops, Lythrypnus, Microgobius, Periophthalmus, Pomatoschistus, Quietula, Sicydium, Tridentiger,* and *Typhlogobius*), with at least 1500 species. Although some species may be placed into synonomy with others there are many undescribed species known to exist (e.g., see Winterbottom and Emery, 1981). Birdsong's (1975) estimate of 2000 species may be a close approximation of the actual number of species which exist.

Family GOBIOIDIDAE—eellike gobies.   Marine, brackish, and freshwater; coastal tropical west Africa, Indo-Pacific, and both coasts of tropical America.

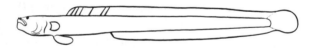

Body eellike; eyes very small; body naked or with cycloid scales; spinous and soft portions of dorsal fin confluent, the latter united or nearly so with the caudal; pelvic fins usually forming an adhesive disc; anal fin with 15–52 rays; no pouchlike cavity in opercular region. Maximum length about 48 cm.

Eight genera (e.g., *Brachyamblyopus, Caragobius, Gobioides, Nudagobioides, Odontamblyopus, Taenioides,* and *Tyntlastes*) with about 19 species.

Family TRYPAUCHENIDAE—burrowing gobies.   Marine, brackish, and freshwater; Indo-Pacific region (Natal, Persian Gulf, India to southern Japan and Philippines).

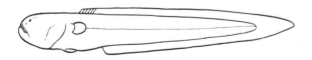

Body eellike; eyes very small to virtually absent; body naked or with cycloid scales; spinous and soft portions of dorsal fins confluent, the latter united or nearly so with the caudal; pelvic fins usually form an adhesive disc; pouchlike cavity in opercular region on each side. Maximum length about 20 cm.

These fish, like the closely related gobioids, live in shallow waters and often burrow in muddy bottoms. Some are virtually blind (e.g., *Ctenotrypauchen microcephalus* of the East Indies and the Philippines).

Five genera (e.g., *Amblyotrypauchen, Ctenotrypauchen,* and *Trypauchen*) with 10 species.

Family KRAEMERIIDAE—sandfishes or sand gobies. Marine (rarely brackish or freshwater); Indo-Pacific (to Hawaii).

Body elongate; tongue bilobed at tip; lower jaw protruding forward with enlarged chin; eyes small; body usually naked; dorsal and anal fins free of caudal; dorsal fin usually single with 4–6 feeble spines and usually 13–18 soft rays; pelvics with one spine and five soft rays, usually separate.

These fishes generally inhabit sandy shallow waters. Many species burrow into the sand with only the head protruding. Maximum length about 6 cm.

Four genera with about 10 species (Norman, 1957, recognized only the wide ranging *Kraemeria samoensis* in the family): *Kraemeria* (= *Psammichthys*) with about seven species; *Kraemericus chapmani* (in which the spiny and soft-rayed portion of the dorsal fins are separated and the body is scaled); *Gobitrichinotus radiocularis* [with fused pelvics, known from the Malabang River, Mindanao, Philippines (Herre, 1953) and Tahiti]; and *Parkraemeria ornata* (with the opercular opening restricted to side of head—Gosline, 1955; Matsubara and Iwai, 1959; Schultz et al., 1966).

Family MICRODESMIDAE (Cerdalidae)—wormfishes. Marine (rarely brackish); tropical waters.

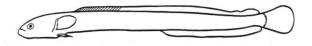

Body elongate to eellike; tongue simple at tip; body with small embedded cycloid scales; lower jaw heavy and protruding; dorsal fin continuous and extending along most of body, with a combination of 10–28 flexible spines and 28–66 soft rays; anal fin with 23–61 soft rays; pelvic fins small, inserted below pectorals, with one spine and 2–4 soft rays; pectoral fin rays 10–16; caudal fin free or united to dorsal and anal fins, with 15 or 17 principal rays; branchiostegal rays 5; vertebrae 42–76.

Wormfishes were once thought to be allied to blennioids but Gosline (1955) showed that they belong in the gobioids. Most of the information on the family is from Dawson (1974b, 1979). Wormfishes often burrow in sand and mud and are known from coral reefs to muddy estuaries and from tidepools to about 40 m depth. Maximum length 30 cm.

Five genera, *Microdesmus* (about 19 diverse Atlantic and eastern Pacific species), *Cerdale* (five eastern Pacific and western Atlantic species), *Clarkichthys* (one eastern Pacific species), *Gunnellichthys* (= *Paragobioides*—with four Indo-Pacific species), and *Paragunnellichthys* (one Red Sea species), with about 30 species. Reasons for removing *Pholidichthys* are given by Springer and Freihofer (1976). Dawson (1974b) notes that *Allomicrodesmus* (known only from a damaged postlarva) does not belong in this family (its relationships, however, are uncertain).

Suborder Kurtoidei

Family KURTIDAE—nurseryfishes.   Brackish and freshwater (rarely marine); in Indo-Malay area and parts of Australia.

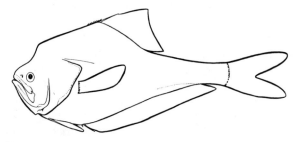

Males with occipital hook, used for carrying eggs; scales small and cycloid; lateral line short and rudimentary; mouth large; dorsal fin single, with spines and soft rays; anal fin with two spines and 31–47 soft rays; pelvic fins with one spine and five soft rays; caudal fin deeply forked; ribs expanded, partly enclosing the anterior portion of the swim bladder and entirely enclosing the posterior portion.

Tominaga (1968) gives additional features for the group and compares it with the beryciforms and perciforms. Maximum length 59 cm, attained in *Kurtus gulliveri*.

One genus, *Kurtus*, with two species. *K. gulliveri* has 44–47 soft rays in anal fin and is found in southern New Guinea and northern Australia; *K. indicus* has 31 or 32 soft rays in anal fin and is found in the Indo-Malay area (India, China, Borneo, etc.).

Suborder Acanthuroidei.   Body deeply compressed; mouth small; swim bladder large; elongate ethmoid and nasal bones give a high-headed appearance; dorsal fin single, with spines and soft rays; gill openings restricted; caudal fin lunate; 22 or 23 vertebrae.

Almost all species are herbivorous, feeding mostly on algae. They pass through a planktonic larval stage, termed the acronurus stage, in which their bodies are transparent.

Twelve genera and about 102 species.

Family ACANTHURIDAE—surgeonfishes.   Marine; all tropical seas.

Pelvic fins with one spine and three or (usually) five soft rays; dorsal fin usually with 4–9 spines and 19–31 (38–42 in *Zanclus*) soft rays; anal fin with two or three spines and usually 19–36 soft rays.

SUBFAMILY ACANTHURINAE (HEPATIDAE, TEUTHIDAE).   One or more spines on caudal peduncle (which, when extended, can form a formidable weapon); premaxilla not protractile. Maximum length about 66 cm.

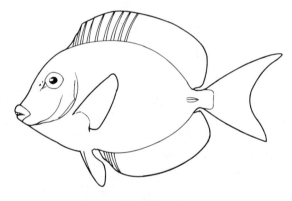

Nine genera with about 76 species. Three tribes can be recognized (regarded as subfamilies in Smith, 1966). The Acanthurini (all tropical seas) with four genera, *Acanthurus, Ctenochaetus, Paracanthurus* (the one species, a popular aquarium fish, is particular striking in color with its blue body, black markings, and yellowish tail), and *Zebrasoma,* and about 53 species; all have three anal spines and one movable spine on the caudal peduncle. Prionurini (primarily Pacific), with *Prionurus* and *Xesurus* and six species (three anal spines and 3–10 bony plates on the caudal peduncle). And Nasini (Indo-Pacific—the unicornfishes), with *Axinurus, Callicanthus,* and *Naso* and about 17 species (two anal spines, three soft pelvic rays rather than five in addition to the spine, one or two plates on the caudal peduncle, and some species with a protuberance on the frontal region developing with age).

SUBFAMILY ZANCLINAE (MOORISH IDOL). Caudal peduncle unarmed; premaxillaries protractile; spine at corner of mouth in juveniles and protuberances in front of eyes in adults.

   The Moorish idol is found in tropical regions of the Indian and Pacific oceans, most commonly in coral reef areas. The extended snout in the adult is well suited for foraging for invertebrates and algae in small crevices. The broad vertical black bars on a largely whitish background and elongated dorsal fin filament make it a very attractive fish. It bears a marked resemblance to the butterflyfish, *Heniochus acuminatus,* another popular aquarium fish.
   One species, *Zanclus canescens (= Z. cornutus).*

Family SIGANIDAE—rabbitfishes.   Marine; Indo-Pacific and eastern Mediterranean.

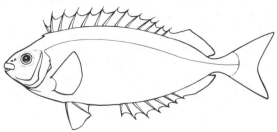

Pelvic fins each with two spines and three soft rays between them; dorsal with 13 strong spines and 10 soft rays; anal fin with seven spines and nine soft rays; spines venomous. Maximum length about 40 cm.

Two genera, *Lo* and *Siganus* (= *Teuthis*), with about 25 species about 15 of which are schooling species with the remainder living among coral (Woodland and Allen, 1977).

Suborder Scombroidei.   Premaxilla fixed [nonprotrusible upper jaw (except in *Scombrolabrax* and *Luvarus*)].

This suborder includes species that are probably the world's fastest swimming fish. Sailfish, swordfish, and bluefin tuna have had speeds between 60 and 100 km/hr attributed to them (for short periods of time).

Gosline (1968) recognizes two suborders in this group: the Xiphioidei (recognized here as a superfamily) and the Scombroidei. According to Gosline (1968) and Johnson (1975) this suborder may have had its origins near the Pomatomidae.

Seven families with 45 genera and about 100 species.

Superfamily Trichiuroidea.   Thirty or more vertebrae; protruding lower jaw; teeth very long. Parin and Bekker (1972) and Tucker (1956) present information on this group.

Family SCOMBROLABRACIDAE.   Marine; deep-water Atlantic, Indian, and Pacific.

Premaxilla protractile; preopercle and opercle serrated; swim bladder with thin, elastic walls and, in adult, with bubblelike evaginations fitting into vertebral bullae; 30 vertebrae, 5th through 12th of adults with expanded parapophyses, called the bullae, that bulge dorsolaterally and with ventral opening. Maximum length about 30 cm. Bond and Uyeno (1981), because of the mixed percoid and scombroid characteristics of the one species (in general appearance it most closely resembles the gempylids), favor placing it in its own suborder, the Scombrolabroidei.

One species, *Scrombrolabrax heterolepis*.

Family GEMPYLIDAE—snake mackerels.   Marine, tropical and subtropical seas, often in very deep water.

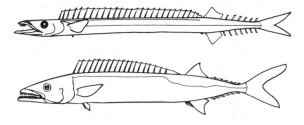

Body oblong or elongate and compressed; maxilla exposed; isolated finlets usually present behind dorsal and anal fins; caudal fin present; pectoral fin low on body; pelvic fin reduced or absent. *Lepidocybium* has many
scombrid characters. *Diplospinus*, which is intermediate between the gempylids and trichiurids in many characters, is placed in the Gempylidae
following Parin and Bekker (1973); it was placed in the trichiurid subfamily Aphanopodinae by Tucker (1956).

Fifteen genera, *Diplospinus, Epinnula, Escolar, Gempylus* (upper figure),
Lemnisoma, Lepidocybium (= *Xenogramma*), *Mimasea, Nealotus, Neoepinnula,
Nesiarchus, Paradiplospinus, Prometichthys, Rexea, Ruvettus,* and *Thyrsites* (lower
figure), with about 22 species.

Family TRICHIURIDAE—cutlassfishes.   Marine; Atlantic, Indian, and Pacific.

Body very elongate and strongly compressed; maxilla concealed by
preorbitals; fanglike teeth usually present; dorsal fin extremely long based,
with spines and soft rays (spinous portion usually shorter than soft rayed
portion, notch between two portions in some species); caudal fin small or
absent; pectoral fin low on body; pelvic fin reduced (with a scalelike spine
and one rudimentary soft ray) or absent; vertebrae 58–192 (34–53 + 24–
151).

Nine genera with about 17 species.

SUBFAMILY APHANOPODINAE.   Caudal fin small, forked; pelvic fin present,
with scalelike spine and one rudimentary soft ray (external fin may be
present only in juvenile); spinous dorsal fin with 38–46 rays, slight notch
at division of spinous and soft portions.

Two genera, the monotypic *Aphanopus* and *Benthodesmus* (seven species),
with eight species.

SUBFAMILY LEPIDOPODINAE.   Caudal fin present (small and forked) or
absent; pelvic fin present, rudimentary; spinous dorsal fin usually with
3–10 rays, spinous and soft portions continuous; lateral line descending
gradually behind the pectoral fin.

Five genera, *Lepidopus, Evoxymetopon, Eupleurogrammus, Assurger,* and
Tentoriceps, with about seven species.

SUBFAMILY TRICHIURINAE.   Caudal fin and hypurals absent; pelvic fin
and skeleton absent; spinous dorsal fin with three or four rays, spinous

and soft portions continuous; lateral line descending steeply from the pectorals and running near ventral profile of body.

Two monotypic genera, *Trichiurus* and *Lepturacanthus.*

Superfamily Scombroidea. Thirty or more vertebrae.

Family SCOMBRIDAE—mackerels and tunas. Marine; tropical and subtropical seas.

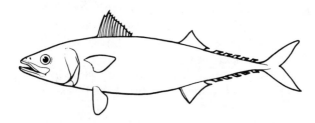

Two dorsal fins (depressible into grooves) with finlets behind second dorsal and anal fins; first dorsal fin origin well behind head; pectoral fins inserted high on body; pelvic fins with six rays, placed beneath the pectorals; gill membranes free from isthmus; scales cycloid and small; slender caudal peduncle with two keels; specialized subcutaneous vascular system in *Thunnus* and its close relatives.

The body temperature of large tunas is warmer than the surrounding water because of their high metabolic rate. These fast-swimming fish constitute a popular sport and valuable commercial fisheries. Length up to 4.2 m, attained by *Thunnus thynnus.*

The placement of certain of the tunas in a separate order by Berg (1940) is ill advised.

Fifteen genera with 48 species (about one-half the species belong to *Scomberomorus* and *Thunnus*).

The following classification is based on Gibbs and Collette (1967), Collette and Chao (1975), and Collette (1979).

SUBFAMILY GASTEROCHISMATINAE. Scales moderate in size, about 80 in lateral series.

One species, the aberrant *Gasterochisma melampus,* of the Southern Oceans.

SUBFAMILY SCOMBRINAE. Scales minute.

TRIBE SCOMBRINI (MACKERELS). Two genera, *Rastrelliger* and *Scomber,* with six species.

TRIBE SCOMBEROMORINI (SPANISH MACKERELS). Three genera, *Acanthocybium, Grammatorcynus,* and *Scomberomorus,* with 20 species.

TRIBE SARDINI (BONITOS). Five genera, *Allothunnus, Cybiosarda, Gymnosarda, Orcynopsis,* and *Sarda,* with eight species.

TRIBE THUNNINI (TUNAS). Four genera, *Auxis, Euthynnus, Katsuwonus,* and *Thunnus,* with 13 species.

Superfamily Xiphioidea. Vertebrae 23–26; dorsal fin origin over back of head except in *Luvarus;* pectorals inserted low on body; pelvics reduced (three rays or fewer) or absent; mouth inferior except in *Luvarus;* two anal fins except in *Luvarus,* in which one is present.

Luvaridae probably bears little or no affinity with xiphioids and is only provisionally retained with them because of the few similarities and lack of a sound basis for placing it elsewhere.

Family XIPHIIDAE—swordfish. Marine; tropical and subtropical seas.

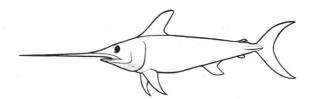

Premaxilla and nasal bones elongated to form a long, pointed, depressed rostrum; gill membranes free from isthmus; scales absent in adult; pelvic fins and girdle absent; jaws toothless in adult; caudal peduncle in adult with single median keel on each side; 26 vertebrae.

Swordfish are a valuable commercial species. Length up to 4.5 m.

One species, *Xiphias gladius.*

Family LUVARIDAE—louvar. Marine; tropical and subtropical seas.

Premaxilla protrusible—no long pointed rostrum (snout blunt); gill membranes broadly joined to isthmus; dorsal fin origin in juvenile well forward, moving back with growth; 22 vertebrae, last two fused. Bolin (1940) gives a detailed description of one specimen.

These fish have an enormous egg production; a 1.7 m individual had an estimated 47.5 million eggs, characteristic of nonschooling oceanic fish. Length up to 1.8 m.

One species, *Luvarus imperialis.*

Family ISTIOPHORIDAE (Histiophoridae)—billfishes. Marine; most tropical and subtropical seas.

Premaxilla and nasal bones elongated to form a long, pointed, rounded rostrum; gill membranes free from isthmus; scales present; pelvic fins elongate; jaws with teeth; caudal peduncle in adult with two keels on each side; dorsal fin with very long base, sometimes saillike, depressible into groove; lateral line retained throughout life; 24 vertebrae.

The bill is used to stun prey fish by slashing back and forth. Billfishes are an extremely popular sportfish. Length up to 4 m.

Three genera with about 10 species.

Istiophorus (sailfishes): first dorsal fin sail-shaped and distinctly taller than body depth; rays of pelvic fin very long. Two species.

Tetrapturus (spearfishes): forward portion of first dorsal fin about as high as body is deep. Six species.

Makaira (marlins): forward portion of first dorsal fin not so high as body is deep (shown in figure). Two species.

Suborder Stromateoidei (see map on p. 423). Toothed saccular outgrowths in gullet behind last gill arch; lachrymal bone covering most of maxilla; scales usually cycloid, weakly ctenoid in some; branchiostegal rays 5–7; hypural plates 2–6; caudal fin with 15 branched rays; vertebrae 25–60. Length up to 1.2 m.

Six families, 16 genera, and about 60 species. All are marine. Classification based on Haedrich (1967) and modifications by Haedrich and Horn (1972) and McDowall (1979b).

Family AMARSIPIDAE. Marine; tropical Indian and Pacific, close to the equator.

Pelvic fins present, jugular, their origin well before the pectoral fins; body translucent, no color pattern; pharyngeal sacs absent; dorsal fin with 10–12 short spines and 22–27 longer soft rays; anal fin with 28–32 soft rays, no spines; pectoral fin with 17–19 rays; vertebrae 45–47. No adults of this pelagic fish are known.

One species, *Amarsipus carlsbergi*, described in 1969.

Family CENTROLOPHIDAE—medusafishes.   Marine; tropical to temperate, all seas except most of mid-Indian and mid-Pacific.

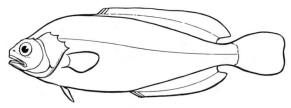

Pelvic fins present in adult; dorsal fin continuous, spines either 0–5, weakly developed and graduating into the soft rays (as in illustration and in the first three genera listed) or 5–9, stout, and considerably shorter than and generally not graduating into the soft rays (in the last three genera listed); total anal fin rays 15–41 (usually three spines).

Centrolophus is the only stromateoid in the far North Atlantic (to Iceland), whereas *Icichthys* is the only stromateoid in the far North Pacific (to Alaska). Both genera are also in southern oceans.

Seven genera, *Centrolophus, Icichthys, Tubbia, Schedophilus, Hyperoglyphe, Psenopsis,* and *Seriolella,* with about 22 species.

Family NOMEIDAE—driftfishes.   Marine; tropical and subtropical seas.

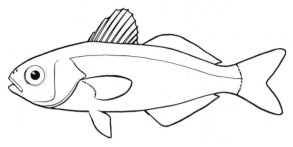

Pelvic fins present in adult; two dorsal fins, the first with 9–12 slender spines and the second with 0–3 spines and 15–32 soft rays; anal fin with 1–3 spines and 14–30 soft rays. Maximum length about 1 m.

The 10 cm *Nomeus gronovii* (man-of-war fish) is circumtropical and usually found with the Portuguese man-of-war *(Physalia)*. The fish swims unharmed among the stinging tentacles.

Three genera, *Cubiceps*, *Nomeus*, and *Psenes*, with about 15 species.

Family ARIOMMATIDAE—ariommatids.   Marine; deep water, tropical and subtropical coastlines of eastern North and South America, Africa, Asia, Kermadec Islands, and Hawaii.

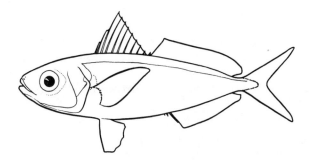

Pelvic fins present in adult; two dorsal fins, the first with 10–12 slender spines and the second with 14–18 soft rays; anal fin with three short spines and 13–16 soft rays; pectoral fin with 20–24 rays; caudal peduncle with two low, fleshy, lateral keels on each side; vertebrae 30–32.

One genus, *Ariomma*, with about six species.

Family TETRAGONURIDAE—squaretails.   Marine; tropical and subtropical seas.

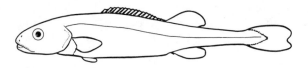

Body elongate; pelvic fins present in adult; two dorsal fins, the first with 10–20 short spines and the second with 10–17 soft rays; anal fin with one spine and 10–16 soft rays; caudal peduncle with a single keel on each side; lateral scales 73–114; vertebrae 40–58. Individuals are thought to feed almost exclusively on coelenterates and ctenophores.

One genus, *Tetragonurus*, with three species. This is the most widely distributed of all the stromateoid genera.

Family STROMATEIDAE—butterfishes.   Marine; coastal North and South America, western Africa, and southern Asia (Indo-Pacific).

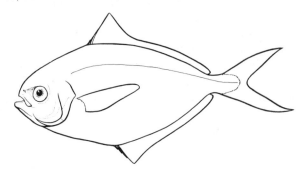

Body usually very deep; pelvic fins absent in adult (present in some young—pelvic bones present); dorsal fin continuous; anal fin usually with 2–6 spines and 30–50 soft rays.

Three genera, *Pampus, Peprilus,* and *Stromateus,* with about 13 species.

Suborder Anabantoidei   (see map on p. 423). A suprabranchial organ present, usually labyrinthine, formed by expansion of first epibranchial; dorsal and anal fins with spines; gill membranes scaly and broadly united; pelvic fins thoracic, usually with one spine and five soft rays; five or six branchiostegal rays; swim bladder divided posteriorly, extending into caudal region; vertebrae 25–31.

The suprabranchial organ is an auxiliary breathing apparatus. Air taken in through the mouth passes through the labyrinth where capillaries absorb oxygen. As air is taken in at various intervals, old air is forced out of the labyrinth through the gill covers. This organ has enabled many species to occupy submarginal or even anoxic waters. Liem (1980) describes the mechanism of ventilation in several anabantoids.

In most anabantoids the male builds a nest of floating bubbles. Eggs are deposited in the bubbles and the male exhibits parental care. Forselius (1957), along with other subjects, gives a detailed description of the behavior of these fishes.

This and the next two suborders, Luciocephaloidei and Channoidei, have been variously classified. Under some schemes (e.g., Jordan, 1923) members of the three suborders were placed together in a separate order, the Labyrinthici. Liem (1963) attributed the possession in all three of a suprabranchial organ to convergent evolution and not phylogenetic relationship. Certainly the first epibranchial becomes variously modified to form the suprabranchial organ. Greenwood et al. (1966), in a fashion similar to Berg (1940), placed the anabantoids and luciocephalids in separate suborders and placed the channids in their own order between

Gasterosteiformes and Synbranchiformes, considering them as preperciforms. Gosline (1968, 1971) placed all three in the same suborder, the Anabantoidei, and, like his suborder Mugiloidei, considered it a "propercoid" in the perciformes. Here all three are recognized as separate suborders and placed consecutively. All are freshwater and indigenous to Africa and southern Asia.

Gosline (1971) believes that the group is an early perciform offshoot with some affinity with the Nandidae (which he suggests may best be placed in the Anabantoidei).

Four families, 16 genera, and about 70 species.

Family ANABANTIDAE—climbing gouramies. Freshwater (rarely brackish); Africa and India to Philippines.

Jaws, prevomer, and parasphenoid with fixed conical teeth; mouth relatively large; upper jaw only weakly protrusile; one genus, *Sandelia,* only with cycloid scales, not ctenoid; gill rakers few and diet generally carnivorous.

Three genera, *Anabas, Ctenopoma,* and *Sandelia,* with perhaps 40 species.

Family BELONTIIDAE (Polyacanthidae)—gouramies. Freshwater; west Africa and India to Malay Archipelago and Korea.

Prevomer and palatine without teeth; upper jaw protrusile; lateral line vestigial or absent; dorsal fin never with more than 10 soft rays; many species with an elongate pelvic ray on each side.

Eleven genera with perhaps 28 species (Liem, 1963, 1965).

Liem (1963) established the following three subfamilies, which represent the three major evolutionary lines of the family.

SUBFAMILY BELONTIINAE (COMBTAIL GOURAMIES). One genus, *Belontia,* with perhaps two species.

SUBFAMILY MACROPODINAE (SIAMESE FIGHTING FISHES, PARADISEFISHES, ETC.)

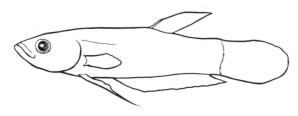

Six genera, *Betta* (shown in figure), *Ctenops, Trichopsis, Macropodus, Pa-rosphromenus,* and *Malpulutta,* with perhaps 14 species. Burgess (1982) comments on a proposal to recognize the bubblenest builders of *Betta* (e.g., *B. splendens*) in a separate genus from the mouthbrooders (e.g., the type species, *B. trifasciata*).

SUBFAMILY TRICHOGASTRINAE (GOURAMIES, ETC.).

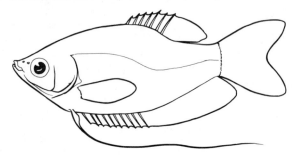

Four genera, *Sphaerichthys, Parasphaerichthys, Colisa,* and *Trichogaster* (shown in figure), with about 12 species.

Family HELOSTOMATIDAE—kissing gourami. Freshwater; Thailand to Malay Archipelago.

Premaxilla, dentaries, palatine, and pharynx devoid of teeth; two lateral lines, the lower commencing below the end of the upper; dorsal fin with 16–18 spines and 13–16 soft rays; anal fin with 13–15 spines and 17–19 soft rays; lateral line scales 43–48; scales on top of head cycloid, others ctenoid. Numerous gill rakers form an elaborate filter apparatus on the gill arches which adapts the fish to filter feeding (horny teeth on the lips also enable the fish to scrape algae off surfaces). Liem (1967a) describes the functional morphology of the head region. Maximum length about 30 cm.
One species, *Helostoma temmincki.*

Family OSPHRONEMIDAE—giant gourami. Freshwater; Thailand to Malay Archipelago.

Prevomer and palatine devoid of teeth; one lateral line, complete and continuous; all scales ctenoid; dorsal fin with 11–13 spines and 11–13 soft rays; anal fin with 9–12 spines and 16–22 soft rays. Maximum length about 60 cm.
One species, *Osphronemus goramy.*

Suborder Luciocephaloidei. See notes under Anabantoidei for taxonomic placement of this group.

Family LUCIOCEPHALIDAE—pikehead. Freshwater; Malay Peninsula and Archipelago.

Suprabranchial organ for air breathing present; no dorsal or anal spines; dorsal fin inserted posteriorly, with 9–12 rays; anal fin with a deep notch and 18 or 19 rays; pelvic fin with one spine and five soft rays (one of which is produced into a threadlike ray); caudal fin rounded; lateral line scales about 40–42; mouth very protractile; gill membranes not united; median gular element present; no swim bladder. Liem (1967b) gives a detailed description of the species. Lauder and Liem (1981) note that it has the most protrusible jaws known among teleosts. The premaxillae can extend anteriorly a distance of 33% of the head length, but prey is not captured by suction but rather by the fish making a rapid lunge and surrounding the prey with the open mouth. Maximum length about 18 cm.

One species, *Luciocephalus pulcher.*

Suborder Channoidei (Ophiocephaliformes). See notes under Anabantoidei for taxonomic placement of this group.

Family CHANNIDAE—snakeheads. Freshwater; tropical Africa and southern Asia (see map on p. 424).

Body elongate; long dorsal and anal fins; pelvic fins usually present, with six rays; no fin spines; cycloid or ctenoid scales; lower jaw protruding beyond upper; suprabranchial organ for air breathing present (the mechanism for air breathing is described in one species by Ishimatsu and Itazawa, 1981). Maximum length about 1.2 m.

One genus, *Channa* (= *Ophicephalus*) with about 12 species. Eight species are found in India (Reddy, 1978).

Suborder Mastacembeloidei (Opisthomi). Body elongate (eellike); no pelvic fins; dorsal and anal fins continuous to or continuous with the small caudal fin; pectoral arch (supracleithrum) attached to the vertebral column by a ligament; no air duct to swim bladder (physoclistic); no posttemporal bone; 70–95 vertebrae.

This group, a perciform derivative, is placed in its own order by many workers.

Family MASTACEMBELIDAE—spiny eels. Freshwater; tropical Africa; through Syria to Malay Archipelago and China (see map on p. 424).

Dorsal fin preceded by a series of isolated spines (usually 14–35); anal fin usually with two or three spines and 30–130 soft rays; fleshy rostral appendage present; body covered with small scales; no basisphenoid. Maximum length up to 0.9 m. In some places mastacembelids are regarded as an excellent food fish; they are occasionally kept as an aquarium fish. They are found in a wide variety of habitats. Some species burrow in the substrate during the day or for certain months and have been found buried in soil in drying ponds (Sufi, 1956).

Two genera, *Macrognathus* (three species in southern Asia, with an elongate rostrum—Roberts, 1980) and *Mastacembelus*, with about 60 species.

Family CHAUDHURIIDAE. Freshwater; northeastern India, Burma, and Thailand.

No dorsal spines; no rostral appendage; body naked; basisphenoid present. Maximum length about 8 cm.

Berg (1940) and Sufi (1956) felt that differences with the mastacembelids were sufficient to place this family in a separate order. R. A. Travers (pers. comm., 1982), who is revising the mastacembeloids, considers the two species of *Pillaia*, placed in their own family, Pillaiidae, by Yazdani (1976), to be congeneric with *Chaudhuria*. The range of the family is extended to Thailand by Roberts (1980).

Two genera, *Chaudhuria* and *Pillaia*, with three species.

Order PLEURONECTIFORMES (Heterosomata). Adults not bilaterally symmetrical; body highly compressed, somewhat rounded on eyed side and flat on blind side; dorsal and anal fins usually long; usually six or seven branchiostegal rays, rarely eight; body cavity small; adults almost always without swim bladder; scales cycloid, ctenoid, or tuberculate.

This is a very distinctive group. Young flatfishes are bilaterally symmetrical and swim upright, but early in their development one eye migrates across the top of the skull to lie adjacent to the eye on the other side. They then lie and swim on the eyeless side. The change involves a complex modification of skull bones, nerves, and muscles and leaves one side of the fish blind (lower side) and the other side with two eyes (upper side). The upper side is also pigmented, whereas the under side is usually white. Asymmetry may also be reflected in other characters such as dentition, squamation, and paired fins. Most species have both eyes on the right side and lie on the left side (dextral) or have both eyes on the left side and lie on the right side (sinistral). In some species both dextral (righteyed) and sinistral (lefteyed) individuals may occur. Among the latter species, the pleuronectid *Platichthys stellatus* (the starry flounder) is especially interesting because of the varying frequency of dextral to sinistral individuals over its range in the North Pacific. Other members of the family are dextral, but almost all starry flounders from Japanese waters are sinistral, while off California the two types are about equal in frequency. Policansky (1982) reports that the difference between sinistral and dextral starry flounders appears to be largely under genetic control. As yet, however, there appears to be no convincing arguments for a direct adaptive advantage for being sinistral or dextral.

Flatfishes are benthic and carnivorous. Maximum length almost 3 m in the halibuts; much smaller in most groups.

Common names for flatfishes include flounder, halibut, sole, plaice, dab, and turbot, which often apply to species in different families. Many species are important in commercial fisheries and are valued as a food source.

About 538 extant species are recognized in approximately 117 genera and six families (some authors recognize seven, giving family status to the Scophthalminae). Norman (1934), Hubbs (1945), Amaoka (1969), and Li (1981b) deal with the classification of this order. The following sequence of families and subfamilies follows the phylogeny presented by Li (1981b) which was based on 84 morphological characters (except that Li gives family status to the Scophthalminae but does show it as at the base of the bothid lineage and does not recognize the Rhombosoleinae). Li (1981b) places the pleuronectiforms between the beryciforms and perciforms (i.e., he considers it a preperciform group).

Suborder Psettodoidei.   Dorsal fin not extending onto head (to or past eye); anterior dorsal and anal rays spinous; palatine with teeth; basisphenoid present; 24 or 25 vertebrae.

Family PSETTODIDAE—psettodids.   Marine; west Africa and Indo-West Pacific.

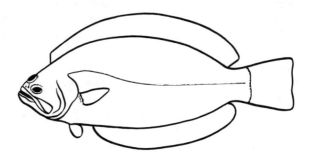

Pelvic fins nearly symmetrical, with one spine and five soft rays; mouth large; eyes sinistral or dextral; preopercular margin distinct, not covered with skin. Maximum length about 60 cm.

One genus, *Psettodes,* with two species: *P. belcheri* from tropical west Africa (eastern Atlantic) and *P. erumei* from eastern Africa and the Red Sea to the western Pacific. Stauch and Cadenat (1965) recognized two west African species, *P. benneti* (coastal Senegal and Mauritania) and *P. belcheri* (coastal Ghana to Angola).

Suborder Pleuronectoidei.   Dorsal fin extending onto head at least to eyes; dorsal and anal fins without spines; palatine without teeth; no basisphenoid; vertebrae 26–70, 10 or more are abdominal; preopercular margin distinct, not covered with skin; one or two postcleithra; optic nerve of migrating eye always dorsal (may be dorsal or ventral in other flatfishes).

Family CITHARIDAE—citharids.   Marine; Mediterranean, Indian Ocean, and Japan to Australia.

Pelvic fins with 1 spine and 5 soft rays; pelvic fin bases short; branchiostegal membranes separated from each other.

Four genera with 5 species.

Subfamily Citharinae.   Eyes sinistral.

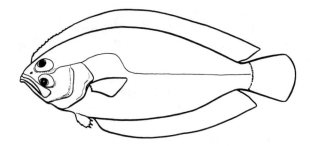

Two genera, *Citharoides* and *Citharus* (= *Eucitharus*), with three species.

SUBFAMILY BRACHYPLEURINAE.   Eyes dextral.
Two monotypic genera, *Brachypleura* and *Lepidoblepharon*.

Family BOTHIDAE—lefteye flounders.   Marine; Atlantic, Indian, and Pacific.

Eyes sinistral; pelvic fins without a spine; branchiostegal membranes connected; egg with a single oil globule in the yolk.
    Thirty-seven genera with about 212 species.

SUBFAMILY SCOPHTHALMINAE.   Both pelvic fin bases elongate. This group,
confined to the north Atlantic and Mediterranean and Black seas, is given
family status by some workers (e.g., Greenwood et al., 1966; Nielsen,
1973; Li, 1981b).
    Five genera, *Scophthalmus, Psetta, Lepidorhombus, Phrynorhombus,* and
Zeugopterus, with about 10 species.

SUBFAMILY PARALICHTHYINAE.   Pelvic fin bases short and nearly symmetrical; pectoral and pelvic rays branched.

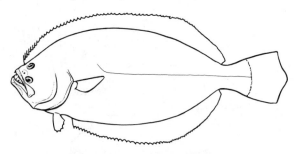

Nineteen genera (e.g., *Ancylopsetta, Citharichthys, Etropus, Gastropsetta, Hip-
poglossina, Paralichthys, Pseudorhombus, Tarphops,* and *Xystreurys*) with about
86 species.

SUBFAMILY BOTHINAE.   Pelvic fin base on blind side shorter than on eyed side; pectoral and pelvic fin rays not branched.

Thirteen genera (e.g., *Arnoglossus, Bothus, Chascanopsetta, Engyprosopon,* and *Taeniopsetta*) with about 116 species.

Family PLEURONECTIDAE—righteye flounders. Marine (occasionally in brackish water, rarely in fresh water); Arctic, Atlantic, and Pacific.

Eyes almost always dextral; no oil globule in yolk of egg.

Forty-one genera with about 99 species.

SUBFAMILY POECILOPSETTINAE.   Origin of dorsal fin above the eyes; lateral line rudimentary on blind side; pelvic fins symmetrical.

Three genera (e.g., *Poecilopsetta*) with 13 species.

SUBFAMILY RHOMBOSOLEINAE.   Pelvic fins asymmetrical (one on the eyed side may be joined to anal fin); lateral line equally developed on both sides; pectoral radials absent. A South Pacific group, occurring primarily around Australia and New Zealand. Some of the species resemble the Soleidae.

Eight genera (e.g., *Ammotretis, Colistium, Peltorhamphus,* and *Rhombosolea*) with 12 species.

SUBFAMILY SAMARINAE.   Origin of dorsal fin in front of eyes; lateral line well developed or rudimentary; pelvic fins symmetrical. An Indo-Pacific group.

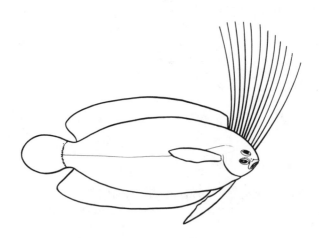

Four genera (e.g., *Paralichthodes, Samaris,* and *Samariscus*) with 14 species.

SUBFAMILY PLEURONECTINAE.   Origin of dorsal fin above the eyes; lateral line well developed on both sides; pelvic fins symmetrical.

TRIBE HIPPOGLOSSINI.   Mouth large and symmetrical; maxillae extending to or behind pupil of eyes; teeth well developed on both sides of jaws. The commercially important and large halibuts belong to this group.
    Ten genera (e.g., *Atheresthes, Eopsetta, Hippoglossoides, Hippoglossus, Lyopsetta, Psettichthys,* and *Reinhardtius*) with about 18 species.

TRIBE PLEURONECTINI.   Mouth small and asymmetrical; maxillae usually not extending to pupil of eye; teeth chiefly on blind side of jaw.

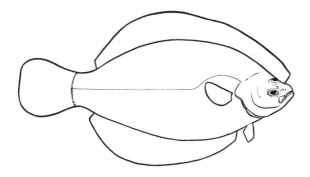

Sixteen genera (e.g., *Embassichthys, Glyptocephalus, Hypsopsetta, Isopsetta, Lepidopsetta, Limanda, Liopsetta, Microstomus, Parophrys, Platichthys, Pleuronectes, Pleuronichthys,* and *Pseudopleuronectes*) with about 42 species.

Suborder Soleoidei.   Preopercular margin not entirely free, covered by skin; vertebrae usually 24–50—10 or fewer are abdominal; no postcleithrum; no basisphenoid; pectoral fins usually absent in adult—right pectoral fin well developed in some; ribs absent; mouth small; jaws on blind side strongly curved and toothed.

Family CYNOGLOSSIDAE—tonguefishes.   Marine (some freshwater); tropical and subtropical seas.

Eyes sinistral; dorsal and anal fins confluent with the pointed caudal fin; usually only left pelvic fin developed; pectorals absent (a fine membrane in *Symphurus*); eyes very small and usually close together; mouth asymmetrical; vertebrae 42–78 (usually 9 or 10 abdominal and 33–66 caudal). Maximum length for most species is less than 30 cm, rarely over 40 cm (up to about 48 cm).

Three genera with about 103 species.

SUBFAMILY SYMPHURINAE.   Snout not hooked; mouth terminal and almost straight; lateral line absent on both sides; pelvic fin free from anal fin. Most are deepwater, occurring about 300–1900 m.

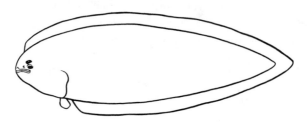

One genus, *Symphurus,* with about 50 species, found on both sides of the Americas and in the eastern Atlantic and Indo-West Pacific (including Hawaii).

SUBFAMILY CYNOGLOSSINAE.   Snout hooked; mouth inferior and contorted; lateral line(s) well developed, at least on eyed side; pelvic fin confluent with anal fin. Most are shallow water burrowing forms; about five species are known primarily from rivers.

Two genera, *Cynoglossus (= Arelia*—lips without fringes) with 49 species and *Paraplagusia* (lips on eyed side with fringes) with four species found in the Old World from the eastern Atlantic to the western Pacific (Menon, 1977).

Family SOLEIDAE—soles.   Marine (some freshwater); tropical to temperate seas.

Eyes dextral.

Thirty-one genera with about 117 species.

SUBFAMILY ACHIRINAE.   Amphi-American, many in fresh water. Margin of preoperculum represented by a superficial groove; dorsal and anal fins free from caudal fin; right pelvic fin joined to anal fin.

Nine genera (e.g., *Achirus*, *Gymnachirus*, and *Trinectes*) with about 28 species.

SUBFAMILY SOLEINAE.   Primarily Europe to Australia and Japan. Margin of preoperculum completely concealed; dorsal and anal fins free from caudal fin or united with caudal; pelvics free from anal fin.

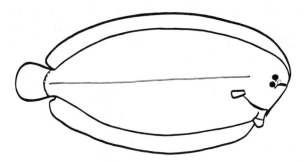

Twenty-two genera (e.g., *Aseraggodes*, *Euryglossa*, *Solea*, *Synaptura*, and *Zebrias*) with about 89 species.

Order TETRAODONTIFORMES (Plectognathi).   No parietals, nasals, or infraorbitals, and usually no lower ribs; posttemporal, if present, simple and fused with pterotic of skull; hyomandibular and palatine firmly attached to skull; gill openings restricted; maxilla usually firmly united or fused with premaxilla; scales usually modified as spines, shields, or plates; lateral line present or absent, sometimes multiple; swim bladder present except in molids; 16–30 vertebrae.

Tetraodontiformes can produce sounds by grinding the jaw teeth or the pharyngeal teeth or by vibrating the swim bladder. The stomach of some tetraodontiforms is highly modified to allow inflation to an enormous size. Fish with this ability, belonging to the two families Diodontidae and Tetraodontidae, are popularly called puffers. Inflation is caused by gulping down water into a ventral diverticulum of the stomach when the fish is frightened or annoyed. Deflation occurs by expelling the water. If the fish is removed from the water, inflation can occur with air. The triodontid and most balistids have another mechanism for slightly enlarging their bodies. They do this by expanding a ventral flap supported by a large movable pelvic bone.

Eight families with approximately 92 genera and 329 extant species.

Two families, Balistidae and Tetraodontidae, have about 77% of the species.

Members of this order are well known in the fossil record beginning in the lower Eocene, and Sorbini (1979) describes a small specimen from the mid-Cretaceous of Lebanon which may be a tetraodontiform. This group is believed to be descended from the ancestral acanthuroid lineage.

Tyler (1980) gives a comprehensive review of the order and much of the information given here is based on his study. Another important study of the group is that of Winterbottom (1974b) who gives a cladistic classification based on myological evidence. Among other differences with the present classification, he proposes that the families Triacanthodidae and Triacanthidae form the sister group of all remaining tetraodontiforms and recognizes the two branches as separate suborders. Other studies of the group include Breder and Clark (1947), Fraser-Brunner (1951), Hutchins (1977), Matsuura (1979, 1980), Tyler (1968), and Tyler and Matsuura (1981).

Suborder Balistoidei (Sclerodermi). Jaws with distinct teeth (i.e., teeth not fused); posttemporal present except in one species; urohyal present; pelvis and pelvic fin usually present.

Superfamily Triacanthoidea. Upper jaw slightly protractile (ascending process of premaxilla well developed); pelvic fin with one large spine and up to two soft rays; dorsal fin usually with six spines; caudal fin with 12 principal rays; 2–6 separate hypurals; 20 vertebrae.

Family TRIACANTHODIDAE—spikefishes. Marine; deepwater benthic; tropical and subtropical western Atlantic and Indo-Pacific.

Dorsal fin rays 12–18; anal fin rays 11–16; caudal fin rounded to truncate.

Fossils include the Eocene *Eoplectus* and *Spinacanthus*.

SUBFAMILY HOLLARDIINAE.   Western Atlantic, one species in Hawaii. Two genera, *Hollardia* and *Parahollardia*, with five species.

SUBFAMILY TRIACANTHODINAE.   Indo-Pacific, one species in western Atlantic.

Nine genera, *Atrophacanthus*, *Bathyphylax*, *Halimochirurgus*, *Johnsonina*, *Macrorhamphosodes*, *Mephisto*, *Paratriacanthodes*, *Triacanthodes*, and *Tydemania*, with 15 species.

Family TRIACANTHIDAE—triplespines.   Marine; shallow benthic; Indo-Pacific.

Dorsal fin rays 19–26; anal fin rays 13–22; caudal fin deeply forked. Maximum length about 28 cm.

Fossils include the Eocene *Protacanthodes* and the balistidlike Oligocene *Cryptobalistes*.

Four genera, *Pseudotriacanthus*, *Triacanthus*, *Tripodichthys*, and *Trixiphichthys*, with seven species.

Superfamily Balistoidea

Family BALISTIDAE—leatherjackets.   Marine; Atlantic, Indian, and Pacific.

Body usually compressed; head and body usually covered with scales (with edges separated from one another or slightly overlapping); no pelvic fins (pelvic spine or tubercle present in balistines and some monacanthines, underlying pelvis present); first dorsal spine with locking mechanism (the small second spine, when present, forms the locking mechanism); upper jaw not protractile; upper jaw with two rows of protruding incisorlike teeth; soft dorsal fin with 23–52 rays and anal fin with 20–66 rays; caudal fin with 12 principal rays; in life the eyes can be rotated independently. Maximum length about 1.0 m, attained in *Alutera (=Aluterus) scripta*.

About 42 genera and 135 species. The two subfamilies are given family status by many authors (e.g., Tyler, 1980).

SUBFAMILY BALISTINAE (TRIGGERFISHES).   Three dorsal spines (third can be minute); all soft fins with branched rays; scales in regular series, platelike; upper jaw usually with four teeth in outer and three in the inner series on each premaxillary, developed more for crushing than for nibbling; 18 vertebrae.

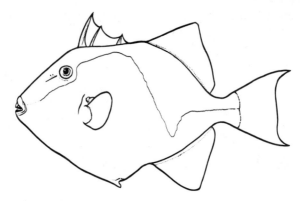

Eleven genera (e.g., *Balistapus, Balistes, Canthidermis, Melichthys, Odonus, Rhinecanthus, Sufflamen,* and *Xanthichthys*), with about 40 species.

SUBFAMILY MONACANTHINAE (FILEFISHES).   Usually two dorsal spines—the second is usually much smaller and it may be absent; soft dorsal, anal, and pectoral rays simple; scales small, in regular series; body prickly or furry to touch; upper jaw usually with three teeth in outer and two in the inner series on each premaxillary, developed for nibbling; 19–31 vertebrae. The greatest number of filefishes, some 54 species, occur in Australia (Hutchins, 1977).

About 31 genera (e.g., *Alutera, Amanses, Cantherhines, Chaetoderma, Monacanthus, Navodon, Oxymonacanthus, Paraluteres, Paramonacanthus, Pervagor, Pseudalutarius,* and *Stephanolepis*) with about 95 species.

Superfamily Ostracioidea (Ostracodermi)

Family   OSTRACIIDAE   (Ostraciontidae)—boxfishes   (cowfishes   and   trunkfishes).   Marine, tropical; Atlantic, Indian, and Pacific.

Body encased in a bony carapace; no pelvic skeleton; no spinous dorsal; dorsal and anal fins each with 9–13 rays; upper jaw not protractile; usually 18 vertebrae. Maximum length about 60 cm.

Some trunkfishes are known to discharge a toxic substance, termed ostracitoxin, which will kill other fishes in confined quarters. The substance is also toxic to the trunkfish, but less so than to most other fishes.

Thirteen genera with about 30 species. Some authors recognize the two subfamilies as separate families (e.g., Tyler, 1980).

SUBFAMILY ARACANINAE.   Carapace open behind the dorsal and anal fins; ventral ridge more or less developed; caudal fin with 11 principal rays. These fishes are found in relatively deep water in the Indo-West Pacific from Hawaii to South Africa; they are most abundant around Australia.

Six genera (e.g., *Anoplocapros, Aracana, Capropygia,* and *Kentrocapros*), with about 10 species.

SUBFAMILY OSTRACIINAE.   Carapace closed, at least behind the anal fin; no ventral ridge; caudal fin with 10 principal rays.

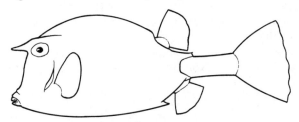

Seven genera, *Acanthostracion, Lactophrys, Lactoria, Ostracion, Rhinesomus, Rhynchostracion,* and *Tetrosomus,* with about 20 species.

Suborder Tetraodontoidei (Gymnodontes). Jaw "teeth" fused (true teeth are absent—the upper and lower jaws have cutting edges; a similar looking beak is found in the Scaridae); depending on the presence or absence of sutures, there may be two, three, or four such "teeth"; upper jaw not protractile; posttemporal absent; urohyal absent except in *Triodon;* pelvis absent except in *Triodon* and pelvic fin (spine and rays) absent.

Superfamily Triodontoidea

Family TRIODONTIDAE—three-toothed puffer.   Marine; Indo-West Pacific.

Three fused teeth in jaws (upper jaw with a median suture, the lower without); pelvis present; dorsal and anal fins usually with 11 rays (a small spiny dorsal fin of one or two rays is present in most specimens from Indonesia to Japan); ribs and epipleurals present; caudal fin with 12 principal rays and numerous procurrent rays, deeply forked. Maximum length about 48 cm.

One species, *Triodon macropterus* (= *bursarius*).

Superfamily Tetraodontoidea.   Body inflatable.

Family TETRAODONTIDAE—puffers.   Marine (several entering and occurring in brackish and fresh water); tropical and subtropical; Atlantic, Indian, and Pacific.

Body naked or with only short prickles (often confined to belly); four fused teeth in jaws (teeth in each jaw fused but separated by a median suture); premaxillaries and dentaries not fused to opposite member at midline; dorsal and anal fins usually each with 7–18 soft rays (many more in *Chonerhinos* and *Xenopterus*); ribs and epipleurals absent; caudal fin with 10 principal rays and no procurrent rays, moderately forked to rounded.

The "flesh" (especially the viscera) of some puffers contains the alkaloid poison tetraodotoxin, produced by the fish, which can be fatal. In at least some species the gonads at spawning time contain the highest concentration of this poison; none occurs in the muscle.

Many species, mostly of *Tetraodon*, occur only in fresh water, primarily in the Congo River and in southern Asia (e.g., Dekkers, 1975). Maximum length 90 cm; most much less.

Sixteen genera with about 118 species.

Subfamily Tetraodontinae. Body broadly rounded in cross section; one or two conspicuous nostrils on each side; lateral line usually conspicuous; gill opening usually extending below midportion of pectoral fin; erectable ridge of skin on dorsal and ventral midline only in *Carinotetraodon* (which is probably relatively closely related to *Canthigaster*, placed in the next subfamily); vertebrae 17–29.

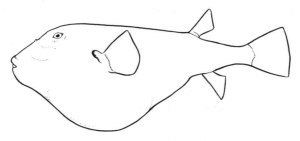

Fifteen genera (e.g., *Arothron, Fugu, Lagocephalus, Sphoeroides, Tetraodon,* and *Torquigener*) with about 95 species.

Subfamily Canthigastrinae (sharpnose pufferfishes). Body laterally compressed (deeper than broad) in uninflated condition; single inconspicuous nostril on each side; lateral line inconspicuous; gill opening restricted, ending ventrally about level of midportion of pectoral fin; snout elongate and relatively pointed; erectable ridge of skin on dorsal and ventral midline; vertebrae usually 17 (8 + 9). Maximum length usually less than 12 cm. Most species of sharpnose puffers occur in shallow water, usually near coral reefs, and feed on benthic organisms. All but one species (which occurs in the Atlantic) occur in tropical Indo-Pacific waters (from the Red Sea and South Africa to Central America).

One genus, *Canthigaster*, with 23 species (Allen and Randall, 1977).

Family DIODONTIDAE—porcupinefishes.   Marine; Atlantic, Indian, and Pacific.

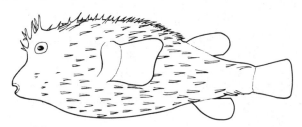

Body covered with well-developed sharp spines (in some species the spines erect only when body is inflated); two fused teeth in jaws (parrotlike); premaxillaries and dentaries completely fused to opposite member at midline.

Adults inhabit inshore waters while the young are pelagic.

Two genera, *Chilomycterus* and *Diodon* (= *Dicotylichthys*), with 15 species.

Superfamily Moloidea

Family MOLIDAE—molas.   Marine; tropical and subtropical; Atlantic, Indian and Pacific.

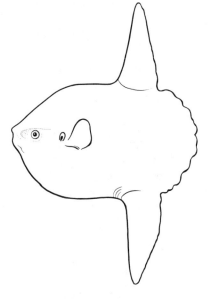

Two fused teeth in jaws; no spines in dorsal or anal fins; no caudal peduncle; caudal fin either absent or formed by a few rays of the pseudocaudal fin (gephyrocercal fin) derived from posteriorly migrated dorsal and anal fin rays; two minute nostrils on each side; lateral line absent; no swim bladder; 16–18 vertebrae.

The major locomotory thrust is provided by the powerful dorsal and anal fins. It has been estimated that up to 300,000,000 eggs can be produced by *Mola mola* (the ocean sunfish), probably making it the most fecund fish species. Maximum length over 2 m with weights up to 1000 kg.

Three monotypic genera, *Masturus*, *Mola*, and *Ranzania*. The first two are considered by some to be synonymous, the two species being placed in *Mola*.

Appendix I

Checklist of the extant classes (numbered), orders (numbered), suborders (not numbered), and families (numbered).

Class 1   Myxini, 30
      Order 1.   Myxiniformes, 30
            Family 1.   Myxinidae, 31
Class 2   Cephalaspidomorphi, 34
      Order 2.   Petromyzontiformes, 34
            Family 2.   Petromyzontidae, 35
Class 3   Chondrichthyes, 43
      Order 3.   Chimaeriformes, 45
            Family 3.   Callorhynchidae, 46
            Family 4.   Chimaeridae, 46
            Family 5.   Rhinochimaeridae, 46
      Order 4.   Hexanchiformes, 49
            Family 6.   Chlamydoselachidae, 49
            Family 7.   Hexanchidae, 50
      Order 5.   Heterodontiformes, 50
            Family 8.   Heterodontidae, 50

Appendix II

The following 45 fish distribution maps are based on information from numerous sources, primarily those acknowledged. Parts of the ranges are often based on scattered populations of a single or a few species. The margins are often generalized.

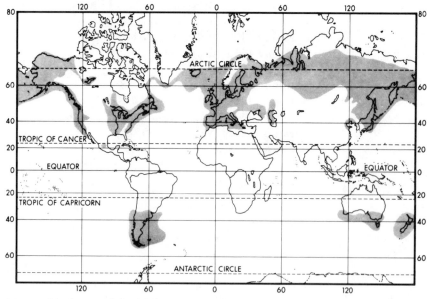

Map 1   Distribution of the family Petromyzontidae, based primarily on Hubbs and Potter (1971).

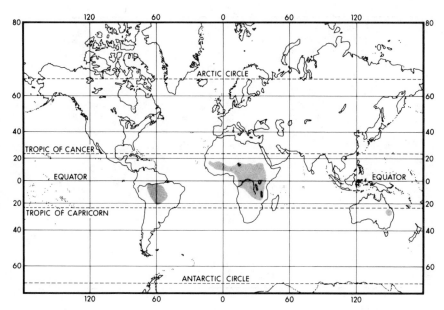

Map 2   Distribution of the subclass Dipneusti, based on Sterba (1966).

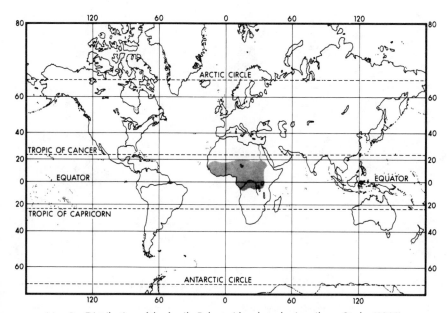

Map 3   Distribution of the family Polypteridae, based primarily on Sterba (1966).

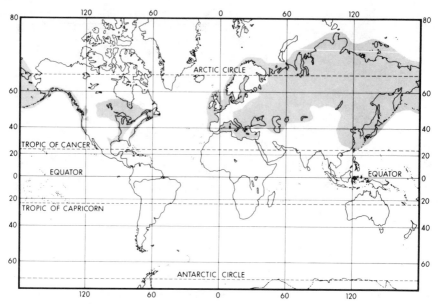

Map 4   Distribution of the family Acipenseridae, based on numerous regional sources.

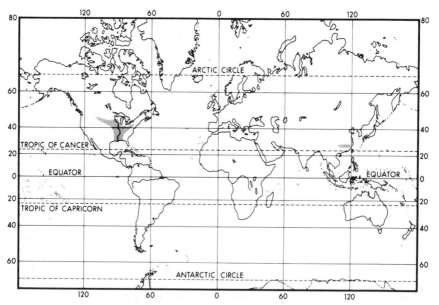

Map 5   Distribution of the family Polyodontidae, based primarily on Nichols (1943) and Trautman (1981).

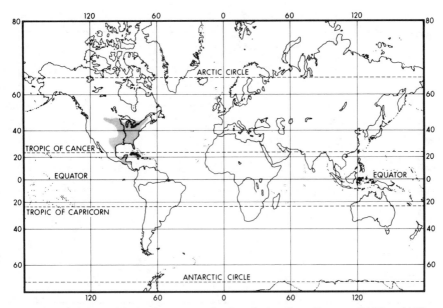

Map 6   Distribution of the family Lepisosteidae, based primarily on Trautman (1981) and Miller (1966).

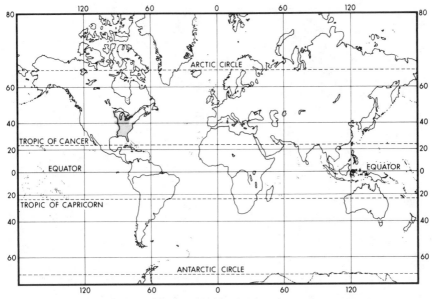

Map 7   Distribution of the family Amiidae, based on Trautman (1981).

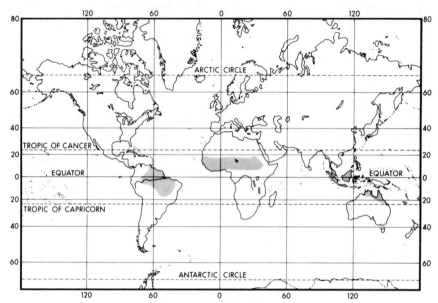

Map 8 Distribution of the family Osteoglossidae, based on Darlington (1957) and Sterba (1966).

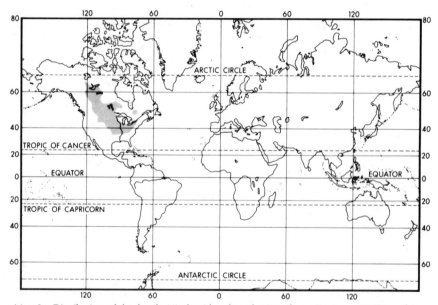

Map 9 Distribution of the family Hiodontidae, based primarily on Trautman (1981) and Mc-Phail and Lindsey (1970).

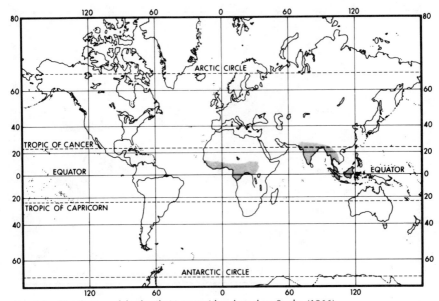

Map 10   Distribution of the family Notopteridae, based on Sterba (1966).

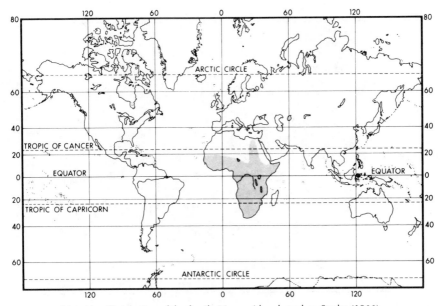

Map 11   Distribution of the family Mormyridae, based on Sterba (1966).

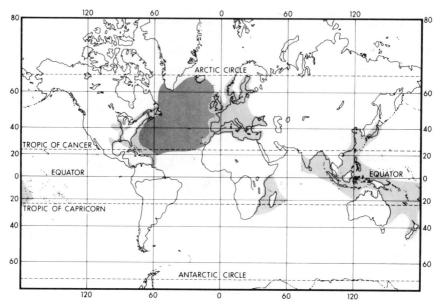

Map 12   Distribution of the family Anguillidae, based on Ege (1939) and regional works. (Dark zone in the Atlantic denotes area of presumed migration.)

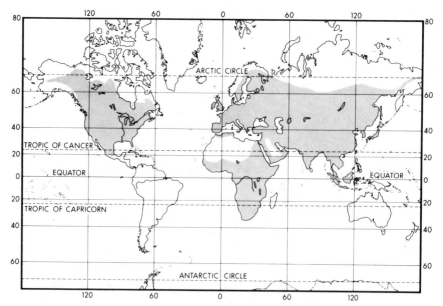

Map 13   Distribution of the family Cyprinidae, based on Lagler et al. (1977).

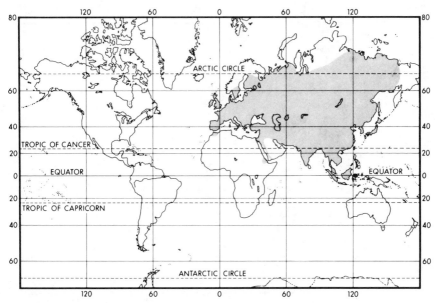

Map 14   Distribution of the family Cobitididae, based primarily on P. Bănărescu, 1964. Pisces: Osteichthyes. *Acad. Republ. Pop. Romine, Fauna* RPR *13*. 959 pp.

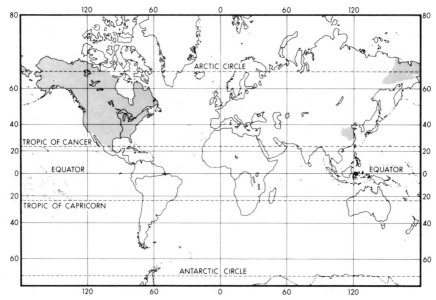

Map 15   Distribution of the family Catostomidae, based on Lagler et al. (1977).

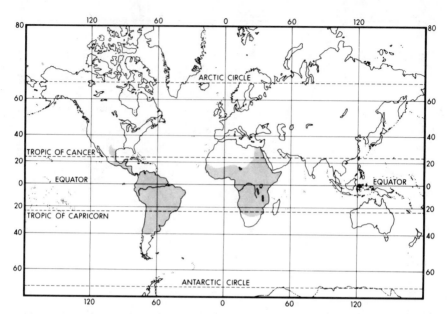

Map 16   Distribution of the family Characidae, based on Miller (1966) and Sterba (1966).

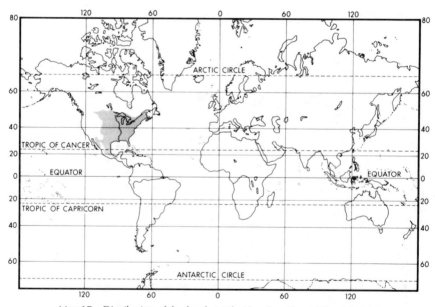

Map 17   Distribution of the family Ictaluridae, based on Miller (1958).

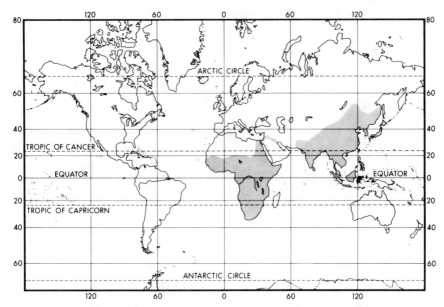

Map 18   Distribution of the family Bagridae, based on Darlington (1957), Sterba (1966), Mirza (1980), and Coad (1981b).

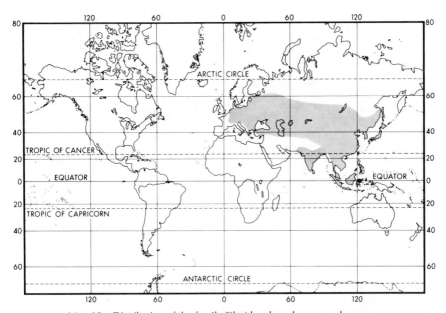

Map 19   Distribution of the family Siluridae, based on several sources.

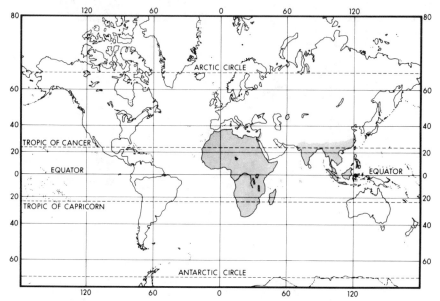

Map 20   Distribution of the family Clariidae, based on Darlington (1957) and Sterba (1966).

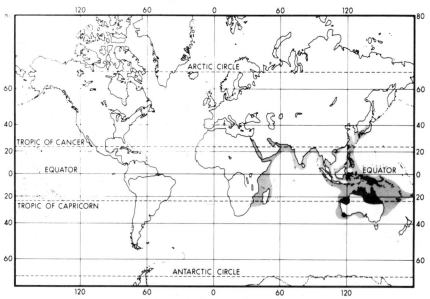

Map 21   Distribution of the family Plotosidae (the dark area is the distribution of freshwater species, the light area is the distribution of brackish water and marine species), based primarily on M.N. Feinberg and G. Nelson (pers. comm. 1982).

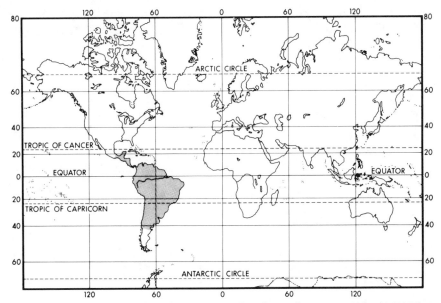

Map 22   Distribution of the family Pimelodidae, based on Miller (1966) and Sterba (1966).

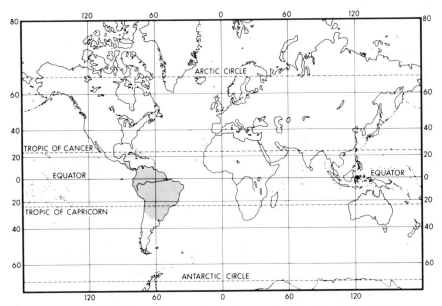

Map 23   Distribution of the superfamily Gymnotoidae, based on Sterba (1966).

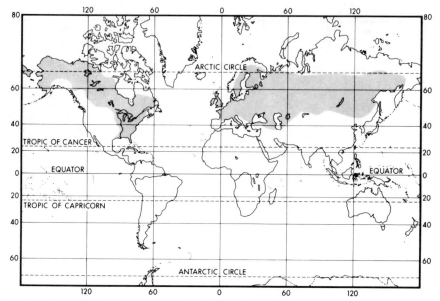

Map 24   Distribution of the family Esocidae, based on Lagler et al. (1977) and McPhail and Lindsey (1970).

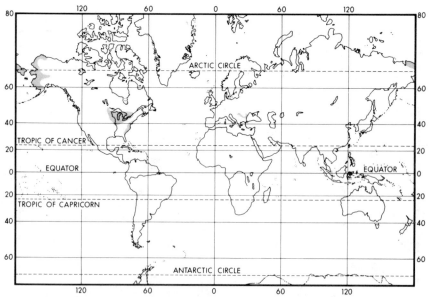

Map 25   Distribution of the family Umbridae, based on Lagler et al. (1977) and McPhail and Lindsey (1970).

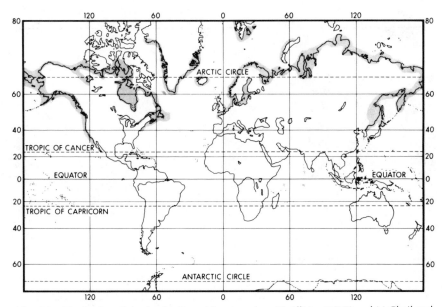

Map 26 Distribution of the family Osmeridae, based on McAllister (1963) and McPhail and Lindsey (1970).

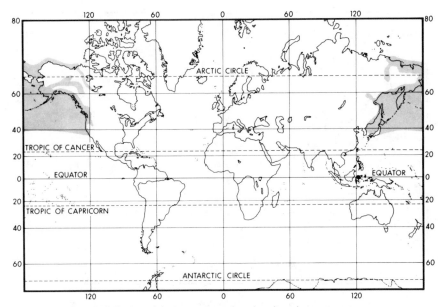

Map 27 Distribution of the genus *Oncorhynchus*, based on numerous sources.

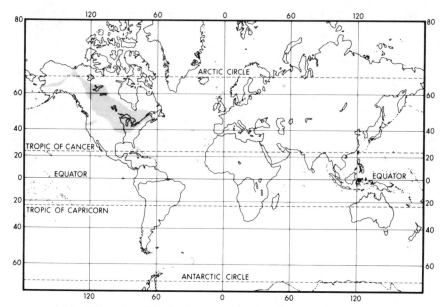

Map 28   Distribution of the family Percopsidae, based on several regional sources.

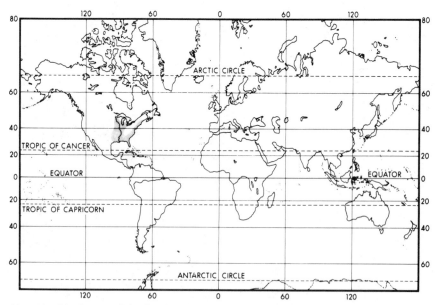

Map 29   Distribution of the family Aphredoderidae, based on Trautman (1981) and Miller (1958).

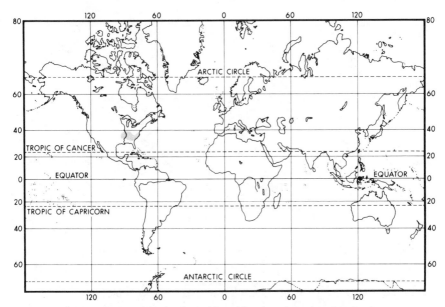

Map 30   Distribution of the family Amblyopsidae, based on several regional sources.

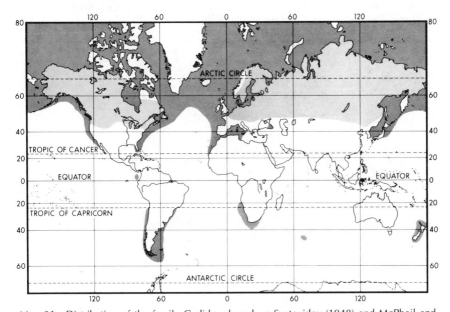

Map 31   Distribution of the family Gadidae, based on Svetovidov (1948) and McPhail and Lindsey (1970). (The light area is the freshwater distribution of *Lota lota*.)

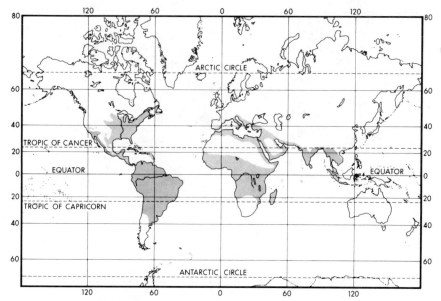

Map 32   Distribution of the families Aplocheilidae and Cyprinodontidae, based primarily on Parenti (1981).

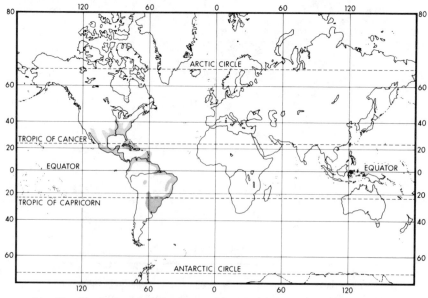

Map 33   Distribution of the family Poeciliidae, based on Rosen and Bailey (1963).

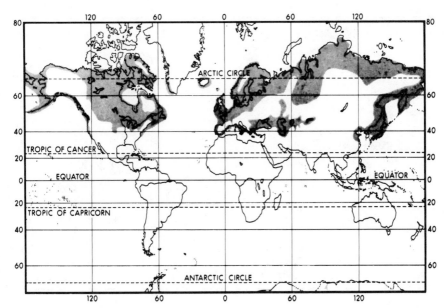

Map 34   Distribution of the family Gasterosteidae, based on numerous regional sources.

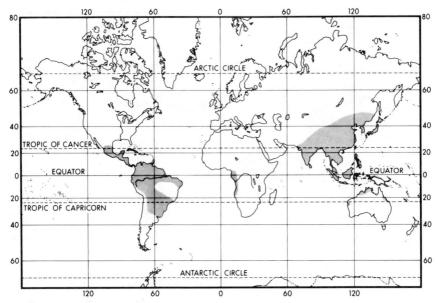

Map 35   Distribution of the family Synbranchidae, based primarily on Lake (1971), Rosen and Rumney (1972), and Rosen (1975).

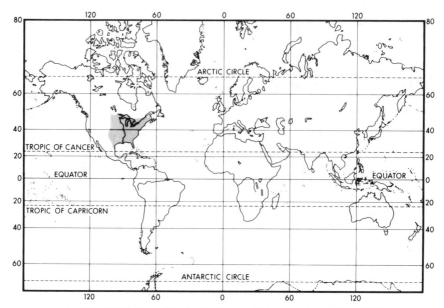

Map 36   Distribution of the family Centrarchidae, based on Miller (1958).

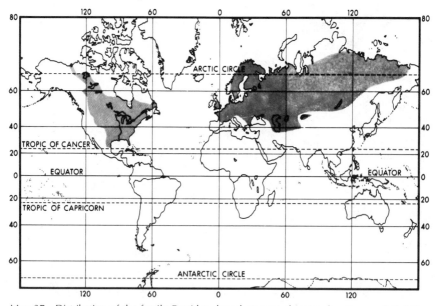

Map 37   Distribution of the family Percidae, based on several regional sources and Collette and Bănărescu (1977).

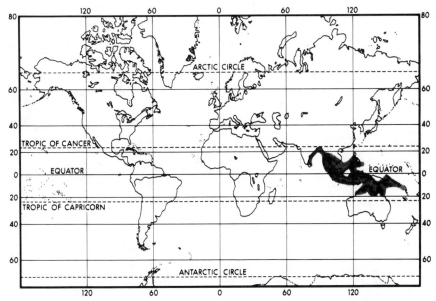

Map 38   Distribution of the family Toxotidae, based on Allen (1978).

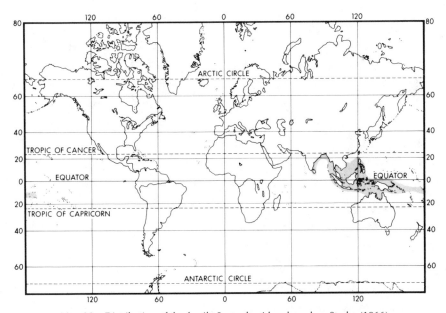

Map 39   Distribution of the family Scatophagidae, based on Sterba (1966).

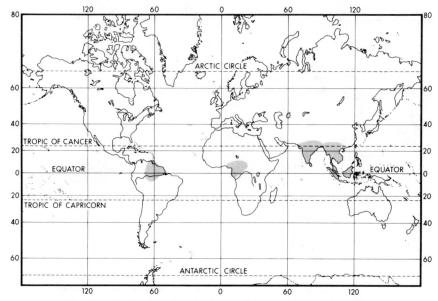

Map 40   Distribution of the family Nandidae, based on Sterba (1966).

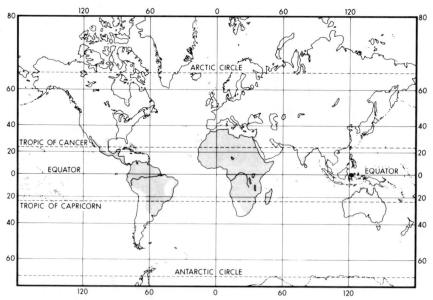

Map 41   Distribution of the family Cichlidae, based on Lagler et al. (1977).

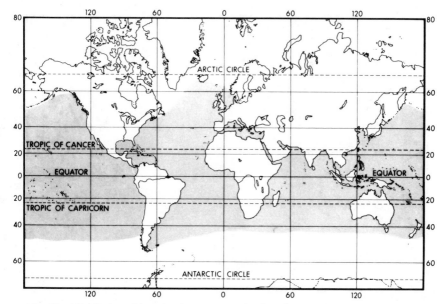

Map 42   Distribution of the suborder Stromateoidei, based on Haedrich and Horn (1972).

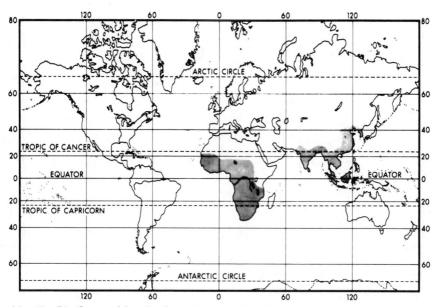

Map 43   Distribution of the suborder Anabantoidei, based on Sterba (1966) and Mirza (1980).

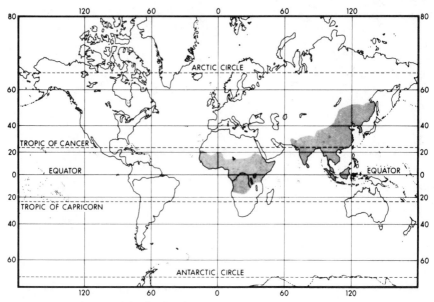

Map 44   Distribution of the family Channidae, based on Sterba (1966), Mirza (1980), and Coad (1981b).

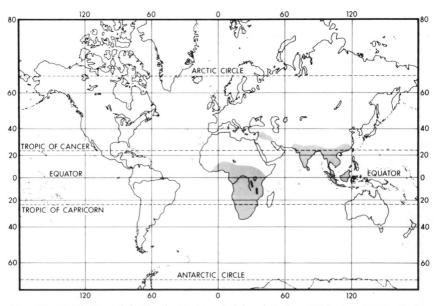

Map 45   Distribution of the family Mastacembelidae, based on Darlington (1957), Sterba (1966), and Mirza (1980).

Bibliography

Abe, T. 1957. Notes on fishes from the stomachs of whales taken in the Antarctic. 1. *Xenocyttus nemotoi*, a new genus and species of zeomorph fish of the subfamily Oreosominae Goode and Bean, 1895. *Sci. Rep. Whales Res. Inst.* **12:** 225–233.

Able, K. W. and D. E. McAllister. 1980. Revision of the snailfish genus *Liparis* from Arctic Canada. *Bull. Can. Fish. Aquat. Sci.* **208.** 52 pp.

Adam, H. and R. Strahan. 1963. Systematics and geographical distribution of myxinoids. In A. Brodal and R. Fänge (Eds.), *The biology of Myxine*. Oslo: Universitetsforlaget: 1–8.

Akihito, Prince and K. Meguro. 1981. A gobiid fish belonging to the genus *Hetereleotris* collected in Japan. *Jap. J. Ichthyol.* **28**(3): 329–339.

Alexander, R. McN. 1964. The structure of the Weberian apparatus in the Siluri. *Proc. Zool. Soc. Lond.* **142**(3): 419–440.

Alfred, E. R. 1969. The Malayan cyprinoid fishes of the family Homalopteridae. *Zool. Meded., Leiden* **43**(18): 213–237.

Allen, G. R. 1975a. *The anemonefishes. Their classification and biology.*, 2nd ed. Neptune City, N.J.: T.F.H. Public. 352 pp.

Allen, G. R. 1975b. *Damselfishes of the South Seas.* Neptune City, N.J.: T.F.H. Public. 240 pp.

Allen, G. R. 1978. A review of the archerfishes (family Toxotidae). *Rec. West. Aust. Mus.* **6:** 355–378.

Allen, G. R. 1980a. A generic classification of the rainbowfishes (family Melanotaeniidae). *Rec. West. Aust. Mus.* **8:** 449–490.

Allen, G. R. 1980b. *Butterfly and angelfishes of the world.* Vol. 2. New York: Wiley: 145–352.

Allen, G. R. and N. J. Cross. 1982. *Rainbowfishes of Australia and Papua New Guinea.* Neptune City, N.J.: T.F.H. Public. 141 pp.

Allen, G. R. and A. R. Emery. 1973. *Pomacentrus exilis,* a new species of damselfish from the central-west Pacific. *Copeia* **1973:** 565–568.

Allen, G. R. and J. E. Randall. 1977. Review of the sharpnose pufferfishes (subfamily Canthigasterinae) of the Indo-Pacific. *Rec. Aust. Mus.* **30:** 475–517.

Amaoka, K. 1969. Studies on the sinistral flounders found in the waters around Japan—taxonomy, anatomy, and phylogeny. *J. Shimonoseki Univ. Fish.* **18**(2): 1–340.

Amaoka, K. et al. 1982. *Fishes of the Kyushu-Palau Ridge and Tosa Bay: the intensive research of unexploited fishery resources on continental slopes.* Tokyo: Japan Fisheries Resource Conservation Association, 436 pp.

Ancona, U. D' and G. Cavinato. 1965. The fishes of the family Bregmacerotidae. *Dana Rep.* **64:** 1–92.

Anderson, M. E. 1982. Revision of the fish genera *Gymnelus* Reinhardt and *Gymnelopsis* Soldatov (Zoarcidae), with two new species and comparative osteology of *Gymnelus viridis. Natl. Mus. Can., Publ. Zool. No. 17.* 76 pp.

Anderson, M. E. and C. L. Hubbs. 1981. Redescription and osteology of the northeastern Pacific fish *Derepodichthys alepidotus* (Zoarcidae). *Copeia* **1981**(2): 341–352.

Anderson, W. D. 1970. Revision of the genus *Symphysanodon* (Pisces: Lutjanidae) with descriptions of four new species. *Fish. Bull.* **68**(2): 325–346.

Andrews, S. M. 1973. Interrelationships of crossopterygians. In P. H. Greenwood, R. S. Miles, and C. Patterson (Eds.), Interrelationships of fishes. *J. Linn. Soc. (Zool.)* **53:** 137–177. Suppl. 1. New York: Academic.

Andrews, S. M. and T. S. Westoll. 1970. The postcranial skeleton of *Eusthenopteron foordi* Whiteaves. *Trans. R. Soc. Edinb.* **68:** 207–329.

Andriashev, A. P. 1965. A general review of the Antarctic fish fauna. In *Biogeography and ecology in Antarctica. Monogr. Biol.* **15:** 491–550. The Hague: Dr. W. Junk.

Andriashev, A. P., A. V. Neelov, and V. P. Prirodina. 1977. On methods of study of the morphology and systematics of the fish family of sea snails (Liparidae). *Zool. Zh.* **56**(1): 141–147. (Translated by D. L. Stein, School of Oceanography, Oregon State University, Corvallis.)

Applegate, S. P. 1967. A survey of shark hard parts. In P. W. Gilbert, R. F. Mathewson, and D. P. Rall (Eds.), *Sharks, skates, and rays.* Baltimore: John Hopkins: 37–67.

Arnold, D. C. 1956. A systematic revision of the fishes of the teleost family Carapidae (Percomorphi, Blennioidea), with descriptions of two new species. *Bull. Br. Mus. Nat. Hist. (Zool.)* **4**(6): 17–307.

Avise, J. C. and R. K. Selander. 1972. Evolutionary genetics of cave-dwelling fishes of the genus *Astyanax. Evolution* **26:** 1–19.

Avise, J. C., D. O. Straney, and M. H. Smith. 1977. Biochemical genetics of sunfish. 4. Relationships of centrarchid genera. *Copeia* **1977**(2): 250–258.

Axelrod, H. R. 1973. *African cichlids of lakes Malawi and Tanganyika.* Neptune City, N.J.: T.F.H. Public. 224 pp.

Axelrod, H. R. and W. E. Burgess. 1982. Loaches of the world. *Trop. Fish Hobb.* **1982**(April): 32–44.

Ayling, A. M. and J. R. Paxton. 1983. *Odax cyanoallix,* a new species of odacid fish from northern New Zealand. *Copeia* **1983**(1): 95–101.

Bailey, R. J. 1936. The osteology and relationships of the phallostethid fishes. *J. Morph.* **59:** 453–478.

Bailey, R. M. et al. 1970. A list of common and scientific names of fishes from the United States and Canada. *Am. Fish. Soc. Spec. Publ.* 6, 3rd ed. 150 pp.

Bailey, R. M. 1980. Comments on the classification and nomenclature of lampreys—an alternate view. *Can J. Fish. Aquat. Sci.* **37:** 1626–1629.

Bailey, R. M. 1982. Reply [to Vladykov and Kott, 1982]. *Can. J. Fish. Aquat. Sci.* **39:** 1217–1220.

Bailey, R. M. and T. M. Cavender. 1971. Fishes. Reprinted from *McGraw-Hill Encyclopedia of Science and Technology.* New York: McGraw-Hill. 34 pp.

Baird, R. C. 1971. The systematics, distribution, and zoogeography of the marine hatchet-fishes (family Sternoptychidae). *Bull. Mus. Comp. Zool.* **142**(1): 1–128.

Ball, G. E. 1981. Current notions about systematics and classification of insects. *Manit. Entomol.* **13** (1979): 5–18.

Balon, E. K. (Ed.). 1980. *Charrs, salmonid fishes of the genus* Salvelinus. The Hague: Dr. W. Junk. 928 pp.

Banarescu, P. and T. T. Nalbant. 1973. Pisces, Teleostei. Cyprinidae (Gobioninae). *Das Tierr.* **93.** 304 pp.

Banarescu, P. M. and T. T. Nalbant. 1975. A collection of Cyprinoidei from Afghanistan and Pakistan with description of a new species of Cobitidae (Pisces, Cypriniformes). *Mitt. Hamburg. Zool. Mus. Inst.* **72:** 241–248.

Banister, K. E. 1970. The anatomy and taxonomy of *Indostomus paradoxus* Prashad and Mukerji. *Bull. Br. Mus. Nat. Hist. (Zool.)* **19**(5): 179–209.

Barbour, C. D. 1973. A biogeographical history of *Chirostoma* (Pisces: Atherinidae): a species flock from the Mexican plateau. *Copeia* **1973:** 533–556.

Barbour, C. D. and R. R. Miller. 1978. A revision of the Mexican cyprinid fish genus *Algansea. Misc. Publs. Mus. Zool. Univ. Mich.* **115.** 72 pp.

Bardack, D. 1965. Anatomy and evolution of chirocentrid fishes. *Paleont. Contr. Univ. Kans.* **40:** 1–88.

Bardack, D. 1979. Fishes of the Mazon Creek fauna. In M. H. Nitecki, (Ed.), *Mazon Creek fossils.* New York: Academic: 501–528.

Bardack, D. and R. Zangerl. 1968. First fossil lamprey: a record from the Pennsylvanian of Illinois. *Science* **1962:** 1265–1267.

Bardack, D. and R. Zangerl. 1971. Lampreys in the fossil record. In M. W. Hardisty and I. C. Potter (Eds.), *The biology of lampreys.* London: Academic: 67–84.

Barel, C. D. N., F. Witte, and M. J. P. van Oijen. 1976. The shape of the skeletal elements in the head of a generalized *Haplochromis* species: *H. elegans* Trewavas 1933 (Pisces, Cichlidae). *Netherl. J. Zool.* **26**(2): 163–265.

Barlow, G. W., K. F. Liem, and W. Wickler. 1968. Badidae, a new fish family—behavioural, osteological, and developmental evidence. *J. Zool.* **156:** 415–447.

Barrington, E. J. W. 1965. *The biology of Hemichordata and Protochordata.* Edinburgh: Oliver and Boyd. 176 pp.

Bartram, A. W. H. 1977. The Macrosemiidae, a Mesozoic family of holostean fishes. *Bull. Br. Mus. Nat. Hist. (Geol.).* **29**(2): 137–234.

Bass, A. J., J. D. D'Aubrey, and N. Kistnasamy. 1976. Sharks of the east coast of southern Africa. 6. The families Oxynotidae, Squalidae, Dalatiidae and Echinorhinidae. *S. African Assoc. Marine Biol. Res. Oceanogr. Res. Inst. Rep.* **45:** 1–103.

Bath, H. 1977. Revision der Blenniini. *Senckenbergiana Biol.* **57:** 167–234.

Bath, H. 1982. Beitrag zur Revalidation von *Parablennius ruber* (Valenciennes 1836) mit kritischen Bemerkungen zur Gültigkeit der Gattung *Pictiblennius* Whitley 1930. *Senckenbergiana Biol.* **62:** 211–224.

Beamish, R. J. 1982. *Lampetra macrostoma*, a new species of freshwater parasitic lamprey from the West Coast of Canada. *Can. J. Fish. Aquat. Sci.* **39:** 736–747.

Beamish, R. J., M. J. Merrilees, and E. J. Crossman. 1971. Karyotypes and DNA values for members of the suborder Esocoidei (Osteichthyes: Salmoniformes). *Chromosoma* (Berlin) **34:** 436–447.

Behnke, R. J. 1968. A new subgenus and species of trout, *Salmo (Platysalmo) platycephalus*, from southcentral Turkey, with comments on the classification of the subfamily Salmoninae. *Mitt. Hamb. Zool. Mus. Inst.* **66:** 1–15.

Behnke, R. J. 1970. The application of cytogenetics and biochemical systematics to phylogenetic problems in the family Salmonidae. *Trans. Am. Fish. Soc.* **99:** 237–248.

Behnke, R. J. 1972. The systematics of salmonid fishes of recently glaciated lakes. *J. Fish. Res. Bd. Can.* **29:** 639–671.

Behnke, R. J. 1979. Monograph of the native trouts of the genus *Salmo* of western North America. Issued by Denver Regional Office, U.S. Fish and Wildlife Service. 215 pp.

Bell, J. D., T. M. Berra, P. D. Jackson, P. R. Last, and R. D. Sloane. 1980. Recent records of the Australian grayling *Prototroctes maraena* Günther (Pisces: Prototroctidae) with notes on its distribution. *Aust. Zool.* **20:** 419–431.

Bell, M. A. 1976. Evolution of phenotypic diversity in *Gasterosteus aculeatus* superspecies on the Pacific coast of North America. *Syst. Zool.* **25:** 211–227.

Bell, M. A. 1977. A late Miocene marine threespine stickleback, *Gasterosteus aculeatus aculeatus*, and its zoogeographic and evolutionary significance. *Copeia* **1977**(2): 277–282.

Bellomy, M. D. 1969. *Encyclopedia of sea horses.* Neptune City, N.J.: T.F.H. Public. 192 pp.

Ben-Tuvia, A. 1966. Red Sea fishes recently found in the Mediterranean. *Copeia* **1966:** 254–275.

Bendix-Almgreen, S. E. 1968. The bradyodont elasmobranchs and their affinities; a discussion. In T. Ørvig (Ed.), *Current problems of lower vertebrate phylogeny.* New York: Wiley-Interscience: 153–170.

Bentivegna, F. 1982. Notes on the taxonomy of the Mediterranean Trachinidae (Pisces, Osteichthyes). *Cybium*, Ser. 3, **6**(2): 41–47.

Berg, L. S. 1940. Classification of fishes, both Recent and fossil. *Trav. Inst. Zool. Acad. Sci. URSS*, **5**(2): 87–517. Also lithoprint, J. W. Edwards, Ann Arbor, Michigan, 1947.

Berg, L. S. 1955. Classification of fishes both Recent and fossil. *Trud. Zool. Inst. Akad. Nauk, SSSR*, **20:** 1–286. 2nd ed. (in Russian).

Berra, T. M. 1981. *An atlas of distribution of the freshwater fish families of the world.* Lincoln: University of Nebraska Press. 197 pp.

Berra, T. M., J. F. Smith, and J. D. Morrison. 1982. Probable identification of the cucumber odor of the Australian grayling *Prototroctes maraena*. *Trans. Am. Fish. Soc.* **111:** 78–82.

Berrill, N. J. 1950. *The Tunicata with an account of the British species.* London: The Ray Society. 354 pp.

Berry, F. H. 1959. Boar fishes of the genus *Antigonia* of the western Atlantic. *Bull. Fla. St. Mus.* **4**(7): 205–250.

Berry, F. H. 1964. Review and emendation of: Family Clupeidae by Samuel F. Hildebrand. *Copeia* **1964:** 720–730.

Bertelsen, E. 1951. The ceratioid fishes. *Dana Rep.* **39:** 1–276.

Bertelsen, E. and N. B. Marshall. 1956. The Mirapinnati, a new order of teleost fishes. *Dana Rep.* **42:** 1–34.

Bertelsen, E. and N. B. Marshall. 1958. Notes on Miripinnati: (An addendum to Dana Rep. 42). *Dana Rep.* **45:** 9–10.

Bertelsen, E., G. Krefft, and N. B. Marshall. 1976. The fishes of the family Notosudidae. *Dana Rep.* **86:** 1–114.

Bertelsen, E. and T. W. Pietsch. 1977. Results of the research cruises of FRV "Walther Herwig" to South America. 47. Ceratioid anglerfishes of the family Oneirodidae collected by the FRV "Walther Herwig." *Arch. Fisch Wiss.* **27**(3): 171–189.

Bertelsen, E., T. W. Pietsch, and R. J. Lavenberg. 1981. Ceratioid anglerfishes of the family Gigantactinidae: morphology, systematics, and distribution. *Contrib. Sci., Nat. Hist. Mus., Los Angeles County* **332:**1–74.

Bertmar, G. 1968. Lungfish phylogeny. In T. Ørvig (Ed.), *Current problems of lower vertebrate phylogeny.* New York: Wiley-Interscience. 259–283.

Bigelow, H. B. and W. C. Schroeder. 1948–1953. Fishes of the western North Atlantic. *Mem. Sears Found. Mar. Res.* Vols. 1 and 2.

Bigelow, H. B. and W. C. Schroeder. 1957. A study of the sharks of the suborder Squaloidea. *Bull. Mus. Comp. Zool.* **117**(1): 1–150.

Bigelow, H. B. and W. C. Schroeder. 1962. New and little known batoid fishes from the western Atlantic. *Bull. Mus. Comp. Zool.* **128**(4): 159–244.

Birdsong, R. S. 1975. The osteology of *Microgobius signatus* Poey (Pisces: Gobiidae), with comments on other gobiid fishes. *Bull. Florida State Mus., Biol. Sci.,* **19**(3): 135–187.

Birkhead, W. S. 1972. Toxicity of stings of ariid and ictalurid catfishes. *Copeia* **1972:** 790–807.

Bjerring, H. C. 1973. Relationships of coelacanthiforms. In P. H. Greenwood, R. S. Miles, and C. Patterson (Eds.), Interrelationships of fishes. *J. Linn. Soc. (Zool.)* **53:** 179–205. Suppl. 1. New York: Academic.

Blot, J. 1975. A propos des Téléostéens primitifs: l'origine des Apodes. *Coll. Internat. C.N.R.S.* **218:** 281–292.

Blumer, L. S. 1982. A bibliography and categorization of bony fishes exhibiting parental care. *Zool. J. Linn. Soc.* **76:** 1–22.

Bockelie, T. and R. A. Fortey. 1976. An early Ordovician vertebrate. *Nature* **260:** 36–38.

Böhlke, J. E. 1956. A synopsis of the eels of the family Xenocongridae (including the Chlopsidae and Chilorhinidae). *Proc. Acad. Nat. Sci. Philad.* **108:** 61–95.

Böhlke, J. E. 1957. On the occurrence of garden eels in the western Atlantic, with a synopsis of the Heterocongrinae. *Proc. Acad. Nat. Sci. Philad.* **59:** 59–79.

Böhlke, J. E. 1966. Lyomeri, Eurypharyngidae, Saccopharyngidae. In Fishes of the western North Atlantic. *Mem. Sears Found. Mar. Res.* **1**(5): 603–628.

Böhlke, J. E. and C. C. G. Chaplin. 1968. *Fishes of the Bahamas and adjacent tropical waters.* Wynnewood, Pa.: Academy of Natural Sciences of Philadelphia, Livingston. 771 pp.

Böhlke, J. E. and C. L. Hubbs. 1951. *Dysommina rugosa,* an apodal fish from the North Atlantic, representing a distinct family. *Stanford Ichthyol. Bull.* **4**(1): 7–10.

Böhlke, J. E. and J. E. Randall. 1981. Four new garden eels (Congridae, Heterocongrinae) from the Pacific and Indian oceans. *Bull. Marine Sci.* **31**(2): 366–382.

Böhlke, J. E. and D. G. Smith. 1968. A new xenocongrid eel from the Bahamas, with notes on other species in the family. *Proc. Acad. Nat. Sci. Phil.* **120:** 25–43.

Böhlke, J. E. and V. G. Springer. 1975. A new genus and species of fish (*Nemaclinus atelestos*) from the western Atlantic (Perciformes: Clinidae). *Proc. Acad. Nat. Sci. Phil.* **127**(7): 57–61.

Bolin, R. L. 1936. The systematic position of *Indostomus paradoxus* Prashad and Mukerji, a freshwater fish from Burma. *J. Wash. Acad. Sci.* **26**: 420–423.

Bolin, R. L. 1940. A redescription of *Luvarus imperialis* Rafinesque based on a specimen from Monterey, California. *Calif. Fish and Game* **26**(3): 282–284.

Bolin, R. L. 1947. The evolution of the marine Cottidae of California with a discussion of the genus as a systematic category. *Bull. Nat. Hist. Mus., Stanford Univ.* **3**(3): 153–168.

Bond, C. E. 1979. *Biology of fishes.* Philadelphia: W. B. Saunders. 514 pp.

Bond, C. E. and T. Uyeno. 1981. Remarkable changes in the vertebrae of perciform fish *Scombrolabrax* with notes on its anatomy and systematics. *Jap. J. Ichthyol.* **28**(3): 259–262.

Bone, Q. 1960. The origin of the chordates. *J. Linn. Soc. (Zool.)* **44**: 252–269.

Boreske, J. R., Jr. 1974. A review of the North American fossil amiid fishes. *Bull. Mus. Comp. Zool.* **146**(1): 1–87.

Bradbury, M. G. 1967. The genera of batfishes (Family Ogcocephalidae). *Copeia* **1967**(2): 399–422.

Bradbury, M. G. 1980. A revision of the fish genus *Ogcocephalus* with descriptions of new species from the western Atlantic Ocean (Ogcocephalidae; Lophiiformes). *Proc. Calif. Acad. Sci.* **42**: 229–285.

Brannon, E. L. 1972. Mechanisms controlling migration of sockeye salmon fry. *Int. Pac. Salmon Fish. Comm. Bull.* **21**. 86 pp.

Brannon, E. L., T. P. Quinn, G. L. Lucchetti, and B. D. Ross. 1981. Compass orientation of sockeye salmon fry from a complex river system. *Can J. Zool.* **59**(8): 1548–1553.

Branson, B. A. and G. A. Moore. 1962. The lateralis components of the acoustico-lateralis system in the sunfish family Centrarchidae. *Copeia* **1962**: 1–108.

Breder, C. M. and E. Clark. 1947. A contribution to the visceral anatomy, development, and relationships of Plectognathi. *Bull. Am. Mus. Nat. Hist.* **88**(5): 287–320.

Breder, C. M. and D. E. Rosen. 1966. *Modes of reproduction in fishes.* New York: Natural History Press. 941 pp.

Briggs, J. C. 1955. A monograph of the clingfishes (Order Xenopterygii). *Stanford Ichthyol. Bull.* **6**: 1–224.

Briggs, J. C. 1974. *Marine zoogeography.* New York: McGraw-Hill. 475 pp.

Briggs, J. C. 1979. Ostariophysan zoogeography: an alternative hypothesis. *Copeia* **1979**(1): 111–118.

Briggs, J. C. and F. H. Berry. 1959. The Draconettidae—A review of the family with the description of a new species. *Copeia* **1959**: 123–133.

Brodal, A. and R. Fänge. 1963. *The biology of Myxini.* Oslo: Universitetsforlaget. 588 pp.

Bullis, H. R., Jr. and J. S. Carpenter. 1966. *Neoharriotta carri*—a new species of Rhinochimaeridae from the southern Caribbean Sea. *Copeia* **1966**: 443:450.

Bullman, O. M. B. 1970. Graptolithina with sections on Enteropneusta and Pterobranchia. In C. Teichert (Ed.), *Treatise on invertebrate paleontology,* Pt. 5. Geological Society of America and University of Kansas. 163 pp.

Burgess, W. E. 1974. Evidence for the elevation to family status of the angelfishes (Pomacanthidae), previously considered to be a subfamily of the butterflyfish family, Chaetodontidae. *Pac. Sci.* **28**: 57–71.

Burgess, W. E. 1978. *Butterflyfishes of the world. A monograph of the family Chaetodontidae.* Neptune City, N. J.: T.F.H. Public. 832 pp.

Burgess, W. E. 1982. *Betta*—one genus or two? *Trop. Fish. Hobb.* **1982:** 28–29.

Burgess, W. and H. R. Axelrod. 1972–1976. *Pacific marine fishes.* Books 1–7. Neptune City, N.J.: T.F.H. Public.

Butter, M. E., M. Wapstra, and E. van Dijk. 1980. *Meandrina meandrites* and *Emblemariopsis diaphana*, first record of an association between a stony coral and a fish, similar to anemone/fish relationships. *Bijdr. Dierk.* **50**(1): 87–95.

Campbell, K. S. W. 1981. Lungfishes—alive and extinct. *Field Mus. Nat. Hist. Bull.* **52**(8): 3–5.

Carroll, R. L. 1982. Early evolution of reptiles. *Ann. Rev. Ecol. Syst.* **13:** 87–109.

Caruso, J. H. 1981. The systematics and distribution of the lophiid anglerfishes I. A revision of the genus *Lophiodes* with the description of two new species. *Copeia* **1981**(3): 522–549.

Castex, M. N. 1967. Fresh water venomous rays. In F. E. Russell and P. R. Saunders (Eds.), *Animal toxins.* Symposium Publ. Div. Oxford: Pergamon: 167–176.

Castle, P. H. J. 1961. Deep water eels from Cook Strait, New Zealand. *Zool. Publ. Victoria University, Wellington* **27:** 1–30.

Castle, P. H. J. 1967. Two remarkable eel-larvae from off southern Africa. *Dept. Ichthyol., Rhodes Univ. Spec. Publ.* **1.** 12 pp.

Castle, P. H. J. 1969. An index and bibliography of eel larvae. *J.L.B. Smith Inst. Ichthyol., Rhodes Univ. Spec. Publ.* **7.** 121 pp.

Castle, P. H. J. 1970. Distribution, larval growth, and metamorphosis of the eel *Derichthys serpentinus* Gill, 1884 (Pisces: Derichthyidae). *Copeia* **1970**(3): 444–452.

Castle, P. H. J. 1972. The eel genus *Benthenchelys* (Fam. Ophichthidae) in the Indo-Pacific. *Dana Rep.* **82:** 1–31.

Castle, P. H. J. 1973. A giant notacanthiform leptocephalus from the Chatham Islands, New Zealand. *Rec. Dom. Mus.* **8**(8): 121–124.

Castle, P. H. J. 1976. The eel *Aotea acus*, a synonym of *Muraenichthys breviceps. Copeia* **1976**(2): 365–366.

Castle, P. H. J. 1977a. Results of the research cruises of FRV "Walther Herwig" to South America. 50. A new genus and species of bobtail eel (Anguilliformes, Cyemidae) from the South Atlantic. *Arch. Fisch Wiss.* **28:** 69–76.

Castle, P. H. J. 1977b. Leptocephalus of the muraenesocid eel *Gavialiceps taeniola. Copeia* **1977**(3): 488–492.

Castle, P. H. J. and G. R. Williamson. 1975. Systematics and distribution of eels of the *Muraenesox* group (Anguilliformes, Muraenesocidae). *J.L.B. Smith Inst. Ichthyol. Rhodes Univ. Spec. Public.* **15.** 9 pp.

Cavender, T. 1966. Systematic position of the North America Eocene fish *"Leuciscus" rosei* Hussakof. *Copeia* **1966:** 311–320.

Cavender, T. 1969. An Oligocene mudminnow (family Umbridae) from Oregon with remarks on relationships within the Esocoidei. *Occ. Pap. Mus. Zool. Univ. Mich. No. 660.* 33 pp.

Cavender, T. M. 1978. Taxonomy and distribution of the bull trout, *Salvelinus confluentus* (Suckley), from the American Northwest. *Calif. Fish and Game.* **64**(3): 139–174.

Cavender, T. M. and R. R. Miller. 1972. *Smilodonichthys rastrosus*, a new *Pliocene* salmonid fish from western United States. *Mus. Nat. Hist. Univ. Oregon Bull.* **18:** 44 pp.

Chalifa, Y. and E. Tchernov. 1982. *Pachyamia latimaxillaris*, new genus and species (Actinopterygii: Amiidae), from the Cenomanian of Jerusalem. *J. Vert. Paleont.* **2**(3): 269–285.

Chandra, R. 1976. On the occurrence of *Psilorhynchus sucatio* (Ham.) in the river Ganga at Allahabad and Buxar with notes on the distribution of *Psilorhynchus* spp. *Matsya* **2:** 81–82.

Chang, M. M. 1982. *The braincase of Youngolepis, a lower Devonian crossopterygian from Yunnan, south-western China.* Stockholm: Dept. of Geology, Univ. of Stockholm, and Section of Palaeozool., Swedish Mus. of Nat. Hist. 113 pp.

Chao, L. N. 1978. A basis for classifying western Atlantic Sciaenidae (Teleostei: Perciformes). *NOAA Tech. Rep. NMFS Circ.* **415.** 64 pp.

Chardon, M. 1967. Réflexions sur la dispersion des Ostariophysi à la lumière de recherches morphologiques nouvelles. *Ann. Soc. R. Zool. Belg.* **97**(3): 175–186.

Chardon, M. 1968. Anatomie comparée de l'appareil de Weber et des structures connexes chez les Siluriformes. *Mus. R. Afr. Cent. Ann. (Ser. 8, Zool.)* **169:** 1–277.

Chen, L. C. 1981. Scorpaenid fishes of Taiwan. *Q. J. Taiwan Mus.* **34:** 1–60.

Chirichigno, N. F. 1974. Clave para identificar los peces marinos del Peru. *Inst. del Mar del Peru, Informe* **44:** 1–387.

Chirichigno, N. F. 1978. Nuevas adiciones a la ictiofauna marina del Peru. *Inst. del Mar del Peru, Informe* **46:** 1–109.

Clark, H. W. 1937. New fishes from the Templeton Crocker Expedition. *Copeia* **1937:** 88–91.

Clausen, H. S. 1959. Denticipitidae, a new family of primitive isospondylous teleosts from west African freshwater. *Vidensk. Meddr. Dansk. Naturh. Foren.* **121:** 141–156.

Coad, B. W. 1981a. A bibliography of the sticklebacks. *Syllogeus 35, Nat. Mus. Canada.* 142 pp.

Coad, B. W. 1981b. Fishes of Afghanistan, an annotated check-list. *Natl. Mus. Can., Publ. Zool.* **14.** 26 pp.

Coad, B. W. 1982. A new genus and species of cichlid endemic to southern Iran. *Copeia* **1982**(1): 28–37.

Cohen, D. M. 1964. Suborder Argentinoidea. In Fishes of the western North Atlantic. *Mem. Sears Found. Mar. Res.* **1**(1): 1–70.

Cohen, D. M. 1970. How many recent fishes are there? *Proc. Calif. Acad. Sci.,* Ser. 4, **38:** 341–345.

Cohen, D. M. 1980. Names of the hakes. *Marine Fish. Rev.* **1980:** 2–3.

Cohen, D. M. and S. P. Atsaides. 1969. Additions to a revision of argentinine fishes. *U.S. Fish. Bull.* **68:** 13–36.

Cohen, D. M. and J. G. Nielsen. 1978. Guide to the identification of genera of the fish order Ophidiiformes with a tentative classification of the order. *NOAA Tech. Rep. NMFS Circ.* *417.* 72 pp.

Cohen, D. M. and C. R. Robins. 1970. A new ophidioid fish (genus *Lucifuga*) from a limestone sink, New Providence Island, Bahamas. *Proc. Biol. Soc. Wash.* **83**(11): 133–144.

Cohen, D. M. and J. L. Russo. 1979. Variation in the fourbeard rockling, *Enchelyopus cimbrius*, a North Atlantic gadid fish, with comments on the genera of rocklings. *U.S. Fish Bull.* **77**(1): 91–104.

Coleman, N. 1980. *Australian sea fishes*. Lane Cove, N.S.W.: Doubleday Australia Pty. 302 pp.

Colin, P. L., D. W. Arneson, and W. F. Smith-Vaniz. 1979. Rediscovery and redescription of the Caribbean anomalopid fish *Kryptophanaron alfredi* Silvester and Fowler (Pisces: Anomalopidae). *Bull. Marine Sci.* **29**(3): 312–319.

Collares-Pereira, M. J. 1980. Population variability of *Pseudophoxinus hispanicus* (Steindachner, 1866) (Pisces, Cyprinidae). *Arg. Mus. Boc.*, Ser. 2, **7**(21): 363–388.

Collette, B. B. 1963. The subfamilies, tribes and genera of the Percidae (Teleostei). *Copeia* **1963**(4): 615–623.

Collette, B. B. 1966. A review of the venomous toadfishes, subfamily Thalassophryninae. *Copeia* **1966**(4): 846–864.

Collette, B. B. 1973. *Daector quadrizonatus*, a valid species of freshwater venomous toadfish from the Rio Truandó, Colombia with notes on additional material of other species of *Daector. Copeia* **1973**: 355–357.

Collette, B. B. 1974. The garfishes (Hemiramphidae) of Australia and New Zealand. *Rec. Aust. Mus.* **29**(2): 11–105.

Collette, B. B. 1979. Adaptations and systematics of the mackerels and tunas. In G. D. Sharp and A. E. Dizon (Eds.), *The physiological ecology of tunas*. New York: Academic: 7–39.

Collette, B. B. 1982a. Two new species of freshwater halfbeaks (Pisces: Hemiramphidae) of the genus *Zenarchopterus* from New Guinea. *Copeia* **1982**(2): 265–276.

Collette, B. B. 1982b. South American freshwater needlefishes of the genus *Potamorrhaphis* (Beloniformes: Belonidae). *Proc. Biol. Soc. Wash.* **95**: 714–747.

Collette, B. B. and P. Bănărescu. 1977. Systematics and zoogeography of the fishes of the family Percidae. *J. Fish. Res. Board Can.* **34**: 1450–1463.

Collette, B. B. and L. N. Chao. 1975. Systematics and morphology of the bonitos (*Sarda*) and their relatives (Scombridae, Sardini). *U.S. Fish Bull.* **73**(3): 516–625.

Collette, B. B. and J. L. Russo. 1981. A revision of the scaly toadfishes, genus *Batrachoides*, with descriptions of two new species from eastern Atlantic. *Bull. Marine Sci.* **31**(2): 197–233.

Compagno, L. J. V. 1973. Interrelationships of living elasmobranchs. In P. H. Greenwood, R. S. Miles, and C. Patterson (Eds.), Interrelationships of fishes. *J. Linn. Soc. (Zool.)* **53**, Suppl. 1: 15–61. New York: Academic.

Compagno, L. J. V. 1977. Phyletic relationships of living sharks and rays. *Am. Zool.* **17**: 303–322.

Compagno, L. J. V. and T. R. Roberts. 1982. Freshwater stingrays (Dasyatidae) of Southeast Asia and New Guinea, with description of a new species of *Himantura* and reports of unidentified species. *Env. Biol. Fish.* **7**(4): 321–339.

Cooper, J. E. and R. A. Kuehne. 1974. *Speoplatyrhinus poulsoni*, a new genus and species of subterranean fish from Alabama. *Copeia* **1974**(2): 486–493.

Cowan, G. I. M. and R. H. Rosenblatt. 1974. *Taenioconger canabus*, a new heterocongrin eel (Pisces: Congridae) from Baja California, with a comparison of a closely related species. *Copeia* **1974**(1): 55–60.

Cressey, R. 1981. Revision of Indo-West Pacific lizardfishes of the genus *Synodus* (Pisces: Synodontidae). *Smithsonian Contrib. Zool.* **342**. 53 pp.

Croizat, L. 1982. Vicariance/vicariism, panbiogeography, "Vicariance biogeography", etc.: a clarification. *Syst. Zool.* **31**: 291–304.

Croizat, L., G. Nelson, and D. E. Rosen. 1974. Centers of origin and related concepts. *Syst. Zool.* **23**: 265–287.

Crossman, E. J. 1978. Taxonomy and distribution of North American esocids. *Am. Fish. Soc. Spec. Publ.* **11**: 13–26.

Daniels, R. A. 1981. *Cryothenia peninsulae*, a new genus and species of nototheniid fish from the Antarctic Peninsula. *Copeia* **1981**(3): 558–562.

Darlington, P. J., Jr. 1957. *Zoogeography: the geographical distribution of animals.* New York: Wiley. 675 pp.

Dawson, C. E. 1974a. Studies on eastern Pacific sand stargazers (Pisces: Dactyloscopidae), 1. *Platygillellus* new genus, with descriptions of new species. *Copeia* **1974**(1): 39–55.

Dawson, C. E. 1974b. A review of the Microdesmidae (Pisces: Gobioidea). 1. *Cerdale* and *Clarkichthys* with descriptions of three new species. *Copeia* **1974**(2): 409–448.

Dawson, C. E. 1975. Studies on eastern Pacific sand stargazers (Pisces: Dactyloscopidae). 2. Genus *Dactyloscopus*, with descriptions of new species and subspecies. *Bull. Nat. Hist. Mus. Los Angeles County, Sci.* **22**. 61 pp.

Dawson, C. E. 1976. Studies on eastern Pacific sand stargazers. 3. *Dactylagnus* and *Myxodagnus*, with description of a new species and subspecies. *Copeia* **1976**(1): 13–43.

Dawson, C. E. 1977. Studies on eastern Pacific sand stargazers (Pisces: Dactyloscopidae). 4. *Gillellus, Sindoscopus* new genus, and *Heteristius* with description of new species. *Proc. Calif. Acad. Sci.*, Ser. 4, **41**: 125–160.

Dawson, C. E. 1979. A new wormfish (Pisces: Microdesmidae) from the eastern tropical Atlantic. *Copeia* **1979**(2): 203–205.

Dawson, C. E. 1980a. *Kimblaeus*, a new pipefish genus (Syngnathiformes: Syngnathidae) from Australia, with a key to genera of pipefishes with continuous superior ridges. *Aust. J. Mar. Freshw. Res.* **31**: 517–523.

Dawson, C. E. 1980b. Synopsis of the pipefishes (Syngnathidae) of New Zealand. *Rec. Nat. Mus. New Zealand* **1**(17): 281–291.

Dawson, C. E. 1981a. Notes on four pipefishes (Syngnathidae) from the Persian Gulf. *Copeia* **1981**(1): 87–95.

Dawson, C. E. 1981b. Review of the Indo-Pacific Doryrhamphine pipefish genus *Doryichthys*. *Jap. J. Ichthyol.* **28**(1): 1–18.

Dawson, C. E. 1982a. Synopsis of the Indo-Pacific genus *Solegnathus* (Pisces: Syngnathidae). *Jap. J. Ichthyol.* **29**(2): 139–161.

Dawson, C. E. 1982b. Atlantic sand stargazers (Pisces: Dactyloscopidae), with description of one new genus and seven new species. *Bull. Marine Sci.* **32**: 14–85.

Dawson, C. E. and G. R. Allen. 1978. Synopsis of the 'finless' pipefish genera (*Penetopteryx, Apterygocampus* and *Enchelyocampus*, Gen. Nov.). *Rec. West. Aust. Mus.* **6**(4): 391–411.

Dekkers, W. J. 1975. Review of the Asiatic freshwater puffers of the genus *Tetraodon* Linnaeus, 1758 (Pisces, Tetraodontiformes, Tetraodontidae). *Bijdr. Dierk.* **45**(1): 87–142.

Denison, R. H. 1971a. The origin of the vertebrates: A critical evaluation of current theories. *Proc. North American Paleontol. Convention.*, Pt. H., pp. 1132–1146.

Denison, R. H. 1971b. On the tail of Heterostraci (Agnatha). *Forma et Functio* **4**: 87–98.

Denison, R. H. 1978. Placodermi. In H. P. Schultze (Ed.), *Handbook of Paleoichthyology*. Vol. 2. Stuttgart and New York: Gustav Fischer Verlag: 128 pp.

Denison, R. H. 1979. Acanthodii. In H. P. Schultze (Ed.), *Handbook of Paleoichthyology*. Vol. 5. Stuttgart and New York: Gustav Fischer Verlag: 62 pp.

de Sylva, D. P. and W. N. Eschmeyer. 1977. Systematics and biology of the deep-sea fish family Gibberichthyidae, a senior synonym of the family Kasidoroidae. *Proc. Calif. Acad. Sci.*, Ser. 4, **41**: 215–231.

DeWitt, H. H. 1969. A second species of the family Cottidae from the New Zealand region. *Copeia* **1969**: 30–34.

DeWitt, H. H. 1971. Coastal and deep-water benthic fishes of the Antarctic. *Amer. Geogr. Soc.*, Antarctic Map Folio Ser. **15**: 1–10.

DeWitt, H. H. 1977. A new genus and species of eelpout (Pisces, Zoarcidae) from the Gulf of Mexico. *U.S. Fish Bull.* **75**: 789–793.

DeWitt, H. H., P. A. Grecay, J. S. Hacunda, B. P. Lindsay, R. F. Shaw, and D. W. Townsend. 1981. An addition to the fish fauna of the Gulf of Maine with records of rare species. *Proc. Biol. Soc. Wash.* **94**(3): 669–674.

Diener, D. R. 1977. Protogynous hermaphroditism in the labrid *Decodon melasma*. *Copeia* **1977**(3): 589–591.

Dillion, L. S. 1965. The hydrocoel and the ancestry of the chordates. *Evolution* **19**(3): 436–446.

Dooley, J. K. 1978. Systematics and biology of the tilefishes (Perciformes: Branchiostegidae and Malacanthidae), with descriptions of two new species. *NOAA Tech. Rept. NMFS Circ.* **411**. 78 pp.

Dooley, J. K. 1981. A new species of tilefish (Pisces: Branchiostegidae) from Bermuda, with a brief discussion of the genus *Caulolatilus*. *Northeast Gulf Sci.* **5**(1): 39–44.

Dutt, S. 1973. Synodidae: correct name for lizardfish family. *J. Mar. Biol. Assn. India* **15**(1): 450–451.

Eakin, R. R. 1981a. Osteology and relationships of the fishes of the Antarctic family Harpagiferidae (Pisces, Notothenioidei). *Biol. Antarc. Seas. 9. Antarc. Res. Ser.* **31**: 81–147.

Eakin, R. R. 1981b. Reports on fishes from the University of Maine Antarctic Biological Research Program. 1. Genus *Pogonophryne* (Pisces, Harpagiferidae) from the South Orkney Islands. *Biol. Antarc. Seas. 9. Antarc. Res. Ser.* **31**: 155–159.

Eastman, J. T. 1977. The pharyngeal bones and teeth of catostomid fishes. *Am. Midl. Nat.* **97**: 68–88.

Eastman, J. T. 1980. The caudal skeletons of catostomid fishes. *Am. Midl. Nat.* **103**: 133–148.

Eastman, J. T. and A. L. DeVries. 1982. Buoyancy studies of notothenioid fishes in Mc-Murdo Sound, Antarctica. *Copeia* **1982**(2): 385-393.

Eaton, T. H. 1970. The stem-tail problem and the ancestry of chordates. *J. Paleontol.* **44**: 969–979.

Ebeling, A. W. and W. H. Weed, III. 1973. Order Xenoberyces (Stephanoberyciformes). In Fishes of the western North Atlantic. *Mem. Sears Found. Mar. Res.* **1**(6): 397–478.

Ege, V. 1939. A revision of the genus *Anguilla* Shaw, a systematic, phylogenetic and geographical study. *Dana Rep.* **16**: 1–256.

Eigenmann, C. H. 1917. Descriptions of sixteen new species of Pygidiidae. *Proc. Am. Phil. Soc.* **56**: 691–703.

Emery, A. R. 1980. The osteology of *Lepidozygus tapeinosoma* (Pisces: Pomacentridae). *Bull. Marine Sci.* **30:** 213–236.

Emery, A. R. and G. R. Allen. 1980. *Stegastes;* a senior synonym for the damselfish genus *Eupomacentrus;* osteological and other evidence, with comments on other genera. *Rec. West. Aust. Mus.* **8**(2): 199–206.

Eschmeyer, W. N. 1969. A systematic review of the scorpionfishes of the Atlantic Ocean (Pisces: Scorpaenidae). *Occ. Pap. Calif. Acad. Sci.* **79.** 143 pp.

Eschmeyer, W. N., T. Abe, and S. Nakano. 1979. *Adelosebastes latens,* a new genus and species of scorpionfish from the North Pacific Ocean (Pisces, Scorpaenidae). *UO* **30:** 77–84.

Eschmeyer, W. N. and B. B. Collette. 1966. The scorpionfish subfamily Setarchinae, including the genus *Ectreposebastes. Bull. Marine Sci.* **16**(2): 349–375.

Eschmeyer, W. M., L. E. Hallacher, and K. V. Rama-Rao. 1979. The scorpionfish genus *Minous* (Scorpaenidae: Minoinae) including a new species from the Indian Ocean. *Proc. Calif. Acad. Sci.,* Ser. 4, **41:** 453–473.

Eschmeyer, W. N., Y. Hirosaki, and T. Abe. 1973. Two new species of the scorpionfish genus *Rhinopias,* with comments on related genera and species. *Proc. Calif. Acad. Sci.,* Ser. 4, **39:** 285–310.

Eschmeyer, W. N. and K. V. Rama-Rao. 1977. A new scorpionfish, *Ebosia falcata* (Scorpaenidae, Pteroinae), from the western Indian Ocean, with comments on the genus. *Matsya* **3:** 64–71.

Eschmeyer, W. N. and K. V. Rama-Rao. 1979. Fishes of the scorpionfish subfamily Choridactylinae from the western Pacific and the Indian Ocean. *Proc. Calif. Acad. Sci.,* Ser. 4, **41:** 475–500.

Eschmeyer, W. N. and K. V. R. Rao. 1973. Two new stonefishes (Pisces, Scorpaenidae) from the Indo-West Pacific, with a synopsis of the subfamily Synanceiinae. *Proc. Calif. Acad. Sci.,* Ser. 4, **39:** 337–382.

Evans, R. R. 1975. Swimbladder anatomy in four species of western Atlantic *Peristedion* (Peristediidae) with notes on its possible classificatory significance. *Copeia* **1975**(1): 74–78.

Fernholm, B. 1981a. Thread cells from the slime glands of hagfish (Myxinidae). *Acta Zool.* **62:** 137–145.

Fernholm, B. 1981b. A new species of hagfish of the genus *Myxine,* with notes on other eastern Atlantic myxinids. *J. Fish Biol.* **19:** 73–82.

Fernholm, B. 1982. *Eptatretus caribbeaus:* a new species of hagfish (Myxinidae) from the Caribbean. *Bull. Marine Sci.* **32**(2): 434–438.

Fernholm, B. and K. Holmberg. 1975. The eyes in three genera of hagfish (*Eptatretus, Paramyxine* and *Myxine*)—a case of degenerative evolution. *Vision Res.* **15:** 253–259.

Fernholm, B. and C. L. Hubbs. 1981. Western Atlantic hagfishes of the genus *Eptatretus* (Myxinidae) with descriptions of two new species. *Fish. Bull.* **79:** 69–83.

Fink, S. V. and W. L. Fink. 1981. Interrelationships of the ostariophysan fishes (Teleostei). *J. Linn. Soc. (Zool.)* **72**(4): 297–353.

Fink, W. L. and S. H. Weitzman. 1982. Relationships of the stomiiform fishes (Teleostei), with a description of *Diplophos. Bull. Mus. Comp. Zool.* **150**(2): 31–93.

Fischer, E. A. 1980. Speciation in the hamlets (*Hypoplectrus:* Serranidae)—a continuing enigma. *Copeia* **1980**(4): 649–659.

Fitch, J. E. 1964. The ribbon fishes (Family Trachipteridae) of the eastern Pacific Ocean, with a description of a new species. *Calif. Fish and Game* **50**(4): 228–240.

Forey, P. L. 1973a. Relationships of Elopomorpha. In P. H. Greenwood, R. S. Miles, and C. Patterson (Eds.), Interrelationships of fishes. *J. Linn. Soc. (Zool.)* **53**. Suppl. 1: 351–368. New York: Academic.

Forey, P. L. 1973b. A revision of the elopiform fishes, fossil and Recent. *Bull. Br. Mus. Nat. Hist. (Geol.).* Suppl. 10. 222 pp.

Forey, P. L. 1980. *Latimeria:* a paradoxical fish. *Proc. R. Soc.,* London B, **208**: 369–384.

Forselius, S. 1957. Studies of anabantid fishes. 1, 2, 3. *Zool. Bid. Från Uppsala* **32**: 93–598.

Fowler, H. W. 1933. Descriptions of new fishes obtained 1907 to 1910, chiefly in the Philippine Islands and adjacent seas. *Proc. Acad. Nat. Sci. Philad.* **85**: 233–367.

Fowler, H. W. 1959. *Fishes of Fiji.* Government of Fiji, Avery Press, New Zealand. 670 pp.

Fowler, H. W. 1972. *A synopsis of the fishes of China.* Reprint of 1930–1962 publications. 2 vols. Netherlands: Antiquariaat Junk. 1459 pp.

Fraser, T. H. 1971. The fish *Dinolestes lewini* with comments on its osteology and relationships. *Jap. J. Ichthyol.* **18**(4): 157–163.

Fraser, T. H. 1972a. Some thoughts about the teleostean fish concept—the Paracanthopterygii. *Jap. J. Ichthyol.* **19**(4): 232–242.

Fraser, T. H. 1972b. Comparative osteology of the shallow water cardinal fishes (Perciformes: Apogonidae) with reference to the systematics and evolution of the family. *Ichthyol. Bull. Rhodes Univ. No. 34.* 105 pp.

Fraser, T. H. and P. Fourmanoir. 1971. The deepwater fish *Scombrosphyraena oceanica.* *J.L.B. Smith Inst. Ichthyol., Rhodes Univ. Spec. Public.* **8**. 7 pp.

Fraser-Brunner, A. 1950. Notes on the fishes of the genus *Antigonia* (Caproidae). *Ann. Mag. Nat. Hist.,* Ser. 12, **3**: 721–724.

Fraser-Brunner, A. 1951. The ocean sunfishes (family Molidae). *Bull. Br. Mus. Nat. Hist. (Zool.)* **1**: 89–121.

Freihofer, W. C. 1970. Some nerve patterns and their systematic significance in paracanthopterygian, salmoniform, gobioid, and apogonid fishes. *Proc. Calif. Acad. Sci.,* Ser. 4, **38**: 215–263.

Freihofer, W. C. 1978. Cranial nerves of a percoid fish, *Polycentrus schomburgkii* (Family Nandidae), a contribution to the morphology and classification of the order Perciformes. *Occ. Pap. Calif. Acad. Sci.* **128**. 78 pp.

Fricke, R. 1981. *Revision of the genus Synchiropus (Teleostei: Callionymidae). Theses Zool. 1.* Braunschweig: J. Cramer. 194 pp.

Fricke, R. 1982. New species of *Callionymus,* with a revision of the *variegatus*-group of that genus (Teleostei: Callionymidae). *J. Nat. Hist.* **16**: 127–146.

Fritzsche, R. A. 1976. A review of the cornetfishes, genus *Fistularia* (Fistulariidae), with a discussion of intrageneric relationships and zoogeography. *Bull. Marine Sci.* **26**: 196–204.

Fritzsche, R. A. 1978. The first eastern Pacific records of bulleye, *Cookeolus boops* (Bloch and Schneider, 1801), (Pisces, Priacanthidae). *Calif. Fish and Game* **64**: 219–221.

Fritzsche, R. A. 1980. Revision of the eastern Pacific Syngnathidae (Pisces: Syngnathiformes), including both recent and fossil forms. *Proc. Calif. Acad. Sci.* **42**: 181–227.

Fryer, G. and T. D. Iles. 1972. *The cichlid fishes of the great lakes of Africa.* Edinburgh: Oliver and Boyd. 641 pp.

Gardiner, B. G. 1967. The significance of the preoperculum in actinopterygian evolution. *J. Linn. Soc. (Zool.)* **47**(311): 197–209.

Gardiner, B. G. 1980. Tetrapod ancestry: a reappraisal. In A. L. Panchen (Ed.), *The terres-*

trial environment and the origin of land vertebrates. Syst. Assoc. Spec. Publ. 15. London: Academic: 177–185.

Garrick, J. A. F. 1951. The blind electric rays of the genus *Typhlonarke* (Torpedinidae). *Zool. Publ. Victoria University College No. 14.* 6 pp.

Garrick, J. A. F. 1960. Studies on New Zealand Elasmobranchii. 12. The species of *Squalus* from New Zealand and Australia; and a general account and key to the New Zealand Squaloidea. *Trans. R. Soc. N.Z.* **88:** 519–557.

Garrick, J. A. F. 1971. *Harriotta raleighana,* a long-nosed chimaera (Family Rhinochimaeridae), in New Zealand waters. *J. R. Soc. N.Z.* **1:** 203–213.

Garrick, J. A. F. 1982. Sharks in the genus *Carcharhinus. NOAA Tech. Rep. NMFS Circ.* **445.** 194 pp.

Garrick, J. A. F. and L. J. Paul. 1974. The taxonomy of New Zealand skates (suborder Rajoidea) with descriptions of three new species. *J. R. Soc. N.Z.* **4**(3): 345–377.

George, A. and V. G. Springer. 1980. Revision of the clinid fish tribe Ophiclinini, including five new species, and definition of the family Clinidae. *Smithsonian Contrib. Zool.* **307.** 31 pp.

Géry, J. 1972. Clé de détermination des familles, sous-familles et tribus des poissons characoïdes néotropicaux. *Zool. Verhand.* **122:** 53–71.

Géry, J. 1976. Les genres de Serrasalmidae (Pisces, Characoidei). *Bull. Zool. Mus., Univ. Amst.* **5**(6): 47–54.

Géry, J. 1977. *Characoids of the world.* Neptune, N.J.: T.F.H. Public. 672 pp.

Gibbs, R. H., Jr. 1964a. Family Astronesthidae. In Fishes of the western North Atlantic. *Mem. Sears Found. Mar. Res.* **1**(4): 311–350.

Gibbs, R. H., Jr. 1964b. Family Idiacanthidae. In Fishes of the western North Atlantic. *Mem. Sears Found. Mar. Res.* **1**(4): 512–522.

Gibbs, R. H. and B. B. Collette. 1967. Comparative anatomy and systematics of the tunas, genus *Thunnus. U.S. Fish. Bull.* **66**(1): 65–130.

Gilbert, C. R. 1967. A revision of the hammerhead sharks (family Sphyrnidae). *Proc. U.S. Natl. Mus.* **119:** 1–88.

Gilbert, C. R. 1968. Western Atlantic batrachoidid fishes of the genus *Porichthys,* including three new species. *Bull. Marine Sci.* **18:** 671–730.

Gilbert, C. R. 1976. Composition and derivation of the North American freshwater fish fauna. *Florida Sci.* **39**(2): 104–111.

Glodek, G. S. and H. J. Carter. 1978. A new helogeneid catfish from eastern Ecuador (Pisces, Siluriformes, Helogeneidae). *Fieldiana Zool.* **72**(6): 75–82.

Goldstein, A. J. 1973. *Cichlids of the world.* Neptune City, N.J.: T.F.H. Public. 382 pp.

Goody, P. C. 1969. The relationships of certain Upper Cretaceous teleosts with special reference to the myctophoids. *Bull. Br. Mus. Nat. Hist. (Geol.)* Suppl. 7. 255 pp.

Goodyear, R. H. 1970. A new species of *Ataxolepis,* a bathypelagic fish from the Gulf of Panama (Pisces, Lampridiformes, Megalomycteridae). *Steenstrupia* **1**(3): 17–20.

Gosline, W. A. 1940. A revision of the neotropical catfishes of the family Callichthyidae. *Stanford Ichthyol. Bull.* **2**(1): 1–29.

Gosline, W. A. 1942. Notes on South American catfishes (Nematognathi). *Copeia* **1942:** 39–41.

Gosline, W. A. 1955. The osteology and relationships of certain gobioid fishes, with particular reference to the genera *Kraemeria* and *Microdesmus. Pac. Sci.* **9:** 158–170.

Gosline, W. A. 1959. Four new species, a new genus, and a new suborder of Hawaiian fishes. *Pac. Sci.* **13:** 67–77.

Gosline, W. A. 1963a. Considerations regarding the relationships of the percopsiform, cyprinodontiform, and gadiform fishes. *Occ. Pap. Mus. Zool. Univ. Mich.* **629:** 38 pp.

Gosline, W. A. 1963b. Notes on the osteology and systematic position of *Hypoptychus dybowskii* Steindachner and other elongate perciform fishes. *Pac. Sci.* **17**(1): 90–101.

Gosline, W. A. 1966. The limits of the fish family Serranidae, with notes on other lower percoids. *Proc. Calif. Acad. Sci.*, Ser. 4., **33**(6): 91–112.

Gosline, W. A. 1968. The suborders of perciform fishes. *Proc. U.S. Natl. Mus.* **124:** 1–78.

Gosline, W. A. 1969. The morphology and systematic position of the alepocephaloid fishes. *Bull. Br. Mus. Nat. Hist. (Zool.)* **18**(6): 183–218.

Gosline, W. A. 1970. A reinterpretation of the teleostean fish order Gobiesociformes. *Proc. Calif. Acad. Sci.*, Ser. 4, **37**(19): 363–382.

Gosline, W. A. 1971. *Functional morphology and classification of teleostean fishes.* Honolulu: University Press of Hawaii. 208 pp.

Gosline, W. A. 1973. Considerations regarding the phylogeny of cypriniform fishes, with special reference to structures associated with feeding. *Copeia* **1973:** 761–776.

Gosline, W. A. 1975a. A reexamination of the similarities between the freshwater fishes of Africa and South America. *Mém. Mus. Natl. d'Hist. Nat.* Sér. A, Zool. **88:** 146–155.

Gosline, W. A. 1975b. The palatine-maxillary mechanism in catfishes, with comments on the evolution and zoogeography of modern siluroids. *Occ. Pap. Calif. Acad. Sci.* **120.** 31 pp.

Gosline, W. A. 1978. Unbranched dorsal-fin rays and subfamily classification in the fish family Cyprinidae. *Occ. Pap. Mus. Zool. Univ. Mich.* **684.** 21 pp.

Gosline, W. A. 1980. The evolution of some structural systems with reference to the interrelationships of modern lower teleostean fish groups. *Jap. J. Ichthyol.* **27**(1): 1–28.

Gosline, W. A. and V. E. Brock. 1960. *Handbook of Hawaiian fishes.* Honolulu: University of Hawaii Press. 372 pp.

Gosztonyi, A. E. 1977. Results of the research cruise of FRV "Walther Herwig" to South America. 48. Revision of the South American Zoarcidae (Osteichthyes, Blennioidei) with the description of three new genera and five new species. *Arch. Fisch Wiss.* **27**(3): 191–249.

Gradwell, N. 1971. Observations on jet propulsion in banjo catfishes. *Can. J. Zool.* **49:** 1611–1612.

Grande, L. 1979. *Eohiodon falcatus,* a new species of hiodontid (Pisces) from the Late Early Eocene Green River formation of Wyoming. *J. Paleont.* **53**(1): 103–111.

Grande, L. 1980. Paleontology of the Green River formation, with a review of the fish fauna. *Wyoming Geol. Surv., Bull.* **63:** 1–334.

Grande, L. 1982a. A revision of the fossil genus † *Diplomystus,* with comments on the interrelationships of Clupeomorph fishes. *Am. Mus. Novit.* **2728.** 34 pp.

Grande, L. 1982b. A revision of the fossil genus † *Knightia,* with a description of a new genus from the Green River formation (Teleostei, Clupeidae). *Am. Mus. Novit.* **2731.** 22 pp.

Grande, L., J. T. Eastman, and T. M. Cavender. 1982. *Amyzon gosiutensis,* a new catostomid fish from the Green River formation. *Copeia* **1982**(3): 523–532.

Graves, J. E. and R. H. Rosenblatt. 1980. Genetic relationships of the color morphs of the serranid fish *Hypoplectrus unicolor. Evolution* **34:** 240–245.

Greenfield, D. W. 1968. The zoogeography of *Myripristis* (Pisces: Holocentridae). *Syst. Zool.* **17:** 76–87.

Greenfield, D. W. 1974. A revision of the squirrelfish genus *Myripristis* Cuvier (Pisces: Holocentridae). *Bull. Nat. Hist. Mus. Los Angeles County, Sci.* **19.** 54 pp.

Greenfield, D. W. and T. Greenfield. 1973. *Triathalassothia gloverensis*, a new species of toadfish from Belize (= British Honduras) with remarks on the genus. *Copeia* **1973:** 560–565.

Greenfield, D. W. and R. K. Johnson. 1981. The blennioid fishes of Belize and Honduras, Central America, with comments on their systematics, ecology, and distribution (Blenniidae, Chaenopsidae, Labrisomidae, Tripterygiidae). *Fieldiana, Zool.*, New Ser., 8, 106 pp.

Greenfield, D. W. and L. P. Woods. 1980. Review of the deep-bodied species of *Chromis* (Pisces: Pomacentridae) from the eastern Pacific, with descriptions of three new species. *Copeia* **1980**(4): 626–641.

Greenwood, P. H. 1961. A revision of the genus *Dinotopterus* (Pisces, Clariidae) with notes on the comparative anatomy of the suprabranchiae organs in the Clariidae. *Bull. Br. Mus. Nat. Hist. (Zool.)*, **7**(4): 215–241.

Greenwood, P. H. 1968. The osteology and relationships of the Denticipitidae, a family of clupeomorph fishes. *Bull. Br. Mus. Nat. Hist. (Zool.)*, **16:** 13–273.

Greenwood, P. H. 1970. On the genus *Lycoptera* and its relationships with the family Hiodontidae (Pisces, Osteoglossomorpha). *Bull. Br. Mus. Nat. Hist. (Zool.)* **19:** 257–285.

Greenwood, P. H. 1973. Interrelationships of osteoglossomorphs. In P. H. Greenwood, R. S. Miles, and C. Patterson (Eds.), Interrelationships of fishes. *J. Linn. Soc. (Zool.)* **53.** Suppl. 1: 307–332. New York: Academic.

Greenwood, P. H. 1974. The cichlid fishes of Lake Victoria, East Africa: the biology and evolution of a species flock. *Bull. Br. Mus. Nat. Hist. (Zool.)*. Suppl. **6.** 1–134.

Greenwood, P. H. 1975. *A history of fishes.* 3rd ed. (revised edition of J. R. Norman's original edition). London: Ernest Benn. 467 pp.

Greenwood, P. H. 1976. A review of the family Centropomidae (Pisces, Perciformes). *Bull. Br. Mus. Nat. Hist. (Zool.)* **29**(1): 1–81.

Greenwood, P. H. 1977. A review of the family Centropomidae (Pisces, Perciformes): an appendix. *Bull. Br. Mus. Nat. Hist. (Zool.)* **31**(6): 297–301.

Greenwood, P. H. 1980. Towards a phyletic classification of the "genus" *Haplochromis* and related taxa, Pt. 2. *Bull. Br. Mus. Nat. Hist. (Zool.)* **39:** 1–99.

Greenwood, P. H. and G. V. Lauder. 1981. The protractor pectoralis muscle and the classification of teleost fishes. *Bull. Br. Mus. Nat. Hist. (Zool.)* **41**(4): 213–234.

Greenwood, P. H., R. S. Miles, and C. Patterson (Eds.). 1973. Interrelationships of fishes. *J. Linn. Soc. (Zool.)* **53.** Suppl. 1. New York: Academic. 536 pp.

Greenwood, P. H., G. S. Myers, D. E. Rosen, and S. H. Weitzman. 1967. Named main divisions of teleostean fishes. *Proc. Biol. Soc. Wash.* **80:** 227–228.

Greenwood, P. H. and D. E. Rosen. 1971. Notes on the structure and relationships of the alepocephaloid fishes. *Am. Mus. Novit.* **2473.** 41 pp.

Greenwood, P. H., D. E. Rosen, S. H. Weitzman, and G. S. Myers. 1966. Phyletic studies of teleostean fishes, with a provisional classification of living forms. *Bull. Am. Mus. Nat. Hist.* **131:** 339–456.

Gudger, E. W. 1926. A study of the smallest shark-suckers (Echeneididae) on record, with special reference to metamorphosis. *Am. Mus. Novit.* **234.** 26 pp.

Haedrich, R. 1967. The stromateoid fishes: systematics and a classification. *Bull. Mus. Comp. Zool.* **135:** 31–319.

Haedrich, R. L. and M. H. Horn. 1972. A key to the stromateoid fishes. Technical Rept. WHOI-72-15. Woods Hole Oceanographic Institution. 46 pp. Unpublished manuscript.

Hagen, D. W. and J. D. McPhail. 1970. The species problem within *Gasterosteus aculeatus* on the Pacific coast of North America. *J. Fish. Res. Bd. Can.* **27:** 147–155.

Hall, B. 1982. Bone in the cartilaginous fishes. *Nature* **298:** 324.

Halstead, B. W. 1967–1970. Poisonous and venomous marine animals of the world. Vols. 2 and 3. *Vertebrates.* Washington, D.C.: U.S. Government Printing Office. Revised 1978 (fishes 298–916). Princeton, N.J.: The Darwin Press.

Halstead (Tarlo), L. B. 1969. *The pattern of vertebrate evolution.* San Francisco: Freeman. 209 pp.

Halstead, L. B. 1982. Evolutionary trends and the phylogeny of the Agnatha. In K. A. Joysey and A. E. Friday (Eds.), *Problems of phylogenetic reconstruction:* 159–196. London: Academic. 442 pp.

Hardisty, M. W. 1979. *Biology of the cyclostomes.* London: Chapman and Hall. 428 pp.

Harper, D. A. T. 1979. Ordovician fish spines from Girvan, Scotland. *Nature* **278:** 634–635.

Harrington, R. W. 1961. Oviparous hermaphroditic fish with internal self-fertilization. *Science* **134:** 1749–1750.

Harrisson, C. M. H. 1966. On the first halosaur leptocephalous, from Madeira. *Bull. Br. Mus. Nat. Hist. (Zool.).* **14:** 441–486.

Harrisson, C. M. H. and G. Palmer. 1968. On the neotype of *Radiicephalus elongtus* Osório with remarks on its biology. *Bull. Br. Mus. Nat. Hist. (Zool.)* **16:** 185–208.

Harry, R. R. 1952. Deep-sea fishes on the Bermuda oceanographic expeditions. Families Cetomimidae and Rondeletiidae. *Zoologica* **37:** 55–71.

Harry, R. R. 1953. A contribution to the classification of the African catfishes of the family Amphiliidae, with descriptions of collections from Cameroon. *Rev. Zool. Bot. Afr.* **47:** 177–232.

Hart, J. L. 1973. Pacific fishes of Canada. *Bull. Fish. Res. Bd. Can.* **180.** 740 pp.

Heemstra, P. C. 1980. A revision of the zeid fishes (Zeiformes: Zeidae) of South Africa. *J.L.B. Smith Inst., Ichthyol. Bull. No. 41.* 18 pp.

Heemstra, P. C. 1982. Taxonomic notes on some triglid and peristediid fishes (Pisces: Scorpaeniformes) from southern Africa. *Copeia* **1982**(2): 291–295.

Heemstra, P. C. and J. E. Randall. 1977. A revision of the Emmelichthyidae (Pisces: Perciformes). *Aust. J. Mar. Freshw. Res.* **28:** 361–396.

Heemstra, P. C. and M. M. Smith. 1980. Hexatrygonidae, a new family of stingrays (Myliobatiformes: Batoidea) from South Africa, with comments on the classification of batoid fishes. *J.L.B. Smith Inst., Ichthyol. Bull. No. 43.* 17 pp.

Heintz, A. 1967. Some remarks about the structure of the tail in cephalaspids. *Coll. Internat. C.N.R.S.* **163:** 21–35.

Hennig, W. 1966. *Phylogenetic systematics.* Urbana: University of Illinois Press. 263 pp.

Herald, E. S. 1959. From pipefish to seahorse—a study of phylogenetic relationships. *Proc. Calif. Acad. Sci.*, Ser. 4, **29:** 465–473.

Herre, A. W. [C. T.] 1939. The genera of Phallostethidae. *Proc. Biol. Soc. Wash.* **52:** 139–144.

Herre, A. W. [C. T.] 1953. Check list of Philippine fishes. *U.S. Fish Wildl. Serv. Res. Rept. 20.* 977 pp.

Herring, P. J. and J. G. Morin. 1978. Bioluminescence in fishes. In P. J. Herring (Ed.), *Bioluminescence in action:* 273–329. London: Academic. 570 pp.

Hesse, R., W. C. Allee, and K. P. Schmidt. 1951. *Ecological Animal Geography.* New York: Wiley. 715 pp.

Hikita, T. 1962. Ecological and morphological studies of the genus *Oncorhynchus* (Salmonidae) with particular consideration on phylogeny. *Sci. Rep. Hokkaido Salmon Hatchery, No. 17:* 1–97.

Hildebrand, S. F. 1938. A new catalogue of the freshwater fishes of Panama. *Zool. Series, Field Mus. Nat. Hist.* **22**(4): 219–359.

Hildebrand, S. F. 1946. A descriptive catalog of the shore fishes of Peru. *Bull. U.S. Natl. Mus.* **189.** 530 pp.

Hoar, W. S. and D. J. Randall (Eds.). 1969–1983. *Fish physiology.* Vol. 1 (1969). Excretion, ionic regulation, and metabolism. Vol. 2 (1969). The endocrine system. Vol. 3 (1969). Reproduction and growth, bioluminescence, pigments, and poisons. Vol. 4 (1970). The nervous system, circulation, and respiration. Vol. 5 (1971). Sensory systems and electric organs. Vol. 6 (1971). Environmental relations and behavior. Vol. 7 (1978). Locomotion. Vol. 8 (1979—with J. R. Brett). Bioenergetics and growth. Vol. 9 (1983—with E. M. Donaldson). Reproduction. New York: Academic.

Hoese, D. F. and R. Winterbottom. 1979. A new species of *Lioteres* (Pisces, Gobiidae) from Kwazulu, with a revised checklist of South African gobies and comments on the generic relationships and endemism of western Indian Ocean gobioids. *R. Ont. Mus. Life Sci. Occ. Pap.* **31.** 13 pp.

Holčík, J. 1982. Review and evolution of *Hucho* (Salmonidae). *Acta Sc. Nat. Brno.* **16**(3): 1–29.

Hollister, G. 1936. A fish which grows by shrinking. *Bull. N.Y. Zool. Soc.* **39**(3): 104–109.

Hora, S. L. 1936. Siluroid fishes of India, Burma and Ceylon. 2. Fishes of the genus *Akysis* Bleeker. 3. Fishes of the genus *Olyra* McClelland. 4. On the use of the generic name *Wallago* Bleeker. 5. Fishes of the genus *Heteropneustes* Müller. *Rec. Indian Mus.* **38**(2): 199–209.

Hora, S. L. and E. G. Silas. 1952. Evolution and distribution of glyptosternoid fishes of the family Sisoridae (Order: Siluroidea). *Proc. Natl. Instit. Sci. Ind.* **18**(4): 309–322.

Howes, G. J. 1976. The cranial musculature and taxonomy of characoid fishes of the tribes Cynodontini and Characini. *Bull. Br. Mus. Nat. Hist. (Zool.)* **29**(4): 203–248.

Howes, G. J. 1978. The anatomy and relationships of the cyprinid fish *Luciobrama macrocephalus* (Lacepède). *Bull. Br. Mus. Nat. Hist. (Zool.)* **34**(1): 1–64.

Howes, G. J. 1980. The anatomy, phylogeny and classification of bariliinae cyprinid fishes. *Bull. Br. Mus. Nat. Hist. (Zool.)* **37**(3): 129–198.

Howes, G. J. 1981. Anatomy and phylogeny of the Chinese major carps *Ctenopharyngodon* Steind., 1866 and *Hypophthalmichthys* Blkr, 1860. *Bull. Br. Mus. Nat. Hist. (Zool.)* **41**(1): 1–52.

Howes, G. 1982a. Anatomy and evolution of the jaws in the semiplotine carps with a review of the genus *Cyprinion* Heckel, 1843 (Teleostei: Cyprinidae). *Bull. Br. Mus. Nat. Hist. (Zool.)* **42**(4): 299–335.

Howes, G. 1982b. Review of the genus *Brycon* (Teleostei: Characoidei). *Bull. Br. Mus. Nat. Hist. (Zool.)* **43**(1): 1–47.

Hubbs, C. L. 1941. A new family of fishes. *J. Bombay Nat. Hist. Soc.* **42**: 446–447.

Hubbs, C. L. 1944. Fin structures and relationships of the phallostethid fishes. *Copeia* **1944**(2): 69–79.

Hubbs, C. L. 1945. Phylogenetic position of the Citharidae, a family of flatfishes. *Misc. Publs. Mus. Zool. Univ. Mich.* **63**. 38 pp.

Hubbs, C. L. 1950. Studies of cyprinodont fishes. 20. A new subfamily from Guatemala, with ctenoid scales and a unilateral pectoral clasper. *Misc. Publs. Mus. Zool. Univ. Mich.* **78**. 28 pp.

Hubbs, C. L. 1952. Antitropical distribution of fishes and other organisms. Symposium on problems of bipolarity and of pantemperate faunas. *Proc. 7th Pac. Sci. Cong.* **3**: 324–329.

Hubbs, C. L. and R. M. Bailey. 1947. Blind catfishes from artesian waters of Texas. *Occ. Pap. Mus. Zool. Univ. Mich.* **499**. 15 pp.

Hubbs, C. L., W. I. Follett, and L. J. Dempster. 1979. List of the fishes of California. *Occ. Pap. Calif. Acad. Sci.* **133**. 51 pp.

Hubbs, C. L., T. Iwai, and K. Matsubara. 1967. External and internal characters, horizontal and vertical distribution, luminescence, and food of the dwarf pelagic shark, *Euprotomicrus bispinatus. Bull. Scripps Inst. Oceanogr.* **10**. University of California Press. 64 pp.

Hubbs, C. L. and T. Iwamoto. 1977. A new genus *(Mesobius)*, and three new bathypelagic species of Macrouridae (Pisces: Gadiformes) from the Pacific Ocean. *Proc. Calif. Acad. Sci.*, Ser. 4., **41**: 233–251.

Hubbs, C. L. and K. F. Lagler. 1964. *Fishes of the Great Lakes region*. Ann Arbor: University of Michigan Press. 213 pp.

Hubbs, C. L., G. W. Mead, and N. J. Wilimovsky. 1953. The widespread, probably antitropical distribution and the relationship of the bathypelagic iniomous fish *Anotopterus pharao. Bull. Scripps Instit. Oceanogr.* **6**(5): 173–197.

Hubbs, C. L., R. R. Miller, and L. C. Hubbs. 1974. Hydrographic history and relict fishes of the north-central Great Basin. *Mem. Calif. Acad. Sci.* **7**. 259 pp.

Hubbs, C. L. and I. C. Potter. 1971. Distribution, phylogeny and taxonomy. In M. W. Hardisty and I. C. Potter (Eds.), *The biology of lampreys*. London: Academic: 1–65.

Hubbs, C. L. and R. L. Wisner. 1980. Revision of the sauries (Pisces, Scomberesocidae) with descriptions of two new genera and one new species. *U.S. Fish. Bull.* **77**(3): 521–566.

Hughes, D. R. 1981. Development and organization of the posterior field of ctenoid scales in the Platycephalidae. *Copeia* **1981**(3): 596–606.

Hulley, P. A. 1972. The family Gurgesiellidae (Chondrichthyes, Batoidei), with reference to *Pseudoraja atlantica* Bigelow and Schroeder. *Copeia* **1972**: 356–359.

Hureau, J. C. 1971. Notes sur la famille des Congiopodidae (Téléostéens, Perciformes): redécouverte de *Zanclorhynchus spinifer* Günther, 1880, aux îles Kerguelen et réhabilitation de *Congiopodus kieneri* (Sauvage, 1878). *Bull. Mus. Natl. Hist. Nat.*, Ser. 2, **42**(5): 1019–1026.

Hutchins, J. B. 1976. A revision of the Australian frogfishes (Batrachoididae). *Rec. West. Aust. Mus.* **4:** 3–43.

Hutchins, J. B. 1977. Descriptions of three new genera and eight new species of monacanthid fishes from Australia. *Rec. West. Aust. Mus.* **5**(1): 3–58.

Hutchins, J. B. 1981. Nomenclatural status of the toadfishes of India. *Copeia* **1981**(2): 336–341.

Ida, H. 1976. Removal of the family Hypoptychidae from the suborder Ammodytoidei, order Perciformes, to the suborder Gasterosteidei, order Syngnathiformes. *Jap. J. Ichthyol.* **23:** 33–42.

Inada, T. and J. A. F. Garrick. 1979. *Rhinochimaera pacifica*, a long-snouted chimaera (Rhinochimaeridae), in New Zealand waters. *Jap. J. Ichthyol.* **25:** 235–243.

Isbrücker, I. J. H. 1978. Descriptions préliminaires de nouveaux taxa de la famille des Loricariidae, Poissons—Chats cuirassés néotropicaux avec un catalogue critique de la sous—famille nominale (Pisces, Siluriformes). *Rev. Fr. Aquariol. Herpétol.* **5**(4): 86–116.

Isbrücker, I. J. H. 1980. Classification and catalogue of the mailed Loricariidae. *Verslagen en Technische Gegevens. No. 22.* 181 pp.

Ishimatsu, A. and Y. Itazawa. 1981. Ventilation of the air-breathing organ in the snakehead *Channa argus. Jap. J. Ichthyol.* **28:** 276–282.

Ishiyama, R. 1967. Rajidae (Pisces). *Fauna Japonica.* Tokyo: Academic Press of Japan. 162 pp.

Iwamoto, T. 1970. The R/V Pillsbury Deep-Sea Biological Expedition to the Gulf of Guinea, 1964–1965. 19. Macrourid fishes of the Gulf of Guinea. *Stud. Trop. Oceanogr.* **4:** 316–431.

Iwamoto, T. 1979. Eastern Pacific Macrourine grenadiers with seven branchiostegal rays (Pisces: Macrouridae). *Proc. Calif. Acad. Sci.* **42:** 135–179.

Iwamoto, T. 1980. *Matsubaraea* Taki, a senior synonym of *Cirrinasus* Schultz (Percophididae). *Jap. J. Ichthyol.* **27**(2): 111–114.

Iwamoto, T., J. E. McCosker, and O. Barton. 1976. Alepocephalid fishes of the genera *Herwigia* and *Bathylaco*, with the first Pacific record of *H. kreffti. Jap. J. Ichthyol.* **23**(1): 55–59.

Iwamoto, T. and J. C. Staiger. 1976. Percophidid fishes of the genus *Chrionema* Gilbert. *Bull. Marine Sci.* **26**(4): 488–498.

Jain, S. L. 1973. New specimens of Lower Jurassic holostean fishes from India. *Palaeontol.* **16**(1): 149–177.

Janvier, P. 1977. Contribution a la connaissance de la systématique et de l'anatomie du genre *Boreaspis* Stensiö (Agnatha, Cephalspidomorphi, Osteostraci) du Dévonien inférieur du Spitsberg. *Ann. Paléont. (Vert.)* **63:** 1–31.

Janvier, P. 1980. Osteolepid remains from the Devonian of the Middle East, with particular reference to the endoskeletal shoulder girdle. In A. L. Panchen (Ed.), *The terrestrial environment and the origin of land vertebrates.* Syst. Assoc. Spec. Publ. 15. London: Academic: 223–254.

Janvier, P. 1981. The phylogeny of the Craniata, with particular reference to the significance of fossil "agnathans." *J. Vert. Paleont.* **1**(2): 121–159.

Janvier, P. and A. Bleick. 1979. New data on the internal anatomy of the Heterostraci (Agnatha), with general remarks on the phylogeny of the Craniota. *Zool. Scripta* **8:** 287–296.

Janvier, P. and R. Lund. 1983. *Hardistiella montanensis* n. gen. et sp. (Petromyzontida) from the Lower Carboniferous of Montana, with remarks on the affinities of the lampreys. *J. Vert. Paleont.* **2**(4): 407–413.

Jarvik, E. 1968a. Aspects of vertebrate phylogeny. In T. Ørvig (Ed.), *Current problems of lower vertebrate phylogeny.* New York: Wiley-Interscience: 497–527.

Jarvik, E. 1968b. The systematic position of the Dipnoi. In T. Ørvig (Ed.), *Current problems of lower vertebrate phylogeny.* New York: Wiley-Interscience: 223–245.

Jarvik, E. 1977. The systematic position of acanthodian fishes. In S. M. Andrews, R. S. Miles, and A. D. Walker (Eds.), *Problems in Vertebrate Evolution.* London: Academic: 199–225.

Jarvik, E. 1981. Review of Lungfishes, tetrapods, paleontology, and plesiomorphy. *Syst. Zool.* **30**(3): 378–384.

Jayaram, K. C. 1968. Contributions to the study of bagrid fishes (Siluroidea: Bagridae). 3. A systematic account of the Japanese, Chinese, Malayan and Indonesian genera. *Treubia* **27**: 287–386.

Jayaram, K. C. 1976. Contributions to the study of bagrid fishes. 13. Interrelationships of Indo-African catfishes of the family Bagridae. *Matsya* **2**: 47–53.

Jayaram, K. C. 1981. *The freshwater fishes of India, Pakistan, Bangladesh, Burma and Sri Lanka— a handbook.* Calcutta: Zoological Survey of India. 475 pp.

Jayaram, K. C. and J. R. Dhanze. 1978. Siluroid fishes of India, Burma and Ceylon. 22. A preliminary review of the genera of the family Ariidae (Pisces: Siluroidea). *Matsya* **4**: 42–51.

Jefferies, R. P. S. 1968. The subphylum Calcichordate (Jefferies 1967) primitive fossil chordates with echinoderm affinities. *Bull. Br. Mus. Nat. Hist. (Geol.)* **16**(6): 243–339.

Jefferies, R. P. S. 1979. The origin of chordates—a methodological essay. In M. R. House (Ed.), *The origin of major invertebrate groups.* Systematic Association Special Vol. 12. New York: Academic: 443–477.

Jefferies, R. P. S. 1981a. In defence of the calcichordates. *Zool. J. Linn. Soc.* **73**: 351–396.

Jefferies, R. P. S. 1981b. Fossil evidence on the origin of the chordates and echinoderms. In L. Ranzi (Ed.), In Origine dei grandi phyla dei Metazoi. *Atti Conv. Accad. Naz. Lincei* **49**: 487–561.

Jefferies, R. P. S. and R. J. Prokop. 1972. A new calcichordate from the Ordovician of Bohemia and its anatomy, adaptations and relationships. *J. Linn. Soc. (Biol.)* **4**(2): 69–115.

Jensen, D. D. 1963. Hoplonemertines, myxinoids, and vertebrate origins. In E. C. Dougherty (Ed.), *The lower metazoa. Comparative biology and phylogeny.* Berkeley: University of California Press: 113–126.

Johnson, G. D. 1975. The procurrent spur: an undescribed perciform caudal character and its phylogenetic implications. *Occ. Pap. Calif. Acad. Sci.* **121**. 23 pp.

Johnson, G. D. 1980. The limits and relationships of the Lutjanidae and associated families. *Bull. Scripps Instit. Oceanogr.* **24**: 1–114.

Johnson, R. K. 1970. A second record of *Korsogaster nanus* Parr (Beryciformes: Korsogasteridae). *Copeia* **1970**(4): 758–760.

Johnson, R. K. 1974a. A revision of the alepisauroid family Scopelarchidae (Pisces: Myctophiformes). *Fieldiana, Zool.* **66,** 249 pp.

Johnson, R. K. 1974b. Five new species and a new genus of alepisauroid fishes of the Scopelarchidae (Pisces: Myctophiformes). *Copeia* **1974**(2): 449–457.

Johnson, R. K. 1982. Fishes of the families Evermannellidae and Scopelarchidae: systematics, morphology, interrelationships, and zoogeography. *Fieldiana Zool.*, New Ser., 12., 252 pp.

Johnson, R. K. and D. M. Cohen. 1974. Results of the research cruises of FRV "Walther Herwig" to South America. 30. Revision of the chiasmodontid fish genera *Dysalotus* and *Kali*, with descriptions of two new species. *Arch. Fisch Wiss.* **25**(1 and 2): 13–46.

Jollie, M. 1982a. What are the "Calcichordata"? and the larger question of the origin of Chordates. *Zool. J. Linn. Soc.* **75**: 167–188.

Jollie, M. 1982b. Ventral branchial musculature and synapomorphies questioned. *Zool. J. Linn. Soc.* **74**: 35–47.

Jones, B. C. and G. H. Geen. 1976. Taxonomic reevaluation of the spiny dogfish (*Squalus acanthias* L.) in the northeastern Pacific Ocean. *J. Fish. Res. Board Can.* **33**: 2500–2506.

Jordan, D. S. 1923. A classification of fishes including families and genera as far as known. *Stanford Univ. Publs., Biol. Sciences* **3**: 77–243.

Jordan, D. S. and B. W. Evermann. 1896–1900. The fishes of North and Middle America. *Bull. U.S. Natl. Mus.* (47), Pt. 1–4: 1–3313.

Jubb, R. A. and G. Bell-Cross. 1974. A new species of *Parakneria* Poll 1965 (Pisces, Kneriidae) from Moçambique. *Arnoldia* (Rhodesia) **6**(29): 1–4.

Kanayama, T. and K. Amaoka. 1981. First record of the scorpaenid fish *Brachypterois serrulatus* from Japan, with a key to Japanese genera of the Pteroinae. *Jap. J. Ichthyol.* **28**(2): 181–183.

Kanayama, T. and S. Maruyama. 1979. Agonid fishes, *Anoplagonus occidentalis* and *Bothragonus occidentalis*, from Japanese waters. *Jap. J. Ichthyol.* **25**(4): 278–282.

Karrer, C. 1968. Über erstnachweise und seltene arten von fischen aus dem Südatlantik (Argentinisch—Südbrasilianische Cüste). *Zool. J. Syst. Bd.* **95**: 542–570.

Kaufman, L. S. and K. F. Liem. 1982. Fishes of the suborder Labroidei (Pisces: Perciformes): phylogeny, ecology, and evolutionary significance. *Breviora* **472**. 19 pp.

Kawaguchi, K. and M. Shimizu. 1978. Taxonomy and distribution of the lanternfishes, genus *Diaphus* (Pisces, Myctophidae) in the western Pacific, eastern Indian Oceans and the Southeast Asian seas. *Bull. Ocean. Res. Inst. Univ. Tokyo* **10**. 145 pp.

Keenleyside, M. H. A. 1979. *Diversity and adaptation in fish behaviour. Zoophysiology. 11*. Berlin: Springer-Verlag. 208 pp.

Kelso, B. W., T. G. Northcote, and C. F. Wehrhahn. 1981. Genetic and environmental aspects of the response to water current by rainbow trout *(Salmo gairdneri)* originating from inlet and outlet streams of two lakes. *Can. J. Zool.* **59**(11): 2177–2185.

Kendall, A. W., Jr. 1976. Predorsal and associated bones in serranid and grammistid fishes. *Bull. Marine Sci.* **26**(4): 585–592.

Kendall, A. W., Jr. 1979. Morphological comparisons of North American sea bass larvae (Pisces: Serranidae). *NOAA Tech. Rept. NMFS Circ.* **428**: 1–50.

Kerkut, G. A. 1960. *Implications of evolution*. London: Pergamon. 174 pp.

Kershaw, D. R. 1976. A structural and functional interpretation of the cranial anatomy in relation to the feeding of osteoglossoid fishes and a consideration of their phylogeny. *Trans. Zool. Soc. London* **33**: 173–252.

Knapp, L. W. 1979. Fische des Indischen Ozeans. A. Systematischer Teil. 22. Scorpaeniformes (4). *"Meteor" Forsch. Ergebnisse* **D29:** 48–54.

Kozhov, M. 1963. Lake Baikal and its life. *Monographiae Biologicae.* Vol. 11. The Hague: Dr. W. Junk. 344 pp.

Kozlowski, R. 1966. On the structure and relationships of graptolites. *J. Paleontol.* **40:** 489–501.

Kramer, D. L. 1978. Terrestrial group spawning of *Brycon petrosus* (Pisces: Characidae) in Panama. *Copeia* **1978**(3): 536–537.

Kramer, D. L., C. C. Lindsey, G. E. E. Moodie, and E. D. Stevens. 1978. The fishes and the aquatic environment of the central Amazon basin, with particular reference to respiratory patterns. *Can. J. Zool.* **56:** 717–729.

Lachner, E. A. 1955. Populations of the berycoid fish family Polymixiidae. *Proc. U.S. Natl. Mus.* **105:** 189–206.

Lachner, E. A. and S. J. Karnella. 1980. Fishes of the Indo-Pacific genus *Eviota* with descriptions of eight new species (Teleostei: Gobiidae). *Smithsonian Contrib. Zool.* **315.** 127 pp.

Lachner, E. A. and J. F. McKinney. 1978. A revision of the Indo-Pacific fish genus *Gobiopsis* with descriptions of four new species (Pisces: Gobiidae). *Smithsonian Contrib. Zool.* **262.** 52 pp.

Lagler, K. F., J. E. Bardach, R. R. Miller, and D. R. M. Passino. 1977. *Ichthyology,* 2nd ed. New York: Wiley. 506 pp.

Lake, J. S. 1971. *Freshwater fishes and rivers of Australia.* Melbourne: Nelson. 61 pp.

Lalmohan, R. S. 1967. *Tentaculus waltairiensis* Rao and Dutt, 1965, a junior synonym of *Pholioides thomaseni* Nielsen 1960 (Pisces: Haliophidae). *Copeia* **1967**(2): 458–459.

Lauder, G. V., Jr. 1979. Feeding mechanics in primitive teleosts and in the halecomorph fish *Amia calva. J. Zool. Lond.* **187:** 543–578.

Lauder, G. V. and K. F. Liem. 1981. Prey capture by *Luciocephalus pulcher:* implications for models of jaw protrusion in teleost fishes. *Env. Biol. Fish.* **6:** 257–268.

Lauder, G. V. and K. F. Liem. 1983. The evolution and interrelationships of the actinopterygian fishes. *Bull. Mus. Comp. Zool.* **150:** 95–197.

Lee, D. S. et al. 1980. *Atlas of North American freshwater fishes.* North Carolina Biological Survey. 854 pp.

Lee, S. C. 1982. The family Monotaxidae (Pisces: Perciformes) of Taiwan. *Bull. Inst. Zool. Acad. Sinica* **21**(2): 155–160.

Lee, S. C. 1983. The family Syngnathidae (Pisces: Syngnathiformes) of Taiwan. *Bull. Inst. Zool. Acad. Sinica* **22**(1): 67–82.

Leim, A. H. and W. B. Scott. 1966. Fishes of the Atlantic coast of Canada. *Bull. Fish. Res. Bd. Can.* **155.** 485 pp.

Lenglet, G. 1973. Contribution à l'étude de l'anatomie viscérale des Kneriidae. *Ann. Soc. R. Zool. Belg.* **103**(2–3): 239–270.

Li, S. C. 1966. On a new subspecies of fresh-water trout, *Brachymystax lenok tsinlingensis,* from Taipaishan, Shensi, China. *Acta Zootax. Sinica* **3**(1): 92–94.

Li, S. Z. 1981a. *Studies on zoogeographical divisions for freshwater fishes of China.* Beijing, China: Science Press. 292 pp.

Li, S. Z. 1981b. On the origin, phylogeny and geographical distribution of the flatfishes (Pleuronectiformes). *Trans. Chin. Ichthyol. Soc.* **1981**(1): 11–20.

Li, S. Z., H. Wang, and Y. Wu. 1981. Observations on the osteology of some holocentrid fishes. *Trans. Chin. Ichthyol. Soc.* **1981**(2): 73–80.

Liem, K. F. 1963. The comparative osteology and phylogeny of the Anabantoidei (Teleostei, Pisces). *Illinois Biol. Monogr. No. 30.* 149 pp.

Liem, K. F. 1965. The status of the anabantoid fish genera *Ctenops* and *Trichopsis. Copeia* **1965**(2): 206–213.

Liem, K. F. 1967a. Functional morphology of the head of the anabantoid teleost fish *Helostoma temmincki. J. Morph.* **121:** 135–158.

Liem, K. F. 1967b. A morphological study of *Luciocephalus pulcher,* with notes on gular elements in other recent teleosts. *J. Morph.* **121:** 103–133.

Liem, K. F. 1968. Geographical and taxonomic variation in the pattern of natural sex reversal in the teleost fish order Synbranchiformes. *J. Zool., Lond.* **156:** 225–238.

Liem, K. F. 1970. Comparative functional anatomy of the Nandidae (Pisces: Teleostei). *Fieldiana, Zool.* **56.** 166 pp.

Liem, K. F. 1978. Modulatory multiplicity in the functional repertoire of the feeding mechanism in cichlid fishes. *J. Morph.* **158**(3): 323–360.

Liem, K. F. 1979. Modulatory multiplicity in the feeding mechanism in cichlid fishes, as exemplified by the invertebrate pickers of Lake Tanganyika. *J. Zool., Lond.* **189:** 93–125.

Liem, K. F. 1980. Air ventilation in advanced teleosts: biomechanical and evolutionary aspects. In M. A. Ali (Ed.), *Environmental physiology of fishes.* New York: Plenum: 57–91.

Liem, K. F. 1981. A phyletic study of the Lake Tanganyika cichlid genera *Asprotilapia, Ectodus, Lestradea, Cunningtonia, Ophthalmochromis,* and *Ophthalmotilapia. Bull. Mus. Comp. Zool.* **149**(3): 191–214.

Liem, K. F. and D. J. Stewart. 1976. Evolution of the scale-eating cichlid fishes of Lake Tanganyika: a generic revision with a description of a new species. *Bull. Mus. Comp. Zool.* **147**(7): 319–350.

Lindberg, G. U. 1971. *Families of the fishes of the world; a checklist and a key.* Leningrad: Zoological Institute, Akademii Nauk SSSR. 472 pp. (in Russian); *Fishes of the World: A Key to Families and a Checklist.* New York: Wiley. 1974. (English translation.)

Lindsey, C. C. and A. N. Arnason. 1981. A model for responses of vertebral numbers in fish to environmental influences during development. *Can. J. Fish. Aquat. Sci.* **38**(3): 334–347.

Lindsey, C. C. and C. S. Woods (Eds.). 1970. *Biology of coregonid fishes.* Winnipeg: University of Manitoba Press. 560 pp.

Lissman, H. W. 1963. Electric location by fishes. *Sci. Am.* **208**(3): 50–59.

Llewellyn, L. C. 1974. Spawning, development and distribution of the southern pigmy perch *Nannoperca australis australis* Gunther from inland waters in eastern Australia. *Aust. J. Mar. Freshw. Res.* **25:** 121–149.

Love, R. M. 1970. *The chemical biology of fishes.* New York: Academic. 547 pp. 1980. Vol. 2. 548 pp.

Løvtrup, S. 1977. *The phylogeny of Vertebrata.* New York: Wiley. 330 pp.

Lowe-McConnell, R. H. 1975. *Fish communities in tropical freshwaters.* London: Longman. 337 pp.

Lubbock, R. 1975. Fishes of the family Pseudochromidae (Perciformes) in the northwest Indian Ocean and Red Sea. *J. Zool., Lond.* **176:** 115–157.

Lubbock, R. 1976a. Two distinctive new Australian *Pseudochromis* (Teleostei: Perciformes). *J. Nat. Hist.* **10:** 57–64.

Lubbock, R. 1976b. Fishes of the family Pseudochromidae (Perciformes) in the central Indian Ocean. *J. Nat. Hist.* **10:** 167–177.

Lund, R. 1977a. A new petalodont (Chondrichthyes, Bradyodonti) from the Upper Mississippian of Montana. *Ann. Carnegie Mus.* **46**(10): 129–155.

Lund, R. 1977b. New information on the evolution of the bradyodont Chondrichthyes. *Fieldiana: Geol.* **33**(28): 521–539.

Lund, R. 1977c. *Echinochimaera meltoni,* new genus and species (Chimaeriformes), from the Mississippian of Montana. *Ann. Carnegie Mus.* **46**(13): 195–221.

Lund, R. 1982. *Harpagofututor volsellorhinus* new genus and species (Chondrichthyes, Chondrenchelyiformes) from the Namurian Bear Gulch limestone, *Chondrenchelys problematica* Traquair (Visean), and their sexual dimorphism. *J. Paleont.* **56**(4): 938–958.

Lund, R. and W. G. Melton, Jr. 1982. A new actinopterygian fish from the Mississippian Bear Gulch limestone of Montana. *Palaeont.* **25**(pt.3): 485–498.

Lundberg, J. G. 1975. The fossil catfishes of North America. *Pap. Paleont.* 11. *Claude W. Hibbard Mem.* Vol. 2. 51 pp.

Lundberg, J. G. 1982. The comparative anatomy of the toothless blindcat, *Trogloglanis pattersoni* Eigenmann, with a phylogenetic analysis of the ictalurid catfishes. *Misc. Publs. Mus. Zool. Univ. Mich.* **163**. 85 pp.

Lundberg, J. G. and J. N. Baskin. 1969. The caudal skeleton of the catfishes, order Siluriformes. *Am. Mus. Novit.* **2398**. 49 pp.

Lundberg, J. G. and E. Marsh. 1976. Evolution and functional anatomy of the pectoral fin rays in cyprinoid fishes, with emphasis on the suckers (family Catostomidae). *Am. Midl. Nat.* **96:** 332–349.

Mago-Leccia, F. 1978. Los peces de la familia Sternopygidae de Venezuela. *Acta Cient. Venez.* **29**(Suppl. 1): 1–89.

Mago-Leccia, F. and T. M. Zaret. 1978. The taxonomic status of *Rhabdolichops troscheli* (Kaup, 1856) and speculations on gymnotiform evolution. *Env. Biol. Fish.* **3**(4): 379–384.

Makushok, V. M. 1958. The morphology and classification of the northern Blennioid fishes (Stichaeoidae, Blennioidei, Pisces). *Proc. Zool. Inst. (Trudy Zool. Inst. Akad. Nauk SSSR),* **25:** 3–129. Translated from the Russian, U.S. National Museum, 1959.

Mansueti, A. J. 1963. Some changes in morphology during ontogeny in the pirateperch, *Aphredoderus s. sayanus. Copeia* **1963**(3): 546–557.

Marino, R. P. and J. K. Dooley. 1982. Phylogenetic relationships of the tilefish family Branchiostegidae (Perciformes) based on comparative myology. *J. Zool., Lond.* **196:** 151–163.

Markle, D. F. 1980. A new species and a review of the deep-sea fish genus *Asquamiceps* (Salmoniformes: Alepocephalidae). *Bull. Marine Sci.* **30**(1): 45–53.

Markle, D. F. 1982. Identification of larval and juvenile Canadian Atlantic gadoids with comments on the systematics of gadid subfamilies. *Can. J. Zool.* **60**(12): 3420–3438.

Markle, D. F. and W. R. Merrett. 1980. The abyssal alepocephalid, *Rinoctes nasutus* (Pisces: Salmoniformes), a redescription and an evaluation of its systematic position. *J. Zool., Lond.* **190:** 225–239.

Markle, D. F. and J. E. Olney. 1980. A description of the vexillifer larvae of *Pyramodon ventralis* and *Snyderidia canina* (Pisces, Carapidae) with comments on classification. *Pac. Sci.* **34**(2): 173–180.

Markle, D. F. and G. R. Sedberry. 1978. A second specimen of the deep-sea fish, *Pachycara obesa*, with a discussion of its classification and a checklist of other Zoarcidae off Virginia. *Copeia* **1978**(1): 22–25.

Marshall, N. B. 1962. Observations on the Heteromi, an order of teleost fishes. *Bull. Br. Mus. Nat. Hist. (Zool.).* **9**(6): 249–270.

Marshall, N. B. 1966a. *Bathyprion danae* a new genus and species of alepocephaliform fishes. *Dana Rep.* **68**: 1–10.

Marshall, N. B. 1966b. The relationships of the anacanthine fishes, *Macruronus, Lyconus,* and *Steindachneria. Copeia* **1966**: 275–280.

Marshall, N. B. and D. M. Cohen. 1973. Order Anacanthini (Gadiformes). Characters and synopsis of families. In Fishes of the western North Atlantic. *Mem. Sears Found. Mar. Res.* **1**(6): 479–495.

Marshall, N. B. and T. Iwamoto (in collaboration). 1973. Family Macrouridae. In Fishes of the western North Atlantic. *Mem. Sears Found. Mar. Res.* **1**(6): 496–665.

Marshall, T. C. 1965. *Fishes of the Great Barrier Reef and coastal waters of Queensland.* Wynnewood [Narberth], Pa.: Livingston. 566 pp.

Masters, C. O. 1968. The most dreaded fish in the Amazon River. *Carolina Tips* **31**(2): 5–6.

Matsubara, K. 1943. Studies on the scorpaenoid fishes of Japan (1 and 2). *Trans. Sigenkagaku Kenkyusyo.* 486 pp.

Matsubara, K. and T. Iwai. 1959. Description of a new sandfish, *Kraemeria sexradiata*, from Japan, with special reference to its osteology. *J. Wash. Acad. Sci.* **49**: 27–32.

Matsubara, K. and A. Ochiai. 1950. Studies on Hoplichthyidae, a family of mail-cheeked fishes, found in Japan and its adjacent waters. *Jap. J. Ichthyol.* **1**(2): 73–88.

Matsui, T. and R. H. Rosenblatt. 1979. Two new searsid fishes of the genera *Maulisia* and *Searsia* (Pisces: Salmoniformes). *Bull. Marine Sci.* **29**: 62–78.

Matsuura, K. 1979. Phylogeny of the superfamily Balistoidea (Pisces: Tetraodontiformes). *Mem. Fac. Fish., Hokkaido Univ.* **26**: 49–169.

Matsuura, K. 1980. A revision of Japanese balistoid fishes. *Bull. Nat. Sci. Mus.,* Ser. A (Zool.), **6**(1): 27–69.

Matsuura, K. and T. Shimizu. 1982. The squirrelfish genus *Adioryx*, a junior synonym of *Sargocentron. Jap. J. Ichthyol.* **29**(1): 93–94.

Maul, G. E. 1969. On the genus *Cetomimus* (Cetomimidae) with the description of a new species. *Bocagiana No. 18:* 1–12.

Mayr, E. 1969. *Principles of systematic zoology.* New York: McGraw-Hill. 428 pp.

Mayr, E. 1981. Biological classification: toward a synthesis of opposing methodologies. *Science* **214**: 510–516.

McAllister, D. E. 1963. A revision of the smelt family, Osmeridae. *Bull. Natl. Mus. Can.* **191**. 53 pp.

McAllister, D. E. 1968. Evolution of branchiostegals and classification of teleostome fishes. *Bull. Natl. Mus. Can.* **221**. 239 pp.

McAllister, D. E. 1971. Old fourlegs. *National Museums of Canada,* Odyssey Ser. 1. 25 pp.

McAllister, D. E. and R. J. Krejsa. 1961. Placement of the prowfishes, Zaproridae, in the superfamily Stichaeoidae. *Nat. Hist. Pap., Natl. Mus. Can.* **11**: 1–4.

McAllister, D. E. and E. I. S. Rees. 1964. A revision of the eelpout genus *Melanostigma* with a new genus and with comments on *Maynea*. *Bull. Natl. Mus. (Zool.), Can.* **199:** 85–110.

McAllister, D. E., M. E. Anderson, and J. G. Hunter. 1981. Deep-water eelpouts, Zoarcidae, from Arctic Canada and Alaska. *Can. J. Fish. Aquat. Sci.* **38:** 821–839.

McCann, C. and D. G. McKnight. 1980. The marine fauna of New Zealand: macrourid fishes (Pisces: Gadida). *New Zealand Oceanogr. Inst. Mem.* **61.** 91 pp.

McCosker, J. E. 1971. A new species of *Parapercis* (Pisces: Mugiloididae) from the Juan Fernández Islands. *Copeia* **1971**(4): 682–686.

McCosker, J. E. 1977a. The osteology, classification, and relationships of the eel family Ophichthidae. *Proc. Calif. Acad. Sci.,* Ser. 4, **41:** 1–123.

McCosker, J. E. 1977b. Flashlight fishes. *Sci. Am.* **236**(3): 106–114.

McCosker, J. E. and M. D. Lagios (Eds.). 1979. The biology and physiology of the living coelacanth. *Occ. Pap. Calif. Acad. Sci.* **134.** 175 pp.

McDowall, R. M. 1969. Relationships of galaxioid fishes with a further discussion of salmoniform classification. *Copeia* **1969**(4): 796–824.

McDowall, R. M. 1970. The galaxiid fishes of New Zealand. *Bull. Mus. Comp. Zool.* **139**(7): 341–432.

McDowall, R. M. 1971a. Fishes of the family Aplochitonidae. *J.R. Soc. N.Z.* **1**(1): 31–52.

McDowall, R. M. 1971b. The galaxiid fishes of South America. *J. Linn. Soc.* **50**(1): 33–73.

McDowall, R. M. 1972. The species problem in freshwater fishes and the taxonomy of diadromous and lacustrine populations of *Galaxias maculatus* (Jenyns.). *J.R. Soc. N.Z.* **2**(3): 325–367.

McDowall, R. M. 1973a. The status of the South African galaxiid (Pisces: Galaxiidae). *Ann. Cape Prov. Mus. (Nat. Hist.)* **9**(5): 91–101.

McDowall, R. M. 1973b. Relationships and taxonomy of the New Zealand torrent fish, *Cheimarrichthys fosteri* Haast (Pisces: Mugiloididae). *J.R. Soc. N.Z.* **3**(2): 199–217.

McDowall, R. M. 1975. A revision of the New Zealand species of *Gobiomorphus* (Pisces: Eleotridae). *Rec. Natl. Mus. New Zealand* **1**(1): 1–32.

McDowall, R. M. 1976a. Fishes of the family Prototroctidae (Salmoniformes). *Aust. J. Marine Freshw. Res.* **27:** 641–659.

McDowall, R. M. 1976b. The taxonomic status of the *Galaxias* populations in the Rio Calle Calle, Chile (Pisces: Galaxiidae). *Stud. Neotrop. Fauna* **11:** 173–177.

McDowall, R. M. 1978a. Generalized tracks and dispersal in biogeography. *Syst. Zool.* **78**(1): 88–104.

McDowall, R. M. 1978b. *New Zealand freshwater fishes.* Auckland: Heinemann Education Books (NZ) Ltd. 230 pp.

McDowall, R. M. 1979a. Fishes of the family Retropinnidae (Pisces: Salmoniformes)—a taxonomic revision and synopsis. *J. R. Soc. N.Z.* **9**(1): 85–121.

McDowall, R. M. 1979b. The centrolophid genus *Tubbia* (Pisces: Stromateoidei). *Copeia* **1979**(4): 733–738.

McDowall, R. M. 1980. Freshwater fishes and plate tectonics in the southwest Pacific. *Palaeogr., Palaeoclimatol., Palaeoecol.* **31:** 337–351.

McDowall, R. M. 1981. The relationships of Australian freshwater fishes. In A. Keast (Ed.) *Ecological biogeography of Australia. Monog. Biol.* Vol. 41. The Hague: Dr. W. Junk: 1253–1273.

McDowall, R. M. and G. A. Eldon. 1980. The ecology of whitebait migrations (Galaxiidae: *Galaxias* spp.). *N.Z. Ministry Agric. Fish., Fish. Res. Bull.* **20.** 172 pp.

McDowall, R. M. and R. S. Frankenberg. 1981. The galaxiid fishes of Australia. *Rec. Aust. Mus.* **33**(10): 443–605.

McDowall, R. M. and A. M. Whitaker. 1975. The freshwater fishes. In G. Kuschel (Ed.), *Biogeography and ecology in New Zealand.* The Hague: Dr. W. Junk: 277–299.

McDowell, S. B. 1973. Order Heteromi (Notacanthiformes). Family Halosauridae. Family Notacanthidae. Family Lipogenyidae. In Fishes of the western North Atlantic. *Mem. Sears Found. Mar. Res.* **1**(6): 1–228.

McEachran, J. D. and J. D. Fechhelm. 1982a. A new species of skate from Western Australia with comments on the status of *Pavoraja* Whitley, 1939 (Chondrichthyes: Rajiformes). *Proc. Biol. Soc. Wash.* **95:** 1–12.

McEachran, J. D. and J. D. Fechhelm. 1982b. A new species of skate from the western Indian Ocean, with comments on the status of *Raja (Okamejei)* (Elasmobranchii: Rajiformes). *Proc. Biol. Soc. Wash.* **95**(3): 440–450.

McKinney, J. F. and V. G. Springer. 1976. Four new species of the fish genus *Ecsenius* with notes on other species of the genus (Blenniidae: Salariini). *Smithsonian Contrib. Zool.* **236.** 27 pp.

McPhail, J. D. and C. C. Lindsey. 1970. Freshwater fishes of northwestern Canada and Alaska. *Bull. Fish. Res. Bd. Can.* **173.** 381 pp.

Mead, G. W. 1957. An Atlantic record of the zeoid fish *Parazen pacificus. Copeia* **1957**(3): 235–237.

Mead, G. W. 1965. The larval form of the Heteromi. *Breviora* **226,** 5 pp.

Mead, G. W. 1972. Bramidae. *Dana Rep.* **81:** 1–166.

Mees, G. F. 1974. The Auchenipteridae and Pimelodidae of Suriname (Pisces, Nematognathi). *Zool. Verhandl.* (Leiden) **132.** 256 pp.

Menon, A. G. K. 1951a. On a remarkable blind siluroid fish of the family Clariidae from Kerala (India). *Rec. Indian Mus.* **48:** 59–66.

Menon, A. G. K. 1951b. Distribution of clariid fishes, and its significance in zoogeographical studies. *Proc. Nat. Inst. Sci. India* **17**(4): 291–299.

Menon, A. G. K. 1977. A systematic monograph of the tongue soles of the genus *Cynoglossus* Hamilton-Buchanan (Pisces: Cynoglossidae). *Smithsonian Contrib. Zool.* **238,** 129 pp.

Miles, R. S. 1973. Articulated acanthodian fishes from the Old Red Sandstone of England, with a review of the structure and evolution of the acanthodian shoulder-girdle. *Bull. Br. Mus. Nat. Hist. (Geol.)* **24**(2): 111–213.

Miles, R. S. 1975. The relationships of the Dipnoi. *Coll. Internat. C.N.R.S.* **218:** 133–148.

Miles, R. S. 1977. Dipnoan (lungfish) skulls and the relationships of the group: a study based on new species from the Devonian of Australia. *Zool. J. Linn. Soc.* **61**(1–3): 1–328.

Miles, R. S. and G. C. Young. 1977. Placoderm interrelationships reconsidered in the light of new ptyctodontids from Gogo, Western Australia. In S. M. Andrews, R. S. Miles, and A. D. Walker (Eds.), *Problems in Vertebrate evolution.* London: Academic: 123–198.

Miller, F. H. 1982. The scientific publications of Carl Leavitt Hubbs: bibliography and index. *Hubbs-Sea World Res. Instit., Spec. Publ. 1.* 258 pp.

Miller, P. J. and P. Wongrat. 1979. A new goby (Teleostei: Gobiidae) from the South China Sea and its significance for gobiid classification. *Zool. J. Linn. Soc.* **67:** 239–257.

Miller, R. J. 1973. The osteology and adaptive features of *Rhyacichthys aspro* (Teleostei: Gobioidei) and the higher classification of gobioid fishes. *J. Zool., Lond.* **171:** 397–434.

Miller, R. R. 1958. Origin and affinities of the freshwater fish fauna of western North America. In C. L. Hubbs (Ed.), *Zoogeography.* Washington, D.C.: Amer. Assoc. Adv. Sci.: 187–222.

Miller, R. R. 1966. Geographical distribution of Central American freshwater fishes. *Copeia* **1966**(4): 773–802.

Miller, R. R. 1979. Ecology, habits and relationships of the Middle American cuatro ojos, *Anableps doui* (Pisces: Anablepidae). *Copeia* **1979**(1): 82–91.

Miller, R. R. 1981. Coevolution of deserts and pupfishes (genus *Cyprinodon*) in the American Southwest. In R. J. Naiman and D. L. Soltz (Eds.), *Fishes in North American Deserts.* New York: Wiley-Interscience: 39–94.

Miller, R. R. 1982. Pisces. In S. H. Hurlbert and A. Villalobos-Figueroa (Eds.), *Aquatic biota of Mexico, Central America and the West Indies.* San Diego: San Diego State University: 486–501.

Miller, R. R. and J. M. Fitzsimons. 1971. *Ameca splendens*, a new genus and species of goodeid fish from western Mexico, with remarks on the classification of the Goodeidae. *Copeia* **1971**(1): 1–13.

Miller, R. R. and G. R. Smith. 1981. Distribution and evolution of *Chasmistes* (Pisces: Catostomidae) in western North America. *Occ. Pap. Mus. Zool. Univ. Mich.* **696.** 46 pp.

Millot, J. and J. Anthony. 1958, 1966. *Anatomie de Latimeria chalumnae.* Vols. 1 and 2. Paris, France: Ed. Centre Nat. Rec. Sci.

Millot, J., J. Anthony, and D. Robineau. 1978. *Anatomie de Latimeria chalumnae.* Vol. 3. Paris, France: Ed. Centre Nat. Rec. Sci.

Mirza, M. R. 1975. Freshwater fishes and zoogeography of Pakistan. *Bijdr. Dierk.* **45:** 143–180.

Mirza, M. R. 1980. The systematics and zoogeography of the freshwater fishes of Pakistan and Azad Kashmir. *Proc. 1st Pakist. Congr. Zool.* **1980:** 1–41.

Misra, K. S. 1976. *Pisces,* Fauna of India and adjacent countries. Vol. 3. Teleostomi: Cypriniformes; Siluri. Delhi: Zool. Surv. India, 2nd ed. 367 pp.

Mizuno, S. and Y. Tominaga. 1980. First record of the scorpaenoid fish *Caracanthus unipinna* from Japan, with comments on the characters of the genus. *Jap. J. Ichthyol.* **26**(4): 369–372.

Mok, H. K. 1981. The posterior cardinal veins and kidneys of fishes, with notes on their phylogenetic significance. *Jap. J. Ichthyol.* **27**(4): 281–290.

Moore, W. S., R. R. Miller, and R. J. Schultz. 1970. Distribution, adaptation and probable origin of an all-female form of *Poeciliopsis* (Pisces: Poeciliidae) in northwestern Mexico. *Evolution* **24:** 789–795.

Morrow, J. E., Jr. 1964a. Family Chauliodontidae. In Fishes of the western North Atlantic. *Mem. Sears Found. Mar. Res.* **1**(4): 274–289.

Morrow, J. E., Jr. 1964b. Family Stomiatidae. In Fishes of the western North Atlantic. *Mem. Sears Found. Mar. Res.* **1**(4): 290–310.

Morrow, J. E., Jr. 1964c. Family Malacosteidae. In Fishes of the western North Atlantic. *Mem. Sears Found. Mar. Res.* **1**(4): 523–549.

Morrow, J. E., Jr. and R. H. Gibbs, Jr. 1964. Family Melanostomiatidae. In Fishes of the western North Atlantic. *Mem. Sears Found. Mar. Res.* **1**(4): 351–511.

Moy-Thomas, J. A. and R. S. Miles. 1971. *Palaeozoic fishes.* London: Chapman and Hall; Philadelphia: Saunders. 259 pp.

Moyle, P. B. and J. J. Cech, Jr. 1982. *Fishes: an introduction to ichthyology.* Englewood Cliffs, N.J.; Prentice-Hall. 593 pp.

Munro, I. S. R. 1964. Additions to the fish fauna of New Guinea. *Papua New Guinea Agric. J.* **16:** 141–186.

Munro, I. S. R. 1967. *The fishes of New Guinea.* Port Moresby, New Guinea: Department of Agriculture, Stock and Fish. 650 pp.

Myers, G. S. 1937. The deep-sea zeomorph fishes of the family Grammicolepidae. *Proc. U.S. Natl. Mus.* **84:** 145–156.

Myers, G. S. 1960a. The genera and ecological geography of the South American banjo catfishes, family Aspredinidae. *Stanford Ichthyol. Bull.* **7:** 132–139.

Myers, G. S. 1960b. A new zeomorph fish of the family Oreosomatidae from the coast of California, with notes on the family. *Stanford Ichthyol. Bull.* **7**(4): 89–98.

Myers, G. S. 1979. A freshwater seahorse. *Pac. Disc.* **32**(1): 30–31.

Myers, G. S. and W. C. Freihofer. 1966. Megalomycteridae, a previously unrecognized family of deep-sea cetomimiform fishes based on two new genera from the North Atlantic. *Stanford Ichthyol. Bull.* **8:** 193–206.

Nafpaktitis, B. G. 1977. Family Neoscopelidae. In Fishes of the western North Atlantic. *Mem. Sears Found. Mar. Res.* **1**(7): 1–12.

Nafpaktitis, B. G. 1978. Systematics and distribution of lanternfishes of the genera *Lobianchia* and *Diaphus* (Myctophidae) in the Indian Ocean. *Nat. Hist. Mus. Los Angeles County, Sci. Bull.* **30:** 1–92.

Nafpaktitis, B. G., R. H. Backus, J. E. Craddock, R. L. Haedrich, B. H. Robison, and C. Karnella. 1977. In Fishes of the western North Atlantic. *Mem. Sears Found. Mar. Res.* **1**(7): 13–265.

Naiman, R. J. and D. L. Soltz (Eds.). 1981. *Fishes in North American Deserts.* New York: Wiley-Interscience. 552 pp.

Nakabo, T. 1982. Revision of the family Draconettidae. *Jap. J. Ichthyol.* **28**(4): 355–367.

Nelson, G. J. 1966. Gill arches of teleostean fishes of the order Anguilliformes. *Pac. Sci.* **20**(4): 391–408.

Nelson, G. J. 1967. Gill arches of teleostean fishes of the family Clupeidae. *Copeia* **1967:** 389–399.

Nelson, G. J. 1968a. Gill-arch structure in *Acanthodes.* In T. Ørvig (Ed.), *Current problems of lower vertebrate phylogeny.* New York: Wiley-Interscience: 129–143.

Nelson, G. J. 1968b. Gill arches of teleostean fishes of the division Osteoglossomorpha. *J. Linn. Soc. (Zool.)* **47:** 261–277.

Nelson, G. J. 1969a. Gill arches and the phylogeny of fishes, with notes on the classification of vertebrates. *Bull. Am. Mus. Nat. Hist.* **141**(4): 475–552.

Nelson, G. J. 1969b. Infraorbital bones and their bearing on the phylogeny and geography of osteoglossomorph fishes. *Am. Mus. Novit.* **2394.** 37 pp.

Nelson, G. J. 1970a. The hyobranchial apparatus of teleostean fishes of the families Engraulidae and Chirocentridae. *Am. Mus. Novit.* **2410.** 30 pp.

Nelson, G. J. 1970b. Gill arches of some teleostean fishes of the families Salangidae and Argentinidae. *Jap. J. Ichthyol.* **17**(2): 61–66.

Nelson, G. J. 1972a. Observations on the gut of the Osteoglossomorpha. *Copeia* **1972**(2): 325–329.

Nelson, G. J. 1972b. Cephalic sensory canals, pitlines, and the classification of esocoid fishes, with notes on galaxiids and other teleosts. *Am. Mus. Novit.* **2492**. 49 pp.

Nelson, G. J. 1973a. Notes on the structure and relationships of certain Cretaceous and Eocene teleostean fishes. *Am. Mus. Novit.* **2524**. 31 pp.

Nelson, G. J. 1973b. Relationships of clupeomorphs, with remarks on the structure of the lower jaw in fishes. In P. H. Greenwood, R. S. Miles, and C. Patterson (Eds.), Interrelationships of fishes. *J. Linn. Soc. (Zool.)* **53**: 333–349. Suppl. 1. New York: Academic.

Nelson, G. J. and N. Platnick. 1981. *Systematics and biogeography.* New York: Columbia University Press. 567 pp.

Nelson, G. J. and M. N. Rothman. 1973. The species of gizzard shads (Dorosomatinae) with particular reference to the Indo-Pacific region. *Bull. Am. Nat. Hist.* **150**: 131–206.

Nelson, J. S. 1968. Hybridization and isolating mechanisms between *Catostomus commersonii* and *C. macrocheilus* (Pisces: Catostomidae). *J. Fish. Res. Bd. Can.* **25**: 101–150.

Nelson, J. S. 1971. Comparison of the pectoral and pelvic skeletons and of some other bones and their phylogenetic implications in the Aulorhynchidae and Gasterosteidae (Pisces). *J. Fish. Res. Bd. Can.* **28**: 427–442.

Nelson, J. S. 1975. Records of a new form of the marine cottid fish *Antipodocottus galatheae* from the east coast of New Zealand. *Rec. Natl. Mus. New Zealand* **1**(4): 80–86.

Nelson, J. S. 1976. *Fishes of the world.* New York: Wiley-Interscience. 416 pp.

Nelson, J. S. 1977. Evidence of a genetic basis for absence of the pelvic skeleton in brook stickleback, *Culaea inconstans*, and notes on the geographical distribution and origin of the loss. *J. Fish. Res. Board Can.* **34**: 1314–1320.

Nelson, J. S. 1978a. The biology of the sticklebacks [book review]. *Copeia* **1978**: 552–554.

Nelson, J. S. 1978b. *Bembrops morelandi*, a new percophidid fish from New Zealand, with notes on other members of the genus. *Rec. Natl. Mus. New Zealand* **1**(14): 237–241.

Nelson, J. S. 1979a. Some osteological differences between the blennioid fishes *Limnichthys polyactis* and *L. rendahli*, with comments on other species of Creediidae. *New Zealand J. Zool.* **6**: 273–277.

Nelson, J. S. 1979b. Revision of the fishes of the New Zealand genus *Hemerocoetes* (Perciformes: Percophididae), with descriptions of two new species. *New Zealand J. Zool.* **6**:587–599.

Nelson, J. S. 1982a. Two new South Pacific fishes of the genus *Ebinania* and contributions to the systematics of Psychrolutidae (Scorpaeniformes). *Can. J. Zool.* **60**(6): 1470–1504.

Nelson, J. S. 1982b. *Pteropsaron heemstrai* and *Osopsaron natalensis* (Perciformes: Percophidae), new fish species from South Africa, with comments on *Squamicreedia obtusa* from Australia and on the classification of the subfamily Hemerocoetinae. *J.L.B. Smith Inst. Ichthyol., Rhodes Univ. Spec. Publ.* **25**. 11 pp.

Nelson, J. S. 1983. *Creedia alleni* and *Creedia partimsquamigera* (Perciformes: Creediidae), two new marine fish species from Australia, with notes on other Australian creediids. *Proc. Biol. Soc. Wash.* **96**(1): 29–37.

Nichols, J. T. 1943. The fresh-water fishes of China. *Natural history of central Asia.* Vol. 9. American Museum of Natural History. 322 pp.

Nicol, J. A. C., H. J. Arnott, and A. C. G. Best. 1973. Tapeta lucida in bony fishes (Actinopterygii): a survey. *Can. J. Zool.* **51**: 69–81.

Nielsen, J. G. 1968. Redescription and reassignment of *Parabrotula* and *Leucobrotula* (Pisces, Zoarcidae). *Vidensk. Meddr. Dansk. Foren.* **131**: 225–249.

Nielsen, J. G. 1973. Scophthalmidae. In J. C. Hureau and T. Monod (Eds.), *Check-list of the fishes of the north-eastern Atlantic and of the Mediterranean.* Clofnam 1. Paris: Unesco. 616–619.

Nielsen, J. G. 1969. Systematics and biology of the Aphyonidae (Pisces, Ophidioidea). *Galathea Rep.* **10**: 1–90.

Nielsen, J. G. and V. Larsen. 1968. Synopsis of the Bathylaconidae (Pisces, Isospondyli). *Galathea Rep.* **9**: 221–238.

Nielsen, J. G. and D. G. Smith. 1978. The eel family Nemichthyidae. *Dana Rep.* **88**: 1–71.

Nijssen, H. and I. J. H. Isbrücker. 1979. Chronological enumeration of nominal species and subspecies of *Corydoras* (Pisces, Siluriformes, Callichthyidae). *Bull. Zool. Mus. Univ. Amst.* **6**: 129–135.

Nijssen, H., I. J. H. Isbrücker, and J. Géry. 1976. On the species of *Gymnorhamphichthys* Ellis, 1912, translucent sand-dwelling gymnotid fishes from South America (Pisces, Cypriniformes, Gymnotoidei). *St. Neotrop. Fauna Env.* **11**: 37–63.

Nishikawa, S., K. Amaoka, and K. Nakanishi. 1974. A comparative study of chromosomes of twelve species of gobioid fishes in Japan. *Jap. J. Ichthyol.* **21**(2): 61–71.

Nolan, R. S. and R. H. Rosenblatt. 1975. A review of the deep-sea angler fish genus *Lasiognathus* (Pisces: Thaumatichthyidae). *Copeia* **1975**(1): 60–66.

Norden, C. R. 1961. Comparative osteology of representative salmonid fishes with particular reference to the grayling (*Thymallus arcticus*) and its phylogeny. *J. Fish. Res. Bd. Can.* **18**(5): 679–791.

Norman, J. R. 1934. A systematic monograph of the flatfishes (Heterosomata). *Br. Mus. Nat. Hist.* **1**: 1–459.

Norman, J. R. 1957. A draft synopsis of the orders, families and genera of recent fishes and fishlike vertebrates. Unpublished photo offset copies distributed by British Museum of Natural History. 649 pp.

Norman, J. R. and P. H. Greenwood. 1963. *A history of fishes.* London: Ernest Benn. 398 pp.

Northcote, T. G. (Ed.). 1969. Symposium on salmon and trout in streams. H. R. Macmillan lectures in fisheries. Institute of Fisheries, The University of British Columbia, Vancouver. 388 pp.

Norton, J. 1982. Angelfish genetics. *Freshw. Mar. Aq.* **5**(4): 15–18; 90–91.

Nursall, J. R. 1981. Behavior and habitat affecting the distribution of five species of sympatric mudskippers in Queensland. *Bull. Marine Sci.* **31**(3): 730–735.

Nybelin, O. 1971. On the caudal skeleton in *Elops* with remarks on other teleostean fishes. *Acta R. Soc. Sci. Litt. Gothoburg. Zool.* **7**: 1–52.

Nybelin, O. 1974. A revision of the leptolepid fishes. *Acta R. Soc. Sci. Litt. Gothoburg. Zool.* **9**: 1–202.

Okada, Y. and K. Suzuki. 1956. On the similarity of the osteological characters found between Owstoniidae and Cepolidae. *Rept. Fac. Fish., Pref. Univ. Mie* **2**(2): 185–194.

Okamura, O. 1970. Macrourina (Pisces). *Fauna Japonica.* Tokyo: Academic. 216 pp.

Olney, J. E. and D. F. Markle. 1979. Description and occurrence of vexillifer larvae of *Echiodon* (Pisces: Carapidae) in the western North Atlantic and notes on other carapid vexillifers. *Bull. Marine Sci.* **29**: 365–379.

Orton, G. L. 1963. Notes on larval anatomy of fishes of the order Lyomeri. *Copeia* **1963**: 6–15.

Page, L. M. 1981. The genera and subgenera of darters (Percidae, Etheostomatini). *Occ. Pap. Mus. Nat. Hist. Univ. Kansas* **90**. 69 pp.

Page, L. M. 1983. *Handbook of darters*. Neptune City, N.J.: T.F.H. Public. 271 pp.

Paine, R. T. and A. R. Palmer. 1978. *Sicyases sanguineus:* a unique trophic generalist from the Chilean intertidal zone. *Copeia* **1978**(1): 75–81.

Palmer, G. 1961. The dealfishes (Trachipteridae) of the Mediterranean and north-east Atlantic. *Bull. Br. Mus. Nat. Hist. (Zool.)* **7**: 335–351.

Palmer, G. and H. A. Oelschläger. 1976. Use of the name *Lampris guttatus* (Brünnich, 1788) in preference to *Lampris regius* (Bonnaterre, 1788) for the opah. *Copeia* **1976**(2): 366–367.

Panchen A. L. (Ed.) 1980. The terrestrial environment and the origin of land vertebrates. *Syst. Assoc. Spec. Publ. 15*. London: Academic. 633 pp.

Parenti, L. R. 1981. A phylogenetic and biogeographic analysis of cyprinodontiform fishes (Teleostei, Atherinomorpha). *Bull. Am. Mus. Nat. Hist.* **168**(4): 335–557.

Parin, N. V. and D. A. Astakhov. 1982. Studies on the acoustico-lateralis system of beloniform fishes in connection with their systematics. *Copeia* **1982**(2): 276–291.

Parin, N. V. and V. E. Bekker. 1972. Classification and distribution data of some trichiurid fishes (Pisces Trichiuroidea; Scombrolabracidae, Gempylidae, Trichiuridae). *Trudy Inst. Okean. SSSR Akad. Nauk* **93**: 110–204.

Parin, N. V. and V. E. Bekker. 1973. Gempylidae. In J. C. Hureau and T. Monod (Eds.), *Check-list of the fishes of the north-eastern Atlantic and of the Mediterranean.* Clofnam I. Paris: Unesco: 457–460.

Parin, N. V., B. B. Collette, and Yu. N. Shcherbachev. 1980. Preliminary review of marine halfbeaks (Hemiramphidae, Beloniformes) of the tropical Indo-West Pacific. *Trudy Inst. Okeanol.* **97**: 7–173 (NMFS Syst. Lab. Trans. 68).

Parin, N. V. and A. W. Ebeling. 1980. A new western Pacific *Poromitra* (Pisces: Melamphaidae). *Copeia* **1980**(1): 87–93.

Parin, N. V. and Y. N. Shcherbachev. 1982. Two new argentinine fishes of the genus *Glossanodon* from the eastern South Pacific. *Jap. J. Ichthyol.* **28**(4): 381–384.

Parr, A. E. 1960. The fishes of the family Searsidae. *Dana Rep.* **51**: 1–109.

Patterson, C. 1964. A review of Mesozoic acanthopterygian fishes, with special reference to those of the English Chalk. *Phil. Trans. R. Soc. London.*, Ser. B, **247**: 213–482.

Patterson, C. 1965. The phylogeny of the chimaeroids. *Phil. Trans. R. Soc. London* **249**: 101–219.

Patterson, C. 1967a. Are the teleosts a polyphyletic group? *Coll. Internat. C. N. R. S.* **163**: 93–109.

Patterson, C. 1967b. A second specimen of the Cretaceous teleost *Protobrama* and the relationships of the sub-order Tselfatioidei. *Ark. Zool.* **19**: 215–234.

Patterson, C. 1968a. *Menaspis* and the bradyodonts. In T. Ørvig, (Ed.), *Current problems of lower vertebrate phylogeny.* New York: Wiley-Interscience: 171–205.

Patterson, C. 1968b. The caudal skeleton in Lower Liassic pholidophoroid fishes. *Bull. Br. Mus. Nat. Hist. (Geol.)* **16**: 203–239.

Patterson, C. 1973. Interrelationships of holosteans. In P. H. Greenwood, R. S. Miles, and

C. Patterson (Eds.), Interrelationships of fishes. *J. Linn. Soc. (Zool.)* **53:** 233–305. Suppl. 1. New York: Academic.

Patterson, C. 1975. The braincase of pholidophorid and leptolepid fishes, with a review of the actinopterygian braincase. *Phil. Trans. R. Soc. London, Series B, Biol. Sci.* **289**(899): 275–579.

Patterson, C. 1977. The contribution of paleontology to teleostean phylogeny. In M. K. Hecht, P. C. Goody, and B. M. Hecht (Eds.), *Major patterns in vertebrate evolution.* New York: Plenum: 579–643.

Patterson, C. 1982. Morphology and interrelationships of primitive actinopterygian fishes. *Amer. Zool.* **22:** 241–259.

Patterson, C. and D. E. Rosen. 1977. Review of ichthyodectiform and other Mesozoic teleost fishes and the theory and practice of classifying fossils. *Bull. Amer. Mus. Nat. Hist.* **158:** 81–172.

Paulin, C. D. 1977. *Epigonichthys hectori* (Benham), the New Zealand lancelet (Leptocardii: Epigonichthyidae). *Rec. Natl. Mus. New Zealand* **1**(9): 143–147.

Paulin, C. D. 1983. A revision of the family Moridae (Pisces: Anacanthini) within the New Zealand region. *Rec. Natl. Mus. New Zealand* **2**(9): 81–126.

Paulin, C. D. and J. M. Moreland. 1979a. Halosauridae of the south-west Pacific (Pisces: Teleostei: Notacanthiformes). *New Zealand J. Zool.* **6:** 267–271.

Paulin, C. D. and J. M. Moreland. 1979b. *Congiopodus coriaceus,* a new species of pigfish, and a redescription of *C. leucopaecilus* (Richardson), from New Zealand (Pisces: Congiopodidae). *New Zealand J. Zool.* **6:** 601–608.

Paxton, J. R. 1972. Osteology and relationships of the lanternfishes (family Myctophidae). *Bull. Nat. Mus. Los Angeles County, Sci.* **13.** 81 pp.

Paxton, J. R. 1974. Morphology and distribution patterns of the whalefishes of the family Rondeletiidae. *J. Mar. Biol. Assn. India* **15**(1): 175–188.

Paxton, J. R. 1975. *Heraldia nocturna,* a new genus and species of pipefish (Family Syngnathidae) from eastern Australia, with comments on *Maroubra perserrata* Whitley. *Proc. Calif. Acad. Sci.,* Ser. 4, **40:** 439–447.

Paxton, J. R. 1979. Nominal genera and species of lanternfishes (family Myctophidae). *Contrib. Sci., Nat. Hist. Mus., Los Angeles County* **322:** 1–28.

Pearson, D. M. 1982. Primitive bony fishes, with especial reference to *Cheirolepis* and palaeonisciform actinopterygians. *Zool. J. Linn. Soc. London* **74:** 35–67.

Pearson, D. M. and T. S. Westoll. 1979. The Devonian actinopterygian *Cheirolepis* Agassiz. *Trans. R. Soc. Edinb.* **70:** 337–399.

Peden, A. E. 1981. Recognition of *Leuroglossus schmidti* and *L. stilbius* (Bathylagidae, Pisces) as distinct species in the North Pacific Ocean. *Can. J. Zool.* **59**(12): 2396–2398.

Peden, A. E. and M. E. Anderson. 1981. *Lycodapus* (Pisces: Zoarcidae) of eastern Bering Sea and nearby Pacific Ocean, with three new species and a revised key to the species. *Can. J. Zool.* **59:** 667–678.

Penrith, M. J. 1969. New records of deep-water fishes from South West Africa. *Cimbebasia,* **A1**(3): 59–75.

Penrith, M. J. 1972. Earliest description and name for the whale shark. *Copeia* **1972**(2): 362.

Penrith, M. J. 1973. A new species of *Parakneria* from Angola (Pisces: Kneriidae). *Cimbebasia,* **A2**(11): 131–135.

Peters, N. Jr. 1967. Opercular—und Postopercularorgan (Occipitalorgan) der Gattung *Kneria*

(Kneriidae, Pisces) und ein Vergleich mit verwandten Strukturen. *Morph. Ökol. Tiere* **59:** 381–435.

Pfeiffer, W. 1963. Alarm substances. *Experientia* **19:** 1–11.

Pfeiffer, W. 1977. The distribution of fright reaction and alarm substance cells in fishes. *Copeia* **1977**(4): 653–665.

Phillipps, W. J. 1926. New or rare fishes of New Zealand. *Trans. Proc. N. Z. Inst.* **56:** 529–537.

Pietsch, T. W. 1972. A review of the monotypic deep-sea anglerfish family Centrophrynidae: taxonomy, distribution and osteology. *Copeia* **1972:** 17–47.

Pietsch, T. W. 1974. Osteology and relationships of ceratioid anglerfishes of the family Oneirodidae, with a review of the genus *Oneirodes* Lütken. *Bull. Nat. Hist. Mus. Los Angeles County, Sci.* **18.** 113 pp.

Pietsch, T. W. 1975. Systematics and distribution of ceratioid anglerfishes of the genus *Chaenophryne* (family Oneirodidae). *Bull. Mus. Comp. Zool.* **147**(2): 75–100.

Pietsch, T. W. 1976. Dimorphism, parasitism and sex: reproductive strategies among deep-sea ceratioid anglerfishes. *Copeia* **1976**(4): 781–793.

Pietsch, T. W. 1978a. A new genus and species of ceratioid anglerfish from the North Pacific with a review of the allied genera *Ctenochirichthys*, *Chirophryne* and *Leptacanthichthys*. *Contrib. Sci., Nat. Hist. Mus., Los Angeles County* **297:** 1–25.

Pietsch, T. W. 1978b. The feeding mechanism of *Stylephorus chordatus* (Teleostei: Lampridiformes): functional and ecological implications. *Copeia* **1978**(2): 255–262.

Pietsch, T. W. 1978c. Evolutionary relationships of the sea moths (Teleostei: Pegasidae) with a classification of gasterosteiform families. *Copeia* **1978**(3): 517–529.

Pietsch, T. W. 1979. Systematics and distribution of ceratioid anglerfishes of the family Caulophrynidae with the description of a new genus and species from the Banda Sea. *Contrib. Sci., Nat. Hist. Mus., Los Angeles County* **310:** 1–25.

Pietsch, T. W. 1981. The osteology and relationships of the anglerfish genus *Tetrabrachium* with comments on lophiiform classification. *Fish. Bull.* **79**(3): 387–419.

Pietsch, T. W. and D. B. Grobecker. 1978. The compleat angler: aggressive mimicry in an antennariid anglerfish. *Science* **201:** 369–370.

Pietsch, T. W. and J. P. Van Duzer. 1980. Systematics and distribution of ceratioid anglerfishes of the family Melanocetidae with the description of a new species from the eastern North Pacific Ocean. *Fish. Bull.* **78**(1): 59–87.

Policansky, D. 1982. The asymmetry of flounders. *Sci. Am.* **246**(5): 116–122.

Poll, M. 1964. Une famille dulcicole nouvelle de poissons africains: les Congothrissidae. *Mém. Acad. R. Sci. Outre-mer, N. S.* **15**(2): 1–40.

Poll, M. 1967. Contribution à la faune ichthyologique de l'Angola. *Compan. Diamant. Angola, Pubic. Culturais (Lisboa). No. 75.* 381 pp.

Poll, M. 1969. Contribution à la connaissance des *Parakneria*. *Rev. Zool. Bot. Afr.* **80**(3–4): 359–368.

Poll, M. 1973. Nombre et distribution géographique des Poissons d'eau douce africains. *Bull. Mus. Natl. Hist. Nat., Ser. 3, Ecol. Gén.* **6**(150): 113–128.

Poll, M. 1976. Poissons. In M. G. F. De Witte (Ed.), *Exploration du Parc National de l'Upemba*. Bruxelles: Fondation pour favoriser les recherches scientifiques en Afrique. 127 pp.

Poll, M. 1977. Les genres nouveaux *Platyallabes* et *Platyclarias* comparés au genre *Gymnal-*

labes Gthr. synopsis nouveau des genres de Clariidae. *Bull. Acad. R. Belg. (Classe Sci.)*, Ser. 5, **63**: 122–149.

Poll, M. and J. P. Gosse. 1969. Revision des Malapteruridae (Pisces, Siluriformes) et description d'une deuxième espèce de silure électrique: *Malapterurus microstoma* sp. n. *Bull. Inst. R. Sci. Nat. Belg.* **45**: 1–12.

Poss, S. G. and W. N. Eschmeyer. 1978. Two new Australian velvetfishes, genus *Paraploactis* (Scorpaeniformes: Aploactinidae), with a revision of the genus and comments on the genera and species of the Aploactinidae. *Proc. Calif. Acad. Sci.* **41**: 401–426.

Poss, S. G. and W. N. Eschmeyer. 1979. *Prosoproctus pataecus*, a new genus and species of velvetfish from the South China Sea (Aploactinidae: Scorpaeniformes). *Jap. J. Ichthyol.* **26**(1): 11–14.

Poss, S. G. and W. N. Eschmeyer. 1980. *Xenaploactis*, a new genus for *Prosopodasys asperrimus* Günther (Pisces: Aploactinidae), with descriptions of two new species. *Proc. Calif. Acad. Sci.* **42**(8): 287–293.

Potter, I. C. 1980. The Petromyzoniformes with particular reference to paired species. *Can. J. Fish. Aquat. Sci.* **37**: 1595–1615.

Poulsen, T. C. 1963. Cave adaptations in amblyopsoid fishes. *Am. Midl. Nat.* **70**: 257–290.

Quast, J. C. 1965. Osteological characteristics and affinities of the hexagrammid fishes, with a synopsis. *Proc. Calif. Acad. Sci.*, Ser. 4, **31**(21): 563–600.

Raju, S. N. 1974. Three new species of the genus *Monognathus* and the leptocephali of the order Saccopharyngiformes. *Fish. Bull.* **72**: 547-562.

Ramaswami, L. S. 1957. Skeleton of cyprinoid fishes in relation to phylogenetic studies. 8. The skull and Weberian ossicles of Catostomidae. *Proc. Zool. Soc., Calcutta, Mookerjee Mem.* **1957**: 293–303.

Randall, H. A. and G. R. Allen. 1977. A revision of the damselfish genus *Dascyllus* (Pomacentridae) with the description of a new species. *Rec. Aust. Mus.* **31**(9): 349–385.

Randall, J. E. 1963. Review of the hawkfishes (family Cirrhitidae). *Proc. U. S. Natl. Mus.* **114**: 389–451.

Randall, J. E. 1978. A revision of the Indo-Pacific labrid fish genus *Macropharyngodon*, with descriptions of five new species. *Bull. Marine Sci.* **28**(4): 742–770.

Randall, J. E. 1979. A survey of ciguatera at Enewetak and Bikini, Marshall Islands, with notes on the systematics and food habits of ciguatoxic fishes. *Fish. Bull.* **78**(2): 201–249.

Randall, J. E. 1980a. Revision of the fish genus *Plectranthias* (Serrandidae: Anthiinae) with descriptions of 13 new species. *Micrones.* **16**: 101–187.

Randall, J. E. 1980b. Two new Indo-Pacific labrid fishes of the genus *Halichoeres* with notes on other species of the genus. *Pac. Sci.* **34**(4): 415–432.

Randall, J. E. 1981a. A review of the Indo-Pacific sand tilefish. *Freshw. Marine Aq.* **4**(12): 39–46.

Randall, J. E. 1981b. Revision of the labrid fish genus *Labropsis* with descriptions of five new species. *Micrones.* **17**: 125–155.

Randall, J. E., K. Aida, T. Hibiya, N. Mitsuura, H. Kamiya, and Y. Hashimoto. 1971. Grammistin, the skin toxin of soapfishes, and its significance in the classification of the Grammistidae. *Publ. Seto Marine Biol. Lab.* **19**: 157–190.

Randall, J. E., K. Aida, Y. Oshima, K. Hori, and Y. Hashimoto. 1981. Occurrence of a crinotoxin and hemagglutinin in the skin mucus of the moray eel *Lycodontis nudivomer.* *Marine Biol.* **62:** 179–184.

Randall, J. E. and J. H. Choat. 1980. Two new parrotfishes of the genus *Scarus* from the Central and South Pacific, with further examples of sexual dichromatism. *Zool. J. Linn. Soc.* **70**(4): 383–419.

Randall, J. E. and P. Guézé. 1981. The holocentrid fishes of the genus *Myripristis* of the Red Sea, with clarification of the *murdjan* and *hexagonus* complexes. *Contrib. Sci. Nat. Hist. Mus. Los Angeles County* **334:** 1–16.

Randall, J. E. and P. C. Heemstra. 1978. Reclassification of the Japanese cirrhitid fishes *Serranocirrhitus latus* and *Isobuna japonica* to the Anthiinae. *Jap. J. Ichthyol.* **25**(3): 165–172.

Randall, J. E. and H. A. Randall. 1981. A revision of the labrid fish genus *Pseudojuloides*, with descriptions of five new species. *Pac. Sci.* **35**(1): 51–74.

Randall, J. E., T. Shimizu, and T. Yamakawa. 1982. A revision of the holocentrid fish genus *Ostichthys*, with descriptions of four new species and a related new genus. *Jap. J. Ichthyol.* **29**(1): 1–26.

Randall, J. E., M. M. Smith, and K. Aida. 1980. Notes on the classification and distribution of the Indo-Pacific soapfish, *Belonoperaca chabanaudi* (Perciformes: Grammistidae). *J.L.B. Smith Institute of Ichthyology, Rhodes University. Spec. Publ.* **21.** 8 pp.

Reddy, W. P. B. 1978. Studies on the taxonomy of Indian species of family Channidae (Pisces: Teleostei) and some aspects of the biology of *Channa punctata* (Bloch, 1793) from Guntur, Andhra Pradesh. *Matsya* **4:** 95–96.

Regan, C. T. 1911. The classification of the teleostean fishes of the order Ostariophysi. 1. Cyprinoidea. *Ann. Mag. Nat. Hist.,* Ser. 8, **8:** 13–32.

Regan, C. T. 1913. The classification of percoid fishes. *Ann. Mag. Nat. Hist.,* Ser. 8, **12:** 111–145.

Regan, C. T. 1929. Fishes. *Encyclopaedia Britannica,* 14th ed. **9:** 305–329.

Reimchen, T. E. 1980. Spine deficiency and polymorphism in a population of *Gasterosteus aculeatus:* an adaptation to predators? *Can. J. Zool.* **58:** 1232–1244.

Repetski, J. E. 1978. A fish from the Upper Cambrian of North America. *Science* **200:** 529–531.

Reshetnikov, Yu. S. 1980. *Ecology and systematics of coregonid fishes* (In Russian). Moscow: Ized. Nauka Press. 300 pp.

Richardson, S. L. 1981. Current knowledge of larvae of sculpins (Pisces: Cottidae and allies) in northeast Pacific genera with notes on intergeneric relationships. *U.S. Fish. Bull.* **79**(1): 103–121.

Ritchie, A. and J. Gilbert-Tomlinson. 1977. First Ordovician vertebrates from the Southern Hemisphere. *Alcheringa* **1:** 351–368.

Rivas, L. R. and S. M. Warlen. 1967. Systematics and biology of the bonefish, *Albula nemoptera* (Fowler). *U.S. Fish. Bull.* **66:** 251–258.

Roberts, T. R. 1969. Osteology and relationships of characoid fishes, particularly the genera *Hepsetus, Salminus, Hoplias, Ctenolucius,* and *Acestrorhynchus. Proc. Calif. Acad. Sci.,* Ser. 4, **36:** 391–500.

Roberts, T. R. 1971a. *Micromischodus sugillatus,* a new hemiodontid characin fish from Brazil, and its relationships to the Chilodontidae. *Breviora* **367,** 25 pp.

Roberts, T. R. 1971b. The fishes of the Malaysian family Phallostethidae (Atheriniformes). *Breviora* **374,** 27 pp.

Roberts, T. R. 1971c. Osteology of the Malaysian phallostethoid fish *Ceratostethus bicornis,* with a discussion of the evolution of remarkable structural novelties in its jaws and external genitalia. *Bull. Mus. Comp. Zool.* **142**(4): 393–418.

Roberts, T. R. 1972. An attempt to determine the systematic position of *Ellopostoma megalomycter,* an enigmatic freshwater fish from Borneo. *Breviora* **384,** 16 pp.

Roberts, T. R. 1973a. Interrelationships of ostariophysans. In P. H. Greenwood, R. S. Miles, and C. Patterson (Eds.), Interrelationships of fishes. *J. Linn. Soc. (Zool.)* **53:** 373–395. Suppl. 1. New York: Academic.

Roberts, T. R. 1973b. Osteology and relationships of the Prochilodontidae, a South American family of characoid fishes. *Bull. Mus. Comp. Zool.* **145**(4): 213–235.

Roberts, T. R. 1974. Osteology and classification of the Neotropical characoid fishes of the families Hemiodontidae (including Anodontinae) and Parodontidae. *Bull. Mus. Comp. Zool.* **146**(9): 411–472.

Roberts, T. R. 1980. A revision of the Asian mastacembelid fish genus *Macrognathus. Copeia* **1980**(3): 385–391.

Roberts, T. R. 1981. Sundasalangidae, a new family of minute freshwater salmoniform fishes from Southeast Asia. *Proc. Calif. Acad. Sci.* **42**(9): 295–302.

Roberts, T. R. 1982a. Review of "The fishes and the forest", "Man and fisheries on an Amazon frontier", and "Man, fishes, and the Amazon". *Quat. Rev. Biol.* **57**(2): 204–206.

Roberts, T. R. 1982b. Unculi (horny projections arising from single cells), an adaptive feature of the epidermis of ostariophysan fishes. *Zool. Scripto.* **11**(1): 55–76.

Roberts, T. R. 1982c. The Bornean Gastromyzontine fish genera *Gastromyzon* and *Glaniopsis* (Cypriniformes, Homalopteridae), with descriptions of new species. *Proc. Calif. Acad. Sci.* **42**(20): 497–524.

Roberts, T. R. 1982d. A revision of the South and Southeast Asian angler-catfishes (Chacidae). *Copeia* **1982**(4): 895–901.

Robertson, D. R. 1972. Social control of sex reversal in a coral-reef fish. *Science* **177:** 1007–1009.

Robertson, D. R. and R. R. Warner. 1978. Sexual patterns in the labroid fishes of the western Caribbean, 2. The parrotfishes (Scaridae). *Smithsonian Contrib. Zool.* **255.** 26 pp.

Robins, C. H. and C. R. Robins. 1971. Osteology and relationships of the eel family Macrocephenchelyidae. *Proc. Acad. Nat. Sci. Philad.* **123**(6): 127–150.

Robins, C. H. and C. R. Robins. 1976. New genera and species of dysommine and synaphobranchine eels (Synaphobranchidae) with an analysis of the dysomminae. *Proc. Acad. Nat. Sci. Philad.* **127:** 249–280.

Robins, C. R. 1966. Additional comments on the structure and relationships of the mirapinniform fish family Kasidoroidae. *Bull. Marine Sci.* **16:** 696–701.

Robins, C. R. 1973. Review of Opredelitel' I Kharacteristika Semeist' Ryb Mirovoi Fauny. *Copeia* **1973:** 635–637.

Robins, C. R. et al. 1980. Common and scientific names of fishes from the United States and Canada. *Am. Fish. Soc. Spec. Publ.* **12,** 4th ed. 174 pp.

Robins, C. R. and J. E. Böhlke. 1970. The first Atlantic species of the ammodytid fish genus *Embolichthys*. *Not. Nat. (Philadelphia)* **430**: 1–11.

Robins, C. R., D. M. Cohen, and C. H. Robins. 1979. The eels, *Anguilla* and *Histiobranchus*, photographed on the floor of the deep Atlantic in the Bahamas. *Bull. Marine Sci.* **29**(3): 401–405.

Robins, C. R. and P. L. Colin. 1979. Three new grammid fishes from the Caribbean Sea. *Bull. Marine Sci.* **29**: 41–52.

Robins, C. R. and J. G. Nielsen. 1970. *Snyderidia bothrops*, a new tropical, amphiatlantic species (Pisces, Carapidae). *Stud. Trop. Oceanogr. Miami* **4**(2): 285–293.

Robins, C. R. and C. H. Robins. 1966. *Xenoconger olokun*, a new xenocongrid eel from the Gulf of Guinea. *Stud. Trop. Oceanogr. Miami* **4**(1): 117–124.

Rofen, R. R. 1959. The whale-fishes: families Cetomimidae, Barbourisiidae and Rondeletiidae (order Cetunculi). *Galathea Report, Scientific results from the Danish deep-sea expedition round the world 1950–52*. Copenhagen. **1**: 255–260.

Rofen, R. R. 1966. Family Paralepididae. Family Omosudidae. Family Anotopteridae. Family Evermannellidae. Family Scopelarchidae. *Mem. Sears Found. Mar. Res.* **1**(5): 205–481; 498–602.

Romer, A. S. 1966. *Vertebrate paleontology*, 3rd ed. Chicago: University of Chicago Press. 468 pp.

Romer, A. S. 1970. *The vertebrate body*, 4th ed. Philadelphia: Saunders. 601 pp.

Rosen, D. E. 1962. Comments on the relationships of the North American cave fishes of the family Amblyopsidae. *Am. Mus. Novit.* **2109**, 35 pp.

Rosen, D. E. 1964. The relationships and taxonomic position of the halfbeaks, killifishes, silversides, and their relatives. *Bull. Am. Nat. Hist.* **127**(5): 217–268.

Rosen, D. E. 1971. The Macristiidae, a ctenothrissiform family based on juvenile and larval scopelomorph fishes. *Am. Mus. Novit.* **2452**, 22 pp.

Rosen, D. E., 1973a. Interrelationships of higher euteleostean fishes. In P. H. Greenwood, R. S. Miles, and C. Patterson (Eds.), Interrelationships of fishes. *J. Linn. Soc. (Zool.)* **53**: 397–513. Suppl. 1. New York: Academic.

Rosen, D. E. 1973b. Suborder Cyprinodontoidei. In Fishes of the western North Atlantic. *Mem. Sears Found. Mar. Res.* **1**(6): 229–262.

Rosen, D. E. 1974. Phylogeny and zoogeography of salmoniform fishes and relationships of *Lepidogalaxias salamandroides*. *Bull. Am. Mus. Nat. Hist.* **153**(2): 265–326.

Rosen, D. E. 1975. A vicariance model of Caribbean biogeography. *Syst. Zool.* **24**: 431–464.

Rosen, D. E. 1978. Vicariant patterns and historical explanation in biogeography. *Syst. Zool.* **27**: 159–188.

Rosen, D. E. 1979. Fishes from the uplands and intermontane basins of Guatemala: revisionary studies and comparative geography. *Bull. Am. Mus. Nat. Hist.* **162**(5): 267–376.

Rosen, D. E. 1982. Teleostean interrelationships, morphological function and evolutionary inference. *Am. Zool.* **22**: 261–273.

Rosen, D. E. and R. M. Bailey. 1963. The poeciliid fishes (Cyprinodontiformes), their structure, zoogeography, and systematics. *Bull. Am. Mus. Nat. Hist.* **126**(1): 1–176.

Rosen, D. E., P. L. Forey, B. G. Gardiner, and C. Patterson. 1981. Lungfishes, tetrapods, paleontology, and plesiomorphy. *Bull. Am. Mus. Nat. Hist.* **167**(4): 159–276.

Rosen, D. E. and P. H. Greenwood. 1970. Origin of the Weberian apparatus and the relationships of the ostariophysan and gonorynchiform fishes. *Am. Mus. Novit.* **2428.** 25 pp.

Rosen, D. E. and P. H. Greenwood. 1976. A fourth neotropical species of synbranchid eel and the phylogeny and systematics of synbranchiform fishes. *Bull. Am. Mus. Nat. Hist.* **157**(1): 1–69.

Rosen, D. E. and L. R. Parenti. 1981. Relationships of *Oryzias,* and the groups of atherinomorph fishes. *Am. Mus. Novit.* **2719.** 25 pp.

Rosen, D. E. and C. Patterson. 1969. The structure and relationships of the paracanthopterygian fishes. *Bull. Am. Mus. Nat. Hist.* **141**(3): 357–474.

Rosen, D. E. and A. Rumney. 1972. Evidence of a second species of *Synbranchus* (Pisces, Teleostei) in South America. *Am. Mus. Novit.* **2497,** 45 pp.

Rosenblatt, R. H. 1959. A revisionary study of the blennioid fish family Tripterygiidae. Ph.D. Thesis. Los Angeles: University of California: 376 pp.

Rosenblatt, R. H. and M. A. Bell. 1976. Osteology and relationships of the roosterfish, *Nematistius pectoralis* Gill. *Contrib. Nat. Hist. Mus. Los Angeles County, Sci.* **279.** 23 pp.

Rosenblatt, R. H. and J. L. Butler. 1977. The ribbonfish genus *Desmodema,* with the description of a new species (Pisces, Trachipteridae). *Fish. Bull.* **75:** 843–855.

Rosenblatt, R. H. and G. D. Johnson. 1976. Anatomical considerations of pectoral swimming in the opah, *Lampris guttatus. Copeia* **1976**(2): 367–370.

Rosenblatt, R. H. and W. L. Montgomery. 1976. *Kryptophaneron harveyi,* a new anomalopid fish from the eastern tropical Pacific, and the evolution of the Anomalopidae. *Copeia* **1976**(3): 510–515.

Rosenblatt, R. H. and I. Rubinoff. 1972. *Pythonichthys asodes,* a new heterenchelyid eel from the Gulf of Panama. *Bull. Marine Sci.* **22:** 355–364.

Rosenblatt, R. H. and J. S. Stephens, Jr. 1978. *Mccoskerichthys sandae,* a new and unusual chaenopsid blenny from the Pacific Coast of Panama and Costa Rica. *Nat. Hist. Mus. Los Angeles Cty. Contrib. Sci. No. 293.* pp. 1–22.

Rothbard, S. 1979. Observations on the reproductive behavior of *Tilapia zillii* and several *Sarotherodon* spp. under aquarium conditions. *Bamidgeh* **31:** 35–43.

Rounsefell, G. A. 1962. Relationships among North American Salmonidae. *U.S. Fish. Bull.* **62**(209): 235–270.

Rutenberg, E. P. 1962. Survey of the fishes of family Hexagrammidae. In T. S. Rass, (Ed.), Greenlings. *Trans. Inst. Oceanol.:* 1–103. Translated from the Russian, *Israel Program for Scientific Translation,* Jerusalem, 1970.

Sawada, Y. 1982. Phylogeny and zoogeography of the superfamily Cobitoidea(Cyprinoidei, Cypriniformes). *Mem. Fac. Fish., Hokkaido Univ.* **28:** 65–223.

Sazima, I. 1977. Possible case of aggressive mimicry in a neotropical scale-eating fish. *Nature* **270**(5637): 510–512.

Schaeffer, B. 1947. Cretaceous and Tertiary actinopterygian fishes from Brazil. *Bull. Am. Mus. Nat. Hist.* **89**(1): 1–40.

Schaeffer, B. 1968. The origin and basic radiation of the Osteichthyes. In T. Ørvig, (Ed.), *Current problems of lower vertebrate phylogeny.* New York: Wiley-Interscience: 207–222.

Schaeffer, B. 1972. A Jurassic fish from Antarctica. *Am. Mus. Novit.* **2495,** 17 pp.

Schaeffer, B. 1973. Interrelationships of chondrosteans. In P. H. Greenwood, R. S. Miles, and C. Patterson (Eds.), Interrelationships of fishes. *J. Linn. Soc. (Zool.)* **53:** 207–226. Suppl. 1. New York: Academic.

Schaeffer, B. 1975. Comments on the origin and basic radiation of the gnathostome fishes with particular reference to the feeding mechanism. *Coll. Internat. C. N. R. S.* **218:** 101–109.

Schaeffer, B. 1981. the xenacanth shark neurocranium, with comments on elasmobranch monophyly. *Bull. Am. Mus. Nat. Hist.* **169**(1): 1–66.

Schultz, L. P. 1957. The frogfishes of the family Antennariidae. *Proc. U.S. Natl. Mus.* **107:** 47–105.

Schultz, L.P. 1958. Review of the parrotfishes family Scaridae. *Bull. U.S. Natl. Mus.* **214.** 143 pp.

Schultz, L. P. 1969. The taxonomic status of the controversial genera and species of parrotfishes with a descriptive list (family Scaridae). *Smithsonian Contrib. Zool.* **17.** 49 pp.

Schultz, L. P. and Collaborators. 1953–1966. Fishes of the Marshall and Marianas Islands. *Bull. U.S. Natl. Mus.* **202:** Vol. 1 (1953), 685 pp., Vol. 2 (1960), 438 pp., Vol. 3 (1966), 176 pp.

Schultz, R. J. 1973. Unisexual fish: laboratory synthesis of a "species." *Science* **179:** 180–181.

Schultze, H. P. 1981. Hennig und der Ursprung der Tetrapoda. *Paläont Z.* **55**(1): 71–86.

Schwartz, F. J. 1972. *World literature to fish hybrids, with an analysis by family, species, and hybrid.* Gulf Coast Research Laboratory, Ocean Springs, Miss. 328 pp.

Schwartz, F. J. 1981. World literature to fish hybrids with an analysis by family, species, and hybrid. Suppl. 1. *NOAA Tech. Rept. NMFS SSRF-750.* 507 pp.

Scott, T. D., C. J. M. Glover, and R. V. Southcott. 1974. *The marine and freshwater fishes of South Australia.* South Australia: A. B. James, Government Printer. 392 pp.

Scott, W. B., A. C. Kohler, and R. E. Zurbrigg. 1970. The manefish, *Caristius groenlandicus* Jensen (Percomorphi: Caristiidae), in Atlantic Waters of Canada. *J. Fish. Res. Bd. Can.* **27:** 174–179.

Seigel, J. A. 1978. Revision of the dalatiid shark genus *Squaliolus:* anatomy, systematics, ecology. *Copeia* **1978**(4): 602–614.

Seigel, J. A. 1982. Median fin-spine locking in the ponyfishes (Perciformes: Leiognathidae). *Copeia* **1982**(1): 202–205.

Selley, L. J. and F. W. H. Beamish. 1977. *The Cyclostomata, an annotated bibliography.* The Hague: Dr. W. Junk. 961 pp.

Shaklee, J. B. and C. S. Tamaru. 1981. Biochemical and morphological evolution of Hawaiian bonefishes *(Albula). Syst. Zool.* **30:** 125–146.

Shaklee, J. B. and G. S. Whitt. 1981. Lactate dehydrogenase isozymes of gadiform fishes: divergent patterns of gene expression indicate a heterogeneous taxon. *Copeia* **1981**(4): 563–578.

Shen, S. C. and Y. H. Choi. 1978. Ecological and morphological study on fish-fauna from the waters around Taiwan and its adjacent islands. 16. Study on the labrid fishes (Labridae). *Rept. Inst. Fish. Biol. Min. Ec. Aff. Natl. Taiwan Univ.* **3**(3): 68–126.

Shen, S. C. and C. Lam. 1979. Intestine coiling patterns of chaetodontids from Taiwan: a preliminary study of their phylogenies. *Acta Oceanogr. Taiwanica* **9:** 111–118.

Silas, E. G. 1953. Classification, zoogeography and evolution of the fishes of the cyprinoid families Homalopteridae and Gastromyzonidae. *Rec. Ind. Mus.* **50**(2): 173–264.

Silas, E. G. 1959. On the natural distribution of the Indian cyprinodont fish *Horaichthys setnai* Kulkarni. *J. Mar. Biol. Assn. India* **1**(2): 256.

Silas, E. G. and E. Dawson. 1961. *Amphipnous indicus*, a new synbranchoid eel from India, with a redefinition of the genus and a synopsis to the species of *Amphipnous* Müller. *J. Bombay Nat. Hist. Soc.* **58**: 366–378.

Sillman, L. R. 1960. The origin of the vertebrates. *J. Paleontol.* **34**(3): 540–544.

Simon, R. C. and P. A. Larkin (Eds.). 1972. *The stock concept in Pacific salmon.* H. R. Macmillan lectures in fisheries. Institute of Animal Resource Ecology, The University of British Columbia, Vancouver. 231 pp.

Singh, B. N. and J. S. Datta Munshi. 1969. On the respiratory organs and mechanics of breathing in *Periopthalmus vulgaris* (Eggert). *Zool. Anz.* **183**: 92–110.

Smith, C. L. 1971. A revision of the American groupers: *Epinephalus* and allied genera. *Bull. Am. Mus. Nat. Hist.* **146**: 69–241.

Smith, C. L. and E. H. Atz. 1969. The sexual mechanism of the reef bass *Pseudogramma bermudensis* and its implications in the classification of the Pseudogrammidae (Pisces: Perciformes). *Z. Morph. Tiere* **65**(4): 315–326.

Smith, C. L., C. S. Rand, B. Schaeffer, and J. W. Atz. 1975. *Latimeria*, the living coelacanth, is ovoviviparous. *Science* **190**: 1105–1106.

Smith, D. G. 1968. The occurrence of larvae of the American eel, *Anguilla rostrata*, in the Straits of Florida and nearby areas. *Bull. Marine Sci.* **18**: 280–293.

Smith, D. G. 1970. Notacanthiform leptocephali in the Western North Atlantic. *Copeia* **1970**: 1–9.

Smith, D. G. 1979. Guide to the leptocephali (Elopiformes, Anguilliformes, and Notacanthiformes). *NOAA Tech. Rept. NMFS Circ. 424.* 39 pp.

Smith, D. G., J. E. Böhlke, and P. H. J. Castle. 1981. A revision of the nettastomatid eel genera *Nettastoma* and *Nettenchelys* (Pisces: Anguilliformes), with descriptions of six new species. *Proc. Biol. Soc. Wash.* **94**: 535–560.

Smith, D. G. and P. H. J. Castle. 1972. The eel genus *Neoconger* Girard: systematics, osteology, and life history. *Bull. Marine Sci.* **22**: 196–249.

Smith, D. G. and P. H. J. Castle. 1982. Larvae of the nettastomatid eels: systematics and distribution. *Dana Rep.* **90**: 1–44.

Smith, H. M. 1945. The fresh-water fishes of Siam, or Thailand. *Bull. U.S. Natl. Mus.* **188**: 622 pp.

Smith, J. L. B. 1940. A living coelacanth fish from South Africa. *Trans. R. Soc. S. Afr.* **28**: 1–106.

Smith, J. L. B. 1950. *The sea fishes of Southern Africa.* South Africa: Central News Agency (5th ed., 1965). 550 pp.

Smith, J. L. B. 1952a. The fishes of the family Batrachoididae from South and East Africa. *Ann. Mag. Nat. Hist.*, Ser. 12, **5**: 313–339.

Smith, J. L. B. 1952b. The fishes of the family Haliophidae. *Ann. Mag. Nat. Hist.*, Ser. 12, **5**: 85–101.

Smith, J. L. B. 1954. The Anisochromidae, a new family of fishes from East Africa. *Ann. Mag. Nat. Hist.*, Ser. 12, **7**: 298–302.

Smith, J. L. B. 1960. A new grammicolepid fish from South Africa. *Ann. Mag. Nat. Hist.*, Ser. 13, **3**: 231–235.

Smith, J. L. B. 1962. Fishes of the family Gaterinidae. *Ichthyol. Bull. Rhodes Univ.* (25): 469–502.

Smith, J. L. B. 1963. Fishes of the families Draconettidae and Callionymidae from the Red Sea and the western Indian Ocean. *Ichthyol. Bull. Rhodes Univ.* (28): 547–564.

Smith, J. L. B. 1964a. The clingfishes of the western Indian Ocean and the Red Sea. *Ichthyol. Bull. Rhodes Univ.* (30): 581–597.

Smith, J. L. B. 1964b. Fishes of the family Pentacerotidae. *Ichthyol. Bull. Rhodes Univ.* (29): 567–579.

Smith, J. L. B. 1964c. An interesting new fish of the family Chiasmodontidae from South Africa, with redescription of *Odontonema kerberti* Weber, 1913. *Ann. Mag. Nat. Hist.*, Ser. 13, **7**: 567–574 (plus plate).

Smith, J. L. B. 1966. Fishes of the sub-family Nasinae with a synopsis of the Prionurinae. *Ichthyol. Bull. Rhodes Univ.* (32): 635–682.

Smith, J. L. B. 1968. A new liparine fish from the Red Sea. *J. Nat. Hist.* **2**: 105–109.

Smith, M. M. 1980. A review of the South African cheilodactylid fishes (Pisces: Perciformes), with descriptions of two new species. *J.L.B. Smith Inst., Ichthyol. Bull. No. 42.* 14 pp.

Smith, R. J. F. 1982. Reaction of *Percina nigrofasciata, Ammocrypta beani,* and *Etheostoma swaini* (Percidae, Pisces) to conspecific and intergeneric skin extracts. *Can. J. Zool.* **60**(5): 1067–1072.

Smith-Grayton, P. K. and M. H. A. Keenleyside. 1978. Male-female parental roles in *Herotilapia multispinosa* (Pisces: Cichlidae). *Anim. Behav.* **26**: 520–526.

Smith-Vaniz, W. F. 1974. A review of the jawfish genus *Stalix* (Opistognathidae). *Copeia* **1974**(1): 280–283.

Smith-Vaniz, W. F. 1975. Supplemental description of rare blenniid fish *Phenablennius heyligeri* (Bleeker). *Proc. Acad. Nat. Sci. Philad.* **127**(6): 53–55.

Smith-Vaniz, W. F. 1976. The saber-toothed blennies, tribe Nemophini (Pisces: Blenniidae). *Acad. Nat. Sci. Philad. Monog.* **19**. 196 pp.

Smith-Vaniz, W. F. 1980. Revision of western Atlantic species of the blenniid fish genus *Hypsoblennius. Proc. Acad. Nat. Sci. Philad.* **132**: 285–305.

Smith-Vaniz, W. F. and F. J. Palacio. 1974. Atlantic fishes of the genus *Acanthemblemaria,* with descriptions of three new species and comments on Pacific species (Clinidae: Chaenopsinae). *Proc. Acad. Nat. Sci. Philad.* **125**: 197–224.

Smith-Vaniz, W. F. and V. G. Springer. 1971. Synopsis of the tribe Salariini, with descriptions of five new genera and three new species (Pisces: Blenniidae). *Smithsonian Contrib. Zool.* **73**. 72 pp.

Smith-Vaniz, W. F. and J. C. Staiger. 1973. Comparative revision of *Scomberoides, Oligoplites, Parona,* and *Hypacanthus* with comments on the phylogenetic position of *Campogramma* (Pisces: Carangidae). *Proc. Calif. Acad. Sci.*, Ser. 4, **39**: 185–256.

Solomon-Raju, N. and R. H. Rosenblatt. 1971. New records of the parasitic eel, *Simenchelys parasiticus,* from the central North Pacific with notes on its metamorphic form. *Copeia* **1971**: 312–314.

Sorbini, L. 1979. Segnalazione di un plettognato Cretacico. *Plectocretacicus* nov. gen. *Boll. Mus. Civ. St. Nat. Verona* **6**:1–4.

Sorbini, L. 1981. The Cretaceous fishes of Nardò. 1° Order Gasterosteiformes (Pisces). *Boll. Mus. Civ. St. Nat. Verona* **8**:1–27.

Spouge, J. L. and P. A. Larkin. 1979. A reason for pleomerism. *J. Fish. Res. Board Can.* **36**: 255–269.

Springer, S. 1979. A revision of the catsharks, family Scyliorhinidae. *NOAA Tech. Rept. NMFS Circ. 422.* 152 pp.

Springer, V. G. 1968. Osteology and classification of the fishes of the family Blenniidae. *Bull. U.S. Natl. Mus.* **284.** 83 pp.

Springer, V. G. 1970. The western south Atlantic clinid fish *Ribeiroclinus eigenmanni,* with discussion of the Clinidae. *Copeia* **1970**(3): 430–436.

Springer, V. G. 1972. Synopsis of the tribe Omobranchini with descriptions of three new genera and two new species (Pisces: Blenniidae). *Smithsonian Contrib. Zool.* **130.** 31 pp.

Springer, V. G. 1978. Synonymization of the family Oxudercidae, with comments on the identity of *Apocryptes cantoris* Day (Pisces: Gobiidae). *Smithsonian Contrib. Zool.* **270.** 14 pp.

Springer, V. G. 1982. Pacific plate biogeography, with special reference to shorefishes. *Smithsonian Contrib. Zool.* **367.** 182 pp.

Springer, V. G. and T. H. Fraser. 1976. Synonymy of the fish families Cheilobranchidae (= Alabetidae) and Gobiesocidae, with descriptions of two new species of *Alabes. Smithsonian Contrib. Zool.* **234.** 23 pp.

Springer, V. G. and W. C. Freihofer. 1976. Study of the monotypic fish family Pholidichthyidae (Perciformes). *Smithsonian Contrib. Zool.* **216.** 43 pp.

Springer, V. G. and M. F. Gomon. 1975. Revision of the blenniid fish genus *Omobranchus* with descriptions of three new species and notes on other species of the tribe Omobranchini. *Smithsonian Contrib. Zool.* **177.** 135 pp.

Springer, V. G., C. L. Smith, and T. H. Fraser. 1977. *Anisochromis straussi,* new species of protogynous hermaphroditic fish, and synonymy of Anisochromidae, Pseudoplesiopidae, and Pseudochromidae. *Smithsonian Contrib. Zool.* **252.** 15 pp.

Springer, V. G. and W. F. Smith-Vaniz. 1972a. Mimetic relationships involving fishes of the family Blenniidae. *Smithsonian Contrib. Zool.* **112.** 36 pp.

Springer, V. G. and W. F. Smith-Vaniz. 1972b. A new tribe (Phenablenniini) and genus (*Phenablennius*) of blenniid fishes based on *Petroscirtes heyligeri* Bleeker. *Copeia* **1972:** 64–71.

Springer, V. G. and A. E. Spreitzer. 1978. Five new species and a new genus of Indian Ocean blenniid fishes, tribe Salariini, with a key to genera of the tribe. *Smithsonian Contrib. Zool.* **268.** 20 pp.

Stahl, B. J. 1967. Morphology and relationships of the Holocephali with special reference to the venous system. *Bull. Mus. Comp. Zool.* **135**(3): 141–213.

Starck, W. A., II and P. L. Colin. 1978. *Gramma linki:* a new species of grammid fish from the tropical western Atlantic. *Bull. Marine Sci.* **28**(1): 146–152.

Stauch, A. and J. Cadenat. 1965. Révision du genre *Psettodes* Bennet 1831; (Pisces, Teleostei, Heterosomata). *Off. Rech. Sci. Tech. Outre-mer., Fort-Lamy Tchad.* **3**(4): 19–30.

Steene, R. C. 1978. *Butterfly and angelfishes of the world.* Vol. 1 Australia. New York: Wiley: 1–144.

Stehmann, M. 1979. Illustrated field guide to abundant marine fish species in Argentine waters. *Mitt. Inst. Seefischerei, Hamburg.* **23.** 153 pp.

Stein, D. L. 1978a. A review of the deepwater Liparidae (Pisces) from the coast of Oregon and adjacent waters. *Occ. Pap. Calif. Acad. Sci.* **127:** 1–55.

Stein, D. L. 1978b. The genus *Psednos* a junior synonym of *Paraliparis,* with a redescription of *Paraliparis micrurus* (Barnard) (Scorpaeniformes: Liparidae). *Matsya* **4:** 5–10.

Stensio, E. [A.] 1968. The cyclostomes with special reference to the diphyletic origin of the Petromyzontida and Myxinoidea. In T. Ørvig (Ed.), *Current problems of lower vertebrate phylogeny.* New York: Wiley-Interscience: 13–71.

Stephens, J. S., Jr. 1963. A revised classification of the blennioid fishes of the American family Chaenopsidae. *Univ. Calif. Publ. Zool.* **68**: 1–165.

Stephens, J. S., Jr. 1970. Seven new chaenopsid blennies from the western Atlantic. *Copeia* **1970**(2): 280–309.

Stephens, J. S., Jr. and V. G. Springer. 1973. Clinid fishes of Chile and Peru, with description of a new species, *Myxodes ornatus,* from Chile. *Smithsonian Contrib. Zool.* **159**. 24 pp.

Sterba, G. 1966. *Freshwater fishes of the world.* London: Studio Vista. 879 pp.

Steyskal, G. C. 1980. The grammar of family-group names as exemplified by those of fishes. *Proc. Biol. Soc. Wash.* **93**(1): 168–177.

Stiassny, M. L. J. 1981. The phyletic status of the family Cichlidae (Pisces, Perciformes): a comparative anatomical investigation. *Netherlands J. Zool.* **31**(2): 275–314.

Strahan, R. 1975. *Eptatretus longipinnis, n. sp,* a new hagfish (family Eptatretidae) from South Australia, with a key to the 5–7 gilled Eptatretidae. *Aust. Zool.* **18**: 137–148.

Strasburg, D. W. 1964. Further notes of the identification and biology of echeneid fishes. *Pac. Sci.* **18**(1): 51–57.

Sufi, S. M. K. 1956. A revision of the Oriental fishes of the family Mastacembelidae. *Bull. Raffles Mus.* **27**: 92–146.

Sulak, K. J. 1977a. *Aldrovandia oleosa,* a new species of the Halosauridae, with observations on several other species of the family. *Copeia* **1977**(1): 11–20.

Sulak, K. J. 1977b. The systematics and biology of *Bathypterois* (Pisces, Chlorophthalmidae) with a revised classification of benthic myctophiform fishes. *Galathea Rept.* **14**: 49–108.

Suttkus, R. D. 1963. Order Lepisostei. In Fishes of the western North Atlantic. *Mem. Sears Found. Mar. Res.* **1**(3): 61–88.

Suzuki, K. 1962. Anatomical and taxonomical studies on the carangid fishes of Japan. *Rep. Fac. Fish. Prefectural Univ. Mie* **4**(2): 45–232.

Svetlov, M. F. 1978. A record of *Xenocyttus nemotoi* Abe in the Southeast Pacific. *Vopr. Ikhtiol.* **18**(3): 544–545.

Svetovidov, A. N. 1948. Gadiformes. In E. N. Pavlovskii and A. A. Shtakel'berg (Eds.), *Fauna of the U.S.S.R., Fishes* **9**(4): 1–304. Zoological Institute, Akademii Nauk SSSR. Translated for the National Science Foundation, and Smithsonian Institution, Washington, D. C., 1962.

Svetovidov, A. N. 1952. Clupeidae. In E. N. Pavlovskii and A. A. Shtakel'berg (Eds.), *Fauna of the U.S.S.R., Fishes* **2**(1): 1–428. Zoological Institute, Akademii Nauk SSSR. Translated for the National Science Foundation, and Smithsonian Institution, Washington, D. C., 1963.

Sychevskaya, Ye. K. and N. I. Grechina. 1981. Fossil sticklebacks of the genus *Gasterosteus* from the Neogene of the Soviet Far East. *Paleont. J.* **1981**(1): 71–80.

Taliev, D. N. 1955. *Sculpins of Baikal (Cottoidei).* Akademii Nauk, USSR, East Siberia Branch, Moscow, Leningrad. 603 pp. (in Russian).

Tandler, G., M. A. Jones, and F. W. H. Beamish. 1979. *The Cyclostomata, an annotated bibliography.* Suppl. 1973–1978. The Hague: Dr. W. Junk. 296 pp.

Taranets, A. Y. 1941. On the classification and origin of the family Cottidae. *Izv. Akad. Nauk*

SSSR Ser. Biol. **1941**(3): 427–447. (Translated from Russian by N. J. Wilimovsky and E. Lanz. Mus. Contrib. 5, Inst. Fish., Univ. Brit. Col., Vancouver).

Tarlo (Halstead), L. B. 1960. The invertebrate origins of the vertebrates. *Int. Geol. Cong.* **21:** 113–123.

Tarp, F. H. 1952. A revision of the family Embiotocidae (the surfperches). *Fish Bull. Calif. Dep. Fish Game* **88.** 99 pp.

Taverne, L. 1968. Ostéologie du genre *Gnathonemus* Gill sensu stricto [*Gnathonemus petersii* (Gthr) et espèces voisines] (Pisces Mormyriformes). *Mus. R. Afr. Cent. Ann. (Ser. 8, Zool.)* **170:** 1–91.

Taverne, L. 1972. Considérations générales sur la systématiques des poissons de l'ordre des Mormyriformes. *Annls. Mus. R. Afr. Centr., Sci. Zool.* **200:** 1–194.

Taylor, W. R. 1969. A revision of the catfish genus *Noturus* Rafinesque, with an analysis of higher groups in the Ictaluridae. *Bull. U.S. Natl. Mus.* **282.** 315 pp.

Tchernavin, V. V. 1944a. A revision of some Trichomycterinae based on material preserved in the British Museum (Natural History). *Proc. Zool. Soc. Lond.* **144:** 234–275.

Tchernavin, V. V. 1944b. A revision of the subfamily Orestiinae. *Proc. Zool. Soc. Lond.* **144:** 140–233.

Templeman, W. 1968. A review of the morid fish genus *Halargyreus* with first records from the western North Atlantic. *J. Fish. Res. Bd. Can.* **25:** 877–901.

Templeman, W. 1973. Description and distribution of new specimens of the fish *Lipogenys gilli* from the western North Atlantic. *J. Fish. Res. Bd. Can.* **30:** 1559–1564.

Tesch, F. W. 1977. *The eel.* London: Chapman and Hull. 434 pp.

Thibault, R. E. and R. J. Schultz. 1978. Reproductive adaptations among viviparous fishes (Cyprinodontiformes: Poeciliidae). *Evolution* **32**(2): 320–333.

Thomson, K. S. 1973. Secrets of the coelacanth. *Nat. Hist.* **82:** 58–65.

Thomson, S. M. 1964. A bibliography of systematic references to the grey mullets (Mugilidae). *Div. Fish. Oceanogr. Tech. Pap. 16, Commonwealth Sci. Ind. Res. Org., Australia.* 127 pp.

Thorp, C. H. 1969. A new species of myrapinniform fish (family Kasidoridae) from the western Indian Ocean. *J. Nat. Hist.* **3:** 61–70.

Thorson, T. B. 1972. The status of the bull shark, *Carcharhinus leucas,* in the Amazon River. *Copeia* **1972:** 601–605.

Thys van den Audenaerde, D. F. E. 1961. L'anatomie de *Phractolaemus ansorgei* Blgr. et la position systématique des Phractolaemidae. *Mus. R. Afr. Cent. Ann. (Ser. 8, Sci. Zool.)* **103:** 101–167.

Tinker, S. W. 1978. *Fishes of Hawaii.* Honolulu: Hawaiian Service. 522 pp.

Tominaga, Y. 1965. The internal morphology and systematic position of *Leptobrama mülleri,* formerly included in the family Pempheridae. *Jap. J. Ichthyol.* **12**(3): 33–56.

Tominaga, Y. 1968. Internal morphology, mutual relationships and systematic position of the fishes belonging to the family Pempheridae. *Jap. J. Ichthyol.* **15**(2): 43–95.

Trautman, M. B. 1981. *The fishes of Ohio,* 2nd ed. Columbus: The Ohio State University Press. 782 pp.

Travers, R. A. 1981. The interarcual cartilage; a review of its development, distribution and value as an indicator of phyletic relationships in euteleostean fishes. *J. Nat. Hist.* **15:** 853–871.

Trewavas, E. 1973a. On the cichlid fishes of the genus *Pelmatochromis* with proposal of a new genus for *P. congicus;* on the relationship between *Pelmatochromis* and *Tilapia* and the recognition of *Sarotherodon* as a distinct genus. *Bull. Br. Mus. Nat. Hist. (Zool.)* **25:** 1–26.

Trewavas, E. 1973b. A new species of cichlid fishes of rivers Quanza and Bengo, Angola, with a list of the known Cichlidae of these rivers and a note on *Pseudocrenilabrus natalensis* Fowler. *Bull. Br. Mus. Nat. Hist. (Zool.)* **25:** 28–37.

Trewavas, E. 1981. Addendum to "Tilapia and Sarotherodon?" *Buntbarsche Bull.* **81:** 12.

Trott, L. B. 1970. Contributions to the biology of carapid fishes (Paracanthopterygii: Gadiformes). *Univ. Calif. Publ. Zool.* **89:** 1–60.

Trott, L. B. 1981. A general review of the pearlfishes (Pisces, Carapidae). *Bull. Marine Sci.* **31**(3): 623–629.

Tucker, D. W. 1954. Fishes, Pt. 1, in the "Rosaura" expedition. *Bull. Br. Mus. Nat. Hist. (Zool.)* **2**(6): 163–214.

Tucker, D. W. 1956. Studies on the trichiuroid fishes. 3. A preliminary revision of the family Trichiuridae. *Bull. Br. Mus. Nat. Hist. (Zool.)* **4**(3): 73–130.

Tyler J. C. 1968. A monograph on plectognath fishes of the superfamily Triacanthoidea. *Acad. Nat. Sci. Philad. Monog.* **16.** 364 pp.

Tyler, J. C. 1980. Osteology, phylogeny, and higher classification of the fishes of the order Plectognathi (Tetraodontiformes). *NOAA Tech. Rept. NMFS Circ.* **434:** 1–422.

Tyler, J. C. and K. Matsuura. 1981. Comments on the osteology of balistoid fishes (Tetraodontiformes), with notes on the triodontid pelvis. *Proc. Biol. Soc. Wash.* **94**(1): 52–66.

Tyler, J. C. and C. L. Smith. 1970. A new species of blennioid fish of the family Notograptidae from eastern Australia. *Notul. Nat. (Philad.)* **431:** 1–12.

Ueno, T. 1970. Cyclopteridae (Pisces). *Fauna Japonica.* Tokyo: Academic. 233 pp.

Uwate, K. R. 1979. Revision of the anglerfish Diceratiidae with descriptions of two new species. *Copeia* **1979**(1): 129–144.

Vari, R. P. 1978. The *Terapon* perches (Percoidei, Teraponidae), a cladistic analysis and taxonomic revision. *Bull. Am. Mus. Nat. Hist.* **159**(5): 175–340.

Vari, R. P. 1979. Anatomy, relationships and classification of the families Citharinidae and Distichodontidae (Pisces, Characoidea). *Bull. Br. Mus. Nat. Hist. (Zool.)* **36**(2): 261–344.

Vari, R. P. 1982. Systematics of the Neotropical characoid genus *Curimatopsis* (Pisces: Characoidei). *Smithsonian Contrib. Zool.* **373.** 28 pp.

Vari, R. P. and J. B. Hutchins. 1978. New species of *Terapon* perches (Percoidei, Teraponidae) from Australia. *Am. Mus. Novit.* **2654.** 8 pp.

Vergara, R. R. 1980. Principales características de la ictiofauna dulceacuícola cubana. *Ciencias Biol.* **5:** 95–106.

Vladykov, V. D. 1962. Osteological studies on Pacific salmon of the genus *Oncorhynchus.* *Bull. Fish. Res. Bd. Can.* **136.** 172 pp.

Vladykov, V. D. 1963. A review of salmonid genera and their broad geographical distribution. *Trans. R. Soc. Can.,* Ser. 4, Sect. 3, **1:** 459–504.

Vladykov, V. D. 1964. Quest for the true breeding area of the American eel (*Anguilla rostrata* Le Sueur). *J. Fish. Res. Bd. Can.* **21**(6): 1523–1530.

Vladykov, V. D. 1973. A female sea lamprey (*Petromyzon marinus*) with a true anal fin, and the question of the presence of an anal fin in Petromyzonidae. *Can. J. Zool.* **51:** 221–224.

Vladykov, V. D. and E. Kott. 1979. Satellite species among the holarctic lampreys (Petromyzonidae). *Can. J. Zool.* **57:** 860–867.

Vladykov, V. D. and E. Kott. 1980. Description and key to metamorphosed specimens and ammocoetes of Petromyzonidae found in the Great Lakes region. *Can. J. Fish. Aquat. Sci.* **37:** 1616–1625.

Vladykov, V. D. and E. Kott. 1982. Comment on Reeve M. Bailey's view of lamprey systematics. *Can. J. Fish. Aquat. Sci.* **39:** 1215–1217.

Vladykov, V. D., C. B. Renaud, E. Kott, and P. S. Economidis. 1982. A new nonparasitic species of Holarctic lamprey, genus *Eudontomyzon* Regan 1911 (Petromyzontidae), from Greece. *Can. J. Zool.* **60:** 2897–2915.

Vorobyeva, E. 1975. Some peculiarities in evolution of the rhipidistian fishes. *Coll. Internat. C.N.R.S.* **218:** 223–230.

Wakiya, Y. and N. Takahasi. 1937. Study on fishes of the family Salangidae. *J. Coll. Agric. Tokyo Imp. Univ.* **14**(4): 265–296.

Walker, B. W. 1952. A guide to the grunion. *Calif. Fish and Game* **38**(3): 409–420.

Walters, V. 1960. Synopsis of the lampridiform suborder Veliferoidei. *Copeia* **1960**(3): 245–247.

Walters, V. 1963. On two hitherto overlooked teleost families: Guentheridae (Ateleopodiformes) and Radiicephalidae (Lampridiformes). *Copeia* **1963**(2): 455–457.

Walters, V. 1964. Order Giganturoidei. In Fishes of the western North Atlantic. *Mem. Sears Found. Mar. Res.* **1**(4): 566–577.

Walters, V. and J. E. Fitch. 1960. The families and genera of the lampridiform (Allotriognath) suborder Trachipteroidei. *Calif. Fish and Game* **46:** 441–451.

Warner, R. R. and D. R. Robertson. 1978. Sexual patterns in the labroid fishes of the western Caribbean, 1: The wrasses (Labridae). *Smithsonian Contrib. Zool.* **254.** 27 pp.

Watanabe, M. 1960. Cottidae. *Fauna Japonica.* Tokyo: Biographical Society of Japan, News Service. 218 pp.

Watson, D. M. S. 1937. The acanthodian fishes. *Phil. Trans. R. Soc. London,* Ser. B, **228:** 49–146.

Weber, M. and L. F. DeBeaufort. 1913–1962. *The fishes of the Indo-Australian Archipelago.* Vols. 2–11 (various authors). Leiden: E. J. Brill.

Weitzman, S. H. 1954. The osteology and the relationships of the South American characid fishes of the subfamily Gasteropelecinae. *Stanford Ichthyol. Bull.* **4**(4): 213–263.

Weitzman, S. H. 1960. Further notes on the relationships and classification of the South American characid fishes of the subfamily Gasteropelecinae. *Stanford Ichthyol. Bull.* **7**(4): 217–239.

Weitzman, S. H. 1962. The osteology of *Brycon meeki*, a generalized characid fish, with an osteological definition of the family. *Stanford Ichthyol. Bull.* **8**(1): 1–77.

Weitzman, S. H. 1964. Osteology and relationships of South American characid fishes of subfamilies Lebiasininae and Erythrininae with special reference to subtribe Nannostomina. *Proc. U.S. Natl. Mus.* **116:** 127–169.

Weitzman, S. H. 1967a. The osteology and relationships of the Astronesthidae, a family of oceanic fishes. *Dana Rep.* **71:** 1–54.

Weitzman, S. H. 1967b. The origin of the stomiatoid fishes with comments on the classification of salmoniform fishes. *Copeia* **1967**(3): 507–540.

Weitzman, S. H. 1974. Osteology and evolutionary relationships of the Sternoptychidae, with a new classification of stomiatoid families. *Bull. Am. Mus. Nat. Hist.* **153:** 327–478.

Weitzman, S. H. 1978. Three new species of fishes of the genus *Nannostomus* from the Brazilian states of Pará and Amazonas (Teleostei: Lebiasinidae). *Smithsonian Contrib. Zool.* **263.** 14 pp.

Wenz, S. 1967. *Compléments á l'étude des poissons actinoptérygiens du Jurassique francais.* Edition du Centre national de la Recherche Scientifique, Paris, 1968. 276 pp.

Wheeler, A. C. 1955. A preliminary revision of the fishes of the genus *Aulostomus*. *Ann. Mag. Nat. Hist.*, Ser. 12, **8:** 613–623.

Wheeler, A. and A. Baddokway. 1981. The generic nomenclature of the marine catfishes usually referred to the genus *Arius* (Osteichthyes—Siluriformes). *J. Nat. Hist.* **15:** 769–773.

Whitehead, P. J. 1962. The species of *Elops* (Pisces: Elopidae). *Ann. Mag. Nat. Hist.*, Ser. 13, **5**(54): 321–329.

Whitehead, P. J. 1963a. A contribution to the classification of clupeoid fishes. *Ann. Mag. Nat. Hist.*, Ser. 13, **5**(60): 737–750.

Whitehead, P. J. 1963b. A revision of the recent round herrings (Pisces: Dussumieriidae). *Bull. Br. Mus. Nat. Hist. (Zool.)* **10**(6): 305–380.

Whitehead, P. J. P. 1967. The clupeoid fishes of Malaya. *J. Mar. Biol. Assn. India* **9:** 223–280.

Whitehead, P. J. P. 1974. Clupeidae. In W. Fischer and P. J. P. Whitehead (Eds.), *FAO species identification sheets for fishery purposes.* Eastern Indian Ocean (fishing area 57) and Western Central Pacific (fishing area 71). 1. Rome: FAO.

Wickstead, J. H. 1974. Cephalochordata. *Encyclopedia Britannica (Macropaedia)*, 15th ed., **3:** 1147–1149.

Wickstead, J. H. 1975. Chordata: Acrania (Cephalochordata). In A. C. Giese and J. S. Pearse (Eds.), *Reproduction of Marine Invertebrates* **2:** 283–319. San Francisco: Academic.

Wickstead, J. H. 1980. The validity of certain species of Acrania (Phylum Chordata). *J. Nat. Hist.* **14.** 453–462.

Wiley, E. O. 1976. The phylogeny and biogeography of fossil and Recent gars (Actinopterygii: Lepisosteidae). *Mus. Nat. Hist. Univ. Kansas Misc. Publ. No. 64.* 111 pp.

Wiley, E. O. 1979. Ventral gill arch muscles and the interrelationships of gnathostomes, with a new classification of the Vertebrata. *Zool. J. Linn. Soc.* **67:** 149–179.

Wiley, E. O. 1981. *Phylogenetics, the theory and practice of phylogenetic systematics.* New York: Wiley. 439 pp.

Wiley, M. L. and B. B. Collette. 1970. Breeding tubercles and contact organs in fishes: their occurrence, structure, and significance. *Bull. Am. Mus. Nat. Hist.* **143**(3): 143–216.

Wilimovsky, N. J. 1979. Provisional key to known genera of living cottoid fishes with a nomenclator of nominal marine forms. Manuscript, Institute of Resource Ecology, University of British Columbia, Vancouver, Canada.

Willmer, E. N. 1974. Nemertines as possible ancestors of the vertebrates. *Biol. Rev.* **49**(3): 321–363.

Willmer, E. N. 1975. The possible contribution of nemertines to the problem of the phylogeny of the protochordates. In E. J. W. Barrington and R. P. S. Jefferies (Eds.), Protochordates. Symposium, *Zool. Soc. London* **36:** 319–345. London: Academic.

Wilson, M. V. H. 1977. Middle Eocene freshwater fishes from British Columbia. *Life Sci. Contrib., R. Ont. Mus.* **113**. 61 pp.

Wilson, M. V. H. 1979. A second species of *Libotonius* (Pisces: Percopsidae) from the Eocene of Washington State. *Copeia* **1979**(3): 400–405.

Wilson, M. V. H. 1980. Oldest known *Esox* (Pisces: Esocidae), part of a new Paleocene teleost fauna from western Canada. *Can. J. Earth Sci.* **17**(3): 307–312

Wilson, M. V. H. 1982. A new species of the fish *Amia* from the Middle Eocene of British Columbia. *Palaeont.* **25**(2): 413–424.

Wilson, M. V. H. 1983. Paleocene amiid fish from Jabal Umm Himar in the Harrat Hadan Area, at Taif Region, Kingdom of Saudi Arabia. *U.S. Geol. Surv., Saudi Arabian Project Rept., Jiddah, Saudi Arabia.* In press.

Wilson, M. V. H. and P. Veilleux. 1982. Comparative osteology and relationships of the Umbridae (Pisces: Salmoniformes). *Zool. J. Linn. Soc.* **76**: 321–352.

Winterbottom, R. 1974a. A descriptive synonymy of the striated muscles of the Teleostei. *Proc. Acad. Nat. Sci. Philad.* **125**(12): 225–317.

Winterbottom, R. 1974b. The familial phylogeny of the Tetraodontiformes (Acanthopterygii: Pisces) as evidenced by their comparative myology. *Smithsonian Contrib. Zool.* **155**. 201 pp.

Winterbottom, R. 1980. Systematics, osteology, and phylogenetic relationships of fishes of the ostariophysan subfamily Anostominae (Characoidei, Anostomidae). *Life Sci. Contrib. R. Ont. Mus.* **123**. 112 pp.

Winterbottom, R. 1982. A revision of the congrogadid fish genus *Halidesmus* (Pisces: Perciformes), with the description of a new species from Kenya and a list of the species included in the family. *Can. J. Zool.* **60**: 754–763.

Winterbottom, R. and A. R. Emery. 1981. A new genus and two new species of gobiid fishes (Perciformes) from the Chagos Archipelago, Central Indian Ocean. *Env. Biol. Fish.* **6**(2): 139–149.

Wirtz, P. 1980. A revision of the eastern-Atlantic Tripterygiidae (Pisces, Blennioidei) and notes on some Westafrican blennioid fish. *Cybium* **11**: 83–101.

Witzell, W. N. 1977. *Apolectus niger* (Family Apolectidae): synonymy and systematics. *Matsya* **3**: 72–82.

Woodland, D. J. and G. R. Allen. 1977. *Siganus trispilos*, a new species of Siganidae from the eastern Indian Ocean. *Copeia* **1977**(4): 617–620.

Woods, L. P. and R. F. Inger. 1957. The cave, spring, and swamp fishes of the Family Amblyopsidae of central and eastern United States. *Am. Midl. Nat.* **58**(1): 232–256.

Woods, L. P. and P. M. Sonoda. 1973. Order Berycomorpha (Beryciformes). In Fishes of the western North Atlantic. *Mem. Sears Found. Mar. Res.* **1**(6): 263–396.

Wootton, R. J. 1976. *The biology of the sticklebacks.* London: Academic Press. 387 pp.

Wu, H. W. 1964. *The cyprinid fishes of China.* Vol. 1. Shanghai: Scientific Technical. pp. 1–228 + 78 pp. plates (in Chinese).

Wu, H. W. 1977. *The cyprinid fishes of China.* Vol. 2. Shanghai: Peoples. pp. 229–598 + 109 pp. plates (in Chinese).

Wu, X., Y. Chen, X. Chen, and T. Chen. 1981. A taxonomic system and phylogenetic relationship of the families of the suborder Cyprinoidei (Pisces). *Sci. Sinica* **24**(4): 563–572.

Wyanski, D. M. and T. E. Targett. 1981. Feeding biology of fishes in the endemic Antarctic Harpagiferidae. *Copeia* **1981**(3): 686–693.

Yabe, M. 1981. Osteological review of the family Icelidae Berg, 1940, (Pisces; Scorpaeniformes), with comment on the validity of this family. *Bull. Fac. Fish. Hokkaido Univ.* **32:** 293–315.

Yarberry, E. L. 1965. Osteology of a zoarcid fish *Melanostigma pammelas. Copeia* **1965:** 442–462.

Yazdani, G. M. 1976. A new family of mastacembeloid fish from India. *J. Bombay Nat. Hist. Soc.* **73:** 166–170.

Yoshino, T. and C. Araga. 1975. Pseudotrichonotidae. In Masuda, H., C. Araga, and T. Yoshino (Eds.), *Coastal fishes of southern Japan.* Tokyo: Tokai University Press: 176–177.

Zahl, P. A., J. J. A. McLaughlin, and R. J. Gomprecht. 1977. Visual versatility and feeding of the four-eyed fishes, *Anableps. Copeia* **1977**(4): 791–793.

Zangerl, R. 1973. Interrelationships of early chondrichthyans. In P. H. Greenwood, R. S. Miles, and C. Patterson (Eds.), Interrelationships of fishes. *J. Linn. Soc. (Zool.)* **53:** 1–14. Suppl. 1. New York: Academic.

Zangerl, R. 1979. New Chondrichthyes from the Mazon Creek fauna (Pennsylvanian) of Illinois. In M. H. Nitecki (Ed.), *Mazon Creek fossils.* New York: Academic: 449–500.

Zangerl, R. 1981. Chondrichthyes. 1. Paleozoic Elasmobranchii. In H. P. Schultze (Ed.), *Handbook of Paleoichthyology.* Vol. 3A. Stuttgart: Gustav Fischer Verlag. 115 pp.

Zangerl, R. and G. R. Case. 1973. Iniopterygia, a new order of chondrichthyan fishes from the Pennsylvanian of North America. *Fieldiana, Geol. Mem.* **6:** 1–67.

Zehren, S. J. 1979. The comparative osteology and phylogeny of the Beryciformes (Pisces: Teleostei). *Evol. Monog.* (University of Chicago) *1.* 389 pp.

Index